spain

GRANIZADOS

TRAVELER

spain

by Fiona Dunlop
photography by Tino Soriano

National Geographic
Washington, D.C.

Qatar
Foundation
21
unicef

CONTENTS

Pages 2–3: An evening stroll in Murcia
Opposite: The FC Barcelona soccer team celebrates a victory.

TRAVELING WITH EYES OPEN

Alert travelers go with a purpose and leave with a benefit. If you travel responsibly, you can help support wildlife conservation, historic preservation, and cultural enrichment in the places you visit. You can enrich your own travel experience as well.

To be a geo-savvy traveler:

- Recognize that your presence has an impact on the places you visit.
- Spend your time and money in ways that sustain local character. (Besides, it's more interesting that way.)
- Value the destination's natural and cultural heritage.
- Respect the local customs and traditions.
- Express appreciation to local people about things you find interesting and unique to the place: its nature and scenery, music and food, historic villages and buildings.
- Vote with your wallet: Support the people who support the place, patronizing businesses that make an effort to celebrate and protect what's special there. Seek out shops, local restaurants, inns, and tour operators who love their home—who love taking care of it and showing it off. Avoid businesses that detract from the character of the place.
- Enrich yourself, taking home memories and stories to tell, knowing that you have contributed to the preservation and enhancement of the destination.

That is the type of travel now called geotourism, defined as "tourism that sustains or enhances the geographical character of a place—its environment, culture, aesthetics, heritage, and the well-being of its residents." To learn more, visit National Geographic's Center for Sustainable Destinations at *www.nationalgeographic.com/travel/sustainable.*

spain

ABOUT THE AUTHOR & THE PHOTOGRAPHER

Fiona Dunlop's peripatetic life has led her from the Australian beaches of her birth to an upbringing in London and subsequent jobs in Europe. During 15 years spent in Paris she was strongly involved in the arts before moving into travel journalism. She has written widely for numerous international art and interior design magazines and national newspapers (including the *Observer, Sunday Telegraph, Guardian,* and *Financial Times*).

A taste for the tropics and ancient cultures led her to spend long research periods in developing countries, producing travel guides to India, Indonesia, Singapore & Malaysia, Vietnam, Mexico, Costa Rica, and southern Africa. Other publications include *In the Asian Style* (on Asian design); *New Tapas,* a book on the Spanish tapas bar tradition; *Medina Kitchen* (exploring the home-cooking of North Africa); and *Viva la Revolucion!,* a food-travel book on Mexico.

She regularly visits her house in the olive groves of Andalucía to write in what she considers to be the optimum conditions, combining *sol y sombra* (sun and shade), not to mention tapas and *ferias.* Her main base is now in London.

The Travelwise chapter has been extensively rewritten and updated by **Xander Fraser,** translator and editor, who lives in Santander, Spain.

Tino Soriano, born and raised in Barcelona, Spain, divides his work between photojournalism and travel photography. He has received awards from the World Press Photo Foundation, UNESCO, Fujifilm, and Fotopres.

Since 1998 Tino has photographed in Spain, France, Italy, Sicily, Portugal, Scotland, and South Africa on assignments for National Geographic. His work has appeared in major magazines around the world including *Der Spiegel, Paris Match,* and *El País.* He also provided photographs for *National Geographic Traveler: Sicily, National Geographic Traveler: Portugal,* and *National Geographic Traveler: Madrid.*

Tino likes to write, and he has published *El Futuro Existe,* a story about children living with cancer. He also regularly lectures and teaches workshops at the University of Barcelona.

Charting Your Trip

Spain offers a mouthwatering range of settings and therefore options. On to its diverse topographical canvas, you can tack excellent regional cuisines, top wines, quirky festivals, deep traditions, and increasingly slick hotels and restaurants. Ultimately, though, Spain is a country with two faces that live comfortably together: one combining centuries of history and foreign input, the other the result of the last three decades of intense cultural and economic development.

Getting Around

There is a lot you can pack in, as Spain's public transport and road network are now excellent. The obvious urban starting points are the international gateways: the capital, Madrid, and its great Catalan rival, Barcelona. Since 2008 the two cities have been less than three hours apart (386 miles/621 km) thanks to the Alta Velocidad Española (AVE) high-speed train network. Madrid is the hub of the network: It takes just 2.5 hours to reach Málaga on the Costa del Sol or the Andaluz capital, Sevilla (Seville), while Córdoba (1.75 hours) and Valencia (1.5 hours), on the Mediterranean coast, are even closer. More AVE rail links are under construction, so keep an eye on the national railway website *(www.renfe.com)*, where you can also book tickets.

Domestic flights (see Travelwise p. 343) open up access to far-flung Galicia, in the northwest, and to the islands–the Balearics and the Canaries–as well as to dozens of cities, although train frequency is often better, and with station locations in town centers, arrival and departure take less time (see Travelwise p. 344). You can take an eight-hour ferry to Mallorca, in the Balearics, from Valencia *(www.aferry.com/valenciaferry.com)*, but otherwise the islands are best reached by plane, using ferries and hydrofoils once there.

Renting a car is a great option for venturing off the beaten path into authentic small towns and rural areas. Highways are first-rate and rarely busy, while secondary roads are well-maintained and nearly always well signposted. Cars with automatic transmissions are rare and therefore more expensive to rent than manual. Dozens of rental companies, both national and international, compete

Paella (rice mixed with vegetables, saffron and meat or seafood) originated in Valencia.

ferociously, so it is always cheapest to book your car in advance (see Travelwise p. 344).

If you like traveling by road but don't want to take the wheel yourself, there are plenty of long-distance buses. These are operated by private, often regional companies so check with the relevant tourist office. They are considerably cheaper than trains or rental cars and the express ones are very comfortable. One of the largest networks is Ansa *(www.ansa.es)*.

NOT TO BE MISSED:

If You Only Have a Week

If you are starting your trip in Madrid, on **Days 1 and 2** see some of the city's excellent museums, stroll in Retiro Park, shop, then dine in style or sample tapas. Use **Day 3** for a day-trip to Toledo from Atocha station (30 min.), but book your train ticket a day in advance as morning trains fill up. An alternative, less crowded day-trip is to the beautiful little town of Cuenca (55 min. by AVE). On **Day 4,** take the AVE from Atocha to Barcelona and spend **Day 5** seeing medieval history, cutting-edge design, and of course Gaudí's architecture: You will need two days to even scratch the surface of this sophisticated Catalan city. Depending on the season, you can spend some of **Day 6** relaxing on the city beaches, or head south to funky Sitges by train (from Passeig de Gracia or Sants station, take the train to Vilanova i la Geltru or St. Vincenç de Calders, 30–40 min.). In cooler months, head for the hills to visit the extraordinary Monastery of Montserrat in dramatic landscapes. On **Day 7,** return to Madrid.

If your international flight arrives in Barcelona, do the same itinerary backward.

From Madrid, an alternative after visiting Toledo is to head south to Andalucía. Take the AVE from Atocha on **Day 4** to Córdoba to spend the afternoon and night there soaking up the atmosphere of this quintessential Moorish city. Continue by AVE on **Day 5** to party-loving Sevilla to enjoy flamenco, tapas, and stunning sights before returning to Madrid.

As high speed connections do not yet encompass Granada, you need to take a domestic flight and spend at least a night there. Remember to book your visit to the

Visitor Information

Prepare your trip well using the websites mentioned throughout this book, as well as the official Spanish Tourism website: *www.spain.info.* On the spot, use the local tourist offices, which are generally helpful and multilingual. Provincial capitals have two types: one which covers the entire province and the other a municipal office. Catalunya sets itself apart with its own official website *(www.catalunyatourism.com),* and for Barcelona see *www.bcn.cat/canalcultura.* For accommodation in *paradores,* mostly beautiful historic buildings at very reasonable rates, see *www.parador.es.* Wildlife enthusiasts should visit *www.iberianwildlife.com.*

Safety

Spain is, overall, a very safe country to travel in with friendly, honest inhabitants. There are a few places where crime is an issue, such as central Barcelona, where pickpockets are rife, Granada (never leave anything visible in a car), and Sevilla (again, pickpockets). Be cautious, and leave your passport and large amounts of cash in your hotel safe; also be careful at any large fiesta.

Alhambra at least a week in advance. Continue to Córdoba by bus *(www.alsa.es)*, which takes about 2.5 hours then return to Madrid by AVE. It would be difficult and too rushed to try and cover the big three Andalusian cities and Madrid in a week.

If you arrive in Barcelona and are averse to changing hotels, you can base your week there and take day-trips to rewarding destinations nearby. Girona (1.25 hrs. by train to the north) is a relaxing, atmospheric city to visit, full of history. Montserrat (1.25 hrs.) spirits you into mountains and fervent Catholicism while Tarragona (less than 1.5 hrs. from Passeig de Gracia or Sants stations) offers a fabulous spectrum of Roman monuments. If you still have time, take in Sitges on the way back from Tarragona or rent a car for the day to tour the blissful Priorat hills. Explore Catalunya *(www.explorecatalunya.com)* makes the logistics easy.

If You Have More Time

The big historical highlights are mostly urban, offering a huge span of history as well as a concentration of contemporary culture. Madrid, Barcelona, Toledo, Valencia, and Donostia (San Sebastián) as well as the great Andalusian triangle of Sevilla, Córdoba, and Granada are all culturally rich destinations. To see them all would require at least three weeks, but if you cover just a few of them spliced with smaller towns and rural areas, you will get a deeper sense of Spanish lifestyle and history, and wonderful memories.

Close to the French border, 218 miles (351 km) north of Madrid, vibrant **Donostia (San Sebastián)** is famed for its pioneering cuisine and *pintxos* (Basque tapas) as well as its majestic seaside setting. The city is just an hour by plane from Madrid or Barcelona. You can also drive (4.75 hrs.) or take a six-hour bus ride *(www.movelia.es)* from Madrid, or drive (5.5 hrs.) from Barcelona. Similarly, in the opposite corner of northern Spain, the delightful pilgrims' city of **Santiago de Compostela** is reached by domestic flight

Climate

Your itinerary should be determined not just by how much time you have available, but also by the season. The climate in Spain differs considerably between north and south, mountain and coast. Avoid Madrid and most of the south (Andalucía, Extremadura, and Murcia) in baking midsummer (July and August) unless you are on a beach holiday. Instead explore the mountains of the north (Picos de Europa and Pyrenees) and "Green Spain," the entire northern strip from Galicia to Catalunya. As this is peak tourist season, however, accommodations fill up and monuments are crowded. Spring and autumn are easily the best times for a holiday in any region, including the lovely Balearics, while Andalucía can be mild in winter, except for January and February, which can be wet. Winter is bitterly cold in Madrid and Castilla. Those months are for visiting the Canary Islands.

Spain boasts more than 2,000 miles (3,500 km) of gorgeous coastline.

from Madrid or Barcelona. In both these cities, you can rent a car on arrival and enjoy several days exploring their bucolic environs. Driving from one to the other, a 430-mile (688 km) trip, would take five to seven days, stopping to see major sights in **Bilbo (Bilbao), Santillana del Mar, Altamira,** and **Oviedo,** with a detour into the breathtaking **Picos de Europa.** With a few more days, you can circle back through Castilla (Castile), taking in wineries near **Valladolid** or in **La Rioja,** visit **León** and **Burgos,** then return to **Donostia** or drive south to **Madrid.** This itinerary requires at least ten days. Two weeks would be better.

Another driving circuit takes you northwest from Madrid through the rugged Sierra de Guadarrama, stopping at **El Escorial,** to the lovely Castilian town of **Segovia.** Continue next day via Ávila to overnight in **Salamanca** (a total of 109 miles/175 km). Then head south through Extremadura to Trujillo and Cáceres. With time, you could also explore the **Sierra de Aracena** or the nature reserve of **Monfragüe.** After seeing the Roman monuments of **Mérida,** it is an easy drive to **Sevilla** (1.75 hrs.) for a couple of days, then continue via Ronda to **Granada** (3 hrs.). After a couple of nights here, drive through olive country to **Córdoba** (2.5 hrs.), where you can drop off the car and return to Madrid by AVE. An alternative, offering some inspiring modern art at the Museo Picasso, would be to drive south to breezy **Málaga** (2 hrs.) and drop the car there before getting the AVE to Madrid. This rewarding circuit needs at least two weeks. ■

Cultural Etiquette & Tipping

The Spanish are less formal than their Latin American counterparts, but always communicative. Learn to say *buenos dias* ("good day") or *buenas tardes* ("good afternoon"). On leaving, *hasta luego* ("see you again") or *adios* ("goodbye") is usual. There is no big tipping culture, but some loose change in a café or bar is appreciated; taxis do not expect tips, but restaurants appreciate up to 10 percent of the bill.

History & Culture

Colorful Spanish fans
Opposite: A Cartujano horse and elegant rider

Spain Today

The stereotypical Spaniard disappeared long ago. In the 19th century, writers and artists wove images of a land inhabited by black-haired, fiery-eyed women and dubious-looking, mustachioed men. Look for them today and you will be disappointed as Spain is firmly within the net of globalization. Yet beneath the surface lies a web of regional differences and deeply embedded traditions that even mobile-phone-clutching young professionals have not forsaken.

Whether Catalan, Basque, Galician, Asturian, Cantabrian, Castilian, Aragonese, Extremaduran, Valencian, Manchegan, Murcian, Andalusian, or from the Balearics or the Canaries, the Spaniard of the 21st century clings adamantly to his or her roots, a habit most colorfully illustrated in local fiestas and even by language itself. After long suppression under the dictator General Francisco Franco, who died in 1975, regional identities have undergone an explosive revival, given impetus by the powers granted to the 17 autonomous communities in the new constitution of 1978. Spain is now Europe's most devolved country. Separatism has provoked terrorist attacks in Euskadi (Basque country), while Catalunya maintains a more pragmatic approach. Regional loyalty fragments further, from province to province, from town to town, and from village to village. There is no Spain or Spaniard as such. Instead, a passionately local spirit is cloaked in the dominant Castilian culture—and in a love of excess that fizzes in the action-packed calendar.

The Spaniard of the 21st century clings adamantly to his or her roots, a habit most colorfully illustrated in local fiestas and even by language itself.

Spain's 40 million people are on the move. You find Andalusians working in Catalunya, unemployed Castilian farmers migrating to Euskadi, and Madrid embraces incomers from every region. Yet deep in the rural countryside, unadulterated relics of distant invaders exist. Descendants of the Romans live in Asturias, and those of the Swabians on the borders of Extremadura and Castilla. Even more determinedly set apart from the mainstream is the 500-year-old Gypsy community, visible above all in Andalucía. Gypsies provoke waves of intolerance, and in the 1990s so did Spain's other highly visible minority—North African migrant workers. However, a vast increase in immigration since 2000 has resulted in far greater racial tolerance (leaping from 2.2 percent to 12 percent of the population).

Language is equally diverse. The language called "Spanish" is actually Castilian, from the central part of Spain. The Basque, Catalan, and Galician languages are utterly distinctive, as are regional accents. Each Canary island has its own accent, and the slurred tones of Andalusians are quite different from the crisp, machine-gun fire of Madrileños, the people of Madrid. This is something that you might not be aware of in Spain's bland coastal resorts, where signs are as likely to be in English and German as in Spanish. The onward march of tourism since the 1960s has created yet another

The bronze "Winged Victory" gazes over Madrid from atop the neoclassical Metropolis.

METROPOLIS

division of Spain, that between the Mediterranean *costas* (coasts) invaded by northern European retirees and summer sun-seekers, and the vast, underpopulated interior. It is in the latter that the reactionary heart of Spain beats, where rural inhabitants may barely know the next town and where population densities descend below 30 inhabitants per square mile. Catholicism rules in these areas—the two Castillas, Aragón, and Extremadura—and the bells peal daily.

In the big cities, it is another story entirely. Barcelona, capital of Catalunya, is one of Europe's top cultural hubs, and its 1.6 million inhabitants exude a prosperity, confidence, and sophistication seen nowhere else in Spain. Although they do not readily embrace foreigners, they exemplify the old adage: Once you get to know them, they are friends for life. Madrid, the capital and Spain's largest city (with three million inhabitants), follows closely in avant-gardism and style, while its businesses and art collections multiply. Its tolerant and relaxed inhabitants have a talent for nocturnal intensity and living on the edge: They were the ones who spearheaded the *movida,* a cathartic surge of hedonism and creativity that seized Spain in the early 1980s with the return of democracy. Sex, drugs, and rock and roll boomed, in tandem with a new wave of artists, filmmakers, and musicians. Spain's third largest city is Valencia, whose people adeptly combine southern laissez-faire with Catalan dynamism. As the site for the America's Cup in 2007 and 2010, it experienced massive regeneration. Sevilla, Zaragoza (home to Expo 2008), Málaga, and Bilbao follow, each with a distinct flavor, culture, and attitude, swinging from high southern exuberance to intelligent urbanism and industrial savvy. However, the boom years ended in 2008 with the global recession: Spain was knocked hard and its economy struggled. Property prices plummeted and unemployment soared to more than 20 percent, with jobless youth around 40 percent, the highest among developed countries. Many have moved to other European countries.

On the environmental front things are rosier. Spain is now a front-runner in renewable energies, with wind power storming ahead to make it the world's third largest producer. Ambitious future targets have been effected by financial constraints, but solar energy is now widespread.

Spain as a nation has undergone a greater social, political, and economic transformation than most other Western European nations. And, despite drinking, eating, and smoking with joyous abandon, Spaniards enjoy an exceptionally long life expectancy of more than 81 years. Perhaps the strength of the family is the reason.

Fiesta del Carmen

Every year on July 16, communities along Spain's spectacular coastline celebrate the patron saint of seafarers, the Virgen del Carmen. Led by sailors and fishermen, the statue of the virgin is carried from the local church to be paraded through the streets and then to the sea. In some places she is taken for a boat trip accompanied by a flotilla of fishing vessels, while in others she is walked into the waves, surrounded by jubilant well-wishers.

In Málaga, on the Sunday after July 16, the local scuba club has its own rite: A bronze statue of the virgin that lives on the seabed is brought ashore to be venerated on the beach. Sixty or so divers then return her to her watery grotto.

Normally reserved Spaniards relish the opportunity to celebrate.

Festivals

The *feria,* or fiesta, of a village or town is the excuse for everyone to let their hair down. This is the zenith of the year, when normally dignified, well-mannered people (which means most Spaniards) take to the streets and dance the night away. Tradition still pulls the heartstrings, despite the radical social upheavals of recent decades, and this is unlikely to change in the near future. Patron saints' days are the most common fiestas, but you also find a multitude of idiosyncratic celebrations stemming from seasonal, historic, or religious events, each one requiring costumed participants, food, drink, music, dance, and fireworks. Stylized battles between Moors and Christians, wine battles in Rioja, the running of the bulls in Iruña (Pamplona), bonfires and satirical figures in Valencia, towering human pyramids in Catalunya, horse-branding and coffin parades in Galicia, men disguised in animal skins and masks in Mallorca, whip-brandishing bogeymen in Extremadura, and a hedonistic pilgrimage to Rocío, in Huelva province, of nearly one million people from all over Andalucía—all are permanent fixtures on the calendar.

Dominating the religious calendar is Semana Santa (Holy Week, see pp. 272–273), the week leading up to Easter at its best in Sevilla, Málaga, and Zamora. Corpus Christi a few weeks later, sees processions of devils, dance groups, dwarfs, giants, and mythological creatures. Sometimes they follow a route of stunningly patterned carpets of flowers, salt, or sawdust. Medieval mystery plays are performed at this and other festivals. Christmas (Navidad), Los Mayos (a spring celebration of love and nature), San Juan (St. John, when pagan rites and bonfires celebrate the summer solstice), and September 8 (an autumn festival) feature among the other general celebrations. Carnival, which takes place around Mardi Gras, brings exceptional outbursts of color, costumes, and offbeat customs, above all in Cádiz, throughout Galicia, and in Santa Cruz de Tenerife, which approaches Rio de Janeiro's Carnival in scale and exuberance.

From Easter to October, every town has a bullfighting season during its *feria* (annual fair)—watch for posters advertising the events.

Bullfighting

Bulls are the best known animal participants in Spain's festivals although these days their popularity is waning. From Easter to October, every town has a bullfighting season during its *feria* (annual fair)—watch for posters advertising the events. The big exception is Catalunya, which banned the "sport" in 2011. Matador prowess reaches a height in the bullrings of Madrid, Málaga, and Sevilla with heroes such as El Juli (Julián López) topping the bill. *Encierros*—the running of the bulls, when bulls are let loose to charge through the streets—lie at the heart of local festivals from Peñafiel to Iruña (Pamplona) and beyond. Bullbaiting is still practiced by Basques. Devotees of bullfighting (primarily Andalusians) are called *aficionados,* and for them bullfighting is not a sport, but an art, both ritualistic and ceremonial, with primitive origins and echoes of Roman gladiatorial combat and medieval jousting.

The *corrida de toros* (bullfight) begins with a procession around the ring of the participants to stirring music from the band. After testing how aggressive the bull is, the matador and his team leave center stage to the horseback *picadores,* who ride out and encourage the bull to charge. The horses are padded to prevent serious injury, and their riders pierce the bull's neck and shoulders with their lances. Next, the *banderilleros* (bullfighters on foot, carrying *banderillas,* colored darts) run at the bull to stick their banderillas into his shoulders. With the bull's energy depleted, the matador enters alone, to demonstrate his skill by making passes with his red cape and steering the bull within inches of his body. Finally, in an intensely dramatic moment, he drives his sword between the bull's shoulders for the kill.

Long reviled by sensitive foreigners and by an increasing number of Spaniards, the bullfight is nonetheless the most perfect expression of Spanishness: pomp and ceremony, *sol y sombra* (sun and shade), a deep sense of drama, tragedy, and fatalism, all orchestrated by the fearless *furia española*–the legendary Spanish fury that made Spain's enemies tremble. Spaniards are not fazed by death, as history from the conquistadores and Inquisition to the Civil War ably demonstrates. Theatricality and pushing to the limit are enduring elements in the national psyche. ■

Bullfighting, considered an art rather than a sport, is a national passion.

The Land

From lush green valley to craggy limestone rockface or barren scrub, the Spanish landscape is a powerful absolute. No other European country rivals the splendor, wildness, and intensity of Spain's landscapes, whether shimmering in scorching heat, softened by drizzle, or swept by glacial winter winds.

From the natural barrier of the Pyrenees and its westerly extension, the Sierra Cantábrica, 197,323 square miles (505,957 sq km) unfold southward through the central *meseta* (tableland) of Castilla to the peaks of the Sierra Nevada and the karstic desert of eastern Andalucía. Spain is Europe's second most mountainous country after Switzerland, boasting the continent's highest village in the Sierra Nevada. This predominance of often spectacular sierra is one of the reasons for the

The Sierra de Tramontana forms the spine of northern Mallorca, one of the Balearic Islands.

strength of tradition in Spain, as isolated valley and mountain communities once had little contact with the sociocultural advances of the cities. Massive improvements in communications and infrastructure over the last 30 years have made most, though not all, of these communities far more accessible.

Like everywhere, the climate is changing: Pyrenean glaciers are melting; snow is less common in the Sierra Nevada, and rainfall is notoriously sparse except in the far north. Water shortages and desertification are a major cause of concern in Andalucía at its narrowest point, only 8 miles (13 km) from Africa. Only five large rivers course across this generous peninsula, each sprouting branches that end in pathetic trickles and often dry up completely. Yet Spain surprises, for it boasts one of Europe's most fertile regions: the rice fields and *huerta* (irrigated land) of Valencia. Naturally verdant havens are found in the meadows of Cantabria and Asturias, and some lusher pockets of the Costa del Sol.

Spain is Europe's second most mountainous country after Switzerland, boasting the continent's highest village in the Sierra Nevada.

Flora & Fauna

An estimated 90 percent of Spain's prehistoric forests disappeared long ago. They gave way to wheat fields, vineyards, olive groves, and fruit orchards, but also to vast tracts of uncultivable scrub and barren shale where only cactuses dare to grow. The remaining forest harbors more than 500 bird species, making it a European hot spot for bird-watching.

After decades of low visibility, wolves and brown bears are multiplying again in the Pyrenees and Cordillera Cantábrica, respectively (as is the Iberian lynx in the south). You are more likely to glimpse chamois, deer, and possibly wild boars among the oak, beech, ash, and lime trees that cover the lower slopes. Spain is also home to about 25 species of birds of prey, including red kites, griffon vultures, and the endangered imperial eagle. Southern Spain is a stopping point on migration routes between Europe, Africa, and Asia, and bird-watchers can spot the greatest number of species in the pine forests of the Sierra de Cazorla, near Úbeda, and in the sand dunes and marshes of the Parque Nacional Doñana, southwest of Sevilla. On inland waters you may see migrating flamingoes and European cranes, while hoopoes, golden orioles, cuckoos, woodpeckers, and bee-eaters frequent the riverbanks and woods.

Flora is another attraction, above all in spring: Spain has an estimated 8,000 species of which one-tenth are endemic. Many of these are alpine varieties that thrive in the highest mountains. ■

Food & Drink

Until the 1990s, Spain was never considered a gastronome's destination, but since Ferran Adrià (Catalunya's revolutionary chef) has become an international star the culinary scene has been transformed. Cuisine is not treated as reverently as in France, but its increasingly refined ingredients are as rich and varied as the climate and terrain.

Chili peppers were brought back from the Americas by Spain's early explorers.

An intimate knowledge of the quality of basic products—for example extra virgin olive oil, *jamón* (ham), cheese, seafood, and the most succulent of lamb—is part of the regional heritage that even city dwellers share. Just as wine has leapt up the quality scale (see pp. 134–135), cooking has developed from simple, hearty fare into sophisticated and inventive dishes.

Revolutionary Chefs

A new generation of chefs leads this gastronomic revolution. Everyone knows veteran *nueva cocina* chef Juan Marí Arzak of Donostia (San Sebastián), but there are others, such as his fellow Basques Pedro Subijana of Akelarré, Martin Berasategui at Lasarte, and Antoní Luis Aduriz at Mugaritz. The Catalans feature Xavier Pellicer in Sant Celoni, Joan Roca in Girona, and Carme Ruscalleda in Sant Pol de Mar. Madrid boasts Catalan supremo Sergi Arola at La Broche, while Valencia trumpets Ca Sento's seafood king Raúl Aleixandre, and Málaga/Marbella share Andaluz star Dani García. With such a galaxy of chefs, the overall standard has soared and firmly established Spain on the world gastro-map.

Tapas

One of Spain's greatest culinary contributions is the tradition of *tapas* (see sidebar this page), appetizers eaten before lunch or in the evening. Tapas let you sample regional specialties and keep you going until dinner (which rarely occurs before 10 p.m.), or even replace it. They are also served in larger *raciones* (sharing plates). Typical tapas are anchovies, *morcilla* (black pudding), hams or cheeses, broad beans cooked with bacon and mint, kidneys sautéed in sherry, or skewers of grilled meat or seafood.

Tapas consumption is invariably linked to socializing in an impromptu, informal way. Customers often move from bar to bar, eating, drinking, and chatting, though many bars are now quite sophisticated with sit-down areas.

The sweet Valencia orange takes its name from the Spanish city renowned for its orange trees.

Enjoying Lunch

Lunch is the most important meal of the day, starting after 2 p.m. In restaurants the *menú del día* (menu of the day) is usually a good choice. Regional specialties include *cochinillo* (roast suckling pig) in Castilla, *rabo de toro* (ox tail) in Andalucía, *fabada* (pork and beans) in Asturias, paella in Valencia, and *pulpo à la Gallega* (boiled octopus) in Galicia. From a basic peasant cuisine, the peninsula's food has evolved into an array of finely orchestrated gastronomic indulgences, all taken with an inimitable Spanish dose of enjoyment.

EXPERIENCE: Time for Tapas

Madrid is a great starting point for sampling tapas (called *pintxos* in the Basque Country) from all over Spain; its restaurants have more geographical and historical scope than any other city.

Sample snails or baby squid at **Antonio Sánchez** *(Meson de Paredes 13, tel 915 39 78 26)*, the capital's oldest tavern, barely changed since 1830, or join the lunchtime throng at **Casa Labra** *(Tetuan 12, tel 915 31 00 81, www.casalabra.es)*, which has been making exquisite *bacalao* (salted cod) and *croquetas* (croquettes) for 150 years. For 19th-century elegance, delicate pastries, and top *caldo* (broth), try **Lhardy** *(San Jerónimo 8, tel 915 32 42 00, www.lhardy.com)*. Less ancient but with bags of eccentricity is **Los Gatos** *(Jesus 2, tel 914 29 30 67)*, good for beer and seafood tapas in the early hours.

Wine diehards should work their way along Cava Baja. **Taberna Tempranillo** *(No. 30, tel 913 64 15 32)* offers hundreds of top Spanish wines to accompany tapas or larger *raciones*. On the parallel street, chic, intimate **Taberna Matritum** *(Cava Alta 16, tel 913 65 82 37, www.matritum.es)* has boutique wines and inventive tapas.

José Luis, an institution with outlets all over the capital, was founded by the eponymous Basque who started his career as a shoe-shiner in a Bilbao café some 70 years ago. His upscale *cervecerias* (beer bars) are renowned for their fresh, top quality pintxos. The flagship is at Serrano 89 *(tel 915 63 09 58, www.joseluis.es)*.

History of Spain

The name Iberia first cropped up in the sixth century B.C. when a Greek writer referred to the people living along the River Ebre, or Ebro (Iberus). Spain's history goes back a lot further, to the time when early people first crossed the narrow Straits of Gibraltar from Africa.

Evidence has been found in the caves of Atapuerca, near Burgos, of human presence (and that of carnivorous mammals) more than one million years ago. By around 25,000 B.C., Paleolithic hunter-gatherers were creating cave paintings of bison and deer. The finest paintings known are in the caves of Altamira in Cantabria and date from around 14,000 B.C., long before the dolmens of Antequera (see p. 280) or the *talayot* of the Balearics (see p. 329) were built, but slightly younger than Lascaux in France.

Settled culture appeared with the Iberians, who may have originated in North Africa.

Settled culture appeared with the Iberians, who may have originated in North Africa. They were later joined by Celts to become Celtiberians. Galicia's *castros* (fortified hill villages) are relics of their advanced hybrid culture. In the western Pyrenees lived another ethnic group, the Basques. Elsewhere, Spain had little sign of an ordered society other than the legendary Tartessos in Andalucía, a sophisticated, hierarchic society between the lower Guadalquivir and Guadiana Rivers.

Phoenicians, Greeks, & Carthaginians

Cultural change came in the first millennium B.C. through the trading network of more sophisticated peoples from the eastern Mediterranean: Phoenicians and Greeks. Spain's extensive mineral resources first attracted Phoenicians to Cádiz in the eighth century B.C. They were followed by Greeks, who spread inland from the Mediterranean coast. The potter's wheel, currency, and iron technology were among Greek contributions to Iberian society. Spain's oldest works of art—"La Dama de Elche" and "La Dama de Baza" (both fifth to fourth century B.C.) display clear eastern Mediterranean influence.

When the sun set for the Phoenicians it rose in turn for their cousins, the Carthaginians (based at Carthage, in modern Tunisia). Rome and Carthage were at loggerheads over control of the Mediterranean, and the Iberian peninsula was a pawn in their game. Greek influence ended as the Carthaginians moved into Tartessos, but native Iberians continued to flourish, exporting wine, olive oil, grain, and their rich mineral deposits. During the Punic Wars (third century B.C.) between Rome and Carthage, Iberians were employed in Hannibal's army, which eventually crossed the Alps into Italy. The Roman response was to obliterate Carthage in 202 B.C. This announced Rome's long hold over Europe—including Hispania, as Roman Spain was known.

Roman Spain

For the next 500 years Rome imprinted its mark on Spain, still distinct today in straight roads, bridges, aqueducts, amphitheaters, urban layouts, and the Latin-based Spanish language. The towns of Córdoba (Corduba), Tarragona (Tarraco), and Mérida (Augusta Emerita) became capitals of the three Roman provinces of

The ruins of a prehistoric Celtiberian *castro* (fortified village) near Coaña in Asturias

Roman emperor Caesar Augustus founded the city of Zaragoza in 24 B.C.

Baetica, Tarraconensis, and Lusitania (Portugal). Other urban settlements—Sevilla (Hispalis), León (Legio), Pamplona (Pompaelo), Zaragoza (Caesar Augusta)—are also Roman. Spain's mines continued to yield gold and silver in vast quantities, much of which was shipped back to Rome in an ironic reversal of Spain's own plundering of the New World more than a thousand years later. Waves of immigrant Romans (and Jews) settled permanently in Hispania and established their customs alongside those of the Iberians. Resistance to Romanization was strongest in the northeast and the northwest. Galicia's Celtiberians preserved their traditions and names, as did the Basques.

Under Roman rule, fish (tuna, mackerel, and sardine) and fish products (salted anchovies, spicy garum sauce) joined the Iberians' already prolific production. Culture blossomed: Hispania produced illustrious Roman emperors such as Trajan and Hadrian, scholars such as the Senecas (father and son), Martial, Quintilian, and the geographer Mela. Yet although born and bred in Hispania, they were all undoubtedly of Roman stock, for the Roman elite kept its distance from the Iberians. Stability and prosperity lasted almost three centuries, until, in the third century A.D., cracks began to appear in the Roman empire as corruption sent it into decline. Spain's weakness was exposed by roving northern tribes of Franks, Vandals, and, in the fifth century, Suebi (Swabians) and Visigoths. Through sporadic raids they gradually broke up the carefully constructed unity. The Roman Empire was in its death throes, and Hispania's economy disintegrated as defense budgets spiraled. By 481, the Visigothic king Euric had replaced the Romans, although he kept Roman structures and order. At that time, the Visigothic kingdom was centered on Toulouse in modern France.

Visigoths

For the next 200 years, the history of Spain became a complex series of regional battles for supremacy, consolidated to a certain extent when the Visigoths established their capital in Toledo and the country was unified under King Leovigild in 584. In 654, King Recceswinth established a single code of law based on that of the Romans. Exceptions to this were the mountain people of the north (Cantabrians, Asturians, and Basques), who temporarily retained their independence, and the south, which had a period of Byzantine rule. Christianity had arrived in the late third century, and the emergence of church councils under the Visigoths established a link between Church and State that was crucial to Spain's subsequent history.

This was a dark period in Spain. The Roman system of huge estates (latifundios) owned by the aristocracy and worked by virtual slaves continued under the new invaders. Cities declined to become mere fortified clusters of churches and convents. Jewish people, who had emigrated to Spain under the Romans, were forced to convert. As a result, many left. Those that stayed welcomed the next invaders: the Moors. A series of raids from North Africa culminated in 711 in an army of Berbers (the indigenous people of North Africa) who landed at Gibraltar. This was to be the beginning of a new era that lasted more than seven centuries.

Moorish Conquest

Since the death of the prophet Muhammad (570–632), much of Arabia and northern Africa had come under the sway of Islam, a new, egalitarian religion. News of rich pickings in anarchic Spain—known as al-Andalus, meaning "isle of Vandals"—reached Ifriqiya, a northern African Islamic province of the Caliphate of Damascus. Once the Berber army crossed the strait, and after a decisive victory over the Visigothic king Roderic, they took barely three years to complete their conquest. Berbers settled in arid areas that resembled their native Atlas Mountains and intermarried. By the ninth century, Arabic and the local Romance language had replaced Latin. This rapid success is not hard to explain, for Islam espoused religious tolerance, allowing Jews and Christians freedom of worship, and the end of Roman law brought liberty for Iberian slaves. Not least, Visigothic opponents of the Moors were embroiled in divisive conflicts that offered little to the average citizen.

Resistance to Romanization was strongest in the northeast and the northwest.

The one reversal in this astounding military advance was the battle of Covadonga in 718 in the mountains of Asturias, where the Visigothic chieftain Pelayo gave the army of the crescent its first whipping. This Moorish defeat was significant, as it left a chink of non-Muslim territory. Over the next century this expanded to cover all of northern Spain, from where it gradually spread south to culminate in the victory of the Catholic Monarchs (see pp. 30–32).

Al-Andalus & Córdoba

The Arab conquerors and their Berber soldiers adopted as their ruler Abd ar-Rahman of the Ummayad dynasty of Damascus, the successors of Muhammad. Fleeing the overthrow of his family, he arrived in Córdoba in 756 and established the emirate of al-Andalus, covering territory as far as the Pyrenees. Thus began the golden period of Islamic Spain, with Córdoba at its heart. Agriculture diversified and prospered as sophisticated irrigation systems were installed. Rice, saffron, cotton, citrus fruits, figs, and dates were successfully introduced. Scholarly pursuits flourished among the philosophers, scientists, and writers who came to Córdoba from all over the Muslim world, and also among Jews, Christians (known as Mozárabes), and local converts to Islam. This socioreligious tapestry was extended by thousands of slaves brought from eastern and northern Europe and the Sudan, who were able to take on important roles in the ruling classes if they converted to Islam. What could have been a hornets' nest actually fused to create one glorious civilization—that of al-Andalus (see sidebar this page).

Not all was milk and honey in the land of al-Andalus. Sporadic raids were made on the infidels of the north in order to exact taxes and tributes under threat of death. Under the despotic rule of al-Hakem I (*R.*796–822), dissenters were decapitated and violence spiraled. After an intervening period of cultural enrichment, unrest and revolts returned at the turn of the tenth century. Once again, a precarious situation was saved by an enlightened ruler—Abd ar-Rahman III (*R.*912–961), whose red hair and blue eyes were inherited from his Basque (or Frank) mother. Severing all ties with Baghdad, he assumed the title of Caliph in 929, took strategic points in North Africa to preempt territorial threats, and reasserted his military strength against the Christian kingdoms of northern Spain. His palatial complex outside Córdoba, the Madinat al-Zahra (see sidebar p. 291), became another of the glories of al-Andalus.

The Glory of al-Andalus

In some respects the medieval Muslim state of al-Andalus was an embellished version of its Roman precursor. Roman foundations were used to rebuild towns that had crumbled under the Visigoths, but Islamic artistry went far beyond mere restoration. Palaces, fortresses, public baths, schools, mosques, fountains, and gardens of incredible beauty were created. At its zenith in the tenth century, when its population reached 100,000, the city of Córdoba was rivaled only by Constantinople and Baghdad. Even today, the Great Mosque (Mezquita, see pp. 286–287) is unsurpassed in vision.

This great show of strength was followed by a period of dynastic weakness under Hisham II (*R.*976–1013), who relied on his ruthless prime minister, Al-Mansur (*R.*940–1002), to such an extent that the latter even took the caliph's mother as his mistress. Al-Mansur's military ambition knew no bounds either, and León, Barcelona, and Santiago de Compostela all bowed temporarily to his might. By the early 11th century, after Al-Mansur's death, the caliphate had fallen prey to factional conflicts that led, in 1031, to its complete breakup into petty *taifas* (kingdoms), and a new wave of Muslim invaders, the Almoravids, had appeared on the horizon.

The Almoravids were a fanatical dynasty of Muslim Berbers who had established a kingdom with Marrakesh their capital. The taifa rulers invited them to Spain to help combat the increasingly successful Alfonso VI of Castilla y León, who conquered Toledo in 1085. The Almoravid leader, Yusuf, took a liking to al-Andalus. After defeating Alfonso in 1086, he decided to stay, so initiating the next Moorish dynasty.

Yet Moorish dominance over Spain was in decline, and for the next 400 years the Christians of the north took the initiative. Raiding Muslim territory from their castles along the Ebro and Duero Rivers, they gradually extended Christian dominion southward. The Way of St. James pilgrimage route (see pp. 86–87) brought a stream of foreign pilgrims and essential revenue to Spain. This stimulated a network of churches and monasteries, and produced a unifying architectural style—the Romanesque.

Christian Spain of the North

In the band of non-Muslim territories across northern Spain, the easternmost was Catalunya, which Charlemagne had established as a buffer zone against the Moors at the turn of the ninth century. Its five counties were ruled by the Counts of Barcelona under a feudal system that concentrated property in the hands of civil and religious authorities. By the 12th century the Catalan identity had crystallized and its French-influenced language had taken root.

Aragón, too, was developing under its own count, and in the early ninth century became linked with neighboring Navarra through marriage. Under Sancho III (*R.*1005–1035), Navarra attained political preeminence but lost it after his death to Aragón and nascent Castilla. The latter was a newly created independent kingdom ruled by ambitious Fernando I, one of Sancho III's four sons. Castilla absorbed León, and Fernando enthroned one of his brothers as puppet ruler of Navarra. He also made vassals of the Muslim kingdoms of Toledo and Zaragoza. In 1085, Alfonso VI of Castilla y León took the prestigious city of Toledo from the Moors and assumed the title Emperor of the Two Religions—a sign of things to come.

In 1085, Alfonso VI successfully captured the city of Toledo from the Moors.

El Cid was born in the town of Burgos, which honored him with a statue.

Reconquest

As the Almoravids were settling comfortably into Andalusian ways, a revivalist Muslim movement led by the Almohads, from the Atlas Mountains, began to threaten their control. By the mid-12th century the Almohads had moved into al-Andalus, bringing a crusading spirit that recovered Extremadura from the Christians and temporarily halted the Christian advance. Christian forces were disorganized and fraught by dynastic crises, and military challenges to the Almohads were left to King Alfonso I of Aragón. He countered their religious zeal with his own, backed by the newly introduced Knights Templar, an order of soldier-monks founded in 1118 during the First Crusade, and resolved to defeat Islam. Zaragoza was one of several Moorish towns to fall into his net, and when his daughter Petronila married Ramón Berenguer of Barcelona, a solid alliance was created.

A major turning point came in 1212 at the battle of Las Navas de Tolosa, when Castilla's Alfonso VIII trounced the Almohads with help from Aragón, Navarra, and France. Yet nothing was straightforward during this period of warlords, mercenaries, knightly orders, militant monks, and warring princes, and the Reconquest moved into its penultimate stages under three different Christian rulers. In the east, Jaume I of Aragón and Barcelona expanded his territory south to incorporate Valencia, Alicante, and the Balearics by 1238. Meanwhile, Fernando III led the armies of Castilla and León to capture Córdoba, Jaén, and Sevilla. Cádiz and Murcia were swept up by his son, Alfonso X (known as "the Wise" for his intellectual and poetic aptitude). Now all that remained of the taifas was Granada, a kingdom that stretched from Tarifa east to Almería. This period, too, saw the Church peaking in strength and status, represented by the massive Gothic cathedrals of Burgos, Toledo, and León. Parallel to this ecclesiastical power came that of the Knights Templar and the Order of Santiago.

In the 1240s the Nazrids, aristocratic Moors driven south from Zaragoza, replaced the Almohads in Granada and oversaw its cultural zenith, epitomized by their palace at the Alhambra (see pp. 298–299, 302–305). Cunning diplomacy ensured Castilla's protection for Granada, and until the mid-14th century most of the peninsula prospered. In eastern Spain, the *cortes* (chamber of representatives) of Catalunya, Aragón, and Valencia instigated a fair system of civil rights accorded by their king in exchange for allegiance. Mozárabes (Christians from formerly Muslim territory) and Muslims were moved to repopulate newly conquered regions, sometimes provoking social tensions. Large-scale Roman-style estates, or latifundios, were allocated to nobility or given as rewards to military orders and prominent knights (hidalgos). The nefarious latifundio system, where large estates are often run by absentee landlords using low-paid laborers, still endures, mainly in Andalucía.

This was the period of Catalan expansion across the Mediterranean, bringing mercantile prosperity reflected in Barcelona's great 14th-century building boom. In 1348 bubonic plague struck, soon followed by famine. The combination drastically reduced Catalunya's population and, to a lesser extent, those of Aragón, Valencia, and the Balearics. By 1412 Castilla's hegemony was complete, and a branch of its ruling Trastámara family provided a new dynasty for eastern Spain.

Unrest continued into the 15th century. Dynastic wars resulted in outright civil war between supporters of Enrique IV's daughter, Juana, and his sister, Isabel, in 1474. Isabel's greatest ally was her husband, Fernando of Aragón. After winning the Battle of Toro in 1476, their collaborative rule transformed the face of Spain, culminating in the momentous events of 1492. That year saw Christopher Columbus landing in the New World, opening up a completely new chapter in Spanish history. Gold and silver were to pour into the national coffers for centuries, while Catholicism and the Spanish language took over the New World. Equally important, Muslim Granada was conquered by Fernando's army after ten years of sieges and rural devastation. Once Navarra had been annexed, Spain's unification was complete.

El Cid: Hero of the Reconquest?

Unlike many medieval knights of European literature, El Cid—who enjoyed a glowing international reputation—really did exist. Rodrigo Díaz de Vivar (his nickname, El Cid, means "the chief" in Arabic) was born around 1040 near the town of Burgos in Old Castile. Less well known is that he spent most of his life fighting as a mercenary in the wars of Reconquest between Christians and Muslims. In 1094, after several years of conflict, El Cid successfully drove the Moors out of Valencia by siege. He then turned the city into his own virtual fiefdom, giving Muslims and Catholics equal status. His died five years later while defending Valencia against the North African Almoravids. His wife later transported his body back to Burgos to be buried in the cathedral. El Cid's literary monument is an anonymous epic poem of the 12th century in which he features as a romantic, courageous figure, loyal to his king and country. Not quite the case.

Catholic Monarchs

Fernando and Isabel's crusade against the Moors was heavily financed by the Church. In return they instigated a long period of religious intolerance. Jews and Muslims were offered the choice of conversion or exile, but converts could still suffer persecution. Confiscated properties were given to nobility, military orders, and town councils. Mosques and synagogues were demolished and rebuilt as churches, and the Inquisition (introduced in 1478) became the central instrument of Catholic and monarchical power using torture and autos-da-fé (burning at the stake).

Culturally Spain prospered, producing an impressive line of Renaissance artists and dramatists.

Fernando and Isabel also expanded their overseas territories. Naples fell to their greatest general, Gonzalo Fernández de Córdoba (known as El Gran Capitán), and Christopher Columbus's pioneering voyage across the Atlantic began to reap rich rewards. Although gold was the chief attraction of the Americas, the conversion of native peoples to Christianity earned Fernando and Isabel the title of Los Reyes Católicos (The Catholic Monarchs) from the Pope himself, a Spaniard of the Borgia family. Apart from this spiritual justification, the Spaniards were also aided by the Castilian language in their expansionism: It had been codified into Europe's first vernacular grammar and became the lingua franca of the Americas. As the conquistadores extended their New World net, indigenous peoples fell before them—prey to Old World diseases and to the sword.

Isabel's death in 1504 announced a completely new twist in Spanish history. Fernando reigned until his death in 1516, by which time his grandson, Carlos, was old enough to inherit the crown. When Flemish-born Carlos I (*R.* 1516–1556) arrived on Spanish soil in 1517, he faced a country wracked by disastrous harvests, plague, and widespread social discontent. Speaking no Castilian, this young Habsburg king was far from ready to manage the complex and disorderly society he had inherited. Yet a new era had begun.

Habsburgs & the Golden Age

The Habsburg dynasty ruled Spain for nearly 200 years. Their monarchs presided over the arrival of untold amounts of bullion from the Americas and ruled Europe's largest empire since that of Charlemagne, but the term "Golden Age" is questionable. Culturally Spain prospered, producing an impressive line of Renaissance artists and dramatists. Politically, however, it was another story. Two years after acceding to the Spanish throne, Carlos inherited the Holy Roman Empire through his father. As Carlos V (Charles V), he ruled a large part of northern Europe, in addition to Spain and the Americas—an unwieldy but unrivaled empire. His loyalties were divided, and regional *cortes* had to lobby intensely to obtain recognition and funds. Insurrections and revolts, notably those of the Castilian *comuneros* and Valencian and Mallorcan *agermanats* (brotherhoods), were brutally crushed by Carlos's German troops. He nonetheless provided Ferdinand Magellan with ships for the first circumnavigation of the globe and dealt successfully with invasion by France. His marriage to Isabel of Portugal brought further wealth to the Spanish Crown and an able replacement during his absences abroad. However, in 1556, weary of the worries of his vast empire, Carlos V abdicated and retired to the monastery of Yuste, in Extremadura (see p. 247). He left a virtually bankrupt kingdom to his son.

Felipe II (Philip II, *R.*1556–1598), fanatically religious and highly cultivated, intensified the Inquisition's activities from his palace-monastery, El Escorial (see pp. 77–79). Heretics were killed in spectacular autos-da-fé. Felipe II won an important naval victory over the Turks in 1571, and in 1588 he sent the Armada to invade Protestant England. When the Spanish fleet suffered catastrophic losses, it lost all international credibility.

Under Felipe III (*R.* 1598–1621), the last 275,000 Moors were expelled from Valencia, a move that ruined local agriculture. This ruthlessness was echoed in Spain's New World activities, where indigenous populations were virtually wiped out by disease and slavery.

Christopher Columbus first sighted Cuba in October 1492.

Felipe IV (*R.* 1621–1665) appeared only slightly more in control than his easily manipulated father. He was an astute patron of the arts, however. Despite his reformist tendencies, his reign saw increasing internal dissent, the loss of Portugal, and the defeats of the Thirty Years War, culminating in the independence of the Netherlands in 1648. Spain's loss of prestige was underlined in the reign of the last and most degenerate Habsburg king, Carlos II (*R.* 1665–1700), whose 35-year rule saw further territorial losses. Spain became an economic wasteland: Once thriving and densely populated Castilla was a bankrupt desert. The only element still to prosper was the Church, and the heavily gilded baroque altarpieces of the time bear witness to its immense wealth.

War of Spanish Succession

Carlos II died childless, but he had appointed an heir: Philippe Bourbon, grandson of his sister María Teresa and the French king Louis XIV. In 1701 this French

17-year-old entered Madrid as Felipe V. However, northern Europe and England supported his rival, the Austrian archduke Charles, and joined Catalunya, Aragón, and Valencia in the 12-year-long War of Succession. England eventually accepted the Bourbon king when it was given Gibraltar (still a thorny point in Anglo-Spanish relations) and Menorca. Stimulated by childhood memories of Versailles, Felipe V (*R.* 1701–1746) spent much of his long reign building sumptuous French-style palaces, a habit continued by more enlightened Carlos III (*R.* 1759–1788).

Other than reveling in baroque artistry, Carlos III continued a centralizing tendency instigated by Felipe V. Steadily, Spain regained its lost prosperity, agriculture recovered, coastal trading companies thrived, and the population expanded. A significant economic move was the Free Trade Act (1778) for the American colonies. Although bread riots ignited Spain in the 1760s, Carlos III found a scapegoat in the Jesuits, who were expelled in 1766. His great love for the arts was expressed by the building of the Prado Museum (see pp. 60–64), Palacio Real (see pp. 54–55), and San Ildefonso de la Granja (see p. 226), near Segovia, monuments to the final moments of an all-powerful monarchy.

War of Spanish Independence

Weak and indifferent, Carlos IV (*R.* 1788–1808) left governing to his wife, María Luisa, and her adviser Don Manuel Godoy. Spain soon found itself enmeshed in the aftermath of the French Revolution. Catapulted into war with Britain, France's arch rival, Spain tumbled into defeat at the sea battle of Trafalgar (1805). On land,

Felipe II's fascination for science and astronomy is well represented by the Armillary Sphere.

Armillary Sphere

In 1582, Antonio Santucci produced an armillary sphere for Felipe II, one of Spain's most intellectual and concerned kings. This ingenious invention, also known as an astrolabe, is an openwork celestial globe showing the solar system according to Ptolemy, the second-century Greek astronomer. The framework of graduated brass rings represents the main circles of the solar system, with the Earth at its center. The earliest Greek armillary sphere is thought to date from the third century B.C., although the Chinese developed something similar even before that. The medieval Islamic world produced improved versions from the eighth century which came to Spain via al-Andalus, in the tenth century.

however, Napoleon was carrying the day. In 1808 he engineered the abdication of Carlos IV and put his own brother Joseph (José I) on the throne. By now the people of Spain had had enough, and the Madrid uprising of May 2 ignited Spain's five-year War of Independence against Napoleon (the Peninsular War).

This produced Spain's first popular united front against a common enemy. Peasant guerrilla fighters played a major role, fragmenting the Napoleonic armies and their supply systems. Guerrillas also cooperated with Spain's former enemies, the British, led by the Duke of Wellington, whose many victories culminated in the Battle of Vitoria in 1813. As a result, José I fled to France. The Spanish crown jewels and Spain's infrastructure lay in ruins, devastated by both French and British troops.

Carlist Wars

In 1812 the *cortes* of Cádiz had worked out the new, liberal Constitution of Cádiz, investing power in a democratically elected chamber. This was soon canceled when despotic Fernando VII (son of Carlos IV) took the throne. As Spain sank yet again under the whims of its king, its American colonies won independence. In 1820 the Constitution of Cádiz was temporarily revived, but a massive French army came to help the king suppress it. On his death in 1833, civil war broke out (the First Carlist War) between supporters of his conservative brother, Carlos, and the liberal promoters of his young daughter, the Infanta Isabel. Isabel's camp won, but her reign (1843–1868) was a troubled one, plagued by successive crises, including the Second Carlist War. In 1874, with Isabel's son Alfonso XII in the driver's seat, the army was assuming increasing power. As a result, Spain's oppressed workers began to organize themselves into trade unions. This was the germination of social conflicts that, around 60 years later, resulted in the rule of the dictator, General Francisco Franco.

Social Transformations

In the late 19th century and early 20th century, Spain experienced a period of relative calm and prosperity. Yet in 1898 its last overseas possessions were lost to the United States (Puerto Rico, the Philippines, and Cuba), and famines wracked Galicia and the south. Huge numbers emigrated: 1.5 million moved to Latin America between 1886 and 1913. The demographic face of the country was changing with a drift to the cities, although Catalunya, Euskadi, and Asturias were the only truly industrialized regions. Ideological differences and regional variations in wealth became

The British fleet's triumph at the 1805 Battle of Trafalgar ran parallel to Napoleon's victories on land, leaving Spain caught between the two rival powers.

more marked, and more than half the population was illiterate. Although the 20th century started with a dazzling cultural renaissance, this was limited to a tiny section of society—the majority languished in poverty.

Barcelona had seen workers' unrest in the mid-19th century, and by the 1880s both here and Andalucía were home to well-entrenched anarchist movements. Marxist Socialism made advances in Madrid, where the PSOE (Socialist Party) was born in 1888. After winning its first parliamentary seat in 1910, it widened its membership in the industrialized north. During World War I Spain remained neutral, and its industry profited for a while from exports to both sides, but in 1917 recession and a draining war in Morocco helped fuel a momentous general strike, which was violently repressed. In 1923 further social unrest caused General Miguel Primo de Rivera to stage a military coup, in cooperation with the incompetent king Alfonso XIII. This led to a military

dictatorship until world depression precipitated the general's resignation in 1930. Within two years, antimonarchist forces won a resounding success in municipal elections, and hapless Alfonso XIII went into exile. He died in Rome in 1941.

Second Republic & Civil War

Euphoria greeted the establishment of the Second Republic on April 14, 1931. At last, Spain was falling into step with democratic movements elsewhere. A new Republican government led by Manuel Azaña soon introduced land reform and civil marriage among other sweeping changes, but political loyalties were becoming dangerously polarized between extreme Republicanism and extreme conservatism. The Church, army, and landowners still wielded enormous economic power. As Socialists, Anarchists, Radicals, and Marxists bickered among themselves, their opponents became organized around the Falange, a fascist youth movement founded by José Antonio Primo de Rivera (son of the dictator). Elections in 1933 gave power to the Right—the Falange and the Monarchists—who revealed their true nature the following year in the bloody suppression of a miners' uprising in Asturias. General Franco's troops killed 3,000 workers.

By 1936, Spain was spiraling into chaos with almost daily assassinations, riots, militia attacks on churches, strikes, and seizures of estates. When victory in the election was won by the leftist Popular Front, it took only five months for the army's response. In July 1936, Franco's troops were airlifted from their garrisons in Morocco by German transport planes and dropped into Spain. The Civil War had begun.

Spain's Civil War was the bloodiest, most tragic period the country ever lived through.

Spain's Civil War was the bloodiest, most tragic period the country ever lived through. It divided families, devastated the countryside, ruined the infrastructure, and left half a million dead and millions starving. Helped by Moroccan mercenaries, Franco's Nationalist army rapidly won control of eastern Andalucía, Extremadura, and Castilla, but it was rebuffed by Madrid, the east, and the north, where Republican sympathies and forces were strongest. Proclaimed Generalísimo of the armed forces and head of state in Burgos, a city with well-entrenched conservative traditions, Franco soon received massive assistance from his Fascist allies in Europe: Germany, Italy, and Portugal. Meanwhile the Republicans received help only from the Soviet Union. Governments of western democracies such as Britain and France did nothing, although about 35,000 foreign volunteers, including George Orwell, Ernest Hemingway, André Malraux, and Willy Brandt, fought for the Republicans with the International Brigade.

The Republicans could not compete with the size and resources of the opposing forces, epitomized by the merciless bombing of Gernika (Guernica) by German planes in 1937. Self-destructive rivalries also existed between Anarchists and Communists within the Republican ranks. All this contributed to the capitulation of the north, and when Franco's offensive in southern Aragón reached the Mediterranean, the Republican forces in the east were divided. In early 1939 Barcelona fell, finally followed by Madrid and Valencia. The game was over, and the Generalísimo took up the reins of power on April 1.

General Franco

Social order and uncontested political authority were the priorities of Spain's new ruler. Franco used firing squads, labor camps, and civic ostracism to quell opposition, and the old adage of "convert or be exiled," used against Jews and Moors centuries before, was now reapplied to other sectors. Many intellectuals fled, about 7,000 teachers were executed, and schoolbooks were rewritten. At the end of World War II, during which Spain remained neutral, Franco was the only Fascist dictator left, ruling over a politically and economically isolated country. Any opposition was quashed, censorship was enforced, and the powers of the Catholic church were restored. Divorce became illegal, church weddings were obligatory, and the confessor was invoked as the ultimate adviser in reading matter.

After Franco, Prime Minister Adolfo Suárez helped restore democracy in Spain.

Change came in the 1950s, when Franco received General Eisenhower and agreed to host American military bases in exchange for massive loans. This opened the floodgates, giving Spain a mask of acceptability, stimulating the economy and propelling Spain into world institutions such as the United Nations (1955). Franco invested in roads, electricity plants, apartment blocks for workers, and other infrastructure. Mass tourism arrived and a booming market economy developed, steered by a new breed of technocrats. Yet this overt prosperity had a flip side: Andalusian peasants worked in miserable conditions, workers continued to flood from the land to the cities and abroad, and political and intellectual repression continued, above all in Catalunya and the País Vasco. Clandestine groups and unions worked behind the scenes, and the Basque separatist group Euskadi Ta Askatasuna (ETA) emerged. In 1973 Franco's expected successor, Admiral Carrero Blanco, was killed by an ETA bomb.

Pacto de Olvido

Long after the Spanish Civil War ended, false allegations and grudges between neighbors and within families continued to fuel conflict. On top of the estimated 365,000 people who died during the Civil War, an additional 50,000–100,000 Republicans were executed or died in prison in the postwar period. Some of them were convicts who had been used to build the infamous Valle de los Caídos memorial, where both Franco and Primo de Rivera, founder of the Falange, are buried. In order to smooth the transition to democracy after Franco's death, the truth was swept under the carpet in an unwritten agreement known as the Pacto de Olvido (Pact of Forgetting).

In the early 2000s, however, family associations began to investigate the deaths of Franco's victims. In 2006, to mark the 70th anniversary of Franco's coup, Zapatero's government passed the "law of historical memory," which allowed previously closed archives to be opened up. Today the pursuit of truth remains a fraught field: Spain's best-known judge, Baltasar Garzón, who led the investigation, was suspended in 2010.

After Franco

When Franco died in 1975, a grandson of Alfonso XIII was crowned King Juan Carlos I. Franco had chosen him as successor partly because he thought that Juan Carlos was a malleable character. He was wrong, and the new king rapidly set about restoring democracy through his prime minister, Adolfo Suárez. Political parties and trade unions were recognized, censorship was lifted, and the 1977 elections brought Suárez and his Christian-Democrat Party to power. With a new, ultra-liberal constitution, parliament set about undoing the knots of Castilian centralism and granting autonomy to the regions. A law of amnesty protected both sides of the conflict.

In 1981, the government survived an attempted military coup thanks to Juan Carlos's firm stand. The following year, Spain entered a new era with the electoral victory of the PSOE (Socialist Party). This brought the youthful and charismatic Felipe González to power and initiated a frenetically optimistic period when anything and everything seemed possible. Advances on every level brought stability, pride, and dynamism, crowned by Spain's entry into the European Economic Community in 1986. European subsidies transformed the country. In 1992 (500 years after Columbus first set foot in the New World), the Olympics were held in Barcelona, Sevilla hosted Expo 92, and Madrid was designated a cultural capital of Europe. Spain's fortunes seemed to be on a roll.

Nothing and nobody is perfect, however, and corruption finally brought down the Socialist government after 14 years in power. José María Aznar's Partido Popular (center-right) was elected in 1996 and survived two terms. Elections in 2004 brought a massive unexpected rejection of Aznar's pro–Iraq War policies and autocratic attitude. He was out, and in came José Luis Rodriguez Zapatero as Socialist prime minister, who rapidly withdrew Spanish troops from Iraq.

In November 2011, as Spain's economy nose-dived further, general elections brought a resounding victory to 56-year-old Mariano Rajoy of the P.P. (Partido Popular), a cautious, uncharismatic conservative. His task is daunting: Huge hurdles, such as endemic corruption and the global credit squeeze, remain. Yet Spain has gained a high standard of living, cultural dynamism, slick city centers, and a viable federal system. ■

The Arts

Spain's art history, one of the oldest in Europe, goes back to the early Stone Age, when hunters started painting on the walls of their caves, but it was to take another 17,000 years for a truly Hispanic style of painting to emerge. Architecture and film are the other major fields of Spanish creative genius.

Painting, Sculpture, & Architecture

The earliest art in Spain probably had a ritualistic role for the Paleolithic hunter-gatherers who painted polychrome bison, wild boars, wolves, horses, and deer with amazing anatomical precision on the walls of their Cantabrian caves. These cave paintings, notably at Altamira, date from 15,000 to 8500 B.C. Later prehistoric art takes the form of copper idol plaques from the fortified settlement of Los Millares, near Almería. Spain's oldest constructions are the megaliths (huge stone monuments) of the Balearics and the dolmens (stone tombs) of Antequera (circa 2500 B.C.).

Nowhere else in Europe had such a wealth of distinctive cultures contributed to artistic development.

Iberian Art: The growth of gold, silver, lead, and tin mines in the Andalusian kingdom of Tartessos, and the subsequent arrival of Phoenician and Greek traders, sparked the next stage in the peninsula's iconography. Sculpture (carved limestone and bronze figurines) is the only relic of the Iberian civilization in central and southern Spain, as the Punic Wars between Carthage and Rome devastated most architectural structures. The most outstanding Iberian works of art are "La Dama de Elche" (sixth–fifth century B.C.), a beautiful bust of a serene, bejeweled lady, and the full-length, seated "La Dama de Baza." Important ceramics, too, have survived the ravages of time. Although influenced by the Greeks, Iberians found their own inventive style of abstract, zoomorphic, or anthropomorphic designs painted on crudely shaped vessels. In the north, Celtiberians produced the magnificent gold jewelry unearthed in Galicia's *castros* (fortified villages).

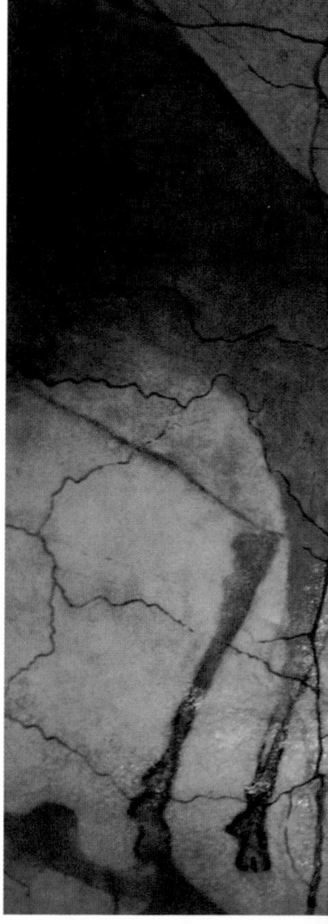

Roman Classicism: Five hundred years of Roman rule steered Hispanic art and architecture into an entirely new phase. Urban design became paramount. Towns centered on the forum (marketplace), around which stood the theater, amphitheater, and temples. The elite lived in magnificently decorated villas where mosaic panels, marble colonnades, and statues created dramatic backdrops. Busts of emperors, magistrates, and governors reflected a taste for realism rather than stylization. At this period in history, Spain was unique. Nowhere else in Europe had such a wealth of distinctive cultures contributed to artistic development.

Visigoths: From the fifth century A.D., the Visigoths introduced their nomadic Scandinavian culture, while southern Spain underwent a century of Byzantine domination (522–621). Outstanding Visigothic craftsmanship is seen in gold- and silverwork of royal crowns and offerings in dignitaries' tombs.

Otherwise all that remains of their 300-year presence in the peninsula is the embryonic structures of Christianity: The seventh-century hermitage of Quintanilla de las

Prehistoric paintings of animals cover the walls of the Altamira caves.

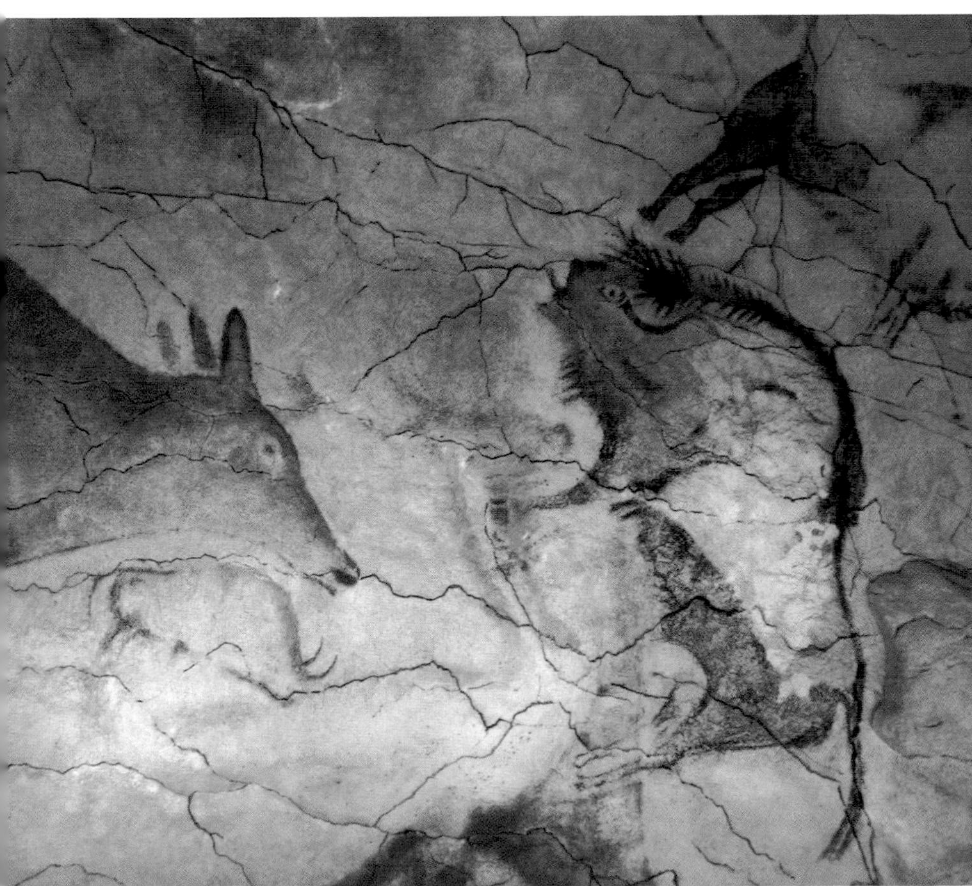

Horseshoe arches typify Islamic architecture in Spain.

Viñas in northern Castilla has primitive, schematized reliefs in carved friezes, and capitals salvaged elsewhere show stylized figures and birds beside floral motifs. This was a far cry from the classical realism of the Romans, and decorative abstraction continued to dominate Spanish art until the flowering of the Romanesque period.

Pre-Romanesque architecture in Asturias, the only kingdom not conquered by Muslims, represents a more sophisticated period before the Romanesque style was imported from France. Soaring barrel vaults, horseshoe arches, ashlar (square-cut stone facings), and illusionist murals were developed in a wide network of surprisingly lavish churches.

Moorish Style: Andalucía, above all, fell under the most concentrated Islamic influence. Fortresses *(alcazabas)*, palaces *(alcázares)*, and mosques *(mezquitas)* became the landmarks of al-Andalus, culminating in Granada's dream-like Alhambra (see pp. 298–299, 302–305). Earlier Islamic legacies date from Córdoba's golden age in the 9th–11th centuries. The spectacularly complex Mezquita (Great Mosque, see pp. 286–287, 290), representing paradise and the holy city, and the caliph's palace (see p. 291) incorporated calligraphic stucco friezes; geometric patterns of brick, stone, and marble; and intricately intertwined plant motifs. Since Islam forbids representation of humans (with some notable exceptions), craftsmen channeled all their imaginative effort into these finely executed embellishments.

Horseshoe arches, cupolas, blind arches, and tracery were the most lasting structural elements, but art evolved considerably during the 700-year Moorish occupation. An early taste for decorative details came from Syria. The later Almoravids and Almohads were more conservative but nonetheless introduced multicolored *azulejos* (tiles) and the techniques of *artesonado* (intricately carved ceilings; see sidebar opposite). Palaces and houses were built around patios (courtyards), an intelligent response to the climate that continues today: Wealthier families escape the heat by living on the lower floors in the summer, then moving upstairs in winter to catch the available sun. Palace gardens had water and fragrant flowers and plants. In all this, the Alhambra represents the zenith of Moorish style, combining unparalleled decorative mastery with perspective and sensuality.

Mozarabic & Mudejar: As the Christians of the north extended their territory south during the Reconquest (see pp. 30–31), their taste was influenced by Mozarabic emigrants—Christians who had lived under Arab rule and who learned Arab techniques and forms. Even after Moorish territories had been conquered and their mosques demolished, talented Moorish artisans continued to work for Christian masters. This was the origin of the Mudejar style, whose enduring influence on Hispanic art cannot be overestimated. Among its creations were Aragón's intricate brick and ceramic towers, Sevilla's Reales Alcázares (see pp. 265–267)—an indulgence of carved wood, stucco, and tilework—and the Gothic Mudejar of Toledo's towers and churches. Synagogues, too, were designed by Mudejar craftsmen, and the three that survive in Toledo and Córdoba are a unique conjunction of Hebrew calligraphy with Arab artistry. Mudejar was a profusely decorative style, and from it emerged an aversion to unadorned space that dominated Spanish art for the following centuries. In architecture, Mudejar forms continued in bullrings and railway stations right up to the beginning of the 20th century.

Romanesque: While the Moors were covering walls and arches in stucco and azulejos, Christian Spain was building its own masterpieces in the north: Romanesque structures designed to inspire every pilgrim who set foot on the long road to Santiago de Compostela (see pp. 88–91). From the mid-11th century, French and Italian religious orders set up monasteries and churches, and their artistic forms soon dominated northern Spain. Yet Spain, as usual, distinguished itself from the rest of Europe, as Visigothic and Moorish influences both played their role. In Catalunya, the Lombards from Italy were another influence, introducing sobriety of form and lofty bell towers.

The cathedral of Santiago de Compostela (see pp. 88–89) retains its original soaring nave, superb reliefs on the Puerta de las Platerías (circa 1100), and, above all, the sculptor Mateo's masterpiece, the high-relief statues of the Pórtico de la Gloria (1188). A few years earlier, an equally magnificent portal was created at the Catalan monastery of Ripoll as a visual Bible for the illiterate. This teaching-through-pictures produced beautifully decorated capitals, cloisters, and portals: Wonderful examples exist

Artesonado

A recurring architectural trademark of Mudejar craftsmen is the *artesonado* (coffered) timber ceiling, carved and inlaid with intricate geometric patterning. Although the remaining Moors had been deported from Spain in the early 17th century, their skills had been absorbed into the Spanish architectural tradition. The prototype of this element is the early 14th-century Salon de Embajadores ceiling in the Nazrid Palace of Granada's Alhambra (see pp. 298–299, 302–305). Other examples can be seen in Sevilla's Alcázar (see pp. 265–267), Zaragoza's Palacio de la Aljafería (see pp. 141–142), and Toledo's Monasterio de San Juan de los Reyes (see p. 240), built in 1478 to commemorate Spain's victory at the Battle of Toro.

Gothic Funerary Sculpture

Like architecture, Gothic sculpture abandoned Romanesque purity in favor of more refined detail such as greater relief and more naturalism in poses and facial features. In terms of funerary art, this change brought more accurate memorials to the dead. With lifelike, individualized features, the sculptures were often moving portraits of the deceased. Skilled artisans, who favored stone, marble, and alabaster, depicted recumbent figures often surrounded by detailed reliefs depicting the funeral or an imaginary ascent to Heaven. By the 15th century, when Flemish artistic influences had replaced Burgundian influences from France, a clear Hispano-Flemish style had developed.

in Girona, Santo Domingo de los Silos, Tarragona, San Juan de la Peña, Sangüesa, Leyre, and Santillana del Mar. The tradition of altar sculptures carved in wood and painted endures in the highly realist *pasos* (floats) of Holy Week processions (see pp. 272–273).

Other forms of Spanish Romanesque art are altarpieces and the dynamic, richly colored frescoes in churches such as San Isidoro in León. Examples from Catalunya's remote parish churches are shown in the museums of Barcelona, Vic, and Jaca. Change came when reforming Cistercian monks brought a taste for austerity and an end to ornate capitals and portals groaning with apostles. Instead huge monastic complexes devoted to prayer and work arose, such as Poblet (see p. 192), Santes Creus (see pp. 192–193), and Santa María de Huerta (see p. 151). Secular constructions of the time multiplied in the frontier castles of Castilla and towns with narrow winding streets, such as Besalú.

Gothic: By the 13th century, the Gothic was making inroads. This was not just an artistic fashion, but represented a new perception of life in which spirituality and culture were transferred from monastic complexes to medieval cities centered on their cathedrals. The three naves of the Romanesque period became one, and the use of stronger pointed arches rather than round ones meant that walls could rise to increasingly lofty ceilings and domes. Many cathedrals bridged these two major medieval styles, but the undisputed stars are the 13th-century cathedrals of León, Burgos, and Toledo, which has a marked Moorish influence.

By the following century the building craze had shifted eastward, producing the great cathedrals of Barcelona, Girona, Palma de Mallorca, and Valencia. As the 14th century gave way to the 15th, Gothic architecture acquired the flowery ornamentation known as Flamboyant Gothic. Two main schools developed. The first, in Toledo, was headed by Juan Guas, who designed San Juan de los Reyes. The second, in Burgos, was led by Juan de Colonia and his son, Simón, who was responsible for the lacelike facade of San Pablo in Valladolid. These examples of the Isabelline style crowned the 15th century, combining the height of Flamboyant Gothic with early Renaissance elements.

By the late 15th century Spanish art had fallen under the sway of Flemish naturalism, a style of remarkably expressive precision. The Catalan Jaume Huguet (circa 1415–1492) was one of its greatest exponents. In sculpture, Gil de Siloé and Pere Joan, respectively, led the Castilian and Aragonese schools. *Retablos* (altarpieces) became towering painted panels with bas-reliefs, wooden sculptures, and heavily gilded frames—Spain's were the most elaborate of their kind in Europe.

Renaissance: With the end of the Reconquest (see pp. 30–31) in 1492, the door closed on medieval Spain and opened to a new philosophy of life—the Renaissance. Scientific discovery and voyages to the New World transformed ideas, and people turned to ancient Greece and Rome for inspiration. Plateresque (meaning "resembling silversmith's work") facades displayed delicate, filigreelike reliefs, best exemplified in Salamanca's superb university facade and Toledo's Santa Cruz hospice. Greater use was made of Renaissance elements from Italy, such as gargoyles, pilasters, and medallions. Diego de Siloé in Burgos, Alonso de Covarrubias of Toledo, and Gil de Hontañón in Salamanca represented the more restrained Renaissance style that emerged in the 1520s, crowned by Pedro Machuca's palace of Carlos V (1526) in Granada, the purest Italianate building in Spain. In the reconquered lands Renaissance mansions mushroomed, with large concentrations in Úbeda and Baeza.

The overriding characteristic of the Gothic style is an abundance of detail.

The Italian aesthetic also came to dominate painting and sculpture. Pedro Berruguete (1450–1504), Juan de Borgoña (1470–1536), and Juan de Juanes (much influenced by Raphael) led the field in painting. In sculpture prolific Damián Forment (circa 1480–1540) bridged the Isabelline-Renaissance period with spectacular altarpieces. Alonso de Berruguete's obsession with dramatic realism anticipated the baroque period, as did the Valladolid-based Frenchman, Juan de Juni (died 1577). One great difference between Italian and Spanish art of the Renaissance stems from simple economics. The Inquisition imposed a 10 percent tax on any work without a religious message, which partly explains the preponderance of saintly and monastic subjects in Spanish art before 1783.

By the late 16th century, Felipe II's patronage of the arts had brought many Italian and Flemish artists to Spain. Domenikos Theotokopoulos, or El Greco—The Greek—arrived in Spain in 1577. His free brushstrokes did not meet with royal approval, forcing him to retreat to Toledo to work on ecclesiastical commissions. Architecture was dominated by Juan de Herrera (1530–1597), whose austere masterpiece, El Escorial (see pp. 77–79), foreshadowed the next century.

Baroque & the Golden Age: The 17th century saw a profusion of civic building, such as Madrid's Plaza Mayor, but it took several decades for Spain to embrace baroque. Exuberant Spanish baroque architecture (Churrigueresque) was named after José de Churriguera (1665–1725) and his brothers, Joaquín and Alberto, although another major protagonist was Pedro de Ribera (1683–1742). Andalucía has abundant Churrigueresque works because Sevilla was the arrival point for the riches of the New World. The Granadino architect, sculptor, and painter Alonso Cano laid the foundation for a new school of three-dimensional work. His pupil Pedro de Mena (1628–1688) created the period's most emotionally expressive sculptures, and in Castilla, Gregorio Hernández (1566–1636) became the master of depicting pain and sorrow. Baroque gilding, salomonic columns (twisted and entwined), and inverted pilasters proliferated in a climax of creative delirium.

Andalucía has abundant Churrigueresque works because Sevilla was the arrival point for the riches of the New World.

The greatest genius of this Golden Age of Spanish art was the painter Diego Velázquez (1599–1660), who emerged from the Sevillian school of Francisco Pacheco (1564–1654). From still lifes and genre paintings his work matured into courtly portraits and royal themes, before reaching its apogee with "Las Meninas" ("The Maids of Honor") and "Las Hilanderas" ("The Spinners"). Master of optical illusions, color, and subtle psychological insights, Velázquez shared the limelight with his contemporaries, the Extremaduran Francisco Zurbarán (1598–1664) and the Valencians Francisco Ribalta (1565–1628) and José de Ribera (1591–1652). Ribalta introduced tenebrism (contrasting light and shadow) to Spain, and Ribera took powerful realism to his adopted Naples. Zurbarán's portraits of monks are unsurpassed in their sobriety of composition, compelling the spectator to focus on the subjects' spiritual passion and personality. Sevilla's other great baroque painters were Juan Valdés Leal (1622–1690) and Bartolomé Esteban Murillo (1617–1682), who respectively produced images of the vanity of the world and diaphanous renderings of beatific Virgins surrounded by cherubim.

In the early 20th century, the work of Pablo Picasso rose to the forefront of Spanish modern art.

18th & 19th Centuries: Excessive ornamentation characterized the French rococo style that dominated the early 18th century, visible in the palaces of the new Bourbon kings at La Granja, Aranjuez, and Madrid. Inevitably, reaction set in: Reason and moderation soon became the ideals of the newly established Academia de Bellas Artes (1752), ushering in the more controlled and sober neoclassic period. In architecture, this was exemplified by Ventura Rodríguez and by Juan de Villanueva, who designed the Prado. In painting, after a period of cold, elegant portraiture, Francisco de Goya (1746–1828) rebelled against neoclassic constraints and developed a style of expressive brushstrokes to depict character and emotions in earthy tones, whether in his later series of "black paintings" stemming from personal depression, or in his vivid portraits and acerbic political commentaries.

Once the 19th century was in full swing, Goya's influence became apparent as the cult of reason was replaced by the notion of human freedom. A stream of academic painters embraced the melodrama of Romanticism, producing often kitsch scenes from Spanish history and *costumbrismo* (depiction of local life and customs). It was only by the start of the 20th century that Spain was belatedly noticing French Impressionism.

20th-Century Modernism: Catalunya's Modernista movement knocked down the barriers of conservatism. Nevertheless, Spain was resistant to the revolution in art (modernism) that was sweeping Europe, despite being the source of some of its greatest protagonists. Pablo Picasso (1881–1973), a native of Málaga, but brought up in Barcelona before moving to Paris, was unquestionably the figurehead, and in later years he used early Spanish art as inspiration. Another Spanish cubist, Juan Gris (1887–1927) worked with Picasso in Paris. Joan Miró (1893–1983) remained faithful to Catalunya and Mallorca, despite international acclaim for his spontaneous, poetic abstraction. This derived from experiments with surrealism, but the latter movement's most colorful Hispanic representative was Salvador Dalí (see pp. 184–185). In both life and artifice, Dalí perfectly exemplified surrealism's obsession with the irrational. In contrast, sculptors such as Pablo Gargallo, Alberto Sánchez, and Julio González excelled in a more sober, abstract field.

For two decades after World War II, abstract expressionism dominated art in Spain. By the more prosperous 1960s, this was led by a rebellious artists' collective known as El Paso, out of which emerged the powerful gestural works of Antonio Saura and the highly influential canvasses of Antoni Tàpies. Subtle color, geometric symbols, and the incorporation of other media (sand, wax) became the hallmarks of the Tàpies school. Its counterpoint was the pop art of Equipo Crónica and the bold narratives of Eduardo Arroyo. Bridging the two was the work of Tàpies's cousin Modest Cuixart (1925–2007). At the same time the purist geometric sculptures of Eduardo Chillida (1924–2002) became virtually the "official" art of his native Basque country. Today the Mallorcan Miguel Barceló produces whimsical, mixed-media paintings as well as large-scale, site-specific works. Susana Solano, Txomin Badiola, Cristina Iglesias, José María Sicilia, Jaume Plensa, Juan Uslé, and Juan Muñoz have all acquired international profiles.

In architecture, style nosedived during the Franco era (other than isolated examples of Josep Luis Sert's modernism). With the return of democracy, Spanish architecture boomed, and Spain is now arguably the European country with the greatest number of civic buildings of quality, beauty, and imagination. Santiago Calatrava is feted for gravity-defying feats of engineering including Valencia's showcase structures, while Pritzker Prize–winner Rafael Moneo is the creator of sensitive, functional, streamlined buildings that are the perfect symbols of this Spanish renaissance and an inspiration to the younger generation.

A flamenco group usually includes a guitarist, singer, hand-clapper, and male and female dancers.

EXPERIENCE: Sport, the Other Art

Eager to catch some of Spain's sporting fever? If cycling is your thing, consider a visit that coincides with the Vuelta a España *(www.lavuelta.com)*, one of the most important bike races in the world. Held annually in mid-August to early September, La Vuelta is a three-week competition involving time trials, road races, and mountain climbs. Spaniard Carlos Sastre is a recent champ.

Spanish spirits are highest—and most deafening—on the football (soccer) pitch, particularly when the match concerns the big rivals at the top of the league, Barcelona *(www.fcbarcelona.com)* and Real Madrid *(www.realmadrid.com)*. If you can, reserve a ticket for a big match to savor one of Spain's greatest passions. The season runs from early August to mid-May, with a short break in December–January.

Music

Perceived as the quintessential music of Spain, flamenco (see pp. 288–289), in fact, has Gypsy, Arab, and Jewish roots. Before this, Spanish music evolved from polyphonic chants of the early Middle Ages, and reached a high point during the Renaissance, when instruments such as the guitar (*vihuela,* with five strings rather than the modern six) proliferated. This distinctive style faded as northern European music became more influential, but a present-day group of musicians called Mudéjar have resurrected its unique sounds and instruments. For centuries, the main forms of homegrown music remained popular ballads and the zarzuela, a form of musical play invented by Pedro Calderón de la Barca in the 17th century. However, Spanish music rebounded under the aegis of composers such as Isaac Albeñiz (1860–1909) and Enrique Granados (1867–1916). Manuel de Falla (1876–1946) represented the psychological duality of Spain with *Nights in the Gardens of Spain:* introspection punctuated by violent outbursts. A still more popular classic is Joaquín Rodrigo's (1901–1999) *Concierto de Aranjuez.*

Spain has produced some of the world's top guitar-players, including the classical performer Andrés Segovia and the flamenco artists Paco Peña and Paco de Lucía. The late Pablo Casals took cello playing to its zenith. Many world renowned opera singers are Spanish: Plácido Domingo, José Carreras, Teresa Braganza, Victoria de los Ángeles, Alfredo Kraus, and Montserrat Caballé. On a lighter note, Julio Iglesias and his son, Enrique, have become household names. Flamenco-rock (see pp. 288–289) and fusion are flourishing with a stream of new talent, and Galician-Celtic groups are also popular; lack of world status is due more to undeveloped marketing than to absence of talent. One big exception is Manu Chao, a musical revolutionary whose first solo album, *Clandestino* (1998), sold five million copies worldwide.

Theater & Literature

Early playwrights Lope de Vega (1562–1635) and Calderón de la Barca (1600–1681) brilliantly mirrored the exploits and optimism of Spain's Golden Age, and Miguel de Cervantes created its universal protagonist, Don Quixote (see pp. 248–249). In theater, Catalunya has always led the way: Barcelona's Teatre Principal was founded in 1603, Frederic Soler created modern Catalan theater, and the 1960s saw political avant-garde productions. Extreme participative form has been perfected by the

Catalan company Fura dels Baus, and Els Joglars, a stable of avant-garde actors, is more than 50 years old. Theater director Calixto Bieito is known for controversial interpretations of classic operas. On a more contemplative note, Santa Teresa de Ávila (1515–1582) and Ignatius Loyola (1491–1556, the founder of the Jesuits) wrote mystic works about their spiritual quests.

The 19th century saw Spanish literature evolving into realism and the satire of Pedro de Alarcón, Leopoldo Alas, and Benito Pérez Galdós. Modern Spanish literature began at the end of the 19th century, when Spain's humiliation by the United States (see p. 35) inspired a quest for identity. This was the Generation of '98, spearheaded by philosopher-essayists Miguel de Unamuno (1864–1936) and José Ortega y Gasset (1883–1955). The following generation included the great poets Federico García Lorca (1898–1936) and Nobel Prize–winning Vicente Aleixandre (1898–1984). In the late 20th century, new registers of irony, drama, and psychology made up for 40 years of Francoist repression. Writers to look out for today are Nobel Prize–winner Camilo José Cela, Javier Marías (and his trilogy *Your Face Tomorrow*), Eduardo Mendoza *(City of Prodigies)*, the thrillers of Juan Madrid, the intellectual fireworks of Juan Goytisolo, Javier Cercas on the Civil War *(Soldiers of Salamis)*, and the bestselling author of contemporary life, Almudena Grandes.

Film

Spanish cinema saw its international genesis in two surrealist films by Luis Buñuel and Salvador Dalí, *Un Chien Andalou* (1928) and *L'Age d'Or* (1930), both filmed in Paris. With the glorious 1930s, when cinema excelled elsewhere, Spain had dived into a morass of sociopolitical upheaval, followed by decades of Franco's censorship.

A defiant new wave emerged in the 1950s and '60s, however. Luis García Berlanga, Juan Bardem, and Carlos Saura created films that artfully sidestepped censorship while maintaining integrity of vision. Buñuel, meanwhile, gravitated between Mexico, Hollywood, and France, writing and directing a succession of masterpieces, including *Viridiana* (1961), which was shot in Spain but also banned there, and the Oscar-winning *Discreet Charm of the Bourgeoisie* (1972). His eventful life covered the rise, fall, and incipient renewal of the Spanish film industry (he died in 1983).

Other than the spaghetti Westerns shot in the Almería desert in the 1950s and 1960s, Spanish cinema stagnated until Franco's death. The next generation of filmmakers includes Oscar-winner Fernando Trueba and Bigas Luna, whose outrageous *Jamón, Jamón* (1992) captivated audiences all over the world. Alejandro Amenábar (*The Others,* 2001) and Isabel Coixet (*The Secret Life of Words,* 2005) represent a younger wave. If one person encapsulates the new Spain it is Pedro Almodóvar (see sidebar this page), though these days all eyes are turning to Catalunya and its award-winning director, Agustí Villaronga. ■

Pedro Almodóvar

From his first international hit, *Women on the Verge of a Nervous Breakdown* (1988), Pedro Almodóvar projected a quirky, frenetic image of Spain onto world screens. His actors Victoria Abril, Carmen Maura, and Antonio Banderas shot to fame, while Almodóvar compounded his success with Oscar-winning *All About My Mother* (1999). Each film is a clever concoction of tragicomedy and high-decibel excess. *Talk to Her* (2002) signaled a more mature, realist approach and gained Almodóvar another Oscar. *Volver* (2006) and *Los Abrazos Rotos* (2009) showcased once again the voluptuous Penélope Cruz.

A city of sizzling nightlife, gastronomic indulgence, good music, fashion, and some of the world's greatest paintings

In & Around Madrid

Plaza de Cibeles, one of Madrid's many beautiful market squares

Madrid

Sprawling over the plateau of central Spain, Madrid is perfectly placed for coordinating the nation's 17 autonomous regions. It does not have a lengthy past—it has been Spain's capital only since 1561, when Felipe II moved his court from Toledo. More recently, it shot into the world psyche following devastating train bombings by Islamic extremists in March 2004 and the economic demonstrations of late 2011.

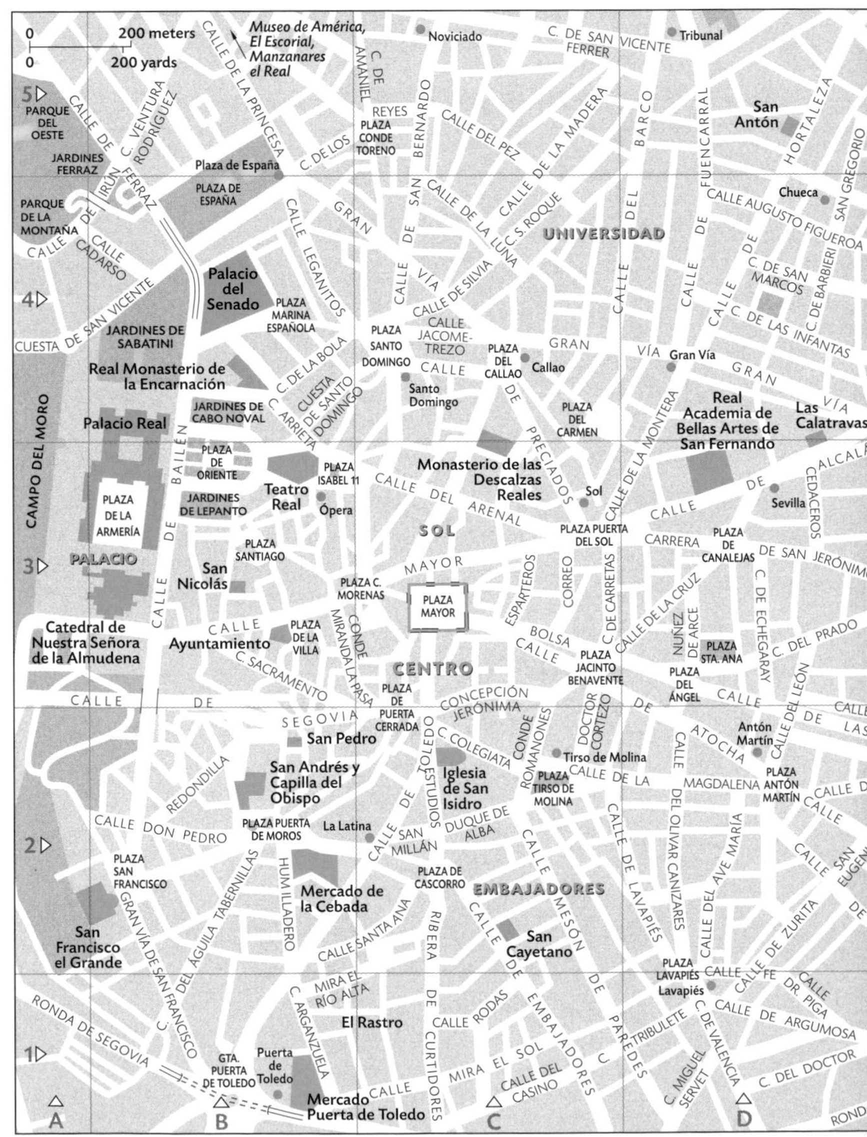

This is Europe's highest capital at 2,120 feet (646 m), and its climate is best in spring or autumn. In winter, Madrid suffers from bitter winds straight off the Sierra de Guadarrama; in summer, it is scorchingly hot.

Madrid's oldest artistic treasures are at the Museo Arqueológico, while the recently expanded Prado spans the Middle Ages to the 19th century. The Thyssen-Bornemisza's selection extends into the 20th century, and the Reina Sofía is the most contemporary. New art centers like the CaixaForum, Conde Duque, and Matadero maintain a healthy rivalry. Smaller collections include the wonderful Monasterio de las Descalzas Reales. The most ostentatious of the city's fine buildings is the Palacio Real.

Chic designer shops line the avenues of Salamanca north of Parque del Retiro. Throbbing clubs and tapas bars fill the narrow streets around Plaza del Ángel, La Latina, Malasaña, and gay Chueca. Northeast, modern office blocks rise on the Paseo de la Castellana, which links with Paseo del Prado to form the city's main north-south axis. Calle de Alcalá, which forms the main east-west axis with the Gran Vía, leads to the heart of Habsburg Madrid, the Plaza Mayor. Stay near any of these roads in order truly to enter the spirit of the "city that never sleeps." ■

Area of map detail

NOT TO BE MISSED:

Palacio Real

Standing on the site of the Moorish ninth-century fortress, the Palacio Real (Royal Palace) became the royal residence in 1561, but was rebuilt after a calamitous fire in 1734. The palace is very much a product of the Bourbon court (see p. 34), and the furnishing is almost all original 18th-century baroque and rococo. King Alfonso XIII lived here until he left Spain in 1931, when the Republicans took control. Today the palace is used only for state ceremonial purposes.

The Real Armería at the Palacio Real boasts a superb collection of ceremonial armor.

Madrid

Visitor Information

✉ Centro de Turismo, Plaza Mayor 27 (Casa de la Panadería)

☎ 915 88 16 36

www.esmadrid.com

From the entrance in front of the cathedral (see p. 59), you go into a vast courtyard, at the back of which a grand staircase leads up to the royal apartments. White stone and granite from the Sierra de Guadarrama are the chief building materials, while inside, marble achieves an impressive acreage.

The **Hall of Halberdiers** (royal guards), with its ceiling painting by Giovanni Battista Tiepolo (1696–1770), leads to the opulent **Hall of Columns,** where 17th-century Flemish tapestries adorn the walls and sculptures symbolize the planets. The dictator General Franco lay in state in the hall in 1975, and in 1985, a formal signing ceremony took place here when Spain joined the European Economic Community.

Throne Rome & King's Rooms

In the sumptuous Throne Room, Tiepolo's ceiling painting **"Apotheosis of the Spanish Monarchy"** looks down on Neapolitan furniture, Venetian chandeliers and clocks from San Ildefonso de la Granja (see p. 226), and bronze lions by Benicelli.

You now move on to the King's Rooms: the Reception Room, Lunch Room, Dressing Room, and Bedroom, each one full of precious objects and furniture. The paintings include portraits by Goya of Carlos IV and his wife, María Luisa. In the **Lunch Room** look out for the astonishing clock made of marble, bronze, and mahogany with a diamond-studded face.

The Italian decorator Gasparini designed the rococo extravaganza of the **Dressing Room.** This riot of silk, gold, and silver wall hangings, an inlaid marble floor swirling with floral designs, and an ornately stuccoed ceiling created a fitting stage for the king to undergo the daily ceremony of being dressed in front of his courtiers.

The **Bedroom,** now furnished as a sitting room with white-and-gold Empire furniture, has a ceiling painting by Vicente López containing numerous references to the religious and honorific order created by Carlos III.

Ballroom & Other Highlights

Next, you see some of the more idiosyncratic rooms, starting with the **Porcelain Room,** a small chamber whose porcelain wall panels were designed for smokers of the time. Grapes, garlands, and flowers decorate the panels. Next door is the **Yellow Room,** lined with fine tapestries, where ladies sat on marquetry chairs by Dugourc and ate chocolates, while the men puffed away in their adjacent smoking room.

Now comes the pièce de résistance, the vast, ornate **Ballroom,** created in 1879 by Alfonso XII out of three smaller rooms built for Carlos III's wife. On her premature death, Carlos closed them up, and so they remained for more than a century. Today the room is used as a banquet hall seating 150 people, who can gaze at the ceiling painting of Christopher Columbus announcing his New World discoveries to Fernando and Isabel. The walls are lined with 16th-century Flemish tapestries and giant vases, both Chinese and French.

The **Music Room** has a rare and unusual collection of stringed instruments by the genius of violin-making, Antonio Stradivari (1644–1737). Watch out, too, for the mother-of-pearl guitar dating from 1796.

INSIDER TIP:

The instruments in the Music Room are occasionally used in private concerts organized by Queen Sofía, a great music lover.

—FIONA DUNLOP
National Geographic author

After the **Silver Room,** you reach the **Capilla Real** (Royal Chapel). Colossal marble columns sustain this neoclassic design, gleaming with gilt. The last four rooms are the apartments of Queen María Luisa and include a porcelain smoking room, a chinoiserie room, and an inspiring study with marble marquetry and painted silk ceiling panels. ■

Palacio Real

52 B4
Calle de Bailén
914 54 88 00
Closed Sun. p.m. & for official ceremonies
$$. Free Wed. p.m. for E.U. citizens. Guided tours in English
Metro: Ópera

www.patrimonionacional.es/preal/preal.htm

A Walk Around Plaza Mayor

This walk takes you to the heart of historic Madrid, where winding streets lead past churches and tapas bars, and give a glimpse of royal history. Follow the trail by day or night—the ambience changes radically.

Shops ring the harmonious Plaza Mayor at the heart of Madrid during Christmastime.

Start your walk at the **Plaza Mayor ❶**, a majestic, porticoed square constructed in the early 17th century as the hub of Habsburg Madrid (see p. 32) under Felipe III. His equestrian statue gazes over the square. The most striking building is the gingerbread-style **Casa de la Panadería** (1672), once home of the Bakers' Guild and now of the tourist office. Opposite is the **Casa de la Carnicería** (Butchers' Guild). Gone are the weekday markets, bullfights, and autos-da-fé (trials and executions of heretics) that once filled the square: Today its cafés are a popular place to meet and celebrate.

NOT TO BE MISSED:

Plaza Mayor • Ayuntamiento • San Pedro • San Francisco el Grande • Calle de Cuchilleros

---

Along Calle Mayor

Leave the square through the arch in the northeast corner leading to Calle de Ciudad Rodrigo. On the left, you see the green wrought-iron facade of the **Mercado de San Miguel.** Once a fresh food market, it is now an upscale food hall. Turn left into the busy Calle Mayor and you soon reach the charming and historic **Plaza de la Villa** ❷. On the right flank of this sloping square stands the **Ayuntamiento** or Casa de la Villa (town hall) designed by Juan Gómez de Mora in 1640 to house the town council and prison. Facing you is the **Casa de Cisneros,** a reconstruction of a 16th-century palace, and on the left is the 15th-century **Torre de los Lujanes,** the birthplace in 1846 of the composer Federico Chueca and now part of the university. The tower has Mudejar (see p. 43) arches at its summit and, opening onto the narrow Calle del Codo, a horseshoe-arched doorway.

Retrace your steps to Calle Mayor and continue to the end. As you walk, the outskirts of Madrid recede in the distance, reminding you of the high altitude of the city. The massive white forms of the **Catedral de Nuestra Señora de la Almudena** *(tel 915 42 22 00),* built in 1985–1992, soon appear. Cross the Calle de Bailén if you want to see the interior—an odd mixture of pure white stone, garish

See also area map pp. 52–53
➤ Plaza Mayor
1.5 hours
1.2 miles (2.4 km)
➤ Plaza Mayor

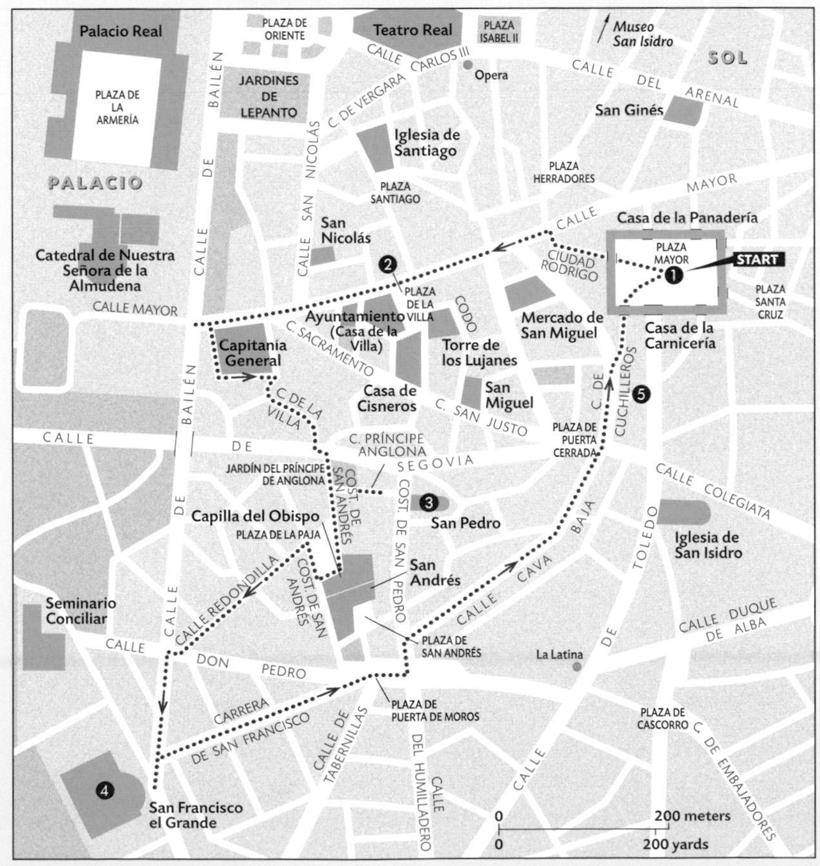

ceiling paintings, and tasteless side chapels. Beside it stands the grandiose **Palacio Real** (see pp. 54–55).

Capitanía General to San Francisco el General

Return to the corner of Bailén and Mayor, and walk down the wide steps beside the Capitanía General, built as a palace in 1611 and now a military establishment. The city drops steeply here: You soon find yourself looking back up at the lofty viaduct (1934) of Calle de Bailén. Circle around the back of the palace through the parking lot, and then turn right down Calle de la Villa to reach Calle de Segovia and an ornate fountain (1850) on Plaza de la Cruz Verde.

Looming uphill opposite is the **Capilla del Obispo** *(Plaza de la Paja, tel 915 59 28 74)*, Madrid's only Gothic chapel. Walk toward it up Costanilla de San Andrés to leafy **Plaza de la Paja.** In the Middle Ages, this was the commercial heart of Madrid. On the corner, enter the shady Jardín del Príncipe de Anglona to admire its rose arbors and 18th-century layout. Make a quick detour into Calle Príncipe Anglona to see **San Pedro** ❸ and its 14th-century Mudejar tower.

Return to Plaza de la Paja, cross over it and turn on Calle Redondilla. This ends at Calle de Bailén, where you turn left to **San Francisco el Grande** ❹, a neoclassical basilica *(tel 913 65 38 00, museum closed Sun.–Mon.)*. Built in 1762–1784, it has a Goya painting of San Bernardino and a lavishly painted cupola.

INSIDER TIP:

Madrid can get hot in the summer, but the evenings are lovely. Pick a café in or near the Plaza Mayor, get a glass (or pitcher) of sangria, and people watch as the Spanish sun sets.

—RACHEL GRAHAM
Director, Digital Publishing & Marketing, National Geographic Books

Café Hopping

Walk along Carrera de San Francisco (away from the basilica), to Plaza de Puerta de Moros. The church of **San Andrés** *(Plaza de San Andrés, tel 913 65 48 71)* overlooks a peaceful square flanked by a fountain and cafés. Go past it to the **Museo San Isidro** *(tel 913 66 74 15, closed Sun. p.m. & Mon.)*, where the saint lived until 1172, although this building dates to the 17th century. Partly closed for renovation, it now covers Madrid city history. Turn left down **Calle Cava Baja.** Stop for refreshments at one of the restaurants and bars that accompany you as far as Plaza de Puerta Cerrada. Or cross to lively **Calle de Cuchilleros** ❺, before going up the arched steps leading into Plaza Mayor.

Fiesta de San Isidro

About two blocks from Plaza Mayor, on Calle Toledo, stands the church of San Isidro. It marks the site where the 11th-century Madrileño purportedly rescued his son from a well by making the water rise. For this miracle, he was canonized and became Madrid's patron saint. Every year, the summer season kicks off in mid-May with a weeklong festival in his honor. The celebration includes the start of the bullfighting season at Las Ventas, with a daily program of parades, exhibitions, and concerts. On May 15, the actual saint's day and climax of festivities, San Isidro's statue is paraded through the streets with fabulous costumed processions, song, and dance. *Cocido* and *callos* (Madrid's trademark dishes of stew and tripe) are distributed freely.

Monasterio de las Descalzas Reales

The royal origins of this Franciscan Convent of the Royal Barefoot Nuns lie in its conversion from a palace into a convent by Felipe II's sister Juana de Austria, who became a nun. Today 28 nuns of the order known as the Poor Clares live in seclusion here, and on your tour you may hear them singing and ringing bells. The magnificent late 15th- to early 16th-century building holds a mass of treasure.

Frescoes by various artists adorn the grand staircase that leads up from the cloisters. The dominant one shows Felipe IV and his family, and opposite is a Crucifixion scene. Off the first-floor cloisters, the remarkable side chapels contain original **Talavera tiled floors,** frescoes, coffered ceilings, and many paintings by anonymous artists. A beautiful recumbent **"Christ"** is the work of 16th-century sculptor Gaspar Becerra. Fra Angelico's masterful "Annunciation" hung here before being moved to the Prado (see pp. 60–64).

The anteroom to the main chapel is packed with silverware, Bohemian crystal crucifixes, and paintings. It leads to the **Choir,** used daily for Mass, where the marble tomb of María stands above that of her daughter, Marguerita. Notice the fabulously realistic and expressive **statue of Mary,** by Pedro de Mena (1628–1688). Back in the cloisters, the next side chapel is devoted to the Virgin of Guadalupe, celebrated in a riot of baroque gilt, with unusual paintings on mirrors. Farther along, look for the **"Madonna and Child"** painted by Bernardino Luini (circa 1480–1532).

The convent houses Renaissance and baroque artwork.

From here you are taken upstairs to the vast **Hall of Tapestries,** lined with 17th-century Flemish tapestries, based on cartoons by Peter Paul Rubens (1577–1640), and packed with other treasures. In the chapter house overlooking the vegetable garden you'll see more works of art, including Gregorio Fernández's **sculpture of Mary Magdalen** and Pedro de Mena's **"Ecce Homo."** The tour ends in splendor in a room hung with paintings by Zurbarán, Titian, Caravaggio, Bruegel the Elder, and Rubens. ■

Monasterio de las Descalzas Reales

- Map: 52 C3
- Address: Plaza de las Descalzas Reales 3
- Phone: 914 54 88 00
- Hours: Closed Fri. & Sun. p.m., & Mon.
- Admission: $. Free on Wed. for E.U. citizens with passport. 50-minute guided tour in Spanish
- Transport: Metro: Sol, Ópera, & Callao

www.patrimonionacional.es/descreal/descreal.htm

Museo del Prado

Spain's premier art museum has a dazzling and selective display of paintings and sculpture spanning some 2,000 years of art history. The core of the collection is Spanish masters but it also encompasses major Italian Renaissance works and Flemish and German paintings, all of superb quality. A massive reorganization between 2009 and 2012 greatly increased the number of works on display, highlighting compelling correspondences and influences.

Madrid's most famous museum has one of the world's greatest collections of classical paintings.

Access to the Prado is now through Rafael Moneo's 2007 extension at the back, the **Puerta de los Jeronimos,** a reference to the church cloister which was dismantled and rebuilt as part of the museum. Modern galleries used for temporary exhibitions and a services area bridge the cloister section with the original **Villanueva building,** named after its architect, Juan de Villanueva (1739–1811). This is where you enter the museum's imposing neoclassical galleries, inaugurated as a national museum of painting and sculpture in 1819 by Fernando VII. Greeting you is a line-up of Roman sculptures, the Muses.

As the original royal collection has been much enriched by other museum collections, donations, bequests, and acquisitions, the scale of the museum appears daunting. The arrangement is essentially chronological, however, making it easy for visitors to find their areas of interest on the two main floors, helped by ample panels in English and Spanish. An audio guide is also available.

Velázquez & the Central Gallery

If you have limited time to spend at the Prado, seek out the great Spanish masters and their Italian and Flemish contemporaries. These are concentrated on the first floor in the redesigned Central Gallery and its adjoining rooms, with Diego Velázquez's works at its heart in an oval gallery **(Room 12).**

The Prado has Velázquez's best paintings, and perhaps the greatest of them all, **"Las Meninas"** ("The Maids of Honor"). Look at this painting from a distance, and you will see Velázquez himself observing you from where he stands beside his easel in the picture. From 1623 until his death, Velázquez worked in Madrid, continuing the tradition of court portraiture that dated back to Titian (died 1576).

Titian's fame during his life nearly matched that of Michelangelo, and it is said that Carlos V once did him the honor of picking up a paintbrush he had dropped. His large format works in the main axis include the dynamic horseback figure of "Carlos V at the Battle of Muhlberg" (1548). Jacopo Tintoretto (1518–1594) appears here, too. Take a look at his "El Lavatorio,"

INSIDER TIP:

Admission to the Prado Museum is free Monday to Saturday from 6–8 p.m. and on Sunday from 5–8 p.m. Entrance is always free with the MadridCard *(www.madridcard.com).* Taking photos inside is forbidden.

—MARY STEPHANOS
National Geographic contributor

Museo del Prado

- Map: 53 E3
- Address: Paseo del Prado
- Tel: 913 30 28 00 (info), 902 10 70 77 (advance tickets)
- Closed Mon., Dec. 25, Jan. 1, Easter Friday, & May 1
- $$
- Metro: Banco de España

www.museodelprado.es

Spain's Royal Art Patrons

The main source of the Prado's incredible collection, which now totals 7,600 paintings (although fewer than a thousand are displayed), as well as 1,000 sculptures and more than 13,000 works on paper, was the Spanish royal family who, over the centuries, commissioned and collected art with passion. Their Habsburg and Bourbon connections introduced numerous other European artists to supplement the Spanish stars such as Velázquez, Goya, Ribera, Zubarán, and Murillo (see p. 46).

Felipe II, an astute art lover with taste strongly influenced by his Flemish aunt, collected many of the Flemish painters. He and his Ghent-born father, Carlos V, also favored Italy's Titian (1490–1576). Felipe IV chose Diego Velázquez (1599–1660) as court painter. Demonstrating admirable perception, Carlos II appointed Francisco de Goya (1764–1828).

a masterpiece of perspective and composition that depicts Jesus washing his disciples' feet.

The works of other Spanish masters hang in **Rooms 10–15.** Look out for the baroque paintings of José de Ribera (1588–1652). While living in Italy, Ribera learned tenebrismo (the art of shadow) from Caravaggio and became a leader of the Neapolitan School. "Jacob's Dream" (1639) highlights his skill.

Caravaggio's works in **Room 4** include his powerful David victorious over Goliath. Ribera's contemporary, Francisco de Zurbarán (1598–1664) was an adept of texture, light, and shadow, as seen in his serene portraits of monks and even his lamb of God, "Agnus Dei" (1640). Here, too, is El Greco (1541–1614), the Greek artist who adopted Toledo as his home. During his Spanish period, his dramatic figures lengthened

Museo del Prado

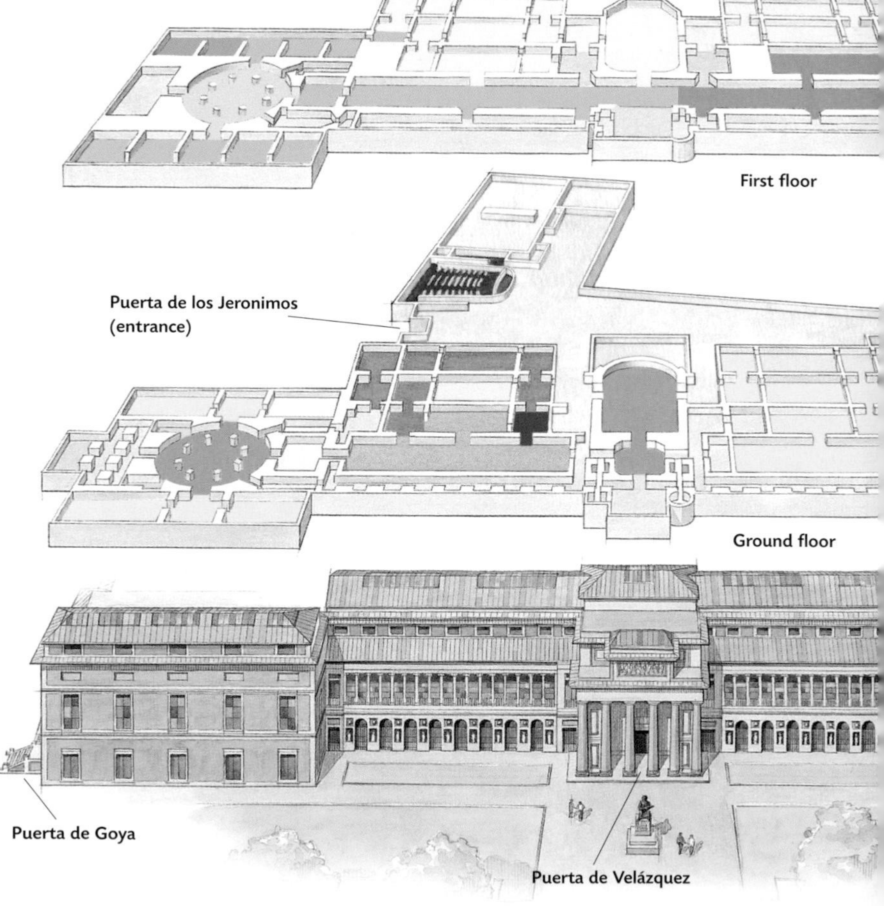

After extensive restoration, Albrecht Dürer's "Adam and Eve" was unveiled at the Prado in 2010.

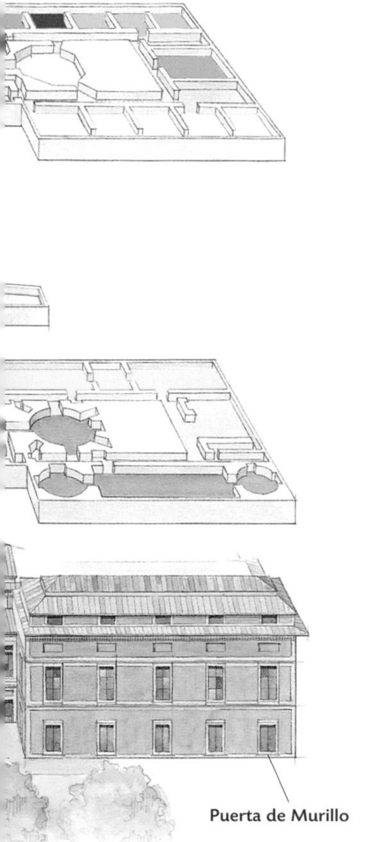

and he adopted a very Catholic concern with Heaven and Earth. "The Nobleman with His Hand on His Chest" (1580) is a startling work of the Spanish Renaissance. More Spanish Baroque comes with Bartolomé Murillo and Alonso Cano, both major figures of the 17th century.

The Central Gallery thus gives a fantastic window on this process of development beginning with Titian and continuing with Velázquez and the majestic works

- Italian paintings
- Spanish paintings
- Flemish paintings
- French paintings
- Sculpture
- German paintings
- New Areas
- Other

of Peter Paul Rubens (1577–1640), a Flemish painter who was a subject of the Spanish Crown. Outstanding paintings by Rubens include the seminal "Adoration of the Magi" (1609) and "The Three Graces" (circa 1635).

Goya

The inspiring route ends in the south block with the 18th century and the works of Goya, whose paintings continue immediately above (early works and tapestry cartoons) and below (his 19th-century works). Goya's world was arguably the most diverse of all Spanish painters, and no other museum in the world can boast a collection that has as much breadth and depth.

Other Masterpieces

Among the beautiful Romanesque and Renaissance works on the Prado's ground floor are Roger Van der Weyden's "Descent from the Cross" (1435), Albrecht Dürer's "Self-Portrait" (1498), "Garden of Earthly Delights" by Hieronymous Bosch (1500–1505), and Raphael's "Cardenal" (1510), resplendent in his scarlet robe. Less well known outside Spain, but not to be missed, are the exquisite late 18th-century still lifes of Luis Menendez, which are almost photographic in their realism.

"The Nude Maja" (1797–1800) in **Room 32** depicts a naked Venus, who in reality was a renowned mistress. His huge political tableaux, "El Dos de Mayo" and "El Tres de Mayo," depict scenes from Spain's War of Independence against France in 1808. Unusually for that time, Goya was not working to commission, so the subject matter was his own choice.

INSIDER TIP:

It is impossible to see everything in the Prado in a day. Choose a few painters, like Goya and Velázquez, and focus on them.

—TINO SORIANO
National Geographic photographer

Don't miss Goya's extraordinary and very strange "black paintings," produced from 1820 to 1823 during a period of deep depression caused by the deaths of his wife and son, and by his own illness. Many of these paintings are grotesque; all are open to interpretation and their titles are conjectural.

"Perro" (1819–1823), seems completely modern in conception, with its extraordinary spatial arrangement of a dog's head against textured space. Some of Goya's earlier court paintings, which are also on display, are just as idiosyncratic and often unflattering due to the emotional approach he had to the characterization of the subjects he chose to paint. ■

Museo Thyssen-Bornemisza

Madrid acquired this exceptional art collection only in 1993, and its quality and scope complement the Prado across the road. The collection was built by two generations of the Thyssen-Bornemisza family, and it is now overseen by the Catalan baroness Carmen Thyssen-Bornemisza. Housed in the 19th-century Palacio de Villahermosa, it represents the best of Western art from the last 800 years.

Large interior murals announce temporary exhibitions at the Museo Thyssen-Bornemisza.

For a chronological tour, work your way down from the top floor. Begin in **Room 1** with the oldest paintings, the Italian primitives, among them "Christ and the Samaritan" by Duccio di Buoninsegna (1278–1319), the only artist known to have signed his work at this time. **Room 3** brings you to early Flemish paintings: Best of these are the black-and-white diptych of the "Annunciation" by Jan Van Eyck (1390–1441), which looks like carved stone, and the incredibly detailed "Enthroned Madonna" by Rogier van der Weyden (1400–1464).

In **Room 5,** which has an exceptional display of Renaissance portraits, you touch on early examples of the modern cult of the personality: Look for Domenico Ghirlandaio's "Portrait of Giovanna Tornabuoni," a representation of perfection, and Hans Holbein's (1498–1543) masterful and much reproduced depiction

Museo Thyssen-Bornemisza

- 52 E3
- Palacio de Villahermosa, Paseo del Prado 8
- 913 69 01 51
- Closed Mon.
- $
- Metro: Banco de España

www.museothyssen.org

of a self-satisfied Henry VIII of England. Next to it hangs the "Infanta" (circa 1496) by Juan de Flandes, a delightful portrait of a youthful Catherine of Aragón, Henry's first wife.

The **Villahermosa Gallery,** adjoining in **Room 6,** displays Raphael's (1483–1520) "Portrait of a Young Man" in a freer style. **Room 7** brings you to larger-format Renaissance paintings. Bernardino Luini's (1486–1532) "Virgin and Child with the Infant St. John" shows wonderful delicacy in the Virgin's face, her veil, and the two babies. "Young Knight in a Landscape" by Vittore Carpaccio (1460–1525) is in a transitional style, part naturalistic, part stylized, and Gothic.

German & Italian Schools

A more exaggerated, and even caricatural, approach characterizes the paintings of the German school on display in **Rooms 8** and **9.** Albrecht Dürer's (1471–1528) "Jesus Among the Doctors" is a compelling composition that draws the eye to the hands at the center. Next door, in **Room 10,** the "Reclining Nymph" by Lucas Cranach the Elder (1472–1553) has a superbly painted transparent veil.

Rooms 11 and **12** represent great artists of the Venetian school (Titian, Tintoretto, Bassano) and other Italians. El Greco appears here because he began his career in Italy, and José de Ribera (1591–1652) has a room to himself. This Spaniard, who worked and died in Italy, combined Spanish drama with Italian techniques, displaying a startling realism.

Baroque

The early baroque section features anguished sculptures

INSIDER TIP:

For a magnificent sunset view of Madrid, head for the rooftop (*$*) of the Círculo de Bellas Artes.

—ALBERTO GIL
Travel Agent, ClickDreaming, Madrid

Círculo de Bellas Artes

Just a five-minute walk from the Museo Thyssen-Bornemisza, the Círculo de Bellas Artes *(Calle de Alcalá 42, tel 933 60 54 00, www.circulobellasartes.com)* is one of Madrid's best kept secrets. This luscious art deco concoction of curvaceous windows, marble staircases, sculptures, and glittering chandeliers stands right in the heart of the city. A private arts club built in the 1920s, it has welcomed luminaries such as Ramón María del Valle-Inclán and even a youthful Picasso. Accolades for the spectacular design go to Antonio Palacios, architect of the 1904 post office on nearby Plaza de Cibeles.

The upper floors are mainly workshops, and below are a cinema, exhibition galleries, dance hall, library, and the grand old café-bar with huge windows overlooking Alcalá. Here you can sip coffee or a cocktail in splendor. You can also visit the roof terrace *($)*.

including, "San Sebastián" and "La Piedad" by Bernini (1598–1680). Other highlights include Luca Giordano's (1634–1705) "Judgment of Solomon," Francisco de Zurbarán's (1598–1664) "Santa Casilda," and radiant views of Venice by Canaletto (1697–1768). Further Flemish and Dutch paintings are in **Rooms 19, 20,** and **21:** Here you'll find superlative works by Van Dyck, Brueghel, and Rubens, especially Rubens's superb "Toilet of Venus." Don't miss Rembrandt's penetrating "Self-portrait."

Dutch 17th-century genre paintings fill a whole wing of the museum's middle level with beautifully observed and composed scenes of daily life, interiors, and landscapes. An unusual still life by William Claesz Heda (1593–1680) depicts a magnificent display of silverware and glass standing beside a half-eaten pie.

Rooms 28, 29, and **30** bring you to English and American artists such as Joshua Reynolds (1723–1792), Thomas Gainsborough (1727–1788), and Thomas Cole (1801–1848), an Englishman who emigrated to America and founded the American school. Apart from a rather fine "Portrait of the Duchess of Sutherland" by John Singer Sargent (1856–1925), this section is more interesting intellectually than artistically. After the Spanish, Flemish, and Dutch works, these portraits seem rather stilted and lifeless. Then comes the shock of European Romanticism, with a wall of Goya, Géricault, and Delacroix in **Room 31,** followed by Courbet and Constable.

The Impressionists are in **Rooms 32** and **33.** Make sure you see Renoir's "Woman with Parasol" (1873), Berthe Morisot's "The Cheval-Glass" (1876), and Edgar Degas's "Swaying Dancer" (1880). Vincent van Gogh's "Les Vessenots" (1890), painted in thick impasto, may have been his last painting before his suicide.

Modernism

The modern art collection begins in **Room 34** with André

Marble and bronze statues accompany the chronologically arranged landscapes.

Derain (1880–1954) and the other Fauves (wild beasts), so-called because they seemed to break all rules. However, the Thyssen-Bornemisza comes into its own with a superlative collection of German expressionists **(Rooms 35–40).** Munch, Kokoschka, Nolde, Schiele, and Beckmann are all here, and Otto Kirchner (1880–1938) is especially well represented. Take a look at his radiating composition in "The Bay" (1914) and "Alpine Kitchen" (1918). Franz Marc (1880–1916) and Wassily Kandinsky (1866–1944) represent the Blaue Reiter group, and the last room has caricatural works by Georg Grosz (1893–1959).

Rooms 41–44 on the ground floor show parallel trends of early modernism, from cubism (Braque, Juan Gris, Picasso) to futurism, constructivism, dadaism, and surrealism. The United States rules supreme in **Room 46,** with abstract expressionism by Rothko, O'Keeffe, and de Kooning. **Rooms 47** and **48** round things off with a general survey of postwar figurative work from late Surrealism to pop art. Look out for Francis Bacon's portrait of his lover George Dyer.

Carmen Thyssen-Bornemisza Collection

In 2004, the museum expanded into two adjoining buildings to accommodate temporary exhibitions and to exhibit the Carmen Thyssen-Bornemisza Collection. The collection starts on the top floor with 17th-century Italian painters, continuing through 18th-century landscapes and portraits to end with Impressionism and Cubism in the early 20th century.

The nucleus of the collection consists of works by Canaletto, Fragonard, Corot, Boudin, Monet, Sisley, Renoir, Toulouse-Lautrec, Degas, Gauguin, Rodin, Matisse, Picasso, and Braque, among others. Subsequently the widowed baroness (and former Miss Spain) acquired less prestigious works by 19th- and early 20th-century Spanish artists; most of these have now been transferred to the Málaga museum that opened in 2011 (see p. 282). ■

EXPERIENCE: Classicism of a Different Sort

For a different kind of gallery hopping, head for Calle de Serrano, Madrid's "golden mile." This is the place to go for tracking down top signatures in the fashion world. Here classicism sits side by side with cutting-edge designs and plenty of Spanish names such as Adolfo Dominguez *(Serrano 18)*, Agatha Ruiz de la Prada *(Serrano 27)*, Pedro del Hierro *(Serrano 24)*, and Manolo Blahnik *(Serrano 58)*. Loewe *(Serrano 26 and 34)* is famed worldwide for its luxury leather goods. Don't miss the ABC shopping mall *(Serrano 61)* in a lavishly tiled 1926 building. To reach Calle de Serrano, head north from Museo Thyssen-Bornemisza to Plaza de Cibeles, about a ten-minute walk. From there, take the N24 bus *($)* north to stop no. 62. Calle de Serrano is just one block west.

Parque del Retiro

Madrid boasts a lovely breathing space in this 350-acre (142 ha) park. In the 17th century, it surrounded Felipe IV's palace. Now it lies conveniently close to the capital's main art museums, and it is the perfect place to recover from them.

A grand monument to Alfonso XII overlooks Estanque Lake in Parque del Retiro.

The Conde-Duque de Olivares laid out the park in 1636, and its formal gardens, copses, fountains, statues, and paths remain. All that is left of the palace is the Casón del Buen Retiro, now a study center and library for the Prado (see pp. 60–64). It stands at the entrance to the park on Calle de Alfonso XII.

In the park itself, you can take a carriage ride, row a boat on the **Estanque Lake,** hear a concert, visit an exhibition, jog, or just stroll. This is a popular meeting point for Madrileños, especially on Sundays. The **equestrian statue** by the lake portrays Alfonso XII (*R.*1874–1885), not Spain's most illustrious ruler but one of its youngest—he died at only 28.

South of the Prado, in the far southwest corner of the park, is the **Real Jardín Botánico** (Royal Botanic Garden), founded in 1774. It has about 30,000 plants, some of them exotic, and aging greenhouses designed by Juan de Villanueva (1739–1811). Also in the southern half are the **Palacio de Velázquez** *(tel 915 73 62 45, closed Tues.)* and the soaring glass walls of the 1887 **Palacio de Cristal** *(tel 915 74 66 14, closed Tues.)*. Both hold exhibitions of contemporary art organized by the Museo Nacional Centro de Arte Reina Sofía (see pp. 71–72). ■

Parque del Retiro

- Map: 53 F2
- Address: Calle de Alfonso XII
- Tel: 915 73 62 45
- Metro: Atocha, Retiro, & Ibiza

Real Jardín Botánico

- Map: 53 E2
- Address: Plaza de Murillo 2
- Tel: 914 20 30 17
- Price: $
- Metro: Atocha & Banco de España

www.rjb.csic.es

Museo Arqueológico Nacional

Standing behind the grandiose Biblioteca Nacional (National Library) in the chic Salamanca district, this museum of ancient art dates from 1867. Over the last few years the museum has been extensively modernized and its displays reorganized; some of the pieces described below may not be exhibited or may be out on loan.

Museo Arqueológico Nacional

- 53 F4
- Calle de Serrano 13
- 91 577 79 12
- Closed p.m. Sun. & Mon.
- $. Free Sat. p.m. & Sun. a.m.
- Metro: Serrano (Line 4) & Retiro (Line 2)

www.man.mcu.es

Some of the museum's oldest objects date from the late Bronze Age (tenth to ninth century B.C.). The **Cuencos de Axtroki,** hammered gold vessels with intricate circular designs, suggest a cult of the sun, while gold collars and bracelets impress by the simplicity of their design. Look, too, for the **Celtiberian silver,** mainly from southeast Spain, and the terra-cotta collar of the sun priestess from the fourth-century B.C. with stylized birds and suns.

Do not miss the outstanding Spanish Islamic exhibits, from an 11th-century **astrolabe** and other exquisite metalwork to an ornate gypsum **archway** from Zaragoza's Aljafería palace (see pp. 141–142).

Iberian Sculpture & Visigothic Jewelry

Pride of place goes to the extraordinary **"La Dama de Baza."** Dated to the early fourth century B.C., this large sandstone figure of a cloaked, seated woman bears traces of polychrome pigments. She sits surrounded by her dowry of terra-cotta vessels, all unearthed at Baza, near Granada.

Slightly older, the limestone bust of the incredibly rare and beautiful **"La Dama de Elche"** probably held human ashes in the shoulder cavity and would also have once been brightly colored. The oldest of all these ladies is the Phoenician **"La Dama de Galera,"** dating from the seventh century B.C. and carved out of alabaster to represent the goddess Astarte.

The dazzling **Tesoro de Javea** (Javea Treasure) includes gold and silver diadems and collars, some with incredible filigree detail. The most sumptuous of all the treasures, however, is the Visigothic **Tesoro de Guarrazar** (Guarrazar Treasure), unearthed near Toledo in 1858–1860. This horde of church decoration that lay hidden for 11 centuries after the Moorish conquest includes gold, silver, rock crystal, and precious stones shaped into the form of crowns, chains, and crosses. ■

INSIDER TIP:

It is worthwhile to combine a trip to the Museo Arqueológico Nacional with a visit to the neighboring Biblioteca Nacional.

—DEAN SNOW
National Geographic grantee

Museo Nacional Centro de Arte Reina Sofía

Home to Picasso's "Guernica" (see sidebar p. 72), the Reina Sofía opened in 1986 in tune with Spain's frenetic *movida* spirit of personal and artistic freedom. In 2005 an expansion devised by acclaimed French architect Jean Nouvel added a triangular-shaped extension for temporary exhibitions, a library, an auditorium, and a restaurant supervised by celebrity chef Sergi Arola around a central atrium topped by a lattice roof.

The main Sabatini building is a converted 18th-century hospital, with immaculate white walls and transparent external elevators. The permanent collection of 20th- to 21st-century art is strong on Spanish art, less so on non-Spanish artists.

Cubism & Surrealism

Start your visit on **Floor 2,** where exhibitions take you from the early 20th century through World War II. **Room 201** showcases the transition from Spanish Postimpressionism—look for Santiago Rusiñol's **"Jardín de Aranjuez"**—to Cubist-influenced works like José Gutiérrez Solana's forceful charcoal drawing.

Early Surrealism follows in **Room 202,** introducing one of Spain's greatest 20th-century artists, Joan Miró, as well as masters of the art of collage such as Francis Picabia. In **Room 203** you will also find exhibits related to Spain's pioneering surrealist filmmaker Luis Buñuel (1900–1983), who had a close connection with art movements of the late 1920s in Paris.

The big hitters, Salvador Dalí and Oscar Dominguez, dominate the surrealist works in **Room 205** before you come to the Reina

Picasso's famous "Guernica" (1937) is one of the star attractions at the Reina Sofía.

Museo Nacional Centro de Arte Reina Sofía

53 E1

Calle de Santa Isabel 52

917 74 10 00, 914 67 02 02 (restaurant)

Closed Sun. p.m. & Tues.

$$. Free Sat. p.m., Sun. a.m., & evenings Mon.–Fri.

Metro: Atocha

www.museoreinasofia.mcu.es

Sofía's most celebrated painting, Picasso's **"Guernica"** (see sidebar this page). It hangs at the center of the back wing of this floor, surrounded by remarkable photos, sketches, sculptures, and other works by Picasso's contemporaries–Torres Garcia, Miró, and Julio Gonzalez–as well as Oskar Schlemmer's **"Triadic Ballet"** (1922). This area also includes architectural documents of the 1930s modernist group G.A.T.E.P.A.C. and a hint of the Bauhaus ideology. Drawings and photos of the Civil War culminate with Basilio Martin Patino's 1971 moving documentary, *Songs for After a War,* composed of mixed footage of the aftermath of the Civil War.

Displays of the cold figurative work of the 1920s contrast with some masterful Cubist paintings made by Juan Gris after he had moved to Paris and met Braque and Picasso.

In **Room 209,** devoted to the surge of creativity in Catalunya in the early 20th century, look for Salvador Dalí's unexpected Cubist self-portrait (1923) as well as Miro's unusual landscape: **"Siurana, el camino"** (1917).

Moving backward in time, the last room on this floor focuses on graphic Constructivism and the genesis of Cubism. Keep an eye out for the strong colors of Sonia Delaunay, as well as works by Picasso and Braque.

"Guernica"

Picasso's tortured, monochromatic painting "Guernica" was created in a white heat of outrage after the brutal bombing of the little town of Gernika (see p. 125), in northern Spain, on April 26, 1937. The three-hour raid was carried out on General Franco's orders by a German squadron and killed more than 2,000 people, most of whom were in Gernika for the weekly market. The painting was commissioned by the Spanish Republicans for Expo 1937 in Paris.

Postwar Abstraction

The museum's third floor is used for temporary exhibitions, so to continue your itinerary through contemporary Spanish art and its international context, take an elevator or the stairs to **Floor 4** to be plunged into postwar effervescence. Here you will find works by artists on both sides of the Atlantic, offering fascinating insight and comparisons. Displays include the European abstraction of Hans Hartung, later surrealist paintings by Dalí, and the political films of Isidore Isou and Maurice Lemaitre.

Particularly fascinating from a historical point of view are the photos on display in **Room 404** by Eugene Smith and Georges Brassai showing life in Spain in the 1950s. Antoni Tàpies (1923–2012), Angel Ferrant, Antonio Saura, Miró (again), and Manuel Millares represent abstraction of the 1950s, echoed in Jorge Oteiza's delicate, graphic sculptures. ■

Museo de América

Madrid had no public museum on Spain's former colonies in Latin America until the Museo de América opened in 1993, bringing together a huge array of scattered documents and exhibits under one roof. The presentation is slick, but you see the colonies only from the colonists' point of view: No mention is made of the atrocities and exploitation wrought by the Spanish, and indigenous peoples appear as mere exotic curiosities.

The 2,500 exhibits are imaginatively displayed. The kernel of the collection came from the Royal Cabinet, but other items have been bought or donated.

Room 1 is devoted to the voyages of discovery, Spanish chroniclers including Christopher Columbus, a reconstructed 18th-century scientific study room, and fascinating old maps. Also here are engravings, paintings, and stunning artifacts such as Amazonian feathered hats, the fantastic feathered Paracas cape, Costa Rican Diquis gold, and colonial antiques.

Most of the pre-Hispanic collection fills **Rooms 2** and **3.** It is arranged in themes like birth and death, ceremonies, and tools and implements. You see ceramic figures from Colima in Mexico, Maya sculptures, Olmec jades, lovely pieces from Mexico's Gulf culture, Inca artifacts, Chilean textiles, ceramics from Ecuador, Colombian and Costa Rican gold ornaments, basketware by Hopi and Chumash Indians, and an enormous Amazonian canoe. Whimsical 18th-century Mexican paintings illustrate the Conquest, while Chinese inlaid furniture indicates maritime links with the Philippines, another Spanish colony.

The museum's most precious items are on the **upper floor** (sometimes closed to make way for temporary exhibitions). Here are the Mayan Stela of Madrid (incised stone), the Colombian gold Quimbayas treasure, the Tudela codex manuscript (1553), and, above all, the Trocortesiano codex (13th–16th century), one of only four Maya manuscripts remaining in the world.

This museum explores the indigenous cultures of Latin America.

Faro de Moncloa

Outside the museum stands the **Faro de Moncloa** (Moncloa Lighthouse), a 250-foot (76 m) cylindrical steel tower designed by Salvador Pérez Arroyo in 1992. Take the elevator up to the observation platform for fantastic views over Madrid. ■

Museo de América

- 53 B5
- Avenida Reyes Católicos 6
- 915 43 94 37
- Closed Sun. p.m. & Mon.
- $. Free on Sun.
- Metro: Moncloa (Line 3)

museodeamerica .mcu.es

Faro de Moncloa (Moncloa Lighthouse)

- Avenida Reyes Católicos
- 917 22 04 00
- Closed Mon.

More Places to Visit in Madrid

CaixaForum Madrid

This latest addition to Madrid's museum mile sits opposite the Real Jardín Botánico and the Parque del Retiro. Echoing the greenery across the road, it displays a vertical garden rising 78 feet (24 m) and counting 15,000 plants of 250 different species, the inspired work of French botanist Patrick Blanc. The building was spectacularly transformed by Swiss architects Herzog + De Meuron by adding a rusted steel crown to the stone facade of a 1900 power station. Apart from airy galleries, the state-of-the-art exhibition center has an auditorium, a specialist bookstore, and a slick restaurant-café on the top floor. Admirably curated exhibitions and free entry have rapidly ensured its success.

53 E2 Paseo del Prado 36 913 30 73 00 Metro: Atocha

Madrid Río

Madrid's latest playground is an ambitious leisure park laid out around the southern perimeter of the city. A section of the M30 highway was buried underground, making way for more than 7 miles (10 km) of walkways and bike paths, as well as a landscaped park, city beach, and iconic bridges crossing the newly liberated Manzanares River. The park's plan also integrates historic buildings, such as the elegant **Arganzuela greenhouse** (1908–1922) and neighboring **Matadero Madrid** *(Paseo de la Chopera 14, tel 915 17 73 09, closed Tues. & a.m. Wed.–Fri., www.mataderomadrid.org),* both situated at the eastern end near the Legazpi metro station. The huge Matadero, once the city abattoir and livestock market, is now a dynamic contemporary cultural center, with ongoing projects.

At the far western end, near the Puerta del Angel metro station, you can admire Madrid's oldest bridge, the **Puente de Segovia,** designed by Juan de Herrera in 1572–1588. Two spiral-shaped walkways form the brand new **Puente de Arganzuela,** designed by French architect, Dominique Perrault.

On Sundays, Madrileños flock to El Rastro flea market looking for bargains.

www.madrid.es/madridrio 53 E1 915 88 36 39/41 12 Metro: Puerta del Angel, Marqués de Vadillo, & Piramides

Museo Nacional de Artes Decorativas

This museum of Spanish decorative arts gives you a taste of the lavish interiors of Spain's many castles and palaces. There are six floors covering furniture, costumes, and objects from the 15th to the 20th century. The top floor houses a wonderful tiled Valencian kitchen. *http://mnartesdecorativas.mcu.es* 53 F3 Calle de Montalbán 12 915 32 64 99 Closed Sun. p.m. & Mon. Metro: Retiro & Banco de España

Museo Sorolla

This charming, highly personal museum was once the home of Valencian painter Joaquin Sorolla (1853–1923) and his family. Apart from Sorolla's luminous post-Impressionist paintings, which hang in a lofty, skylit hall, you can admire furniture and ceramics of the period and a typical Andalusian-style patio with tiled fountain and soaring palms. Altogether it makes an elegant escape from the bustle of the nearby Castellana. *http://museosorolla.mcu.es* 53 E5 Calle General Martinez Campos 37 913 10 15 84 Closed Sun. p.m. & Mon. $ Metro: Iglesia & Gregorio Marañon

El Rastro

If you are in Madrid on Sunday morning, don't miss this vast flea market. Goods for sale vary from dusty, rusty bric-à-brac to high-quality antiques, in addition to the usual motley array of T-shirts, ethnic imports, cheap shoes, and bags. Stalls invade the old streets of La Latina district, stretching from Plaza de Cascorro to the Puerta de Toledo. The best area for antiques and secondhand knickknacks is the **Calle Mira el Río Baja** and its offshoots.

INSIDER TIP:

For high-quality flamenco shows at affordable prices, featuring some of the best and most prestigious artists, Villa Rosa on Plaza Santa Ana is definitely the place to be. Don't be deterred by its touristic appearance.

—YUKO AOYAMA
National Geographic grantee

Old books are piled up in the **Plaza del Campillo del Mundo Nuevo,** and superior antique shops are concentrated on **Calle Ribera de Curtidores.** A word of warning: As in any market, beware of pick-pockets. The Rastro is notorious for them, although a greater police presence means things have improved in recent years. 52 C1 Metro: La Latina & Puerta de Toledo

Real Academia de Bellas Artes de San Fernando

Despite its prime position on the stately Calle de Alcalá, this art museum is often overlooked by visitors intent on the art giants down the road (the Prado and Thyssen-Bornemisza, see pp. 60–68). Housed in the grandiose rooms of the former Palacio Goyeneche, the remarkable collection spans five centuries of Spanish painting, ending with 20 Picasso etchings. Look for Zurbarán's eight superb life-size **portraits of monks,** works by Alonso Cano (1601–1667), and Goya's **"Burial of the Sardine."** Other European artists include Paolo Veronese and Peter Paul Rubens. The museum also has displays of sculpture and porcelain. *http://rabasf.insde.es* 52 D3 Calle de Alcalá 13 915 24 08 64 Closed Sun. p.m. & Mon. $ Metro: Sol & Sevilla

Around Madrid

After hotfooting it around the sights of Madrid, if you feel you need some air, Aranjuez is the place to go. Strawberries and cream are a local specialty sold in season at every corner. Or venture 30 miles (50 km) northwest of the capital to another world: Built for Felipe II on a personally chosen site, El Escorial is a summer palace, monastery, and mausoleum combined.

The ceiling frescoes in the beautiful library at El Escorial depict the seven liberal arts.

Aranjuez
77 B1
Visitor Information
Aranjuez Turismo, Plaza San Antonio 9
918 91 04 27
www.aranjuez.com

Palacio Real
Plaza de Parejas, Aranjuez
91 891 07 40
Closed Mon.
$ guided tour. Free Wed. for E.U. nationals
www.patrimonionacional.es

Aranjuez

This genteel royal town 30 miles (48 km) south of Madrid may remind you of the French royal palace of Versailles near Paris. Its elegant grid pattern, the lateral wings of the royal palace, and the delightful Casa del Labrador were all commissioned by the Bourbon kings of the late 18th century—the heyday of Versailles. Even the formal gardens were the work of a French landscape designer.

The **Palacio Real** (Royal Palace) was built for Felipe II by Juan Bautista de Toledo and Juan de Herrera. The grand staircase, rococo Salón del Trono (Throne Room), Sala de la China (lined with whimsically decorated porcelain tiles), Sala Árabe (inspired by the Alhambra, see pp. 298–299, 302–305), and Salón de los Espejos (Hall of Mirrors) are just some of the palace's wonders.

From here you can take a leisurely walk through the 370-acre (150 ha) **Jardín del Príncipe** to the far more harmonious **Casa del Labrador** (Laborer's House), built for Carlos IV. The most scintillating room is the **Gabinete del Platino** (Platinum Room), with walls encrusted with gold, platinum, and bronze.

If you don't want to walk, a **visitor train** *(tel 902 08 80 89, closed Mon.)* makes regular circuits of the town, starting from the Palacio Real and stopping at the main sights.

El Escorial

Felipe II's palace-monastery looms over the little town of **San Lorenzo de El Escorial.** The king wanted the palace to reaffirm the glory of the Habsburg dynasty, but also to be a retreat where he could lead a more contemplative existence than was possible in Madrid.

The building was started by Juan Bautista de Toledo in 1563 and rapidly completed by his pupil, Juan de Herrera, in 1584, with constant input from the king himself. Grandiose but austere, it suits its bleak setting.

If you visit in winter, snow may be on the ground, for you are at 3,370 feet (1,028 m). Whatever the season, the views from the 2,673 windows are sublime, sweeping over manicured hedges to the mountains beyond. The small town of San Lorenzo has a number of hotels and restaurants. You may be glad of these, as the Escorial is a vast labyrinth of patios, corridors, halls, staircases, and chapels, requiring at least three hours to visit.

You have to follow a set route around the building: It is well signed, and information panels give good descriptions in Spanish and English of the main features in each room. Your first sight on entering the palace is the series of tapestries called the **Golden Tapestry** (circa 1502) and El Greco's massive **"Martyrdom of St. Matthew"** (1580–1582).

From here you descend to the **Museo de Arquitectura,** which displays architectural drawings, models, and examples of carpentry methods. Next is the **Museo de Pintura** (Painting Museum), with masterpieces by Titian, Tintoretto, Veronese, Van Dyck, and Rubens. Look for the powerful light in Luca Cambiaso's (1527–1585) **"Archangel St. Michael"** and the **triptych** by Michel Coxcie (1499–1592). Place of honor goes to van der Weyden's **"Calvary,"** which Felipe II inherited from his aunt, Mary of Hungary. Compare the original, and its extraordinary shadows and perspective, with the two Juan Fernández Navarrete (circa 1520–1579) copies flanking it. José Ribera (1591–1652), the great protagonist of tenebrism (depiction of shadows), is well represented by his dramatic and luminous **"St. Jerome Penitent"** and **"Aesop."**

Casa del Labrador

Calle de la Reina, Aranjuez
91 891 03 05
Closed Mon.
$. Free Wed. for E.U. nationals. Reservations required.

www.patrimonionacional.es

San Lorenzo de El Escorial

77 A2

Visitor Information

Oficina de Turismo, Calle Grimaldi 4
918 90 53 13

www.sanlorenzoturismo.org

Real Monasterio de San Lorenzo de El Escorial

77 A2

918 90 59 03 or 918 90 59 02

Closed Mon.

$$. Free Wed. for E.U. nationals

Stairs lead up to Felipe II's palace, partly remodeled by Carlos III. Here you glimpse the more intimate side of royal life, including the bedroom where Felipe II died in 1598. In between is the **Strolling Gallery,** an immense hall with windows on three sides, old maps, and countless paintings of 17th-century battle scenes. The curious sundial inlaid in the floor by the south window is a "solar adjuster," an 18th-century system for checking clocks.

INSIDER TIP:

Visit El Escorial early in the day, before the crowds. The Pantheon Real is very small and often overwhelmed by lots of visitors.

—TINO SORIANO
National Geographic photographer

Pantheon Real: Inside the baroque Pantheon Real a staircase lined with jasper and gilt leads to a circular chamber full of marble caskets. These contain the remains of nearly all the kings of Spain from Carlos V onward. A series of nine adjoining chambers contains the tombs of princes and princesses.

From the Pantheon, steps rise to the vast **Salas Capitulares** (chapter houses), where you are confronted by a superb El Greco (1541–1614) painting: **"St. Peter."** Here, too, are Titian's **"Last Supper"** and Hieronymus Bosch's **"Christ Carrying the Cross"** and **"The Crown of Thorns."** The delicate ceiling paintings of these rooms date from the 1580s.

Next you reach the **cloister,** blanketed with fresh-colored frescoes, mainly the work of Pellegrino Tibaldi in the late 16th century, and housing the monastery's magnificent main staircase. Above hovers a spectacular **ceiling fresco** by Luca Giordano (1632–1705), glorifying the Habsburg monarchy; on the walls are more Tibaldi frescoes. The cloister encloses the

El Escorial

Evangelist Courtyard, with a temple (designed by Herrera) flanked by four pools.

Basilica & Library: The basilica stands at the center of El Escorial and dazzles with its 45 side chapels, as well as a monumental marble **"Christ"** by Benvenuto Cellini (1500–1571). The choir stalls were designed by Juan de Herrera, and the beautiful ceiling frescoes are the work of Luca Giordano and Cambiasso. From the church you cross the Kings' Patio to ascend to the vast **royal library** (above the main entrance), with 45,000 books from the 15th and 16th centuries, and 5,000 Arab, Latin, and Castilian manuscripts. Don't miss the ceiling frescoes, again by Tibaldi. Felipe II's fascination for science and astronomy is well represented by various globes and the **Armillary Sphere,** made around 1582 (see sidebar p. 35). ■

More Places to Visit Around Madrid

Alcalá de Henares

The first planned university town in the world lies just 20 miles (33 km) east of Madrid and is easy for visitors to reach by train, bus, or car. In its 16th-century heyday, the university produced the Complutensian Polyglot Bible with four original language texts side by side. Today, despite industrial areas, Alcalá remains a fascinating town, deserving of its World Heritage status accorded in 1998.

Three monuments in town stand out: the **Monasterio de Religiosas Bernardas,** with its baroque extravaganza of a church; the illustrious **university,** centering on the fine plateresque (see p. 45) college of San Ildefonso; and, in contrast, the small **Museum of Miguel de Cervantes,** dedicated to Alcalá's most famous offspring (see pp. 248–249).

From Madrid, you can catch the train to Alcalá at the Atocha station. The ride takes about 45 minutes. *www.turismoalcala.com* ▲ 77 B1 **Visitor Information** ✉ Callejón Santa María 1 ☎ 918 89 26 94

Chinchón

The town of Chinchón is a quaint, relaxing place, nestling on a hillside 28 miles (45 km) southeast of Madrid. Its only real sight, the **Plaza Mayor,** charms by its total irregularity, with three-story medieval houses rising above porticoes and the church of La Asunción standing at one end. In August, the plaza is transformed into a bullring, but otherwise life here goes on quietly, despite the quantities of anise, gin, and other spirits brewed locally to accompany its wholesome food.

In the 17th century, the Countess of Chinchón caught malaria in Peru, where her husband was viceroy, and cured herself using the bark of a tropical tree that she subsequently brought back to Spain. This was later named *chinchona* in her honor.

To get to Chinchón, less than an hour from Madrid, take bus no. 337 from Conde de Casal. *www.ciudad-chinchon.com* ▲ 77 B1 **Visitor Information** ✉ Plaza Mayor 6 ☎ 918 93 53 23

Manzanares el Real

The **castle** *(closed Mon.)* that towers over this small town 31 miles (50 km) north of Madrid featured in *El Cid,* the 1961 movie starring Charlton Heston and Sophia Loren. An imposing (though heavily restored) example of 15th-century military architecture, it once belonged to one of Castilla's most powerful families, the Mendozas. Inside you can see armor, 17th- and 18th-century tapestries and furniture, as well as a display on the castles of Spain. Overlooking the vast Santillana reservoir, the castle is framed by the dramatically craggy landscape of La Pedriza, once favored by bandits and now dotted with climbers and hikers. The trip on bus no. 724 from Plaza de Castilla, Madrid, takes less than an hour. *www.manzanareselreal.org* ▲ 77 A2 **Visitor Information** ✉ Plaza Puebla 1 ☎ 639 17 96 02

Guided Tours

You can visit Aranjuez, El Escorial, Valle de los Caídos, Toledo, Segovia, La Granja, or Ávila on guided day trips from Madrid. Three companies offer comparable services and rates: Julià Tours *(Gran Vía 68, tel 915 59 96 05, metro Plaza de España, www.juliatours.es)*, Pullmantur *(Plaza de Oriente 8, tel 915 41 10 66, metro Ópera, www.pullmantur.es)*, and Trapsatur *(Calle San Bernardo 5, tel 915 42 66 66, metro Santo Domingo, www.trapsatur.com)*. Also check *www.city-discovery.com/madrid.*

A bucolic region with prehistoric cave paintings, ancient churches, exquisite seafood, and Spain's premier pilgrimage site

Northwest Spain

A cross dedicated to sailors who died at sea

Northwest Spain

Santiago de Compostela, Spain's greatest pilgrimage site and westernmost city, is the magnificent capital of Galicia. Once you have been to Santiago, you understand more about the rest of northern Spain and the spiritual fervor behind its Romanesque and Gothic monuments. You won't be alone either, as in recent years the Camino de Santiago (Way of St. James) has undergone an incredible revival.

The awesome granite peaks of the Cordillera Cantábrica helped protect the region from the Moorish advance, and Asturias and Cantabria are the only parts of Spain without any Muslim influence. The northwest does, however, have Paleolithic cave paintings; Celtic, Roman, and Visigothic remains; and a culture that may remind you of Cornwall in western England, Brittany in western France, or Ireland. Even the mild, often drizzly climate resembles that of its Celtic cousins.

Cider, rather than wine, is the local tipple in Asturias, and cheese comes in numerous shapes and flavors. The northwest is also grain-growing country, and the grain (either corn, originally brought from America, or wheat) ends up

NOT TO BE MISSED:

Attending Mass at the cathedral of Santiago de Compostela **88–89**

Eating *pulpo a feira* (octopus) anywhere in Galicia **93**

The blissful beaches on Galicia's Illas Cíes **96**

Sampling Asturian cheeses with a glass of local cider **102**

Oviedo's medieval heart and legendary Cámara Santa **102–103**

Santillana del Mar's cobbled streets and Romanesque gems **105–106**

Looking above the clouds in the Picos de Europa **106–108**

The Paleolithic caves and inspiring museum at Altamira **109**

in all sorts of dairy-based cakes. Throughout Galicia and Asturias you see picturesque *hórreos,* grain-stores on stilts to keep rodents at bay. For centuries people in Galicia painstakingly gleaned a living from fishing or from tiny farms. Hardship prompted emigration to Andalucía and Latin America. Some emigrants returned once they had made money, and you can easily identify their more gracious houses by the symbolic palm trees growing in front.

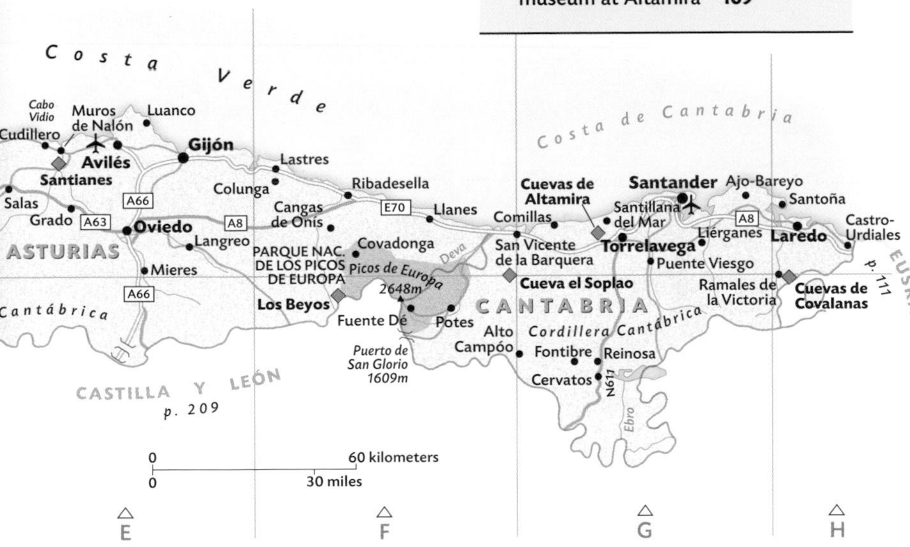

Galicia has 805 miles (1,289 km) of *rías* (sea inlets) and rocky cliffs; Asturias and Cantabria have sandy beaches, with the Picos de Europa mountains rising dramatically in the background. Fishing is the main industry, although this has suffered from the drop in sea stocks and E.U. quotas. Tourism is increasing, and the fashion industry is booming.

Relaxed Santander and breezy A Coruña are the only large coastal towns; otherwise the coast has just a string of fishing villages, low-key resorts, and a handful of industrial towns in Asturias. Remember when touring, you will cross and recross breathtaking mountains, so journeys might take longer than you expect. ■

Galicia

Spain's most remote region is a wildly beautiful windswept land, squeezed into the peninsula north of Portugal and bordered by the Atlantic on two sides. Celtic culture arrived here around 1000 B.C. Bagpipes are the most obvious sign of Celtic influence, their strident wail still heard in every Galician festival. A deep sense of melancholy and mysticism, a love of poetry, but also a great joie de vivre are present.

Despite emigration and pockets of industry, Galicia's interior is still essentially agricultural.

Galicians have their own language, *gallego,* a combination of Spanish and Portuguese spoken by nearly 70 percent of the 3 million population. Street names, public information, and museum captions are increasingly only in gallego. Thwarted by the Civil War and Franco's centralism, nationalism raised its head in the late 19th century and simmers again today, just as it does in Euskadi (País Vasco) or Basque country and Catalunya.

For centuries Galicia was Spain's poorest region, whose rural inhabitants suffered frequent famines as they eked out a living, either farming on the harsh terrain or fishing. As a result, Galicians were Spain's most enthusiastic emigrants to Latin America, where the term "Gallego" is interchangeable with "Spanish." In the 1980s and '90s, Galicia greatly benefited from E.U. subsidies, and today it has a much more prosperous face, as people give up farms and settle in expanding towns on the coast.

Galicia's capital city of Santiago de Compostela has been a magnet for European pilgrims since the Middle Ages. This is a city you must not miss, with its Romanesque architecture and unique atmosphere, but don't ignore charming smaller towns such as Pontevedra, Ourense, and Tui, or the sharply indented coastline and verdant inland hills. Here are remote hermitages, deserted beaches, and dramatic canyons, and all over Galicia you find the region's own wines and divinely fresh seafood.

A Coruña (La Coruña)

Galicia's former capital was demoted in 1982. It now concentrates its energies on deep-sea fishing and cargo activities. Everything here evokes the sea: The city stands on a peninsula and has salty air, Atlantic beaches, and a Roman lighthouse (the city's emblem). The ill-fated Armada of 1588 set off from here, and its defeat by the English spelled the end of Spanish maritime power.

The most interesting part of the city starts at the well-defined neck of the peninsula, where La Coruña's nickname of "crystal city" originated. Street after street is lined with houses that have several stories of glassed-in balconies to protect people from the wind while they enjoy the sun. From a distance this looks like modernist architecture of the 1960s, but at closer quarters you can see distinctive 19th-century styles. Here, too, is **Plaza de María Pita,** the arcaded main square, named for a local heroine who saved the town from an English invasion in 1589 by raising the alarm during the night.

Dominating one side of the square is the ornate **Palacio Municipal** that also houses a small **museum of clocks** *(tel 981 18 42 26, closed a.m. & weekends).* Calle Franja, which leads off the western side, is packed with specialist shops and tapas bars. Two blocks south lies the **marina,** and immediately east is the old quarter, which meets the waterfront at **Castillo de San Antón.** This castle is a museum with exhibits on Galicia's Roman culture, and beautiful Iberian and Celtic metalwork.

Two streets away is the harmonious collegiate church of **Santa María del Campo.** Built by the guild of seafarers, it has a beautiful carved Romanesque portal beneath its rose window. In front of the church is a 15th-century

(continued on p. 88)

A Coruña (La Coruña)
82 B3

Visitor Information

Oficina de Turismo, Dársena de la Marina s/n

981 22 18 22

www.turismocoruna.com

Castillo de San Antón & Museo Arqueológico

Paseo Marítimo del Parrote, A Coruña

981 18 98 50

Closed Sun. p.m. & Mon.

$

www.sanantón.org

Santa María del Campo

Calle Damas, A Coruña

981 20 31 86

Galician Fashion

One of the most successful global marketing phenomena of the late 20th century started life in A Coruña in 1985. The empire was the brainchild of a local fashion entrepreneur, Amancio Ortega, and his ex-wife, Rosalía Mera. Their company, **Inditex** *(www.inditex.com),* now encompasses eight different brands, with Zara its mid-market arm and Massimo Dutti the higher-end label.

Inditex is based on the outskirts of Ortega's home town, where he still lives. His unquestionable prowess in the garment industry has its roots in Galician tradition. While their fishermen husbands were away for weeks on end, the wives would sew clothing to earn extra money. In this indirect way, a modest cottage industry blossomed into a lucrative international industry.

Way of St. James

For ten centuries pilgrims have been doggedly treading the long path to Santiago de Compostela in a protracted ritual of self-purification. Their goal is the immense cathedral built to house the remains of St. James (Santiago). The relics may or may not be there, but they have had immense symbolic significance for Spain.

Tourists of all kinds come to Santiago de Compostela to reenact the medieval pilgrimage.

It is said that the apostle preached widely in Roman Spain before returning to Judea to face execution, after which his body was allegedly brought back by followers to Galicia. After long oblivion, its discovery in the ninth century inspired not just a cathedral and pilgrimage route, but also the infrastructure to serve it and the spread of Christian culture throughout northern Spain. In turn, this gave impetus to and funds for the fight against the Moors of al-Andalus.

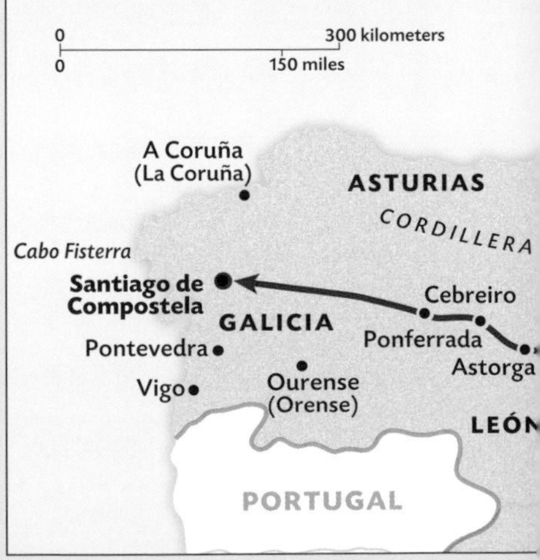

Originally just a simple monastic complex, the subsequent grandiose cathedral of Santiago rapidly became a magnet for pilgrims, bringing them along fixed routes lined with hospices, sanctuaries, and increasingly sophisticated cathedrals. From Tours, Vézélay, and Le Puy in France, pilgrims crossed the Pyrenees via Roncesvalles or Somport, meeting at Puente La Reina to continue together in 13-day stages along the "French Way." This became so popular that in the 12th century a type of pilgrim's guide (Book V of the Liber Sancti Iacobi, or Book of St. James) was written, detailing the characteristics of the regions and people en route. After giving the Basques and people of Navarra a poor press, it becomes more lyrical when describing Castilla and even more so with Galicia—"a land made pleasant by its rivers, meadows and marvelous orchards, its fine fruits and crystal springs . . . Abundant too are gold and silver, textiles and furs and other riches, particularly Saracen treasures." With such worldly enticements, pilgrims flocked to Santiago from Portugal, Germany, the Low Countries, Italy, and, by maritime routes, England and Scandinavia. However, the French Way predominated, and it is still followed in today's revival of the medieval trail. Many of today's "pilgrims" are not religious but use it for self-discovery and challenge for the sense of community among walkers and cyclists. See *www.xacobeo.es* and *www.turgalicia.es.*

Along the route Romanesque and Gothic architecture blossomed. In addition to hospices and monasteries, pilgrims also needed protection from brigands, and this was provided by military-religious orders such as the Knights of Santiago. Secondary cults associated with the Way of St. James also proliferated.

To show their status, pilgrims adopted the scallop shell as a symbol. The reasons for this are clouded in mystery and legend, although it had a practical purpose, too: to scoop water from a fountain or use as a plate. Whatever the origin, the symbol endures and the way itself goes from strength to strength.

INSIDER TIP:

Every day, the first ten pilgrims to arrive in the hall of the Hostal de los Reyes Católicos *(Praza do Obradoiro)* at 9 a.m., noon, and 7 p.m., will enjoy a free meal. This is an old custom that dates back to the time when the hotel was a pilgrim's refuge.

—ALFONSO PARDO
Professor, Universidad de Zaragoza

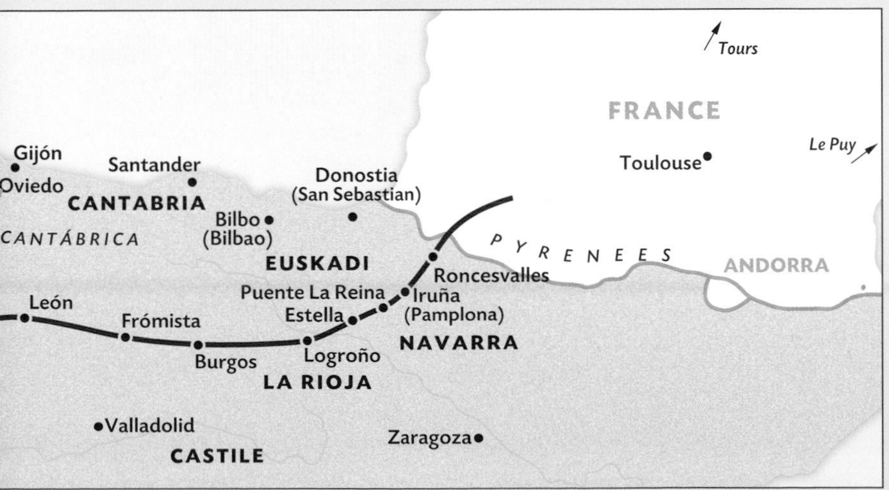

Torre de Hércules
Carretera de la Torre, A Coruña
981 22 37 30

Domus
Rúa Santa Teresa, A Coruña
981 18 98 40

Santiago de Compostela
82 B2

Visitor Information
Oficina Municipal de Turismo, Rúa do Vilar 63
981 55 51 29

www.santiagoturismo.com

Calvary (representation of the Crucifixion). One mile north of this atmospheric area looms the **Torre de Hércules,** built by the Romans in the second century A.D., but considerably remodeled in 1790. Said to be the world's oldest working lighthouse, it rises to a lofty 341 feet (104 m). You can climb to the top for the view. Do not miss the outdoor sculpture park at its base overlooking the ocean. The ultramodern building on the west of this promontory is **Domus,** an interactive museum of mankind designed in the 1990s by the Japanese architect Arata Isozaki.

Santiago de Compostela

Santiago has been drawing pilgrims from all over Europe for more than a millennium. Today, visitors still pour in, but the second-most visited site after the cathedral is now the Mercado de Abastos, a cornucopian food market. Santiago exudes an inimitable atmosphere, with wonderful old buildings, great seafood restaurants, and winding medieval streets.

Start at the **cathedral,** a massive edifice that rises between four squares. Its ornate towers, carved doorways, and facade are a visual symphony of styles. The cathedral was first built in Romanesque style in the 11th to 13th centuries, but much of it was subsequently modified. Look at the main western facade from the vast **Praza do Obradoiro** and you see a baroque masterpiece (1750) by Fernando Casas y Novoa. Behind this is the magnificent Romanesque inner facade, the **Pórtico de la Gloria,** which was the work of Master Mateo in 1188. Unfortunately it is now encased in scaffolding as part of a meticulous restoration program. Above the triple-arched doorway, the carvings of the central tympanum show Christ in Majesty flanked by the four evangelists with the 24 Elders of the Apocalypse. Above the central pillar is a seated figure of Santiago (St. James); crouched behind it is the **Santo dos Croques,** meaning "saint of the bumps," which may be a self-portrait of Master Mateo himself. A side door here gives you access to the roofs of the cathedral, made of granite and stepped, with panoramic views.

You enter the cathedral from the south facade (on **Praza das Praterías**) through the stunning **Puerta das Praterías.** Its low-relief sculptures (1103) illustrate biblical scenes from Adam and Eve to the flagellation of Christ.

Despite visitors, the **cathedral interior** has a working atmosphere.

The baroque facade of Santiago's cathedral

EXPERIENCE: Transcantabrico Trains

Experience northern Spain the unusual way: by taking a narrow-gauge sleeper train through the mountains and along the coast. FEVE trains *(www.trenesturisticosdelnorte.com)* run from Leon, Santiago de Compostela, and San Sebastián, winding their way along the Basque coast, down into the plains of Castilla y León, and farther west through Cantabria, Asturias, and Galicia.

There are three grades of train: the **Expreso de la Robla,** the **Transcantabrico Clasico,** and the latest, the super-luxury **Gran Lujo.** The first is the most affordable and offers short routes of two or three days in fairly cramped en suite compartments. The Clasico covers week-long trips in greater comfort, while the Gran Lujo covers the same itinerary but with panoramic lounge-cars, double the compartment space, and five-star treatment. Side-trips by bus take in regional highlights. Meals showcase local foods.

The 3-foot-wide (0.9 m) FEVE was initiated in the 1890s to transport coal and iron ore from the mines of León province over the mountains to Bilbao, the industrial heart of Spain.

INSIDER TIP:

When the moon is full over the cathedral in Santiago de Compostela, and the ground is moist from rain, the reflection is divine.

—ENRIQUE SEOANE
Concierge, Hostal de los Reyes Católicos, Santiago de Compostela

During major celebrations the ***botafumeiro,*** a gigantic incense burner, is swung like a pendulum in front of the dazzling baroque high altar.

Don't miss the treasury, the 16th-century cloister, or the museum: One ticket gets you into all three. The **treasury** (off the south aisle, on the right as you face the altar) has a bust (1332) of St. James Alpheus, a lesser apostle, that contains his relics. You reach the 16th-century cloisters from the transept. The upper floors have Flemish tapestries and give wonderful views. Entered to the right of the main facade, the **museum** has contemporary versions of the zithers, fidulas, viols, and lutes played by the Elders on the Pórtico de la Gloria and medieval artwork. Best of all is the reconstruction of Mateo's original choir structure, destroyed in 1603.

To the left is the **Palacio Gelmírez,** the former archbishop's palace, a rare example of a civil Romanesque building. Inside is the magnificent **Salón Sinodal,** more than 98 feet (30 m) long, that has unusual rib-vaulting. On the square outside, admire the **Colegio de San Jerónimo** (1501) to the south, the **Pazo Raxoi** (1766) to the west, now the City Hall, and, to the north, the spectacular **Antiguo Hospital Real,** founded in the 16th century as a hospice for sick pilgrims but now a luxury parador.

At the back of the cathedral are two interconnecting squares. **Praza das Praterías** was the home of the silversmiths' guild, and **Praza da**

Catedral
✉ Praza do Obradoiro, Santiago de Compostela
☏ 981 58 11 55
www.archicompostela.org/Catedral/catedral.htm

Museos de la Catedral
✉ Praza do Obradoiro, Santiago de Compostela
☏ 981 56 05 27
$ $ (Treasury, crypt, & cloisters)

Palacio Gelmírez
✉ Praza do Obradoiro, Santiago de Compostela
☏ 981 55 29 85
🕒 Closed Sun. Book for guided tour.

Museo de Arte Sacro

Praza da Quintana, Santiago de Compostela
981 58 31 27
Closed Sun. a.m.

Quintana used to be a cemetery. You can enjoy the majestic setting at several outdoor cafés: This is a wonderful spot from which to admire the cathedral entrance known as the **Puerta Santa** (Holy Door) or **Puerta del Perdón,** only opened during Holy Year.

Opposite is the **Monasterio de San Paio de Antealtares** *(Praza da Quintana),* founded in the ninth century to house the tomb of St. James, and its church, dating from 1707. Inside, the **Museo de Arte Sacro** displays sculpture, paintings, gold, and silverwork.

One former monastery, the Convento de Santo

Praza do Obradoiro

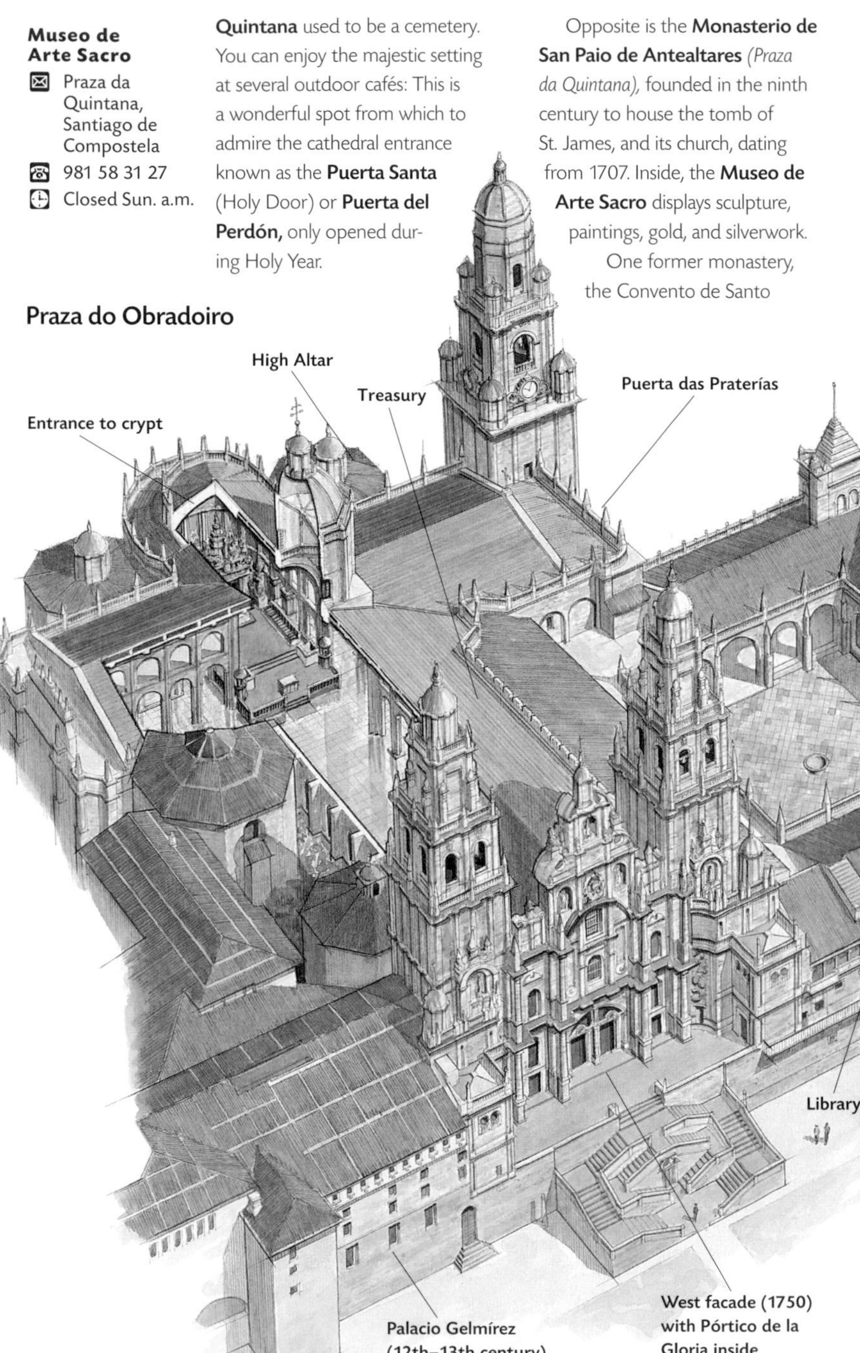

Domingo de Bonaval, ten minutes' walk northeast of the center, is now the **Museo do Pobo Galego** (Museum of the Galicians). Set around verdant cloisters, the rooms are packed with traditional handicrafts, costumes, agricultural implements, and musical instruments. The visit is worthwhile if only to climb the remarkable triple spiral staircase designed by Domingo de Andrade in the 17th century. Next door to the museum, in complete contrast, stands Galicia's slick contemporary art center, **Centro Galego de Arte Contemporánea,** built in 1993 to a minimalist design by Portuguese architect Alvaro Siza.

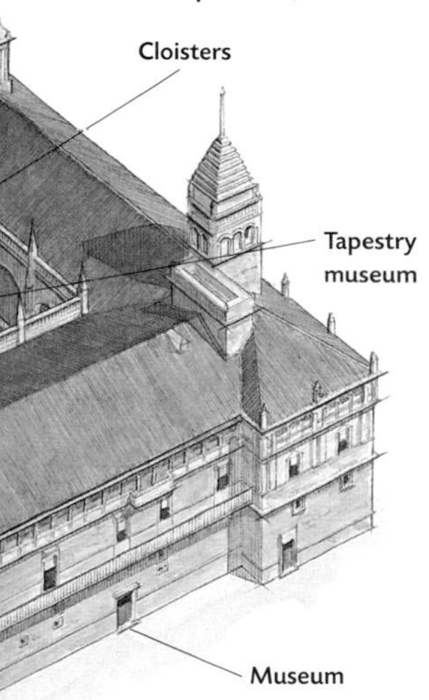

Partly housed in a Gothic tower, the **Museo de las Peregrinaciones** tells the fascinating story of the Santiago pilgrimage. Exhibits include jet jewelry, one of the city's traditional crafts, which is still produced and sold in jewelry shops. The museum will eventually move to Praza das Platerías.

A few yards downhill from the museum you will find the church of **San Martín Pinario** *(Plaza de San Martín),* now functioning as a museum, built in 1597, with gracefully curved steps leading down to its plateresque (see p. 45) facade. Inside are a breathtaking baroque altarpiece and finely carved 17th-century choir stalls. It is part of the massive seminary (and part hostel) of San Martín Pinario.

Just south of the religious epicenter, a must-visit is the **Mercado de Abastos** *(Praza de Abastos, tel 981 58 34 38, closed Sun.),* the city's main food market, which dates from 1873. Seventy traders sell a cornucopia of Galician shellfish, fish, beef, *pimientos de Padrón,* cheeses, chorizos, wines, and tarts. On busy Thursdays and Saturdays, dozens of country women sit behind baskets of homegrown produce and plants.

Like the rest of Spain, Santiago de Compostela boasts an ambitious

(continued on p. 95)

Museo de Pobo Galego (Museum of the Galicians)

✉ Convento de Santo Domingo, Santiago de Compostela
☎ 981 58 36 20
🕒 Closed Sun. p.m. & Mon.

Centro Galego de Arte Contemporánea

✉ Rúa Ramón del Valle-Inclán, Santiago de Compostela
☎ 981 54 66 19
🕒 Closed Mon.

Museo de las Peregrinaciones

✉ Praza do San Miguel, Santiago de Compostela
☎ 981 58 15 58
🕒 Closed Sun. p.m. & Mon.

Las Tunas

At night in Santiago de Compostela, traditional bands of students, *las tunas,* head for the arcades of the Praza do Obradoiro to sing and play music for tips or the sale of CDs. The tradition goes back to the 13th century, when poorer students became troubadours to earn pocket money and a plate of soup in the bars. For that they always had a spoon and fork attached to their clothes, joined by several belts, each one representing an amorous conquest. Today's student-formed *tunas* dress in dashing medieval costumes and play instruments of the period such as lutes and mandolins.

Drive: The Hórreo Trail from Santiago to Cabo Fisterra

This circuit takes you west to the wild reaches of Galicia's Atlantic coast. It encompasses the characteristic scenes of Spain's most remote province, from rural landscapes to empty beaches and historic fishing villages. You also see plenty of Galicia's *hórreos* (pitched-roof grain-stores on stilts), now more decorative than functional.

Sunny Playa de San Francisco, in the coastal town of Louro

Leave Santiago de Compostela (see pp. 88–91) by following the signs to Noia (AC543), turning right at the traffic circle on the outskirts. At Bertamiráns, turn right to drive through eucalyptus and pine forests to Negreira, where you turn left toward Muxia (AC546). Rolling farmland and hórreos recur along this stretch. At Pereira, the road becomes AC441. On reaching a major junction at Berdoias, turn left on the AC552 to Corcubión.

Corcubión to Cabo Fisterra

The AC552 takes you past the industrial town of Cée, then 1.8 miles (3 km) farther to **Corcubión ❶**. This charming fishing village has fine emblazoned houses with glazed balconies. At low tide you see people collecting shellfish.

Continue by following signs to Fisterra (Finisterre), 9 miles (14 km) farther. On the way you round a headland with stunning views through pines to the Atlantic Ocean below, and you pass the half-moon beaches of Praia de Estorde, Praia de Langosteira, and Praia de Sardiñeiro.

At **Fisterra ❷**, follow the sign marked Faro (lighthouse) through the town. Stop

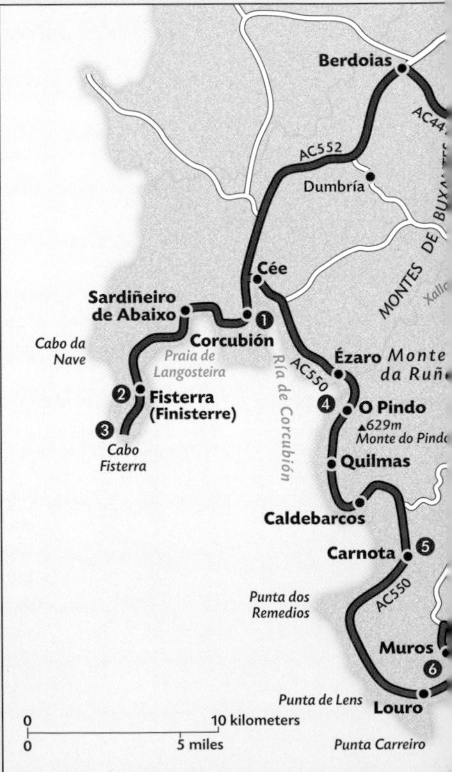

NOT TO BE MISSED:

Cabo Fisterra • Carnota • Muros • Santa María a Nova, Noia • San Martiño, Noia

at the lovely 12th-century church of **Santa María des Areas** *(closed in winter)*, on the main road at the edge of town, to see its much revered statue of Christ with a golden beard, before continuing to the lighthouse.

The lighthouse stands on Europe's westernmost point, **Cabo Fisterra** ❸. Magnificent panoramas open up over the rocky bay, and a path around the lighthouse gives vertiginous views of the surf below.

Octopus

In deeply traditional Galicia, you can hardly move without eating octopus. To make *pulpo a la gallega* (in Spanish) or *pulpo a feira* (in Galician), simmer the octopus for two hours in a copper pan, remove, then chop or snip into bite-size pieces. These are then sprinkled with olive oil, sea salt, and paprika and served on a wooden platter. Contrary to popular belief, the texture of octopus is not rubbery if it is fresh, as it always is in Galicia. Eat it with boiled potatoes and another Galician classic: *pimientos de Padrón,* baby green peppers lightly fried in olive oil then sprinkled with coarse sea salt.

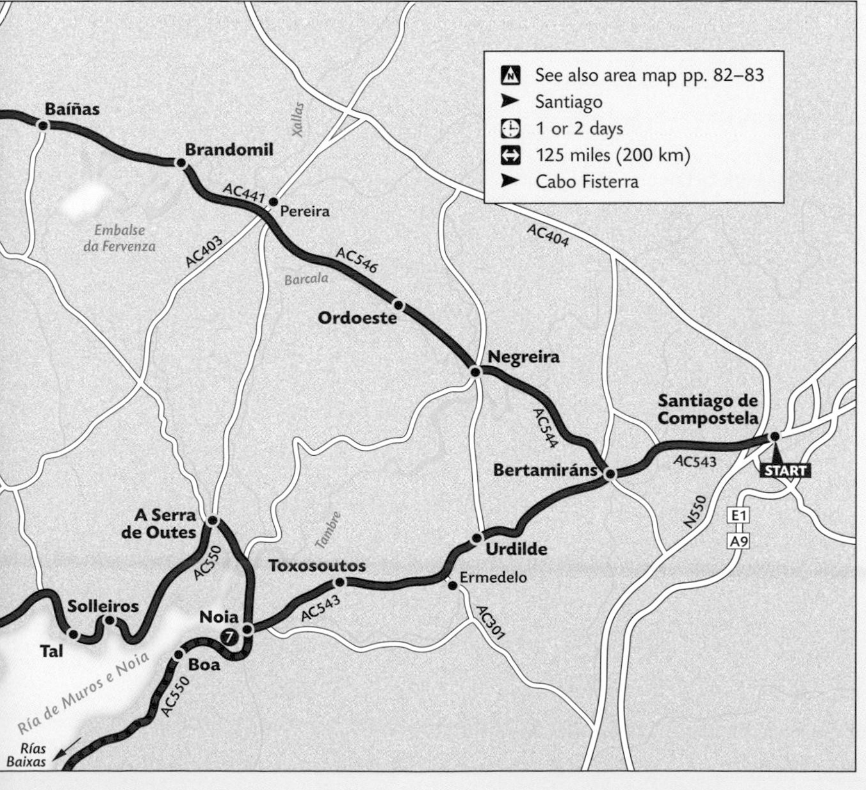

South Along the Coast

Retrace your route back to Corcubión and Cée. At Cée, turn right on the AC550 and head toward Muros. After crossing the estuary of Ézaro you reach **O Pindo ❹,** another stunning beach, before passing the rock formations of the 2,063-foot (629 m) **Monte do Pindo,** also known as the Celtic Olympus.

The next stop on your drive is **Carnota ❺,** which has the longest hórreo in Galicia. On entering the village turn right at the main square, circle left around the church, and there you'll see it—a grain-store of 1763 that stretches 78 feet (24 m) in length. Six miles (10 km) farther are Carnota's magnificent wild sand dunes and beach.

Go back to the main road, and continue to **Muros ❻** *(Visitor information, Casa del Ayuntamiento, Curro da Praza, tel 981 82 60 50),* a surprisingly grand town with arcaded buildings facing the bay. In 1544, a French fleet was sunk offshore, and in 1809 French troops burned 185 houses in the town. Walk up through the labyrinth of picturesque lanes to see **Santa María do Campo** (1400), a blend of Romanesque and Gothic, then head for the **Pescadería Vella** to see a curious turtle-topped fount.

Rapa das Bestas

If you are visiting during the summer months, consider extending your drive to take in Rapa das Bestas, the Galician version of the rodeo. From Santiago drive about 1.5 hours southwest to the village of Sabucedo, in the province of Pontevedra. Literally meaning "capturing the beast," the Rapa das Bestas takes place here on the first weekend of July and involves rounding up wild horses and herding them into corrals, where *agaradorres* (grapplers) wrestle them to the ground, brand them, and cut off their manes and tails. Once all the horses have been tamed in this way, the usual riotous festivities kick in. Sabucedo's stone corral is centuries old.

Noia

From Muros, the road snakes around forested promontories overlooking the bay. It then crosses a high bridge to make a dramatic arrival at the historic little port of **Noia ❼** *(Visitor information, Casa de la Cultura, Rúa Luis Cadarso 6, tel 981 82 41 69).* Noia's lovely Romanesque church of **Santa María a Nova** *(Carreiriña do E. Ferreiro, closed p.m. Sat. & Sun)* was built in 1327 and has a unique collection of more than 300 tombstones from the 10th to the 16th centuries, each one carved with symbols of the deceased's trade. The **medieval quarter** radiates from the Praza do Tapal, with its Galician Gothic church of **San Martiño** (1434). The magnificent carved portal may remind you of Master Mateo's work at Santiago, and Mateo was, in fact, a strong influence. Noia has many fine old mansions as well as some beautiful sandy beaches.

INSIDER TIP:

While touring Spain's sleepy northwest, you will see the humble scallop shell just about everywhere, including on road signs and even on your dinner plate. Santiago means "St. James," and medieval pilgrims to his shrine adopted the scallop shell as their symbol.

—MARY STEPHANOS
National Geographic contributor

From Noia you can return 21 miles (34 km) to Santiago on the AC543 or continue south to the Rías Baixas (see p. 96).

mega-project, the **Cidade de Cultura de Galicia** *(tel 881 99 75 84, www.cidadedacultura.es)*. This lies southeast of town at Monte do Gaias. Designed by the American architect Peter Eisenman, the 173-acre (70 ha) arts complex of local stone ripples over the hillside. Not without controversy, the budget has quadrupled and budget restrictions have left the project only half complete.

In & Around Pontevedra

Pontevedra is one of Galicia's most seductive small towns. According to legend it was founded by the Greek warrior Teucro, who fought at Troy. More prosaic history records that it prospered on sardine fishing until the mid-16th century, when its port silted up.

As a result of its former prosperity, Pontevedra has numerous fine old buildings of local granite, especially in the old town. This is now a lively pedestrianized zone. Pretty little squares such as **Praza do Teucro** and **Praza da Verdura** are still used by traditional specialist markets. The more grandiose **Praza da Herrería** has gardens overlooked by the 14th-century monastery and church of San Francisco. Opposite stands the unusual neoclassic church of the Virgen la Peregrina, built to an elliptical form to house a statue of the city's patron saint. To the west in the old fishermen's quarter stands the plateresque church of **Santa María la Mayor,** erected by the powerful seamen's guild in the 16th century. Low-relief biblical scenes adorn the western facade.

The excellent **Museo de Pontevedra** is housed in five different sites, three of which face the delightful arcaded **Praza da Leña.** The 18th-century mansion of **Castro Monteagudo** displays magnificent Celtic jewelry from 800 to 700 B.C. and a collection of medieval and Renaissance paintings. The museum continues in the beautifully conserved neighboring house of **García Flórez,** with precious metalwork, religious statuary, and reconstructed period interiors, including one of a ship. Galician art and Spanish paintings of the 19th and 20th centuries are displayed in the **Edificio Sarmiento** and **Edificio Fernández López.** Don't miss the fifth section, however: This is the evocative Gothic **ruin of Santo Domingo,** next to the leafy gardens of the Alameda, where architectural fragments and sculptures are exhibited. The **Alameda** is a popular spot for the paseo.

Just 4 miles (6 km) west from Pontevedra is the Benedictine

Religious sculptures decorate Pontevedra's cathedral.

Pontevedra
82 B2

Visitor Information
Oficina de Turismo, Marqués de Riestra, 30 Baixo
986 85 08 14

www.visit-pontevedra.com

Santa María la Mayor
Avenida Santa María 24, Pontevedra
986 86 99 02

Museo de Pontevedra
Pasantería 2–12, Pontevedra
986 85 14 55
Closed Sun. p.m. & Mon.

www.museo.depo.es

Illas Cíes

82 B1

Naviera Mar de Ons, Estación Marítima de Ría, Vigo

986 22 52 72

Boats hourly: Easter & July–Sept. Also Ría de Vigo day-cruises

www.turismodevigo.com
www.mardeons.com

Vigo

82 B1

Visitor Information

Oficina de Turismo, Cánovas del Castillo 22

986 43 05 77

Baiona

82 B1

Visitor Information

Oficina Municipal de Turismo, Paseo da Ribeira s/n

986 68 70 67

www.baiona.org

Monasterio de Poio *(with suitably austere accommodation, tel 986 77 00 00)*. The medieval monastery is rather forbidding, but the 1708 church is a fine example of late Galician classicism. Portuguese architect Mateo López designed the 16th-century cloister.

Rías Baixas

The long inlets of the Galician coast are known as *rías*. Those between Noia and Vigo are called the Rías Baixas—the lower rías—to distinguish them from the Rías Altas on the rockier northern coast. The milder Rías Baixas enjoy most of Galicia's tourism.

Fortified Roman-Celtic villages *(castros)* and dolmens (prehistoric slab tombs), hórreos (grain-stores), *pazos* (mansions), and Romanesque churches are plentiful. Some spots are overrated, like the island of Arousa, despite its bird sanctuary, the resort of O Grove, and the island of A Toxa.

Head instead for the delightful town of **Cambados.** Dominating the main square is the 16th-century **Pazo de Fefiñanes,** a Renaissance palace carved with stone busts and heraldic arms, and an arched footbridge leading to the San Sadurniño tower. Across the square stands the church of **San Benedict.** Vineyards around town produce a light, slightly fruity and sparkling white Albariño wine. Bodegas (wine cellars) abound, and good local bars face the Pazo de Fefiñanes.

The **Illas Cíes** are three beautiful uninhabited islands off the Ría de Vigo, with white beaches, pine forests where rare seabirds nest, and Celtic remains. In summer, you can take a 40-minute boat trip from Vigo, Baiona, or Cangas to this national park and stay at a campsite *(tel 986 43 83 58/22 55 82)*. The much industrialized fishing port of **Vigo** (Spain's largest) has pockets of interest around the harbor, a hilltop castle with wonderful views, a cutting edge **marine museum** *(Av. Atlantida, tel 986 24 77 50, closed Mon., www.museuodomar.com)*, and **MARCO** *(Rúa do Principe, tel 986 11 39 00, closed Mon., www.marcovigo.com)*, an impressive museum of contemporary art.

Baiona, the southernmost town of the Rías Baixas, has massive fortified walls of the **Castelo de Monte Real,** where the townspeople sheltered from pirate attacks in earlier centuries.

(continued on p. 98)

Rías Baixas Wines

In 1988 a brave group of growers and winemakers in Cambados, near the city of Pontevedra, established the DO *(denominación de origen)* Rías Baixas and its regulating council. By 2007, just before the global economic crisis sabotaged business, it looked like unstoppable growth, with 53 countries importing the wine. The Albariño grape, the queen of the Rías Baixas crop, is sometimes said to have derived from the Riesling grape brought by Cistercian monks, but tests now reveal that viticulture existed well before the monks arrived. Other native grapes used for white wine are Loureiro, Treixadura, and Caíño Blanco. To find local wineries, consult *www.rutadelvino riasbaixas.com*.

EXPERIENCE: Fish Like a Galician

Spain is the largest consumer of seafood per capita in the European Union, and more than half its fishing industry is concentrated in Galicia, where this age-old activity continues to flourish along the intricately indented coastline. Marine tourism, an innovative development that aims to counter the problems of diminishing catches and reduced quotas, is also now growing. Learn to buy fish like a local or, better yet, head out on the water yourself.

The most widely fished species is the sardine, followed by mackerel, blue whiting, jacks, hake, and albacore (a kind of tuna). Then there are the legions of molluscs and crustaceans: oysters, clams, crabs, scallops, lobsters, *coquinas* (a tiny clam), cockles, mussels, and shrimp: The gourmet options are endless.

One of the most sought after specimens is the goose barnacle. Barnacle buffs distinguish two types: the highly prized *de sol,* which grow on sunny, wave-thrashed rocks, and the less prized *de sombra,* whose shady existence leaves less flavor. In the fall and winter, when they are at their best, prices soar. Barnacles are collected by strictly regulated *perceberos* (*percebeiros* in Galician), one of the most dangerous jobs in Europe.

Visiting the Fish Market

Visit the fish market in any of the fishing harbors and watch how the day's catch is auctioned: Try the markets in O Grove, A Coruña, or Vigo. Auctions are usually held in the afternoon, once the boats have returned to port after collecting the *nasas* (a narrow-necked, baited trap) that were set the previous day.

Fishing flourishes along Galicia's 930-mile (1,500 km) coast.

Fish with Galicians

Best of all though, is to join the fishermen on the water. **Pescanatur** *(www.pescanatur.es),* an association of six fishing and shellfish collecting guilds in the Rías Baixas, offers the chance to set off with fishermen or collect shellfish. You can experience half a day at sea in search of sea urchins, razor clams, and barnacles and then tour the estuary before returning with your skipper to the fish auction.

If you prefer to remain ashore, the *sequeiras* (women who gather shellfish at low tide on a specific patch of beach) show how to collect cockles and clams on the beautiful Rías Baixas sands. These tours last two to three hours and depend on tides.

What to Expect

If you decide to become a crew member, your day will start at 5 or 6 a.m. Expect to fish octopus from July to November and more general catch from April to June. O Grove, Pontevedra, and Cangas de Onís are the main fishing harbors in Rías Baixas.

Farther south, Arcade is famed for its oysters and A Guarda for its lobster, while the rough seas of the rugged Costa da Morte, to the north, are said to foster the world's best seafood: Lira (Lires) is the port to go to.

No matter where you go, you can rely on the fisherfolks' recommendations for a top place to eat seafood. Some knowledge of Spanish and, even better, a few words of Galician is helpful.

Set in a fertile river valley, Ourense is at the heart of this region's wine country.

Ourense (Orense)

82 C1

Visitor Information

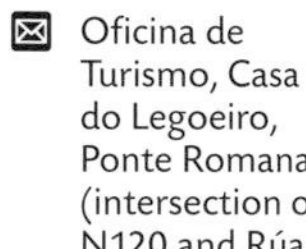

Oficina de Turismo, Casa do Legoeiro, Ponte Romana (intersection of N120 and Rúa Progreso)

988 37 20 20

www.turismourense.com

Catedral

Praza do Trigo, Ourense

988 22 09 92

Museo Arqueológico

Plaza Mayor

988 20 33 58

Closed Mon. & Sun. p.m.

In & Around Ourense (Orense)

This inland town rimmed by mountain ranges is noticeably poorer than Galicia's prosperous seaboard, although Ourense is rich in natural resources. Here the Miño River, which crosses Ourense on its way south to the Portuguese border, creates an extensive, fertile valley, the heart of Ribeiro wine country.

The city of 100,000 inhabitants has a confrontational past: It was attacked by Romans, Visigoths, Swabians (who destroyed the town in A.D. 463), Moors, and Normans (responsible for further destruction in 970). Today, it proudly conserves a **Roman bridge,** rebuilt in the Middle Ages for pilgrims going to Santiago, and other monuments in the pedestrianized ***casco viejo*** (old town). The **catedral,** originally Romanesque, has three exceptional portals. The best is the west-facing **Pórtico del Paraíso,** which is decorated with polychrome sculptures. The harmonious **interior** has carved choir stalls, suspended lanterns, gilded statues, carved sarcophagi set into niches, a very ornate retable (1520), and the cloister houses a museum.

Walk east of the cathedral to see the charming **Praza do Ferro,** lined with timbered medieval houses. Then walk down from the cathedral to the sloping, arcaded **Praza Maior.** On one corner, the excellent **Museo Arqueológico** is in a 12th-century archbishop's palace with an ornately emblazoned Renaissance facade. The intelligently laid out collection (with fleeting views over internal patios) is strong on Gallic-Roman pieces, and has Romanesque and Gothic statuary. Notice the fine granite statue of a Roman warrior and the polychrome Romanesque figure of **Nuestra Señora del Refugio,** which shows a strong Byzantine influence.

Ourense's origins were the thermal springs, known as **Las Burgas,** now on the square of the same name. The water (which heats up to 153°F/ 67°C) erupts into a neoclassical fountain and pools surrounded by contemporary sculptures. The entire Ourense region is famed for its spas, including Galicia's oldest, **Caldas de Portovía,** which dates from Roman times.

Ribadavia: It's an easy excursion 18 miles (30 km) west to Ribadavia, a pretty riverside town and the center of Ribeiro wine. Bodega tours can be booked through the tourist office. Old stone houses cluster around Praza Magdalena, once home to a large Jewish community that specialized in the wine trade. Among the churches, 13th- to 14th-century **Santo Domingo** has a Romanesque-Gothic interior. Rising beside the road, crumbling walls of the **Castillo de los Condes de Ribadavia** enclose tombs and towers.

Canyon del Sil: Venture 12 miles (20 km) northeast of Ourense and you could spend an entire day exploring the otherworldly canyon of the Río Sil, whose confluence with the Miño has been tapped to create two reservoirs. This wild, thickly forested region of oaks, pines, and ferns harbors unique historical sights. Hike the trails or take a two-hour boat trip across the river's dark green waters.

Known, too, as Ribeira Sacra ("sacred ravine"), the canyon has three monasteries. **San Estevo** is the most overwhelming in scale, style, and history. It was founded in the sixth century, but the earliest parts are a Romanesque **cloister** and **church.** The other two cloisters date from the 16th and 17th centuries, and there is a monumental staircase dating from 1739. This vast edifice has been extensively restored and is now a wonderfully remote and atmospheric parador.

The 9-mile (14 km) drive from Loureiro, 2.5 miles (4 km) east of the monastery, to the village of Parada do Sil gives the most spectacular views over the canyon. Teetering on the brink 3 miles (5 km) north of Parada is the melancholically beautiful, part ruined **monastery of Santa Cristina.** What you see dates from the 12th and 13th centuries. Trails make this perfect hiking terrain.

Castro Caldelas is a ruined castle 25 miles (40 km) farther east, crowning a hilltop town. Medieval ramparts give huge views, and inside is an illuminating history museum. Don't miss the **Torre del Reloj** where you get a close view of a 1760 clock that functions with stone weights. Continue 20 miles (30 km) farther and you reach Manzaneda, Galicia's only ski resort. ■

Santa Marta

Galician traditions can be extreme, but little beats the eccentric procession that takes place in As Neves, a small town lost in the hills above the Miño River. Every year on July 29, in honor of Santa Marta, the patron saint of resurrection, grateful survivors of accidents and illnesses are carried in open-topped coffins around town, followed by crowds clutching candles. Offerings are made to the saint's statue before the festival culminates in deafening fireworks.

Ribadavia

82 B1

Visitor Information

Oficina Municipal de Turismo, Parroquia Ribadavia (San Domingos), Lugar Ribadavia, Praza Maior 7

988 47 12 75

Closed Oct.–May

www.ribadavia.com

Viajes Pardo (boat trips through Canyon del Sil)

Juan XXIII, 1 Ourense

988 21 51 00 or 902 21 51 00

www.riosil.com

As Neves

82 B1

More Places to Visit in Galicia

Betanzos

This delightful town lies 14 miles (23 km) southeast of A Coruña. By the 14th century the commercial talents of its inhabitants had earned them the nickname the "Genoese of Spain." They used their wealth to build its medieval streets and buildings, including the pleasingly asymmetrical 14th- to 15th-century church of **Santa María del Azogue** and the neighboring church of **San Francisco** (1387). This lovely Gothic structure has tombs in niches in the walls and sculptures of wild boar. Best of all is the tomb of the town's powerful 14th-century ruler, Count Fernán Pérez de Andrade. His extraordinary sarcophagus is raised on the backs of his heraldic animals, a boar and a bear. Betanzos holds fairs on the first and sixteenth day of every month, when crowds of locals sell homemade baskets, cheese, and furniture. More historic in character is the Medieval Fair held every July. *www.betanzos.es* 82 B3 **Visitor Information** Oficina Municipal de Turismo, Praza de Galicia 1 981 77 66 66

A Guarda (La Guardia)

Venture to this remote town on the Portuguese border to see **Monte de Santa Tegra.** This legendary hill has the restored remains of a Celtic-Roman *castro* (see sidebar this page) dating back to 600–200 B.C. The rebuilt circular stone dwellings occupy an impressive strategic location, and the mirador (viewing point) that crowns the hill gives fantastic views: The best are south across the Río Miño to Portugal and west across the Atlantic. Just below stands a small **museum** *(tel 986 61 00 00)* with stone inscriptions, Roman amphorae, and other artifacts. From the castro, a path lined with stone crosses leads to the hermitage of Santa Tegra. *www.aguarda.es* 82 B1 **Visitor Information** Oficina de Turismo, Praza do Reloxo s/n 986 61 45 46

Tui

The medieval quarter of this charming small town is clearly defined by a sharp rise in level along Rúa Ordoñez. Above lies a web of atmospheric cobbled streets dominated by the 12th-century **Catedral San Telmo,** which looks like a fortress because its other role was to fend off attacks from Valença, in Portugal. The beautifully sculpted main portal is said to be the earliest example of Gothic architecture in Spain. The **museum treasury** leads to the **cloisters,** from which you reach the corner tower. Climb this to the ramparts for views to Portugal. Opposite the cathedral is the **Museo Diocesano** *(tel 98 660 31 07, closed Oct.–Easter),* with exhibits from the Roman to baroque periods. At the **Convento de las Encerradas** (Convent of the Cloistered Nuns, *Rúa das Monxas*), nuns sell cookies through a swiveling counter. *www.concellotui.org* 82 B1 **Visitor Information** Praza do Concello 1 677 41 84 05

Castros

The long Celtic history of northwestern Spain is exemplified by its hilltop settlements, or *castros,* whose structures evolved over a thousand years or so. The Romans integrated their own systems into the castros, which by the last few centuries B.C. had become sophisticated defensive towns or *oppida,* with populations of several thousand. The often circular buildings rarely rose higher than 6 feet (2 m). Walls were of slate with clay used as cement, and roofs were thatched. Saunas, or bathhouses, were public and relied on fireplaces, boilers, and water channels. About 3,000 castros have been discovered in Galicia and around 200 in Asturias.

Asturias & Cantabria

Squeezed between some of Spain's highest mountain ranges and the Cantabrian Sea, these two regions are a seductive combination of magnificent landscapes richly spiked with history. Traveling by car is momentous, with vast vistas over emerald green valleys, precipitous ridges, and narrow, gushing ravines. Lush pastures and solid stone houses are other hallmarks of Spain's most bucolic region, which also has sandy beaches, fishing ports, and ski resorts.

Together Asturias and Cantabria make up Spain's most bucolic region.

About 12,000 years ago, Paleolithic (Old Stone Age) people painted the caves that riddle Cantabria's limestone terrain. The cave paintings of Altamira are world famous and their replica almost as good. Millions of years earlier, dinosaurs roamed here and the new Museo Jurasico at Colunga does them imaginative justice. Much later, mountains rearing behind the Cantabrian coast protected the last Christian enclave in Spain: In 718, a Visigothic nobleman named Pelayo halted the Moorish advance north in the Picos de Europa. These spectacular mountains now form Europe's largest national park.

Oviedo, the part-industrialized Asturian capital, has three beautiful pre-Romanesque churches and a stunning medieval center. The undisputed star of Romanesque in Cantabria is at Santillana del Mar, but the roads of this region are dotted with signs pointing travelers to lesser known structures built for pilgrims on the Way of St. James (see pp. 86–87).

In contrast, Santander, the Cantabrian capital, is a lighthearted 19th-century resort that makes a relaxing stopover. Westward from here, a string of small coastal

EXPERIENCE: Gijón's Cider Fiesta

Asturias is the center of Spain's apple orchards. In Gijón *(visitor information, Oficina de Información Turística, Calle Rodriguez Sampedro, tel 985 34 17 71, www.gijon.info, map 83 E3)*, the capital of cider-making, more than 300 *sidrerías* (cider bars) are said to sell some 10 million gallons (10 million liters) a year.

Since cider has no additives or chemicals, it is considered a healthy tipple. At less than €3 per bottle, it is also inexpensive. Its alcohol content is barely five percent, so a local will easily drink his way through a bottle or more over dinner. In order to preserve the natural gas, a waiter will pour the cider theatrically from far above his head. When the stream of cider hits the inner side of the glass the drink is aerated and so slightly fizzy. Only a couple of inches are poured at a time, known as *un culín*, and traditionally this should be drunk in one go before going flat.

Easter sees big celebrations for the first cider of the year. But to really understand this Asturian obsession, visit Gijón in the last week of August for the cider fiesta *(http://en.turismo.gijon.es)*. Four days of related events include a cider-waiters' competition and selection of the year's best brew.

Oviedo

83 E3

Visitor Information

Oficina Municipal de Información Turística, Plaza Constitución 4

984 08 60 60

www.oviedo.es

Catedral

Plaza de Alfonso II, Oviedo

985 20 31 17

Closed Sun. (Cámara Santa, Claustro, & Museo Diocesano)

$. Free Thurs. p.m.

www.arsvirtual.com/monum/oviedo.htm

resorts dish up generous portions of seafood and shellfish. Try white beans *(fabes)* with clams, and wash them down with Asturias's specialty: local cider (see sidebar this page).

The Asturian triangle of Avilés, Gijón, and Oviedo is busy with industry, as well as coal and iron mines. Move inland, however, and you find age-old traditions, such as clogmaking, and wild countryside. In Cantabria, many of the half million inhabitants live in rural communities where livestock farming predominates. Exquisite Tudanca beef is one gastronomic result, while Asturias is famed for its many cheeses, topped by pungent blue-veined Cabrales.

Oviedo

Set in a saucer of land that is often shrouded in low cloud, Oviedo is Christian Spain's oldest city, and a good proportion of the 200,000 inhabitants seem to celebrate nightly in the town's ***sidrerías.*** The harmonious architecture of the old quarter is one of northern Spain's jewels, while cultural life is lively.

Rising above the elegant **Plaza Alfonso II,** named after the ninth-century founder of the town, is the **catedral,** a sprawling edifice in Flamboyant Gothic style. It towers over the remains of the church of San Tirso (its ninth-century predecessor), the former monastery of San Vicente, and the Benedictine monastery of San Pelayo. Inside the cathedral is the venerated **Cámara Santa,** with remarkable statues, capitals, and relics, including the Holy Shroud and Oviedo's symbol: the Cross of the Angels. You reach it from the corner of the nave that also gives access to the 14th-century cloisters and the **Museo Diocesano.** This has splendid processional crosses, chalices, and Romanesque statues.

A few steps from the cathedral, the **Museo de Bellas Artes**

(Palacio de Velarde, Santa Ana 1, tel 985 21 30 61, closed Sun. p.m. & Mon., www.museobbaa.com) is richly stocked with art from the 16th to the 20th centuries. Emphasis is on Asturian and Spanish painting, but Flemish and Italian works are also here. In the web of streets extending south from here baroque stone mansions are juxtaposed with Asturian timbered buildings and the 1882 iron and glass market, El Fontán, brimming with produce.

Just outside Oviedo are three rare pre-Romanesque churches. Closest to the center is ninth-century **San Julián de los Prados** *(tel 985 28 55 82, closed Sun.)*. Squeezed between the Gijón highway and the Campus Universitario, it is a strikingly serene, vaulted structure with extraordinary frescoes. Two and a half miles (4 km) northwest of Oviedo at Monte Naranco is **Santa María,** built in A.D. 848 as the king's summer palace before becoming a church a century later. This beautifully proportioned two-story structure has open loggias and a vaulted crypt, originally built as a guardroom. Immediately uphill stands its contemporary, **San Miguel de Lillo.** The capitals and reliefs are very delicately sculpted. These two churches are called the **Iglesias Prerrománicas de Monte Naranco,** and visits are by guided tour only.

Los Oscos

Spaniards from farther south visit Asturias for one reason: to escape the unrelenting dryness. Los Oscos, 60 miles (100 km) west of Oviedo, makes the classic destination. The valleys of this biosphere reserve have lush, untouched scenery, rivers and waterfalls, strong folk traditions, and hearty food.

The warmhearted inhabitants who inherit their strong, dark features from Roman ancestors were drawn here by gold. Growing rural tourism gives ample opportunities for hiking, horseback riding, and trout fishing, and encourages traditional crafts. Accommodations are simple, but hospitable.

Three villages bear the name Oscos (Santa Eulalia, Villanueva, and San Martín), but **Taramundi** is the best place to start exploring.

Iglesias Prerrománicas de Monte Naranco

- ☎ 985 29 56 85 & 676 03 20 87
- ⌚ Closed Sun. & Mon. p.m.
- $ $ (30-minute guided tour); free Mon. a.m.

Taramundi

- Map 82 D3

Visitor Information

- ✉ Oficina de Turismo, Calle Solleiro 14
- ☎ 985 64 68 77
- ⌚ Closed Mon.

www.taramundi.net

Santa Eulalia is one of three villages comprising Los Oscos.

Steep hills surround the colorful (and busy) harbor in the little village of Luarca.

Santa Eulalia
82 D3
Visitor Information
Oficina de Turismo, Carretera General s/n
985 62 12 61
Closed Mon. & winter
www.oscos-eo.es

San Martín
82 D3
Visitor Information
Oficina de Turismo, Carretera General s/n
664 11 38 15
Closed winter
www.oscos-eo.es

It was a center of knifemaking, as iron was worked in local forges using water power. Several old watermills show 18th-century technology, notably that of **Teixois,** a dizzy 20-minute drive southeast.

From Taramundi the narrow road winds southeast to the three Oscos, passing 3,330-foot (1,015 m) Pico de Ouroso. Stunning **Santa Eulalia** is the most modernized but has exemplary 18th-century rural architecture. A road through pristine forest leads to **Villanueva,** with its partly ruined Benedictine monastery, where one barrel-vaulted room exhibits information on the region.

The last village, **San Martín,** has the most tortuous access roads, as it lies huddled between two mountains. Next to the church is an impeccable slate-and-thatch-roofed hórreo (grain-store), the best of the many in the region. The baroque archway leads to the former palace of the Guzmanes. A few miles on at **Mon** you will find the turreted, emblazoned 16th- to 18th-century palace of the Mon y Velarde family.

Costa Verde

The "Green Coast" edges Asturias, from the Río Eo on the Galician border to Llanes close to the border with Cantabria, 125 miles (200 km) east. Other than the industrialized port of Avilés, it is characterized by low-key resorts, fishing villages, sandy beaches, and strong traditions.

Moving from west to east, the lively fishing port of **Luarca** is shaped by the sinuous Río Negro, which winds through to the picturesque harbor lined with cider bars below the steep slopes of the old town. Walk or drive up the hill at the end of the harbor to the elaborate marine cemetery and church for wonderful views. Good beaches are easily reached to the west and farther east at Cabo Busto.

The lighthouse at **Cabo Vidio** gives dramatic views before the next essential stop: **Cudillero,** its tiny harbor sandwiched between cliffs in a cove. A cluster of outdoor restaurants serve seafood and cider. The beach, Playa de Aguilar, stretches to a rocky headland. Immediately beyond that is **Muros de Nalón,** which has large elegant residences of the 15th and 16th centuries and the popular Playa de Aguilar.

At **Colunga,** overlooking the beaches of Lastres and Griega in an area rich in dinosaur tracks, the ambitious **Museo Jurasico** *(tel 902 30 66 00, closed Mon. & Tues.)* displays lifesize copies beside real remains and fossils.

Lastres is a picturesque clam-fishing port, with the harbor and noble mansions nestling beneath a cliff, while **Llanes,** a delightful historic port full of character, has a dozen sandy beaches close by. **Ribadesella** has the paleolithic cave network of **Tito Bustillo** *(tel 985 86 11 20, closed Mon. & Tues., winter),* which rivals Altamira, and a new center of cave painting *(tel 985 18 58 70).*

In & Around Santillana del Mar

It is said that the name of this noble village incorporates three lies. It is not saintly *(sant),* nor is it flat *(llana),* nor is it by the sea *(el mar),* which is 2 miles (3 km) away. But what does this matter when a village has a 1,200-year history and a unique mix of architecture. Just 12 miles (20 km) west of Santander, Santillana attracts hordes of visitors. In summer they throng the narrow cobbled streets; July and August are best avoided.

The main sight, the **Colegiata,** once a 9th-century monastery, was transformed in the 12th century into a Romanesque masterpiece. Its intricately sculpted main portal, interior friezes, and the 42 capitals of the magnificent cloisters depict lions, doves, snakes, pelicans, and plant motifs. The entrance to the **cloisters** is from the side—don't miss them, nor the beautifully carved stone **fount** at the back of the nave, nor the early 16th-century **altarpiece** honoring the relics of St. Juliana, whose tomb stands in the transept.

From the Colegiata, the main street runs through the village to the **Museo Diocesano** *(tel 942 84 03 17, closed Mon. in winter, $),* located in a converted convent.

INSIDER TIP:

Playa de Santa Justa, one of the lovely beaches in Cantabria, is easily reached from Santillana del Mar. Just head west for half a mile (0.8 km) and then turn right.

—JOSÉ CARLOS CAMPOS REGALADO
Santillana del Mar parador manager

The museum has a fine collection of medieval and baroque sculptures, silver, carved ivory, and enamelwork. Between the Colegiata and museum a web of delightful streets winds through the Gothic towers, houses in the

Luarca
82 D3
Visitor Information
Oficina de Información Turística, Palacio del Marqués de Gamoneda, Plaza Alfonso X El Sabio s/n
985 64 00 83
www.valdes.es

Cudillero
83 E3
Visitor Information
Oficina de Turismo, Puerto del Oeste
985 59 13 77
www.cudillero.org

Muros de Nalón
83 E3
Visitor Information
Oficina de Información Turística, Avenida Fierros s/n
985 58 03 79
www.bajonalon.es

Santillana del Mar
83 G3
Visitor Information
Oficina de Turismo, Calle Jesús Otero 20
942 81 82 51
www.turismo cantabria.com

San Vicente de la Barquera

83 G3

Visitor Information

Oficina de Turismo, Avenida del Generalísimo 20

942 71 07 97

www.sanvicentedela barquera.org

Parque Nacional de los Picos de Europa

83 F2

Visitor Information

National Park Reception Center, Casa Dago, Cangas de Onís

985 84 86 14

www.picosdeeuropa .com

Potes

83 F2

Visitor Information

Oficina de Turismo, Plaza Independencia s/n

942 73 81 26

Potes

The lively market town of Potes sits at the crossroads of four valleys, where a relatively mild climate nurtures the outlying cherry orchards and grapevines. This center for climbers, mountain bikers, canoeists, and hikers has specialist equipment shops, and guides abound. The warm, friendly restaurants serve sausages, cheeses, cheesecakes, and milk-based desserts, evidence of delicious mountain cooking.

Calle del Cantón, the Renaissance palace of Velarde behind the Colegiata, and many baroque mansions. Local fine-food stores fill in the gaps.

West of Santillana are Comillas and San Vicente de la Barquera. **Comillas** *(visitor information, tel 942 72 03 39)* has the neo-Gothic **Palacio de Sobrellano** *(Plaza Joaquín del Piélago 1, tel 942 72 25 91)*, designed by Catalan Modernista architect Joan Martorell. It stands on a hilltop beside the marquis's chapel and a folly designed in 1883 by the architect Gaudí (see pp. 172–175). Comillas also has popular beaches.

San Vicente de la Barquera is an animated fishing port below a castle, now a museum and exhibition center, and a 13th-century fortified church. The town attracts masses of visitors in summer, and make sure you're among them—local restaurants serve spectacularly good seafood. One mile (1.6 km) south lie the world-famous caves of **Altamira** (see sidebar p. 109).

Picos de Europa

Cantabria's idyllic rolling pastures lead to breathtaking mountains: the limestone massif of the Picos de Europa that is shared with Asturias and Castilla y León. They rise to more than 8,500 feet (2,600 m) just 15 miles (25 km) from the coast and are riddled with caves. Some 273 square miles (700 sq km) form Spain's first national park, inhabited by brown bears, chamois, wild boar, wolves, and royal eagles. In restaurants, game and organic veal top the menu, while cheeses are varied and delicious.

Long isolated by its rim of peaks, the succession of valleys known as **Liébana** successfully repelled Romans, Arabs, and French. Cutting through it is the Río Deva, which has carved a spectacular gorge, the **Desfiladero de la Hermida.** Only one road (N621) runs into Liébana from the Cantabrian coast, and it follows the gorge, so be prepared for tortuous bends. Craggy, eroded pinnacles rise above, and below is the boulder-strewn torrent of the Deva, teeming with salmon and trout. Two other access roads are the N621 from the province of León, south over the San Glorio Pass (5,278 feet/1,609 m), and the C627 southeast from Palencia. Both have incessant switchbacks and spectacular scenery.

Liébana has lovely churches and hermitages, above all **Nuestra**

Señora de Lebeña *(1.8 miles/3 km north of Cillorigo-Castro, tel 942 74 43 32, closed in winter),* a tenth-century Mozarabic structure.

The road west out of Potes (see sidebar opposite) to Fuente Dé (12 miles/19 km) is worth taking. Just outside Potes, turn left at the signpost and go 2.5 miles (4 km) to the Franciscan **monastery of Santo Toribio de Liébana** *(tel 942 73 05 50).* This is the most important religious site in the region, prompted in the eighth century when a fragment of the True Cross (allegedly) was brought here from Jerusalem. A large gold-plated cross contains the holy relic, in the **Capilla del Lignum Crucis** (Chapel of the Wood of the Cross).

The main road ends abruptly at a cluster of restaurants and a parador that form **Fuente Dé,** sitting at the base of a dramatic sheer rock face. A cable car takes you up to a lookout at 6,058 feet (1,847 m), with spectacular views. From there, a 1.8-mile (3 km) path leads to the **Puerto de Aliva,** remote haunt of brown bear, chamois, and capercaillie (a large grouse).

On the Asturian (western) side of the mountains the most historic site is **Cangas de Onís** (see p. 110), Spain's first Christian capital 1,300 years ago and now a major canoeing center. Driving south on the main N625, you go through the gorge of **Los Beyos,** flanked by multiple limestone strata. About 6 miles (10 km) farther is the **Mirador de Oseja de Sajambre,** one of the region's panoramic lookout points. The road from here to Potes (via the LE244 and N621) is for diehards only as it entails no fewer than four mountain passes. Another

Fuente Dé
- 83 F2
- Teleférico (cable car)
- 942 73 66 10
- Closed weekdays in Jan.
- $$$

From the Picos de Europa you can look down on the clouds.

Liérganes
83 G3
Visitor Information
Oficina de Turismo, Paseo del Hombre Pez
942 10 16 24

route from Cangas de Onís, equally spectacular, follows the AS262 to Covadonga (see p. 110), site of Pelayo's famous victory over the Moors. From here the road narrows as it climbs spectacularly to the Lago de Enol.

Palacio de la Magdalena, Santander

INSIDER TIP:

For a little something sweet, head 19 miles (30 km) southeast of Santander to the town of Liérganes, which is surrounded by steep pastures. Here the most popular desserts are *sacristanes,* local puff pastries.

—LAWRENCE GUY STRAUSS
National Geographic grantee

Santander

The genial capital of Cantabria swings around a huge bay backed by mountains. Santander has its own charm, mixing chic shoppers, shady bars, and stylish cafés. The architectural style, from the late 19th and early 20th centuries, is typified by the wedding-cake casino overlooking the beaches. Much regeneration has transformed Santander into a very popular resort and home to 180,000 people.

The Península de la Magdalena separates the elegant resort area of **El Sardinero** from the bustling commercial town and port. It is crowned by the incongruous, Scottish-style **Palacio Real** (late 19th century), built for King Alfonso XIII and his British wife, Victoria Eugenia, by public donation, to encourage the king's pioneering habit of sea-bathing in their town. The palace is not open to the public, but the surrounding park with a small zoo and restaurants is accessible from

EXPERIENCE: Explore Cantabria's Prehistoric Caves

Discovered in 1879, **Altamira,** 1 mile (1.6 km) inland from Santillana del Mar (see pp. 105–106), was the first example of Paleolithic cave-painting found in Spain. The sophistication of the polychrome art—which includes expressive renderings of animals and handprints—confounded historians and scientific evaluation for decades, but it is now accepted that the paintings are 25,000 to 35,000 years old. (Paintings at France's famed Lascaux are estimated to be 17,000 years old.)

The cave is closed to the public, but you can see an exact replica at the **Museo de Altamira** *(tel 942 81 88 15, www.museodealtamira.mcu.es, closed Mon. Advance booking recommended in holiday season: tel 902 24 24 24, www.bancosantander.es).* The fascinating displays cover the stages of early man (in Spanish and English) using video, interactive display, and animation.

Farther south at Puente Viesgo, about 17 miles (27 km) from Santander, **El Castillo** *(tel 942 59 84 25, http://cuevas.culturadecantabria.com/castillo.asp.)* boasts five caves with outstanding Paleolithic paintings of animals (including mammoths), handprints, and abstract signs. Guided visits lasting 45 minutes are available year-round.

Red deer and dots monopolize the cave-paintings at **Covalanas** *(tel 942 64 65 04, http://cuevas.culturadecantabria.com/covalanas.asp),* a small cave located southeast of Santander near Ramales de la Victoria. Discovered in 1903, this art may be more than 20,000 years old.

A different cave experience awaits at **El Soplao** *(tel 902 82 02 82, closed Mon. Oct.–June, www.elsoplao.es. Book in advance through www.cajacantabria.com),* where you can take a one-hour trip on a mining train through tunnels and caverns.

the beaches on either side. The venerable and still heaving Playa Sardinero stretches north from here, highlighted by an ornate belle epoque casino. The large villas of this enclave include the home of Emilio Botín, president of Spain's biggest bank, Santander.

The **catedral** in central Santander is in fact two buildings, one superimposed on the other. The lower church dates from the 12th century although displays Roman origins. Within a few decades it was joined by the upper one. External steps lead up to this more ostentatious section. It was rebuilt in the 17th century but was damaged by a dynamite explosion in the harbor in 1893 and again in 1941, after a devastating fire. This led to extensive reconstruction of the center.

Don't miss a breezy stroll along Santander's seafront avenue, which edges the animated pedestrianized shopping area. Note the ornate **Correos** (post office), **Palacete del Embarcadero** (Jetty Mansion), and excellent **Museo Marítimo** (Maritime Museum; *tel 942 27 49 62*). The **Museo de Prehistoria y Arqueólogia** *(Calle Casimiro Saínz 4, tel 942 20 71 05, closed Sun. p.m. & Mon.)* outlines Cantabria's extensive prehistoric past. The small collection includes mysterious inscribed circular stones from the fourth to first centuries B.C. ■

Santander

83 G3

Visitor Information

Oficina Municipal de Turismo, Jardines de Pereda s/n

942 20 30 00 or 942 20 30 01

www.turismo.cantabria.com

Catedral

Plaza Obispo y Trecu, Santander

942 22 60 24

More Places to Visit in Asturias & Cantabria

Cangas de Onís

In the eighth century, the town of Cangas de Onís became the capital of Christian Spain when Pelayo was proclaimed king after he defeated the Moors at Covadonga. The **chapel of Santa Cruz** was built to mark that victory, but was rebuilt in the 15th century. It incorporates a Bronze Age *dolmen* (stone tomb). The town also has a medieval humpbacked bridge mistakenly labeled Roman. Three miles (5 km) east at Cardes is the **Cueva del Buxu** with its Paleolithic cave paintings. Less than 2 miles (3 km) north by the Sella River you will find the 12th-century Benedictine **monastery of San Pedro,** now a parador. *www.cangasdeonis.com/turismo* 83 F3 **Visitor Information** Oficina de Turismo, Casa Riera, Avenida de Covadonga 1 985 84 80 05

Covadonga

This major pilgrimage site is a picturesque mountain sanctuary on the northern flanks of the Picos de Europa where Pelayo started the Christian Reconquest (see pp. 27–30) in 722. A statue of the legendary hero stands in front of the 1800s **basílica.** Inside the adjoining **Museo de la Virgen** are items given to the Virgin of Covadonga, including a priceless diamond-studded crown. Pelayo's sarcophagus is in the neighboring cave, the **Santa Cueva,** where he retreated. Here, too, is the much venerated **statue of the Virgin,** patron saint of Asturias.

From Covadonga a steep road twists 12 miles (20 km) up to a limestone plateau and the beautiful lakes of **Enol** and **Ercina,** a good starting point if you are interested in hiking in the mountains. 83 F3 **Visitor Information** Oficina de Información, Explanada de la Basílica 985 84 60 35

Santa Cueva, Covadonga

Reinosa

This lively market town on Santander's main road link with Castilla y León makes a good base for visitors to the region, as it lies on the slopes of the Cantabrian Mountains. The ski resort of **Alto Campóo** is located 16 miles (25 km) west, just beneath the towering peak of **Pico de Tres Mares** (7,136 feet/2,175 m). You can reach the summit by chairlift. There you will enjoy magnificent views over the Picos de Europa.

On the C628 road to Alto Campóo, stop at **Fontibre** where a scenic footpath leads to the source of the Ebro River. This whole lush valley has great natural beauty and numerous dolmens (prehistoric stone tombs) lie hidden in remote corners. Immediately east of Reinosa is the immense **Embalse del Ebro,** a reservoir that attracts a wide variety of waterfowl (and bird-watchers). On its banks cows gently chew their cud..

Four miles (7 km) south of Reinosa is **Cervatos,** which has a 12th-century Romanesque **collegiate church** *(tel 942 75 41 42 or 679 21 09 49, keys available next door).* Wonderful carvings of lions and more unusual, blatantly erotic figures decorate the capitals of the church's apse and corbels. *www.turismoreinosa.es* 83 G2 **Visitor Information** Oficina de Turismo, Avenida del Puente de Carlos III 23 942 75 52 15

One of Spain's most diverse regions, from fishing villages and farming communities to vast sweeps of vineyards and the Pyrenees

Northeast Spain

Sunset over picturesque Hondarribia (Fuenterrabía)

Northeast Spain

Four autonomous regions nudge the mountain barrier separating Spain and France: Euskadi (Basque Country), Navarra, Aragón, and Catalunya (see pp. 180–198). Nestling south of the three is La Rioja. They present very different faces of the Spanish character.

Traditionally, this region never had as many foreign visitors as other parts of Spain, but its main towns are now firmly on the trail. On the coast are the hip resort of Donostia (San Sebastián) and the burgeoning city of Bilbo (Bilbao), still experiencing a boom spearheaded by the Guggenheim Museum. Inland are the monasteries and sierra of La Rioja, Navarra, and Aragón, and the nature reserves of the Pyrenees. In Aragón especially, where the Moors held sway until the 12th century, you find tiny historic towns with elaborate Mudejar architecture and open, rolling landscapes.

Be prepared for a new vocabulary, as the Basques, like the Catalans and Galicians, use their own language on every sign. Explore the coastal towns, but go inland to experience rural life and delightful small towns. Although Euskadi led Spain's industrial revolution, which accounts for much of its wealth and self-esteem, unspoiled nature is never far away. The best areas in northeast Spain are in the Pyrenean foothills, and the most beautiful stretch of these is in Aragón's Parque Nacional de Ordesa y Monte Perdido.

Navarra has Iruña (Pamplona), world famous for bullrunning, but it also has some of the major stopping points on the Way of St. James (see pp. 86–87), hence the string of superb Romanesque constructions that continue through La Rioja. Palaces, castles, and churches are scattered through the region. ■

NOT TO BE MISSED:

of Biscay
Hondarribia (Fuenterrabía)
Irún
Getaria
Donostia (San Sebastián)
Zarautz
Azkoitia
Azpeitia
Guipuzcoa
Peñas de Aia 1018m
Santuario de San Miguel de Excelsis
Orreaga (Roncesvalles)
FRANCE
0 60 kilometers
0 40 miles
Iruña (Pamplona)
Monasterio de Irantzu
NAVARRA
Estella (Lizarra)
Monasterio de Iratxe
Monasterio de Leyre
Ansó
Hecho
Puerto de Somport
Parque Nacional de Ordesa y Monte Perdido
Torla
3355m Monte Perdido
Pico Posets 3371m
Pico de Aneto 3404m
Bielsa
Revilla
Benasque
Jaca
Sangüesa (Zangoza)
Castillo de Javier
Sos del Rey Católico
San Juan de la Peña
Sabiñánigo
Aínsa
El Pont de Suert
Olite
Riglos
Castillo de Loarre
Calahorra
Monasterio de la Oliva
Sádaba
Ayerbe
Bolea
Huesca
Graus
Arnedo
Enciso
Corella
Bardenas Reales
Tudela
Ejea de los Caballeros
Fitero
Almudévar
Barbastro
Tarazona
Zuera
Binéfar
2316m
Monasterio de Veruela
Utebo
Sariñena
Sierra del Moncayo
ZARAGOZA
Los Monegros
La Almunia de Doña Godina
Fraga
Bujaraloz
Quinto
Embalse de Mequinenza
Calatayud
ARAGÓN
Maluenda
Cariñena
Fuendetodos
Monasterio de Santa María de Huerta
Caspe
Híjar
Monasterio de Piedra
Daroca
Alcañiz
Calanda
Valderrobres
Calamocha
Montalbán
Monreal del Campo
CASTILLA-LA MANCHA p.233
CATALUNYA (CATALUÑA) p. 177
Mirambel
La Iglesuela del Cid
Sierra de Albarracín
Albarracín
Teruel
Mora de Rubielos
VALENCIA p.177
Sarrión
Sierra de Javalambre
A8
A15
A12
AP68
A23
E90
A2
N330
Ebro
Aragón
Gállego
Jalón
Jiloca
Guadalope
Turia
Cinca
Alcanadre
Ésera
Ara
Bidasoa
3 2 1
C D E F

Euskadi & Navarra

Euskadi (as the Basques call their country) and Navarra have long been linked by their common language, *euskera,* still widely spoken in varying dialects throughout the region. When Castilla wrested control from the kings of Navarra in the 13th century, the Basque identity and sense of civic rights strengthened. Seven centuries later, with grievances exacerbated by Franco's repression, this became a bitter separatist struggle that continues today. There is generally no threat to visitors, however, as targets are political.

Permanent sculptures outside Bilbo's Museo Guggenheim include "Tulips" by Jeff Koons.

The 2,800 square miles (7,200 sq km) of Euskadi divide into three historical territories: Vizcaya to the northwest, around Bilbo (Bilbao); Guipúzcoa to the northeast, with Donostia (San Sebastián) as its capital; and the inland region of Álava to the south, surrounding Gasteiz (Vitoria). The latter borders Navarra, 4,056 square miles (10,400 sq km) of diverse landscapes, from Pyrenean peaks and green valleys to southern plains.

You may find Euskadi's prosperous cities of Bilbo and Donostia more exciting than Iruña (Pamplona), the capital of Navarra. The Basque coast has a history of seamanship and fishing. Donostia and Hondarribia (Fuenterrabía) are established resorts; elsewhere are surfing beaches and low-key fishing villages strung along 125 miles (200 km) of rugged coastline.

Common to both Navarra and Euskadi are rolling green hills and valleys clad in beech, oak, and chestnut forests. Here are nature reserves, solid stone houses, pastoral scenes, and stark mountains. This is where the Sierra Cantabrica meet the Pyrenees.

Navarra's 56,810 acres (23,000 ha) of vineyards have progressed by leaps and bounds since the late 20th century and now produce highly regarded wines. Euskadi's *pintxos* (appetizers) and internationally applauded cuisine are as good as its traditionally excellent wines from the Rioja Alavesa (which neighbors La Rioja). Signature bodegas are the latest development here, part of the renewal that has infused this corner of Spain since Bilbo's massive facelift in the late 1990s.

Bilbo (Bilbao)

Ever since the Museo Guggenheim opened in 1997, Bilbo has experienced a cultural renaissance and consequent surge in tourism. Nearly half the population of Euskadi lives in greater Bilbo (one million people), and the city is vital to the Spanish economy. Architects Cesar Pelli, Calatrava, Isozaki, Legorreta, Foster, and Zaha Hadid have all left their mark.

In 1300 the city, which sits on the navigable estuary of the Río Ibaizabal, became the export hub for Castilian goods. Today the old shipbuilding and dock area of **Abandoibarra** is the cultural hub with a 2-mile (3 km) sculpture walk, the Guggenheim, Pedro Arrupe's footbridge, and Calatrava's glass-floored bridge.

On the other side of Bilbo, the winding streets of the ***casco viejo*** (old town) around the **cathedral** *(closed Sat. & Sun.)* have been injected with new life. The **Museo Vasco** gives background on the culture and economy of the Basque region. A few steps away is the lively **Plaza Nueva,** lined with cafés and food shops. Foodies should not miss Europe's largest market, the **Mercado de la Ribera** *(Ribera 20, closed Sun. & Mon.–Fri. 2 p.m.–5 p.m.)*, a soaring 1930s structure on the riverbank. Beside the Puente del Arenal stands the **Teatro Arriaga** and across the river the ornate 1902 railway station. Most of the casco viejo is pedestrianized and packed with tapas bars.

INSIDER TIP:

The Museo de Bellas Artes, just southwest of the Guggenheim, boasts an excellent collection of Spanish and Basque paintings. Don't miss it.

—LAWRENCE GUY STRAUSS
National Geographic grantee

A riverside tramway links this quarter with Abandoibarra. In between stretches Bilbo's **19th-century quarter** and the Gran Vía—home to Bilbo's financial institutions and upscale shops. It ends in the west at the **Parque Doña Casilda de Iturriza,** a park next to the **Museo de Bellas Artes.** Its paintings by Zurbarán, Ribera, El Greco, van Dyck, Goya, Gauguin, Chillida, Tàpies, and

Bilbo (Bilbao)
112 B6
Visitor Information
Bilbao Turismo, Plaza del Ensanche 11
944 79 57 60
Closed Sat. & Sun. p.m.
www.bilbao.net

Museo Vasco
Plaza Unamuno 4, Bilbo
944 15 54 23
Closed Sun. p.m. & Mon.

Museo de Bellas Artes
Plaza del Museo 2, Bilbo
944 39 60 60
Closed Sun. p.m. & Mon.
$$
www.museobilbao.com

The "Guggenheim Effect"

In the late 1980s, the city of Bilbo was decidedly unseductive, but the construction of Frank Gehry's Guggenheim in the 1990s changed that completely. Star architects flocked to the city. British architect Sir Norman Foster, for example, designed the tubelike subway entrances affectionately known as ***Fosteritos.*** Inaugurated in 1995, they were the first element in the city's massive investment in infrastructure. Santiago Calatrava's **Campo Volantin footbridge** followed soon after.

More recently, in 2008, came the **Isozaki Atea,** Bilbo's 22-story twin towers, the tallest buildings in Basque country and the work of Japanese architect Arata Isozaki. The **University Library** by Rafael Moneo was completed the same year. In the burgeoning Abandoibarra district you can see the streamlined forms of Alvaro Siza's **Auditorium** and Cesar Pelli's **Iberdrola Tower.** Still taking shape is a huge project for Zorrotzaurre, a peninsula jutting into the Nervion River that will become an island complex for residential and business use. The masterplan is by Zaha Hadid, the Iraqi-British architect.

Bilbo's heritage has not been ignored, either. French star Philippe Starck has transformed one of the city's most loved buildings, the 1909 Alhóndiga, from an old wine warehouse into the spectacular cultural and leisure center, the **Alhóndiga-Bilbao** *(www.alhondigabilbao.com),* with 43 stunningly decorated columns.

Museo Guggenheim

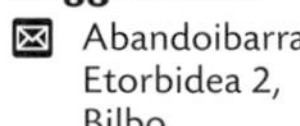

Abandoibarra Etorbidea 2, Bilbo

944 35 90 80

Closed Mon. Sept.–June

$$$. Guided tours in English available.

www.guggenheim-bilbao.es

Bacon are often overlooked due to the "Guggenheim effect" (see sidebar this page).

Museo Guggenheim: However many photographs you may have seen of this building, the reality is still a visual shock. Its curved steel and titanium planes beside the Puente de la Salve reflect the hills, sky, and river of Bilbo in an endless play with light that defies all logic. Architect Frank Gehry's masterwork has put Bilbo firmly on the world cultural map and is one of the icons of 20th-century Spain. One million visitors per year now come to admire it.

The idea of the museum arose in the late 1980s when the Basque government decided to diversify the city's economic base by redeveloping the derelict shipbuilding area as part of a coordinated revamp. By 1992, the Solomon R. Guggenheim Foundation had been signed up to manage this important new institution, and in October 1997 the innovatively designed museum opened to world applause.

The nucleus of Gehry's design is a soaring 164-foot-high (50 m) atrium, around which are interconnected blocks housing 19 galleries, an auditorium, a restaurant, and offices, in steel, glass, and limestone. Transparent elevator shafts, curving walkways, and terraces all add to the vertiginous sense of excitement in this rule-breaking building—an apt expression of Basque audacity.

Since its inauguration, neighboring structures have matched Gehry's imagination, notably Federico Soriano's Congress Hall and Music Centre and Ricardo Legorreta's Melía Hotel.

The Guggenheim's total floor area is 260,000 square feet (24,000 sq m), and just under half that is exhibition space, including the world's largest exhibition hall, a staggering 426 feet (130 m) in length. This now displays the museum's greatest work, a gravity-defying installation of eight rolled steel sculptures by Richard Serra. Walk inside them, and then admire their stupendous curves from the balcony above.

Along with its sister museums in New York and Venice (the Solomon R. Guggenheim Museum and the Peggy Guggenheim Collection), the Bilbo museum has access to an impressive sweep of 20th-century artworks that form a shared permanent collection. These are presented on a rotational basis and offer contrasting perspectives on seminal movements and artists from the U.S. and Europe. The Bilbo collection has its regulars, from Basque sculptor Eduardo Chillida to Tapiès, Warhol, and U.S. abstract expressionists and Pop artists.

Leading contemporary Spanish and Basque artists are also featured, and an exciting program of temporary exhibitions and installations highlights current trends in Spanish art. Galleries on the top floor are reserved for temporary exhibitions, often of a historical nature.

Much emphasis is placed on new forms of medium, bringing installations together with videos and paintings. Multimedia and site-specific commissions include a witty LED installation by Jenny Holzer in a corner of the atrium. One unmissable piece is the gigantic, flower-studded **"Puppy"** by Jeff Koons that sits outside the museum entrance. Equally arresting

(continued on p. 119)

The bold titanium planes of Frank Gehry's Guggenheim overlook the Río Nervion.

EXPERIENCE: Basque Cooking

Something quite exhilarating has been taking place in the province of Guipúzcoa. In Donostia (San Sebastián) and other Euskadi cities, chefs have returned to their roots, developing less heavy and sauce-dependent dishes using regional produce, including vegetables and olive oil. Known as *nueva cocina* (new cooking), this new style, which also includes the innovative combination of ingredients, began in the mid-1970s and has since taken the country by storm. Put yourself right at the forefront of Basque cooking with a class or specialized tour.

Learn Basque Cooking

The **Basque Culinary Center** in Donostia *(Paseo Juan Avelino Barriola 101, www.bculinary.com)* is dedicated to training the chefs of the future. It offers a master's degree in Basque cooking yet also has courses for interested nonprofessionals, too. These include half-day sessions on cooking with spring vegetables *($$$$)* to five-day courses devoted to rice dishes *($$$$$)*.

Learn how to prepare some of the region's quintessential seafood dishes at a four-hour class *($$$$)* given by **San Sebastián Food** *(Calle Aldamar 30, Donostia, tel 634 75 95 03, www.sansebastian.com)*. You will visit the three-Michelin star restaurant **Akelarre** *(Paseo Padre Orcolaga 56, Donostia, tel 943 31 12 09, www.akelarre.net)*, where friendly, experienced chef Alex Barcenilla leads students in this hands-on session. After class, enjoy a gourmet lunch with wine. Or sign up for the half-day *pintxo* (tapas) cooking class *($$$$)*, after which you'll have the opportunity to savor the fruits of your effort. Longer options include a three-day Basque cooking class *($$$$$)* as well as a special spa and cooking course weekend *($$$$$)*.

Walking & Tasting Tours

If you're more interested in eating than cooking Basque food, try one of the half-day walking and tasting tours sponsored by **Tenedor Tours** *(tel 609 46 73 81, http://tenedortours.com)*. The **Culinary Walking Tour** *($$$$)* begins in the morning at Donostia's farmers market with an introduction to the region's seasonal produce. This is followed by a walking tour of the city's old quarter, with stops at fish stands, wine cellars, and gourmet shops for tastings of local meats and cheeses. Or fill up on pintxos at bars in the old quarter during the **Tapas Tour** *($$$$)*.

Nearly all top Basque chefs confess that their earliest culinary influences came from their families. You can see Basque tradition up close by joining the **Farm Tour** *($$$$$)*, a full-day excursion that begins at Donostia's farmers market and includes stops at shops in the old quarter, an organic vegetable farm overlooking the Cantabrian Sea, an anchovy producer, a winery, and a mountain cheesemaker. The price includes a guide, wine and cheese tastings, and lunch—with wine. The full-day **Basque Gastronomic Immersion** *($$$$$)* will take you up to isolated mountain villages, where you will meet local bakers, cheesemakers, and craftsmen. A village lunch is included.

Bogavante coralino: sesame crisps, lobster, and onions

is Louise Bourgeois's bronze **"Maman,"** a giant spider on the riverside esplanade.

Vitoria-Gasteiz

Vitoria-Gasteiz is the Basque country's capital. The medieval streets of the old part ring the hilltop cathedral, and their picturesque slopes have endless nooks and crannies to explore. The town was fortified in 1181 by Sancho III, king of Navarra, as a stronghold against Castilla, and flourished as a trading crossroads.

Much of the town is pedestrianized, reinforcing the air of placid provincialism so evident in the formal gardens of the **Parque de la Florida** (1820) and stately **Plaza de España.** This square, **Los Arquillos,** and **Plaza del Machete** form an intriguing bridging area between the medieval hilltop town and the flat, largely 19th-century city below. Just east of here is the **Artium** *(tel 94 520 90 20, closed Mon., www.artium.org),* a stunning new museum devoted to contemporary Basque and Spanish art.

Walk from Plaza del Machete along Calle de Santa María and you pass the **Palacio de Montehermoso** (1524) and, a block to the west, the plateresque **Palacio de Escoriaza-Esquivel.** At the end stands the 14th-century **cathedral of Santa María** *(tel 945 25 51 35, daily visits by appointment, www.catedralvitoria.com)* and a cluster of medieval and Renaissance buildings.

This historic nucleus includes **El Portalón,** built in timber and brick, the **Torre de los Anda** (a fortified house), and a modern intruder, Bibat. This houses the **Museo de Arqueología** and encompasses the exceptional **Museo Fournier,** devoted entirely

(continued on p. 122)

Vitoria-Gasteiz

112 B5

Visitor Information

Oficina Municipal de Turismo, Plaza de España 1

945 16 15 98 or 945 16 15 99

www.vitoria-gasteiz.org

The crowds in lively Plaza de la Virgen Blanca, Vitoria-Gasteiz, make for perfect people-watching.

Museo de Arqueología

Calle Cuchillería 54, Vitoria-Gasteiz

945 20 37 07

Closed Sat. & Sun. p.m. & Mon.

www.catedralvitoria.com

Basque Identity

The mysterious origins of the Basques help to make Euskadi, as they call their country, one of Spain's most beguiling regions. Green valleys and a dramatically indented coastline do not, however, capture the headlines. Far more prominent is the Basque role as a thorn in the flesh of central government.

Basques in traditional garb celebrate Carnival with lively town processions.

Numerous hypotheses have linked the Basque language, which predates Indo-European, to Caucasian languages of Central Asia and Berber, the language of the pre-Arab inhabitants of North Africa. Diverse studies eventually produced one common theory: The Basques have inhabited their remote, verdant valleys since the Stone Age. Today 30 percent of Basques are fluent Basque speakers, a proportion on the increase due to school curriculums.

The fiercely independent Basques converted to Christianity only in the ninth and tenth centuries, and were the last to adopt urban living–as late as the 14th century. The lack of towns did not stop the Basques forging ahead to establish elective assemblies in the provinces of Vizcaya and Guipúzcoa, however. Their ongoing battle with the central Spanish government dates from the days of the *fueros,* codes of traditional laws that were respected by the Catholic Monarchs and the Habsburgs, but were repeatedly revoked in the 19th century in order to create a more centralized Spain.

Separatist Politics

The man who catalyzed Basque resentment was Sabino de Arana Goiri (1865–1903). After coining the word "Euskadi" to encompass the four Spanish Basque territories of Álava, Guipúzcoa, Vizcaya, and northern Navarra, where Basque is spoken, he founded the Basque National Party (PNV). By the time of his death his avowed aim had swung from independence to autonomy.

Francisco Franco (dictator from 1939 to 1975) aroused intense bitterness after colluding in the bombing of the Basque town of Gernika in 1937; he later repressed Basque identity and abolished all remaining fueros. In 1960, Basque separatists founded ETA (an acronym meaning Euskadi and Freedom), which started a campaign of terrorism against Madrid.

Euskadi (or Basque Country) gained autonomy in 1979, but ETA bombs, assassinations, and 800 deaths continued to make headlines, goading the rest of Spain into massive demonstrations of outrage. Over four decades, cease-fires came and went. In May 2011, elections brought Bildu, a coalition of separatists, to power, a source of concern for many non-Basques. However, in October, a beleagured ETA declared a total cease-fire and called for dialogue.

Basque Culture & Traditions

Having been an agrarian society, Euskadi rapidly became Spain's most competitive industrialized region. Yet, like all Spaniards, the Basques cling to their roots. Some of the most genuine expressions of Basqueness come from *bertsolaris,* poets who improvise in local competitions, *pelota* (a ball and bat game), and *harriketa,* a more primitive pastime of lifting stones of up to 660 pounds (300 kg).

Basque gastronomy has propelled chefs such as Juan Marí Arzak, Andoni Luis Aduritz, and Martín Berasategui to the forefront of Spanish cuisine. Their emphasis on ultra-fresh ingredients and innovative combinations has spread like wildfire (see sidebar p. 118). The Basques even have gastronomic clubs *(txokos).*

Despite its apparently inward-looking nature, Euskadi has also been a region of maritime explorers (Sebastián Elcano, Lope de Aguirre) and of spiritual philosophers (Ignatius de Loyola, Francis Xavier).

Performers such as this dancer help keep Basque folk traditions alive.

Donostia's centuries of history edge the regal sweep of the Playa de la Concha.

Donostia (San Sebastián)
113 C6
Visitor Information
Oficina de Turismo, Boulevard 8
943 48 11 66
www.sansebastianturismo.com

to tarot and playing cards and displayed in the Renaissance mansion of Bendaña.

Donostia (San Sebastián)

The dynamic, outgoing queen of Euskadi's coast, also called the "pearl of the ocean," surrounds a stunning bay and spans the estuary of the Río Urumea. A fishing village that grew into a port, it is now a prosperous resort town of 180,000 people. All of them seem to gravitate nightly to the old quarter, with allegedly the greatest concentration of bars in the world.

After surviving no fewer than 12 major fires since the 13th century, Donostia's zenith came in the 19th century. Queen Isabel II (*R.*1843–1868) was the catalyst: She chose this spot when her doctor advised her to frequent the Cantabrian coast. For more than 20 years she returned each summer, and in 1863, by agreeing to the demolition of the old town walls, she unleashed Donostia's expansion. The result is the 19th-century city, a harmonious grid of streets stretching south from the old quarter, west around the Bahía de la Concha, and eventually east across the river. Donostia may be poor in monuments, but it has plenty of other good things, from public sculpture to excellent cuisine and beaches.

The coastline is punctuated by three hills. **Monte Igueldo** has a belle epoque amusement park and is reached by cable car *(tel 943 21 05 64, cars run every 15 minutes during daylight)* from the Plaza del Funicular. The old town grew at the foot of **Monte Urgull,** now a park, with a castle at the top. In the far east, **Monte Ulía** has fabulous views. Go by bus, car, or taxi from the old town to the base of the hill, then walk or drive about a mile (1.5 km) up the hill.

A 7-mile (12 km) waterfront promenade dotted with contemporary sculpture takes you the length of the city, and three city beaches give good swimming. Queen Isabel II's favorite was the lively **Playa de la Concha,** where her mock-English manor house, **Palacio de Miramar,** still stands.

In the old quarter, one of the nicest strolls is along Paseo del Muelle, at the back of the harbor. At the far end stands the **Aquarium,** modernized in 1998, with a transparent tunnel for close views of creatures of the deep. Packed into the little **harbor** are fishing trawlers, tour boats, the fish market, and a string of outdoor seafood restaurants. The **Museo Naval** displays items from the city's seafaring past.

Penetrate the labyrinth of streets behind the harbor packed with pintxo bars and you soon see the heavy baroque facade of the church of **Santa María** *(Calle 31 de Agosto).* The vaults beneath the organ hold a sculpture by Eduardo Chillida (1924–2002), Euskadi's great artist, whose funeral was held here in 2002.

Continue along Calle 31 de Agosto to reach another historical hulk: **San Telmo.** This 16th-century Dominican convent has been recently renovated and ambitiously expanded to become an avant-garde landmark for Basque culture. **San Telmo Museoa** displays ethnographic, archaeological, photographic, and art historical exhibits in a seamless transition from the original building. Do not miss the 11 extravagant murals by Catalan artist José Maria Sert (1874–1945) in the old church, or the blooming vertical garden of the new facade.

Also in this quarter look for the **Plaza de la Constitución,** an arcaded square lined with outdoor cafés. The numbered balconies above were once the seats of spectators for the square's original function as a bullring.

Opposite the emblematic 1912 theater, **Teatro Victoria Eugenia,** a bridge crosses the Urumea River to the 20th-century residential quarter of Gros. Impossible to miss are the geometric planes of Rafael Moneo's 1999 convention center,

Film Festival

Donostia has a flourishing cultural life, but the biggest event of the year is the international film festival in September. It was first held in 1952. Screenings are shared at Rafael Moneo's state-of-the-art convention center, the Kursaal, whose spectacular translucent cubes rise on the eastern tip of the estuary, and the recently restored Teatro Victoria Eugenia. Stars prefer to stay at the regal-looking María Cristina hotel next to the theater.

INSIDER TIP:

When going out for *pintxos* in Donostia, the tradition is to bar hop all night. For the freshest food, select from the offerings listed on the chalkboard menus rather than off the preprinted one at the bar.

—JON WARREN
Managing Director & Founder, San Sebastián Food

Aquarium
Plaza Carlos Blasco de Imaz, Donostia
943 44 00 99

Museo Naval
Paseo del Muelle 24, Donostia
943 43 00 51
Closed Sun. p.m. & Mon.

San Telmo Museoa
Plaza Zuloaga 1, Donostia
943 48 15 80
Closed Sun. p.m. & Mon.

www.santelmomuseoa.com

Tabakalera
- Duque de Mandas 52, Donostia
- 943 01 13 11

www.tabakalera.eu

Getaria
- 113 C6

Visitor Information
- Oficina de Turismo, Parque Aldamar 2
- 943 14 09 57
- Closed winter

www.getaria.net

Zarautz
- 113 C6

Visitor Information
- Oficina de Turismo, Calle Nafarroa Kalea 3
- 943 83 09 90

www.turismo zarautz.com

the **Kursaal,** superb when lit at night. The eastern side of town is also home to Donostia's latest project, **Tabakalera,** an old tobacco factory transformed into a contemporary art center. It is located just behind the railway station.

Explore the art deco streets nearer Zurriola beach and you will find upscale restaurants and sophisticated pintxos, but for more boisterous nocturnal sampling washed down with cider and/or *txakoli* (local white wine), head back to the old quarter.

Donostia has been selected as the 2016 European Capital of Culture, so things should sharpen up even further.

Costa Vasca

Stretching from the Pyrenees at the French border, an enticing, often wild coastline of nearly 125 miles (200 km) stretches west to Bilbo. Most resorts are small, squeezed between rocky cliffs and the thundering surf of the Cantabrian Sea. Town outskirts may be marred by high-rises and light industry, but the coast has good opportunities for board sailing, surfing, scuba-diving, and sailing.

West of Donostia, a string of resorts starts with one of the busiest, **Zarautz,** which has this coastline's longest beach (2 miles/3 km), a favorite with surfers. The access road from the hills goes past modern buildings that do not auger well, but the old quarter claims a 16th-century Luzea tower, Palacio de Narros, a Franciscan convent, and grand 19th-century villas.

From Zarautz the coast road (N634) twists around the indented shore to the town of **Getaria,** a real charmer. The old quarter lies on a promontory ending at **Monte San Antón,** nicknamed the "mouse of Getaria." The main attraction is the seafood restaurants lining the lively port, the perfect place to sip a glass of txakoli in honor of two of Getaria's most illustrious sons: fashion designer Cristobal Balenciaga (1892–1972) and Juan Sebastián Elcano, second-in-command to the Portuguese navigator Ferdinand Magellan on his great voyage around the world. Eight years late and way over budget, the sleek new **Cristóbal Balenciaga Museoa** *(Parque Aldamar 6, tel 917 87 46 00, closed Mon., www.cristobalbalenciagamuseoa.com)* opened its doors in 2011.

The corniche road soon comes to **Zumaia** *(visitor information, Plaza Kantauri, tel 94 314 33 96, closed winter, www.zumaia.es/turismo),* a friendly town on Mon in an estuary, with a lovely medieval quarter and a breezy

Lovely resorts like Mundaka dot Spain's Costa Vasca.

promenade. Zumaia has two good beaches, **Itzurun** and **Santiago;** surfers prefer the pounding surf at **San Telmo,** to the west.

Ten miles (16 km) inland of Zumaia are the neighboring towns of Azpeitia and Azkoitia. On the outskirts of **Azpeitia** stands the sanctuary of St. Ignatius de Loyola, philosopher and founder of the Jesuits, now a major pilgrimage spot. Next to his family's tower-house stands the **Basílica de Loyola** *(tel 94 302 50 00, www.sanctuariodeloyola.org),* designed by Carlo Fontana, a disciple of the Italian sculptor Bernini, with a striking baroque facade and 196-foot (60 m) cupola.

Back on the coast, **Deba** is the next fishing port west of Zumaia, with a good beach and dramatic cliffs. It lies at the mouth of the river of the same name and was important in the heyday of the Castilian wool trade–hence the surprisingly grandiose 16th-century church of **Santa María la Real.**

West of Deba, the coast road becomes increasingly scenic as it edges cliffs with plunging views over **Mutriku,** the rugged **Playa Saturraran,** and **Ondarroa.** Lookout points let you stop to admire the scene in safety, before the road reaches **Lekeitio,** in its lovely bay setting. The protected beaches here have safe swimming, and the seafood restaurants are predictably good.

Sixteen miles (25 km) to the west, houses at **Elantxobe**—the attractive marine extension of Ibarrangelu—seem to tumble down the steep hillside to the harbor and fishing boats. West of Elantxobe's rugged headland, **Cabo Ogoño,** are the area's two main beaches, **Playa de Laida** and **Playa de Laga,** both at the mouth of the lovely **Mundaka estuary.** Declared a biosphere reserve in 1984, the estuary has rich plant life and birdlife, beaches, and the prehistoric **caves of Santimamiñe.**

The town of **Gernika (Lumo)** lies at the southern end of the estuary. The name is immortalized by Picasso's painting (see sidebar p. 72) and commemorated in Gernika's park with sculptures by Eduardo Chillida and British sculptor Henry Moore. Of vital symbolic importance for Basque political identity is the oak tree under which the medieval Lords of

Hondarribia

The prettiest coastal town by far is Hondarribia (Fuenterrabía), a picture-postcard town looking across the Bidasoa estuary to Hendaye in France. This strategic site was heavily fortified, and 15th-century ramparts still enclose the austere Castillo de Carlos V, now a parador. The steep narrow streets around it have several baroque mansions. Down at the marina, painted wooden balconies brimming with flowers overlook lively bars and outdoor restaurants. Toward sunset, drive west about 4 miles (7 km) to the mirador (lookout point) at Jaizkibel, for polychrome views.

Deba
- Map: 112 B6

Visitor Information
- Oficina de Turismo, Calle Ifar Kale 4
- Tel: 943 19 24 52

www.deba.net

Lekeitio
- Map: 112 B6

Visitor Information
- Oficina de Turismo, Plaza Independencia s/n
- Tel: 946 84 40 17

www.lekeitio.com

Caves of Santimamiñe
- Centro de Interpretación, Barrio Basondo, Kortezubi
- Tel: 944 65 16 57 or 944 65 16 60
- Closed Mon.
- $

Gernika (Lumo)
- Map: 112 B6
- Artekale 8
- Tel: 946 25 58 92

www.gernika-lumo.net

Hondarribia (Fuenterrabía)
- Map: 113 C6

Visitor Information
- Plaza Arma 9
- Tel: 943 64 54 58

www.bidasoaturismo.com

Museo de la Paz

Gernika
946 27 02 13
Closed Mon.
$

www.museodelapaz.org

Bergara

112 B6

Visitor Information

Oficina de Turismo, Plaza San Martín de Agirre 1
943 77 91 28

www.bergara.net

Oñati

112 B5

Visitor Information

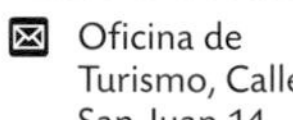

Oficina de Turismo, Calle San Juan 14
943 78 34 53

www.oinati.org

Vizcaya (Biscay) would periodically vow to uphold Basque privileges. The original tree died in 2004 but an offshoot has been planted; its green shoots represent new hope for the Basques. Nearby stands the **Museo de la Paz** and the **Casa de Juntas** where, since 1979, Vizcaya representatives meet once more.

INSIDER TIP:

Santimamiñe, near the historic town of Gernika, is one of the few Paleolithic cave art sites in the region open to the public.

—LAWRENCE GUY STRAUSS
National Geographic grantee

Valley Towns

Despite Euskadi's high level of industrialization, its green valleys encompass vast swaths of unadulterated nature and fascinating small towns. Northern Navarra has these, too, with the added bonus of Romanesque relics of the Way of St. James.

Bergara: In the valley of the Deba River, 34 miles (54 km) southeast of Bilbo, Bergara has harmonious Renaissance buildings behind its industrialized outskirts. You may arrive during one of its many music festivals.

The heart of Bergara is **Plaza San Martín Agirre,** where the arcaded baroque town hall faces the former royal Jesuit seminary. Also on the square are three Renaissance palaces with emblazoned facades. Immediately uphill, the church of **San Pedro de Ariznoa** has a 17th-century statue of Christ by Juan de Mesa and a painting by José Ribera. Don't leave Bergara without tasting the local *errellenoak* and *tostoiak* sweets.

Of the 20 hermitages dotting the countryside, the most venerated is that of **San Miguel de Aritzeta,** 1 mile (1.6 km) south of Bergara. It gives wonderful views over this lush region.

Oñati: Seven miles (12 km) south through the hills lies the noble town of Oñati. Its monuments make it the most historically rich town in the province of Guipúzcoa, and the calendar is studded with local fiestas that usually involve the populace parading in Basque costumes. **Sancti Spiritu University,** started in 1540, has a beautiful plateresque facade and a courtyard decorated in coffered Mudejar style. On the main square stands the church of **San Miguel Arcángel,** originally Gothic but with an 18th-century baroque-rococo tower, the work of Martin Carrera, who was also responsible for the rococo **Casa Consistorial** (Town Hall).

The monastery of Bidaurreta (1510) is on the southern edge of town. About 5 miles (9 km) on is Guipúzcoa's most important shrine, dedicated to **Arantzazu** *(tel 94 878 09 51),* the region's patron saint. The 1955 building was a collaboration between architects Sainz de Oiza and Laorga, and sculptors Eduardo Chillida, Lucio Muñoz, and Jorge Oteiza.

Estella: Strong Basque traditions continue 27 miles (43 km) southwest of Iruña (Pamplona) at Estella (Lizarra), the 12th-century capital of the kings of Navarra. It became a center of the Carlists (see p. 35) seven centuries later. It flourished because it was on the Way of St. James (see pp. 86–87) and also enjoyed privileges granted by King Sancho Ramirez—hence its fine medieval buildings.

The **Palacio de los Reyes de Navarra**—the royal palace—dates from the 12th century and is a rare example of civic Romanesque architecture. It is now the **Museo Gustavo de Maeztu.** Close by stands the 12th-century church of **San Pedro de la Rúa,** built in Cistercian style (see pp. 150–151). Two sides of the cloisters were blown up in the 16th century, but what is left is very beautiful. Cross the Río Ega, by the Puente de la Cárcel, and you find an old quarter of winding medieval lanes and the Romanesque church of **San Miguel,** with its intricately carved northern portal.

Outside town, in wild, bucolic surroundings, is the Cistercian **Monasterio de Irantzu** *(6.8 miles/11 km north of Estella on N120, tel 94 852 00 12, www.monasterio-iranzu.com)*, now a college. The even older **Monasterio de Iratxe** *(1.8 miles/3 km southwest of Estella, tel 94 855 44 64, closed Mon. & p.m. Tues.)* is on the old pilgrimage route. It has magnificent plateresque **cloisters** and a **church** combining Cistercian and Romanesque features. Since 1985 it has been unoccupied, inspiring projects for a museum and parador.

Sangüesa: Less atmospheric, and in the much more arid area bordering Aragón, Sangüesa (Zangoza) has a remarkable church, **Santa María la Real** *(open in summer; for guided visits, call Sangüesa Tour 620 11 05 81)*, which looms above the Aragón River. It was begun in the early 12th century, and final touches, such as the octagonal tower, the south portal, and spire, date from the middle of the 13th century.

The highlight is the **south portal,** which contains an astonishing number of sculptures by the master of San Juan de la Peña (see p. 147) and Leodegarius. Close by, on Calle Alfonso el Batallador, is **Palacio de Vallesantoro,** with an unusual baroque facade: It has projecting carved eaves and elaborately carved columns inspired by Spanish colonial art in Latin America.

Modern life and Renaissance heritage mix well in Bergara.

Estella (Lizarra)
113 C5
Visitor Information
Oficina de Turismo, Calle San Nicolás 1
948 55 63 01
www.estella-lizarra.com

Sangüesa (Zangoza)
113 D5
Visitor Information
Oficina de Turismo, Calle Mayor 2
948 87 14 11
www.turismo.navarra.es

Monasterio de Leyre
113 D5
2.5 miles (4 km) northeast of Yesa on N240
948 88 40 11
$

www.monasteriodeleyre.com

Navarra's Spiritual Lookouts

Northern Spain's monasteries and other holy sites are often in remote and beautiful settings, and Navarra's are no exception.

Monasterio de Leyre: The Monasterio de Leyre stands in the rugged, pine-clad Sierra Errando, 31 miles (50 km) southeast of Iruña, and has sweeping views of the **Yesa Reservoir.** Benedictine monks returned here in 1954; arrive early or stay late in order to hear their Gregorian chants *(daily at 7:30 & 9 a.m. and 7 & 9 p.m.)* in the serene Romanesque church of San Salvador. You can stay at the monastery hotel *(tel 94 888 41 00)*, or visit from Sos del Rey Católico (see p. 152) or Iruña.

The church entrance, known as the **Porta Speciosa,** has complex carvings; inside is the mausoleum of the kings of Navarra. Visit the unique **crypt** (1057), where vaults and pillars spring from low, carved capitals of extraordinary dimensions—some are up to 3 feet (1 m) in width.

Castillo de Javier: A few miles southwest of Leyre, the much rebuilt Castillo de Javier *(tel 948 88 40 24, www.santuariodejavier.org)* was the birthplace of the great Jesuit missionary Saint Francis Xavier (1506–1552). He is Navarra's patron saint, and the castle has spawned a basilica, a Jesuit retreat, and a mission.

Inside the castle, exceptional exhibits include a Gothic sculpture of Christ carved in walnut and a 15th-century wall painting of the Dance of Death (both in the Holy Christ Tower). From the crenellated walls on the terrace you look north

Throughout history monarchs have taken refuge at the peaceful Monasterio de Leyre.

toward Leyre and south to Aragón (see pp. 139–152). Javier itself has rather commercialized cafés and souvenir shops.

Santuario de San Miguel de Excelsis: To reach this remote site, you drive through lovely holm-oak and beech forests, up to wild heath that inspired legends of dragons. The area has the largest concentration of Stone Age structures in northern Spain and is popular with trekkers. Ask about trails at the **Casa Forestal** on the road to the sanctuary.

The church is perched on a promontory with dizzying views over the Sierra de Aralar, about halfway between Donostia and Iruña. It has a Visigothic (9th century) apse and an enclosed Romanesque chapel. The fabulous gilded and enamel 12th-century altar front, almost certainly from Limoges, was brought here from Iruña cathedral in 1765.

Iruña (Pamplona)

Outside of the festival of Sanfermines (see sidebar this page), Iruña is a quiet, even colorless little city, where life revolves placidly around the porticoed **Plaza del Castillo** on the edge of the old quarter. North of this are dark narrow lanes that date from when Iruña was the fortified capital of the kingdom of Navarra. Today they are lined with five-story houses and specialist shops.

Close to the old city walls, the Gothic **cathedral** has delicately structured cloisters. The old refectory and kitchen (1330) are now the **Museo Diocesano,** which displays religious objects. For an idea of Navarra's long and complex history, visit the **Museo de Navarra,** housed in a 16th-century hospital with an impressive Renaissance frontage. It has Roman mosaics (Pamplona was founded by the Romans in 75 B.C. on the Basque settlement of Iruña), Romanesque capitals from the former cathedral, Renaissance paintings, and frescoes gathered from all over the province.

The **bullring** lies immediately southwest of the old quarter on **Paseo Hemingway,** a broad leafy promenade. Follow the example of Hemingway himself and retire to the chandeliered 19th-century splendor of the **Café Iruña** on the Plaza del Castillo. ■

Sanfermines

Every July 6–14, Iruña holds its Sanfermines festival, marked by the *encierro,* the bullrunning immortalized by Ernest Hemingway in *The Sun Also Rises.* Intended to honor Iruña's patron saint, the encierro has become a test for daredevils. It starts daily at 8 a.m., when bulls are let loose to charge along a fenced route through town on their way to the bullring. Hundreds of people run into the street to pit their wits and speed against the bulls. Bullfights take place every day and celebrations continue long into the night.

Santuario de San Miguel de Excelsis

- Map 113 C5
- 10 miles (18 km) SW of Lekunberri
- 948 37 30 13

www.turismo.navarra.es

Iruña (Pamplona)

- Map 113 C5

Visitor Information

- Oficina de Turismo, Avenida Roncesvalles 4
- 948 42 04 20

www.pamplona.net

Cathedral & Museo Diocesano

- Dormitalería 3–5, Iruña
- 848 22 29 90
- Closed Sun.
- $

www.catedraldepamplona.com

Museo de Navarra

- Cuesta de Sto. Domingo, Iruña
- 848 42 64 92
- Closed Sun. p.m. & Mon.

More Places to Visit in Euskadi & Navarra

Olite

Olite's castle is a massive affair with crenellated towers and battlements. It dates from 1407 and had numerous Moorish elements such as hanging gardens, *azulejos* (tiles), and stucco work, but much of this vanished during multiple renovations and a devastating fire in 1813. Part of the castle is now a parador. The neighboring 14th-century church of **Santa María la Real** has a remarkable Renaissance altarpiece, but Olite's other medieval church, **San Pedro,** retains only a Romanesque doorway. From Olite, it's a 19-mile (30 km) drive to the 12th- to 15th-century Cistercian **Monasterio de la Oliva** *(tel 948 72 50 06, www.monasteriodelaoliva.eu)*, where cultivating the vineyards is an integral part of the monks' faith. *www.turismo.navarra.es* 113 C5 **Visitor Information** Oficina de Turismo, Plaza de los Teobaldos 948 74 17 03

EXPERIENCE: Desert Hiking

Parque Natural de Bardenas Reales *(Centro de Información, NA 134, km 15.1, tel 948 82 00 20, www.bardenasreales.es)*, a UNESCO biosphere reserve just 9 miles (15 km) northeast of Tudela, is a vast uninhabited wilderness, where wind and water have sculpted clay, chalk, and sandstone into magical forms. The 3-mile (4.6 km), one-way **Walking Route D** *(N126, km 22)* takes you up Cabezo de Fraile, a 1,824-foot (556 m) rise in the remote southern end of the park. At the top explore the remains of an old fort and then soak in the panoramic views. **Walking Route A** (0.6 miles/1 km) begins at Castildetierra and affords a closer look at one of this desert region's hidden ravines.

Orreaga (Roncesvalles)

This mountain pass in the Pyrenees has a special place in history and poetry: It was here that the Navarrese Basques unleashed their terror on the rear guard of Charlemagne's army in A.D. 778.

Over the centuries, thousands of pilgrims trudged through the pass on their way to Santiago de Compostela (see pp. 88–91). Landmarks include a 12th-century **hostelry,** the overrestored **collegiate church,** and its Gothic **chapter house,** which contains the tomb of Sancho VII (1154–1234) beside his queen. Don't miss the **museum** *(tel 948 79 04 80)* in the old stables. Among other wonders it contains an emerald from a Sultan's turban, worn during his fatal battle against King Sancho at Navas de Tolosa in 1212, and a 14th-century enameled reliquary dubbed **"Charlemagne's chessboard"** because of its checkered design. From the village, you can walk up an easy trail to **Puerto Ibañeta,** the top of the pass (3,466 feet/1,057 m), for good views. *www.roncesvalles.es* 113 D5 **Visitor Information** Oficina de Turismo, Antiguo Molino 948 76 03 01

Tudela

Ruled by Moors for several centuries, Navarra's second largest city lies at the center of a fertile agricultural region, the source of Tudela's hearty vegetable soup and its robust red wine, la Ribera del Queiles. The old Moorish quarter, the **Morería,** is an atmospheric labyrinth of winding lanes lined with Mudejar-style houses; also here is the 12th- to 13th-century **cathedral,** built on the site of a mosque. Its carved **Portada del Juicio** (Last Judgment doorway) fronts a Romanesque-Gothic interior and the tranquil cloisters. Tudela's patron saint, Santa Ana, is honored in an exuberantly decorated baroque side chapel. *www.tudela.es* 113 C4 **Visitor Information** Oficina de Turismo, Calle Juicio 4 948 84 80 58

La Rioja

To most non-Spaniards the word "Rioja" means Spain's most prestigious and internationally famous wine. But this small province of 1,950 square miles (5,000 sq km) sandwiched between Navarra and Castilla y León has a lot more. A combination of mountains, fertile farmland, and a mild climate has given rise to a cheerful population and a rich, delicious cuisine. Between hearty Riojan meals you can explore monasteries, churches, or chase dinosaur paths.

The Sierra de la Demanda rises behind La Rioja's beautiful rolling landscape.

The Ebro River marks the northern border with Euskadi (Basque Country), and a tributary, the Río Oja, gave the province its name. Rioja's main towns sit along the Ebro's fertile banks: Logroño, the modern provincial capital, Calahorra, and Haro, the center of the wine industry.

To the south loom Rioja's two mountain ranges, the Sierra de la Demanda and the Sierra de Cameros. This mountainous area is the Rioja Alta–Upper Rioja, as opposed to the flatter Rioja Baja in the northeast–with skiing, mountaineering, hunting (red and roe deer, wild boar), and fishing (river trout, crab, and carp). Low-key spas have grown up around the therapeutic springs at Arnedillo and Arnedo to the east on the bank of the Río Cidacos. The peaks have snow from late October until May and good hiking the rest of the year.

As you climb south into the sierra, churches and monasteries multiply. So do the flocks of sheep and cattle–Rioja's cuisine is largely meat based, with succulent lamb the main specialty. Vegetarians

La Rioja

113 C4

Visitor Information

Oficina de Turismo, Calle Salvador Pereda s/n, Hórreo de Pradillo, Pradillo

941 46 21 51

www.turismorioja.com

Sierra de la Demanda
112 B5
Visitor Information
Calle Sagastia 1, Ezcaray
941 35 46 79
www.sierradela demanda.com

won't go hungry: The Ebro Valley produces abundant artichokes, asparagus, peppers, and beans, for the famous Riojan vegetable stew.

Sierra de la Demanda

Rising to more than 6,500 feet (2,000 m) in western Rioja and western Castilla y León, the Sierra de la Demanda is ruggedly beautiful. This is a place for hikers. The Way of St. James (see pp. 86–87) runs below the northern flanks (now the N120 route), and part of the western side is a nature reserve.

Good walking trails on the Burgos (western) side of the mountains start from the villages of Pradoluengo, Pineda de la Sierra, Quintanar de la Sierra, and Neila. The last gives access to the **Parque de las Lagunas Altas,** a series of high-altitude lakes in stark, moody surroundings.

The Riojan side is crowned by the pine forests of **San Lorenzo** (7,450 feet/2,271 m) and the ski resort of **Ezcaray** *(Map 112 B4, www.ezcaray.org),* also a hub for Spanish hunters. The nature reserve of rivers and forest, which covers 200,800 acres (81,270 ha) has wolves, deer, mountain cats, eagles, and wild boars.

Santo Domingo de la Calzada's cathedral

Santo Domingo de la Calzada: Nudging the northern flanks is the pilgrimage town of Santo Domingo de la Calzada, situated where a Riojan holy man, Domingo, built a hospice for pilgrims. The Romanesque cathedral was completed shortly before his death in 1109. The ornamental baroque steeple (1765) that rises 230 feet (70 m) above the cathedral is actually the third version.

Inside the cathedral is its oddest feature, a late-Gothic **henhouse,** where a white cock and hen are kept to remind worshippers of a miracle that took place here: A roast chicken jumped up and crowed to prove the innocence of the pilgrim hanged for stealing it (the pilgrim was also revived).

Across the nave, look for the side chapel holding the stunning

The Birth of Written Spanish

The earliest known example of written Castillian (Spanish) dates from the ninth or tenth century, when an anonymous monk in the Monasterio de Suso (*suso* meaning "upper" as opposed to *yuso*, "lower," in archaic Castillian) wrote out the Codex Aemilianensis 60 in the monastery's scriptorium. He added marginal notes in Castillian to clarify passages in the Latin text, as well as shorter annotations in Basque. He also included a prayer in Castillian that was called by one Spanish philologist "the first cry in the Spanish language." This marked a watershed for Spanish culture.

Later, in the early 13th century, the same area saw the first poet to write in Castillian, Gonzalo de Berceo. The universities of Valladolid and Salamanca gave the Spanish language further authority until it reached today's status of being the fourth language of the world (after English, Chinese, and Hindu), spoken by some 400 million people.

main altarpiece, moved in 1994 to reveal the Romanesque chapel that it concealed. Unique in its profuse depiction of mythological and fantastical figures, the altarpiece is the last work of the prolific sculptor Damián Forment (circa 1480–1540). The sensitive polychrome painting of this 42-foot (13 m) masterpiece is by Andrés de Melgar.

The church's restored early 14th-century cloisters and Sala Capitular are now a **museum** *(closed Sun.)*, with treasures such as three Flemish triptychs and mid-17th-century Mexican silver. In the Sala Capitular the coffered ceiling and **choir stalls** (1668) were carved by Santiago Allona and his son, Juan Baptista.

San Millán de la Cogolla:

Southeast of Santo Domingo is San Millán de la Cogolla, named for the sixth-century Visigothic shepherd who retreated to this spectacular valley. Countless miracles were attributed to him. Pilgrims on their way to Santiago would make a detour into the hills above Santo Domingo de la Calzada to pay homage to him at two monasteries 1.5 miles (2 km) apart. Today they are both World Heritage sites.

The tenth-century Mozarabic **Monasterio de Suso** is a pretty, tiered structure, built above the cave where San Millán had his retreat. Lines are lengthy (only 20 enter at a time) to see its graceful horseshoe arches, Visigothic capitals, and the saint's alabaster tomb.

In complete contrast is the massive 16th- to 18th-century **Monasterio de Yuso** in the valley below. It's a popular Sunday outing for Riojans, and the Benedictine monks have converted part of the monastery into a four-star hotel. The church itself is an unsuccessful mixture of styles from Renaissance to baroque, but the monastery **treasury** has exceptional pieces, including carved ivory reliquaries and 12th-century processional crosses. Considered the cradle of written Castillian, the **library** contains Spain's best monasterial collection of medieval books.

(continued on p. 137)

Santo Domingo de la Calzada

112 B5

Visitor Information

Oficina Municipal de Turismo, Calle Mayor 33

902 11 26 60

www.lacalzada.com

San Millán de la Cogolla

112 B4

Visitor Information

Oficina de Turismo, Monasterio de Yuso, Planta Baja

941 37 32 59

www.najerasanmillan.com

Monasterio de Suso

941 37 30 82

Closed Mon.

Monasterio de Yuso

941 37 30 49

Closed Mon.

A Spanish Wine Renaissance

About 2.7 million acres (1,100,000 ha) of vineyards make Spain the country with the largest productive area, and it is the world's third largest producer after France and Italy. The delectable and highly diverse range of Spanish wines is causing concern among Europe's other big producers. From sparkling cava to smooth Riojan vintages, full-bodied Ribera del Duero, and light, fruity Galician whites, the choice seems endless.

Spain now has more than 60 official wine-producing areas, each one a Denominación de Origen.

Spanish winemaking dates back to the Phoenicians in Cádiz and to the Romans' need to fuel their legions. According to Roman chroniclers Pliny and Martial, the wine of Tarragona vied with that of Sevilla as the finest wine of the Roman Empire. After centuries of Arab domination, production was revived by thirsty medieval monks and pilgrims on the Way of St. James and was subsequently boosted by English merchants in Galicia and Jerez. The biggest impetus came in the 19th century when Bordeaux vintners were ruined by the grape scourges of oidium and phylloxera. They set up in Rioja instead, where many of their companies still figure among the elite of today's producers.

Aging

One of the fundamental differences between French and Spanish wines is the Spanish system of aging. Whereas in France the consumer takes the risk by choosing and investing in young wines, in Spain it is the vineyard that selects wines deemed most promising for aging.

Crianzas must be at least two years old and have spent a minimum of six months in a cask (one year in La Rioja). **Reservas** undergo a minimum of a year in an oak cask followed by two in the bottle, and **Gran Reservas** require two years in oak casks followed by at least three years in the bottle.

This vigil in shady cellars at constant temperatures intensifies the character of each wine, as the wood adds aromatic qualities while its tannin is blended with that of the wine. For white and rosé wines aging periods are shorter, and oak is replaced with stainless-steel vats.

INSIDER TIP:

Locals enjoy *tinto de verano* (literally, "red wine of the summer"), which is a refreshing mixed drink made of red wine with fizzy lemonade. Beer blended with fizzy lemonade, a concoction known as *clara,* is also popular.

—YUKO AOYAMA
National Geographic grantee

Spanish Innovation

Vintners are now experimenting with mixing native varieties of grapes such as Tempranillo, Garnacha, Graciano, Palomino, and Albariño, with imported ones (Cabernet Sauvignon, Merlot, Pinot Noir, Chardonnay, Syrah), a system that was frowned upon until recently. A revolution in quality has swept Spanish vineyards since the 1980s, and greater use has been made of varieties that were once minorities—notably the Tempranillo grape. Although it has always been Spain's best-known variety outside the peninsula because of its primordial role in Riojan wines, it is no longer exclusive to that region. It now figures in wines from Navarra to La Mancha and forms the basis for almost half of Spain's Denominaciones de Origen. This has given rise to the following regional synonyms for cloned varieties adapted to local terrain: Cencibel, Tinto Fino, Tinta de Toro, Tinta del País, and Ull de Llebre. Although the grape is basically the same, wide variations in climate and soil produce quite different personalities.

Wines to Look For

An example of Spain's new wave wines is the *denominación* of **Priorat** (see pp. 196–198), a

EXPERIENCE: Visit a New Wave Bodega

The latest trend to hit Spain's wine industry is innovative bodega architecture. The most famous example is at Elciego, near Laguardia (see sidebar p. 136), where the **Marqués de Riscal** *(Rioja Alavesa, tel 945 18 08 88, www.marquesderiscal.com)* bodega designed by Frank Gehry opened in 2006. The building houses a hotel, wine-spa, and restaurant run by Riojan chef Francis Paniego.

Equally arresting is Santiago Calatrava's cathedral for **Bodega Ysios** *(Laguardia, tel 945 60 06 40, www.bodegasysios.com)* and the ground-breaking zinc-and-glass **Bodega Baigorri** *(Rioja Alavesa, tel 945 60 94 20, www.bodegasbaigorri.com)* by local architect, Iñaki Aspiazu. Near Logroño (see p. 137), **Bodegas Viña Real** *(tel 945 62 52 55, www.cvne.com)* features a design by French architect, Philippe Mazières. In Haro (see p. 138), Zaha Hadid has designed a tasting room and shop inside 130-year-old **López de Heredia** *(tel 941 31 02 44, www.lopezdeheredia.com).*

Other innovative bodegas in the region include **Bodegas Campo Viejo** *(near Logroño, tel 941 27 99 00, www.bodegasjuanalcorta.com),* **Bodegas Darien** *(Logroño, tel 941 25 81 30, www.darien.es),* and **Bodegas Campillo** *(Laguardia, tel 945 60 08 26, www.bodegascampillo.com).* See also *www.vinoturismorioja.com.*

region of Catalunya where winemaking dates from the 12th century. In the early 1980s, a group of innovative young vintners came, attracted by the slate soil and terraced terrain. For seasoned winemakers such as René Barbier, it provided a perfect combination of ancient Garnacha and Cariñena vines with soil that has no need of fertilizers or chemicals and easily absorbs water. By introducing Cabernet Sauvignon, Syrah, and Merlot (and new French barrels), they were producing highly rated wines within a decade.

Other contenders in Spain's new wine stakes include Aragón's lesser known **Somontano.** In the mid-1980s it was producing bulk wines for export, but it is now experimenting with international grape varieties that thrive in its relatively high terrain and cool nights.

Apart from this vastly improved wine produced in the foothills of the Pyrenees near Huesca, Aragón has three other Denominaciones de Origen. **Cariñena,** the oldest, lies just south of Zaragoza and produces remarkable reds; lesser known **Campo de Borja** to the west uses the Garnacha grape for delicious reds and some rosés, and **Calatayud,** located between the two, is another resurgent tipple to watch out for (it actually goes back to Roman times).

Increasingly recognized abroad are the muscular, complex reds of **Toro** and **Bierzo,** both of which are neighbors of the award-winning **Ribera del Duero** east of Valladolid. Highly regarded whites are **Rueda** in Castilla, **Penedés** in Catalunya, and the fresh, crisp **Albariño** wine of Galicia's Rías Baixas. The latter, said to have originated in the Riesling grape, has helped reverse the previous reputation of Spanish white wines.

Laguardia

One of the most attractive places to sample Riojan wine is Laguardia *(visitor information, Oficina Municipal de Turismo, Casa Garcetas, Calle Mayor 52, tel 945 60 08 45, www.laguardia-alava.com),* which produces Tempranillos flavored with Mazuelo and Graciano. Bodegas built into the walls of this fortified village give an atmospheric introduction to Spain's most famous wine.

In 2010–2011, Spanish wine exports broke the record of two million euros.

Monasterio de la Valvanera: Due south of here, over the sierra, lies the Monasterio de la Valvanera. Part of its attraction is the access along the winding LR113, which follows every bend of the Río Najerilla. A narrow turnoff snakes 3 miles (5 km) up through oak and beech forest to this peaceful monastery perched on the hillside with terraced vegetable gardens below.

Dedicated to Santa María, the patron saint of Rioja, it was rebuilt in the 15th century after the original structure burned down, but the lofty church still contains the precious 12th-century **sculpture of the Virgin Mary,** allegedly carved out of an oak tree by a repentant thief. You can taste the monks' produce and liqueur in the monastery restaurant. Downhill is a little stone hermitage and the fountain of **Fuensanta.**

Logroño

The prosperous riverside capital of La Rioja is not the most picturesque or historical town, yet it has a dynamism and friendliness that make up for this as well as being king of tapas. Slicing through the center is the modern Gran Vía, which separates the new city to the south from the pedestrianized old quarter that ends at the Ebro River.

Just off the access road to the Puente de Hierro (iron bridge) you find Logroño's oldest church, **Santiago el Real** *(Barriocepo 6)*, originally a Gothic structure but rebuilt in 1500. Look above the main portal for the **statue of St. James** astride a chubby horse, slaying Moors. Opposite stands a 16th-century **pilgrims' fountain.**

A few steps away looms Logroño's cathedral, **Santa María de la Redonda** *(Plaza del Mercado).* The twin baroque towers, sometimes topped by storks' nests, can be admired from sidewalk cafés in front. The third church to see is **Santa María del Palacio** *(Calle Marqués de San Nicolás 30),* remarkable above all for its soaring pyramidal spire, 146 feet (45 m) high. The old **pilgrims' hostel** stands close by on Ruavieja, Logroño's oldest street.

Nobody should leave Logroño without touring the **Mercado San Blas,** an art deco market building that brims with La Rioja's finest and shiniest produce. Better still, sample it at restaurants and the dozens of specialty tapas bars in nearby **Calle Laurel** and **Calle San Juan**—a Riojan must-do and one of Spain's great tapas itineraries. ■

INSIDER TIP:

During Logroño's grape-picking festival of San Mateo in the second half of September, bullfights, parades, folklore, a wine fountain, and night-long tapas bar crawls take over.

—FIONA DUNLOP
National Geographic author

Monasterio de la Valvanera
941 37 70 44
Closed Dec. 20–Jan. 7
www.valvanera.com

Logroño
112 B5

Visitor Information
Oficina de Turismo, Calle Portales 50
941 27 33 53
www.logroturismo.org

Mercado San Blas
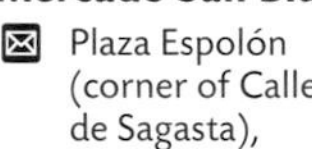
Plaza Espolón (corner of Calle de Sagasta), Logroño
Closed Sat. p.m. & Sun.

More Places to Visit in La Rioja

Calahorra

The far east of Rioja province, known as Rioja Baja, is a region of orchards and fields watered by the Alhama and Cidacos Rivers. The Romans built Calahorra (Calagurris), and by the fifth century A.D. it had gained episcopal status. The **cathedral,** originally Gothic, has a neoclassic facade and Renaissance cloisters. The remains of the old Roman walls are most visible in the lower town at the **Arco del Planillo,** the only surviving gateway. Just west of here are the narrow streets of the old Jewish quarter, the second largest community in northern Spain until 1492.

www.ayto-calahorra.es 113 C4 **Visitor Information** Oficina de Turismo, Calle Ángel Oliván 8 941 10 50 61

INSIDER TIP:

Rioja Baja boasts the largest number of dinosaur footprints *(ichnites)* in Europe. The best place to see them is at Enciso, about 22 miles (35 km) southwest of Calahorra. The Centro Paleontologico *(tel 941 39 60 93, www.dinosaurios-larioja.org)* explains their history.

—FIONA DUNLOP
National Geographic author

Haro

Many of the world-famous Riojan wines originate from the prestigious bodegas of Haro, a strategic market town on the banks of the Ebro, 22 miles (35 km) west of Logroño. Its economy blossomed with the growth of the wine industry in the late 19th century, and by 1890, Haro was the first town in Spain to install electric streetlighting. Monuments include the elegant **Casa Consistorial** (1775) designed by Juan de Villanueva, architect of the Prado, and a former Augustinian convent (1741), now a hotel. The town makes an atmospheric setting for visiting bodegas (the tourist office publishes a useful guide to them; see also sidebar p. 135), sampling Riojan cuisine, and enjoying the cafés of the sloping **Plaza de la Paz.** At the southern end of town, the **Centro de Interpretación del Vino** *(Calle Bretón de los Herreros 4, tel 941 30 57 19, closed Mon.–Thurs. & Sun. p.m.)* illustrates the latest processes of winemaking and aging. At Haro's Wine Battle, held every June 29, the ammunition is Riojan wine. **Dinastia Vivanco,** another wine museum, is at Briones, just outside Haro *(tel 941 32 23 32 or 902 32 00 01).*

www.haroturismo.org 112 B5 **Visitor Information** Oficina de Turismo, Plaza Monseñor Florentino Rodríguez s/n 941 30 33 66 Closed Sun.

Nájera

This industrialized town was once the capital of the kings of Navarra and an important halt on the road to Santiago. The rather unattractive center conceals one architectural gem, the **monastery of Santa María la Real** *(tel 941 36 36 50, closed Mon.).* Legend says it was founded in 1044 by King García Sánchez III after his falcon led him to a statue of the Virgin in a cave; the present church dates from 1516. The **royal pantheon** is next to the cave and contains the tombs of kings of Navarra, Castilla, and León. The delicately carved sarcophagi date from the 12th century and earlier. A 13th-century **statue of the Virgin** is at the center of the plateresque (see p. 45) altarpiece. Don't miss the masterly choir stalls (1495) or the lacelike stonework of the cloisters.

www.najerasanmillan.com 112 B5 **Visitor Information** Oficina de Turismo, Plaza San Miguel 10 941 36 00 41

Aragón

Aragón has incredible diversity: the stark, snowcapped peaks of the Pyrenees in the north, rich green valleys, desolate sierra, and arid plains. Cutting through the middle is the placid Ebro River. This vast area of 18,720 square miles (48,000 sq km), nearly one-tenth of Spain, harbors an abundance of artistic riches from Roman, Moorish, and medieval times, when the region reached its zenith. It is often, mistakenly, missed by visitors.

Stone houses give the town of Fragen, in the province of Huesca, a fairy-tale feel.

Created in the 11th century and unified with Catalunya in 1150, the kingdom consolidated its power and influence under Jaime I (1213–1276), who drew even Naples, Sicily, and Sardinia into the Aragonese net. This lasted until 1469, when the marriage of King Fernando II of Aragón and Isabel of Castilla led to Spain's virtual unification.

One of Aragón's most outstanding characteristics is its high level of culture and tolerance, assets that led to a fruitful coexistence of Catholics, Jews, and Muslims until the days of the Inquisition. Out of this peaceful coexistence sprang the Mudejar architectural style (see p. 43). The province also has exceptional monasteries, just as diverse, from remote and rocky San Juan de la Peña to peaceful Cistercian-style Veruela. Even Zaragoza, the ungainly and industrialized provincial capital, has unique sights such as the Moorish Aljafería, two

Aragón

113 D3

Visitor Information

Oficina de Turismo, Avenida César Augusto 25, Zaragoza

976 28 21 81

www.turismodearagon.com

Zaragoza
113 D4
Visitor Information
Patronato Municipal de Turismo, Calle Eduardo Ibarra 3
976 72 13 33
There are information booths around the city, and a tourist bus (*$$*) makes 15 stops along two different routes, April–Oct.
www.zaragoza.es

Roman Forum
Plaza de la Seo, Zaragoza
976 39 97 52
Closed Sun. p.m. & Mon.

vast cathedrals, and several striking Mudejar towers.

The real magic of Aragón, however, lies in its small towns and villages, which may nestle in verdant valleys beside rushing streams, huddle in the shadow of a ruined castle, or look out over placid artificial lakes rimmed by sierra. Public transportation does not bring you easily to these places, so rent a car and head into the hills to explore the likes of the Sierra del Moncayo, south of Tarazona; the sleepy charms of Sos del Rey Católico; or the walled splendor of Daroca and Albarracín.

Aragón has excellent cross-country and alpine skiing from November to April, followed in the warmer months by canyoning (climbing up and down canyons), kayaking, and hiking. The province also makes excellent wines.

Basílica de Nuestra Señora del Pilar, Zaragoza

Zaragoza

The appearance of this city of more than 650,000 inhabitants is due to extensive reconstruction in the 19th century, after it was devastated by Napoleon's troops. Industry has played a major role, and until Expo 2008, unattractive outskirts sprawled beside the Ebro River. In the center, you find wide boulevards and squares, and a dynamic commercial life.

Zaragoza's history kicked off with the Romans, whose name for their settlement, Cesaraugusta, became today's Zaragoza. Remains from that time include the **Roman Forum,** in front of La Seo cathedral, and parts of the third-century A.D. wall on Avenida César Augusto. Four centuries of Moorish rule from 714 saw the city flourishing. The most outstanding monument is the beautiful Aljafería palace. Muslims, Jews, and Christians continued to coexist peaceably, leaving the skyline spiked with Mudejar towers, until the Inquisition arrived (see p. 32). As capital of Aragón, Zaragoza continued to prosper, but half the population died in the Napoleonic siege of 1808–1809.

Zaragoza's two cathedrals rise over the vast, paved **Plaza del Pilar,** which lies between the old quarter and the river. The older and more interesting of the two is **La Seo.** Its extraordinary mix of styles includes original Gothic, later Mudejar, and finally baroque of the ornate Spanish sort known as

Francisco Goya

Francisco Goya, arguably Spain's most intriguing Old Master (and regarded by some as the first of the Moderns), was born in 1746 in the little farming village of Fuendetodos in Aragón. His father soon moved the family to Zaragoza, where Goya was apprenticed to a painter.

In 1771, after studying in Madrid and Rome, Goya returned to Zaragoza, where he painted the cupola of the Basilica del Pilar. Within a decade he had achieved royal recognition in Madrid and acquired a network of patrons. By the 1790s, Goya was Court Painter and the commissions flowed, despite his tendency to satirize and avoid flattery. But increasing deafness isolated him and, combined with a mental breakdown, inspired groundbreaking etchings of a dark, alienating world. He died in Bordeaux in 1828.

You can visit Goya's boyhood home and view some of his etchings at the compelling **Museo del Grabado** *(Calle Zuloaga 3, Fuendetodos, tel 976 143 830).*

Churrigueresque. The gigantic edifice has been extensively restored and its interior gleams. The fantastic altarpiece was initially carved by the Catalan sculptor Pere Johan in 1434–1445, and 30 years later was reworked by Hans Piet d'Anso. A Mudejar dome crowns the **Parroquieta,** a Gothic chapel in the chancel; also Mudejar is the northern brick facade inlaid with geometric ceramics, in high contrast to the 18th-century baroque of the main western facade.

At the back of La Seo is the entrance to the **Museo de Tapices** and **Museo Capitular.** This stunning collection of 60 tapestries, mainly 15th-century Flemish, is one of the best in the world. The huge, fine weavings measure up to 36 feet (11 m) long and are displayed beside beautiful antiques. Don't miss the **Arco del Dean** (Dean's Arch), four brick arches spanning the alleyway that were built in Mudejar style in the 16th century.

Dominating the northern flank of the Plaza del Pilar is the other cathedral, **Basílica de Nuestra Señora del Pilar** *(tel 976 29 12 31),* a real hodgepodge of styles and materials built around a legendary pillar on which the Virgin Mary is said to have appeared to St. James. There is little of interest other than the huge **Capilla del Virgen** where the pillar and a statue of the Virgin are displayed. Her embroidered mantle is ceremoniously changed daily, and a constant stream of admirers kiss the pillar. Look, too, at the frescoes painted by Goya (see sidebar this page) inside the cupolas, and then take an elevator to the top of the tower for city panoramas.

Just east of the basilica and the 20th-century Town Hall stands one of Zaragoza's most important civic buildings, the Renaissance **La Lonja de Mercaderes,** symbolizing economic influence. West of here, along Calle de Viena, visit the dazzling food market housed in an elaborate 1903 iron-and-glass building.

Among Zaragoza's Moorish monuments, the jewel in the crown is the fully restored fortified **Palacio de la Aljafería,** which

La Seo

- ✉ Plaza de la Seo, Zaragoza
- ☎ 976 39 38 56
- 🕒 Closed Mon.

www.redaragon.com/cultura/laseo

Museo de Tapices & Museo Capitular

- ✉ Plaza de la Seo, Zaragoza
- ☎ 976 29 12 31
- 🕒 Closed Sun. p.m. & Mon.

La Lonja de Mercaderes

- ✉ Exchange Palace, Zaragoza
- ☎ 976 39 72 39
- 🕒 Closed Sun. p.m. & Mon.

Palacio de la Aljafería

- ✉ Av. Madrid, Zaragoza
- ☎ 976 28 96 85
- 🕒 Closed Fri. a.m. & Thurs., & Sun p.m. in winter
- $ $
- 🚌 Bus 32/36 from Plaza del Pilar

stands 2 miles (3 km) west of the old quarter. Originally built in the ninth century, it surrounds a central patio rich in carved stuccowork. The most exceptional sight is the **musallah,** an intimate mosque, which is a visual feast of Moorish craftsmanship. After the Reconquest (see pp. 30–31),

A Mudejar tower dominates Monterde, near Daroca.

Fernando and Isabel could not resist using this stunning palace, and this is reflected in the Flamboyant Gothic of the upper floor.

The infrastructure built for Expo 2008 transformed this western side of town, connecting it to the center with about 2 miles (3 km) of riverside walkway and a cable car. It is now a gigantic water park highlighted by the **Water Tower,** freshwater **Aquarium,** said to be Europe's largest, and Zaha Hadid's **Pabellon Puente.** Rent a bike to get around the center, and use the Zaragoza card (*www.zaragozacard.com*) for discounts and free museum entrance.

Mudejar Towns

A unique fusion of Islamic and Western styles developed in the wake of the Reconquest (12th–16th centuries). This style was created by the remaining community of Arab craftsmen to meet the needs of Catholic Spain. Aragonese Mudejar is characterized by brickwork bell towers, decorated with glazed ceramic tiles.

Daroca
113 D3
Visitor Information
Oficina de Turismo, Plaza de España 4
976 80 01 29
www.daroca.es

Daroca: The delightful little town of Daroca huddles beneath the roaring traffic on the N330 southwest of Zaragoza, but remnants of its Moorish origins are still visible. Symbolic of its illustrious past is the ruined hilltop castle, originally an 11th-century Moorish fortress of which the keep, the **Torre del Homenaje,** remains, though much altered.

Encircling the town below are 2 miles (4 km) of walls punctuated by towers and three surviving gateways (*puertas*). You can take a scenic three-hour walk around the walls starting at the **Puerta Alta,** climbing to the castle, then continuing around the northern and western perimeters to end at the crenellated and intricately worked **Puerta del Arrabal.** This walk gives wonderful views over Daroca's pretty tiled roofs, pinkish stone houses, and verdant surrounding countryside.

Walk through the **Puerta Baja** to find atmospheric cobbled alleyways and graceful mansions. Also here is Aragón's first Mudejar tower, the belfry of **Santo Domingo.** A Muslim mason completed the upper part in the early 14th century, but when fire destroyed much of the church interior, the Gothic-Mudejar structure was replaced by 18th-century baroque. Next door the **Museo Parroquial** *(tel 976 62 02 47, closed Sun. p.m. & Mon.)* displays gold and silver plate made in Daroca beside other ecclesiastical objects. A few steps northeast is stunning **San Juan,** begun in Romanesque style in the 12th century and completed by Muslim craftsmen a century later with a flourish of Mudejar brick pilasters.

Tarazona: Northwest of Zaragoza lies Tarazona, the medieval home of the kings of Aragón. Between the 13th and 16th centuries Tarazona excelled in Mudejar craftsmanship, and numerous bell towers spike the clifftop site overlooking the Río Queiles. Of these, the one at the church of **La Magdalena** is particularly striking. The complex architecture of Tarazona's **cathedral** makes extensive use of brickwork and inlaid ceramic tiles beside its minaret-like belfry. Don't miss the **cloisters,** where niches are filled with delicate stucco tracery made in the 16th century. Tarazona's other curiosity is its arcaded old bullring, now transformed into a residential square, **Plaza de Toros Vieja.**

Teruel: Southern Aragón's main town of Teruel has its own version of Mudejar towers: square in form, decorated with green and white glazed tiles, and sometimes incorporating a passageway at the base. Teruel stands on a high plateau, and its harmonious group is visible from miles around.

Teruel has five Mudejar towers, four of which are alongside equally exceptional churches. The most impressive are 13th-century **Torre de San Martín** (slightly leaning) and **Torre del Salvador,** both of which rise majestically over streets, leaving access through the arched base. The sprawling **cathedral** *(tel 978 60 22 75)* has a magnificent coffered ceiling painted with portraits, hunting scenes, and decorative patterns. The last tower of note, **Torre de San Pedro** is above the mausoleum of Teruel's star-crossed lovers, Diego de Marcilla and Isabel de Segura, the Aragonese Romeo and Juliet.

EXPERIENCE: Geological Walk

For a total contrast to the exquisite man-made structures of the Mudejar towns, travel 44 miles (70 km) north of Teruel to Aliaga, a valley flanked by mountains. Here you can hike amid the extraordinary formations of Aliaga Geoparque *(visitor information, tel 978 77 10 09, www.parquegeologicoaliaga.com)*, Spain's first geological park. From a signpost on the road to Villaroya, take a 30-minute (one way) walk through gorse and poplars, up an easy hill to La Clara, one of the park's prettiest waterfalls. Or head for the park's power station and follow the dirt road up the peak (about 30 min., one way). Watch for vulture nests along the way. At the top marvel at the Hoz Mala Gorge below and soak up the panoramic view of the entire region.

Tarazona

113 C4

Visitor Information

Oficina de Turismo, Plaza de San Francisco 1

976 19 90 76 or 976 64 00 74

www.tarazona.es

Teruel

113 D2

Visitor Information

Oficina de Turismo, Calle San Francisco 1

978 64 14 61

www.teruel.es

Huesca
113 E4
Visitor Information
Oficina de Turismo, Plaza de Luis López Allué s/n
974 29 21 70
www.huescaturismo.com

Cathedral
Plaza de la Catedral, Huesca
974 22 06 76

Museo Diocesano
Plaza de la Catedral, Huesca
974 23 10 99
Closed Sat. p.m., Sun., & p.m. daily in winter

Iglesia de San Pedro El Viejo
Plaza San Pedro, Huesca
974 22 23 87

Jaca
113 D5
Visitor Information
Oficina de Turismo, Plaza de San Pedro 11–13
974 36 00 98
www.jaca.es

Diego returned from his quest to make his fortune, to find Isabel had been forcibly married to someone else. He died of grief, and at his funeral Isabel kissed his lips and fell dead beside him.

Huesca

This unassuming town is in fact a major crossroads of Aragón, the last of the plains before the Sierra de Guara and the foothills of the Pyrenees. Called Osca by the Romans, Wasqa by the Arabs, and Vesca or Huesca in the local Iberian language, it reached its zenith in the Middle Ages when it was home to the royal court.

INSIDER TIP:

Huesca's cuisine features *pollo al chilindrón* (chicken with peppers) and Moorish-style sweets of marzipan and chestnuts.

—FIONA DUNLOP
National Geographic author

By 1354 Huesca had its own influential university, but decline followed and it was not until the late 19th century that its prosperity revived. Among its more illustrious recent sons are the artist Antonio Saura and the filmmaker Carlos Saura. This city has been dynamized by the AVE high-speed rail link, leaving Madrid just 2.5 hours away.

The **old town** lies on a hill at the center. Flanking the Plaza de la Catedral are the **Ayuntamiento** (Town Hall), a striking example of Aragonese Renaissance style, and the **cathedral.** This towering 13th- to 16th-century structure has an ornately carved **portal** (1302) sheltered by a wood and tiled gable that is typical of Aragón (added in 1574). The interior is Gothic and austere, but with an alabaster altarpiece (1533), intricately carved by Damián Forment (circa 1480–1540). Another exceptional alabaster altarpiece is in the cathedral's **Museo Diocesano;** this one, dating from 1512, is by Gil Morlanes el Viejo.

More poignant still is Huesca's oldest church, **San Pedro El Viejo,** a real marvel of Romanesque style with a beautifully restored cloister, where King Ramiro II spent his final years in retreat. Started in 1116 on the site of a Visigothic church, San Pedro has a fortresslike tower that was once much higher. In its gloomy interior, look for the beautifully restored late 13th-century **frescoes** and several impressive Renaissance **altarpieces.** The Romanesque capitals of the cloisters are carved with apocalyptic monsters, devils, musicians, and dancers.

Don't miss the **San Bartholomé chapel,** reached from Calle de Cuatro Reyes, where Ramiro II lies in a Romanesque alabaster sarcophagus opposite Alfonso I.

Jaca

Lying in the shadow of the Pyrenees at an altitude of 2,690 feet (820 m), the lively little town of Jaca is Aragón's prime base for winter skiers, with plenty of

You can visit the tourist office or relax at a café in Huesca's Plaza de Luis López Allué.

bars, hotels, and restaurants. It also boasts one of Spain's most important displays of Romanesque frescoes and an imposing citadel built by Philip II. If you come from the south, you notice a distinct change in architectural style, with timbered chalet-style interiors and high-gabled houses.

Jaca is well organized for outdoor pursuits, with mountain guides, adventure sports agencies, hunting and fishing equipment, and buses to ski resorts. The town was the first capital of the kingdom of Aragón, and the gateway for the French Romanesque style (see pp. 43–44) that was to spread across northern Spain to Santiago de Compostela.

Aragón's first king, Ramiro I, commissioned the **cathedral,** built 1076–1130. Unusual for a cathedral, it is not easy to find as the low structure is tucked away in Jaca's narrow streets. The Romanesque portal, with its capitals and complex stone carving shaded by a carved wooden Aragonese overhang at the base of a squat stone tower, is obvious. Inside the Gothic style wins, for example at the doorway to the cloisters. These have been transformed into the exceptional **Museo Diocesano,** with Romanesque and Gothic frescoes transferred for conservation from remote village churches. Some are breathtaking, above all those from Bagües, and, together with remarkable 12th-century wooden sculptures, form a rare collection. The museum reopened in 2010 after extensive renovation, doubling its exhibition space.

Jaca's pride and joy is the late 16th-century **Ciudadela** with its moated-and-walled exterior, the only one still standing in Spain.

Aragonese Pirineos (Pyrenees)

This is the place to come to escape all imprints of modern civilization. The Pyrenees, and particularly the central section that lies in Aragón, have unadulterated wilderness beyond their tiny slate-roofed hamlets, spas, ski runs, and

(continued on p. 148)

Cathedral
- ✉ Calle de la Catedral, Jaca
- ☎ 974 35 62 41

Museo Diocesano
- ✉ Calle de la Catedral, Jaca
- ☎ 974 35 63 78
- Closed Sun. p.m. & Mon.
- $ $

www.jaca.com/museodiocesano.htm

Drive: Castles & Eyries

Drive through wheat fields and pine forests to see stunningly sited relics of Aragonese history before ending at the influential monastery of San Juan de la Peña.

Riglos nestles at the foot of Los Mallos.

NOT TO BE MISSED:

Colegiata de Bolea • Castillo de Loarre • Monasterio de San Juan de la Peña

Leave **Huesca** by following signs to Iruña (Pamplona) (A132) as far as Esquedas, where a signed turnoff to the right leads across farmland to the hill village of **Bolea** ❶. Turn into the village and drive up to park on the main square. Walk up to the **Colegiata** *(tel 649 65 51 25)*, a Renaissance church built on the ruins of an Arab castle in 1556. Inside is a main altarpiece of 77 paintings by the anonymous "master of Bolea," with carvings and sculpture by Gil de Brabante. The altar of Santiago (1530) is attributed to the prolific Damián Forment (circa 1480–1540). Just downhill is the church of **Santo Tomás** *(open only Sat. & Sun. June–Aug.)*, with an old covered fountain in the garden at the back.

Leave Bolea by the same road, then turn right at a junction below the village, following signs to Loarre. The road winds through the hills, passing the occasional shepherd, fruit orchards, and wheat fields. After 5 miles (8 km) a signed turnoff to the right twists precipitously up to **Castillo de Loarre** ❷ *(tel 974 34 21 61)*, a dramatic walled-and-turreted castle perched on a towering rock. Built on Roman walls in the 11th century by the king of Navarra, Sancho Ramírez, it may be the oldest castle in Spain. Not surprisingly it has featured in many movies. Exploring it entails climbing narrow staircases in the three towers and crossing ruined ramparts, but it is well worth the effort. The beautiful Romanesque **chapel** is in excellent condition.

Drive back down to the village of Loarre, skirting around it to rejoin the main road (A1206) where you turn right. Continue 4 miles (6 km) to Ayerbe, and turn right on the A132 (direction of Iruña). Soon, on your right, the pink, eroded cylindrical rocks of **Los Mallos** ❸ come into sight and dominate the landscape for several miles. For a closer view turn right to the village of Riglos, just after Concilio.

Return to the A132, which runs through a gorge next to the torrential waters of the Río Gállego, passing the pretty village of Murillo de Gállego, before crossing a bridge over the **Embalse de la Peña** (reservoir). Immediately after, take a right turn marked San Juan de la Peña. The long and winding road (A1205) parallels the reservoir then climbs through beautiful wild pine forests. You may see falcons and eagles soaring above. After 21 miles (34 km), at the village of Bernués, turn left, again following signs to San Juan de la Peña. The road twists upward for 11 miles (18 km) until it finally reaches the grounds of the **Monasterio de San Juan de la Peña** ❹ *(tel 974 35 51 19, closed Mon., $$).*

An ideal place to stop for lunch, the grounds are a highly organized park with hiking trails, a small bar, and picnic tables in front of the partly ruined 18th-century monastery. You can walk or take a bus half a mile (0.8 km) downhill to the much older **monastery,** set under an enormous projecting rock. Although only about a quarter of the original structure remains, this monastery (founded in 1025) has frescoes, an open-air **cloister** with superb capitals sheltered by the rock, the sarcophagi of Aragonese kings (the last, Pedro I, was buried here in 1104), a pantheon of nobles, and a vaulted **Romanesque church.** Much has been restored, but this has been done in a sympathetic way.

Leave the park by driving downhill past the old monastery (where parking is forbidden) and continuing 3 miles (5 km) to the N240 where you turn right to reach Jaca in 6 miles (10 km).

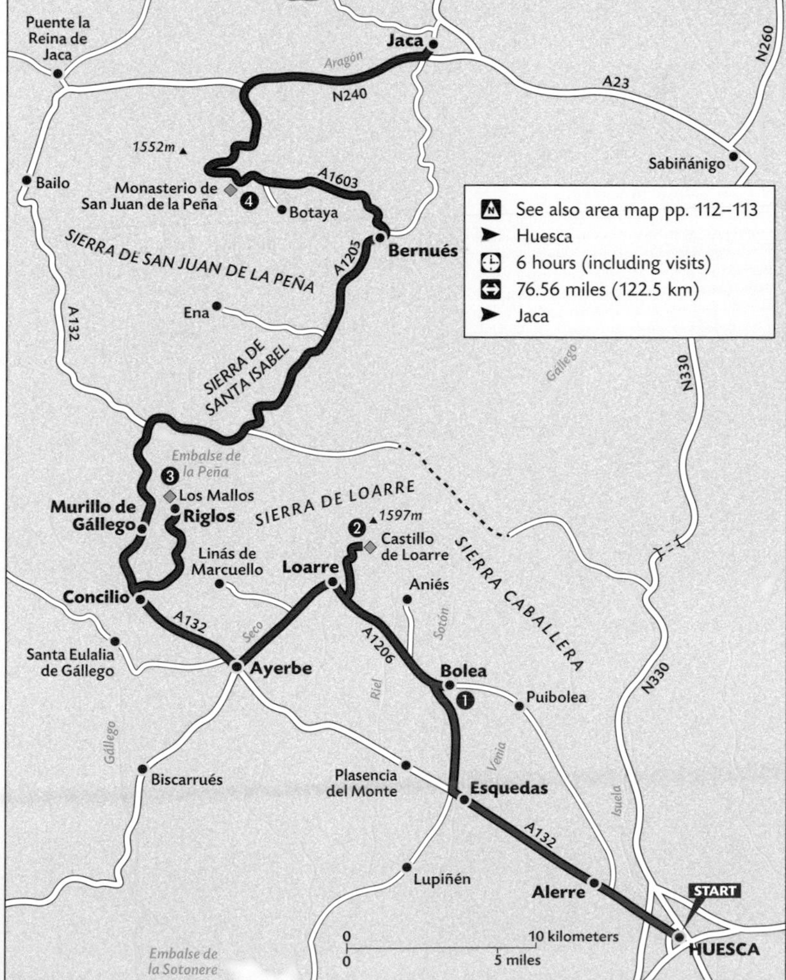

shepherds. This mountain range is Spain's natural barrier with France. Aragón has its highest peaks, the loftiest being Pico de Aneto (11,170 feet/3,404 m), and much harsher, more rugged landscapes than the Pyrenees in Navarra or Catalunya.

Between the peaks lie lakes, canyons, glaciers, gorges, sculptural limestone outcrops, and sparsely forested foothills that are encompassed by a national park, up in the east, near Parque Posets Maladeta. Outside the national park are villages where stone houses still have *cadieras* (wooden benches set around a cooking fire). The area used to be inaccessible, but tourism is making inroads.

Parque Nacional de Ordesa y Monte Perdido: This 38,568-acre (15,608 ha) national park encompasses virtually every aspect of Pyrenean

The slopes of the Pyrenees attract dedicated hikers in summer and skiers in winter.

Parque Nacional de Ordesa y Monte Perdido. Its wild beauty is best in summer and fall. From October to May snow blocks the high roads and they are officially closed, leaving the terrain to climbers and cross-country skiers.

The starting points for exploring are Jaca (see pp. 144–145) in the west, Aínsa (see p. 150) in the center, and Pont de Suert, higher

nature, and has unique species of flora and fauna. Rising over its northern perimeter is **Monte Perdido** (11,007 feet/3,355 m), a peak of sharply eroded limestone and glaciers. It overlooks the Ordesa valley, a canyon sliced by the Arazas River whose course is punctuated by waterfalls, notably **Cascada de Tamborrotera** and the 230-foot (70 m) **Cola de Caballo** (Horse's Tail). Beeches, maples, willows, and, higher up, silvester pines and firs are the dominant trees here. Eagles and vultures soar above and trout fill the water below.

This popular hiking area is easily reached by car from Aínsa via the pretty village of Torla. The road ends at Cascada de Tamborrotera, from where several hiking routes are laid out, the easiest along the river. Detailed route maps are available at the visitor center and cover more strenuous hikes such as the one to **Circo de Soaso,** a full-day trek with steep climbs and fantastic panoramas. Camping in small tents is allowed but only at the four camping grounds. Refuge huts also provide for overnight treks.

To the east of this valley on the other side of the mountains is the **Cañon de Añisclo,** reached by car from Aínsa via Bielsa. This is a much narrower gorge than Ordesa and has sheer cliffs striped with gray and red-ocher strata. The walk beside the Río Vellos (allow about five hours) is not difficult and takes you through woods of ilex and beech. Farther east still, on the edge of the park, is the **Valle de Escoaín,** best reached from Revilla on a turnoff from the A138. You can follow a trail from Revilla down to the Río Yaga and see the village of Escoaín across the river, high up on the flanks of Mt. Castillo Mayor.

From Bielsa it is also well worth driving beside the Río Cinca to the **Balcón de Pineta,** near the parador (state-run hotel) at the base of Monte Perdido. The views from here are quite spectacular. Beyond lie the French Pyrenees: You can reach them through the **Bielsa tunnel,** 7 miles (11 km) north of Bielsa.

INSIDER TIP:

Certified scuba-divers should not miss the opportunity to dive any of the 197 glacial lakes (called *ibones* in Aragonese) in the Pyrenees. Ice-diving skills are required in winter, and the use of a dry-suit is highly recommended even in summer.

—ALFONSO PARDO
Professor, Universidad de Zaragoza

Parque Nacional de Ordesa y Monte Perdido Pirineos

113 E5

Visitor Information

Calle Fatas
974 48 63 78

Plaza de Luis López Allué, Huesca
974 29 21 70

Av. Ordesa 1, Broto
974 48 64 13

www.pirineo.com

Hikers' Tips

Before embarking on any long hike, get reliable weather and geographical information from the nearest tourist office or visitor center. The Pyrenees are notorious for potentially dangerous storms and rising river levels. In a storm, do not stay on ridges or isolated outcrops, nor shelter under trees.

Be prepared for cooler temperatures as you rise in altitude, but remember that in summer the karstic (limestone) surrounds increase the aridity of the air, so take plenty of water. Start early, not only to catch the good morning light but also to grab a space at one of the official parking lots.

Aínsa

113 E5

Visitor Information

Oficina de Turismo, Avenida Pirenaica 1

974 50 00 67

www.ainsa-sobrarbe.es

Benasque

113 F5

Visitor Information

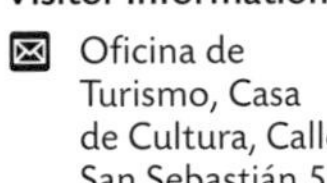

Oficina de Turismo, Casa de Cultura, Calle San Sebastián 5

974 55 12 89

www.turismobenasque.com

Monasterio de Piedra

113 C3

Nuévalos

902 19 60 52

$$ (monastery); $$$ (monastery & park)

www.monasteriopiedra.com

Aínsa & Benasque: The charming old town of **Aínsa** stands on a promontory at the meeting point of the Cinca and Ara Rivers, and of two main roads that twist up through the mountains—the A138 to France and the N260. The latter curves through stunning landscapes around the southern edge of Ordesa National Park. Aínsa's houses of golden stone, brimming with geraniums, surround the arcaded, cobbled Plaza Mayor, which is overlooked by the 12th-century church of **Santa María,** a lovely example of Aragonese Romanesque.

Benasque lies higher up and west, in a striking setting at 3,743 feet (1,138 m). The wide Benasque valley opens out at the base of the rugged Maladeta range that includes the Pyrenees' highest peak, **Pico de Aneto,** with the popular ski resort of Cerler on its slopes. Benasque is a favorite hiking destination, but you should also take a stroll around the old quarter, which is lined with elegant mansions. Immediately west, trails lead into the **Parque Posets Maladeta,** surrounding the Pyrenees' second highest peak, **Pico de Posets** (11,060 feet/3,371 m). Lakes abound in this area. To the south, the Ésera River enters the dramatic **Congosto de Ventamillo,** 2 miles (3 km) of sheer limestone cliffs.

Cistercian Monasteries

The Cistercian order came to northern Spain from France in the mid-12th century to build a series of monasteries in isolated sites. Cistercians devoted themselves to God and physical work. Their architecture is suitably devoid of decoration.

One of Aragón's most beautiful parks harbors the remains of the **Monasterio de Piedra,** a Cistercian abbey built with the stones of a Moorish castle. It lies near the village of Nuévalos about 75 miles (120 km) southwest of Zaragoza. The monks remained in this verdant oasis for 640 years, until the closure of monasteries in 1835. Since then, Piedra has been privately owned and converted into a hotel with a mediocre,

Pyrenean Fauna & Flora

Of all the wildlife that haunts these imposing rocky mountains, the Pyrenean ibex is the rarest: It once inhabited the higher slopes but was officially declared extinct in January 2000. You may still spot marmots, chamois (a goatlike antelope), foxes, and mink. The cold rivers have otters, trout, and the Pyrenean newt. Among 65 species of birds nesting here are golden eagles, bearded vultures, lioned vultures, various sorts of falcon, and capercaillies (a large form of grouse). The 1,500 species of flora are a delight, especially in May and June when the snows have melted and brilliant primulas, edelweiss, and gentians carpet the slopes.

motley assembly of wine museum, restaurants, and carriage collection. The vast **church ruins,** open to the sky, are nonetheless impressive, and the surrounding **park** is a magnificent mixture of waterfalls, lakes, grottoes, and woods.

The beautiful **Monasterio de Santa María de Huerta** lies to the west, just over the border of Castilla y León, but it is best visited together with other Aragonese sights. Founded in 1162, it was inhabited continuously by monks until 1835 and was reestablished in 1930. The first sight as you enter is the 16th-century **cloister,** now the monks' quarters. Behind an older Gothic cloister are the **refectory** and enormous **kitchen.** These two rooms give you a vivid picture of monastic daily life: You can imagine monks eating in silence while listening to texts being read from the carved stone pulpit, or cooking communal meals in the kitchen's central oven. The original purity of the **church** was enlivened by frescoes (1580) by Bartolomé de Matarana and gilded baroque altarpieces, and you will no doubt spot a few of the 20 white-robed monks. Do not miss the monks' shop, which sells homemade jams and liqueurs.

Ten miles (16 km) south of Tarazona (see p. 143) in the verdant Huecha Valley is the fortified Cistercian **Monasterio de Veruela** (1171–1224). The vast Romanesque and early Gothic church has an unusual green-and-blue **tiled floor** beneath its massive pointed vaults, and the ornate 14th-century **cloisters** writhe with carvings of gargoyles, plant motifs, and human heads. The **chapter house,** a more perfect example of Cistercian sobriety, contains the tombs of early abbots. ■

Monasterio de Santa María de Huerta

- 113 C3
- Santa María de Huerta (Soria)
- 975 32 70 02
- $

www.monasteriohuerta.org

Monasterio de Veruela

- 976 64 90 25
- Closed Tues.

The Cistercian Monasterio de Piedra is spectacularly set among lakes and waterfalls.

More Places to Visit in Aragón

Albarracín

Lower Aragón's most spectacularly sited town lies in the arid Sierra de Albarracín overlooking the Guadalaviar River, 28 miles (45 km) west of Teruel. If you are in Teruel, this is an essential detour. Albarracín has been declared a national monument, and restoration work has been sensitive. Originally built by the Moors, the ruined, turreted **ramparts** are visible for miles. In the center of the town, cobbled medieval streets twist up past pink, part-timbered houses with tiled roofs, then go through archways to eventually reach the Renaissance **cathedral** *(tel 978 71 00 93)*. The cathedral museum has 16th-century Flemish tapestries and beautiful liturgical objects. Around Albarracín are pine forests with good walks, mountain-biking, and horse-trekking. You can see prehistoric **rock paintings** 3 miles (5 km) southeast of town toward Bezas. *www.turismoalbarracin.com* 113 C2 **Visitor Information** Oficina Comarcal de Turismo, Calle San Antonio 2 978 71 02 62 Closed Mon.

INSIDER TIP:

The glaciers at Parque Posets-Maladeta, near the town of Benasque [see p. 150], are more than 10,000 years old.

—ALFONSO PARDO
Professor, Universidad de Zaragoza

Ansó

One of the prettiest Pyrenean towns lies in splendid isolation in northwestern Aragón, 5 miles (7 km) from the Navarra border. This remoteness led to Ansó's own dialect and traditions. The small **Museo Etnológico** *(Inside San Pedro, tel 974 37 00 22)* tells you more. Ansó lies between the equally attractive **Valle del Roncal,** to the west, and **Valle de Hecho,** to the east. **Hecho** (4 miles/7 km from Ansó) is a lovely town, though somewhat marred by its popularity; from there you can take an easy walk to the **monastery of San Pedro,** in Siresa, in the hills to the north. This entire area is ideal for hikes. *www.valledeanso.com* 113 D5 **Visitor Information** Oficina de Turismo, Plaza Domingo Miral 1 974 37 02 25 Closed Mon.

Sos del Rey Católico

This delightful walled town studded with towering gateways acquired its name because it was the birthplace of King Fernando of Aragón (see pp. 31–32). Sos del Rey Católico is in the bleak Sierra de la Peña and easily visited from the Monasterio de Leyre (see p. 128) and Sangüesa (see p. 127) in neighboring Navarra. The road from the reservoir Embalse de Yesa (A1601, the route from Jaca) has beautiful scenery.

Sos was a medieval stronghold against the kingdom of Navarra, and its shady lanes wind along a strategic hilltop between two promontories. Crowning the eastern end are the ruins of the **castle,** and just below is the 12th-century church of **Sant Esteban.** Inside are amazing things: the late-Renaissance **Capilla del Pilar** (with a stunning baroque altarpiece), Mudejar floor tiles, a 12th-century statue of a swarthy Christ, and an 8th-century font. You can visit the **crypt** *($)*, which has unusual frescoes in Byzantine style and beautifully carved capitals.

Sos also has fine Renaissance houses: the **Palacio de los Sada,** where Fernando was born, and harmonious mansions linked by arches around the tiny Plaza Mayor. A few steps north of here, off the Calle Pérez de Biel, the medieval **corn exchange** has graceful pointed arches and a stone well. *www.sosdelreycatolico.com* 113 D5 **Visitor Information** Oficina de Turismo, Palacio de Sada, Plaza Hispanidad s/n 948 88 85 24 Closed Mon. & Tues. in winter

A proud, self-sufficient city exuding style, with enticing shops, innovative museums, and great restaurants

Barcelona

Hand-painted tiles used as decoration by architect Antoni Gaudí

Barcelona

Catalunya's vibrant capital rooted itself in the global psyche with its spectacular staging of the Olympic Games in 1992 and has not looked back since. Before that the city struggled to keep its own culture and politics alive despite vindictive repression from the central government. Today Barcelona is among the front-runners of Spanish business, theater, cuisine, and design while Catalan identity is constantly expressed.

Barcelona's heritage ranges from Roman ruins to state-of-the-art contemporary architecture, with a good dose of Gothic and Modernista (Catalan art nouveau) mixed in. Start in the Barri Gòtic (Gothic quarter), where the cathedral, palaces, and museums all echo the zenith of Catalan trading prowess. In the 1990s the port area was transformed from a grimy, neglected quarter into a glossy new window on culture and gastronomy. The main artery in this area is La Rambla, a long avenue stretching from Plaça de Catalunya to the statue of Christopher Columbus by the harbor. South of La Rambla is the funky and fashionable Raval district, home to the contemporary art museum (MACBA), while to the north, La Ribera and El Born offer history and gastronomy. Seafront development continues northward

NOT TO BE MISSED:

Enjoying tapas in El Born **161**

Salivating at all the food offered in the Mercat de la Boquería **163**

The breathtaking cable-car ride across the harbor **165**

Marveling at the art and architecture of Fundació Miró **168**

Precious Romanesque and Gothic art at the Museu Nacional d'Art de Catalunya **168–169**

Rooftop views from La Pedrera **171**

Gaudí's brilliance at Parc Güell **171**

past the 2004 Forum building, now a science museum. A fresh architectural landmark is Jean Nouvel's Torre Agbar.

To the west lie Eixample and Gràcia. Most of Barcelona's art nouveau monuments are here, standing beside designer shops and restaurants. This, too, is where you see the unmistakable spires of the Sagrada Familia, Gaudí's masterwork, and, farther inland, his Parc Güell. More of Barcelona's 40-odd museums lie in Montjuïc's hilltop setting, which you can reach via a cable car ride from the main harbor. Public transport, notably the metro, is very user friendly, restaurants are of high quality, and the surrounding hills and sea give a clear sense of the layout of this culturally rich city. ■

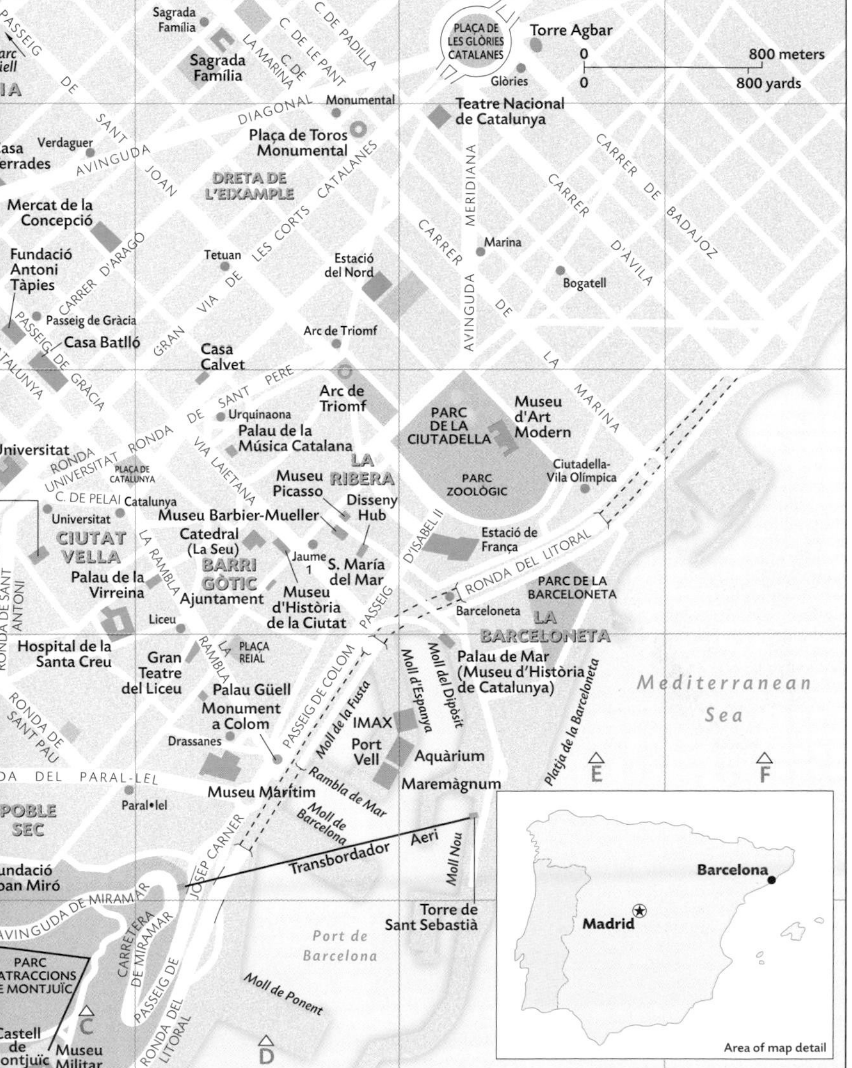

Catedral (La Seu)

The imposing facade and spires of this massive cathedral may look Gothic, but they actually date from the 19th century when they were added to the existing 14th- to 15th-century structure. Luckily the original 1408 designs by Charles Galtès from Rouen were used, which ensured overall visual harmony. Before this Gothic edifice came into existence in 1298, the site was occupied by a Romanesque church, a mosque, and a Roman basilica.

Memorial candles available in front of Barcelona's cathedral, commonly referred to as La Seu.

Crypt

Penetrate the interior and you are in a lofty single nave whose vast space is broken midway by the elaborate choir. This, in turn, fronts stairs leading down to the crypt. Here in a low-vaulted chamber beneath the main altar stands the carved marble **sarcophagus of Santa Eulalia,** a locally born virgin martyr who was executed by the Romans in the fourth century and who subsequently became Barcelona's patron saint. From the sunken steps you have a magnificent view of the soaring vaulted ceiling supported by ribbed columns.

The **choir** is among the cathedral's many masterpieces. Its white marble screen depicts Santa Eulalia's life (sculpted from designs by Bartolomé Ordóñez) and encloses beautifully carved Renaissance choir stalls. These were later decorated with the coats of arms of European kings.

Chapels

No fewer than 29 side chapels line the nave and apse, nearly every one of them containing an altarpiece or sculpture of interest. On your immediate right as you enter the main doors is the large **Capella del**

Festes de la Mercè

Every September 24, the Catalan capital celebrates the Virgen de la Mercè, the city's patron saint. Events kick off on September 22, and the *cava* continues to flow and Catalans revel in distinctive traditions until September 26. The festivities include parades of human-operated, giant wooden figures *(gegants)*, a dragons and devils race, outdoor movies, sports events, jazz concerts, street theater, dancing, and fantastic fireworks displays. One highlight to look out for is the *castellers* competition on Plaça de Sant Jaume. Participants in traditional costume climb on top of each other to create the highest possible tower *(casteller)*: Eight levels are common. There are also plays and concerts at the Greek theater in Montjuïc (see pp. 168–169). Check the packed program in advance at *www.bcn.cat/merce* or visit the tourist office for more information.

Santissim Sagrament, whose 16th-century crucifix with its twisted Christ is alleged to have adorned the prow of Don Juan of Austria's flagship during the Battle of Lepanto (1571). In the opposite corner, a side chapel contains a huge marble font (1433) and a historic plaque recording the baptism of six Carib Indians brought back by Christopher Columbus in 1493.

INSIDER TIP:

The cloister's 13 geese mark the 13 years of the life of Santa Eulalia, to whom the cathedral is dedicated.

–CHRISTINE O'TOOLE

National Geographic contributor

At the back of the cathedral look at the first side chapel to the left of the altar to see the alabaster tomb of Ramon d'Escales, Count of Barcelona, sculpted by Antoni Canet in 1409. Farther around the ambulatory, **Chapel VI** contains a lovely 1390 painting of St. Gabriel on 18 panels, by Lluís Borrassa. Between these is the **Capella de Sant Benet,** dedicated to the Benedictine Order, which is celebrated by an altarpiece (1452) painted by Bernat Martorell. This corner of the apse also gives access to the elevator for the rooftop. Look for two surprisingly modest coffins attached to the transept wall that belong to Ramon Berenguer I (Count of Barcelona) and his wife.

Cloister

Another surprise lies in store in the Gothic cloister (1498), which you can also enter directly from Carrer del Bistre through the Porta de Santa Eulalia: A gaggle of geese roams between a palm tree, potted plants, and a fountain mounted with a statue of Sant Jordi (St. George), Catalunya's patron saint. Huge vaulted chapels line the cloister, each dedicated to a saint, and the **chapter house** has a small museum. The font in the lobby was salvaged from the original Romanesque cathedral. ■

Catedral (La Seu)

- Map: 155 D3
- Pla de la Seu
- 933 42 82 60
- Closed Sun. p.m.
- $ (choir & elevator to rooftop); $ (chapter house museum)
- Metro: Jaume I

www.catedralbcn.org

Barri Gòtic Walk

This walk takes you through the evocative narrow alleyways of Barcelona's oldest quarter, passing major monuments, such as the cathedral and medieval palace, while touching the pulse of the city.

The large annual Festes de la Mercè celebrations begin in Plaça de Sant Jaume.

Leave **Plaça Reial** by the northeast corner, Carrer del Vidre, and then cross Ferran to walk up the alley of Carrer d'en Quintana. Turn right onto Boquería and immediately left to emerge in Plaçeta del Pi. In front of you is the apse of **Santa María del Pi** ❶ and its 177-foot (54 m) octagonal tower. Walk around the church to the main plaza, backed by ornately decorated 18th-century houses, and admire the huge rose window. Turn into narrow, tile-studded **Carrer de Petritxol,** then right onto Carrer Portaferrissa. Walk straight into **Plaça Nova,** where the cathedral looms behind the Casa de l'Ardiaca (Archdeacon's house).

Turn right here, past remains of the Roman wall, onto Carrer del Bisbe, where ahead of you is a surprising neo-Gothic **covered bridge** (1929) linking the medieval Casa dels Canonges (Canons' Residence) to the Palau de la Generalitat (Parliament Building). Turn right again onto Carrer de Montjuïc del Bisbe to see the baroque church of **Sant Felip Neri** ❷ in a delightful little square. On the corner is the idiosyncratic **Museu del Calçat** (Shoe Museum; *tel 933 01 45 33, closed Mon. & p.m.*), a must for shoe fanatics.

Returning to Carrer del Bisbe, enter the **Catedral (La Seu)** ❸ (see pp. 156–157) through the cloister doorway. Leaving the main door, turn right past the **Museu Diocesà** *(tel 933 15 22 13, closed Mon.)* to walk beside a monumental section of the **Roman wall** and sections of the medieval royal palace that lead to impressive **Plaça Ramon Berenguer el Gran,** named after the Catalan ruler who is honored by an equestrian statue. Turn right off the main avenue, Via Laietana, onto Carrer

NOT TO BE MISSED:

Catedral • Museu d'Història de la Ciutat • Museu Frederic Marès

Llibreteria, past a candlemakers' shop dating from 1761.

Turn right again onto Carrer del Veguer, where you reach the **Museu d'Història de la Ciutat ❹** *(Plaça del Rei, tel 933 15 11 11, closed Sun. & public holidays p.m., & Mon. Oct.–April).* This Museum of the History of the City overlooks the evocative 14th- to 16th-century Plaça del Rei. Among rare displays are Jewish and Arab artifacts, a large underground section showing Roman foundation walls and water channels, as well as Roman sculptures, the lovely 14th-century **Capella de Santa Àgata,** and, at the back of the square, the vast **Saló del Tinell,** a majestic construction of semicircular arches. Adjoining it is the five-story **Torre del Rei Martí:** Climb this for fine views of the entire Barri Gòtic.

On the left (southwest) of the square stands the Gothic-Renaissance palace used by Catalan viceroys. Walk around this to the back of the cathedral and turn right to reach Plaça de Sant Lu. In front is the renovated **Museu Frederic Marès ❺** *(tel 932 56 35 00, closed Mon.).* This exceptional collection has Spanish sculpture from pre-Roman times to the 19th century. The "Collector's Cabinet" displays thousands of curios assembled by Frederic Marès (1893–1991).

Return to Carrer Llibreteria and turn right to reach the administrative heart of Barcelona, the **Plaça de Sant Jaume ❻.** On the right is the **Palau de la Generalitat,** home to the Catalan government, and on the left the **Ajuntament** (City Hall; *tel 934 02 70 00, closed Mon.–Sat.* Guided tours show the remarkable Saló de Cent and Saló de Crònique, and Catalan artworks.

See also area map pp. 154–155
Plaça Reial
1–2 hours (without visits)
1.25. miles (2 km)
Plaça de Sant Jaume

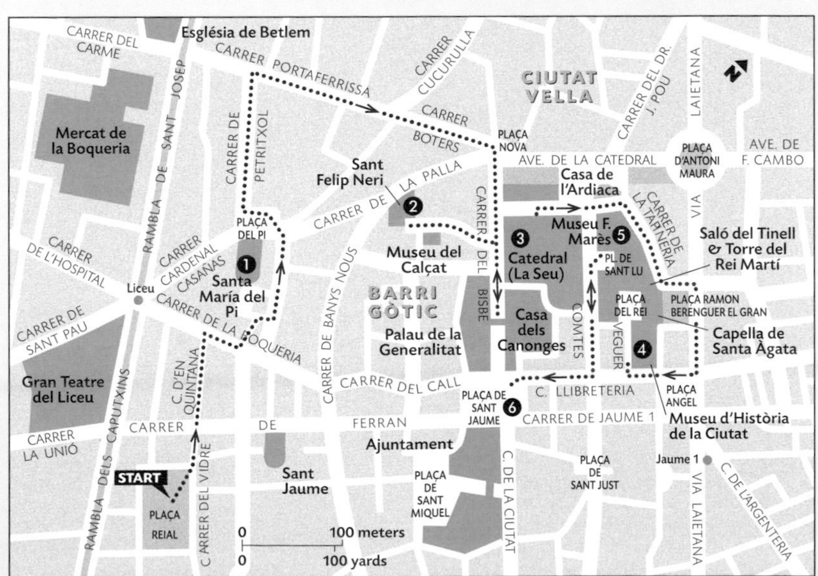

La Ribera & El Born

If you enjoyed the Gothic quarter, then neighboring La Ribera, which extends east of Via Laietana, should prove even more fascinating. Carrer de Montcada, with wall-to-wall art galleries, craft shops, Gothic palaces, and museums slices through here to reach the funky Born district.

Museu Picasso
- 155 D3
- Carrer de Montcada 15–23
- 932 56 30 00
- Closed Sun. p.m.
- $$
- Metro: Jaume 1, Line 4

www.museupicasso.bcn.es

La Ribera

La Ribera has been a residential quarter since medieval times. Any detour down its shady side streets takes you beneath balconies festooned with laundry, past neighborhood bars and Chinese-owned shops. The entire port area used to look like this before it was transformed for the Olympic Games. Since then, designers and restaurateurs have made it one of Barcelona's hippest neighborhoods, especially around lively Passeig del Born.

Museu Picasso: This museum may not have the world's finest or most comprehensive collection of Picassos, but it certainly has the most illuminating. The richest sections here cover Picasso's early years, his "Las Meninas" series, and his last burst of creativity, expressed in engravings. All this and more is displayed in the neighboring Gothic palaces of **Berenguer de Aguilar** and **Barón de Castellet.**

At the top of the beautiful courtyard staircase, the collection moves chronologically through Pablo Picasso's life (1881–1973). Sketches he produced as a ten-year-old prodigy show his lively imagination and academic prowess. Skillful portraits and oil landscapes of A Coruña, painted when his family moved there from Málaga, demonstrate his early application and humor (look for his self-portrait in a wig, 1897). These are followed by stylistic experiments, much influenced by a visit to Paris in 1900.

After a room devoted to his **Blue Period** (1901–1904), the

The Museu Picasso in La Ribera district celebrates the ever-changing work of the great artist.

INSIDER TIP:

Join Catalan society by taking in a performance at El Born's Palau de la Música Catalana. Decorated in stained glass and mosaics, the building alone is a marvel.

—RACHAEL JACKSON
Research Manager, National Geographic Channels

collection leaps to 1917, when Picasso's artistic freedom was in full flower, then to his **"Las Meninas" series** (1957). These 57 oils, inspired by Velázquez's painting "Las Meninas" (see p. 61), are astounding in their deconstructed abandon. The last rooms on this floor display landscapes of Cannes and ceramics made at Mougins.

Upstairs is Picasso's twilight masterpiece, **"Suite 156"** (1969–1972), a series of engravings that were the culmination of both his cultural inspirations and strong erotic impulses.

Museu Barbier-Mueller: Virtually opposite the Museu Picasso, the medieval Palau Nadal houses this choice collection of pre-Columbian art. Every exhibit is a masterpiece in perfect condition, so you have a real feast of the best of Latin America's indigenous cultures. Eight rooms take you from Mesoamerica's mother culture, the Olmec, through the classic period of Teotihuacán, the Aztec, the Maya, as well as rare pieces from Central and South America. Chavin, Moche, Nazca, and Inca pieces represent Andean culture beside pottery from the Lower Amazon. Admire the complex Zapotec god in feathered headdress and the fearsome, cross-eyed Maya mask of jade.

Santa María del Mar: At the end of Montcada you cannot miss the popular Gothic church of Santa María del Mar, founded by local sailors in the 14th century to rival the extravagance of the bourgeois cathedral and known as the People's Cathedral. It has perfect proportions and a lovely 15th-century **rose window** above the western portal. An incongruous modern window (1997) at the other end celebrates the Olympics.

El Born

North of here is the Passeig del Born, once used for jousting at the center of a delightful medieval merchants' quarter, El Born. Today this forms a maze of enticing fashion and design shops, as well as lively tapas bars and affordable young restaurants. Gourmet stores, art galleries, and more upscale restaurants are booming.

Finally, by following the Via Laietena northwest, you reach the landmark Modernista building, **Palau de la Música Catalana,** a concert hall designed by Lluís Domènech i Montaner in 1908. Guided tours are offered daily. ■

Museu Barbier-Mueller
- Map: 155 D3
- Address: Carrer de Montcada 14
- Phone: 933 10 45 16
- Hours: Closed Mon., Sun. p.m., & p.m. on public holidays
- Price: $

www.amicsmuseuprecolombi.org

Santa María del Mar
- Map: 155 D3
- Address: Plaça de Santa María del Mar 1
- Phone: 933 10 23 90

Palau de la Música Catalana
- Map: 155 D3
- Address: Calle Sant Francesc de Paula 2
- Phone: 932 95 72 00
- Price: $$$

www.palaumusica.org

A Walk Down La Rambla

Soak up the many variations on Barcelona's 21st-century spirit by exploring the animated Rambla and its side streets. These harbor a wealth of historical and contemporary interest in an inspirational mix of styles, as well as endless street theater.

Take a walk down La Rambla to set your eyes—and feet—on mosaics designed by Joan Miró.

NOT TO BE MISSED:

Museu d'Art Contemporani de Barcelona • Mercat de la Boquería • Palau Güell • Plaça Reial

With your back to the modern fountain **"Homenatge a Francesc Macià"** ❶ on the southwest corner of Plaça de Catalunya *(visitor information, Plaça de Catalunya 17-S, tel 807 11 72 22)*, cross to the central pedestrian walkway of **La Rambla.** This immediately gives you a taste of Barcelona's most famous avenue with sidewalk cafés, street performers, flower sellers, and people strolling. At the sign pointing to Anteneu, cross to the left and take a sharp left into the pedestrianized Carrer de Santa Anna. At No. 32, walk into the courtyard where the charming Romanesque church of **Santa Ana** ❷ *(tel 933 01 35 76, open a.m. & 6:30–8.30 p.m., closed Sun. p.m.)* now stands jammed between 19th- and 20th-century buildings.

Retrace your steps to La Rambla. Cross to the other side, noting the ornate pharmacy, and walk down Calle d'Elisabets. This street crosses the Plaça del Bonsuccés before reaching a junction at Carrer dels Angels. Immediately visible on your right are the contemporary forms of the **Museu d'Art Contemporani de Barcelona** or **MACBA** ❸ *(Plaça dels Àngels 1, tel 934 12 08 10, closed Sun. p.m. & Tues., www.macba.es)*, a stone, glass, and metal-plated building designed by Richard Meier that opened in 1995. The permanent collection starts in the late 1940s with artists such as Jean Dubuffet, Alexander Calder, and Marcel Broodthaers, and ends with contemporaries such as Christian Boltanski, Rosemary Trockel, Richard Long, and Jaume Plensa. The museum has inspired a rash of art and design-related shops in the surrounding streets of El Raval.

From here, turn right down tree-lined Carrer dels Angels until you come to Carrer del Carme. Opposite stands the massive Gothic-style **Hospital de Santa Creu,** which currently houses the **Biblioteca de Catalunya** ❹ *(tel 933 17 07 78)*. It is worth walking around to **Carrer de l'Hospital 56** to enter the courtyard and Gothic patio.

Continue across the pretty little square named for Alexander Fleming (the Scottish bacteriologist who discovered penicillin) and return to La Rambla. On your left is the rusticated baroque facade of the **Església de Betlem.** The interior of the church dates from a 1930s renovation after a fire and is of little interest. Turn right into the lively **Rambla de Sant Josep,** monopolized by a **bird market,** where caged parrots squawk beneath the chestnut trees.

Rambla de Sant Josep

On the right is the imposing **Palau de la Virreina 5** (1778), whose baroque and rococo interior now hosts photography exhibitions. Next comes the cornucopian **Mercat de la Boquería** (also called Mercat de Sant Josep; *closed Sun.*), where foodstuffs are sold beneath a soaring wrought-iron and glass roof. Flower stands on La Rambla partly conceal a **Joan Miró design** on the sidewalk as it widens into Plaça de la Boquería. Look, too, at **No. 77,** its facade decorated in art nouveau mosaics. Almost opposite is a kitsch example of the 1920s chinoiserie craze that bristles with dragons and parasols.

See also area map pp. 154–155
- ➤ Plaça de Catalunya
- 1–2 hours (without visits)
- 1.75 miles (2.8 km)
- ➤ Plaça Reial

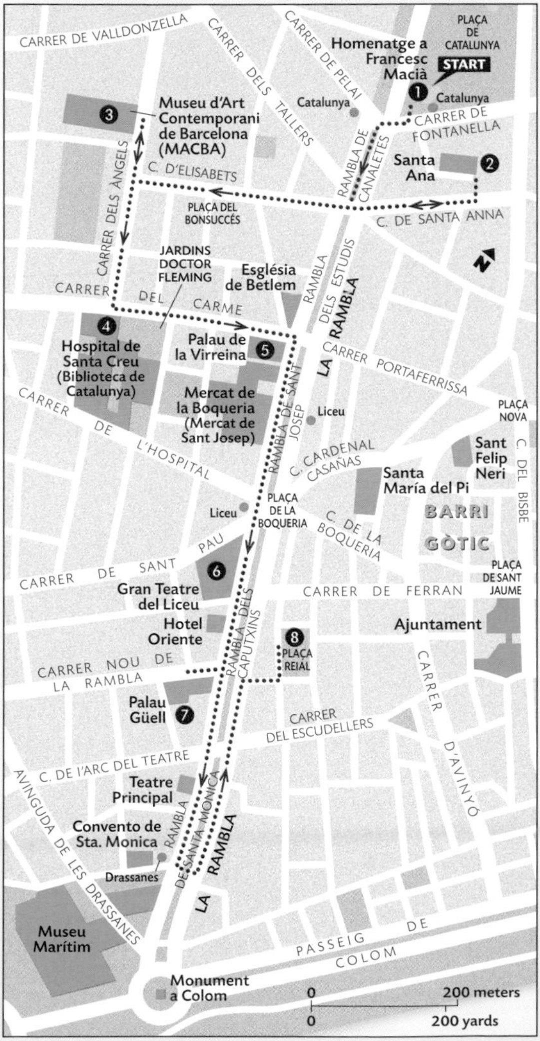

Rambla dels Caputxins

On the right stands the **Gran Teatre del Liceu 6**, Barcelona's most prestigious theater. After the Hotel Oriente turn right into Carrer Nou de la Rambla to see Gaudí's extraordinary **Palau Güell 7** *(Carrer Nou de la Rambla 3, tel 933 17 39 74, closed Mon., guided visits only)*, built 1885–1890. Back on La Rambla you pass the curved facade of Barcelona's oldest theater, **Teatre Principal** (1847), opposite which stands a statue of the founder of modern Catalunyan theater, Frederic Soler.

Rambla de Santa Mònica

The 17th-century **Convento de Santa Mònica** hides behind the nondescript facade of a cultural center. Cross over and walk back up La Rambla to No. 42 and enter a covered passageway. This leads to the elegant **Plaça Reial 8**, where overpriced cafés overlook palm trees and lampposts designed by Gaudí.

Waterfront

Completely transformed since the 1990s, Barcelona's harbor (Port Vell) now bristles with marinas, leisure facilities, state-of-the-art museums, restaurants, and plenty of viewing points. Alongside the spanking new is the illustrious old, nearly all of it connected with the city's maritime history. Not least, 4 miles (7 km) of golden sand run from here to the Forum park.

Barcelona's Aquàrium has a special tunnel for viewing sharks.

Monument a Colom
- 155 D2
- 933 02 52 24

Museu Marítim
- 155 D2
- Avinguda de les Drassanes
- 933 42 99 20
- $$
- Metro: Drassanes, Line 3

www.museumaritimbarcelona.com

The symbolic Columbus Lookout or **Monument a Colom** makes a good starting point. Take the elevator up this 160-foot (50 m) iron column to join the statue of Christopher Columbus surveying the harbor. In front is the mooring for trimarans *(Las Golondrinas, tel 934 42 31 06)* that tour the harbor to the **Vila Olímpica.**

You also look down on the world's largest **medieval shipyards,** a unique complex of 13th-century vaulted halls built around a central courtyard large enough to contain galleons. Luckily for Barcelona they were saved from demolition and in their refurbished form make a fitting background for the **Museu Marítim,** where model ships, paintings, prowheads, navigational instruments, maps, and charts illustrate Barcelona's maritime history. Exhibits also give a wider picture of the evolution of seafaring, ending with submarines before you are plunged into an aquatic virtual reality show. The café-restaurant overlooks orange trees in the sunken courtyard.

Another successful conversion houses the **Museu d'Història de Catalunya,** a lively chronological survey of Catalan history using interactive exhibits, information panels, charts, audiovisuals, photos, reconstructions, and models. Texts are in Catalan, but you can borrow a translation brochure at the ticket desk. The illuminating display covers two remodeled floors of the 1900 **Palau de Mar,** the former main warehouses of the Barceloneta wharf. The most interesting section is on **Floor 2,** showing man's origins in Catalunya, the Iberians, and Romans. It also covers the short Moorish occupation, medieval times, and the Habsburg Empire. Don't miss **Floor 4,** where the café opens onto a terrace with fabulous port views.

A boardwalk, **Rambla de Mar,** leads from the Monument a Colom to **Port Vell** and the **Moll d'Espanya** (Jetty of Spain), devoted to entertainment. Here the Maremàgnum mall and cinema complex jostle with the **IMAX theater** *(tel 932 25 11 11)* and the **Aquàrium** *(tel 932 21 74 74).*

La Barceloneta & Port Olímpic

The 18th-century grid of streets known as La Barceloneta was traditionally the sailors' quarter. To the south looms the rusty **Torre de Sant Sebastià** from where you can catch a cable car, **Transbordador Aeri** *(Teleférico de Miramar, tel 934 30 47 16, $$),* with heart-stopping views over the harbor to Montjuïc (see pp. 168–169). Seafood restaurants abound, and sandy beaches stretch northward. Two high-rises tower over Port Olímpic. One houses the avant-garde Hotel Arts, fronted by a giant metallic fish designed by Frank Gehry.

The beaches end at the junction with the lengthy Avinguda Diagonal, now graced by the controversial Fòrum, which houses the **Museu Blau,** an innovative museum of natural sciences. ■

Museu d'Història de Catalunya

155 E2

Palau de Mar, Plaça Pau Vila 3

932 25 47 00

Closed Sun. p.m., & Mon.

$

Metro: Barceloneta, Line 4

www.mhcat.net

Museu Blau

Plaça Leonardo da Vinci

932 56 60 02

EXPERIENCE: Cooking Catalan

Why not carry the Catalan culinary experience home with you by taking a cooking class or two while you're in town? **Cook&Taste Barcelona** *(Carrer Paradis 3, tel 933 02 13 20, www.cookandtaste.net)* offers two classes a day in Spanish and English for individuals or groups. Customized private sessions *(fee negotiable)* are also available.

The half-day class *($$$$)* begins with an optional walking tour *($)* of the huge **Mercat de la Boquería** (see p. 163; *tel 934 12 13 15, closed Sun., www.boqueria.info*), where the mouthwatering displays are as unbeatable as the sheer variety of available produce. The school's chefs will give you tips about selecting and buying the best on offer.

Back at the school's well-equipped kitchens, you will learn how to prepare some of Spain's most authentic dishes, like tapas, gazpacho, and paella, each shaped by Spain's varied traditions, including ancient Roman, Muslim, and Jewish. Later enjoy the result of your hard work with a relaxed meal in the comfortable dining room.

Cook&Taste Barcelona also offers a Foodies Stroll. Sign up for the lunch or dinner session and be treated to an expert walking and tasting tour, including the Boquería market. Sample local cheeses, artisanal hams, and even hot chocolate and pastries in cafés, shops, and bars across the city. Tours are customized to your interests and require a minimum of two people.

Catalan Pride

At the heart of Catalunya lies Barcelona, "a city of merchants, conquerors and people of good upbringing, refined, well educated and luxurious." Little has changed since these words were written in a 19th-century travel guide, and Catalunya still spearheads Spain's commercial development, culture, and cuisine.

Pride, an integral part of the individualistic Catalan character, manifests itself first in the language, which stirs Provençal French and Castilian Spanish into a unique cocktail, and second in a strong attachment to regional customs. Whether dancing the sardana, a slow-moving circular dance, or creating gravity-defying human pyramids *(castellars)*, the seven million or so Catalans have defied all attempts to quash their identity.

This individualism stems from the early ninth century when Charlemagne successfully besieged Barcelona and then divided the surrounding land into feudal kingdoms ruled by counts. By the 12th century, Catalan had become a written language, and the word "Catalunya" was mentioned explicitly. For two centuries Catalunya remained at its zenith. Its seamen and merchants dominated trade in the Mediterranean, and its citizens enjoyed a unique system of privileges. Although Catalan trading prominence was later usurped by Castilian and Andalusian monopolization of New World routes, Catalans never lost their strong sense of civil rights, something that has irritated every Madrid-based ruler since.

The 19th and 20th centuries saw decades of industrial revolt and anarchism, and Catalunya was at its lowest ebb under General Franco's dictatorship (1939–1975), when the Catalan language itself was banned, as were books in Catalan and even the sardana.

Behind the scenes the radical spirit never died, and Catalan entrepreneurs now once more lead the way. Pragmatism (some would say mercantile obsession) is another enduring Catalan characteristic. Although one-third of Spanish wine is produced in Catalunya, it is textiles, chemicals, cars, and planes that form the backbone of the healthy economy.

Culturally, this region long dominated the Spanish avant-garde. Although Madrid and regional cities have caught up since the 1980s, Barcelona still boasts Spain's liveliest cultural calendar and a string of 20th-century luminaries. It is no surprise that Spain's greatest living writer, Juan Goytisolo, was born in Barcelona.

Catalunya's proximity to France encourages high standards in gastronomy, art, and design, but French influence is tempered by habits that can only be termed Spanish, such as the relaxed

Curious Catalan Fiestas

Catalunya has just as many fiestas as the rest of Spain, but a few are particularly striking. Every September in Escala on the Costa Brava, for example, boats loaded with salt for curing anchovies sail into the harbor, announcing the **Festa de la Sal** (Salt Festival). In Begur, on the same coast, the **Fira dels Indians** (West Indian Festival) on the first weekend of September celebrates the city's links with Cuba. Cuban bands join locals who sing sea shanties and dance the sardana, the ubiquitous Catalan folk dance. The eerie **Dansa de la Mort** (Dance of Death) held in Verges (near Girona) is one of Spain's more original Easter celebrations. At midnight on Maundy Thursday, a procession winds through the town with Jesus carrying his cross, a weeping Mary, Roman soldiers, hooded penitents, and people dressed as skeletons cavorting to drumbeats.

The spectacle of human pyramids *(castellars)* is an ancient Catalan tradition.

post-meal chat *(sobretaula)*, which can last several hours. On the table itself, refined, Mediterranean dishes are served with an elegant flourish, and restaurants may display audacious contemporary architecture and designer furniture.

With dozens of Catalan newspapers and an exciting arts scene, Catalan pride is unlikely to fade anytime soon. Meanwhile, the buzzword "separation" comes and goes: in Catalan, *Independentism català*.

Montjuïc

Easily accessible from the city below, Montjuïc (meaning "Mount of the Jews") is an essential destination for its culture, gardens, and panoramic views. The bucolic setting of the 1929 World's Fair, it was revitalized in 1992, when the stadium was remodeled for the Olympics.

Calatrava's telecommunications tower crowns Montjuïc.

Montjuïc
- Map 154 C1

Fundació Joan Miró
- Map 154 C1
- Parc de Montjuïc
- 934 43 94 70
- Closed Sun. p.m., Mon., & public holidays
- $$
- Bus 50 or funicular

www.bcn.fjmiro.es

You can reach Montjuïc by **cable car** from La Barceloneta (see p. 165) or by **funicular railway** from Paral•lel metro station. Another cable car links the Montjuïc funicular station with the castle at the top of the hill and Montjuïc's best view. In summer outdoor movies play in the castle moat *(tel 933 02 35 53, www.salamontjuic.org)*.

Fundació Joan Miró

Near the funicular terminus is the Fundació Joan Miró, set up by Catalan artist Joan Miró (1893–1983) in 1971 to conserve his work and promote contemporary art. It remains popular thanks to excellent temporary exhibitions and a lovely setting overlooking the city. Josep Luis Sert's architecture creates luminous free-flowing spaces with changing vistas. The permanent collection is concentrated on the upper floor, leaving most of the ground floor for temporary exhibitions.

On the ground floor don't miss Alexander Calder's spellbinding **"Mercury Fountain,"** made in 1937 for the Paris World's Fair. Beside this are wonderful, playful Miró sculptures and a large room showing his early work from the 1930s and '40s, with the **"Constellations"** series. Upstairs is the main body of work from the 1950s to '60s. The last, equally revealing section is comprised of works donated by friends, from Henry Moore to Henri Matisse. Look for Arnold Newman's 1979 photograph of Miró, which spells out the intense humanity of this man.

Museu Nacional d'Art de Catalunya

The **Palau Nacional** was Spain's national pavilion at the 1929 World Fair. This extravagant building now houses the world's largest collection of Romanesque art, an equally impressive Gothic section, the Cambó collection of Renaissance and baroque paintings, a large section on Catalan art, and a recently added section of the Thyssen-Bornemisza Collection.

The **Romanesque section** is largely composed of church interiors salvaged from remote churches in the Pyrenees. Their murals have been beautifully remounted here. Also look for the late 12th-century altar frontals, notably those from Avia and Baltarga.

The **Gothic section,** dazzling with gilt and multipaneled altar paintings, includes a row of lifesize saints by Pere Llobet (circa 1387). Look for the fine double portrait of John the Baptist and St. Estève from Santa Maria de Puigcerdà (1445–1453), the room devoted to Bernat Martorell, and Jaume Huguet's magnificent paintings.

Below is the **Poble Espanyol** *(Avinguda Marquès de Comillas, tel 933 25 78 66),* an architectural composite of regional Spanish styles. Inside are dozens of craft shops, bars, restaurants, and a flamenco *tablao.*

Other Sites

At the base of the wide steps to the Palau Nacional, beside the 1929 **Font Màgica** (Magic Fountain), stands the serene **Pavelló Mies van der Rohe**—the pavilion designed by modernist Mies van der Rohe for the 1929 World's Fair. The inner pool comes to life with a copy of Georg Kolbe's sculpture "Morning." Inside are examples of the Barcelona chair.

Down the avenue, stands a beautifully restored art nouveau factory that since 2002 has been a showcase for the contemporary art collection of **CaixaForum** *(tel 934 76 86 00, closed Mon.)*—a bank foundation—and a popular venue for concerts and talks. ■

Museu Nacional d'Art de Catalunya

154 B1

Palau Nacional, Parc de Montjuïc

936 22 03 76

Closed Sun., Mon., & p.m. on public holidays

$$

Metro: Espanya, Lines 1 & 3

www.mnac.es

Pavelló Mies van der Rohe

154 B2

Avinguda del Marquès de Comillas

934 23 40 16

$

Metro: Espanya, Lines 1 & 3

www.miesbcn.com

EXPERIENCE: Relive the Civil War in Poble Sec

As a predominantly left-wing city, Barcelona experienced merciless, indiscriminate bombing (initially by Mussolini's planes) during the Civil War. Bloody fighting took place, too, not just between Republicans and fascists but also between the numerous left-wing factions.

When British writer George Orwell (1903–1950) arrived in Barcelona in late 1936, he and his wife Eileen stayed at the Hotel Continental on Las Ramblas while fighting raged in the streets below. After joining the Marxist workers' party, Orwell served as a corporal until June 1937, when he had the choice of escape or prison. The result of his experience was the stirring book, *Homage to Catalonia* (1938).

Today Barcelona offers little information about the Civil War, as many people would like to forget it. An exception is the barrio of Poble Sec, where you can visit **Refugio 307** *(Carrer Nou de la Rambla 169, tel 932 56 21 22, metro Paral•lel, daily guided tours in Spanish and Catalan),* one of hundreds of air-raid shelters in the city dug into the hillside by local residents in 1938. The grim castle crowning Montjuïc above was used as a political prison and execution site until 1940.

For a half- or full-day English-language tour that focuses on the Civil War and its key sites in Barcelona, contact local British expert Nick Lloyd *(tel 633 47 60 09, e-mail: Nick.iberiannature@gmail.com).*

Eixample

This neat grid of streets, whose name means "new extension," dates from the late 19th century, when booming Barcelona expanded westward from the Barri Gòtic. It is the place to go for Modernista follies, designer shopping, art, and sophisticated dining. On the western side is Gai-Eixample, the hub of Barcelona's gay nightlife.

Casa Batlló, with its lavish baroque face, is a Gaudí redesign of a typical Eixample apartment block.

Sagrada Familia

Chief among Eixample's architects is Antoni Gaudí (see pp. 172–175), and here you find his unfinished masterpiece, the gigantic, unorthodox Sagrada Familia (see pp. 173–175). The cathedral's steeples, surrounded by cranes and a builders' site below, have become the emblem of Barcelona's individualism. Like it or not, the story behind the ambitious structure is of an architect's total, and ultimately tragic, dedication to his greatest work.

Building started in 1882, but was interrupted by World War I. When Gaudí died in 1926, only the **Nativitat** (Nativity) **facade** was complete. Since then, work has continued sporadically, fraught by personality clashes, controversy, and, above all, a total absence of plans, as was Gaudí's modus operandi. In 1986 the **Passion** (western) **facade** was commissioned from Josep Maria Subirachs, who added yet another thorny aesthetic issue with his stiff, stylized sculptures.

Gaudí is buried in the **crypt,** and a small museum relates the complexities of the cathedral's history and Gaudí's role. In 2010 the roof over the apse and the transept was completed, forming the

INSIDER TIP:

Want to escape the city? Take the metro north of Parc Güell to the Montbau stop. From there walk through maquis and forest to the Collserola ridge. You might even spot a wild boar.

—NICK LLOYD
Barcelona tour guide

base of the central tower. Brave the crowds at the tower elevator on each facade for stunning views. Tickets have time slots.

Other Gaudí Designs

Far more successful as a Gaudí memorial is **La Pedrera** or **Casa Milà** *(Carrer de Provença 261–5, tel 934 84 59 00)*, in the heart of Eixample. This innovative apartment block was built in 1906–1912, defying all architectural norms. On its top floor is the **Espai Gaudí,** an interactive display of Gaudí's designs and models. This gives access to the extraordinary roof terrace crowned with organically shaped ventilation shafts. The Caixa, the dynamic Catalan bank that runs the space, organizes high-profile art exhibitions on the first floor (the adjoining gift shop and snack bar are excellent, too).

Other Gaudí designs in the neighborhood are **Casa Batlló** (1906) at Passeig de Gracia 43, **Casa Calvet** (1899) at Casp 48, the **Torre de Bellesguard** (1909) at Bellesguard 16–20, and **Casa Vicenç** (1888) at Carolines 24.

Parc Güell

One of Gaudí's most expansive designs is Parc Güell, at the foot of Mont Carmel, just outside Eixample. This massive project (1900–1914) was originally intended as a garden city for 60 houses, but when the plots did not sell, Count Eusebi Güell, the promoter, allowed the architect to let his fantasies fly. The result is a labyrinth of textured viaducts, pavilions, stairways, fountains, benches, curved columns, and arches upon which he developed his characteristic use of randomly fragmented ceramics. The **Casa-Museu Gaudí** (where Gaudí lived) is of less interest. Join a one-hour guided tour of the park at the ticket office to understand the concepts behind it all. ■

Sagrada Familia

- 155 D5
- Carrer de Mallorca
- 932 07 30 31
- $$$
- Metro: Sagrada Familia, Lines 2 & 5

www.sagradafamilia.org

Parc Güell & Casa-Museu Gaudí

- 155 C5
- Carrer d'Olot 7
- 932 19 38 11
- $
- Metro: Lesseps, Line 3

www.casamuseugaudi.org

Antoni Tàpies

Antoni Tàpies (1923–2012) was a Catalan artist with the status of a regional institution. He instigated the **Fundació Antoni Tàpies** *(Aragó 255, tel 934 87 03 15, closed Mon., www.fundaciotapies.org)* in 1984 to promote contemporary art, preserve a representative body of his own work, and create an impressive reference library of modern and Oriental art. All this is installed in an extensively converted Modernista building designed by Lluís Domènech i Montaner (1850–1923).

Tàpies first erupted onto the art scene in the 1950s when he incorporated old paper, rags, and mud into his artworks. All his signature canvases have tactile sand or other elements.

Gaudí & Modernism

The barriers of Spain's artistic conservatism were shattered in the early 20th century when Antoni Gaudí (1852–1926) and others, including Lluís Domènech and his son Pere Domènech, turned architectural tradition on its head. Their organically inspired structures, extensive use of decorative brickwork, and design "follies" were Spain's answer to art nouveau.

Fanciful chimney pots cap one of Gaudí's inventive designs in Parc Güell.

The Catalan version of art nouveau, *modernismo,* became the most extreme form and Gaudí its most controversial and intuitively brilliant protagonist. Through his complete dedication to organic forms, he revolutionized architecture in Catalunya.

Gaudí originated from Reus, near Tarragona, where he showed a precocious fascination with natural forms found in zoology, botany, and anatomy. This, combined with a taste for craft techniques inherited from his father (a coppersmith), became the unifying thread running through his work. For Gaudí, structure was inseparable from form, color, and texture, a holistic approach inspired by the Arts and Crafts movement. He transformed these ideas into reality with the assistance of architectural training and an enlightened backer.

Gaudí's Influence & Approach

Gaudí's early designs in the 1880s incorporated Mudejar and Gothic influences, using ornamental brickwork, ceramic tiling, parabolic arches, turrets, and domes. By the 1900s he had developed his inimitable, curvilinear style in ambitious, ground-breaking **Parc Güell** (see p. 171) in Barcelona. This project was financed by Eusebi Güell, a local industrialist who became his faithful patron. Free-flowing, organic form and extensive use of fragmented ceramic tiles became the hallmarks of Gaudí's complex, playful style.

Other examples in Barcelona are in the **Casa Batlló** (see p. 171), nicknamed the "house of the emaciated tibia," and **La Pedrera** (Casa Milà, see p. 171), where chimney pots and access staircases on the roof were transformed into colorful, surrealistic sculptures. This rooftop fantasyland is still a popular meeting place for Barcelona's art-oriented youth.

Gaudí's approach to construction was equally unorthodox: He never used plans, instead depending on sketches, elevations, and models. This deliberate nonrationality may have predated the surrealists but later produced insurmountable difficulties in completing Gaudí's last project, Barcelona's Sagrada Familia cathedral (see pp. 170–171), after his death.

Gaudí's sculptural roof overlooks the organic forms of La Pedrera.

Sagrada Familia

Begun by Francisco Villar in 1882, this project was taken over by Gaudí a year later. He planned to create a church in the form of the Latin Cross, with four towering spires over each of the three facades to represent the 12 Apostles and a central cluster of five more to symbolize Christ and the Evangelists. Much

The magnificent though incomplete towers of Gaudí's Sagrada Familia mark the Barcelona skyline.

of the structural inspiration came from trees, leading to branching columns.

The architect intended this neo-Gothic church to synthesize his deepening sense of spirituality, developed in mystical theories of symbolic structure while he lived as a virtual recluse during the latter part of his life. His

INSIDER TIP:

Don't miss the Nativity facade on the east side of Sagrada Familia. Its riot of ornament—with more than 40 animal species depicted—highlights Gaudí's love of the natural world.

—MARY STEPHANOS
National Geographic contributor

work on the church became so obsessional that when funds were low Gaudí even sold his possessions and begged money from friends.

On his death, just one spire, the crypt, the apsidal walls, and the Nativity facade had been completed. Work continued under Domènec Sugrañes until 1938, and since 1984 under

Interior of Sagrada Familia

Jordi Bonnet i Armengol. In 1936, during the Civil War, much of the workshop and models were destroyed. Since the outset, it has been built from donations.

Death of an Eccentric Genius

Gaudí's life came to an end in a tragic, though fittingly unconventional way: When he was knocked over by a tram in 1926, Gaudí's appearance was so tramplike that nobody recognized him. Since then his star has risen, and the still incomplete Sagrada Familia has become the architectural symbol of Barcelona.

Disseny Hub & Torre Agbar

As of 2013, Barcelona at last has a spectacular design center to reflect the city's pioneering role in the world of decorative arts. The new building, Disseny Hub *(Plaça de les Glories, metro Glories, www.dhub-bcn.cat),* was designed by MBM of Barcelona to utilize underground space beneath a striking parallel-piped section projecting above the street. Inside, three major collections are combined: the **Museu Textil i d'Indumentària** (fashion design), the **Museu de les Arts Decoratives** (product design), and the **Gabinet de les Arts Gràfiques** (graphic design). Until 2013, these collections will remain in their original locations at Montcada 12 *(tel 932 56 23 00)* and the Palau de Pedralbes *(Avenida Diagonal 686, tel 932 56 34 65).*

Soaring behind this new structure is Jean Nouvel's unmissable phallic **Torre Agbar** (2005), the 466-foot-high (142 m) headquarters of Barcelona's municipal water company. Its glittering outer skin, said to have been inspired by architect Antoni Gaudí, is spectacular when illuminated at night (Friday, Saturday, and Sunday only).

More Places to Visit in Barcelona

Monestir de Santa María de Pedralbes

On the flank of the Collserola hills, west of Eixample, drift back to medieval times at the Monestir de Santa María de Pedralbes. The walled Gothic convent was founded in 1326 by the widowed fourth wife of Jaume II, Elisenda de Montcada, who spent her last 37 years living here. Her companions were Clarissa nuns whose tiny cells surround a beautiful three-story **cloister**. A small chapel, **Capella de Sant Miquel,** is faced in exquisite frescoes (1346) by Ferrer Bassi, a follower of Giotto. The former **dormitory, kitchen, pharmacy,** and **church** give fascinating insight into the cloistered life. In 1983 the community moved to an adjoining building, opening this Gothic jewel to the public. *www.museuhistoria.bcn.es/cat/centres/pedralbes* 154 A4 Baixada del Monestir 9 932 56 34 34 Open Tues.–Sun. a.m. $ Metro: Maria Cristina, Line 3

EXPERIENCE: Camp Nou

Few people can ignore the talent of Barcelona's great soccer team and its legendary players, regularly top of the national and European leagues. The club was founded in 1899 by a Swiss, and its first president was an Englishman. Since 1957, Camp Nou *(Av. Arístides Maillol, access 9, Les Corts, tel 934 96 36 00, www.fcbarcelona.com, closed Sun p.m., $$$, metro Coll Blanc, Les Corts, & Maria Cristina, map 154 A3)* has been Barça's home pitch and it makes an inspiring pilgrimage for sports enthusiasts. If you can't make a match day, it is well worth seeing the club museum and following the excellent audio-guide tour from the players' changing-room to the President's box. The tentacles of Catalan design reach even here; in 2010 the museum underwent a complete makeover to include state-of-the-art multimedia sections. Full of emotion for some, a visit to the stadium is now termed a Camp Nou Experience.

Palau Reial de Pedralbes

Originally a farm, the Palau Reial de Pedralbes was bought by Eusebi Güell (the patron of Gaudí) in 1882 and remodeled by the architect Joan Martorell i Montells into an incongruous-looking palace together with a **neo-Gothic chapel.** Gaudí contributed to the work and partially designed the magnificent **gardens** with fountains, a pergola, and Mediterranean plants. After it was donated to the royal family, the palace was again remodeled, bringing lavish interior decoration that zigzags crazily from Louis XIV to art nouveau. In 1932 it became a decorative arts museum. 154 A4 Avinguda Diagonal 686 932 80 13 64 Closed Sun. p.m. & Mon. $ Metro: Palau Reial

Parc de la Ciutadella

Barcelona's largest park lies north of La Ribera on the site of the 1888 World's Fair. Between the paths, lawns, and ponds stand buildings from that period: the **Umbracle** (tropical greenhouse), the **Hivernacle** (winter glasshouse), and the **Castell dels Tres Dragons** (designed as an elaborate restaurant by Domènech i Montaner), all now sections of the **Museu de Ciencies Naturals** *(www.bcn.es/museuciencies)*. The neoclassical **Museu Martorell** (1878) was Barcelona's first custom-built museum and is also part of the natural sciences network. These locations are now supplemented by the Museu Blau (see p. 165), with its user-friendly, interactive exhibits. 155 E3 Metro: Ciutadella–Vila Olímpica, Arc de Triomf, & Barceloneta

Endless beaches, remote inland sierra, and Spain's third largest city, Valencia—with inventive rice dishes and sparkling *cava* in the bargain

Eastern Spain

Cadaqués, one of many harbor towns dotting Costa Brava

Eastern Spain

Eastern Spain encompasses a vast swath of land from the Pyrenees on the French border south to the carefree beach resorts of Costa Blanca. Its landscapes vary from chilly mountain villages to mellow sandy beaches, rugged interior sierra, and valleys clad in almond and citrus trees. You can experience huge climatic variations in a day, but almost everywhere, with only a few exceptions, you also sense a strong Catalan work ethic.

The Santuari dels Angels offers panoramic views of the region around Girona.

Of the cities, Barcelona (see pp. 153–176) has the highest profile, but Valencia, Spain's third largest city, has been hard on its heels in recent years. It is an increasingly strong cultural center, with plenty of spruced-up monuments and dazzling new buildings. Between the two is Tarragona, giving an unparalleled vision of Roman Spain. The design-conscious town of Girona (Gerona) is to the north, and in the deep south the mirage of Alacant (Alicante) rises from arid hills over a generous bay and rampant tourism along the Costa Blanca.

Seafaring has been king since the Greeks and then the Romans crossed the Mediterranean to colonize Spain. Charlemagne left his mark in the ninth century, creating the County of Barcelona and a feudal system that persisted for several centuries. The Moors came and went fast from the north of this region, but more slowly from Valencia. By 1443, Catalunya, Aragón, Valencia, and the Balearic Islands had created one powerful kingdom including Sardinia, Sicily, and southern Italy and was soon united with Castilla. Many of the monuments date from this prosperous Renaissance period, and huge areas were repopulated by northerners to replace the victims of the Spanish Inquisition.

Agriculture is still important—obviously so in Valencia's vast inland *huerta* (vegetable "garden," a nickname for its irrigated land), and more discreetly in Catalunya's interior. The region is also highly industrialized.

A major source of income is tourism, above all along the *costas*, home to a high proportion of northern Europeans. The most venerable,

NOT TO BE MISSED:

the Costa Brava, saw its first waves of foreign visitors in the 1950s. The disproportionate development of the 1960s and '70s now seems a mistake, yet vacationers still flock here. Despite this, you still see dramatic natural beauty. If you visit only one stretch of coast, the Costa Brava should be your choice. Farther south, the Costa Blanca has pockets of outstanding scenery and is famed above all for that quintessential Spanish dish—paella, a fragrant blend (with variations) of rice, saffron, shellfish, chicken, and vegetables. ■

Catalunya (Cataluña)

Together with the Madrid region and Euskadi (Basque Country), Catalunya is economically the most dynamic part of Spain and long stood on its own as the most avant-garde. With the global recession, unemployment rose to 18 percent and the economy stuttered. It still clings jealously to its Catalan language, sometimes to the detriment of universal communication.

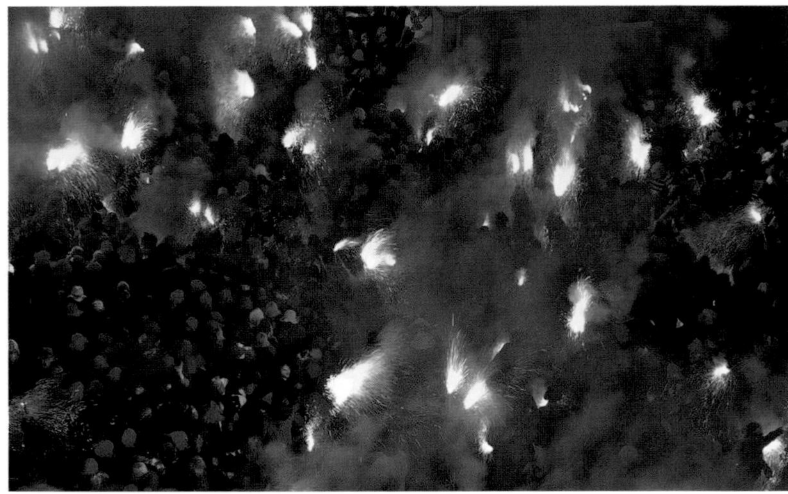

Torches flicker among the crowd at the flamboyant Patum de Berga celebration.

This clear sense of identity dates from the ninth century, when Charlemagne established Catalunya as a buffer zone. The region has close linguistic and cultural links with southern France, although this did not protect it from destructive French troops during warfare between France and Spain in 1714 and in 1808. Close connections continue today, and for inhabitants of northern Catalunya, France is more easily accessible than the Spanish capital.

The Moorish occupation was short, enabling the counts of this feudal region to finally crystallize Catalan identity in the 12th century, crowned by the marriage of Count Ramon Berenguer IV with the Aragón heiress Petronila in 1137. This was the beginning of a golden age for Catalan merchants that peaked in the 14th century, when Catalunya and Aragón controlled a huge Mediterranean empire. Despite their alliance, each of these regions kept its traditional civic privileges, and the Catalans' proud sense of justice, expressed in strikes and industrial unrest, was one of the biggest thorns in Franco's side.

Catalunya has widely diverse attractions, from gastronomy to history, wine to contemporary design, and volcanoes to sun-drenched beaches and crisp ski slopes. Highlights include historic monasteries in Pyrenean valleys and coastal sierra, spectacular Roman remains at Empúries and Tarragona, and Girona–Catalunya's most enjoyable, forward-looking town outside Barcelona. You can pick up the threads of Salvador Dalí's eccentricities in Cadaqués and Figueres, or take a drive into the hills to hike and taste wine and *cava* (the Spanish equivalent of champagne) before collapsing on a beach to digest it all. On the down side, Catalunya's greatest economic asset, its industry, does not always make for scenic landscapes.

Costa Brava

From the French border at Portbou south to Blanes stretch 125 miles (200 km) of rugged coastline, coves, and beaches that still possess magic and beauty despite vigorous development in the 1960s and '70s. Dalí, Picasso, Chagall, and Man Ray were among the many artists captivated by the coast's fishing villages and limpid sky. More recently, Ferran Adrià placed molecular gastronomy on the map at El Bullí near Roses.

The Costa Brava has black spots such as the package vacation resort of Lloret de Mar, but its highlights include the inland medieval villages of **Pals** and **Peratallada,** the nature reserve of **Les Medes** (islands reached by glass-bottomed boat from L'Estartit), and, in the south, the picturesque walled town of **Tossa de Mar.**

Empúries: Empúries (Ampurias) was the site of a Greek and Roman settlement that held sway over the area for more than seven centuries from 600 B.C. The location encapsulates the original untouched beauty of this coast, with magnificent views across the Golf de Roses and a lovely beach. Wander through the Greek and Roman ruins, looking at the mosaics of the villas, then see the dramatic audiovisual show at the **Museu d'Arqueologia.** Even the anchovy industry at nearby L'Escala dates to the Romans.

INSIDER TIP:

Located 1 mile (1.6 km) offshore from L'Estartit in the province of Girona, the Illes Medes marine reserve is open to scuba divers and features karstic caves, groupers, red coral—in short, Mediterranean life at its best.

—ALFONSO PARDO
Professor, Universidad de Zaragoza

Cadaqués: One of the coast's most popular towns is Cadaqués, which, unlike more commercialized resorts, still has a distinctive atmosphere out of season. This whitewashed fishing port huddles in a cove at the end of a tortuous road across the hilly promontory and nature reserve of **Cap de Creus.** Seafood restaurants *(reservations necessary in summer)* and art galleries are abundant, and Salvador Dalí's fascinating

Costa Brava
179 C5
www.costabrava.org

Empúries (Ampurias)
179 C5

Museu d'Arqueologia
L'Escala, Empúries
972 77 02 08
www.mac.cat/seus/empuries

Cadaqués
179 C5
Visitor Information
Oficina Municipal de Turismo, Calle des Cotxe 2A
972 25 83 15
www.cadaques.cat

Casa-Museu Salvador Dalí

Portlligat, Cadaqués

972 25 10 15

Reservations required

www.salvador-dali.org

Begur

179 C5

Visitor Information

Oficina Municipal de Turismo, Avenida Onze de Setembre 5

972 62 45 20

www.begur.cat

Girona (Gerona)

179 C5

Visitor Information

Oficina de Turismo, Joan Maragall 2

872 97 59 75

Closed Sun. p.m.

www.girona.cat

house, **Casa-Museu Salvador Dalí,** awaits over the hill.

Begur: The most exclusive resort is Begur, 30 miles (50 km) east of Girona. Crowned by castle ruins and backed by wooded hills, it lies within a couple of miles of idyllic sandy coves lapped by crystalline water. From here to the lighthouse of Llafranc is arguably the most beautiful stretch of the Costa Brava that you can explore on foot or by car before visiting delightfully well-preserved **Palafrugell,** preferably for its Sunday market.

Girona (Gerona)

With budget flights from all over Europe landing at its airport, the lovely old town of Girona has undergone a minor boom. This, combined with its strategic location, makes it a stimulating base from which to explore the region. In some ways Girona is a mini-Barcelona, its characteristic river frontage replacing the Catalan capital's seafront. It even has its own equivalent of Gaudí, embodied in his contemporary, Rafael Maso (1880–1935), whose Modernista buildings pepper the center.

Iberians built Girona as a military fortress at the confluence of the Ter and Onyar Rivers. Romans, Jews, and Arabs all left their mark, and Charlemagne's army was not the only one to besiege it. The Onyar River clearly divides the medieval town from the 19th- and 20th-century quarter that spreads to the west, and the numerous **footbridges** give you lovely views of colorful old houses with laundry-draped balconies lining the banks. One of the best viewpoints is the **Pont de Peixateries Velles,** built in 1877 by Gustave Eiffel's company.

Back on the historic east (or right) bank, head for the social focal point, porticoed **Rambla de la Llibertat,** with a Saturday flower market, sidewalk cafés, and boutiques. From here it is a gentle uphill climb into the heart of medieval Girona, which culminates at the Roman walls and their highest point, the medieval **Torre Gironella,** where you have panoramic views and a rampart walk. Skirting around the walls you come to the magnificent **Roman north gate,** which opens onto a wide esplanade in front of the **cathedral** *(www.catedraldegirona.org)*. The baroque facade conceals a Gothic interior of one single nave, an astonishing 94 feet wide (23 m), which caused controversy

INSIDER TIP:

While in Girona, take a side trip to Lago de Banyoles, only about 8 miles (13 km) away. Here you can follow a path around the lake spotting waterbirds. Later stop at a restaurant, swim, or take a boat ride on the lake.

—TINO SORIANO
National Geographic photographer

when it was designed in the 14th century. The trapezoidal cloister and chapter house museum house the original Romanesque section including Charlemagne's tower. The museum, the **Tresor Capitular** *(tel 972 21 44 26, closed Sun. p.m. & Mon.)*, displays the **Tapestry of the Creation,** a Romanesque masterpiece, alongside sacred art and manuscripts (look for the Codex del Beatus). See more Catalan art at the **Museu d'Art** *(tel 972 20 38 34, closed Sun. p.m. & Mon., www.museuart.com)* in the superb 12th- to 14th-century Episcopal Palace.

Just outside the north gate stand the **Banys Àrabs** (Arab Baths), built in 1194 in Moorish style but based on Roman design. The *frigidarium* (cold bath) has a colonnaded octagonal pool beneath a skylight. Immediately downhill, you can't miss the unfinished Gothic bell tower of **Sant Feliu** church, which contains sarcophagi from the Roman and early Christian era, some from Italy. Another major site is the beautiful Romanesque monastery that now houses the **Museo Arqueológico de Sant Pere de Galligants.**

Girona's newest jewel is in the renovated Jewish quarter, **El Call,** just a few steps south of the cathedral square along Carrer de la Força. The Jewish community that had lived here for six centuries was expelled in the 15th century, when part of this web of lanes was bricked up. Today, El Call is not only one of the most fashionable places to live, but is also home to the **Bonastruc ça Porta,** a study center and museum. It has been rebuilt from a synagogue and named for the 13th-century rabbi, scholar, and kabbalist Nahmánides. The museum illustrates rituals and daily life, giving insight into

(continued on p. 186)

Banys Àrabs

- ✉ Carrer Ferrán al Católic, Girona
- ☎ 972 21 32 62
- 🕒 Closed Sun. p.m.

Museo Arqueológico de Sant Pere de Galligants

- ✉ Plaza Santa Lucia, Girona
- ☎ 972 20 26 32
- 🕒 Closed Sun. p.m & Mon.
- $ $

Bonastruc ça Porta

- ✉ Carrer de la Força 8, Girona
- ☎ 972 21 67 61
- 🕒 Closed Sun. p.m. & public holidays

The Onyar River flows past central Girona's colorful houses.

Salvador Dalí

Salvador Dalí's image transcended nationality, as did his trademark mustache, dreamlike paintings, and unsurpassed megalomania. Seduced by fame, he expertly cultivated his status whether in his garden in Cadaqués, at the Hotel Meurice in Paris, or the St. Regis in New York. In 1958 he wrote, "It is difficult to hold the world's interest for more than half an hour at a time. I myself have done so successfully every day for twenty years."

Andy Warhol predicted that everyone would be famous for 15 minutes, but Dalí made his fame last a lifetime, from the day he joined the surrealist movement in Paris in 1929 until his death in 1989. Nor did his cult end there, for Dalí's posthumous legacy was a minefield of unauthenticated works and question marks over his chosen burial place and will that provided headlines for years after.

Dalí had a talent for drama, provocation, and exhibitionism, held together by unbridled imaginative genius. These qualities came at the perfect moment, propelling him to the forefront of the surrealist movement, although its founder, André Breton, later labeled him in disgust "Avida Dollars" (dollar greedy). Dalí's principles were questionable: He veered between anarchism, Marxism, monarchism, and Catholicism, and he did not hesitate to embrace Francoism when it suited him. Yet this extravagant opportunist was no empty bubble, and his earlier works reveal a consummate draftsman and expert weaver of Freudian dreams and neuroses. From **"Metamorphosis of Narcissus"** (1936–1937) to **"Galarina"** (1944–1945), he showed off classical oil-painting techniques with mythological, sexual, and psychoanalytical references in a virtuoso body of work. Before that, his talents extended to collaborating with the filmmaker Luis Buñuel on two seminal surrealist films: ***Un Chien Andalou*** (1928) and ***L'Âge d'Or*** (1930).

At the center of Dalí's existence and of many of his paintings was his seductive, strong-willed Russian wife, Gala. From 1930 onward they led an unconventional existence between globe-trotting winters and summers at their fisherman's cottage at Port Lligat, near Cadaqués. In 1970 Gala moved to a transformed castle ruin, Castell Pubol, to which Dalí was admitted only by written invitation. Here she entertained young lovers until her death in 1982, while Dalí dallied with the transsexual Amanda Lear. This arrangement is typical of their offbeat yet impassioned relationship.

Figueres

Located only 12.5 miles (20 km) from the Costa Brava, the pleasant small town of Figueres *(visitor information, Plaça del Sol, tel 972 50 31 55, www.figueres.cat, closed Sun. Oct.–June, p.m. Oct.–Feb., map 179 C5)* is the birthplace of surrealist artist Salvador Dalí. Since 1974 the town has also been home to the provocative **Dalí Theater-Museum** *(Plaça Gala-Salvador Dalí 5, tel 972 67 75 00, closed Mon. except June–Sept., $$$, www.salvador-dali.org)*. From its inception in 1961, Dalí was closely involved in the development of the museum, and he created many works especially for it. In the Mae West room he used a red sofa to portray the actress's lips, yellow curtains for her hair, framed paintings for her eyes, and a fireplace for her nose. If you pass through Figueres, don't miss seeing this uniquely kitsch museum. The charming **Museu del Joguet** (Toy Museum; *tel 972 50 45 85, closed Sun. p.m. & Tues.*) displays trains, teddy bears, and doll furniture.

Dalí's last years were taken up with obsessional work on his museum (see sidebar opposite). This converted theater was to be a monument to his life and "paranoiac-critical" stance, blurring the boundaries between fiction and reality. A coin-operated Cadillac sprayed by a fountain, articulated bronze sculptures, the Mae West room, a bed from a brothel, and facades studded with models of eggs and bread-rolls provide the context for hundreds of his works. Dalí's tomb is under the central stage, marked by a simple gravestone–unexpected for someone who once declared "I have always considered myself to be a genius."

Costumed children bring the surreal world of Salvador Dalí to life in the town of Figueres.

Museu del Cinema
Carrer Sèquia 1
972 41 27 77
Closed Sun. p.m. & Mon.
$
www.museudelcinema.cat

this community's role in Spanish Girona's history.

A final glimpse of Girona's illustrious past can be had in **Pujada de Sant Domènec** at the **Palau dels Agullana.** The unusual oblique archway of this 14th- to 17th-century mansion flanks a picturesque stairway, one of the city's most photographed corners.

Cinema buffs should not miss the **Museu del Cinema,** once a private collection covering hundreds of years of moving images.

Mist cloaks the valleys of the Pirineos near Girona.

Pirineos (Catalan Pyrenees)
179 B5–C5

Parque Nacional d'Aigüestortes
973 62 40 36 or 973 69 61 89
Number of visitors limited in summer
www.reddeparquesnacionales.nma.es

Pirineos (Catalan Pyrenees)

The Catalan Pyrenees are more developed than their counterparts in Aragón and Navarra, but you still find fortified medieval villages, remote monasteries and hermitages, and flocks of sheep and cattle grazing in meadows. Looming in the far west is the highest peak, Aneto (11,200 feet/3,408 m); 83 miles (230 km) east after skirting the Andorra, the last bumps descend into the Mediterranean at Portbou, on the French border.

The **Parque Nacional d'Aigüestortes** covers 34,500 acres (14,000 ha) and is a perfect destination for hiking outside winter. The national park, whose name means "winding waters," is a heady mountain mix of glacial lakes, waterfalls, and rushing streams, spiked by towering granite peaks with flanks clad in pine and fir forests.

One of the most popular places is the **Estany de Sant Maurici** (Estany meaning "lake"), which you can reach by car from Espot (on the C147) in the east. Access from the west is from Boí (via Pont de Suert on the N230), and a trail connects the two villages. Paths are well marked, and there are refuge huts for longer treks. Driving from the south, on the N260, you can't miss the spectacular **Estret de Collegats,** a narrow gorge gouged by the torrential Noguera River. A rock face dripping with icy stalactites here is named the **Roca de l'Argentaria.**

At the spa town of **Caldes de Boí,** on the western perimeter of Aigüestortes park, you can recover in hot springs. Reproductions now replace unique frescoes that were painstakingly moved to Barcelona's Museu Nacional d'Art de Catalunya (see pp. 168–169). If you are short of time, go straight to **Taüll** to see the lovely churches of **Santa Maria** and **Sant Climent,** both with Lombard-style bell towers rising above slate roofs, in a setting of verdant meadows backed by craggy peaks. In winter this area becomes the domain of skiers at **Boí-Taüll** resort, which reaches 8,060 feet (2,457 m). The Vall de Boi also boasts the most important group of Romanesque churches in the world, their tall, slender bell towers spiking the valley floor.

The easternmost area of interest in the Pyrenees is the county of **Ripollès,** where towering peaks of 9,850 feet (3,000 m) dominate two valleys, **Camprodon** and **Ribes.** Their access point is **Ripoll,** a sleepy town at the confluence of two rivers that you will want to visit for its Romanesque monastery, **Monestir de Santa Maria,** a landmark in Catalan history (see sidebar this page).

North of Ripoll, the mountain area of **Núria** can be reached only by rack railway (with a cogged rail between the bearing rails), the

Ripoll

179 C5

Visitor Information

Oficina de Turismo, Plaça de l'Abat Oliba s/n

972 70 23 51

www.ajripoll.org

Sant Joan de les Abadesses

179 C5

Visitor Information

Oficina de Turismo, Plaça de l'Abadia 9

972 72 05 99

www.santjoandeles abadesses.com

The Monasteries of Guifré the Hairy

Born in southwest France, Wilfred or Guifré el Pilós (Guifré the Hairy) ruled as Count of Barcelona from 878 to 898. He founded the **Monastir de Santa Maria** *(Plaça de l'Abat Oliba, Ripoll, tel 972 70 02 43)* in 880 and was martyred in 898. The monastery housed the royal pantheon until the focus moved to Barcelona in 1162. Its scriptorium produced illuminated masterpieces such as the Ripoll Bible (1015–1020), now housed in the Vatican, while the monastery's library was said to be one of Europe's top four in the Middle Ages.

The monastery itself lost all of its charm during 19th-century alterations, but the **basilica** and **cloister** remain outstanding. Pick up a leaflet at the ticket office to help identify the monastery's countless fascinating details, and be sure to admire the basilica's structure from the garden at the back, where you can see the seven apses that end the single nave, four aisles, and transept. Santa Maria's masterpiece is the **front portal** (built around 1150), a monumental gateway sculpted with a multitude of scenes, figures, and symbols. Take time to sit in the glassed-in lobby and follow its intricacies.

Guifré the Hairy was responsible for another remarkable monastery, **Sant Joan de les Abadesses,** only 6 miles (10 km) farther up the Ter River. His daughter Emma became its first abbess. A 15th-century earthquake caused the steeple to collapse, but the pure Romanesque interior remains a serene backdrop to rarities such as the **Santissim Misteri,** a 13th-century group of sculptures depicting Christ's removal from the cross.

Estació de Muntanya
Queralbs
972 73 20 30
www.valldenuria.cat

Volcanoes of Olot (Garrotxa)
Visitor Information
Casal dels Volcans, Avinguda Santa Coloma, Olot
972 26 62 02
www.turisme garrotxa.com

Olot
179 C5
Visitor Information
Oficina Municipal de Turismo, Calle Hospici 8
972 26 01 41
www.olot.org

Besalú
179 C5
Visitor Information
Oficina Municipal de Turismo, Calle de la Llibertat 1
972 59 12 40
www.besalu.cat

Cremallera. This lifts you 7.5 miles (12 km) from Ribes de Freser to Núria's ski station, **Estació de Muntanya,** 3,280 feet (1,000 m) higher up.

Volcanoes of Olot (Garrotxa)

Spain's greatest volcanic landscape is somewhat illusory. Ever since the last eruption more than 10,000 years ago, these 46 square miles (120 sq km) of valleys, plains, rivers, and volcanoes have been transformed into well-irrigated cropland and grazing pastures. The craters are mostly visible from the volcano summits, and the walls of river valleys reveal spectacular basalt strata created by lava flows.

In 1985 the **Garrotxa** became a protected natural park, and visitor facilities make it a popular weekend hiking destination *(routes: www.senderisme.turismedecatalunya.com).* Start in the town of **Olot,** within easy striking distance of the scenic beech woods of Jordà and the neighboring volcanoes of Croscat and Santa Margarita. The latter, reached by an almost vertical path, has a hermitage that sits picturesquely in its crater. Croscat (17,000 years old) has a less strenuous trail past fissured rock and lava blocks. Garrotxa's diverse woodland provides habitats for beech marten, wildcats, genets, badgers, wild boar, otters, and 143 bird species.

Three of the villages are exceptional. **Castellfollit de la Roca** perches dramatically on 197-foot (60 m) walls of basalt prisms, with the Fluvia River at its feet. It is best seen from the N260. Head east to explore **Besalú,** a stunning medieval village where a Romanesque bridge and four churches stand beside a Jewish quarter with baths and a restored synagogue. In **Santa Pau,** walk through cobbled medieval streets to the sloping main square bordered by Gothic arches (each one a different shape) where a cattle market was once held. Looming above is an 11th-century baron's castle that was later used as a Dominican monastery before being abandoned.

Vic

At first sight Vic is a dark, uninviting industrial town, not helped by a microclimate of high rainfall and fog, and surrounding pig farms. Other

La Patum de Berga

In the Pyrenean foothills, 38 miles (60 km) northeast of Vic, the small town of Berga makes a very big noise during the festival of Corpus Cristi, celebrated in May–June (the date varies) from Wednesday to Sunday. Dating from the 15th century, the flamboyant Patum de Berga fused popular culture with religious beliefs. The result is an extraordinary series of dances and jumps by costumed devils, giants, angels, Moors, and dragons, accompanied by a mesmerizing drumbeat *(tabal)* or band. Bonfires and incredible fireworks light up the sky, flaming torches flicker, and smoke fills the air as the locals act out this primitive street theater.

Catalan towns may appear livelier, but don't be put off—the old town center has been renovated and now displays numerous architectural jewels.

Vic has a long mercantile tradition (and tanning and sausagemaking industries), and the twice-weekly market *(Tues. & Sat.)* has been held on **Plaça Major** for centuries. This porticoed square lined with cafés exemplifies the historical continuity of the town: Gothic houses stand next to baroque and 1900s extravaganzas. The prize for true Modernista excess must go to the **Casa Comella,** a neo-Gothic folly on the southwest corner.

Walk along the narrow streets that run southeast of the square and you come to the oldest building in town, a restored second-century **Roman temple** that stands beside the ruins of the **Palau dels Montcada.**

Downhill from here stands the hulk of Vic's **cathedral**—a mixture of styles from Romanesque to neoclassic. Inside are the theatrical murals in dark gold and red by Josep Maria Sert (1876–1945), painted twice over owing to a devastating Civil War fire, and completed shortly before his death. Every surface of the vast nave writhes with Sert's powerful figures illustrating both biblical subjects and the history of Catalunya. His modest tomb stands in the lovely Gothic **cloister** beside the ostentatious tomb of Vic's homegrown philosopher, Jaume Balmes (1810–1848).

Other unusual features are the beautiful 10th- to 11th-century capitals of the **crypt** and the main **altarpiece,** which now stands at the back of the apse—feed the light-meter a coin to illuminate Pere Oller's 1427 alabaster masterpiece, carved with scenes of the life of Christ and Mary.

The **Museu Episcopal de Vic** has one of the most important and complete collections of medieval Catalan art in Spain beside works from the 16th to 18th centuries. Since 2002 it has been housed in a luminous new building designed by Federico Correa and Alfonso Milá. Another striking modern building is **Atlàntida** *(tel 937 02 72 57, www.latlantidavic.cat),* an asymmetrical theater and music school by Josep Llinas.

Three Monasteries

Of the many monasteries in eastern Catalunya, three are outstanding. Montserrat is the most popular, Poblet the most beautiful, and Santes Creus the most instructive.

A craftsman in Olot skillfully sculpts figures for use in nativity scenes and other Christian tableaux.

Vic

179 C5

Visitor Information

Oficina de Turismo, Carrer de la Ciutat 4

938 86 20 91

www.ajvic.net

Cathedral

Plaça de la Catedral, Vic

938 86 44 49

$

Museu Episcopal de Vic

Plaça del Bisbe Oliba 31, Vic

938 86 93 60

Closed Mon. & Sun. p.m.

$

www.museuepiscopalvic.com

Monestir de Montserrat: Whatever way you choose to reach Montserrat (meaning "serrated mountain"), whether by road, cable car, or rack railway from Monistrol (see sidebar opposite), the journey is unforgettable. For a thousand years pilgrims have been drawn to the spectacular pinnacles crowning the rugged sierra that is home to Catalunya's holiest site: the Benedictine monastery, chapels, and caves of Montserrat. About 80 monks live here, but don't expect a sense of deep spirituality. The entire complex is heavily commercialized and very crowded on Sundays and public holidays. That said, facilities are excellent, with funiculars to the hermitage of Sant Joan and grotto of Santa Cova, a museum, restaurants, hotel, shops, and well-marked paths through the sierra.

For many, the main priority is to see the carved wooden statue of the Virgin of Montserrat, popularly known as **La Moreneta** (the dark one), due to her black face. Legend has it that the statue was carved by St. Luke and then miraculously found in 880 in Santa Cova, but scientific testing has proved that it is 12th century. La Moreneta's status was enhanced in 1881 when she became patron saint of

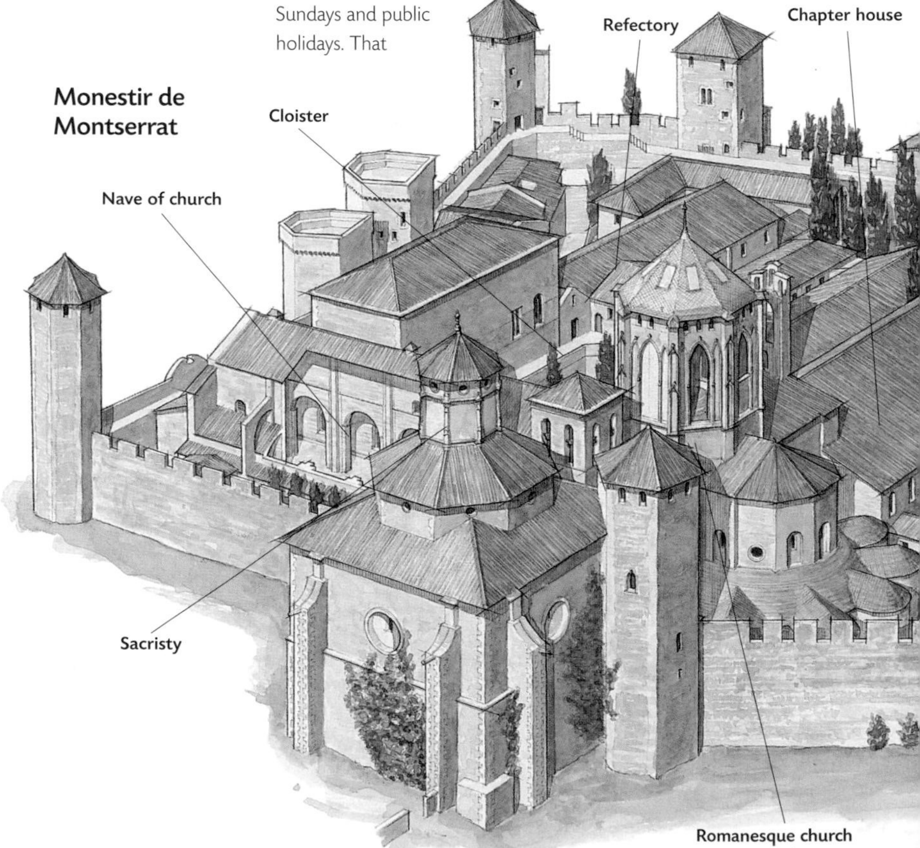

Catalunya. See her up close by following a passage *(tel 938 77 77 66, closed 10:30 a.m.–noon)* to the right of the main doors to her jewel-studded eyrie behind the altar.

The basilica was much transformed in the early 19th century following destruction by French troops, and the facade dates from 1901. Try to coincide your visit with **L'Escolania** *(Mon.–Fri. 1 p.m. & Sun. 12 p.m. & 6:45 p.m.)*, Europe's oldest boys' choir.

Beneath the esplanade in front of the basilica, the museum displays pieces ranging from a 4,000-year-old Egyptian mummy to classical and Impressionist paintings, and a touching collection of votive offerings to La Moreneta.

Getting to Montserrat

It is easy to visit Montserrat on a day trip from Barcelona. At Espanya station, take a Manresa train, Line R5, to the base of the mountain. This train leaves roughly hourly, and the trip takes just over an hour. On arrival you have two options: the cable car, Aeri *($)*, or the slower funicular, Cremallera *($)*, which you board at Monistrol. The cable car to the monastery takes five minutes, while the funicular (in which you can sit) takes 15 minutes. Views are better from the Aeri, but the funicular is a more comfortable ride.

Monestir de Montserrat

- 179 C4
- Montserrat
- 938 77 77 01
- $$$ (museum); $ (parking)

www.abadiamontserrat.net
www.montserratvisita.com

Santa María de Poblet
179 B4
Poblet
977 87 02 54
$$
www.poblet.cat

Santes Creus
179 B4
Santes Creus
977 63 83 92
Closed Mon.
$. Free Tues.
www.altcamp.info/eng/santescreus.htm

For magnificent views of the Pyrenees, make the gentle climb to the **shrine of Sant Miquel** or follow the longer **Way of the Rosary,** lined with Modernista sculptures, to **Santa Cova.** Wilder in spirit but kinder to the leg muscles is the **Cami des Degotalls** that skirts around the mountain.

Santa María de Poblet: Named for the surrounding poplar trees, this tranquil, harmonious monastery (1151), the largest inhabited Cistercian monastery in Europe, lies near medieval **Montblanc** *(www.montblancmedieval.cat),* which is also worth seeing. Poblet gives a wonderful sense of Cistercian purity (see p. 44) within its walled precinct. Monks returned in 1940 after a century-long absence, and parts of the monastery are out of bounds, but you can peer through the library doors, for instance, to see these theologians working at computers. The beautiful, contemplative Gothic **cloister** encloses a pretty washing pavilion connected to the kitchen, a vaulted **refectory** where monks eat and drink in silence, and the **chapter house** with its palm tree vaults and tombstones of past abbots.

The cloister also leads to the Romanesque **church,** where attention focuses on the exceptional alabaster altarpiece carved by Damián Forment in 1527 and the elaborate royal tombs, dating from the 14th century but extensively restored in 1950. The stairs to the left of the altar lead up to the monks' vast dormitory—no longer in use—and out to the upper gallery of the cloister. The tour ends in the **wine cellars** below, a reminder of the Cistercians' involvement in viticulture and agriculture, which in medieval days gave a huge boost to the local economy.

Poblet was founded on land conquered from the Moors.

Santes Creus: Founded shortly after Poblet by French Cistercians from Toulouse, Santes Creus has a similar layout to its sister monastery but is no longer in use. The austere **church,** on the other hand, never stopped functioning, and here you see a lovely rose window and royal tombs beneath elaborate Gothic canopies.

There are two cloisters. The so-called **old cloister** was built in the 17th century on the site of the original one, and leads to the kitchen, refectory, wine cellars, and royal palace. The 14th-century **Gran Claustro** (Great Cloister) is lined with beautifully carved capitals and leads to the chapter house. Above this, the lofty dormitory is now used for summer concerts.

EXPERIENCE: Ebro Birdlife

The low-lying Ebro Delta offers birders the potential of sighting up to 300 species—six percent of the total bird species found in Europe. Kingfishers, seven species of gull (including Audouin's), ospreys, egrets, purple gallinules, godwits, ibis, and pink flamingos all thrive in this complex range of habitats that includes rice fields, lagoons, marshes, salt pans, sand dunes, and reed beds. The north and south sides of the Ebro River differ greatly in landscapes and birds, the south being more scenic and interesting.

If you want to stay in the middle of it all, **Poblenou del Delta** is a delightful village sprawled beside the southernmost, flamingo-rich lagoon with a modern, family-run hotel *(www.hotelalgadirdelta.com)*. For tours visit *www.birdinginspain.com*, run by Steve West, a British bird specialist based in Catalunya.

An innovative **audiovisual circuit** guides you through the monastery, reconstructing its atmosphere and life. If you want the English version, make sure you arrive promptly at either 10 a.m. or 3 p.m.

Costa Daurada & Ebro Delta

Costa Daurada is not one of Spain's most appealing coastlines, but it has long golden *(daurada)* beaches and unusual spots. Cosmopolitan Sitges, an offshoot of Barcelona, is known as the gay beach resort of Spain, Port Aventura is a must for anyone with children, and the Ebro Delta is the second largest in the Mediterranean.

Sitges: Sitges lies just half an hour's drive southwest of Barcelona airport, and crowds from all over Europe throng its bars, nudist beaches, and palm-lined promenade. Its reputation flowered in the 1960s when it nurtured an arty counterculture and antagonized Franco. An outrageous February carnival continues the traditions of the heady past.

Sitges lies beside a beautiful stretch of high, rocky coastline. There enlightening windows on Sitges's history are at the **Museu del Cau Ferrat,** once the home of the eccentric painter Santiago Rusinyol (1861–1931), who created a haven for artist friends, and the neighboring **Museu Maricel,** an old hospital that was lavishly refurbished for the American millionaire Charles Deering.

Port Aventura: Barely 5 miles (8 km) south of Tarragona lies **Port Aventura,** Spain's largest theme park. Packed with high-adrenaline rides and entertainment, it is ideal for anyone with children in tow.

Ebro Delta: The string of family resorts fades away in the south at the large and peaceful peninsula formed by the Ebro Delta. These 124 square miles (320 sq km) of wetlands, partly protected as a reserve, come third only to France's Camargue and Andalucía's Parque Nacional

Sitges
179 C4
Visitor Information
Oficina Municipal de Turismo, Calle Sinia Morera 1
938 94 50 04
www.sitgestur.com

Museu del Cau Ferrat & Museu Maricel
Carrer Fonollar s/n
938 94 03 64
Closed Sun. p.m. & Mon.
$

Port Aventura
179 B4
Avinguda Pere Molas, Vila-Seca
902 20 22 20
www.portaventura.es

Deltebre
179 B3
Visitor Information
Oficina de Turismo, Calle Martín Buera 22
977 48 96 79
www.deltebre.cat

Eco-Museu (Ecological Museum)
Carrer Marti Buera 22, Deltebre
977 48 96 79

Tarragona
179 B4
Visitor Information
Oficina de Turismo, Calle Major 39
977 25 07 95
www.tarragona turisme.es

Passeig Arqueològic
Tarragona
977 24 57 96
Closed Mon.

Pretori & Circ Romans
Plaça del Rei, Rambla Vella, Tarragona
977 24 19 52
Closed Sun. p.m. & Mon.
$ (combined ticket for Pretori & Circ Romans)

NOTE: The Tarragona Card gives free admission to all sights.

de Doñana (see sidebar p. 271) for Mediterranean aquatic wildlife. Diverse ecosystems include rice fields, lagoons, and salt pans, all favored by flamingoes, Audoin's gulls, and more than 350 other migratory bird species from April to late August and October to February. You can bird-watch, fish, ride, kayak, sail, cycle, or scuba dive in the delta. The starting point is the village of **Deltebre,** site of the **Eco-Museu,** or **Ecological Museum.**

Tarragona

Pronounced "the most pleasant spot for resting" by the Roman poet Virgil (70–19 B.C.), Tarragona now has more than 150,000 inhabitants, whose livelihoods oscillate between the petrochemical industry and tourism. Spain's deepest port and Catalunya's most productive fishing harbor first attracted the Romans in the third century B.C. Three centuries later this city, known to the Romans as Tarraco, was the capital of the vast Imperial Hispania Tarraconensis. It was granted world heritage status by UNESCO in 2000.

Contemporary Tarragona spreads west of the hilltop cathedral and Roman remains into a grid of 19th- and 20th-century streets. It is very much a provincial town, lacking the designer buzz of Barcelona or Girona, but compensated for by its fabulous archaeological finds, wonderfully mild climate, sandy beaches, and bountiful seafood. Go to the newly gentrified port area of **El Serrallo** for upscale fish restaurants.

Once you climb to the **walls** (third- to second-century B.C.) and follow the **Passeig Arqueològic** around their perimeter, you begin to understand the importance of the largest and oldest Roman settlement in Iberia. These fully restored, 40-foot-high (12 m) sandstone blocks once enclosed three terraced levels: a massive temple, the forum (marketplace), and vast **Circ Romans** (circus or chariot stadium), which could accommodate 30,000 of Tarraco's 40,000 inhabitants. A Romanesque cathedral replaced the temple, but much of the lower walls and structures were incorporated into houses and public buildings.

For the best view head for the **Pretori** (Praetorium), a stone tower and former palace of the counts of Barcelona that rises beside the circus at the base of the Rambla Vella. An elevator speeds you to the rooftop. Roman remains lie at your feet, literally—beneath the tower, two of many vaulted tunnels have been excavated to reveal the sophistication of Roman engineering. Don't miss the model of Tarraco displayed

INSIDER TIP:

Tarragona's packed festival calendar peaks at Carnival, which starts up in February, and Santa Tecla, in mid-September.

—FIONA DUNLOP
National Geographic author

here, and stop at the first floor to admire a superbly sculpted sarcophagus showing the legend of Hippolytus. From the rooftop you also have a good aerial view of the much restored **amphitheater,** where gladiator fights were held.

Continue to the neighboring **Museo Arqueològic** to see exceptional Roman artifacts. There is a fine mosaic **head of Medusa** in Room 3 and, on the top floor, arches enclose rounded Romanesque ones with Moorish-inspired tracery above. The 1430 masterful altarpiece of alabaster and wood by Pere Joan illustrates in detail the life of Tarragona's patron saint, Santa Tecla. Look out for minutely carved animals and insects, and extremely realistic human expressions. The 330-foot-long (100 m) nave has wonderful proportions, enhanced by Flemish tapestries.

Amphitheater

✉ Parc del Miracle, Tarragona
☎ 977 24 25 79
🕒 Closed Mon.

Museo Arqueològic

✉ Plaça del Rei 5, Tarragona
☎ 977 23 62 09
🕒 Closed Mon.

Tarragona's Plaça del Forum once served as the town's ancient Roman marketplace.

a copy of an articulated ivory doll whose original is exhibited at the **Necropolis** west of town. Tarragona's magnificent **aqueduct** can be seen off the N240 motorway, 3 miles (5 km) north of town.

Back at the summit, the **cathedral** beckons, its curious facade combining Romanesque and Gothic portals beneath a huge rose window and two unfinished steeples. Enter through the **cloister,** where pointed Gothic

When you leave the cathedral, walk around the back to see the beautifully sculpted 12th- to 14th-century arches of the former **hospital of Santa Tecla,** and then go down the wide steps in front of the cathedral. At the bottom of the steps you will find **Carrer La Merceria.** Here Gothic market arcades that replaced the Roman forum colonnade are still used on Sunday mornings for a bustling antique market. ■

Cathedral

✉ Plaça de la Seu, Tarragona
☎ 977 23 86 85
🕒 Closed Sun.

Drive: Priorat Vineyards & Templars

This inland circuit takes you through rugged sierra ("serra" in Catalan) to a little-visited wine-producing region and to the impressive castle of Miravet. This was a stronghold of the Knights Templar, a religious military order of knighthood that was originally formed during the Crusades. The drive ends at Tortosa on the Ebro Delta.

Leave Tarragona on the A2/T11 heading toward the airport and Reus, through a flat, semi-industrial area. Stay on this road, skirting around Reus, and continue on the N420 to Falset. You soon see the distant outline of the Serra de la Mussara with vineyards in the foreground. After climbing 1,800 feet (548 m), the road winds down through pine-clad limestone hills to **Falset** ❶ *(visitor information, Avinguda Catalunya 6, tel 977 83 10 23)*. Crowned by a castle, the baroque church of Santa Maria, and arcaded Plaça Quartera, this pretty medieval town is a major wine-producing center. You can visit the impressive **wine-cooperative building** *(tel 977 83 03 63, closed Jan.–Feb.)* designed by Cesar Martinell, a disciple of Antoni Gaudí (see pp. 172–175). Park your car below the **old town** and walk up from there.

Leave Falset to tour the heart of the Priorat wine-producing area by following the continuation of the access road, now the T710, to Gratallops. Enjoy this good road while it lasts for the next 6 miles (10 km), and when **Gratallops** ❷ appears on its striking hilltop site, circle around the village to turn right at the sign for Centre Urba. You enter Calle Piro, in the shadow of the church, where there are three wine cooperatives, at any of which you can taste and buy different varieties of wine and olive oil. Try the **Celler Cecilio** *(Carrer Piró 28, tel 977 83 91 81, www.cellercecilio.com)*, which still uses time-honored methods. Continue your route on

---

NOT TO BE MISSED:

Falset old town • Gratallops wineries • La Cartoixa, Escaladei • Castell de Miravet • Tortosa cathedral

---

the T710, and then, after 1 mile (1.6 km), turn right onto the much narrower T711, toward Torroja del Priorat.

As the road twists through wild, semiarid landscapes where pine and olive trees grow, with glimpses of the lovely pink-ocher Serra de Montsant in the distance, you feel far from civilization. Three miles (5 km) of bends farther you reach the picture-postcard vision of **Torroja del Priorat** ❸, perched high on an isolated hilltop. Cross the bridge to drive up behind the tiny village for a view over its tiled roofs and cobbled streets. It is inhabited by only 140 people. Return to the T711 and turn right toward **Escaladei** ❹, 4 miles (7 km) ahead.

This beautiful village, also written **Scala Dei,** is the historic and spiritual focal point of the Priorat area because monks from the 12th-century Carthusian monastery here introduced the techniques of vine cultivation and wine-aging. Follow the sign beside the bridge (La Cartoixa) to drive half a mile (0.8 km) beyond the village to the picturesquely ruined and very extensive monastery of **La Cartoixa** *(tel 977 82 70 06, closed Mon.).* Escaladei itself

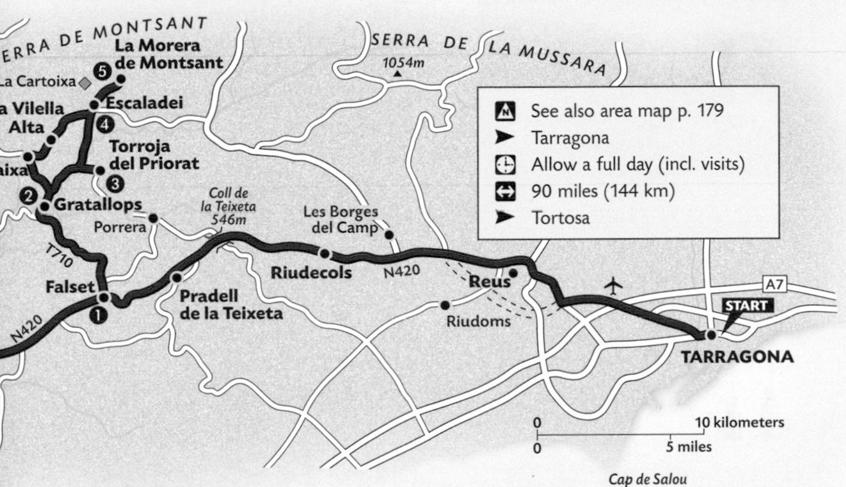

EXPERIENCE: Priorat Wine-Tasting

The tradition of wine-making in Priorat began with medieval French monks in the delightful hamlet of Escaladei. Today Priorat's terraced vineyards grow local grapes as well as imported varieties.

The region's wineries are concentrated in Falset and Gratallops, notably Costers del Siurana *(Manyetes s/n, Gratallops, tel 977 83 92 76, www.costersdelsiurana.com),* **where Carles Pastrana has created the highly rated Clos de l'Obac label and pioneering René Barbier set up Clos Mogador in the 1970s. In the village of Poboleda, by the Siurana River, taste the dry red wine at Mas Doix** *(Calle Carme 115, Poboleda, tel 639 35 61 72, e-mail: info@masdoix.com).*

Investigate the region's other famous wineries—and some avant-garde ones, too—with Cellar Tours *(tel 911 43 65 53, www.cellartours.com, $$$$$),* **which offers customized itineraries, including hotel and transportation, based on your interests. Or go it alone. For information on wineries and routes, see** *www.turismepriorat.org/en/what-to-do/wine-route.*

is an idyllic stone village with a restaurant and well-organized **winery** *(Cellers Scala Dei, Rambla de la Cartoixa s/n, tel 977 82 70 27)*. Don't miss the exquisite Siurana olive oil.

Further stunning landscapes unfold by following the sign to La Morera de Montsant

Finca el Tancat winery near Tarragona

along a 3-mile (5 km) road. This route takes you up through the hills to the spectacularly sited village of **La Morera de Montsant** ❺ *(visitor information, Carrer Major 4, tel 977 82 73 10)*, which nestles beneath the 3,660-foot (1,115 m) Seyalets peak, part of the "blessed mountain" (Montsant). The village is a popular starting point for climbing, hiking, and horseback riding in the Serra de Montsant. Return by the same road to Escaladei, where you turn right on the T702 to drive beside the scenic sierra to La Vilella Baixa. Rejoin the T710 back to Falset, 9 miles (15 km) away.

Drive through Falset, following signs for Móra d'Ebre on the N420, to follow a less dramatic but still pretty 20-mile (32 km) road through the agricultural plain. Pass by the unappealing town of Móra la Nova, cross over the Ebro River, and then, at a traffic circle, turn left to Miravet on the T324. On entering the village of **Miravet** (see sidebar this page), follow the signs to Castell that lead you uphill to the forbidding ruins of **Castell de Miravet** ❻ *(tel 977 40 73 68, closed Mon.)*. This was the castle of the Knights Templar, an order of medieval soldier-monks (see p. 30). There are panoramic views from the castle over the river valley. From here you can either hike down a cliff path to the **Casc Antic** (old quarter), or drive back down, following signs to Casc Antic. Park on the shady, riverside square, visit the pottery workshops, and walk through the old town before continuing by car along the river to **Pas de Barca.** Here a simple **ferry** *(closed 1–3 p.m. & in bad weather)*, powered only by the swift-flowing current, takes up to three cars at a time across the Ebro. On the opposite bank you join the C12, a good road that for 20 miles (32 km) slices through forested sierra, follows the peaceful meanders of the river, and finally passes through extensive groves of orange trees to reach Tortosa.

In **Tortosa** ❼, do not miss a visit to the three soaring Gothic naves of the **cathedral** *(tel 977 44 96 48)*. After this go for a well-deserved drink at the hilltop castle of **La Zuda,** now an impressive *parador* (state-run hotel). This magnificent building echoes with the ghosts of three former kings: Abd-ar-Rahman III, who ordered the construction of the *zuda* (well); Count Ramon Berenguer IV, who reclaimed Tortosa from the Moors in 1148; and Jaime I of Aragón, who used it as his royal residence.

Miravet Potteries

In the early 19th century, the traditional potters of Miravet were moved out of the village center to their own quarter, the Raval dels Canterers. Eight workshops still exist where you can see potters making pieces by hand using the wheel. The traditional shapes and glazes of these water pitchers, vats, and oil jars were introduced from the Islamic world. Decoration is sparse as these simple pieces were destined for the agricultural world. Memories of colorful El Cid, who captured the castle from the Moors in 1090, seem to have long faded.

Valencia

Valencia has an indented coastline backed by hills and the inland *huerta,* said to be Europe's most fertile land. Contrary to what you might expect, this region is not always scenic, but you do see terraced orchards and rice fields stretching to the horizon. Particularly striking is the immense palm grove of Elx (Elche), an oasis in the increasingly arid terrain that borders Murcia to the south and source of the symbolic palm fronds used in Holy Week processions.

For beach lovers the Costa Blanca has highlights at Dénia, Xàbia (Jávea), and Calp (Calpe). Best of all is the seaside capital of Valencia itself, where Renaissance and baroque buildings stand as testimony to the region's long history. Over the last 15 years the city has reinvented itself through dazzling architecture and a sophisticated new seaside quarter.

The kingdom of Valencia's first golden age started in 1238 and nurtured the independent streak that remains at its heart. Depression followed in the 17th century when Madrid forced Valencia to expel its Moriscos—baptized Moors—who made up almost one-third of the population. This economic disaster was compounded by the War of Spanish Succession (see pp. 33–34), when Valencia picked the losing side.

The Valencian language may vary only slightly from Catalan, but a quite different, easygoing character comes to the fore in the province's imaginative fiestas. It is here that a whole day is spent pelting friend and foe with tons of ripe tomatoes. This takes place at Buñol, 25 miles (40 km) southwest of the capital on the last Wednesday of August. Nor does the capital rest in the wings, for this is

Valencia City's Ciudad de las Artes y las Ciencias includes a museum, IMAX theater, and aquarium.

Las Fallas: Valencia Burns

Valencia's biggest and noisiest festivities come every March, beginning officially on the 15th and reaching their fiery culmination at midnight on the 19th. In reality, celebrations kick off weeks before, with the entire city throwing itself into the riotous annual fiesta, originally in honor of Saint Joseph, patron saint of carpenters. At the heart of Las Fallas are giant satirical figures *(ninots)*, expertly made in papier-mâché but destined to be burned on the last night. Earth-shattering gunpowder explosions *(mascleta)* start at 2 p.m. every day outside City Hall, and parades, street performances, dances, sports events, and spectacular fireworks last all week.

Valencia City
179 A2

Visitor Information

- Oficina de Turismo, Plaza del Ayuntamiento s/n
- 963 52 49 08
- Closed Sun. p.m.

www.turisvalencia.es

the home of Las Fallas (see sidebar this page), an ear-shattering fiesta of image-burning and fireworks.

Valencia City

Spain's third largest city is not enticing at first sight, but with a sunny climate, excellent restaurants, a hopping nightlife, and the makeover crowned by hosting the America's Cup in 2007 and 2010, it is a city on the move. Wide avenues lined with upscale shops and palm trees lead to the new marina area and landscaped beach promenades. After the sun has set, the superb monuments are spotlit, lending the city an evocative atmosphere as nightclubs and tapas bars move into high gear. One-way streets make driving difficult, so if you are in a car, head for a parking lot then use your feet.

Valencia's history dates back to the Greeks, Carthaginians, Romans, Visigoths, and, in A.D. 714, the Arabs. Legendary El Cid conquered the city in 1094, but it was retaken by the Moors (the Almoravids), whose rule lasted until King Jaime I of Aragón's conquest in 1238. This marked the start of a golden age when Valencia became one of the strongest Mediterranean powers, prospering from trading links with possessions in Italy. Hard times followed, culminating in the Civil War (1936–1939), when Republican forces retreated to Valencia after Franco took Catalunya. After intense bombardment, Valencia gave in to the Nationalists on March 30, 1939.

Today, Valencia's economy is based on agriculture, industry (with Ford and IBM factories), and the service industry. The city demonstrates a strong sense of art and design symbolized by the internationally acclaimed Ciudad de las Artes y las Ciencias. Precursors are the **IVAM** (Instituto Valenciano de Arte Moderno), a contemporary art center (see sidebar p. 203), and the glass-fronted **Palau de la Música y Congresos,** a congress center designed in 1977 by British architect Norman Foster.

Despite this dynamism, Valencians retain strong traditions. Numerous shops sell ornate mantillas, hand-painted fans, hand-embroidered silk shawls, and ceramics from outlying Paterna. Paella is on every menu, for this is where it originated.

The historic sights lie close to each other, within the area once enclosed by the city walls. Demolished a century ago, only two impressive gateways remain. North of this area are the **Jardines**

del Turia, landscaped gardens in the old riverbed that offer a welcome splash of greenery. In the old center, the Gothic **cathedral** *(Plaza de la Reina, tel 96 391 81 27)* is flanked by **El Miguelete,** an octagonal bell tower. Climb to the top of this for sweeping views over Valencia's glazed ceramic domes and labyrinthine streets.

The main sight inside the cathedral is the **Capilla del Santo Cáliz** (Chapel of the Holy Grail), a Flamboyant Gothic chapel with a superb alabaster altarpiece carved with biblical scenes by the Florentine sculptor Giuliano Poggibonsi. This enshrines the cathedral's marvel, a first-century **agate goblet** said to be the one used by Christ at the Last Supper. Before reaching the cathedral in 1437, it transited via Rome, the monastery of San Juan de la Peña (see p. 147), and Zaragoza (see pp. 140–141). The chapel leads to the museum.

In front of the cathedral overlooking the Plaza de la Reina, you can't miss the **baroque bell tower** of **Santa Catalina.** Northeast one

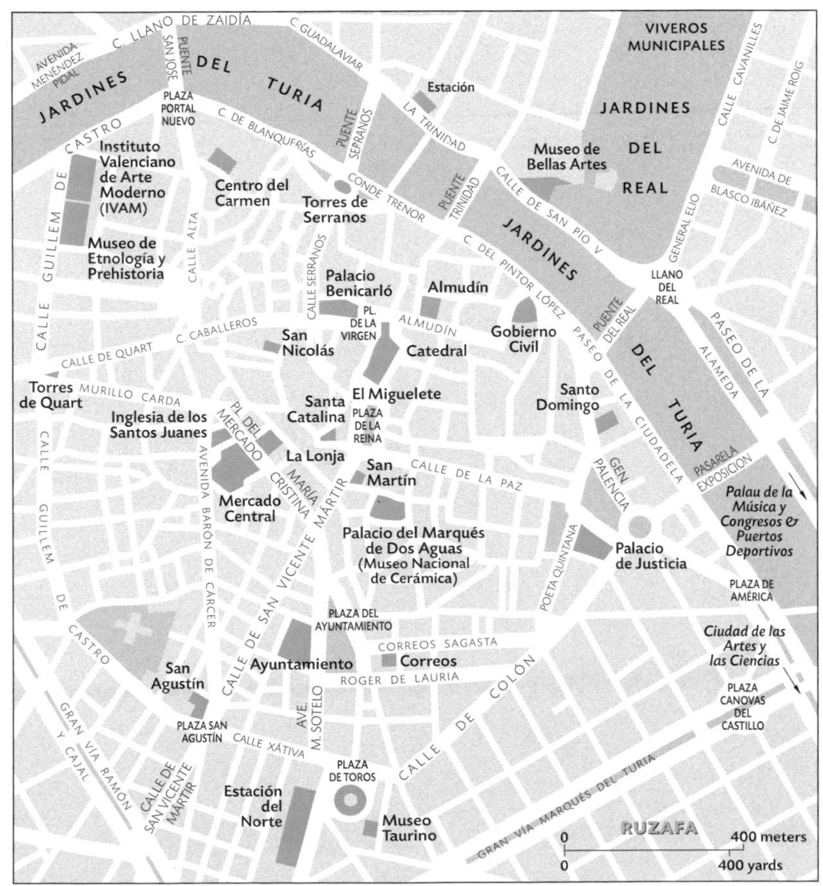

Head to Valencia City's old town for a taste of doughnuts dipped in milky, sweet *horchata*.

Palacio del Marqués de Dos Aguas

Poeta Querol 2, Valencia

963 51 63 92

Closed Sun. p.m. & Mon.

www.mnnceramica.mcu.es

block lies the beautiful 13th- to 14th-century **Almudín** *(Plaza San Luis Bertran 1, tel 963 52 54 78, closed Sun. p.m. & Mon.)*, the city's former granary, now used for art exhibitions. Note the sober stone interior enhanced by whimsical 17th-century wall paintings. Outside, a large archaeological site shows Roman and Moorish ruins. A few steps north of the cathedral is the **Palacio Benicarló** *(Calle Santa Ana)*, a striking Gothic structure of two arcaded stories—once the residence of the Dukes of Gandia—now the seat of the Valencian parliament.

For Valencia's greatest vision of excess, visit the **Palacio del Marqués de Dos Aguas,** a wedding cake of a building with what is arguably Spain's most ornate domestic facade. The building dates from the 15th century but was heavily restructured in 1740. Don't miss the **cupola painting** by Hipolito Rovira (1693–1765), the **Chinoiserie Room,** the inlaid ivory and ebony furniture of the **Smoking Room,** or the **marquis's bedroom** with carved marble bath. On the top floor, the **Museo Nacional de Cerámica** gives an excellent overview of the development of Spanish ceramics, from early Arab pieces through the 18th century. The collection ends with six superb Picasso works and contemporary pieces.

INSIDER TIP:

Half an hour south of Valencia lies the Parque Natural de la Albufera. Whether you spend the day hiking or sailing the lagoon, or both, make sure to stick around for a peaceful and spectacular sunset.

—MARY STEPHANOS
National Geographic contributor

Valencia's palatial railway station, the **Estación del Norte** *(Calle Xàtiva)*, is an artistic treasure of a different sort—a fine example of the use of illustrative *azulejos* (tiles) and decorative woodwork in a purely functional building. It dates from 1910–1917, the creative period that also produced the central market. Valencia's **Mercado**

Central (central market) occupies a vast Modernista (see pp. 47–48) building and is worth a morning visit to see the incredible wealth of produce from the *huerta.*

The **Iglesia de los Santos Juanes** is next to the market. Opposite stands **La Lonja,** the Silk Exchange building *(Plaza del Mercado, tel 963 52 54 78, closed Sun. p.m. & Mon.),* commissioned in the 15th century by the city's wealthy silk merchants. It is an exceptional Flamboyant Gothic building, from the imposing crenellated exterior to the vast interior hall of pillars, their twisted spirals rising to tracery high up in the vaults. Take the stairs from the orange-tree patio to the upper floor to admire a masterfully carved and gilded ceiling that has been resurrected from the old town hall.

In 1989 Valencia's cultural riches were enhanced with the **Instituto Valenciano de Arte Moderno** or IVAM. The modern galleries complex stands in the northwest corner of the old town.

You can find the city's main art collection at the **Museo de Bellas Artes** *(Calle San Pío V, tel 963 87 03 00, closed Mon., www.museobellasartesvalencia.gva.es),* on the far side of the old riverbed. This large and important collection has paintings that range from Valencian primitives, through the Renaissance, and up to the early 20th century. Watch for the Valencian painters Juan de Juanes (died 1579) and Francisco Ribalta (1565–1628), and also for Hieronymus Bosch, Ribera, van Dyck, Murillo, Goya, and a wonderful self-portrait painted by Velázquez.

Due west of here is the city's latest innovation, **Bioparc** *(tel 902 25 03 40, www.bioparcvalencia.es),* a region in which African savannah comes to the riverbed, complete with animals.

The area around Valencia's port was revamped for the America's Cup in 2007, bringing modern hotels and the **Veles e Vents,** a spectators' building by David Chipperfield and Fermín Vázquez. **Playa Malvarrosa,** the popular beach north of the marina, is home to some of the city's best paella restaurants, joined by tapas bars in the atmospheric old fishermen's quarter, **El Cabañal,** now under threat of redevelopment.

Ciudad de las Artes y las Ciencias

Follow the old riverbed southeast through Valencia and you soon see the futuristic forms of the Ciudad de las Artes y las Ciencias (City of Arts and Sciences). Completed in 2003, the four components of this ambitious cultural complex are the Hemisféric, showing IMAX films; the Science Museum; the Palace of the Arts, where concerts and opera are staged; and finally the Oceanogràfic—Europe's largest seaquarium, a universe of lakes and islands complete with an "underwater" restaurant. The entire complex has become a magnet for Valencianos who stroll beside mosaic-clad pools of water or beneath the palm trees of the Umbracle, a raised walkway. The latest iconic structure, the Agora, is a soaring multipurpose hall used for fashion week, concerts, and sports events. Besides attracting world attention, the project has successfully regenerated an entire district.

Instituto Valenciano de Arte Moderno (IVAM)

- Calle de Guillem de Castro 118, Valencia
- 963 86 30 00
- Closed Mon.

www.ivam.es

Ciudad de las Artes y Ciencias

- Avenida Autopista de El Saler, Valencia
- 902 10 00 31
- $$

www.cac.es

Costa Blanca
179 B1
www.costablanca.org

WARNING: Avoid driving along the coast road N332, as its many bends get choked with traffic. Stick to the Autovia and drive into specific coastal spots from there.

Valencia offers great shopping in and around the renovated **Mercado de Colón** *(Jorge Juan 19)*, an iconic Modernista building that now houses select boutiques and cafés. In the traditional center, the **Barrio del Carmen,** northwest of the Plaza de la Reina, fascinating artisan workshops alternate with funky, alternative fashion and bars. Keep an eye, too, on the arty emerging district to the south, the **Barrio Ruzafa.**

Costa Blanca

Halfway between Valencia and Alacant on the map, the Costa Blanca still has immense natural drama. Moody mountains loom just a few miles inland, and the exceptionally mild climate nurtures lush vegetation. Many of the beaches are now full of high-rise hotels. Worst of all is Benidorm, give it a wide berth.

The city of **Calp (Calpe)** *(visitor information, Plaça del Mosquit, tel 965 83 85 32, closed Sun. p.m. in winter)* has high-rises, but it also has a beautiful wide bay backed by sierra, a sandy beach, a working fishing harbor, and the **Peñón de Ifach,** a huge rock rising 1,090 feet (332 m) above the Mediterranean. A **nature reserve** *(tel 965 83 69 20, closed on rainy days)* here protects about 300 species of flora and a large number of seabirds that nest there in spring. Just inland is the hilltop **old town,** with the restored remains of a 16th-century castle.

North of Calp is the popular beach resort of **Moraira.** Far more scenic is **Xàbia (Jávea)** *(visitor information, Plaça de la Iglesia 6, tel 965 79 43 56, closed Sat. p.m. & Sun.)*, on the north side of the Costa Blanca peninsula, near its point. El Arenal beach draws the sun lovers here.

A peaceful corner in Dénia in the province of Alacant, Costa Blanca's tourist hub

The attractive, partly walled old town was built inland around the fortified church of **San Bartolomé** for fear of pirates, and this is where you find its history explained at the small **Museo Arqueológico** *(tel 965 79 10 98)*. Today tourism has meant expansion, but the rocky capes and lovely beaches still hold their own.

The same goes for **Dénia,** 5 miles (8 km) northwest, a popular retirement area for northern Europeans. Its illustrious Greek, Roman, and Moorish past, is illustrated at the **Museo Arqueológico** *(Castillo de Dénia, tel 966 42 06 56)*, inside a stunning 17th-century castle.

Alacant (Alicante)

Sprawling around a huge bay, Alacant is a thriving, ever expanding port city with few historic sights other than its magnificent castle. You could spend a happy couple of hours exploring the backstreets of the old town, which burst into long nocturnal life on Friday and Saturday nights. Then head for one of the beaches.

In the **old town,** just behind the marina, have a look at the 18th-century **Ayuntamiento,** with its beautiful baroque facade. A few steps away, Alacant's ambitious **MACA** (Museo de Arte Contemporáneo; *tel 965 21 31 56*) opened in 2011. Sol Madridejos and Juan Carlos Sancho restructured a baroque edifice to house an impressive 20th-century art collection (Picasso, Dalí, Miró) that belonged to local artist Eusebio Sempere (1923–1985).

From here, take a stroll south along the **Explanada de España,** with its majestic banyan trees, past the marina to the **Lonja del Pescado** *(tel 965 92 23 06, closed Mon.)*. This former fish market,

INSIDER TIP:

You will find Alacant's best swimming in the marine reserve of the Isla de Tabarca, a delightful archipelago one hour away by boat *(Empresa Kontiki, tel 965 21 63 96).*

—FIONA DUNLOP
National Geographic author

designed in Modernista style, is now used for temporary exhibitions. More contemporary culture including a vertical garden is at Alacant's latest venue, **Centro Cultural Las Cigarreras** *(Calle San Carlos 78, tel 965 20 66 74)*, a converted tobacco factory.

For magnificent views, take the elevator built into the rockface opposite El Postiguet beach to the **Castillo de Santa Bárbara,** a fortress built by the Carthaginians. A large collection of 20th-century sculpture is dotted around the ramparts and in the halls. The oldest buildings, dating from the Middle Ages, are found at the top of the elevator. Halfway down is the 16th-century section, and the lowest level is 17th century. Walk down the access road, circle left along a path and go down steps to return to the old quarter. ■

Dénia

179 B2

Visitor Information

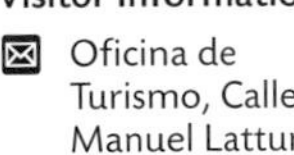

Oficina de Turismo, Calle Manuel Lattur 1

966 42 23 67 or 902 11 41 62

www.denia.net

Alacant (Alicante)

179 B1

Visitor Information

Oficina de Turismo, Avenida Salamanca s/n

965 12 56 33

Closed Sun.

www.alicanteturismo.com

Castillo de Santa Bárbara

Alacant

965 16 21 28

Exhibitions closed Sun. p.m. & Mon.

$ (elevator)

Drive: Into the Sierra

Leave the coastal crowds behind to head into the welcome emptiness of the sierra (called "serra" in Catalan). The Moors originally carved out the terraced hillsides, now covered in olive and almond trees, and orange and lemon groves. Guadalest attracts visitors from the coast because of its dramatic site, but it is worth visiting for the magnificent views over the surrounding mountains.

Depart from the resort of **Altea** on the Valencia road (N332) following the bay. Turn left toward Callosa d'en Sarrià (A150), and then left again onto CV755. The Serra de Guadalest looms ahead, with terraced orange and lemon groves in the foreground. You soon come to **Callosa d'en Sarrià ❶,** an agricultural town with a medieval arch and old walls around **Plaza del Castell.** As an antidote to the dry sierra, make a 2-mile (3.2 km) detour on the CV715 (direction Bolulla) to **Fonts de l'Algar ❷** *(tel 965 88 01 53),* an area of rushing springs with environmental exhibits and small restaurants.

From Callosa, follow signs to Guadalest (CV755) and drive 8 miles (12 km) through rugged limestone hills clad in pine trees and maquis. Your first sight of **Guadalest ❸** is extraordinary: Granite pinnacles topped by towers stand out of the valley, and in fact it was once accessible only through a tunnel. Drive into the village to the parking lot. From there wander through narrow streets lined with souvenir shops to the tunnel that leads into the old part of Guadalest. (Follow signs to "Museo.")

The castle ruins above are reached via 18th-century **Casa Orduña,** Guadalest's noble mansion, now the **Museo Municipal** *(Calle Iglesia 2, tel 965 88 53 93).* This was built after a devastating earthquake in 1644 destroyed most of the original castle, and was subsequently rebuilt after being burned during the 1708 War of Succession. Inside, it retains the Orduña family's furnishings, paintings (look at the anonymous double-sided "Ecce Homo"), and vast library. From the garden, steps lead up to the ruins of **Sant Josep castle,** now partly a cemetery, which give fantastic panoramic views. Other sights in this popular village are the church and a small **ethnological museum** *(opposite church, tel 661 15 27 74, closed Sat.),* with displays on Guadalest's chocolate-making industry.

Leave Guadalest on the same road, which winds around the flanks of the valley through terraced almond trees (a magnificent sight in February when the trees are covered in a mass of pink and white blossoms) and tiny villages. When you reach the pretty village of

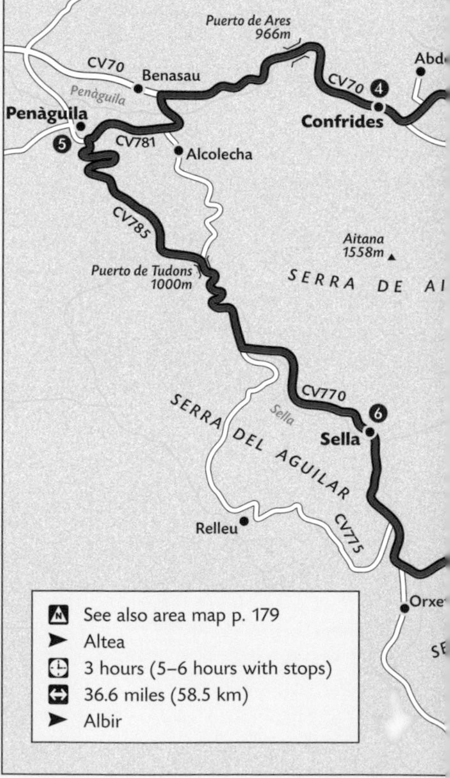

NOT TO BE MISSED:

Fonts de l'Algar • Guadalest • Confrides • Finestrat

Confrides ❹ *(visitor information, tel 965 88 58 04)*, source of the Guadalest River, stop to enjoy the magnificent views and the monumental walnut tree on the main square. From here to Penàguila, the road winds through 6 miles (10 km) of rocky moor and over the 3,170-foot (966 m) pass. Turn left onto the CV781, and then make a stop at **Penàguila** ❺ to look at its medieval gateway and noble mansions.

Leave this village on the CV785 in the direction of Sella (14 miles/22 km), driving through the beautiful, densely forested **Serra de Aitana,** with the 4,626-foot (1,410 m) silhouette of Puig Campana a permanent companion. **Sella** ❻ has Roman ruins and the remains of a medieval castle at the top of the town, and is a good starting point for hikes. Keep going toward Finestrat, where you return to terraced agriculture and orchards. Stop in **Finestrat** ❼ *(visitor information, Avenida Marina Baixa 14, tel 966 80 12 08)* to walk up to the **church and hermitage of the Remedio,** built over a Moorish castle, which gives fine views toward the Mediterranean.

The CV758 finally joins the busy CV70, from which you turn off on the N332 to **Alfaz del Pi.** The pretty beach at **Albir** ❽, overlooked by the rocky outcrop of Serra Helada, is another good spot for hiking, this time with a sea breeze.

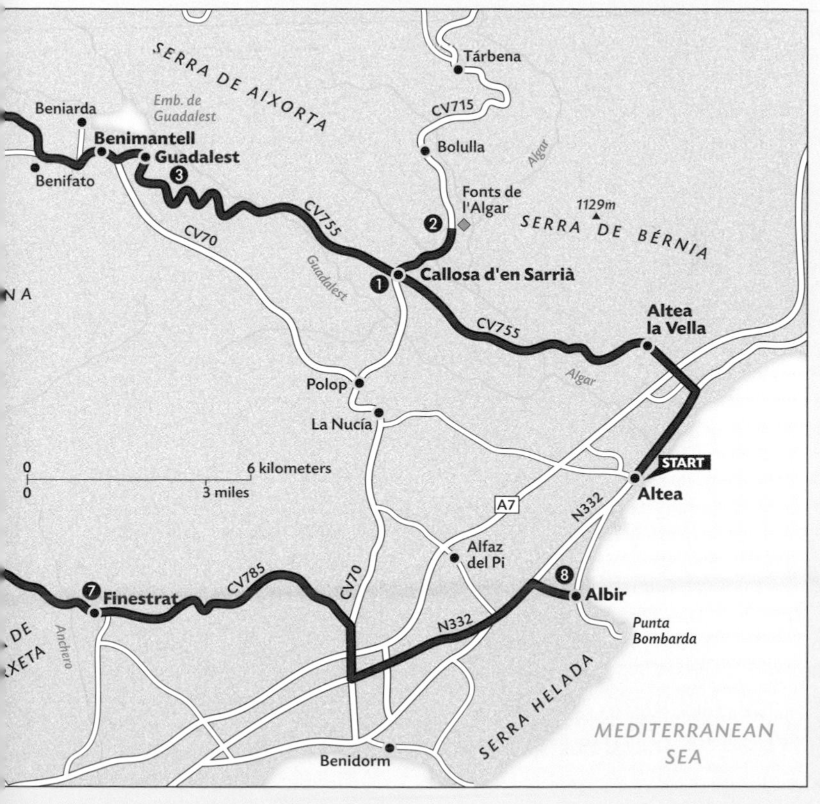

More Places to Visit in Valencia

Elx (Elche)

Twenty-five miles (32 km) southwest of Alacant lies the small town of Elx, known for three things: the Iberian sculpture, "La Dama de Elche," found here and now displayed at Madrid's Museo Arqueológico Nacional (see p. 70); the medieval mystery play enacted every August 14–15; and the largest **palm grove** in Europe, thought to have been planted by Phoenicians. Growing alongside canals of brackish water on the eastern side of the Vinalopo River, the palms reach heights of up to 78 feet (24 m). Do not miss the beautiful house and ponds of the **Huerto del Cura** *(Porta de la Morera, tel 965 45 19 36, www.huertodelacura.com)*, one of a series of plantations. Reigning supreme here among flowers and cactuses is the bizarre **Palmera Imperial,** which has seven secondary trunks. *www.turismedelx.com* 179 A1 **Visitor Information** Oficina de Turismo, Plaça del Parc 3 966 65 81 96

Sagunt (Sagunto)

Hannibal is best known in Spain for his failure to defeat Rome, which led to Roman dominance of the peninsula. The city of Sagunt, a Roman ally, put up a heroic fight against Hannibal in 219 B.C. The best of the Roman remains is the controversially restored **amphitheater,** used during the city's annual drama festival. You can visit the ruins of the old hilltop **fortress** *(tel 962 66 55 81, closed Mon. & Sun. p.m.)*, as well as the **Judería,** one of Spain's oldest Jewish quarters. *www.sagunt.es* 179 A2 **Visitor Information** Oficina de Turismo, Plaza Cronista Chabret s/n 962 65 58 59

Xàtiva

Xàtiva is a picturesque hill town set among vineyards where the crenellated **ramparts** of a ruined 15th-century castle give sweeping views toward the sea. Just below, the Mozarabic church of **Sant Feliu** houses Renaissance paintings. In the main historic center, head for **Plaza del Seo,** dominated by the bulky **Colegiata** (1596), standing opposite a delicately decorated plateresque building, the former **hospital.** Most interesting is the **Museo del Almudín** *(Carrer de la Corretgeria 46, tel 962 27 65 97, closed Sun. p.m. & Mon.)*, housed in a former granary. Here, the portrait of Felipe V, who sacked most of the town in 1707, hangs upside down. *www.xativaturismo.es* 179 A2 **Visitor Information** Oficina de Turismo, Avenida Selgas 2 962 27 33 46

EXPERIENCE: Savor Paella

The Moors introduced rice into the region in the eighth century. Soon the huge, flat frying pan gave its name to a delectable mixture of seafood, poultry, and/or game, vegetables, and saffron: paella.

Start your self-guided tour of the history of this delectable dish at the **Museo del Arroz** *(tel 963 52 54 78, www.museoarrozvalencia.com)*, a converted rice mill in Valencia's Cabanyal district. Then head for the converted farm of **La Matandeta** *(Alfafar, tel 962 11 21 84, www.lamatandeta.es)*, right in the middle of the rice fields outside the city. Here paella is still cooked over open fires of orange wood. Chef Rafael Alvez will even teach you the tricks of this delicious trade if there are ten in your group.

Tours Valencia *(www.toursvalencia.com)* also offers paella cooking lessons *($$$)* and a traditional lunch near the Ciudad de las Artes y de las Ciencias.

Plains punctuated by castles, superlative cathedrals, numerous monasteries, and golden-stone Renaissance monuments

Castilla y León

Peaceful fields belie a history of religious clashes.

Castilla y León

This is arguably the quintessential region of northern Spain. Here you can explore secret villages, contemplate Romanesque monasteries and churches, drive across endless plains, or clamber over medieval battlements. Salamanca, Valladolid, and León are convivial, attractive cities and some of Spain's greatest wines are produced beside the Duero River.

Most of the nine provinces of Castilla y León are on the meseta, an arid, often barren plateau that lies between 2,300 feet (700 m) and 3,600 feet (1,100 m) above sea level. The climate is extreme, with fierce summer temperatures and long harrowing winters. Simple farming villages where life has hardly changed in centuries stud the countryside.

Castilla y León is Old Castile, the original kingdom of Madrid. Castilla-La Mancha is New Castile, reconquered much later from the Moors. Dominating the landscape of Old Castile are the castles that gave the region its name in the ninth century, reminders of constant battles between Moors and Christians. In the towns are the emblazoned mansions of the ruling nobles, called *hidalgos.* Catholicism and conservatism are still deeply rooted. The Way of St. James (see pp. 86–87) pilgrimage route crossed the north of Old Castile, resulting in monumental cathedrals and a string of monasteries and sanctuaries.

The kingdoms of Castilla and León first united in 1037, a territorial marriage that was not fully consummated until the 13th century. Old Castile is the proud mother of the purest Castilian Spanish. The purest form of all is spoken in Burgos, seat of the first counts of Castilla. This region was also the source of the Spanish culture that conquered the New World. Salamanca has some of Spain's finest Renaissance architecture and its first university. Ávila produced the feminist mystic Santa Teresa. The legendary hero El Cid came from near Burgos, and Segovia has the archetypal, multiturreted royal castle.

Follow the course of the Duero River, from Zamora in the west to Peñafiel in the east, and you can sample Castilla y León's best wines (see pp. 134–136), organic sausages, cheese, and a wide variety of beans. Despite their reputation, Castilians are welcoming to visitors. With city centers renovated, modern architecture and standards of living vastly improved since the 1980s, Castilians are proud of their heritage. ■

NOT TO BE MISSED:

The stunning sculpture at the Museo Nacional de Escultura **215**

Salamanca's magnificent, arcaded Plaza Mayor at night **218**

Walking around the massive medieval walls of Ávila **223**

The cathedral and animated Barrio Húmedo in León **212–213**

Listening to Gregorian chants at Santo Domingo de los Silos **229**

The old Roman gold mines of Las Médulas **232**

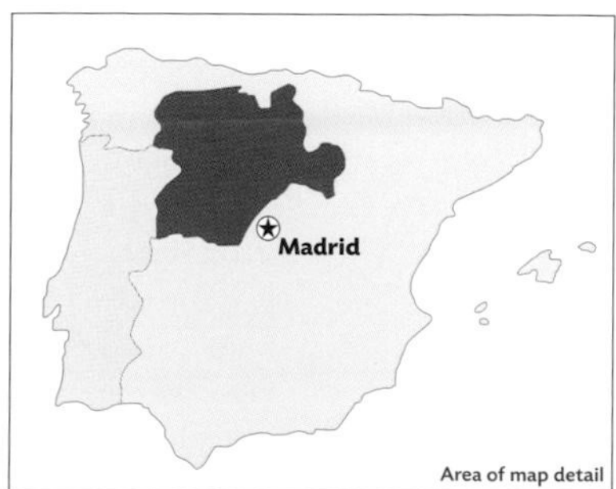

León

Lively and attractive, León has an easily negotiated scale. Much of the old center—the *casco viejo*—is now pedestrianized and renovation has made it a fabulous showpiece. Historic buildings have been converted into apartments, and bars and restaurants pack the Barrio Humédo quarter. The modern city spreads westward along and over the banks of the Río Bernesga, but still León's population barely tops 160,000.

León's contemporary art museum was designed by Madrid-based architects Mansilla & Tuñón.

León

210 C4

Visitor Information

Consorcio Patronato Provincial de Turismo, Plaza de la Regla s/n

987 29 21 89

www.turismocastillayleon.com

Catedral de León

The spires of the mighty Catedral de León, founded by Alfonso IX, guided weary pilgrims for centuries. Built between the mid-13th and late 14th centuries, this Gothic masterpiece has more than a hundred **stained-glass windows,** which cover an area of 19,375 square feet (1,800 sq m) and are considered second only to Chartes Cathedral in France. For searing color, go late in the afternoon, when sunlight pierces the rose window above the magnificently sculpted western portal. Other things to look for are the **Renaissance choir,** with four alabaster reliefs by Juan de Badajoz; the Gothic tombs and statue of pregnant Mary of the **ambulatory chapels;** and the **high altar painting** by Nicolás Francés (died 1468).

The lofty vaults of the **nave** are breathtaking, but they are easily rivaled by the **cloisters.** Enter through a plateresque (see p. 45) doorway that doubles as the entrance to the **museum** *(closed Sun.)*. Frescoes by Nicolás Francés and 16th-century keystone vaulting in the galleries add to the impact of this monumental courtyard.

Basílica San Isidoro

The Basílica San Isidoro abuts the Roman ramparts at the northern perimeter of the old town. As harmonious as the cathedral, its construction ranged from the late 11th century through to a baroque mid-18th century.

Entered from beside it is the remarkable **Panteón de los Reyes** (Kings' Pantheon) and a selective **museum.** Superb exhibits include the jewel-encrusted gold and agate chalice of Doña Urraca (11th century) and the silver reliquary of San Isidoro. A spiral staircase goes down to the vaulted pantheon, which holds the **sarcophagi** of 23 kings and queens. Unique and still fresh 12th-century **frescoes** blanket the vaults.

Other Sites

León's main pedestrianized artery, Calle Ancha, which leads to the cathedral, starts at dreary **Casa de Botines,** a castle designed by Antoni Gaudí (see pp. 172–175) and now a bank and exhibition hall.

South of Calle Ancha, a web of narrow streets makes up the lively **Barrio Húmedo,** an essential destination for sampling León's *cecina* (cured beef) and nightlife: The center is Plaza Mayor, lined with baroque buildings including the Town Hall. Every Saturday morning a huge farmers market fills the square.

León's other major sight, the Renaissance **Convento de San Marcos,** lies west of the center on the banks of the Río Bernesga. The Convento, founded for the Knights of the Order of St. James, extends more than 109 yards (100 m). Inside are a parador (see p. 366), church, cloisters, and a small archaeological display.

The city's latest addition is the innovative **MUSAC** (Museo de Arte Contemporaneo de Castilla y León; *Avenida Reyes Leoneses 24, tel 987 09 00 00, www.musac.es, closed Mon.*). The award-winning, multicolored cubes house diverse activities from art to cinema.

Thirty miles (47 km) north of the city in region of waterfalls and forests lie the cave formations of the **Cuevas de Valporquero.** The seven vast subterranean spaces with stalactites and stalagmites have humidity at 99 percent and a constant temperature of 45°F (7°C)—so be prepared, and take a sweater and walking shoes. ■

Catedral de León

- Plaza de Regla
- 987 87 57 70
- Closed 1:30–4:00 p.m.

www.catedraldeleon.org

Basílica San Isidoro

- Plaza San Isidoro 4
- 987 87 61 61
- Closed Sun. p.m.
- $; museum free Thurs. p.m.

Cuevas de Valporquero

- 987 57 64 08
- Closed Jan.–Feb., Mon.–Thurs. March–mid-May & Oct.–Dec.

EXPERIENCE: Sampling Regional Foods

Home to everything from the latest tapas bars to family-run restaurants, León's Barrio Húmedo is heaven for foodies. Prized specialties include *cecina* (cured beef), red peppers from the Bierzo region, Valdéon blue cheese, *morcilla leonesa* (León's blood sausage, resembling a porridge), tongue, chorizo, and stewed pig's ear. Dishes here are humble but flavorful.

One of the best places in León to sample much of what the region has to offer, either as *raciones* (sharing plates) or as a full meal, is Nuevo Racimo de Oro *(Plaza San Martín 8, tel 987 21 47 67, www.racinodeoro.com)*, in Barrio Húmedo. At Cocinandos *(Calle de la Campanillas 1, tel 987 07 13 78, www.cocinandos.com)* the chefs serve an inventive set menu that changes weekly.

Zamora

Sometimes called a living museum of Romanesque art, Zamora predates the Romanesque period. Its history goes back to the Celts and Romans who occupied this strategic site overlooking the Duero River. For most of the year, a charming, small-town atmosphere prevails, but in Holy Week Zamora's unique collection of *pasos* (sculpted floats) appears in fervent processions.

Zamora

210 B2

Visitor Information

Oficina Municipal de Turismo, Plaza Arias Gonzalo 5

980 53 36 94

www.ayto-zamora.org

Cathedral & Museo Catedralicio

Plaza del Pío XIII

980 53 18 02

Closed Mon.

$

Cathedral

Zamora's unusually squat 12th-century cathedral has a beautiful **dome,** which has been clad in scalloped tiles, and a Romanesque **bell tower** and south portal. Inside, look at the elaborately carved **choir stalls** and the anatomically perfect statue of Christ in the **Capilla de San Bernardo.**

INSIDER TIP:

The verb *invitar* can mean "to treat someone." So if you happen to be out at dinner or a bar and a Spaniard says, "I invite you," he or she might really be saying, "It's on me!"

—RACHAEL JACKSON
Research Manager, National Geographic Channels

The cathedral's 17th-century cloisters give access to the charming **museum,** where exquisite 15th-century **Flemish tapestries** include four illustrating the Trojan War. Behind the cathedral, peaceful **gardens** of the former castle abutting the old city walls give good views.

Romanesque Churches

Zamora has 16 Romanesque churches, each one different and many of them still functioning. At the beautifully proportioned **Santa María Magdalena** *(Rúa de los Francos, closed Mon.),* look at the delicately sculpted tomb of an unknown lady (1190) and intricate carvings in the southern portal. **San Cipriano** *(Plaza Claudio Moyano, closed Mon.)* has a single nave with ornamentation only in the carved capitals flanking the altar. Zamora's oldest church, **Santa María la Nueva** *(Calle Motín de la Trucha),* rebuilt in 1158, played an important role as both a refuge and a forum for nobles and their workforce.

Other Sights

Impressive 16th-century civic buildings include the **Palacio de Los Momos** *(Plaza Zorilla, not open to the public)* with its exuberant Isabelline windows and the masterly **Palacio del Cordón.** Part of the **Museo de Zamora** *(Plaza de Santa Lucia 2, tel 980 51 61 50, closed Mon.)* is housed here. For more imaginative displays visit the **Museo Etnográfico** *(tel 980 53 17 08, closed Sun. p.m. & Mon., www.museo-etnografico.com)* near the 500-year-old Plaza Mayor. ■

Valladolid

Overtly modern Valladolid plays a leading industrial role as Spain's chief car manufacturer but still has some intriguing secrets tucked away. With a population of 320,000, it is one of northern Spain's larger cities, but the partly pedestrianized center is easy to find your way around and borders a vast central park, Campo Grande.

Valladolid's history is symbolized by the **Plaza Mayor,** rebuilt in 1631 after a fire, and the dazzling sculpture collection of the **Museo Nacional de Escultura** *(Calle Cadenas de San Gregorio 1, tel 983 25 03 75, www.museosangregorio.mcu.es, closed Sun. p.m. & Mon.).* The museum's setting, the **Colegio de San Gregorio** is a remarkable example of Spanish Gothic (1496). The entrance gateway is a riot of sculpture, rivaled in splendor by the patio, staircase, and funerary chapel of Fray Alonso. Sculptures on show, mainly in polychrome wood, cover the 13th to 18th centuries. Some of the finest pieces are Alonso Berruguete's (circa 1488–1561) 16th-century altarpiece for San Benito and the "Burial of Christ" by Juan de Juni (died 1577). Adjoining the museum is the church of **San Pablo,** with a beautiful late Gothic facade by Simon of Cologne.

The city's **cathedral** is a mixture of styles, but it has elaborate baroque decoration by the influential Alberto Churriguera (see p. 46) and a striking altarpiece by Juan de Juni. The **Museo Oriental** *(Paseo Filipinos 7, tel 983 30 69 00, closed Mon.–Sat. a.m. & Sun. p.m.),* housed in a neoclassical Augustinian seminary, is an excellent antidote to a surfeit of Castilian religious art: It shows a priceless collection of ivory figures, tribal pieces from the Philippines, and Chinese decorative arts. Equally escapist is the **Casa-Museo Colón** *(Calle Colón, tel 983 29 13 53, closed Sun. p.m. & Mon.)* dedicated to Christopher Columbus, who died in Valladolid in 1506.

One of Europe's best private collections of African art, the **Fundación Alberto Jiménez,** is exhibited at the **Palacio de Santa Cruz** *(Plaza Santa Cruz 8, tel 983 18 45 30, closed Sun.).* On a more hedonist note, every mid-October Valladolid hosts Spain's national tapas competition. ■

The best way to experience fast-growing Valladolid is on foot.

Valladolid

210 C3

Visitor Information

Oficina de Información Turística, Pabellón de Cristal, Acera de Recoletos s/n

983 21 93 10

www.info.valladolid.es

Castles in Castilla y León

Old Castile is liberally studded with castles. Celtiberian fortified settlements were built over by Roman military outposts. Moors built castles to defend their kingdom against the Christians of Asturias. As the Reconquest advanced, Christian nobles rebuilt these and used them as bases for pushing farther south. Others were built completely afresh—nearly 90 survive today in Castilla y León.

Site of clashes between Christian and Moorish kingdoms, Old Castile has more than 600 castles.

Castillo de Coca
- 210 C2
- Coca, Segovia province
- 617 57 35 54
- Closed first Tues. of month
- $ (40-min. guided tour)

www.castillodecoca.com

Castillo de Coca

The crenellated ramparts and polygonal turrets of Castillo de Coca rise majestically from the plains about 30 miles (45 km) northwest of Segovia. It was built in Gothic Mudejar style for Alonso de Fonseca, archbishop of Sevilla, in 1453, and then given to the Marquis of Ayala and later the Duke of Alba (whose family still owns it). An outer square bailey encloses an inner one, both executed in decorative brickwork. The **Pedro Mata Tower** has a circular room where a secret whispered into a wall can be heard on the opposite side. Here, too, the **dungeon** is a cruel reminder of the days when prisoners endured a long, slow death.

Castillo de Cuéllar

Set high on a citadel and incorporated into the town

walls, Castillo de Cuéllar (mid-15th century) has been much lusted after. The original owner, Juan II, bequeathed the castle to his daughter Isabel, but her stepbrother, Enrique IV, grabbed it and passed it to his favorite, Beltrán de la Cueva. Inside the castle is an extensive collection of antique arms.

Castillo de Frías

Castillo de Frías *(Frías, Burgos province, tel 947 35 80 11, www.ciudaddefrias.es, map 211 E4)* is one of Castilla's most dramatically placed castles: It perches high on a craggy rock that towers over a charming medieval village. Construction spanned the 13th to 16th centuries, a period echoed in the village's church of **San Vicente.** Below is a medieval fortified bridge.

INSIDER TIP:

Although Castillo de Frías is now mainly in ruins, you can climb up to the ramparts for stunning views north over the Ebro River.

—MARY STEPHANOS
National Geographic contributor

Castillo de la Mota

Castillo de la Mota is one of Castilla y León's greatest castles, with crenellated walls and a towering keep on a hilltop. Started by the Moors in the 13th century, it was much extended by Fernando and Isabel in the 15th century. Their daughter Juana the Mad was another royal resident. It became a state prison, and Cesare Borgia was one of its political and military prisoners.

Castillo Pedraza de la Sierra

The austere 14th- to 16th-century **Castillo Pedraza de la Sierra** contrasts with one of Castilla's prettiest and best conserved medieval towns, its steep, narrow streets lined with atmospheric mansions, porticoes, and balconies. The castle belonged to the counts of Castilla, the Fernández de Velasco family. Its present owners are the descendants of the painter Ignacio Zuloaga (1870–1945), some of whose works are exhibited beside antiques and engravings. The castle moat is cut into the rock, with circular and square towers rising above.

Castillo de Peñafiel

The elongated white stone Castillo de Peñafiel looms high above the plain and the charming wine-producing town at its feet. The castle was built in the 15th century, and the keep was remodeled in the following century for the Girón family, with walls 11 feet (3.5 m) thick and eight side-turrets. Visit the castle's **wine museum,** and don't miss the rest of this unusual town. **Plaza del Coso** is surrounded by timbered houses, and the church of **Santa María** has a museum of religious art. ■

Castillo de Cuéllar

- 210 D2
- Cuéllar, Segovia province
- 921 14 22 03
- Closed Mon. p.m. Guided visits: call for an appointment.

www.aytocuellar.es/turismo

Castillo de la Mota

- 210 C2
- Medina del Campo, Valladolid province
- 983 81 27 24
- Closed Sun. p.m.

www.castillodelamota.es

Castillo Pedraza de la Sierra

- 210 D2
- Pedraza de la Sierra, Segovia province
- 921 50 98 25
- Closed Mon. & Tues., & when family is in residence

www.pedraza.info

Castillo de Peñafiel

- 210 D3
- Peñafiel, Valladolid province
- 983 88 11 99
- Closed Mon.

www.museodelvinovalladolid.com

Salamanca

Spend a couple of days in Salamanca to get an insight into Spain's academic life and a complete picture of the evolution of Spanish architecture. Salamanca's university, one of Europe's earliest, was founded in 1218. Over the centuries, this lively town has hardly stood still, and today its university population combines with a steady flow of visitors and Spanish language students to create a cosmopolitan atmosphere in which traditions are nonetheless respected.

Salamanca's prestige was built upon its university, which opened in 1218.

Salamanca

210 B2

Visitor Information

Oficina Municipal de Turismo, Plaza Mayor 14

923 21 83 42 or 902 30 20 02

www.salamanca.es

Plaza Mayor

Designed by the Churriguera brothers (see p. 46) in the 1720s, Salamanca's Plaza Mayor is one of the most beautiful squares in Europe. Look for the sculpted portraits of Christopher Columbus, El Cid, Cervantes, and a string of Spanish kings. At night musicians and other street performers invade the square.

Rúa Mayor

The main monuments lie west and south of Plaza Mayor. The **Casa de las Conchas,** or House of Shells, was once a palace and is now a public library. The stone Renaissance facade comes alive with 400 sculpted scallop shells, the symbol worn by pilgrims to Santiago de Compostela (see pp. 88–91). Inside the courtyard are delicately carved balustrades and lions' heads.

The pedestrianized Rúa Mayor is the most commercial street in Salamanca, and it leads straight to the cathedral, which dominates broad Plaza de Anaya. Turn down any side street, however, and you are projected back in time.

Cathedral

The massive cathedral is in fact two buildings: the Catedral

Nueva (New Cathedral) and the Catedral Vieja (Old Cathedral). The **Catedral Nueva** dates from 1513, and additions over the next two centuries created a mixture of styles from late Gothic through Renaissance and plateresque to baroque. Its immense scale is striking, with soaring carved arches, ribbed columns, and the ornately carved choir, another work of the Churriguera brothers. Here, too, you see one of Spain's most famous organs, the work of Pedro de Echevarría in 1745.

You must go behind the main altar to see the much revered 11th-century figure of Christ set into an exuberant Churrigueresque altarpiece. And don't miss the **Patio Chico,** through a door in the south aisle, a terrace which gives an all-encompassing view of the old cathedral, cupola, and baroque tower of the new cathedral.

The entrance to the Romanesque **Catedral Vieja** (*$*) is also off the south aisle. Light stone columns lead your eye to an early Renaissance **altarpiece** comprised of 53 exquisitely painted panels surrounding a bejeweled statue of the Virgin of the Vega, patron saint of Salamanca. This gilded sculpture dates from the late

Casa de las Conchas
✉ Calle Compañía
☎ 923 26 93 17

Catedral Nueva
✉ Plaza de Anaya
☎ 923 21 74 76
$ $ (Catedral Vieja)

www.catedralsalamanca.org

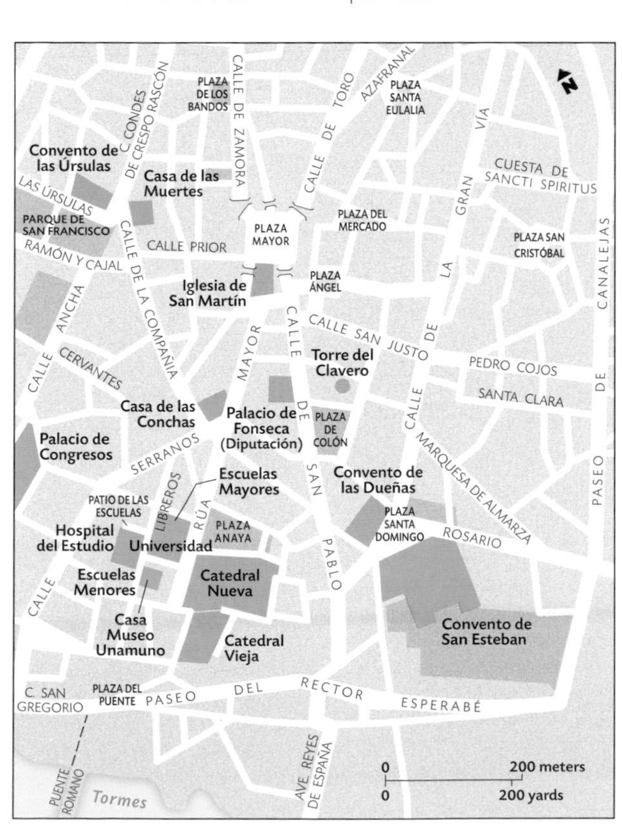

Convento de San Esteban

Plaza del Concilio de Trento s/n

923 21 50 00

Convento de las Dueñas

Plaza del Concilio de Trento s/n

923 21 54 42

Universidad de Salamanca

Libreros, s/n

923 29 44 00

Closed Sun. p.m.

$

www.usal.es/webusal/visita/index.htm

12th century, as does the cathedral. Other outstanding features are the frescoes (1262) by Antón Sánchez de Segovia, the beautiful dome above the transept, the part-Romanesque cloisters, and the **Capilla de Talavera,** with its Mudejar dome.

San Esteban & Las Dueñas

Head 200 yards (183 m) east to the church of San Esteban and the convent of Las Dueñas. San Esteban's facade (1524–1610) is a stunning example of fine plateresque carving. Inside, the luminous single nave focuses on a fabulous Churrigueresque altarpiece, 98 feet (30 m) in height, that surrounds a painting of the martyrdom of St. Stephen (San Esteban). For an even better view, look from the elevated choir above the nave. You reach this through the **King's Cloister,** notable for medallions depicting prophets. Climb the magnificent **grand staircase** to the upper gallery and the **biblioteca** (library), which exhibits lovely 17th-century ivory statues from the Philippines, and then on to the choir viewpoint.

Dominican nuns still live in the **Convento de las Dueñas,** where the main attraction are the pretty Renaissance cloisters. The lattice screens of their cell windows are visible from the gardens. Go around the side of the convent to see the **Torre del Clavero,** an octagonal tower that is the only remnant of a medieval castle. ■

Universidad de Salamanca

Salamanca's university is one of the world's oldest, a contemporary of the universities of Paris and Bologna. Its various buildings are clustered around Calle Serranos and Calle Libreros, immediately west of Rúa Mayor. The most spectacular facade is that of the **Escuelas Mayores,** a plateresque masterpiece completed in 1533 for the original Gothic university behind. Inside, the modernized patio (with a Mudejar wooden ceiling) is surrounded by the old lecture halls where literati such as the philosopher Miguel de Unamuno (see p. 50) once held sway. A beautiful carved stone staircase leads to the upper floor, where you can peer at the library through a glass vestibule. The shelves contain some 2,770 manuscripts, 483 *incunabula* (early books), and 62,000 pre-19th-century publications.

Flanking this building to the south is the **Casa Museo Unamuno,** the home of the writer Miguel de Unamuno, who taught here. Opposite, overlooking a small square, are the **Hospital del Estudio** (Students' Hospice) and neighboring **Escuela Menores** (for pre-university studies). Here you discover a delightful Gothic patio and, in the **Museo Universitaria,** an extraordinary ceiling decoration, the Cielo de Salamanca (Salamanca Sky), transferred from the old library. Only a third of it is here, but it is enough to convey the finesse of Fernando Gallego's 1473 illustration of the cosmos and celestial beings. Other Renaissance exhibits include a collection of walnut sculptures by Felipe Bigarny, paintings, and dazzling silverwork. Next door, the curious **Sala de las Tortugas** (Tortoise Room) shows the world's second largest fossil collection.

EXPERIENCE: Enjoy *La Vendimia,* or Grape Harvest

Castilla y León's most globally acclaimed product is wine: Its current ten classified areas or D.O.'s *(denominación d'origen)* and four *vinos de la tierra* provide a fantastic quality choice. Top reds such as Ribera del Duero easily rival the better known Riojas, while mellow white wines from Rueda are increasingly sought after and Cigales looks after the rosés. What they all share is the proximity of the Duero River, stony limestone soil, and low rainfall.

Traveling through these landscapes in fall, when the vine leaves turn yellow, orange, and russet, is sheer visual delight. Even better are the harvest festivals that propel visitors into centuries-old traditions.

The grape harvest is one of the most important Spanish festivals.

Every town has its own customs, but all *fiestas de la vendimia* must start with the treading of the first grapes and the tasting of the first grape must (the fresh juice containing the pips and skin). Veterans nod wisely as they savor what will become that season's big money-earner.

Where to Enjoy the Grape Harvest

One of the most scenic settings to witness the celebration is in **Peñafiel** (see p. 217; *www.turismopenafiel.com*), a stunning town crowned by an elongated white castle, with bodega chimneys poking out of the hillside. At its heart is the striking Plaza del Coso, an irregular-shaped square flanked by wooden buildings, a perfect backdrop for jousts, plays, music, and dancing. Stalls heave with excellent tapas, and bottles of Ribera del Duero wine are emptied with alacrity.

In **Cigales** *(www.turismocigales.blogspot.com),* over the first weekend of the harvest, grape-treading is followed by wine-tasting and folkloric dancing. A parade of wine-producers *(el desfilé de las bodegueras)* culminates in the rapturous election of the year's best winemaker in the Plaza de Lujano. The main square sees partying late into the night, overlooked rather sternly by the church of Santiago Apostol. Athletic visitors can take part in a bike ride of about 50 miles (80 km) to every town along the Cigales wine route.

White wine lovers should head for **Rueda,** southeast of Valladolid and just south of the Duero, on the second weekend of October. Tastings of the town's highly rated Sauvignon Blanc and Verdejo wines are perfect fuel for energetic music and dancing, for washing down a portion of gigantic paella prepared for the town, and, maybe, for watching a bullfight.

Producers in **Toro,** west of Valladolid, time their festival to coincide with Valladolid's big Puente del Pilar festival in October. A major attraction is the procession of old carts pulled by oxen or horses and decorated with farming and harvesting utensils. A medieval market, painting competition, music, food, and dance round off the festivities.

For more information on regional wine routes and places to stay, consult *www.turismocastillayleon.com, www.haciendas-espana.com,* and *www.winetourismspain.com/wine-hotel.*

Ciudad Rodrigo

The fortified town of Ciudad Rodrigo is one of northern Spain's delightful secrets, redolent with history without being affected by mass tourism. This is slowly changing with new highway connections to Portugal and northern Spain. It comes to life every year at the start of the bull-fighting season, during Carnival in February, when the *encierro*—the running of the bulls—takes over the streets. Easter week is another highlight.

Ciudad Rodrigo
210 B1
Visitor Information
Oficina de Información Turística, Plaza de las Amayuelas 5
923 46 05 61

The surrounding agricultural region is by no means prosperous—you might guess this from Ciudad Rodrigo's rather dubious speciality, *el farinato,* a sausage made from flour and lard, generally eaten with fried eggs. The town's illustrious past is recalled by a string of palaces. The town was named for Count Rodrigo González Girón, who resettled it after driving out the Moors in the 12th century. In 1812, the Duke of Wellington took Ciudad Rodrigo from Napoleon's forces after a bloody siege. Ciudad Rodrigo's strategic position on the frontier is symbolized by its massive **ramparts**. Several stairways lead to the one-mile (1.6 km) sentry path—and very good views.

This sleepy town near Portugal was a once a key fortress.

Rising above the town is the keep of the 14th-century **castle of Enrique II de Trastámara,** now a parador (see p. 366). The crenellated towers are spectacularly illuminated at night. The **cathedral** *(Plaza San Salvador, tel 923 48 14 24, $ cloisters)* has features from the 12th century in addition to a beautiful 13th-century portal, Portada de la Virgen, Isabelline choir stalls exuberantly carved by Rodrigo Alemán and an alabaster Renaissance altarpiece. Richly ornamented tombs of noblemen and women add to its interest. Next door the more sober Capilla de Cerralbo is worth a visit for its altar-painting by José Ribero.

Walk south to reach the town's main social gathering place, arcaded **Plaza del Buen Alcalde,** where the Tuesday market is held. Then continue to the sloping Plaza Mayor to sample a farinato. ■

Ávila

The walled town of Ávila is one of Spain's most spectacular urban sights, but within Spain it is more famous for just one person. The mystic Santa Teresa was born here in 1515, and convents and churches devoted to her grace its streets. It is a small town of 50,000 inhabitants perched on a spur above the Río Adaja at an altitude of more than 3,700 feet (1,130 m). Winters are particularly harsh, but in any other season, it's a joy to explore on foot.

Ávila's perfectly preserved **walls** date from the 11th century, when the 88 cylindrical towers and 9 gateways were built to fend off the Moors. Abutting the walls at the older, eastern end is the 12th- to 15th-century **cathedral.** Look for the tomb of El Tostado (a 15th-century bishop nicknamed "the toasted one" for his dark complexion). There are also finely carved plateresque choir stalls, two unusual wrought-iron pulpits, and a Renaissance altarpiece. Don't miss the 13th-century **sacristy** with its octagonal vaulted ceiling. In the **museum,** you will find a gigantic silver monstrance (1571). The delicate Gothic **cloisters** lie next to the museum.

INSIDER TIP:

In Ávila, be sure to sample *yemas,* the candies made from egg yolks and sugar that originated here.

—RACHAEL JACKSON
Research, Manager, National Geographic Channels

You can walk 1.5 miles (2.5 km) beside Ávila's walls for panoramic views.

Turn right on leaving the cathedral to reach the Puerta de San Vicente and, just outside the walls, the Romanesque-Gothic **Basílica de San Vicente** *(Plaza San Vicente, tel 920 25 52 30),* with an exceptional sculpted west portal. Inside is the canopied **sarcophagus** of San Vicente and his sisters.

Santa Teresa was a great mystic, rebel, and writer, and founder of the barefoot Carmelite order. Her birthplace in Ávila is marked by the **Convento de Santa Teresa** *(Plaza de la Santa).* The **Convento de la Encarnación** *(Paseo de la Encarnación, tel 920 21 12 12),* where she lived for 27 years, has a rather dull museum dedicated to her far-from-dull life. ■

Ávila

Map 210 C1

Visitor Information

Centro de Recepción de Visitantes, Avenida Madrid 39

920 22 59 69

www.avilaturismo.com

Cathedral

Plaza de la Catedral

920 21 16 41

$ (museum)

In & Around Segovia

Like a huge ship moored on the plain of Old Castile, Segovia is one of northern Spain's most seductive towns. Depending on where you come from, your first sight may take in the Roman aqueduct, cathedral, and fantasy palace of the Alcázar, all clustered around the prominent limestone outcrop on which the old town stands. In addition to the monuments that have made it a World Heritage city, Segovia has a healthy cultural life and gastronomy.

Segovia's Roman aqueduct brought water from the Río Frio, several miles away.

Segovia

210 D2

Visitor Information

Patronato Provincial de Turismo, Plaza Mayor 9

921 46 60 70

www.segoviaturismo.es

In summer or winter you can feel the climate change as you approach the city, for Segovia lies at 3,300 feet (1,000 m). The Romans were the first to recognize the site's attractions: The 95-foot-high (29 m) aqueduct spanning Plaza de Azoguejo still stands as proof of their superior engineering.

After Visigothic and Moorish domination, Segovia came into its own in 1088, when the Castilian king Alfonso VI installed his court here and initiated a prosperous period represented by the construction of more than 40 Romanesque churches.

The city reached its zenith in 1474, when Isabel la Católica was proclaimed Queen of Castilla in the church of San Miguel. The town declined under the Habsburg kings (16th and 17th centuries) but enjoyed an 18th-century renaissance.

Old Town

Segovia's old town is very much a place to explore, so arm yourself with a map from the visitor center and head for the backstreets, all of which contain notable churches, towers, and mansions enlivened by numerous storks. The hub of the old town is semiporticoed **Plaza Mayor,** lined with lively cafés and dominated by the huge, rhythmical hulk of the **cathedral.** This Flamboyant Gothic extravaganza houses some rarities in its lofty interior, notably the baroque main altarpiece by Andrea Sabatini (circa 1480–1530) and the "Entombment" sculpture by Juan de Juni (died 1577) in a side chapel off the south aisle. The choir stalls and the cloisters were saved from the old cathedral, which was destroyed by fire during the Revolt of the Communeros (1520–1521).

From the Plaza Mayor, follow Calle Infanta Isabel to reach Segovia's most striking square, **Plaza de San Martín.** This terraced area surrounds a statue of local hero Juan Bravo in the shadow of the magnificent church of **San Martín.** Like most of Segovia's churches, this is open only for services, but you can admire the Mudejar tower and Romanesque capitals of the porch. Next door stands the elegant 17th-century **royal prison,** now a public library. Across the square looms a 14th-century tower, the **Torreón de Lozoya** *(Plaza de San Martín, tel 921 46 24 61, open from 7 p.m.),* flanked by the **Museo de Arte Contemporáneo Esteban Vicente** exhibiting works by this abstract expressionist painter who died on Long Island in 2001 *(tel 921 46 20 10, closed Mon.).*

Downhill from here is the **Casa de los Picos** *(Calle Juan Bravo 33),* a 15th-century mansion with a remarkable facade of diamond-shaped granite studs. This is now the School of Applied Arts. Facades decorated in plaster relief patterns *(esgrafiados)* abound in this quarter, including that of the **Alhóndiga,** meaning "public granary," now home to the Municipal Archives. Both the Alhóndiga and the neighboring **Palacio de Aspiroz** *(Plaza Platero Oquendo)* are typical of 15th-century local architecture.

Building the Alcázar

The Habsburg king Felipe II was responsible for the building of this unexpected sight. During his reign major additions were made to the original medieval castle. But thank also the 19th-century restorers who enhanced the castle's theatricality in the 1880s after a fire. It was then handed over to the Royal Artillery, who have a museum inside.

Alcázar

Without a doubt, Segovia's greatest landmark is the Alcázar, the turreted castle that rises like a mirage at the western tip of the outcrop above the

Cathedral

- Calle Marqués de Arco I
- 921 46 22 05
- $ (cloisters, chapter house, museum)

www.turismodesegovia.com

Alcázar

- Plaza de la Reina Victoria Eugenia
- 921 46 07 59
- $

www.alcazardesegovia.com

San Ildefonso de la Granja

- 210 D2
- Plaza de España San Ildefonso
- 921 47 00 19, 921 47 00 20
- Closed Mon. all year & Sun. p.m. Oct.–March
- $$. Free on Wed. p.m. for E.U. nationals.

Real Palacio de Riofrío

- 210 D1
- Bosque de Riofrío
- 921 47 00 19, 921 47 00 20
- Closed Mon. all year & Sun. p.m. Oct.–March
- $$. Free on Wed. p.m. for E.U. nationals.

confluence of the Clamores and Eresma Rivers (see sidebar p. 225). Ask at the ticket office for a leaflet with detailed descriptions of the interior, although the itinerary tends to change. Arrows guide you through, from the medieval entrance hall with original mullioned windows to the elaborate throne room that dazzles with restored Mudejar decoration. Tapestries, antique furniture, paintings, beautiful coffered Mudejar ceilings (look in particular at the one in the chapel), and suits of armor accompany you throughout. Don't miss the panoramic views from the roof of the keep, reached by more than 150 narrow steps in a tower beside the ticket office, and notice the half-formed turrets of its ramparts—truly theatrical!

Royal Environs

Segovia's environs are also replete with royal memorabilia. The finest is **San Ildefonso de la Granja,** 7 miles (11 km) southeast on the N601, in a stunning location at the foot of the Guadarrama Mountains. Begun in 1721, the palace reflects the nostalgia of the Bourbon king Felipe V for his grandfather's palace—Versailles in France. Several architects contributed to La Granja, producing a blend of Spanish baroque and French neoclassic styles. Marble, gilded stucco, and velvet surround predictably lavish furnishings such as beautiful 16th-century Flemish tapestries and scintillating chandeliers. The latter were made at the nearby glass factory, the **Real Fábrica de Cristales** *(Paseo del Pocillo, tel 921 01 07 00 or 921 47 00 20, closed Sun. p.m. in winter & Mon.),* where you can watch glassblowing and see a display of antique glass. The palace also has exceptional, extensive formal gardens, the work of French landscape gardeners, which, again like Versailles, are strewn with statues and fountains.

Felipe V's second wife, Isabella Farnese, was responsible for the royal retreat at **Riofrío,** 4 miles (7 km) south of Segovia off the N603. More a country mansion than a palace, it is surrounded by 1,700 acres (700 ha) of holm-oak woods. The pink Italianate building houses valuable paintings (by Ribera, Velázquez, and Rubens), plus a hunting museum. ■

EXPERIENCE: Sierra de Guadarrama

Slicing across the border between Madrid and Castilla y León, this 62-mile (100 km) mountain range of granite outcrops, streams, and oak and pine forests attracts hordes of Madrileños in summer. **Hiking in Madrid** *(tel 915 19 03 10, www.hikinginmadrid.es)* offers guided treks *($$)* that include an ascent up **Peñalara,** at 7,970 feet (2,429 m) the highest peak in the range. Experienced climbers will also enjoy a five-hour guided scramble over the rocks *($$).* Snow hikes and winter climbing tours are also available. Transportation can be arranged.

Soria

Although not the most compelling of the provincial capitals, Soria is known for its "liquid gold" garlic soups. Above all, it lies at the heart of some beautiful landscapes. This province is a region of transition wedged between Castilla, Aragón, and La Rioja. Northwest is the magnificent Sierra de Urbión, known for prolific game and trout. East is the dramatically rugged Sierra de Moncayo.

Plaza Mariano Granados marks the eastern tip of Parque Alameda.

The red-tiled roofs of golden sandstone houses, lauded by poet Antonio Machado (1875–1939), slot into the streets of this town center. South from the formal **Parque Alameda de Cervantes** through squares and pedestrian streets is **Plaza Mayor,** the hub of the town. In the web of streets that lies between, centering on **Calle Aduana Vieja,** emblazoned Renaissance facades lead you to the Romanesque church of **Santo Domingo,** with statues of its founders flanking the richly carved portal, a rose window, and tiers of niches.

Other churches lie south, near the Duero River. The **cathedral of San Pedro** *(Plaza de San Pedro s/n, closed April-Oct. Mon. p.m., & Nov.–March Tues.–Sun. p.m. & Mon.)* is mainly Gothic but has pure Romanesque cloisters. Across the Duero are the remains of the **Monasterio de San Juan de Duero** *(Camino Monte de las Animas, tel 975 23 02 18, closed Sun. p.m. & Mon.),* built with Moorish influence in the 13th century. From here you can see the **Parque del Castillo,** a landscaped hill.

The Romans rebuilt **Numancia** *(4 miles/7 km NE of Soria)* in 133 B.C. after its Celtiberian inhabitants destroyed it to avoid capture. The ruins are of interest only for enthusiasts, but in town the **Museo Numantino** *(Paseo del Espolón 8, tel 975 23 24 56, closed Sun. p.m. & Mon.),* beside the Alameda de Cervantes park, has Roman artifacts. ■

INSIDER TIP:

Vineyards line the Duero River, and regional wines rule in Soria. Local food like wild mushrooms is just as delectable.

—LAWRENCE GUY STRAUSS
National Geographic grantee

Soria

211 E3

Visitor Information

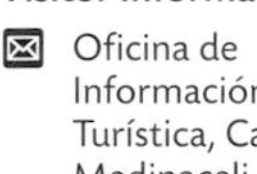

Oficina de Información Turística, Calle Medinaceli 2

975 21 20 52

www.sorianitelaimaginas.com

Drive to Arlanza: Valley of Towers

From its source in the Sierra de Urbión, the Arlanza River meanders through a dramatic valley west to Lerma. This drive takes you through beautiful, often wild countryside, much of it ideal hiking territory and recently classified as a protected area. On the way visit jewel-like churches, each one in a different architectural style.

The Monasterio de Santo Domingo de Silos boasts one of the world's most beautiful cloisters.

Leave Burgos on the A1/E5 in the direction of Madrid. After 22 miles (36 km), cross the Arlanza River and turn off the highway at Lerma–Estacion. Follow the signs into **Lerma ❶**. The stone arch, **Arco de la Cárcel,** is all that remains of the medieval town walls. Proceed uphill to Plaza Mayor.

In front stands the **Palacio Ducal,** austere symbol of the extensive political power of Francisco Gómez, Duke of Lerma, who virtually ruled Spain from 1598 to 1618. This is now a parador. Downhill lies the old quarter, best seen on foot. From the square, walk down Calle de la Audiencia past the former convent of Santa Teresa, now the town hall and tourist office *(Casa Consistorial, Calle de la Audiencia, tel 947 17 70 02, closed Sun. p.m. & Mon.).* The **Plaza de Santa Clara** is flanked by the monastery of La Ascensión and a balcony with sweeping views. Lerma's most important ecclesiastical monument, the 1617 church of San Pedro, or **Colegiata** *(by guided tour only),* houses one of Spain's oldest organs.

NOT TO BE MISSED:

Colegiata, Lerma • Monasterio de Santo Domingo • Colegiata, Covarrubias • San Pedro de Arlanza • Ermita Visigótica

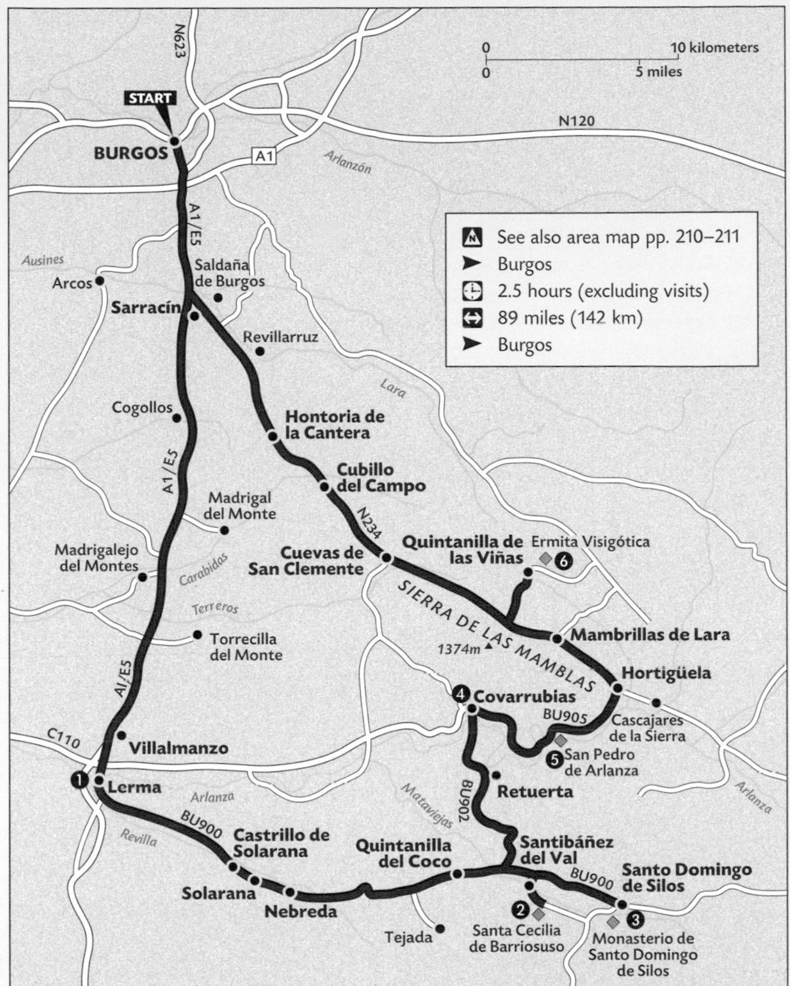

Leave Lerma by continuing across the Plaza Mayor (following signs "Todas direcciones"), and turn right downhill to take the left turnoff signed Santo Domingo de Silos. This road (BU900) passes stone villages typical of the Arlanza, such as **Castrillo de Solarana.** Turn right at the next junction (signed Santo Domingo), and after 1 mile (2 km) turn right into Santibañez del Val. Follow signs for the Ermita Mozárabe, past the church, and left at a junction to continue beyond the hamlet, parallel to the Ura River, for half a mile (0.8 km). Cross a bridge to reach the charming stone hermitage of **Santa Cecilia de Barriosuso** ❷, which dates from the 10th to 13th centuries. Below is a restored Roman bridge and spring.

Return to the BU900 to drive 3 miles (5 km) to **Santo Domingo de Silos.** This idyllic medieval village is the home of the **Monasterio de Santo Domingo de Silos** ❸ *(tel 947 39 00 68, www.abadiadesilos.es, closed Sun. a.m., Mon., & public holidays)*, famous for the hugely successful recordings made by the monks. You can hear their melodic Gregorian chants during Mass *(check daily schedule)* in the 18th-century church. Take time to explore the village's cobbled streets, and then visit the **cloisters.** The lower floor has carved 11th- to 12th-century capitals decorated with harpies and griffons. The ceiling is pure 14th-century Mudejar artistry, and the corner pillars have eight superb Romanesque bas-reliefs illustrating the life of Jesus. Of the many treasures in the **museum,** look for the 11th-century chalice of Santo Domingo, the Romanesque woman's head, the manuscript of the Mozarabic rite (10th–11th century), and the old pharmacy with fine Talavera jars.

From Santo Domingo backtrack 4 miles (6 km) along the BU900, and turn right to Covarrubias. After 7 miles (11 km) you will descend to the village of **Covarrubias** ❹ *(visitor information, tel 947 40 64 61, closed Mon. & Sun. p.m., & mid-Dec.–mid-March),* huddled at the base of the Sierra de las Mamblas. Wander the streets past impeccably maintained medieval houses. The church of San Cosme y San Damián, or **Colegiata** *(tel 947 40 63 11, closed Tues., guided tour only)* is a harmonious white stone Gothic structure begun in 1474. The 400-year-old organ still functions. The delicately carved cloisters, dating from 1528–1535, surround a lovely patio with a fountain and lead to the museum, a treasure trove of statues, papal bulls (documents), and 150 magnificent bishop's capes. The artworks include a painting by Jan van Eyck (circa 1390–1441) and a 16th-century triptych of the Adoration of the Magi.

Leave Covarrubias by following signs to San Pedro de Arlanza, 4 miles (6 km) away on the CL110. Now an evocative ruin undergoing renovation, **San Pedro de Arlanza** ❺ *(tel 689 59 60 64, closed Mon.–Tues., & last weekend of month)* was one of Castilla's largest Benedictine monasteries. The church dates from 1080.

The road continues through a delightful valley, crisscrossing the Arlanza River before joining the N234 at Hortigüela. Turn left here and drive 4.4 miles (7 km) to a turnoff marked Quintanilla de las Viñas. Once you reach the village of Quintanilla de las Viñas, take a right fork marked Ermita Visigótica. A few more bends and you come to the **Ermita Visigótica** ❻ *(tel 626 49 62 15, closed Mon.–Tues., & last weekend of month),* the region's oldest religious structure. It is a simple stone hermitage of the late seventh century, decorated with Visigothic carved friezes.

Return to the N234, turn right and after 2.5 miles (4 km) pass the cave houses of **Cuevas de San Clemente** before returning to Burgos, reconnecting with the A1/E5 at Saldaña de Burgos.

Fields of vivid sunflowers light up the Castillian landscape in summer.

Burgos

This prosperous and ultraconservative city on the Way of St. James has one of Spain's greatest Gothic cathedrals, making it is an essential stop in the barren *meseta* (plateau). Its other Gothic treasures are the monasteries of Las Huelgas and Miraflores, just outside town. Burgos also has the ghost of the heroic warrior and mercenary El Cid, whose legendary exploits ended in death at the hands of the Moors in 1099. His body was entombed in the cathedral in 1921.

Burgos is strung out on both banks of the Arlanza River, but the atmospheric old town lies to the north and can be easily toured on foot. Towering above everything are the lacelike steeples of the **cathedral,** commenced in 1221 and extended over the next five centuries by some of Spain's most outstanding craftsmen. Third in size after the cathedrals of Sevilla and Toledo, it presents an overwhelming display of Flamboyant Gothic design, sculpture, funerary art, carved Renaissance choir stalls, and baroque wrought iron. A rich treasury is housed in the sacristy, the 14th-century **Capilla de Santa Catalina,** and the chapter house, all of which lie off the cloisters. Admission to this area includes access to the main side chapels and the high altar. Look for the "Virgin and Child" by Hans Memling (circa 1430–1494) and Diego de Siloé's "Christ at the Column."

Each of the side chapels is a work of art. Above all is the **Capilla del Condestable,** designed by Simon of Cologne in 1482. West of the nave is the **Capilla de Santa Ana** and the rococo **Capilla de Santa Tecla.**

Just east of the cathedral in the heart of the old quarter is the pedestrianized, arcaded **Plaza Mayor** with its terrace cafés, overlooked by the **Town Hall** (1791).

Cutting-edge architecture surrounds the new **Museo de la Evolucion Humana** (Museum of Human Evolution; *tel 902 02 42 46, closed Mon., www.museoevolucionhumana.com*). Interactive exhibits on early man are inspired by the ongoing archaeological excavations in the **Atapuerca** hills *(tel 902 02 42 46 www.visitasatapuerca.com),* about 14 miles (22 km) east of Burgos.

Toward sunset, when your energy is flagging, take Burgos's tourist train to coincide with the dramatic illumination of 32 monuments along the **Ruta de la Luz** *($, see tourist office for times).* ■

Fiesta de la Matanza

If you happen to find yourself in the bleak midwinter near Burgos, on the third weekend of January, then head for the village of Covarrubias *(visitor information, Oficina de Turismo Municipal s/n, tel 947 40 64 61, www.ecovarrubias.com, map 210 D3)* on the southwestern edge of the beautiful Sierra de la Demanda. This is the site of the age-old *matanza,* or pig slaughter, celebrated by the entire community in the main square at midday. Wine, dancing, music, and, of course, food all day long in the plaza help warm up the crowds.

Burgos
Map: 210 D3
Visitor Information
Address: Centro de Recepción de Turistas, Calle Nuño Rasura 7
Tel: 947 28 88 74
www.aytoburgos.es

Cathedral
Address: Plaza de Santa María
Tel: 947 20 47 12
Fee: $ (cloisters area & chapels)
www.catedraldeburgos.es

More Places to Visit in Castilla y León

EL Burgo de Osma

This delightful town has an air of faded grandeur, especially in the medieval streets surrounding the Gothic **cathedral** *(Plaza de San Pedro 2, closed Mon.)*. Originally built for the Cistercians, it acquired late Gothic cloisters and also has a baroque bell tower and ambulatory. The main attraction of Burgo de Osma are its placid streets, lined with 16th-century porticoes, and majestic buildings such as the **Hospital de San Agustín** (1694) on Plaza Mayor. The hospital was built outside the town wall, but in the late 18th century it was incorporated into a new quarter. Today it is used as an exhibition center. In the arcaded **Calle Mayor,** explore the food shops for local fare: cakes, pâté de foie gras, blood-pudding, and ewe's cheese.

www.burgosma.es 211 E2 **Visitor Information** Oficina de Turismo, Plaza Mayor 9 975 36 01 16

Las Médulas

Added to UNESCO's cultural heritage list in 1997, the Roman gold mines of Las Médulas are this region's most spectacular sight. These remnants of first-century Roman occupation produced five tons of gold in two centuries. They lie 14 miles (22 km) southwest of Ponferrada, close to the Galician border and the Sil River, and cover a vast, desertlike area, interrupted only by gnarled chestnut trees. The reddish ocher crags are most striking toward sundown, when their contours seem to catch fire. A visitor center explains the sophisticated system of hydraulics, tunnels, and channels set up by the Romans, and you can follow trails or drive effortlessly to a viewpoint at Orellán to admire this surreal landscape.

www.fundacionlasmedulas.org 210 B4 619 25 83 55

Tordesillas

The friendly little town of Tordesillas is famed for the 1494 Treaty of Tordesillas, which carved up the New World between Spain and Portugal. Head for the 14th-century **Monasterio de Santa Clara** *(tel 983 77 04 63, closed Mon., guided tour)*, one of Old Castile's best examples of Mudejar art. This includes Sevillian *azulejos* (tiles) and an arched patio. Outstanding features are the church's carved Mudejar ceiling and the 43 paintings of saints. A Gothic side chapel housed the tombs of the Catholic Monarchs, Fernando and Isabel, before they were moved to Granada; its gilded altarpiece is superb. Unusual musical instruments include a portable organ used by Juana the Mad. After the death of her husband, she was declared insane and shut away in Tordesillas for 46 years.

www.tordesillas.net 210 C2 **Visitor Information** Oficina de Turismo, Casas del Tratado 983 77 10 67

San Martín de Frómista

Known by the thousands of people who walk the Camino Francés to Santiago every year, the wheat fields of Palencia are home to some spectacular structures, particularly San Martín de Frómista *(Plaza San Martín s/n, Frómista, tel 979 81 01 28, www.fromista.com, $, free on Wed.)*, one of the most exquisite Romanesque churches in northern Spain. Although heavily restored, the proportions of the golden stone and the detail in its intricately carved capitals are exceptional.

The name Frómista derives from the surrounding wheat fields that made the town's fortune in the tenth century. Its strategic position soon made the town a major stage on the long and lonely trail across Castilla.

A region for heading off the beaten path—from bucolic hills to historic sights and urban surprises like Toledo, Cuenca, and Cáceres

Castilla-La Mancha & Extremadura

In Badajoz, east of Mérida

Castilla-La Mancha & Extremadura

Castilla-La Mancha, that great swath of land that lies between Madrid and Andalucía, seems drab compared with its neighboring regions on all sides—including Extremadura, which is a place of rural delights. For many people Extremadura represents the last bastion of old Spain, sidelined by the dynamism of the country's other autonomous communities, and still an enclave of tradition, Catholicism, and unspoiled countryside.

Castilla-La Mancha does have two points of major interest: Toledo and Cuenca. Toledo, just south of Madrid, is one of Spain's great museum cities. Despite being entirely geared to tourism, it maintains an affable and still individualistic attitude. It was the center of multireligious learning during the Middle Ages, before a long period of intolerance, and is one of those places you simply have to see.

A long leap to the east is Cuenca, perched picturesquely on a cliff and edged by spectacular rock formations. Exhilarating for its setting and for its fantastic museums of abstract art, it is now easy to reach by AVE train from Madrid and Valencia. The area north of Cuenca has beautiful landscapes and the charming town of Sigüenza. The region's central plains are empty except for fields of saffron, the "poor man's gold," and the wetlands of Daimiel. Interest picks up again at Sierra de Alcaraz, which borders Andalucía. La Mancha is the largest vineyard in the world, producing half of Spain's wine. It also grows *ajo morado,* the gourmet garlic tinged with purple.

In Extremadura you enter verdant valleys of olive and cherry trees, rolling wheat fields, sheep pastures, and the Dehesa (wooded hills home to Iberian pigs), an intensely rural land that in the 16th century produced the conquerors of the New World. Two towns are especially redolent of the past: Cáceres, with its monumental upper town of silent Renaissance mansions, and Mérida, once the heart of Roman Lusitania, whose Roman remains are quite exceptional. You can complete a triangular itinerary by also visiting Trujillo, a real charmer of a town

0 80 kilometers
0 40 miles

where historic monuments are integrated into daily life. Extremadura's big religious center is the magnificent monastery of Guadalupe. Emperor Carlos V spent his last contemplative days in the monastery at Yuste, in the north of Extremadura. This is the most bucolic part, where fertile undulating terrain gives good hiking, and villages have unique rural architecture.

Extremadura has cool, wet winters and hot summers, and the plains of La Mancha (whose name derives from the Arabic *manxa,* meaning "dry land") become a furnace in midsummer. Neither region is renowned for innovative gastronomy, but both have an honest cuisine of dishes such as goat or lamb stew, exquisite *pata negra* ham (the best), fresh river trout, game, and La Mancha's vegetable *pisto.* Perhaps the most outstanding characteristic of this part of Spain is its unspoiled nature—here the visitor becomes a benign conquistador. ■

NOT TO BE MISSED:

Cuenca and the otherworldly Ciudad Encantada **236**

Viewing El Greco's glorious paintings in Toledo **238–241**

The Valle del Jerte's springtime cherry blossoms **246–247**

Hiking in the magnificent Parque Nacional de Monfragüe **247**

The lovely, intimate town of Trujillo **251–252**

Soaking up Mérida's Roman heritage **254–255**

Cuenca

Cuenca is Castilla-La Mancha's greatest surprise. It is set spectacularly on a cliff between the Huécar and Júcar Rivers, northeast of the central plains, where the Serranía de Cuenca rises to become a natural frontier with Aragón. The equally dramatic surroundings helped lure dozens of artists here in the 1960s.

Cuenca *(visitor information, Centro de Recepción de Turistas, Avenida de la Cruz Roja 1, tel 969 24 10 50, www.turismocuenca.com, map 235 E3)* is famous for its vertiginous ***casas colgadas*** (hanging houses), best viewed from the Puente de San Pablo. One contains the **Museo de Arte Abstracto Español** *(Calle Canonigos, tel 969 21 29 83, closed Sun. p.m. & Mon., $, www.march.es/cuenca).* On the other side of the bridge stands the **Monasterio de los Paúles,** a parador (see p. 369) and art foundation.

Cuenca's towering houses cling to a rocky precipice.

A few steps away looms the beautiful Gothic-Norman and Renaissance **cathedral** *(Plaza Mayor, tel 969 22 25 06).* Look for the carved walnut door leading to the chapter house and the stained-glass windows. Outside is the trapezoidal **Plaza Mayor.**

At the top of town, in a converted 17th-century convent, the **Fundación Antonio Pérez** *(Convento de las Carmelitas Descalzas, Ronda de Julián Romero, tel 969 23 06 19)* exhibits a vast collection assembled by artist Antonio Pérez.

Ciudad Encantada

The region's most striking spot is the **Ciudad Encantada** (Enchanted City), a surrealistic landscape of eroded rocks 15 miles (25 km) northeast of Cuenca. Three miles (5 km) north lies the **Garganta del Júcar** (Júcar Gorge), best seen through a rock opening nicknamed the **Ventana del Diablo** ("devil's window"). ■

Albacete

Isolated Albacete, in eastern La Mancha, has no great monuments, but lies at a crossroads for routes between central Spain, Valencia on the east coast, and Andalucía. Its name refers to its flat setting, now the scene of intensive cultivation of vines, artichokes, and profitable saffron, introduced by the Moors.

Arabs also brought the art of knife-making, and the quality of Albacete's steel knives and daggers has long been admired. Workshops use time-honored techniques to make knives in all shapes and sizes, so this is the perfect place to restock your kitchen. The new **Museo de la Cuchilleria** *(Plaza de la Catedral, closed Sun. p.m. & Mon., $)* displays old and new designs.

The sleek, modern **Museo de Albacete** *(Parque de Abelardo Sánchez, tel 967 22 83 07, closed Sun. p.m. & Mon., $)* houses prehistoric objects like an Iberian sphinx from Haches and a lion from Bienservida, and Roman artifacts uncovered at the fourth-century necropolis of Ontur. The museum also has a substantial art collection.

Drive 31 miles (50 km) northeast to **Alcalá del Júcar,** a cliff village dominated by a Moorish castle. South of Albacete is **Liétor,** another spectacularly sited village perched above the Mundo River. Narrow medieval streets reflect the village's Moorish past. Do not miss **Chinchilla de Monte Aragón,** with its well-conserved medieval quarter, 15th-century castle, noblemen's houses, and Arab baths. An important potterymaking center, it also has a ceramics museum. Try the provincial specialties, notably partridge, hare, snails, and rabbit. ■

Albacete

235 E2

Visitor Information

Oficina de Turismo, Posada del Rosario, Calle del Tinte 2

967 58 05 22

www.turismocastillalamancha.com

EXPERIENCE: Mad About Saffron

Saffron—the most expensive spice in the world—was first brought to this region by the Romans, then reintroduced by the Moors on a much larger scale. In autumn, fields of purple saffron crocuses blanket the horizon, but as they only flower for a day, harvesting is short-lived and intensive. Handpicking takes place each morning over a couple of weeks between late October and November. The crimson stamens are laboriously removed by expert older women called *mandadoras.* The pistils are then dried and toasted, becoming luscious orange threads.

A perfect place to sample the creative use of saffron is at Michelin-starred **Restaurante Las Rejas** *(General Borrero s/n, Las Pedroñeras, tel 967 16 10 89, www.lasrejas.es),* where chef Manuel de la Osa has concocted a pickled partridge and saffron dish that is simply divine. Or try to catch the rousing **Fiesta de la Rosa del Azafrán,** which marks the end the harvest in Consuegra. The celebration takes place the last weekend in October.

As you savor the saffron, remember that it takes at least 80,000 flowers to produce one pound, which costs about €1,500 ($2,000). With such figures, shady dealing inevitably surrounds the product, and some brands contain a high percentage of other ingredients.

Toledo

Toledo's proximity to Madrid makes it a classic day-trip destination (trains take 30 minutes to reach the stupendous neo-Mudejar station), but its many monuments and eerie nocturnal atmosphere warrant an overnight stay. It is one of Spain's great historic cities, spectacularly sited on a hilltop and practically encircled by the Tajo River. The Greek painter El Greco lived and worked in Toledo until his death in 1614, and left an overwhelming pictorial legacy.

Dominated by the much-reconstructed Alcázar, Toledo was long the spiritual capital of Spain.

Toledo
235 C3
Visitor Information
Oficina de Turismo, Plaza del Consistorial 1
925 25 40 30
Oficina de Turismo, Puerta de Bisagra s/n
925 22 08 43
www.turismocastillalamancha.com

Toledo became the Visigothic capital in A.D. 554 and played a major role for the next eight centuries. It was a flourishing trading center under Moorish rule, when Jews, Muslims, and Christians worked side by side. The three communities continued to prosper peaceably under Christian rule until the mid-14th century, when persecution of the Jewish community began. From 1492, decline set in with the expulsion and repression of Jews and Muslims.

Modern Toledo depends above all on tourism, and you may become jaded at the sight of many multilingual menus and tourist souvenir shops. Plot your route carefully: Toledo is a labyrinth of steep cobbled streets.

The Cathedral

The extraordinary cathedral is the obvious starting point, a symphony of Gothic spires and pinnacles rising over the Plaza del Ayuntamiento. Construction began in 1226, but it took more than 250 years to complete, resulting in a bizarre convergence of styles and artists. Look at the **western portal,** consisting of three heavily sculpted doors (Hell, Pardon, and Judgment), the

Flamboyant Gothic **spire** to the left, and to the right the Renaissance **dome** by the son of El Greco, Jorge Theotocópuli (who also designed the elegant town hall opposite). Access is from the side, in the Calle Cisneros, where you should buy a ticket from the shop opposite to visit the cathedral's treasures.

Inside, between the lofty ribbed columns and 800 stained-glass windows, your first sight is the immense, elaborately sculpted choir. The **choir stalls** are masterpieces, especially the lower, 15th-century ones, carved by Rodrigo Alemán with mythical beasts and battle scenes of the conquest of Granada. Above are 16th-century alabaster seats separated by columns of jasper.

Go around the outer walls of the choir (depicting Old Testament scenes) to the High Altar: The **altarpiece** is a gigantic Flamboyant Gothic polychrome carving of the Life of Christ. To your right is another outsize work, a 30-foot (9 m) mural depicting St. Christopher. Behind the altar is the cathedral's most remarkable architectural and artistic feature, the **Transparente** (1732). This baroque folly was designed by Narciso Tomé to allow light to penetrate from the ceiling and illuminate the tabernacle. It requires a real neck bend to admire the incredible feat of sculptures looking down from the painted dome, where the Virgin evaporates into a cloud of saints and angels.

To the right is the ***sala capitular*** (chapter house), where both the antechamber and main hall have magnificent coffered ceilings, the main one heavy with gold leaf. Below are lovely frescoes by Juan de Borgoña, and a bottom row of portraits of Toledo's powerful archbishops—leaving space for those of the future. Look, too, at the delicately carved wardrobes in the antechamber.

Your next surprise comes in the **sacristy** and **museum.** This is an art galley in itself, rich in El Grecos and work by Zurbarán, Juan de Borgoña, and Goya (note the light and expressions of his "Capture of Christ"). El Greco's dramatic **"El Expolio"** demands attention, but don't miss the exhibits flanking it: a superb Romanesque "Virgin and Child" in silver with a gold filigree crown, and to the right a beautiful 12th-century silver casket that contains the relics of St. Eugenio. The vestry displays more masterpieces—Van Dyck, Velázquez, Titian, and

Cathedral

- ✉ Calle Cisneros
- ☎ 925 22 22 41
- Closed Sun. a.m. & Mon.
- $ $$ (museum, chapter house, treasury, & choir)

Toledo's Sweetest Treat

Of the many Moorish traditions that have survived in Toledo, the most seductive is marzipan. Brought to the city as a delicacy in the eighth century, marzipan was the main treat here until Columbus brought back chocolate from the New World. Today one of the best places to buy it is Santo Tomé *(Calle Santo Tomé, tel 925 22 37 63, www.mazapan.com)*, a family business that has flourished since 1856. At the back of the shop Spanish almonds are combined with sugar, honey, and water to make a thick paste. Once hardened, the marzipan is sculpted into ingenious shapes. You can also buy marzipan at Toledo's many convents.

Alcázar
Calle Union
925 23 88 00
Closed Sun. p.m. & Mon.
$
www.ejercito.mde.es

Hospital y Museo de Santa Cruz
Miguel de Cervantes 3
925 22 10 36
Closed Sun. p.m.

Monasterio de San Juan de los Reyes
Calle de los Reyes Católicos 21
925 22 38 02
$
www.sanjuandelosreyes.org

Rubens—and leads to rooms filled with sumptuous clerical robes, altar dressings (look for the one of silver thread and coral), and embroidered Moorish banners from the 14th century.

In the **treasury** is a 10-foot-high (3 m) gold and silver monstrance made by Enrique de Arfe in the 1520s. Despite its immense weight of almost 400 pounds (180 kg), it is paraded through Toledo during Corpus Christi (May/June). Assorted items around it include the finely illustrated Bible of St. Louis (13th century) and a 15th-century calvary cross painted by Fra Angelico.

East of the Cathedral

Dominating Toledo's skyline, the **Alcázar** is a massive fortress that dates from the Middle Ages but retains little of its original structure. Successive fires in the 18th and 19th centuries wrought havoc with the fabric. Even greater damage came during the Civil War (see pp. 37–38), when Franco's forces withstood a siege and bombardment for ten weeks. Since being rebuilt, the Alcázar has become the headquarters of military organizations, and its exhibits demand a keen interest in army history.

Downhill and just north of the Alcázar you reach the touristic hub of the **Plaza de Zocadover.** Go through the horseshoe arch to reach Toledo's most beautiful Renaissance building, the **Hospital y Museo de Santa Cruz** (1524), a former orphanage. Its delicately carved facade, cloisters, and staircase are plateresque masterpieces by Alonso de Covarrubias (1488–1570), and the patio garden makes a wonderfully serene retreat. It is now Toledo's main museum of art, industrial arts, and archaeology. The lower floor is worth visiting if only to see the giant tusks of a Paleolithic mammoth; also here are Roman mosaics and pottery. The upper floor has paintings by El Greco (including "The Assumption of the Virgin"), Flemish tapestries, sculptures by Pedro de Mena, and local crafts.

West of the Cathedral

The west side of Toledo has a cluster of monuments that demonstrate the medieval coexistence of three cultures. The Franciscan **Monasterio de San Juan de los Reyes** is a massive Flamboyant Gothic construction by Juan Guas (died 1496), with a north portal by Covarrubias. Commissioned by the Catholic Monarchs (see p. 32), it bears traces of their royal patronage. The superb **cloisters** are a harmonious mixture of ornate pinnacles, balustrades, and arches with a Mudejar ceiling on the upper gallery. The **church,** much rebuilt following a French attack in 1808, combines royal escutcheons with Gothic stone tracery.

Close by are two highly significant buildings, former synagogues that are the only reminders of Toledo's once flourishing Jewish community and Jewish quarter, most of which was destroyed in 1491. The **Sinagoga del Tránsito** was commissioned in 1336–1357 by Samuel ha-Leví, a distinguished court adviser. It finally closed in

1494 after Jews were expelled from Spain. Subsequently it functioned as a hospital and a church, but is now the **Museo Sefardí** (Sephardic Museum). It has been completely restored to reveal its original use, with additional rooms illustrating Jewish traditions and the history and presence of Sephardic Jews. The main worship hall, a sumptuous example of Mudejar artistry, incorporates Hebrew and Kufic inscriptions and heraldic shields. Look in particular at the spectacular cedarwood ceiling and intricate stuccowork around the *hejal* (Jewish altar).

In contrast, the **Sinagoga de Santa María la Blanca** *(Calle de los Reyes Católicos 4, tel 925 22 72 57)* has an immaculately restored and whitewashed interior, almost devoid of any exhibits or furnishings. Five aisles are divided by rhythmical horseshoe arches (reminiscent of Córdoba's Mezquita, see pp. 286–287) with identical capitals adorned with plant motifs. By 1405, the synagogue had been converted into a church and had acquired its present name. The three altars were decorated by Covarrubias.

Just behind the Transito synagogue is Toledo's latest must-see, the stunning **Museo del Greco,** reopened in 2011 following an ambitious four-year makeover and after being known for a century as Casa de El Greco ("house of El Greco"—in fact he lived nearby in a far more modest house). The beautiful garden is now connected to the original house by a luminous glass pavilion. The jewels of the collection are the Apostolado, El Greco's series of portraits of the Apostles, and his outstanding "Las Lagrimas de San Pedro." In the library hangs "Vista y plano de Toledo," an extraordinary aerial view of his adopted city. Backing up these masterpieces are more than a hundred paintings by Spanish masters of the 16th and 17th centuries, and a display on the Marquis of Vega-Inclán (1858–1942), a key patron of the arts who was responsible for the revival of El Greco's painting. Uphill from here, the church of **Santo Tomé** *(Plaza del Conde, tel 925 25 60 98)* houses El Greco's masterpiece, the **"Burial of the Count of Orgaz"** (1586), an unmissable site.

Museo Sefardí (Sephardic Museum)

- ✉ Calle Samuel Leví
- ☎ 925 22 36 65
- 🕒 Closed Sun. p.m. & Mon.
- $ $. Free Sat. p.m. & Sun. a.m.

Museo del Greco

- ✉ Paseo del Tránsito
- ☎ 925 22 36 65
- 🕒 Closed Sun. p.m. & Mon.
- $ $

www.museodelgreco.mcu.es

Celebrating Corpus Christi in Toledo's cathedral

Opposite the Tránsito, the **Museo de Escultura Victorio Macho,** set in gardens overlooking the Tagus River, makes a delightful escape. Inside are works by the figurative artist Victorio Macho (1887–1966), who, after political exile in South America, spent the last years of his life in Toledo. ■

Museo de Escultura Victoria Macho

- ✉ Plaza de Victorio Macho
- ☎ 925 28 42 25
- 🕒 Closed Sun. p.m.
- $ $

A Walk Around Toledo

This walk takes you through the characteristically steep, high-walled streets of Toledo's convent neighborhood, stopping at intriguing churches, convents, and even a mosque—a synopsis of this once spiritual city.

The typically tall buildings of Toledo are at their best during festival season.

Start from the **cathedral** ❶ and walk up the slope beside the **Palacio Arzobispal** (Archbishop's Palace) opposite. On the pretty Plaza Consistorial at the top, turn right and walk up Cuesta de la Ciudad. Turn right and then left into narrow Callejón de Jesus María beside ECAT, a contemporary art center. At the top turn right, where you will see the imposing baroque facade of **San Ildefonso.**

Turn left beside the church into Calle de San Román, which leads to **San Román** ❷; the entrance is around the corner in Calle San Clemente. San Román is Toledo's oldest church. Of Visigothic origin, it was later used as a mosque before being rebuilt in Mudejar style in the 13th century. Now it is a museum of Visigothic culture, the **Museo de los Concilios y de la Cultura Visigoda** *(Iglesia de San Román, Calle de San Román, tel 925 22 78 72, closed Sun. p.m. & Mon.).* The unusual interior combines Caliphal arches, Roman columns, Visigothic and Mozarabic capitals, and wonderful frescoes.

On leaving the church, walk down the street opposite and turn left at the bottom into Plaza de Padilla. Cross the square diagonally past the Convento San Clemente, where you can buy marzipan (see sidebar p. 239). Descend the steps, and then turn right to skirt **Santo Domingo el Antiguo** ❸ *(tel 925 22 29 30, closed Sun. a.m.),* Toledo's first convent, founded in 1085 by Cistercians. The church is neoclassical inside and has three paintings by El Greco, as well as several copies. Two of the originals (depicting John the Baptist and San Bernard) are part of the altarpiece; the third is the exceptional **"Resurrection of Christ"** hanging to the right of this area. Switch on the lights to peer through a grille at the coffered ceiling of the chapter

NOT TO BE MISSED:

San Román • Santo Domingo el Antiguo • Mezquita del Cristo de la Luz.

house and through the floor at El Greco's tomb. The choir and adjoining antechamber have a superb coffered ceiling, a carved head of John the Baptist by Pedro de Mena (see p. 46), a painting by Luca Giordano (1634–1705), and richly embroidered altar dressings.

Walk down Calle de Santa Leocadia and turn right into Calle Real, passing the provincial council building. Turn right and immediately left at the end through a typically narrow, high-sided lane, Calle Buzones. This brings you to baroque **Santo Domingo el Real,** one of several convents around the square. Walk through the *cobertizo* (a bridged-over passageway), turn right up another, and you come to the 13th-century Mudejar church of **San Vicente.** On your left is **Las Gaitanas,** a cloistered convent; beyond San Vicente is the neoclassic **Palacio de Lorenzana.** Turn left into Calle de los Alfileritos, and then take the third lane on your left, Calle del Cristo de la Luz. This brings you downhill to the **Mezquita del Cristo de la Luz** ❹ *(Calle del Cristo de la Luz, tel 925 25 41 91)*, an exquisite restored mosque dating from A.D. 999, with a 12th-century Romanesque sanctuary.

See also area map pp. 234–235
➤ Plaza del Ayuntamiento
1.5–2 hours
1.7 miles (2.7 km)
➤ Mezquita del Cristo de la Luz

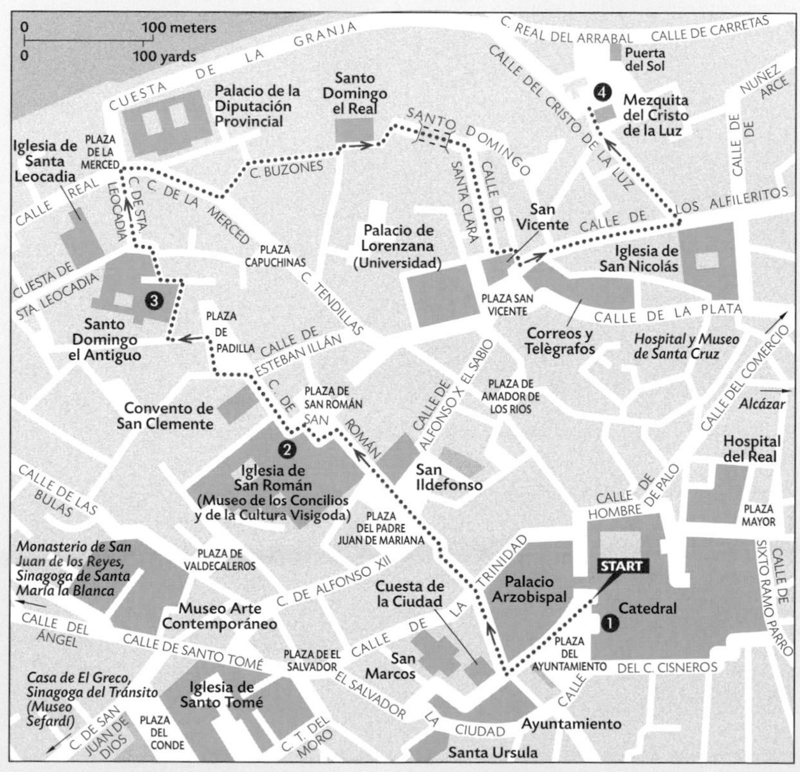

Guadalupe

Mexico's much revered patron saint, the Virgin of Guadalupe, originated here, a village in the remote green hills of Extremadura, where a miraculous image of the Virgin was found seven centuries ago. This black-faced Virgin became the patron of "all Spains," the very essence of Spanishness, and her shrine continues to attract streams of pilgrims.

The sanctuary of the Real Monasterio de Santa Maria

Guadalupe
234 B2
Visitor Information
Oficina de Turismo, Plaza de Santa María de Guadalupe s/n
927 15 41 28

A huge monastery and church dominate the pretty hillside village, where medieval streets lined with flower-filled balconies radiate from a wide plaza in front of the church. The 12th-century statue of the Virgin, allegedly carved by St. Luke, inspired the building of the Hieronymite **Real Monasterio de Santa María** *(tel 927 36 70 00, $, guided tours only, www.monasterioguadalupe.com)* in 1340. It is now run by Franciscans, who have undertaken extensive restoration. There is a very pleasant guesthouse in the Gothic cloisters.

The golden-stone church facade rises between crenellated towers. In the church all attention is focused on the altarpiece and its diminutive, caped figure of the Virgin. You get a closer look in the Camarín above, a small, highly decorated 18th-century chapel. This is where your guide spins the image around to face the crowd of expectant pilgrims. In the nearby **Relicario** are the Virgin's rich wardrobe and crown, reserved for processions.

The **Museo de Bordados** is an embroidery museum, with monks' needlework from the 15th to 19th centuries. In the **Museo de Pinturas y Esculturas** (paintings and sculptures), look for an ivory sculpture of Christ, said to be by Michelangelo, and the beautiful small portraits of monks by Zurbarán. The **chapter house** has a dazzling collection of illuminated psalmbooks. Structurally the most interesting section of the monastery is the **Claustro Mudejar,** an unusually large, two-story cloister of horseshoe arches. ■

Sierra de la Peña de Francia

This range is part of the rugged Cordillera Central that continues into the craggy Sierra de Gredos, and is a natural border between Castilla y León and Extremadura. The highest peak, Peña de Francia, rises to 5,682 feet (1,732 m), and its tortuous access road gives panoramic views west toward Portugal, east to the Sierra de Gredos, and north over the Castilian meseta.

The most interesting place to head is **La Alberca** in Castilla y León, a charming, restored mountain village of stone and half-timbered houses on cobbled streets. For centuries its remoteness preserved local traditions and religious zeal, but national monument status has resulted in a steady stream of visitors in summer. If you can, time your visit for August 15, when villagers don exuberantly embroidered costumes to enact a mystery play celebrating the triumph of the Virgin over the Devil.

Immediately south, over the Portillo pass, the dramatic road (SA201) descends into the bucolic valley of **Las Batuecas**—protected as a nature park. Rock formations in startling shapes harbor prehistoric cave paintings.

Las Batuecas is located on the edge of **Las Hurdes,** a region brought to fame by Luis Buñuel in his 1932 film *Tierra Sin Pan (Land Without Bread),* which portrayed its extreme hardship and poverty. Today life in Las Hurdes has improved, but there remains a distinctive wildness in the landscape, and a time-warped atmosphere in the tiny whitewashed hamlets and stone farmhouses.

Follow the C515 to see attractive **Miranda del Castañar** before reaching **Béjar,** a fortified hilltop town, and then go southeast to **Hervás.** This village preserves a remarkable old **Jewish quarter** among its leaning, half-timbered houses. The maze of narrow streets with a backdrop of snowcapped peaks makes a rewarding stroll. ■

Béjar

234 B3

Visitor Information

Oficina de Turismo, Carretera de Salamanca s/n

923 40 30 05

www.aytobejar.com

Hervás

234 B3

Visitor Information

Oficina de Turismo, Calle Braulio Navas 6

927 47 36 18

www.hervas.com

The Mesta

In Spain, transhumance (the seasonal movement of livestock) became a structured part of life in medieval Castilla. Too insecure for settled farming, the no-man's-land that existed between Christian and Moorish Spain was used only by shepherds and drovers. Once reconquered by the Christians, however, the land was settled and a powerful group of sheep owners, the Mesta, funded by the immense profits from merino wool, took shape. As the first and most influential agricultural union in medieval Europe, the Mesta enjoyed privileges granted by the kings of Castilla. Even today, although sheep may be transported by rail, the ancient *cañadas* (traditional rights of way for sheep) are protected by law. The entire network zigzags an incredible 78,000 miles (125,529 km) from Andalucía north to Castilla. Even some Madrid streets, notably La Castellana, still see sheep migration through them as a reminder of ancient rights.

In & Around Plasencia

Dramatically sited on a hilltop above the Jerte River, against a backdrop of jagged limestone outcrops, the "pearl of the Jerte" is a fine base for explorations of the beautiful Valle del Jerte. South are the rural delights of the Valle de la Vera, and the monastery to which Carlos V retired in 1556, exhausted from the burden of being Holy Roman Emperor.

Valle de la Vera is a major producer of tobacco, vegetables, goat cheese, and *pimentón* (paprika).

Plasencia
234 B3
Visitor Information
Oficina de Turismo, Plaza Santa Clara 2
927 42 38 43
www.plasencia.com

Valle del Jerte
234 B3
Visitor Information
Oficina de Turismo Mancomunidad, Paraje de Peñas Alba s/n
927 47 25 58
www.turismovalledeljerte.com

Plasencia

Plasencia's star attraction is the **cathedral,** which, like Salamanca's (see pp. 218–220), combines two distinct periods and buildings: the old Romanesque-Gothic cathedral, dating from the 13th and 14th centuries, and, linked to it by cloisters, the **new cathedral.** Completed in Renaissance style in the early 16th century by some of Spain's best architects of the time, the latter is Extremadura's most ornate church. Look in particular at the **dome** of the chapel of San Pablo, the beautiful plateresque north **portal,** the **sculptures** by Gregorio Fernández for the main altar (1634), and the carved **choir stalls** (1520).

Handsome mansions line the streets around the **Plaza Mayor,** where every Tuesday sees a bountiful food market dating from the Middle Ages. The Casa del Dean, Palacio Episcopal, and Casa de las Dos Torres are worth finding, and the **Museo la Etnográfico** *(Plaza Marqués de la Puebla, tel 927 42 18 43, closed Sun. p.m., Mon., & Tues.)* gives insight into the area's rural traditions, above all textiles.

Valle del Jerte

The beautiful Valle del Jerte is rich in cherry trees: More than 30 varieties of cherries are grown here on an estimated one million trees, the biggest production area in Europe, peaking with the prized picota cherry. Imagine the blossom in spring, or, better still, be here to see it. It only lasts ten days, a movable feast from mid-March to early April. From May to July, visit any of the 11 towns in the valley for a close-up on cherry-related activities: Families pick and sort them, and you can take guided tours of the cooperatives where cherries are bottled and turned into liqueurs.

Near the village of Jerte is the **Reserva Natural Garganta de los Infiernos,** a stunning nature reserve of torrential waterfalls that gives really scenic, though tough, hiking, and extends to **Tornavacas.** This is the last village before the border with Castilla y León, 4 miles (6 km) away at the Puerto de Tornavacas mountain pass (4,183 feet/1,275 m). Slotted between the towering sierras of Gredos and Béjar, Tornavacas has only one main street, Calle Real. At **No. 23** is the inn where Carlos V spent the night on his way to the monastery at Yuste in 1556.

Valle de la Vera

To the south is Valle de la Vera, reached on the EX203 west from Plasencia. The main historical interest is at Jarandilla and Yuste, but you find traditional architecture at any of the rural villages. One of the prettiest is **Cuacos;** walk or drive 1 mile (1.6 km) uphill to the monastery.

Carlos V, depressed with court life and political intrigues, chose to retire to the simple Hieronymite **Monasterio de Yuste** in 1556. He stayed until his death in 1558.

To complete this imperial tour, visit **Jarandilla,** just 3 miles (5 km) northeast of the monastery, where the magnificent 15th-century **castle** welcomed Carlos V while he awaited the completion of his quarters at Yuste. The **church of Jarandilla** was built by the Knights Templar, and the castle stands on the ruins of the Templar fortress. Although austere from the outside, this Renaissance edifice conceals a gracious home centered on a verdant courtyard, and has become, not surprisingly, a parador (see p. 348).

INSIDER TIP:

To party like a Spaniard, consider sampling some *calimocho.* This mixture of red wine and Coca Cola is very popular at festivals across the country.

—RACHAEL JACKSON
Research Manager, National Geographic Channels

Parque Nacional de Monfragüe

Southeast of Plasencia lies the Parque Nacional de Monfragüe, sliced by the Tajo River and blanketed in Mediterranean scrub and forest. Created to protect the rare flora and fauna of this region, notably Iberian lynxes, boars, badgers, imperial eagles, black storks, and numerous vultures, it offers fantastic hiking opportunities. In 2003 the park was enlarged to 453 square miles (1,175 sq km) and in 2007 became a national park. ■

Monasterio de Yuste

- Cuacos de Yuste
- 927 17 21 97
- Guided tour only. Closed Mon.

Jarandilla

- Plaza de la Constitución
- 927 56 04 60

www.jarandilla.com

Parque Nacional de Monfragüe

- 234 B3

Visitor Information

- Centro de Información, Villareal de San Carlos (on Plasencia-Trujillo road)
- 927 19 91 34

www.monfrague.com

Miguel de Cervantes & Don Quixote

Trotting across the plains of La Mancha are the ghosts of Don Quixote and his faithful squire, Sancho Panza, two comical but darkly allegorical figures created by Miguel de Cervantes (1547–1616). From its initial aim to be a parody of traditional romantic ballads and tales of knights errant, this book became a universally popular synthesis of the Renaissance. It is also a racy adventure story crammed with amusing, earthy characters.

Born in Alcalá de Henares, Cervantes started adult life as a soldier. He participated in the naval victory of Lepanto (1571) against the Ottoman Turks, where injuries left him with a crippled arm. He then ran into trouble when captured by pirates on his return to Spain in 1575. Enslaved for five years in Algiers, he made several unsuccessful attempts to escape before he was ransomed by his family.

Cervantes led a disillusioned, outsider's life, not helped by an unhappy marriage or the menial jobs with which he made a living. He wrote when he was in prison, and from 1608 he was able to devote himself entirely to literary pursuits while living in Madrid. Little is known about the man himself except that he was reserved, cautious, and at times aggressive. He was 50 before he realized his own talent for narrative, first glimpsed in his unsuccessful pastoral novel, *La Galatea* (1585), and later in his short stories, *The Exemplary Novels* (1613).

Don Quixote perceived windmills as giants.

The multiple dimensions of Don Quixote stretched Cervantes's imaginative powers to the fullest and brought him instant success. Publication of the first part of the book in 1605 was followed rapidly by pirate editions within just a few weeks, and made the public avid for more. This finally appeared ten years later, just one year before the author's death, and was a much deeper and more subtle text. Described at this point by a French visitor as "old, a soldier, a gentleman and poor," Cervantes nevertheless died knowing that his creation had become famous, with translations into French and English.

In Don Quixote's illusory, innocent world, the windmills of La Mancha become giants, and heroic misadventures are inspired by his parallel vision of reality. The knight's noble, eccentric generosity, set against the commonsensical, often skeptical attitudes of his faithful servant, Sancho Panza, becomes an allegory about human perception: Things can be real or ideal, feasible or fantastic, sane or insane. Don Quixote's descent into madness, accentuated by his awareness of it, is finally cured only by death. Ironically it is Sancho who has the hero's return. In the words of the English writer V. S. Pritchett, "The extreme strains of the Spanish nature are celebrated in these two characters: the passionate tendency to fantasy, the fatal reaction into skepticism, realism, and cynicism." Four hundred years after the publication of his masterpiece, Cervantes's analysis still holds true.

Cáceres

This is stork city, where white storks nest on towers, chimneys, and TV antennae in spring and summer. They are visible all over Extremadura and La Mancha. Cáceres displays its noble past in a walled hilltop quarter where emblazoned facades, lofty towers, archways, and winding cobbled streets create an inimitable atmosphere. Walk around it at night to admire spotlit history in peace.

The town hall dominates generous Plaza Mayor in Cáceres.

To taste real life in this provincial capital you have to explore the **lower town,** which centers on Plaza Mayor. Steps here lead up to **Moorish walls,** some of their rubble masonry towers still intact. At the **Arco de la Estrella,** an 18th-century arch, enter the **Torre de Bujaco** to see a display on Cáceres history and climb to the ramparts for good views *(tel 927 24 67 89, closed Mon.)*.

Then enter the venerable old quarter at its heart, **Plaza de Santa María.** Go inside the cathedral of **Santa María** *(tel 927 24 52 50)* to admire the Gothic vaulting, serene proportions, and Renaissance details. Just behind is the **Palacio de Carvajal,** home of the local tourist board. Enter the lovely courtyard, see the garden at the back, and don't miss the Moorish tower with fragments of 16th-century frescoes. In the lobby a model of old Cáceres gives a clear idea of the various palaces.

Facing the cathedral across the square are three beautiful Renaissance mansions, all of the honey and gray stone typical of Cáceres: the **Palacio de Hernando de Ovando,** the **Palacio de Mayoralgo,** and the **Palacio Episcopal.** The first was built by the Ovando family. Nicolás Ovando was

Cáceres

234 B2

Visitor Information

Oficina de Turismo, Calle Ancha 7

927 24 71 72

www.turismo.ayto-caceres.es

Palacio de Carvajal

Calle Amargura 1

927 25 55 97

Closed Sun. p.m.

San Francisco Javier
Plaza de San Jorge 8
927 24 51 71

San Manteo
Open only for 12 p.m. & 8 p.m. Mass

appointed governor of the Indies by the Catholic Monarchs, taking over from Christopher Columbus and Francisco de Bobadilla. Closed to the public, the palace now houses administrative offices.

Stepped back from the cathedral to the south is the magnificent **Palacio de los Golfines de Abajo,** whose tower overlooks Plaza San Jorge. The facade combines late-Gothic and plateresque decoration of the 15th and 16th centuries: Look in particular at the rooftop balustrade of carved birds and the medieval tower. Looming above the little plaza is a very different style of building, the whitewashed 18th-century church of **San Francisco Javier.** Art and photography exhibitions are regularly held here.

At the top of the wide steps flanking the church is another delightful square, **Plaza de las Veletas,** centering on the church of **San Mateo.** Next to it stands the crenellated tower of **Casa de las Cigüeñas** (House of Storks), the only tower in this quarter not to have been lopped off—a sign that its owner, Diego de Ovando, was a supporter of Isabel in the civil war of the 1470s (see p. 31). Behind these monuments stretches the old Jewish quarter, now the Barrio San Antonio: A chapel has replaced the old synagogue.

On the south side of the square, is the elegant Casa de las Veletas, now the excellent **Museo de Cáceres.** Here you find a good collection of prehistoric and Roman artifacts, and regional ethnographic exhibits including beautiful weavings, lace, costumes, and ceramics. Downstairs is the star exhibit, an Arab *aljibe* (cistern) with perfectly conserved horseshoe arches. Across the garden a modernized **annex** displays fine art, a rather motley collection including etchings by Picasso and Miró, and "Jesus Salvador" by El Greco.

Before leaving this square, notice the ivy-draped **Torre de los Plata,** behind San Mateo, then descend Calle Ancha past more emblazoned palaces to the parador (see p. 348), the former mansion of the Marquises of Torreorgaz. This is the perfect place to have a drink or a meal. ■

EXPERIENCE: Bird Festivals

Extremadura is widely regarded as one of Europe's best birding regions, and the cities of Cáceres and Trujillo in particular are recognized as ornithological paradises. Here you see flocks of screeching swifts, acrobatic kestrels, flycatchers, and jackdaws, among others. In mid-May, Cáceres hosts the **Festival de las Aves** *(www.festivaldelasavescaceres.com)*, which includes city bird-watching, bird-banding, and even a photography marathon: Snappers are given 24 hours to photograph birds in the city and its environs. In early December, Extremadura as a whole celebrates the **Festival de las Grullas** *(www.festivaldelasgrullas.com)*, which marks the arrival of 80,000 cranes *(grullas)* that have winged their way 2,500 miles (4,000 km) to their winter quarters, north of the Tagus River. For other birding events in the region, consult *www.birdingextremadura.com.*

Trujillo

This delightful little town is a pleasure to visit, with a network of fine old buildings, exuberant vegetation—cactuses, palms, olives, oranges, and magnolias—and plenty of life. Trujillo's renown, however, is due to one man: the conquistador Francisco Pizarro, who conquered the Incas of Peru. His statue (erected in 1927, and identical to one in Lima) reigns supreme over the Plaza Mayor, surrounded by palaces paid for with plunder from Latin America.

Trujillo's church of Santa María la Mayor was once a Muslim mosque.

All Trujillo's narrow, winding streets eventually lead to this large, irregular square (actually more of a triangle). **Plaza Mayor** is the social hub of the town, lined by sidewalk cafés, restaurants, and illustrious palaces. It is flanked by wide steps leading up to their porticoes, and the rather severe church of San Martín rises in the north corner. Opposite the church is the **Palacio Carvajal-Vargas** (or Palacio de Duques de San Carlos), a sober late Renaissance building. It was handed over to Hieronymite nuns (hermits of St. Jerome—a medieval religious order also called Jeronymite) in the 1960s, so public access is unfortunately restricted. Pull the bell chain in the entrance hall and a nun will open up, attempt to sell you cakes, and then wave you across the handsome patio toward the palace's most curious feature. The steps of this 17th-century staircase are not attached to the wall but held together by an interlocking structure, which has earned it the name "flying."

Trujillo

Map 234 B2

Visitor Information

- Oficina de Turismo, Plaza Mayor s/n
- 927 32 26 77
- $ ($ combined ticket includes 4 monuments)

www.ayto-trujillo.com

Francisco Pizarro

The actions of this illiterate, illegitimate son of a captain eventually led to the death of an estimated five million Incas. In 1513, Pizarro (ca 1478–1541) accompanied another Extremaduran explorer, Vasco Núñez de Balboa, on his expedition to the Pacific, and in 1524 began searching the coasts of Ecuador and Peru for the legendary Inca empire.

He discovered it in 1532, had the Inca emperor Atahualpa treacherously killed in 1533, and founded the city of Lima two years later. Pizarro's ambition and ruthlessness eventually turned against him, when he was assassinated by the followers of Diego de Almagro, a fellow explorer whom Pizarro had double-crossed.

At the other end of the square, the more ornate **Palacio del Marqués de la Conquista** was built by Hernando Pizarro, Francisco's brother. Its richly emblazoned corner, added in the 17th century, displays busts of the two brothers and their wives. From here you can walk up to explore the upper town by following the Cañon de la Cárcel, a passageway in the corner of the Palacio de la Justicia next to the Pizarro mansion.

Go around the corner to your right and you come to the harmonious facade of the 16th-century **Palacio Orellana-Pizarro,** now a convent school. Francisco de Orellana was another of Trujillo's conquistadores, the first European to explore the Amazon. You can enter the beautiful patio for a small fee and look for the ghost of Miguel de Cervantes, author of *Don Quixote* (see sidebar p. 248), who once stayed here.

By circling this mansion into the Cuesta de la Sangre, you pass another imposing Renaissance palace, before turning left through the archway of Santiago. This brings you to the charming **church of Santiago,** where a Romanesque bell tower stands beside a basically Gothic structure. The scenic path beside the church takes you along the old **town walls,** built by the Moors in the 13th century to defend their 10th-century castle from Christian attacks. Views take in Trujillo's abundant stork population nesting on every available tower. The **castle** stands above, an imposing sight of crenellated walls and sturdy towers. There is little inside, however, except the revered statue of the Virgen de la Victoria, the patron saint of Trujillo, who can easily be seen from outside in her glassed eyrie.

Take Calleja de los Martires to the left and you soon come to the **Casa-Museo Pizarro,** a 15th-century house where the conquistador was born. Inside, period furniture and conquistador memorabilia are shown with Inca artifacts. A few steps farther bring you to the Gothic **church of Santa María la Mayor,** which holds the tombs of Trujillo's explorers. It also has a lovely main altarpiece painted by Fernando Gallegos. Climb the Romanesque bell tower for sweeping views over Trujillo's tiled roofs to the distant Sierra de Guadalupe. ■

EXPERIENCE: The Heart of *Jamón*

Millions of Spaniards love *jamón,* cured ham with historic roots in Extremadura. Velvety, top-grade *jamón ibérico de bellota* is irresistible and experiencing a boom worldwide, easily beating its Italian rival, *prosciutto di Parma,* in flavor and, some say, in purity. (The more common *jamón serrano,* from the white pig, keeps Spain's tapas bars and corner shops in business.) To sample this regional delicacy join a specialized tour or create your own itinerary.

In the 1970s, the pure Iberian pig was virtually extinct, replaced by northern European breeds of white pig that could be industrially farmed. Luckily, the Iberian pig was saved by the first *denominaciones de origen* or D.O. (regional food classification) in the late 1980s and eventually made a triumphant recovery.

Land of Jamón Ibérico

For an in-depth and expert introduction to Iberian ham, consider the four-day regional tour *($$$$)* offered by **A Taste of Spain** *(Calle Alonso Cano 8, Cádiz, tel 856 07 96 26 or 956 23 28 80, www.atasteofspain.com).*

Beginning in Sevilla, you will travel northwest through the **Dehesa,** where rolling meadows dotted with ancient holm oaks provide essential autumnal fodder for the pigs. See them up close and learn about how they are raised at one of the area's private farms.

Charcoal-colored with floppy ears and long snouts, the pigs totter around freely, snuffling for the sweet acorns whose flavor finds its way into their fat. (Never discard the fat when eating: It is delicious, nutritious, and may even lower cholesterol.)

The *montanera,* or main feeding period, lasts roughly from October to February. The pigs must devour enough acorns to reach the 353 pounds (160 kg) necessary to be recognized as Iberian. Once the pigs have fattened up, the *matanza,* or slaughter, a collective endeavor takes place, usually on local farms.

In the small town of **Jabugo,** a master *jamonero* (ham specialist) will show you how the ham is cured. Following the slaughter, legs are packed in sea salt for 10–12 days, then rinsed and hung under controlled conditions for 18 months to as many as three years. Finally, it is ready for consumption. In **Zafra** (see p. 257), you will enjoy a meal of Iberian delicacies and local wines.

Where & When to Find the Best Jamón

The town of **Jerez de los Caballeros** (see pp. 256–257) holds its Feria del Jamón in the second week of May, while **Monasterio** holds its festival *(www.jamondemonesterio.org)* in early September. In early December, **Montánchez** puts on the Jornadas Gastronomicas del Cerdo Ibérico. Other centers of Extremaduran ham are **Fregenal de la Sierra, Cabeza la Vaca,** and **Oliva de la Frontera.**

The progression of *jamón* from pig to plate is a highly regulated process.

Mérida

With a street named after John Lennon, Mérida, capital of Extremadura, is not exactly buried in its past. It is a lively town that has been developing on the eastern bank of the Guadiana River ever since 25 B.C., after which it became capital of the Roman province of Lusitania. It has more Roman remains than any other Spanish town except Tarragona, and since 1986, a superlative museum has displayed the best of its Roman artifacts. Avoid the city in midsummer.

Ancient Romans worshipped the emperor not the goddess in Mérida's Temple of Diana.

Mérida

234 B2

Visitor Information

Oficina Municipal de Turismo, Calle José Sáenz de Buruaga s/n

924 33 07 22

Closed Sat. & Sun. p.m.

www.merida.es

The most impressive sights in Mérida are the **Teatro Romano y Anfiteatro** (Roman theater and amphitheater), both built of blocks of granite. The majestic colonnaded levels of the theater facing the semicircular terraced seats are absolutely magnificent. Visit in July or August to watch Mérida's theater festival, when the entire structure returns to its original function. It holds 6,000 spectators. A few yards away is the vast amphitheater, with a capacity for 14,000 people. This was used for gladiator combats, chariot races, and mock sea battles, for which the arena was flooded.

Close by, the **Casa del Anfiteatro** displays the ruins of a third- to fourth-century villa still being excavated. Note the mosaic floors. Another villa, **Casa de Mitreo** *(Calle Oviedo, tel 924 30 15 04)*, a five-minute walk southwest, displays the beautiful Mosaico Cosmológico, a lyrical mosaic rendering of the Roman gods. The fifth-century **basilica of Santa Eulalia** contains the relics of the martyr, Santa Eulalia. Since 1990, major excavations have revealed the successive stages of its long history. It stands east of the Plaza de España *(Avenida de Extremadura).*

The star of today's show is the **Museo Nacional de Arte Romano** opposite the theater and amphitheater. This brilliantly conceived design by Rafael Moneo evokes Roman architecture in a purist, sympathetic style. Captions are in Spanish, but ask for a leaflet in English at the ticket desk. The vast, skylit main hall exhibits superb sculptures, architectural details, and mosaics, with two mezzanine galleries rising to one side. The first mezzanine concentrates on daily objects (glass, pottery, lamps, coins, dice) and the second, not to be missed, has thematic displays, including an exceptional section of sculpted heads. Huge **mosaic panels** add to the general impact. In the main hall, don't miss the beautiful **seated figure of Ceres,** goddess of agriculture, or the trio of the imperial family (Augustus, Tiberius, and Drusus, in the end alcove). In Section IX, look especially for the **torso of Thorocatus,** with its remarkable depiction of movement in the tasseled strips of his uniform.

End your visit in the **crypt** below, where ruins of first- and second-century houses with murals and tombs were found during construction of the museum. From here, a tunnel leads directly into the amphitheater precinct.

From the museum, walk downhill (northwest) to the town center and turn left into Calle Sagasta. On your right you soon see the ruins of the **Forum** and then the magnificent **Temple of Diana.** Although named after the goddess of hunting, it was in fact dedicated to the cult of the emperor. Immediately behind is the Renaissance mansion of the counts of Corbos. Two blocks farther is the **Plaza de España,** dotted with orange and palm trees. The **Town Hall** (1883) and the ceramic-faced folly of the **Palacio de la China** are particularly striking. The square has outdoor cafés, and is a good spot to relax before you visit the riverside **Alcazaba** *(Calle Graciano s/n, tel 924 00 49 08),* a ninth-century Moorish fortress incorporating Roman and Visigothic details. It has a majestic cistern built into the rock. From the Alcazaba you get wonderful views of the **Roman bridge,** its 60 arches stretching 866 yards (792 m) across the river. ■

INSIDER TIP:

While in Spain, don't pass up an offer of homemade paella. Each dish usually has its own delicious secret ingredient.

—ALED GREVILLE
National Geographic operations staff

Teatro Romano y Anfiteatro

- ✉ Paseo José Álvarez Sáez de Buruaga
- ☎ 924 31 25 30
- $ $$ ($$ combined ticket includes Casa de Mitreo, Alcazaba, & Santa Eulalia excavations)

www.merida.es/guiaturistica/monumentos

Museo Nacional de Arte Romano

- ✉ Calle José Ramón Mérida
- ☎ 924 31 16 90
- ⌚ Closed Sun. p.m. & Mon.
- $ $. Free Sat. p.m. & Sun. a.m.

www.arteromano.mcu.es

Frontier Towns

The towns of Olivenza, Jerez de los Caballeros, and Zafra in southern Extremadura are close to two borders: that of Portugal across the Guadian River, and that of the vast sweep of Andalucía to the south. History here is inextricably linked to this strategic position and to the Christian Reconquest of Muslim land. As a result this pastoral landscape is dotted with fortresses.

The sumptuously carved bell tower of San Miguel (1749) rises over the Plaza de España in Jerez de los Caballeros.

Olivenza

Nudging the Portuguese border, the fortified town of Olivenza was actually in Portuguese hands for 600 years. This has left it with an interesting dual character. The castle, with a mighty keep rising nearly 100 feet (30 m), was built by Juan II of Portugal in the 15th century; this and the former royal bakery now house the **Museo Etnográfico** *(tel 924 49 02 22, closed Sun p.m. & Mon.)*. The **church of Santa María Magdalena** is Spain's only example of 16th-century Manueline Gothic, a Portuguese style. The spiraling columns, slender rib-vaulting, *azulejos* (tiles), and genealogical tree of the Virgin crowning the altar are outstanding features. Close to the Puerta de los Angeles stands the **Casa de la Misericordia,** notable for a chapel faced in azulejos.

Seven miles (11 km) north of Olivenza stand the ruins of the 1,246-foot (380 m) **bridge of Ajuda** across the Olivenza River. Built by Manuel I of Portugal, it frequently became a battleground in the wars fought over this region.

Jerez de los Caballeros

About 50 miles (80 km) southeast, Jerez de los Caballeros became a stronghold of the Knights Templar after being captured from the Moors in 1230. In the hilltop town center is the Templar castle, with Moorish remains still visible in the renovated structure. Other landmarks are the 1759 **church of San Bartolomé** *(Plaza de San Bartolomé)*, a dazzling combination of inlaid ceramic and gilt, and **Santa María** *(Llano de Santa María)*, both with baroque towers. Keys for both churches are at the tourist office. The pretty whitewashed streets produced one of Extremadura's adventurers, Vasco Núñez de Balboa (1475–1517), the first European to cross the Central American isthmus and see the Pacific.

Jerez is famous for colorful celebrations during Semana Santa (Holy Week), and for its pork festival in May (see p. 253). Several dolmens (prehistoric stone tombs) are in the area. The most striking is the **Dolmen del Torriñuelo** *(5 miles/8 km northeast of town at La Granja)*.

Zafra

About 30 miles (50 km) east of Jerez de los Caballeros is Zafra, which some call a miniature Sevilla. Zafra has a wonderfully homogeneous 18th-century center full of whitewashed houses and large mansions, their architectural details picked out in saffron yellow.

The town's history started with the Moors, but fame and fortune came in the 1440s following construction of a massive stone castle, the **Alcázar,** by the Dukes of Feria. Although this is now a parador (see p. 348), you can visit the vast, graceful Renaissance patio (the work of Juan de Herrera, architect of El Escorial, see pp. 77–79). Ask to see the superb gilded *artesonado* ceiling of the chapel, and have a drink beneath the more sober Mudejar ceiling of the bar. In front, the **Plaza Corazón de María** descends to a web of streets leading to the interconnecting **Plaza Grande** and **Plaza Chica.** These charming arcaded squares are the sleepy heart of Zafra. Palm trees dominate the former, and the old town hall (1750) the latter.

Rising above the roofs one block west is the unmistakable bell tower of the Renaissance **church of La Candelaria** *(Calle Tetuán, tel 924 55 01 28)*. Inside are altarpieces by Francisco de Zurbarán (1598–1664), who was born nearby, and Juan Ramos Castro. Zafra's other architectural jewel, **Plaza del Pilar Redondo,** is dominated by the present **town hall** *(tel 924 55 45 01)*, which occupies a 16th-century Franciscan convent. Enter the patio to admire the arcaded structure, and then, for a contrast, look at No. 14 on the square, an idiosyncratic art nouveau house completely faced in turquoise tiles. ■

INSIDER TIP:

In Jerez de los Caballeros, climb to the roof of La Posada de las Cigüeñas (Hotel of the Storks; *Calle Santiago 5–7*) for a grand view of the city.

—TINO SORIANO
National Geographic photographer

Olivenza
234 A2
Visitor Information
Oficina de Turismo, Plaza de España s/n
924 49 01 51
Closed Sun. p.m.
www.olivenzavirtual.com

Jerez de los Caballeros
234 A1
Visitor Information
Oficina de Turismo, Avenida de la Constitución 4
924 73 03 72
Closed Sun. p.m.
www.jerezdeloscaballeros.es

Zafra
234 B1
Visitor Information
Oficina de Turismo, Plaza de España 8B
924 55 10 36
www.zafraturismo.com

More Places to Visit in Castilla-La Mancha & Extremadura

Almagro

Smack in the middle of Don Quixote country, Almagro is a small town with a long history and theatrical bent. Mansions, monasteries, and churches surround the **Plaza Mayor.** At No. 18 is Europe's oldest continuously used theater, the 16th-century **Corral de Comedias** *(tel 926 86 15 39, closed Mon., $).* You can look inside, or, better still, see a play here during the festival of classical drama every July. Not surprisingly, Spain's only theater museum, **Museo Nacional de Teatro** *(Calle Gran Meastre 2, tel 926 26 10 14, closed Sun. p.m. & Mon.),* is here, too.

In the 13th century, Almagro became the base of the Knights of Calatrava, one of the military orders that fought for the Reconquest. Their seat was the stunning castle of **Calatrava la Nueva** *(19 miles/30 km S of Almagro on Carretera de Calzada de Calatrava, tel 926 22 13 37, closed Mon., $).* Extensive vineyards have replaced the battlefields of old, and red peppers, tomatoes, and eggplant are grown for the vegetable dish *pisto manchego.*

www.almagro.es 235 D2 **Visitor Information** Oficina de Turismo, Plaza Mayor 1 926 86 07 17

Parque Nacional de las Tablas de Daimiel

Nineteen miles (30 km) northeast of the city of Ciudad Real is Tablas de Daimiel, an area of marshy wetlands formed by the Guaiana River. This ornithologists' paradise of breeding aquatic birds and huge flocks of migrants has been under serious environmental threat. The lagoons are suffering from thousands of illegal agricultural wells. You can still see various species of duck, purple heron, and great crested grebes. Guided visits are on foot or by jeep. In Daimiel itself, look out for the 1,100-year-old olive tree on the main square.

www.lastablasdedaimiel.com 235 D2 11 miles (18 km) N of Daimiel 926 69 31 18 or 902 52 02 00

Talavera de la Reina

Talavera is renowned for one thing: ceramics. Be prepared for the feast of color, above all in the form of the *cacharro* (drinking jar). Talavera's production of handpainted glazed *azulejos* (tiles) blossomed in the 15th century, and Talaveran techniques were taken to Mexico by Spanish colonists. West of the center are workshops where you can buy domestic ware, or go to the shops on Avenida de Portugal. Other sights in town include a Roman wall, four Gothic-Mudejar churches, and the **Basílica de la Virgen del Prado** *(tel 925 80 14 45),* a showcase of azulejos inside and out. *www.turismotalaveradelareina.org*

235 C3 **Visitor Information** Oficina de Turismo, Calle Palenque 2 925 82 63 22

Sigüenza

The lovely hilltop town of Sigüenza *(visitor information, Oficina de Turismo, Calle Serrano Sanz, tel 949 34 70 07, www.siguenza.com, map 235 E4)* lies in the far north of Castilla-La Mancha, near the border with Aragón. It is dominated by its castle (now a hotel) and fortresslike Romanesque cathedral. The old town is a labyrinth, but if you keep going up you eventually reach the 16th-century Plaza Mayor and the cathedral. Look for the poignant alabaster sculpture on the tomb of El Doncel, Isabel I's page, and the countless cherubim decorating the sacristy ceiling by Alonso de Covarrubias (1488–1570).

Rugged sierra, verdant valleys, dazzling white hill villages, and a succession of Moorish castles and Renaissance mansions

Andalucía & Murcia

Sunset over the Córdoba plains

Andalucía & Murcia

Together with neighboring Murcia, Andalucía covers 38,063 square miles (98,583 sq km), sweeping across from the Portuguese border and the Atlantic Ocean past the towering Sierra Nevada peaks to the lunar landscapes of southeastern Spain. Andalucía's southernmost tip is a mere 9 miles (14 km) from Morocco, so it is not surprising that their culture, climate, and topography are so similar.

All the stereotypical images of Spain come from Andalucía: fiestas, siestas, flamenco, bullfights, and a relaxed approach to life—and there is some truth in them. The flip side of an easygoing attitude is corruption, which in Andalucía has spawned Spain's worst coastal eyesores and a few politicians in jail. Nonetheless, Andalucía has a string of unmissable cities: Sevilla, Córdoba, Granada, and Málaga, each with spectacular (and well-maintained) monuments, superb tapas, beautiful old hotels, and modernized services. Smaller towns, too, such as, Jerez de la Frontera, Ronda, Antequera, Úbeda, and Priego, not only reflect Spain's so-called Golden Age, when the booty from the New World financed Andalucía, but are also highly rewarding.

When you become monument weary, refresh your eyes in this region's virgin landscapes, from

the marshes and dunes of Doñana to the Alpujarras (the lovely foothills of the Sierra Nevada), the green Sierra de Cazorla, and the undulating desert of the southeast corner, home of spaghetti Westerns. The high-speed AVE train helps, connecting Madrid with Cordoba, Sevilla, Málaga, and Cádiz.

Lowland Andalucía divides into two halves, with Granada at its midpoint. To the west lies the fertile Guadalquivir basin, virtually one huge tract of cultivated land dotted with *fincas* (farms), bulls, and horses. To the east around Cordoba and Jean, olives take over: This is the world's largest production area. Almeria province is made up of karst and shale, with minimal rainfall making cultivation an uphill struggle except at El Ejido. Here acres of plastic greenhouses force-grow vegetables tended by North African workers. ■

NOT TO BE MISSED:

Easter procession in any major Andalusian town 272–273

Ronda's awe-inspiring gorge and mountains 277

Driving through the hills of the *pueblos blancos* 278–279

Málaga's Museo Picasso 282

Córdoba's mesmerizing Mezquita and flowery patios 286–287

Flamenco in Sevilla 289

Moorish artistry of Granada's Alhambra 298–299, 302–305

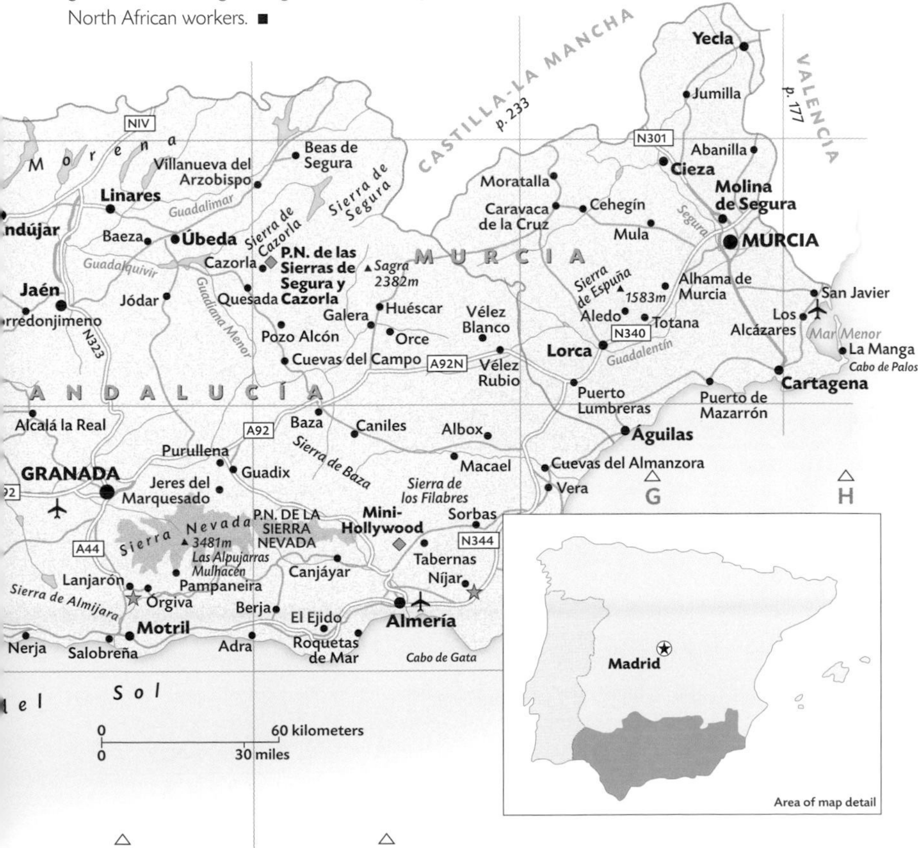

Sevilla (Seville)

Sevilla is a city of 700,000 extroverts who revel in flamenco, bullfighting, processions, fiestas, and tapas. The town center resembles a mosaic of stage sets, each plaza prettier than the next, with its colorful baroque church and orange trees. Alcove shrines and shady tiled patios point to a more secret life, but the overwhelming characteristic is one of openness and conviviality.

Colorfully painted *azulejo* tiles adorn Plaza de España.

Sevilla (Seville)
260 C3
Visitor Information
Oficina de Turismo, Avenida de la Constitución 21B
954 78 75 78
Closed Sun. p.m.
www.andalucia.org

The negative side of Sevilla's charm is the inevitable commercialization of the center. In the Barrio de Santa Cruz district (see p. 265), steer clear of the more touristy restaurants and watch your wallets, bags, and cameras. That said, relax and take your time. Lose your way in the whitewashed streets, and enjoy the daily life of the shops, markets, music, and bars that boom into the night.

Sevilla's history began with the Romans. Extensive ruins of Itálica, where the emperors Hadrian and Trajan were born, lie 6 miles (10 km) northwest. Remnants of Hispalis, the Roman settlement here, include the aqueduct (best seen in the Callejón del Agua, in the Barrio de Santa Cruz), and the columns and statues of Hercules and Julius Caesar on the Alameda. Hercules was Sevilla's legendary founder, Julius Caesar the real one.

The Moors disembarked in 711. It took four centuries for Sevilla to reach its zenith under the rule of the Almohad dynasty, who left a lasting influence on architectural style. Most visible is the Torre del Oro, a dodecagonal watchtower rising over the river. From the sumptuous royal palace (Reales Alcázares) and the Casa de Pilatos to endless tiled walls, Sevilla is a dazzling window on an artistry still practiced today.

The end of this golden period came in 1248 when King Fernando III of Castilla captured Sevilla from the Moors, but Sevilla soon prospered again following the European discovery of America in 1492. The Atlantic Ocean is only 56 miles (90 km) away down the Guadalquivir River, and Sevilla's port saw Ferdinand Magellan, Juan Sebastián Elcano, and Christopher Columbus set sail. The immense riches brought back in their holds financed many of the city's monuments.

The 20th century had two high points: the 1929 Ibero-American Exhibition and the 1992 World's Fair. The first has survived best. The latter on the Isla de la Cartuja is now a technology park. Sevilla's

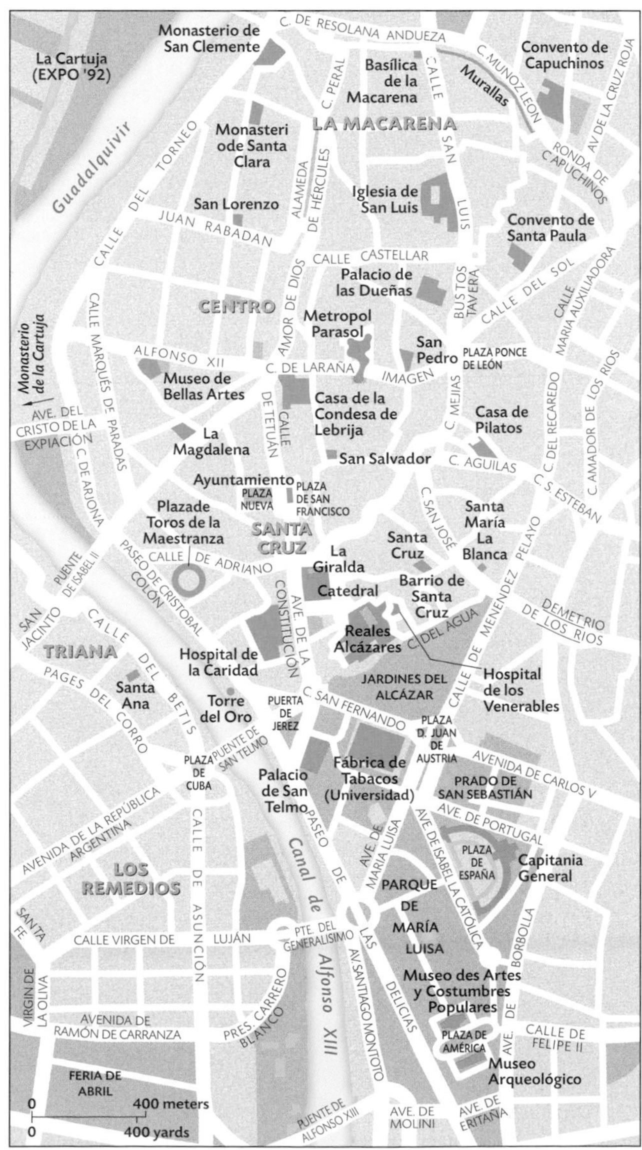

Escaping the Sun—in Style

The **Metropol Parasol** is a collection of 100-foot-high (30 m), curvaceous timber structures that bloom out of the ground, offering shade to Plaza de la Encarnación. Construction was jump-started by the discovery of Roman ruins here while digging an underground parking lot. Work began in 2005, and by spring 2011, the instant cultural icon was complete. Its nickname—*las setas*, or "mushrooms"—quickly followed. Aboveground are a farmers' market, shops, restaurants, and a concert podium. Belowground you can visit the **Museo Arqueológico Antiquarium,** which showcases the extensive ruins and mosaics of Roman houses found here, as well as Almohad (Moorish) elements. Finally, high on the roof, a restaurant, viewing gallery, and winding, undulating **walkway** *(tel 954 78 75 78)* give views over the rooftops of the city. The views are particularly stunning at night, but for Sevillians in high summer, the best part is the afternoon shade down below.

Catedral de Sevilla & La Giralda

263
Plaza del Triunfo
95 421 49 71
Closed Sun. p.m.
$$

www.catedraldesevilla.es

latest innovation is the Metropol Parasol (see sidebar this page), in a rather run-down area. Bike lanes are also multiplying; try a saddle-bound guided tour.

Catedral & La Giralda

Though ungainly, the cathedral has many treasures, not least being the emblematic Giralda tower rising majestically on one side. This, Sevilla's finest relic of the Almohad dynasty, served as the minaret for the mosque on the site on which the cathedral was built.

Completed in 1198 by architect Ali de Gomara, La Giralda suffered damage from an earthquake in 1365, then in the 16th century acquired a Renaissance belfry with 25 bells, and finally the weather vane, from which its name derives. Inside the 322-foot (98 m) tower is a ramp that enabled the muezzin, a Muslim crier whose job is to call the faithful to prayer, to go up on horseback. Lesser mortals must climb up on foot, but the effort is repaid by stupendous views over Sevilla.

Enter both La Giralda and the cathedral through a large patio dotted with orange trees and edged by horseshoe arches on two sides, which is all that remains of the mosque. From here a double arch, one Arab and one Gothic, leads inside the world's third largest cathedral (after St. Peter's in Vatican City and St. Paul's in London), an overpoweringly scaled combination of late Gothic and Renaissance styles. It took more than a century to build, from 1403 to 1506. Start at the **high altar,** a staggering work of Flemish art incorporating 2.5 tons (2.4 tonnes) of gold from Mexico and Peru. This alone took 35 years to complete. The detailed carving is magnificent but difficult to see from a distance, so take binoculars.

Behind you, the **choir** is another artistic feat, with beautifully carved 15th- and 16th-century choir stalls of Cuban mahogany. Look up into the transept dome to see ornate stonework dating from after the Lisbon earthquake of 1778, when this section collapsed and was rebuilt. The vivid stained-glass windows are Gothic in the upper row and Renaissance below.

To the right of the transept stands the tomb of Christopher Columbus; after years of controversy, DNA testing proves his remains lie here, not in the vast mausoleum in the Dominican Republic. In the sacristy rooms is the cathedral's dazzling **treasury,** with paintings by Murillo, Zurbarán, and Goya (the only Goya in Sevilla), silver and gold chalices, reliquaries, and processional crosses laden with jewels, a beautiful 12th-century portable altar, and a massive monstrance. The oval **chapter house** was the first such construction in Europe. The cathedral's last surprise is the **Capilla Real,** entered separately from the plaza, which houses the much revered 12th-century statue of the Virgen de los Reyes, the patron saint of Sevilla.

From here walk west to the river to visit the **Torre del Oro** *(tel 954 22 24 19, closed p.m. & Mon.);* climb 91 steps for views.

Barrio de Santa Cruz

Immediately east of the cathedral lies a charming web of streets and little squares. The Barrio de Santa Cruz developed as the Jewish quarter in the 13th century, after Sevilla was taken from the Moors, and remained so until a massacre of its inhabitants in 1391. Around 400 families lived here in a self-contained ghetto with their own judiciary and synagogue. Today, Santa Cruz has a very different image, being a desirable residential quarter and, above all, heavily geared up for visitors, with a mouthwatering choice of tapas bars and restaurants.

It makes an attractive stroll, though, and you pass typical flower-filled Sevillian patios and orange trees on the way, particularly along the **Callejón del Agua.** Head for **Plaza de Santa Cruz,** the site of the main synagogue, which was later converted into a church and, in turn, destroyed by Napoleon's troops. Between this plaza and the cathedral is the impressive baroque **Hospital de los Venerables,** founded as an asylum for priests, with superb frescoes by Valdés Leal and his son Lucas in the church. The hospital is owned by the Focus cultural foundation and stages concerts and exhibitions.

Reales Alcázares

Sevilla's rulers did themselves proud, as this royal palace complex displays a masterful

Hospital de los Venerables

- 263
- Plaza de los Venerables
- 95 456 26 96

Reales Alcázares

- 263
- Plaza del Triunfo
- 95 450 23 24
- $$

www.patronato-alcazarsevilla.es

Sevilla's favorite taxi service is a horse-drawn carriage.

combination of Moorish techniques and Catholic symbols: the ultimate example of Mudejar architecture. One of Europe's oldest royal palaces, it is still used by the king of Spain.

The earliest surviving parts of the Alcázar were built by the Almohad dynasty, but long before that the Roman acropolis was here, then an early Christian basilica, and a Moorish castle.

Sevilla's Torre del Oro houses a small naval museum.

What you see today is essentially the work of Pedro I, who ordered its construction in 1362, about the same time as the Nazrid Palace was being built in Granada's Alhambra (see pp. 298–299, 302–305). A century or so later Isabel I added a wing, and a century later Emperor Carlos V built an adjoining palace.

From the entrance (where it is advisable to rent audioguide headphones), you enter the **Patio de las Doncellas,** a beautiful arcaded patio of exquisite cedarwood marquetry, original *zelij* tiling, and intricate stucco. The upper story, now the king's official residence, and the adjacent **Salón de Carlos V,** with its beautiful mahogany *artesonado* (coffered Mudejar ceiling), are both 16th-century additions. Whenever you see red-and-gold paintwork, you are seeing 19th-century restoration. The Moorish and Mudejar palette was essentially blue and green.

The most masterfully worked rooms lie off the far side of the patio, a maze of interconnecting bedrooms and reception rooms. At their center is the stunning **Salón de Embajadores** (Ambassadors' Hall), topped by an exceptional cedarwood cupola. Horseshoe arches lead to a luminous dining room overlooking the garden: Note the more delicate decoration here, the work of Persian artists after the original hall burned down in a fire. Next is the delightful **Patio de las Muñecas** (Dolls' Patio, so called for its diminutive size), also known as the Patio de la Reina (Queen's Patio) because it has pierced screens for court women to look through, just as harems did. The open upper gallery was for musicians. Off this lie the modest bedrooms of Fernando and Isabel and their son, Don Juan.

From the tiled chapel flanking Pedro I's palace, you cross gardens to enter **Palacio de Carlos V,** a complete contrast in scale, with lifeless decoration dominated by tapestries (1740) of the Conquest of Tunisia. Keep moving, however, and you enter the magnificent **Jardines del Alcázar** (gardens) beside Mercury's Pool, backed by decorative volcanic rock. This is the perfect place to wander, among the perfumes of aromatic plants, magnolias or orange trees in flower, and the sounds of trickling water. If you are here during Sevilla's sultry summer, don't miss a late evening concert *(nightly at 10:30 p.m.)* in this magical setting.

Parque de María Luisa

In 1893, María Luisa, Duchess of Montpensier, gave most of the vast grounds of Palacio San Telmo to the city. The 1929 Ibero-American Exhibition was staged here, so the 94-acre (38 ha) park is riddled with architectural curiosities.

Enter from the **Palacio de San Telmo,** built in 1734 as the first nautical school in the world and later the palace of the Dukes of Montpensier. It is now home to the Andalusian government. Just beyond looms the imposing **Fábrica de Tabacos** (Tobacco Factory, now part of Sevilla University), the setting of Prosper Mérimée's story *Carmen* (1845), on which Bizet's opera was based.

The park is crisscrossed with roads and paths connecting the numerous structures that were built here for the 1929 Ibero-American Exhibition. Each building has found a subsequent function, whether as consulate, museum, art school, flamenco school, or police station (the Brazil pavilion). Spain's national pavilion reigns in splendor around the semicircular **Plaza de España.** Designed by Aníbal González, this outsize masterpiece of neo-Andalusian baroque uses brick and handpainted tiles (from Valencia, Toledo, and Sevilla) with generous abandon. Each Spanish province is represented in a tiled illustration of its historical high point, and three pretty bridges span the surrounding water channel. Don't miss the fabulous *artesonado* (marquetry) ceilings above the lateral staircases into the pavilion, but give the wily Gypsy fortune-tellers a wide berth.

Walk 300 yards (275 m) south to Plaza de América, site of two museums. The **Museo de Artes y Costumbres Populares** in the grandiose Mudejar Pavilion has a worthwhile ceramics exhibit on the lower floor. The display of costumes and furniture above is currently closed. The superb **Museo Arqueológico** in the plateresque Pavilion has Phoenician statuary, the gold Carambolo Treasure, Roman works, and Mudejar ceramics. ■

Feria de Abril

A quintessential Andalusian event, the weeklong Feria de Abril marks the beginning of Sevilla's bullfighting season. Men in short, tight jackets and black gaucho hats strut about with women dressed to kill in the season's latest style. Some ride on horseback, others in horse-drawn carriages. The rest simply swagger through the city streets. The heat really rises in Los Remedios, the fairground southwest of the city center, across Triana Bridge. Here, row after row of *casetas* (square, partially open-air tents) come alive with parties; many are private (and increasingly corporate), though some are open to the public. Find one and join the fun: Drink some sherry, dance the *sevillana,* and let the city's carnival atmosphere reign supreme.

Museo de Artes y Costumbres Populares

Map 263
Plaza de América
954 71 23 91
Closed Sun. p.m. & Mon.

Museo Arqueológico

Map 263
Plaza de América
954 78 64 74
Closed Sun. p.m. & Mon.

More Places to Visit in Sevilla

Casa de Pilatos

Another fantastic example of Mudejar architecture, the intriguing Casa de Pilatos lies northeast of the Alcázar and cathedral. Built by the Marqués de Tarifa in the 15th to 16th centuries, it was erroneously thought to be a copy of Pontius Pilate's villa, hence the name.

The main patio presents an exceptionally harmonious combination of stuccowork, tiles, *artesonado* (coffered) ceilings, and marble and tiled floors. In the garden to the left of the main patio, an incongruous Italian loggia is the wing of the palace where the 18th Duchess of Medinacelli and her family still live. Here and throughout the palace are numerous very fine Roman busts and statues, most brought from Rome. The peaceful and well-tended garden to the right of the patio makes a wonderful spot for relaxing beside the fountain during Sevilla's long hot afternoons. Don't miss the gilded artesonado ceiling in the neighboring study, nor the spectacularly worked dome above the main staircase. On the upper floor, wait for a guide to walk you through a completely different universe, that of the Spanish Renaissance.

www.fundacionmedinaceli.org/monumentos/pilatos 263 Plaza de Pilatos 954 22 52 98 $$. Free Wed. p.m. for E.U. citizens

Hospital de la Caridad

The Hospital of Charity is a few steps west of the cathedral, behind the Teatro de la Maestranza, Spain's prestigious operatic and musical venue. In 1625, a repentant, formerly dissolute aristocrat, Miguel de Mañara, became head of the brotherhood of La Caridad and founded the hospital and church. Both are wonderful examples of Sevillian baroque.

In the church you can see the paintings Mañara commissioned: seven superb works by Murillo created for the site (four others were looted by Napoleon's troops), and two compelling paintings by Valdés Leal.

263 Calle Temprado 3 954 22 32 32 Closed Sun. p.m. $. Free Sun. a.m. for Spanish citizens

INSIDER TIP:

Don't pass up the chance for a hot-air balloon ride. Green Aerostación *(tel 669 80 90 55, www.globo.info)* in Gines, just outside Sevilla, offers spectacular flights over the city.

—JAVIER VAZQUEZ DE PRADA
Environmental officer, Sevilla

Monasterio de la Cartuja & Centro Andaluz de Arte Contemporáneo

The Isla de la Cartuja, site of Expo '92, is home to a vast and venerable Carthusian monastery that has stood here since 1428. Once visited by every Spanish monarch who came to Sevilla, it lost its function in 1836 when Church property was seized by the state. In 1841, Charles Pickman, an Englishman, set up a porcelain factory on the site, which remained active until 1982. Since then, La Cartuja has become government property and extensive restoration has created a unique place. A pristine contemporary art center installed beside the orchards stages innovative shows and events, and the Mudejar church successfully displays contemporary works beside beautiful original features and the monks' quarters. In 2011, the old Pickman factory reopened under new ownership.

www.juntadeandalucia.es/cultura/caac 263 Isla de la Cartuja, Avenida Américo Vespucio 2 95 503 70 96 Closed Sun. p.m. & Mon.

Museo del Baile Flamenco

Opened in 2006 by the great flamenco dancer Cristina Hoyos, this high-tech museum is a real eye-opener on the tradition. Interactive exhibits, costumes, projections, photos, paintings, and sound tracks of the inimitable rhythms and voices all create an evocative universe. Sign up for a class or hire a flamenco group from the museum's extensive database for an evening.
www.flamencomuseum.com 263
Calle Manuel Rojas Marcos 3
954 34 03 11 $$

Museo de Bellas Artes

This outstanding yet uncrowded museum, transformed from a 17th-century convent in 1841, displays some of Spain's greatest old masters. It is laid out around three patios with two floors connected by an imperial staircase. The Aljibe cloister is particularly interesting for its central well and Sevillian tilework. Although the nucleus of the collection is the Sevillian school of painting that flourished in the 17th century, you can sidetrack to look at medieval art.

Rooms 3 and **4** on the lower floor are crucial—they hold mannerist works by Francisco Pacheco, who exerted great influence on his students Diego Velázquez (1599–1660) and Alonso Cano (1601–1667). Cano's wonderful painting of the "Souls of Purgatory" and Velázquez's "La Casulla a San Ildefonso," in which the Virgin was modeled on Juana Pacheco, his wife and the daughter of his teacher, hang there also.

Room 5 moves into the baroque world of Murillo, perfectly represented in the reconstructed altar of the Convento de los Capuchinos, and the subtly executed "Virgen de la Servilleta" (Virgin of the Napkin, so called because it was allegedly painted on Murillo's dinner napkin). Head for the upper floor to see the intense, colorful canvases of Juan de Valdés Leal (1622–1690) in **Room 8,** and the great spiritual master of monks, Francisco de Zurbarán, represented in **Room 10** by monastery altarpieces.
www.juntadeandalucia.es/cultura/museos/mbase
263 Plaza del Museo 9 95 478 65 00 Closed Sun. & Mon. $. Free for E.U. citizens

Sevilla's Museo de Bellas Artes collection includes "Penitente" (1605) by Juan Martínes Montañés.

Jerez de la Frontera

This lively little town may smack of Sevilla (only 62 miles/100 km to the north), but it has its own raisons d'être: sherry, horses, flamenco. No fewer than 16 sherry bodegas are open for visits, the Royal Andalusian School of Equestrian Art is world famous for equestrian shows, and two Gypsy quarters (San Miguel and Bulería) perpetuate the traditions of the legendary flamenco dancer Lola Flores, a native of Jerez.

Jerez's Royal Andalusian School of Equestrian Art offers frequent performances.

Jerez de la Frontera

260 B2

Visitor Information

Oficina Municipal de Turismo, Alameda Cristina s/n (Claustros de Santo Domingo)

956 34 17 11

www.turismojerez.com

Jerez also has an impressive old walled **Alcázar** *(Alameda Vieja, tel 956 14 99 55)*, containing a well-conserved mosque, beautifully restored baths, and shady gardens. This abuts the baroque **Villavicencia palace,** where you can climb up to a camera obscura projecting a bird's-eye view of the townscape below. The lovely Palacio Atalaya houses a clock museum, the **Palacio del Tiempo** *(Calle Cervantes 3, tel 902 18 21 00, closed Sun. p.m. & Mon., $$)*, where 302 17th- to 19th-century clocks and watches from all over Europe strike in unison every noon. The pedestrianized center has numerous beautiful baroque mansions and old churches. The dignified **cathedral** *(Plaza de la Encarnación, tel 956 16 90 59, closed Sun.)* combines baroque styles.

You will find flamenco (see pp. 288–289) everywhere, nurtured at the **Centro Andaluz de Flamenco** *(Palacio Pemartín, Plaza San Juan 1, tel 856 91 41 32, closed Sat. & Sun., www.centroandaluzdeflamenco.es)*, a dance school and museum. Come to Jerez in late February to see top performers during the Feria Flamenca.

Bulls and horses are part and parcel of the Jerez landscape. Jerez even has a bull museum, **Museo Taurino** *(Calle Pozo del Olivar 6, tel 956 32 30 00, closed p.m. & Sun., $)*, but your priority should be the **Real Escuela Andaluza del Arte Ecuestre.** This equestrian academy was founded in 1973 to train dressage riders mounted on the Andalusian horse, the Cartujano, originally bred in the 18th century by Carthusian monks. You can watch morning training sessions on Mondays, Wednesdays, and Fridays (plus Tuesdays in winter), and then visit the stables and saddlery. Don't miss the Thursday performance (also on Tuesdays in summer) of dancing horses mounted by riders in stunning 17th-century costumes. Visits to stud farms and estates are also available. Jerez's greatest show is the Horse Fair in May, with horse shows, dancing, and parades of horse-drawn carriages.

Andalucía takes great pride in sherry, as you might guess from the huge sherry barrels sitting outside bars here and in Sevilla. Sherry (the English corruption of "Jerez") is a blended wine made from palomino grapes and then aged in casks of American oak. The four main categories are: *fino,* the driest and lightest in color; *amontillado,* still dry but with greater body and more depth; *oloroso,* medium dry and a rich golden color; and *dulce,* the sweetest of all, whose color resembles a port.

Sandeman, Pedro Domecq, Harvey, and González Byass are all mainstays of Jerez's economy. A visit to a bodega is enlightening. The classic is the 170-year-old **Bodega González Byass** near the Alcázar, where you see barrels signed by the likes of Orson Welles, Winston Churchill, and the entire Spanish royal family. All visits are followed by a tasting. ■

Real Escuela Andaluza del Arte Ecuestre

- Avenida Duque de Abrantes
- 956 31 80 08
- Closed Sat.–Sun.
- $ (training); $$/$$$ (dressage show)

www.realescuela.org

Bodega González Byass

- Calle Manuel M. González 12
- 956 35 70 16
- Closed Sun. p.m.
- $$

www.gonzalezbyass.es

EXPERIENCE: Seaside Horse-Trekking

Just 14 miles (22 km) northwest of Jerez lies Spain's largest national park, **Parque Natural de Doñana** *(visitor information, Centro de Visitantes, Carretera A-483, km 37.5, El Rocío, tel 959 43 04 32 or 959 44 87 39, www.donanavisitas.es, map 260 B2).* Covering 195 square miles (500 sq km), Doñana was created in 1969 to protect wetlands edging the Guadalquivir River, 31 miles (50 km) of coastal sand dunes, and inland pastures.

One of the best ways to experience the park's coastal wilds and diverse vegetation is on horseback. **VisitHuelva** *(tel 959 82 11 08, www.visithuelva.com)* offers one-, two-, and three-hour guided tours, as well as half-day treks. Begin in the village of El Rocío then head into the park, where you ride through low pine trees and down to the beach. Walk your horse along the sand or break into a trot and let the water splash.

Offered year-round, the tours *($$–$$$$ depending on duration)* are suitable for riders of all levels, even beginners. The price includes the services of a guide and the rental of a horse and helmet; transportation and meals are not included. Select the start time when making a reservation.

DiscoverSevilla *(Calle Joiquín Guichot 6, Sevilla, tel 954 22 66 42, www.discoversevilla.com)* offers two-hour guided horse treks *($$$$)* in the park. Round-trip bus transportation from Sevilla is included.

Semana Santa

Spain's most important festival is Semana Santa (Holy Week), a spectacular demonstration of mourning that lasts from Palm Sunday to Easter Sunday. In any village of Andalucía you might encounter midnight processions with hooded, torch-bearing penitents, or, in brilliant sunlight, see crowds of villagers clutching palm fronds before a venerated statue of Christ.

Women in *mantillas* (hair combs with black lace) ask prayers of the Virgin Mary.

In the words of the travel writer Jan Morris, "There are few spectacles on earth to match the holy parades of Málaga or Seville." The main protagonists are parish brotherhoods *(cofradías)*, whose penitential origins go back to the 15th century and who spend the preceding year preparing costumes and floats. The floats, or *pasos,* feature highly realistic figures in theatrical poses and are the focal point of Semana Santa, although in some places the week culminates in the ceremonial burning or exploding of an effigy of Judas. The sculptures of the elaborate floats, usually focusing on a sorrowful Virgin Mary and a tortured Christ, are life-size figures (some dating from the 16th and 17th centuries) dressed in embroidered robes and surrounded by flowers, palm fronds, and candles. Beneath them labor the cassocked *costaleros* (carriers), accompanied by hooded *nazarenos* (penitents; see sidebar this page) atoning for their year's errors.

Sevilla has 57 brotherhoods, 116 floats, and more than 50,000 nazarenos, who slowly advance in turn along a preset route from their *barrio* (quarter) to the cathedral. The weeklong commemoration reaches a climax early on Good Friday, when the most venerated statues of the Virgin Mary and of Christ are carried by six specific brotherhoods.

With the penitents, worshippers, and onlookers come the inevitable bands. Usually composed of wind and percussion instruments led by an obsessive drum beat, these bands are sometimes interrupted by the penetratingly deep wail of a *saeta,* a song that

Penitents

Although a royal decree in 1777 banned acts of medieval penitence and self-abasement, many have survived. In San Vicente de la Sonsierra (Rioja), you see penitents indulge in self-flagellation using strips of linen to beat their bare backs, pricked to facilitate bleeding and avoid blood congestion. Equally extreme are the acts of the *empalaos* in Valverde de la Vera (Extremadura) who cover their backs, torsos, and arms with thick rope before being bound to a cross-shaped plow and dragged through the stages of the Passion.

Hooded penitents follow a *paso* (float) that bears a statue of the crucified Christ.

originates in flamenco. Traditionally, these agonized notes from the crowd impose an immediate silence and halt—signs both of respect for the vocalist and solidarity in his or her prayer. However, the saeta is often prearranged, giving the costaleros a break for a drink and cigarette. Although religious passions run deep, the Sevillian Semana Santa is also about enjoyment, a prelude to the hedonistic Feria that takes place two weeks later.

Cádiz & Costa de la Luz

Cádiz is truly out on a limb. It sits on a narrow tongue of land curving northward on the Costa de la Luz—the coast of light. Over the millennia, this seagirt site was much coveted by Phoenicians, Greeks, Romans, Visigoths, and Arabs. Even today, Cádiz has an end-of-the-world feel, although recent regeneration is changing this. The opening of the high-speed AVE train line, in 2010, has played a key role.

Europe's oldest city, Cádiz was Spain's main trading port with the New World.

Cádiz

 260 B1

Visitor Information

- Patronato Provincial de Turismo, Plaza de Madrid s/n, Estadio Ramón de Carranza (Fondo Sur)
- 956 80 70 61 or 956 80 72 23
- Closed Sun.

www.cadizturismo.com

Cádiz

Cádiz has few great sights, but it makes a relaxed stopover where traditions are still strong. Penetrate the city's peripheral shell of modernity to find a harmonious old center of baroque churches and elegant mansions, many of them painted in delicate pastel colors and sporting ornate wrought-iron balconies.

Artisans carve wooden furniture and gild baroque frames, cafés align bottles of olive oil to drizzle over morning toast, and in the old part of the town, a network of narrow alleyways reeks of Arab urbanism, particularly in **Barrio de la Viña,** an excellent area for flamenco and seafood restaurants. In summer, when the wind drops, head for the beaches of fine white sand on the west coast of the peninsula.

The most visible of Cádiz's churches is the **cathedral** *(Plaza de la Catedral, tel 956 28 61 54, closed Mon., Sat., & Sun. p.m., $),* whose tiled dome towers over the Plaza de la Catedral. The resulting mix of styles is not the most compelling, although it displays some impressive baroque paintings. You can climb the Poniente bell tower for inspiring views over the city and ocean. Close by are the remains of a first-century B.C. **Roman theater** *(tel 956 26 47 34, closed Tues.)*, another sign of the city's great age.

West of here, the seawall leads to an unusual bastion with a castle, the **Castillo de San Sebastián,** jutting out into the sea.

Museo de Cádiz: The Museo de Cádiz has an impressive collection of archaeology and fine arts. Head straight for **Room 2** to see a pair of fifth-century B.C. Phoenician marble sarcophagi. These magnificent life-size tombs lie in serene splendor beside sophisticated terra-cotta busts of gods, amphorae, and Etruscan pieces. Next door, bright, skylit **Room 4** exhibits fine Roman statues including one of the emperor Trajan, dating from A.D. 98 to 117.

The painting collection on the upper floors includes Zurbarán's series of portraits of monks. Murillo, Rubens, and a string of 20th-century artists from Joan Miró to Chema Cobo (born in 1952 in Tarifa) occupy the other rooms of this grandiose mid-19th-century building.

Outside, on the southwestern flank of the lush and shady Plaza de la Mina, stands the birthplace of Spanish composer Manuel de la Falla (1876–1946) whose tomb is in the cathedral crypt. Follow Calle Zorrilla from the northeastern corner to discover some of Cádiz's best tapas bars before ending at the Alameda gardens overlooking the Atlantic.

Costa de la Luz

South of Cádiz stretches a coastline of golden beaches and dunes backed by inland pastures grazed by bulls. Shady trails cut through pine forests with tantalizing glimpses of the ocean below. Kitesurfing is king in these choppy waters, above all close to Tarifa, the southernmost point, while surf- and body-boarding come in a close second at El Palmar beach. The one drawback is the wind, which at certain times of the year becomes irritating. This does not put off hundreds of illegal African immigrants who land at night in tiny fishing boats.

Wind aside, this coast has attractive villages, beautiful scenery, and, as yet, little beach development except around **Conil**

Cádiz Carnival

If sleepy most of the year, Cádiz really makes up for it in February—Carnival time. The party starts on Shrove Tuesday and ends with the Burial of the Sardine, when hundreds of "mourners" follow the papier-mâché fish while loudly lamenting its passage. In between are processions, dance, and above all music. Brimming with ingenuity, satire, and song, costumed Carnival groups called *chirigotas* flock to the more traditional barrios, such as La Viña, El Pópulo, Santa María (near the cathedral), and Mentidero, singing satirically about everything from politicians to celebrities. More organized are the extravagantly dressed *coros* (choirs) who ride in open carts playing guitars and lutes. Calle Ancha and Calle Columela see masses of action, and the Plaza de la Catedral hosts top Spanish rock bands. The celebration is popular, so reserve your hotel early.

Museo de Cádiz

- Plaza de Mina, Cádiz
- 956 20 33 68
- Closed Sun. p.m., Mon., & Tues.
- $. Free for E.U. citizens

www.juntadeandalucia.es/cultura/museos

Conil de la Frontera

260 B1

Calle Carretera 1

956 44 05 01

www.conil.org

Tarifa

260 C1

Paseo de la Alameda

956 68 09 93

www.cryttotarifa.com

de la Frontera and Tarifa. Conil, a once elegant, traditional town has spawned a sprawling family resort due to its calm, shallow water. Immediately south stretches the beautiful **El Palmar** beach, where surfers' cafés and a few restaurants nestle behind the dunes. At the southern headland a lighthouse marks **Cabo Trafalgar** (Cape Trafalgar) where British admiral Horatio Nelson trounced the French-Spanish fleet in 1805 and died in the process.

EXPERIENCE: Whale-Watching

Whale Watch Tarifa *(Avenida de la Constitución 6, Tarifa, tel 639 47 65 44 or 956 62 70 13, www.whalewatchtarifa.net)* **has offered trips on the Strait of Gibraltar since 1996. Join one of the two-hour whale- and dolphin-watching trips** *($$$)* **available between April and October, or sign up for the three-hour killer whale trip** *($$$$)* **in July and August. If you don't see at least one bottlenose dolphin, pilot whale, or other cetacean, you will receive a voucher for a free trip. Wear waterproof clothing and sneakers. Trips are subject to change due to weather conditions.**

Vejer de la Frontera

260 C1

Avenida de los Remedios 2

 956 45 17 36

www.turismovejer.es

About 5 miles (8 km) inland is the stunning hill village of **Vejer de la Frontera.** Although the city is much targeted by Northern Europeans for holiday homes, a potent medieval atmosphere prevails in the walled upper part surrounding the old **castle,** the attractive church of **San Salvador,** and well-preserved **Jewish quarter.** Some aristocratic mansions have become boutique hotels while bars and restaurants monopolize the **Plaza de España** down below, with its ornately tiled fountain. Just outside town, contemporary art is scenically presented at the **NMAC Foundation** *(Carretera A48/ N340, tel 956 45 51 34, $$).* Head north of Vejer to **Arcos** to connect with the *pueblos blancos* circuit (see pp. 278–279).

To the south, between Cabo Trafalgar and Barbate lies a 4,940-acre (2,000 ha) nature reserve, the **Parque Natural La Breña y Marismas de Barbate,** where pines, junipers, scrub, and salt flats are much favored by gulls, rock doves, kestrels, barn owls, and cattle egrets. Barbate itself, once a major tuna fishing port, suffers from unemployment and drug-trafficking is rife. A blissful 4 miles (6 km) of beach, Caños de Meca, stretch to the west. Farther south, beyond another popular resort, **Zahara de los Atunes,** and one of Spain's largest wind-farms, lies **Playa de Bolonia,** a beautiful sweep with the Roman ruins of **Baelo Claudia** *(tel 956 68 85 30, closed Mon.).* Founded in the second century B.C., this fish-salting town traded with North Africa.

Overlooking the Strait of Gibraltar, **Tarifa** is rimmed by cheap apartment blocks but that doesn't deter the wind- and kite-surfers who flock to this hip resort and the dune-backed **Playa de los Lances.** Tarifa was the first Arab settlement in Spain, in 711, and the plazas and alleys of the old-walled town still have character. Ferries run to Morocco, only 9 miles (14 km) away, and there are plans for a future railway tunnel. ■

Ronda

Ronda, Andalucía's great cliff-hanger, straddles a gorge with a sheer 325-foot (100 m) drop to the Guadalevín River. Over the gorge (known as El Tajo), the Puente Nuevo, or "new bridge," connects the old and new parts of town—"new" being only relative as it dates from the 18th century. The popular town has extensive tourist facilities, including numerous "antique" shops, yet the old port retains a powerful atmosphere. Avoid the crowded summer months.

Among the evocative secret plazas and cobbled streets of **Old Ronda** you can visit several mansions. The recently restored **Casa del Gigante** *(tel 678 63 14 45)* has a richly decorated Nazrio (11th–12th century) patio, and a short film gives a stirring introduction to Ronda's history.

Built in 1314 as the residence of the great Moorish king Abb el Malik, the **Palacio de Mondragón** *(Plaza de Mondragón, tel 952 87 84 50, closed Sat. & Sun. p.m.)*—the prettiest and most intimate of the mansions—now houses a small museum. Fernando and Isabel stayed here in 1485, and the palace acquired its present facade in the 18th century. From the Mudejar courtyard, rich in craftsmanship in brick, marble, tiles, and wood, a horseshoe arch leads to a charming garden. A few steps away is the stately **Parque Duquesa de Parcent,** overlooked by the church of **Santa María la Mayor** *(tel 952 87 40 48)*, and the Renaissance **town hall,** with an impressive loggia.

Downhill (east) from here on the main road looms a Nazari-style **minaret** that now belongs to the church of San Sebastián. To the south stands a section of the old Arab walls with their double gateway: the Moorish **Puerta de Almocabar** and the Renaissance **Puerta de Carlos V.** At the bottom of the hill to the east lie the restored **Baños Árabes** (Arab Baths; *Calle San Miguel, tel 656 95 09 37, www.turismoderonda.es*). Walk down to them on Calle Santo Domingo past the beautiful **Palacio del Marqués de Salvatierra.**

In the new town, don't miss the venerated bullring, the **Plaza de Toros** *(Calle Virgen de la Paz, tel 952 87 41 32, www.rmcr.org, closed for bullfights, $$)*, which was built in 1785. On display in the **Museo Taurino** inside are dazzling toreadors' jackets and capes encrusted with beading, sequins, and braids, beside photos of matadors, fights, deaths, and aficionados such as Orson Welles. ■

Bandits held court in Ronda between the 18th and 20th centuries.

Ronda

260 C2

Visitor Information

Oficina Municipal de Turismo, Paseo Blas Infante s/n

952 18 71 19

Closed Sun. p.m.

$$ (1 ticket covers 5 sites)

www.turismoderonda.es

A Drive Through *Pueblos Blancos*

This drive takes you through the dramatic Sierra de Grazalema Natural Park from west to east, stopping at typical white villages *(pueblos blancos)* before arriving at Ronda, the most inviting of them all.

NOT TO BE MISSED:

Arcos de la Frontera • El Bosque • Puerto del Boyar • Grazalema

Arcos de la Frontera ❶ *(visitor information, Cuesta del Belén 5, tel 956 70 22 64),* first settled by the Romans, is the western gateway to this region, with roads radiating in all directions from its spectacular clifftop site. Negotiating the narrow, winding streets by car is an art, so allow time to climb up on foot to the main square. On one side is the beautiful Gothic-Mudejar **church of Santa María;** on the other is a mirador (lookout point) with views over orchards and olive groves. Here, too, are the Moorish walls of the **Castillo de los Duques** and numerous baroque and Renaissance facades.

Leave Arcos on the beltway by following signs for the A372 to **El Bosque,** 17 miles (27 km) away. Scenery becomes increasingly spectacular as you arrive at **El Bosque** ❷, huddled at the base of the Sierra de Grazalema. This center for hikers, rock climbers, trout fishers, and hang gliders consists of a handful of cafés and a waterwheel grouped around a bridge over El Bosque River. Cross this and turn right after the bar to reach the parking lot, from where you can walk to the visitor center of the **Parque Natural de la Sierra de Grazalema** *(tel 956 71 60 63).*

Leave El Bosque on the A372 and after 1 mile (1.6 km) watch for a turnoff on the left to Grazalema. From here the road climbs immediately through eucalyptus and pine trees, and the soil becomes chalkier. You soon see the village of **Benamahoma** ❸ on your left. Views of the stark, granite-capped peak of **Monte Simancón** (5,134 feet/1,565 m) accompany you to the pass, the **Puerto del Boyar** ❹ (3,618 feet/1,103 m), where you can park to admire the superb perspective of mountain ridges receding to the west and buy honey

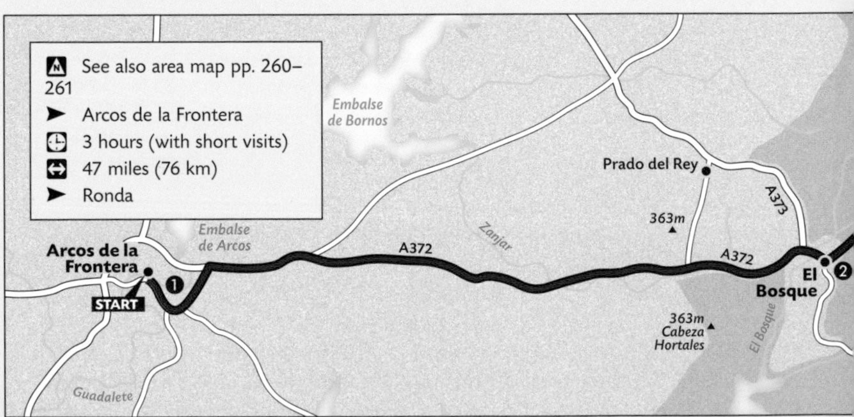

Grazalema is a dazzling sight of whitewashed houses, tile roofs, and church towers.

from local vendors. This is classic territory for roe deer, mountain goats, Griffon vultures, and eagles. Also here is the rare Spanish fir *(pinsapo)*, a survivor from the forests of the Tertiary era, which grows only above 3,280 feet (1,000 m).

As the road snakes down, you can see **Grazalema** ❺ *(visitor information, Plaza de España 11, tel 956 13 22 25)*, wedged between the sierras of El Pinar and El Endrinal. Opposite is the rocky outcrop of El Reloj ("the clock"). Drive down into the village, cross the main square, and turn right at the church into the parking lot (invaded by a market on Tuesday mornings). Then start exploring this immaculate village, its houses thick with layers of whitewash and its streets well endowed with bars, restaurants, and churches. The neoclassical **church of La Aurora** has an octagonal tower. Built over a mosque, the **church of San José** was once a Carmelite monastery.

Leave Grazalema by continuing on the A372 marked Ronda (20 miles/33 km). After 1 mile (1.6 km) a turnoff to the left, signed to **Zahara,** is a worthwhile detour if you can face more than an hour of truly tortuous bends. Otherwise continue on the A372 through a rock-strewn valley with striking views of Grazalema perched high above. Cork- and holm-oak forests line the road as you cross into the province of Málaga, and views gradually open up to farmland. Turn right toward Ronda when you reach the first junction, and then right again onto the A376. As this twists rapidly downward past steep granite cliffs on the right, **Ronda** (see p. 277), set dramatically over a gorge, appears on the horizon.

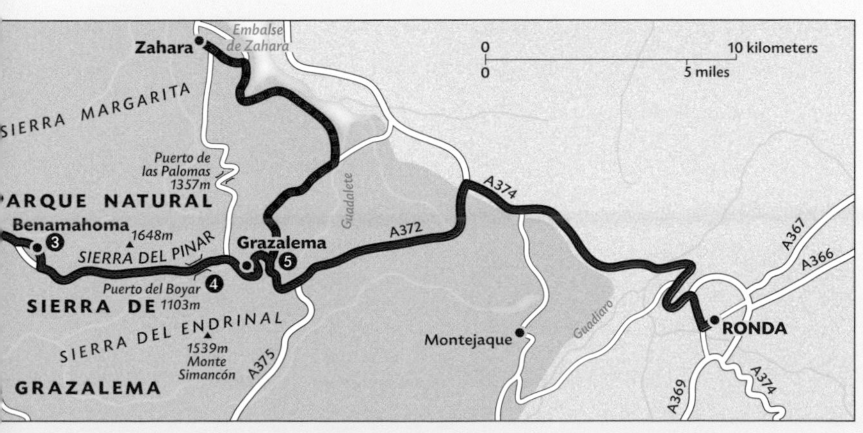

Antequera

It seems apt that the town at the geographical heart of Andalucía also claims the greatest number of churches of any town in Spain. Thriving Antequera lies in an exceptional spot, between the spectacular rock formation of El Torcal to the south and Europe's most important dolmens.

Antequera
260 D2
Visitor Information

Oficina Municipal de Turismo, Plaza San Sebastián 7
952 70 25 05
Closed Sun. p.m.
www.antequera.es

El Torcal
260 D2
Visitor Information
Centro de Interpretación
952 24 33 24
www.torcaldeantequera.com

Crowned by the **Alcazaba,** or Moorish castle, the white houses of Antequera spill down the hillside, their tile roofs spiked with some 30 church steeples. The **church of El Carmen** *(Plaza del Carmen, tel 952 70 25 05, closed Sun. p.m.)* has a masterfully carved main altarpiece, one of Andalucía's finest baroque works.

Walk uphill, through the 16th-century **Arco de los Gigantes,** to the **Colegiata de Santa María** *(closed Sat. & Sun. p.m., & Mon.)*, an early example of Andalusian Renaissance architecture. From here you can walk up through the gardens of the Alcazaba to the tower, **Torre del Homenaje** *(closed Mon.)*, for wonderful views, or continue around the walls.

Back in the center of town, don't miss the graceful Palacio de Nájera, now the **Museo Municipal** *(Plaza Coso Viejo, tel 952 70 40 21, closed Sat. & Sun. p.m., & Mon.)*. The main exhibit is a superb first-century Roman bronze statue of a boy. Antequera's ornate 19th-century **Plaza de Toros** *(tel 952 70 40 52)* is unmissable at the end of Paseo María Cristina.

Take the Málaga road out of town to three dolmens (stone tombs). The **Cueva de Menga** and **Cueva de Viera** *(Carretera de Málaga, closed Sun. & Tues. p.m.)*, the most impressive, date from about 2500 B.C. One mile (1.6 km) farther on is the slightly younger **Romeral** *(closed Sun. & Tues. p.m.)*.

Older than all of these is **El Torcal,** 8 miles (13 km) south, where 6.5 square miles (17 sq km) of calcareous rock have been eroded into extraordinary shapes. Hiking trails lead through this fantasy landscape with sea views. ■

EXPERIENCE: Commune With Wolves

In the mood for something just a little bit wild? Venture 5.5 miles (9 km) south and west of Antequera to Lobo Park ***(Ctra. Antequera-Álora, A343, km 16, tel 952 03 11 07, www.lobopark.com)***, **a 100-acre (40 ha) wolf sanctuary in the heart of Andalucía.**

One-hour guided tours ***($)***, **in Spanish and English, are offered throughout the day** ***(last tour at 4:30 p.m.)***. **As you walk through the park, which affords terrific views of El Torcal, your expert guide will teach you about wolf behavior. Observation platforms along the way allow you to come in close contact with the animals.**

Special Wolf Howl Nights ***($$)*** **are offered one or more times per month, depending on the time of year, and last from 7:30 p.m. to midnight. Eat dinner as the sun sets over El Torcal, and then enjoy a walk through the park among the most primal of sounds.**

Málaga

Picasso is the buzzword in this city of more than half a million people. The working port once attracted Phoenicians, Romans, and Moors, but today it is art lovers who flock to enjoy its museums, restaurants, tapas bars, and beaches. It is a lighthearted city that likes to party, and Malagueño exuberance peaks during the August feria.

The 14th-century castle of Gibralfaro gives sweeping views over the town and harbor.

Crowning a hilltop in the center of town is the Moorish **Alcazaba.** Its many towers and walls enclose the former palace, which is now the **Museo Arqueológico.** Go inside to see the Mudejar-style carved and painted ceilings, fine Roman pottery, mosaics, and Arab ceramics, appropriate echoes of the mixed architectural elements of the fortress. At the entrance below is a **Roman theater**—a venue for summer concerts.

Much of Málaga's attraction lies in its breezy walking areas, from the **Paseo Marítimo** beside the town beach to the luxuriant gardens, tiled benches, and duck ponds of the **Paseo del Parque** leading to the leafy **Alameda.** As pony carts trot by, flower vendors set up their stands under towering centennial trees in front of elegant 19th-century buildings.

Running north from the Alameda is the marble-paved shopping street, **Marqués de Larios,** which ends at the Plaza de la Constitución. The web of narrow pedestrian streets on both sides bristle with little restaurants, bars, and small shops. Three blocks west of Marqués de Larios, the bustling mock-Mudejar market, **Mercado de Atarazanas,** has wonderful fresh produce and an unexpected 14th-century stone arch.

Málaga

Map: 260 D2

Visitor Information

Address: Oficina Municipal de Turismo, Plaza de la Marina 11

Phone: 951 92 60 20

www.malagaturismo.com

Alcazaba & Museo Arqueológico

Address: Calle Alcazabilla

Phone: 952 22 72 30

Closed Mon.

Price: $

Cathedral
Calle Molina Larios
932 21 59 17
Closed Sun.

Museo Picasso
Palacio de Buenvista Calle San Agustín 8
952 12 76 00
Closed Mon.
$$

www.museopicassomalaga.org

Casa Natal de Picasso
Plaza de la Merced
952 06 02 15

www.fundacionpicasso.es

CAC
Calle Alemania
952 12 00 55
Closed Mon.

www.cacmalaga.org

Museo Carmen Thyssen
Plaza Carmen Thyssen
Closed Mon.

www.carmenthyssenmalaga.org

Finca de la Concepción
Carretera de las Pedrizas (Km 166)
952 25 07 45
Closed Mon.

Inside the must-see **cathedral** cupolas crown the three naves, with spectacular choir stalls carved by Pedro de Mena. In the **gardens** out back, the church of **El Sagrario** has a magnificent plateresque altarpiece by Juan Balmaseda and an ornate Isabelline-Gothic portal.

INSIDER TIP:

On December 28, Málaga celebrates the Fiesta Mayor de Verdiales, an energetic dance competition.

—CHRISTINE O'TOOLE
National Geographic contributor

Museo Picasso

A short walk northeast of here is Málaga's artistic jewel, the Museo Picasso. This homage to the town's native son, Pablo Picasso (1881–1973), is housed in a beautifully renovated Renaissance mansion, the Palacio de Buenavista, with a sleek modern extension. The collection stems from Picasso's daughter-in-law, Christine Ruiz Picasso, and his grandson, Bernard, who together donated 155 works, as well as 89 long-term loans. The result is an electrifying display, hung chronologically. Many of the works have never been on public display before—look out for **"Olga Seated"** (1923) and **"Geometrical Still Life with Music Score"** (1921). Relevant temporary exhibitions are displayed in a vast hall in the annex. A café and a leafy patio offer welcome respite.

Picasso's childhood home is just a five-minute walk away along a winding pedestrianized street. The **Casa Natal de Picasso** is an elegant house on a rather scruffy square. The pristine, renovated interior displays ceramics, enlarged photos, and small-scale works.

Other Art Venues

The controversial **Museo Carmen Thyssen,** which opened in 2011, is a five-minute walk west of the Museo Picasso. Here, in the converted Palacio de Villalón, hang 230 paintings from the baroness's private collection. It includes some greats (Zurbarán, Juan Gris, Sorolla) but also many mediocre 19th- and 20th-century clichés of Andalusian life. The collection is on a 15-year loan to the city of Málaga.

Málaga's contemporary venue is the **CAC** (Centro de Arte Contemporáneo), a dynamic exhibition center modeled out of an old market building beside the river. Artists featured in the permanent collection include Roy Lichtenstein, Frank Stella, Susana Solano, and Juan Uslé, and there is a lively program of cutting-edge exhibitions.

Finca de la Concepción

Four miles (7 km) north of Málaga on the A45 is a botanical garden, **Finca de la Concepción,** a vast collection of palms and exotic plants that was started in the 1850s and has flourished in the mild, humid climate. Pools and Roman statues add to the charm, and a mirador (lookout point) gives views across the city to the Mediterranean. ■

Costa del Sol

Stretching from Gibraltar to Almería, this much visited coast, backed by rugged sierra, has its highs and its lows. Intense development is concentrated west of Málaga, but there is glamour at the resort of Marbella. To the east, Nerja and Salobreña perch spectacularly above the sea.

San Pedro de Alcántara has a lovely beach and several golf courses.

Nerja *(visitor information, Calle Carmen 1, tel 952 52 15 31)* is an attractive resort town 33 miles (53 km) from Málaga, with a cave complex, **Cuevas de Nerja** *(Carretera de Maro, tel 952 52 95 20)*. The chambers, of stalactites and stalagmites, and a few Paleolithic rock paintings, stretch for 2,625 feet (800 m). Fifteen miles (24 km) farther, **Salobreña** *(visitor information, tel 958 61 03 14)* appears like a mirage, a huddle of white houses clinging to an outcrop.

Southwest of Málaga is **Torremolinos,** a jumble of high-rises packed with bars, shops, discos, and other facilities for vacationers. **Fuengirola** has more of the same, but it also has the ruins of a Moorish castle and nearly 4 miles (6 km) of beach. If you like water sports, this is a good place to be. Five miles (8 km) inland, the beautiful and well-preserved hill village of **Mijas,** once a haunt of artists, now suffers from a tidal wave of visitors from the coast. Sights include old Arab walls and the 17th-century hermitage of the Virgen de la Peña, but the chief attractions are the town's geranium-laden balconies, craft shops, and wonderful views, easily seen by donkey taxi.

Next stop west along the coastal highway is **Marbella,** the most glitzy and upscale resort in Spain, and its offshoot, **Puerto Banus,** famed for its marina. Cars cruise along the "Golden Mile" past endless bars, discos, a modern mosque, and chic hotels. The old center radiates from the Plaza de la Constitución, with a 16th-century town hall and a castle, **Castillo de Madera.** Its nightlife is the hottest on the costa.

San Pedro de Alcántara *(visitor information, Oficina Municipal de Turismo, Avenida Marqués del Duero 69, tel 952 78 52 52, map 260 D1)* was the Roman colony of Silniana, destroyed by an earthquake in A.D. 365. You can see well-restored structures and a sixth-century **Visigothic basilica** amid rampant development. San Pedro is the start of the tortuous, but magnificent 31-mile (50 km) drive up into the Serranía de Ronda. ■

Fuengirola
260 D1
Visitor Information
Oficina Municipal de Turismo, Paseo Jesús Santos Rein 6
952 46 76 25
www.visitafuengirola.com

Marbella
260 D1
Visitor Information
Oficina Municipal de Turismo, Plaza de los Naranjos s/n
952 77 36 21
www.marbella.com

Córdoba

There is something very special about Córdoba. At its heart, a labyrinth of narrow streets lined with whitewashed houses, flower-filled patios, and secret corners surrounds one of Spain's greatest monuments: the Mezquita. Souvenir shops crowd the immediate environs, but strike out farther and you discover quaint old taverns, craft workshops, flamenco performers—and the true spirit of Andalucía.

Once the largest city in the world, delightful Córdoba lies slightly off the Andalusian tourism trail.

Córdoba
260 D3

Visitor Information
Oficina de Turismo, Calle Torrijos 10
957 35 51 79

www.turismodecordoba.org

Straddling the Guadalquivir River between the wild Sierra Morena to the north and the agricultural plains to the south, this city of 325,000 people is developing a cultural dynamism to match its illustrious past. You can watch dancing horses in the old royal stables, or visit the 14th-century synagogue or the Alcazar (royal palace), before sampling *salmorejo* (Cordoba's version of gazpacho), white wine from Montilla to the south, and Iberico ham from Los Pedroches, to the north. Then take a bus out to the museum and palatial complex of Madinat al-Zahra, spectacular symbol of Córdoba's role as caliphal capital, holding sway over most of the peninsula. Allegedly it was the most populous city in the world, as well as an intellectual hotbed.

The city endures baking temperatures in July and August, when shady patios become essential oases. This climactic adversity has not prevented a string of festivities. During Holy Week (see pp. 272–273) processions invade the narrow streets. In May, the Feria (festival) takes place, and the entire population seems to be involved in crucifix-decorating, patio contests, and pilgrimages. Córdoba's legendary bullfighters and flamenco performers spring into action. Sultry summer evenings bring flamenco music to various gardens of the city.

The Romans founded the town in 169 B.C. and left a temple as proof, but it was under Islamic dominance that Córdoba reached its zenith. In 756, Abd ar-Rahman I founded Córdoba as the capital of Moorish Spain. By 929, when Abd ar-Rahman III declared himself caliph, it had become the envy of Europe. About 1,000 mosques, 600 public baths, public street lighting, and a renowned university graced the city, where philosophers, poets, mathematicians, and doctors (including the great Jewish thinker, Maimónides) created an intellectual ferment.

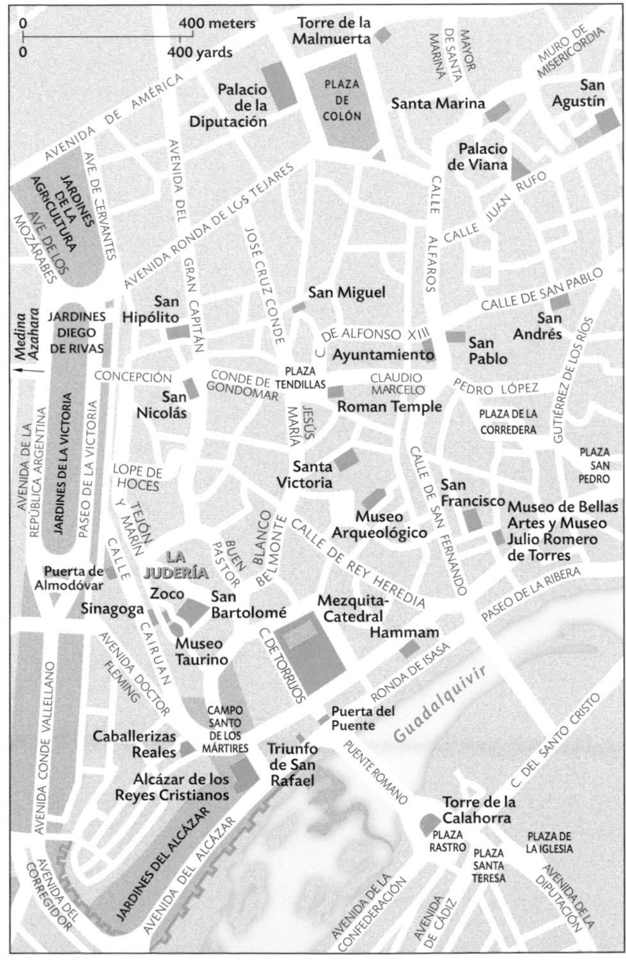

EXPERIENCE: Tasting Olive Oil

Spain has the world's greatest number of olive trees (more than 300 million) and 50 different types of olives. It is also the world's leading producer of olive oil, with the province of Córdoba leading the way. Spend a day learning all about this most basic of Mediterranean ingredients on a tour led by **A Taste of Spain** *(Calle Alonso Carro 8, Cádiz, tel 856 07 96 26 or 956 23 28 80, www.atasteofspain.com, $$$$$).*

Beginning in the city of Córdoba, you will travel through the region's olive groves—many of them organic—to the town of Baena. Along the way, you'll learn how to distinguish Picual olives (the most common) from Arbequina olives and other varietals. You may also catch a glimpse of olive pickers, harvesting the olives by hand or by hitting branches with a long pole. You'll visit two of the region's leading olive oil producers, **Luque** *(www.alcubilla2000.com)* and the famed **Núñez de Prado,** as well as an olive mill in **Baena.** Then it's on to a relaxed traditional Andalusian lunch (with select regional wines, of course) at a rustic and atmospheric old olive mill in Castro del Río. After lunch, you return to Córdoba.

Tours of Córdoba's olive groves are available year-round and include an expert guide, all transportation, one private olive oil–tasting session, and lunch (wine included). Tours starting from Sevilla are also available.

Mezquita

- Map 285
- Cardenal Herrero 1
- 957 47 05 12
- Closed Sun. a.m.
- $$

www.turismodecordoba.org/mezquita.htm

Alcázar de los Reyes Cristianos

- Map 285
- Calle Caballerizas Reales
- 957 42 01 51
- Closed Sun. p.m. & Mon.
- $. Free on Fri.

www.turismodecordoba.org/alcazar.htm

Decline came in the 11th century after the skillful but ruthless reign of al-Mansur, although intellectual life continued until 1236, when Córdoba was conquered by Fernando III. From then on it was a steady downward slide. Ingenious Moorish waterworks were abandoned and every mosque except the Mezquita was replaced by a church. In the 16th and 17th centuries, Córdoba's artisans of embossed leather and silver were much sought after, but plague decimated the population in the 17th century.

Córdoba is an easy city in which to orient yourself, although you may get lost in the Judería, the old Jewish quarter north of the Mezquita. It is worth exploring the barrios to the east and north, beyond the striking Plaza de la Corredera: Their more modest houses have produced famous bullfighters and flamenco artists.

Mezquita

The jewel in Córdoba's crown is still called by its Arabic name, Mezquita, meaning "mosque," despite the extraordinary intrusion of a Catholic cathedral in its midst. It is the only mosque left from medieval Spain, and it is one of the largest in the world.

The huge structure covers 258,330 square feet (24,000 sq m). Building started in 785, it was extended in 848 and 961, then almost doubled in size in 987. Your first sight is from the **Puerta del Perdón,** an immense gateway beside the baroque belfry that encloses the old minaret. In front is the beautiful **Patio de los Naranjos,** dotted with orange trees whose fragrant blossoms in April are unforgettable. Once you enter the oldest part of the mosque, you understand why Charles V ordered that the building be saved, despite immense pressure from the Church to demolish it. It is a visual masterpiece of rhythmical horseshoe arches that somehow gives the sense of infinity that underlies Islamic belief. Each of the 824 columns is different, as are their capitals, since they were mostly salvaged from previous Roman and Visigothic structures. The two-tiered arch was copied from Roman aqueducts for structural purposes and to increase the light. Notice the alternating bands of red brick and white stone, and their painted imitations in the later, northern section, built with inferior materials under power-crazy Prime Minister Al-Mansur.

Penetrate the interior, passing the cathedral on your left, and you come to the end wall, the **Kibla,** which should face Mecca (southeast of Córdoba) but actually faces due south. The Mezquita's most stunning piece of craftsmanship is here, the **mihrab,** or prayer niche, from which the imam (Muslim prayer leader) would lead worshippers in prayer. Look carefully at the exquisite mosaics and dome decorated by Byzantine craftsmen, and the entire *maqsura,* the marble-flagged space that was once reserved for the caliph and his courtiers. Koranic texts are engraved into marble cornices, and you can see Spain's earliest stucco tracery—later to become a major feature of Nazrid and Mudejar architecture.

From here you move to the **Tesoro,** a comparatively heavy baroque chapel containing Córdoba's massive silver and gold monstrance, made by Enrique de Arfe in 1516. Next comes the 14th-century **Capilla Real** (Royal Chapel), built under Alfonso X and sympathetically decorated in Mudejar-style stucco. Finally you get to the carbuncle of the Mezquita, the Renaissance-baroque **cathedral** (1523–1617) that was plunked down in the center of the mosque. On leaving, take time to

(continued on p. 290)

INSIDER TIP:

For something a little different in the Córdoba area, visit Lagar La Primilla *(www.laprimilla.es)*, a *lagar,* or small winepress, in the vineyards of Montilla near Córdoba. You can taste the wines with a selection of excellent tapas.

—TERESA REDONDO
Director, Bacus Travel & Tours

Montilla

Map pp. 260–261

Visitor Information

Oficina Municipal de Turismo, Calle Capitán Alonso de Vargas 3, Casa del Inca

957 65 23 54

www.montilla.es

The Mezquita's interior creates a spatial sense of infinity.

Flamenco

Flamenco is a form of song, guitar playing, and dance that epitomizes the complex soul of Andalucía. Arab, Oriental, and Gypsy influences mingled to produce this extraordinarily characteristic sound, which in its rawest, most authentic state is a spontaneous outburst late at night in a backstreet bar. The shows put on for tourists can be disappointingly mechanical. Nonetheless, true flamenco is alive, well, and reinventing itself.

Enjoy foot-tapping flamenco performances in the caves of Sacromonte.

Most experts believe that the roots of flamenco lie in the 15th century, when Gypsies arrived from north India via Egypt and eastern Europe, and fused their music with that of the Moors and Jews in Andalucía. The word "flamenco" probably derives from the Arabic "felag mengu," meaning "fugitive peasant"—a reference to Gypsies and perhaps also Moriscos (baptized Moors). Since then it has evolved into several branches, notably the *soleá* of Sevilla's Triana district, the *bulería* of Jerez de la Frontera, and the *cantes festeros* (festive styles) of Cádiz. Granada's Sacromonte district fine-tuned the zambra gitana, gypsy festivity, while Córdoba has produced fantastic artists such as Fosforito (a legend) and Luis de Córdoba. The different styles, or *palos,* have a common rhythmical cycle of 12, like the blues, but differ in key and harmonic progression.

For all its variations, the bottom line of flamenco is to attain *duende* (soul), an intense communication with the audience, which participates with interjected cries of appreciation. Flamenco song can be modified according to need and context. Often performed a cappella, the *cante jondo* (deep song), reserved for virtuosos, is the oldest form, in which the singer's emotional expression of loss, grief, or injustice is considered more important than tonal clarity.

Solo guitar playing evolved from providing the singers with a break to becoming an art in itself. Guitarists such as Paco Peña, Paco de Lucía, and Tomatito have become world famous, often more so than their singing companions. A notable exception was El Camarón de la Isla (1950–1992). The total performing art of song, music, and dance came together in the late 19th century and was crowned by Manuel de Falla's flamenco ballet, *El Amor Brujo,* in 1915. Since the 1950s, *tablaos* (specialized flamenco bars) have encouraged exponents of all three elements.

In dance, it is mesmerizing footwork that is primordial, hence the flounced, long-trained dresses cut high at the front. In the 1970s, the Sevillian dancer Manuela Carrasco carried this technique to its greatest heights. Anyone who saw Carlos Saura's film *Carmen* (1983) must remember the fabulous footwork of Cristina Hoyos dancing with Antonio Gades. Their torch is carried forward by Joaquin Cortés, Eva "La Yerbabuena," and Niño de los Reyes.

Flamenco still has traditional interpreters, most of whom are Gypsies. With women singers such as Aurora Vargas and Rosario La Tremendita and the impetus of *nuevo flamenco* (new flamenco) groups such as Ketama, Pata Negra, Radio Tarifa (fusing flamenco with Arab music), Ojos de Brujo (mixing in Latin rhythms and electronics), and Chambao (flamenco "chill"), flamenco is gaining wider audiences and, again, evolving.

Many flamenco troupes also offer classes where you can learn the evocative dance.

EXPERIENCE: Joining in Flamenco

You often hear a flamenco performance before you see it: the syncopated hand-clapping or *compas,* the anguished wails, the phenomenal guitar playing, the rapid-fire heel-stomping, and the "olé olé" from an excited audience. Every big Andalusian city stages performances at *tablaos,* which, even if superficially touristy, usually feature top artists. For the real deal, look for a *peña* or flamenco club for aficionados. Most towns have at least one *peña flamenca,* and cities have up to thirty. Peñas are far more traditional: You will witness the most orthodox tones of *cante jondo* accompanied by the purest flamenco guitar.

Learn flamenco yourself and you will gain far greater insight. Granada's traditional Albaicín quarter (see pp. 306–307) offers weeklong classes in rhythm or dance that can be combined with Spanish language classes *(www.golearnto.com).* The highly regarded Taller de Flamenco *(www.tallerflamenco.com)* in Sevilla has an even fuller array, from weekend-long dance classes to guitar, compas, singing, and percussion with or without Spanish language thrown in. Sevilla's Museo del Baile Flamenco *(www.museoflamenco.com)* also holds classes and workshops. For flamenco products visit *www.flamencoshop.com* and *www.flamenco-world.com.*

Museo Arqueológico

- Plaza de Jerónimo Páez 7
- 957 35 55 17
- Closed Sun. p.m. & Mon.
- $. Free for E.U. citizens

www.turismodecordoba/museos.htm

look at the exquisitely carved outer doorways on Calle de Torrijos (by the Mezquita's western wall), where an elevated walkway once joined the caliph's palace.

A few steps southwest of the Mezquita lies the **Alcázar de los Reyes Cristianos** (Fort of the Christian Kings), which was built in 1328 after the Christian Reconquest of Córdoba. Fernando and Isabel used this fortified palace as their base in 1491–1492 while plotting their attack on Granada, the last Moorish stronghold of Andalucía. After that its functions became less glorious: It was the Court of the Inquisition until the early 19th century and then a prison. Today, the interior has a few interesting features, but it is the **water gardens** that are superb. They were re-created in Moorish style in the 1960s, and every July are the setting for Córdoba's guitar festival.

The water garden at the Alcázar de los Reyes Cristianos

Just behind the garden are the spectacular royal stables, **Caballerizas Reales** *(tel 957 49 78 43, closed Mon., www.caballerizasreales.com)*, built in 1570 on the order of the horse-loving Felipe II. From here came the Andalusian horse, bred by royal order. Equestrian shows include flamenco.

Cross the Roman bridge from here to reach the **Torre de la Calahorra** *(Puente Romano, tel 957 29 39 29)*, an Arab tower that replaced a Roman gateway and was rebuilt in 1369. From the roof you have spectacular views of Córdoba across the river; inside is an audiovisual display on Moorish culture.

Museums & Palaces

Two blocks northeast of the Mezquita, on one of Córdoba's most delightful squares, the **Museo Arqueológico** is as interesting for its setting as for its collection. The collection is imaginatively distributed throughout the four patios and galleries of a lovely Renaissance mansion with a magnificent sculpted gateway. In 2011, a sharply designed extension opened next door, built over Roman remains that include a theater. **Patio II** has a superb Roman statue of a crouching Aphrodite, copied from a Greek piece. In **Patio III** the remains of Roman steps face a mosaic panel of the Nile River. Fragments of stone inscriptions, columns, and capitals in **Room V** lead you to a model of the Roman temple standing on Calle Claudio Marcelo and a superb statue of Hermaphroditos.

As you climb the Renaissance staircase examine the carved *artesonado* ceiling before moving clockwise around the upper galleries devoted to Moorish artifacts. Among them are a lovely capital sculpted with four figures of musicians and, in **Room VII,** the incised bronze of a fawn: This and the surrounding glass and ceramic all came from Medina Azahara. Also outstanding is the rare collection of terra-cotta wells.

Just beside the museum is the **Zoco,** or souk, a small artisans' market where some of Córdoba's many silversmiths and ceramicists practice their trade. Beside it is the tiny yet exquisitely crafted **Sinagoga** *(Calle Judíos, tel 957 20 29 28, closed Mon.),* built in 1315.

Opposite is the newly opened **Casa de Sefarad** *(Calle Judios, tel 957 42 14 04, $)* in which five rooms explain the history of Spain's Sephardic Jews and exhibit related objects. Fourteenth-century architectural details reveal the age of this remarkable street, the best preserved of Spain's many medieval Jewish quarters. A little farther stands the 12th-century **Casa Andalusí** *(tel 957 29 06 42, $),* with a sympathetic reconstruction of a typical interior and display on paper manufacture.

Right by the northeastern corner of the Mezquita is a renovated mansion devoted to the craft of embossed leather, the **Museo Arte sobre Piel.** This craft was originally developed under the Caliphate in the tenth-century and still survives today.

Well outside the Judería but still within walking distance, the **Palacio de Viana** is a fine and substantial aristocratic mansion. The one-hour guided tour (in Spanish but with an explanatory leaflet in English) whisks you through a labyrinth of halls and rooms, all stuffed with valuable antiques, chandeliers, paintings, and tapestries. Like the Casa de Pilatos in Sevilla (see p. 268), it makes a fascinating eye-opener on the lifestyle and means of the Spanish nobility. Twelve gardens surround the mansion, each one perfumed by aromatic plants. If you miss Córdoba's fabulous Festival of Patios, held in May, this makes an excellent substitute. ■

Madinat al-Zahra

Madinat al-Zahra is one of Spain's most important archaeological sites, and it is a must on your Andalusian journey. It lies on a hillside 7 miles (11 km) west of Córdoba off the C431. A little bus ferries visitors from the superbly designed museum uphill to the ruins, or you can walk. The Medina stood for only 70 years before it was destroyed by North African Berbers in 1010. The main sight is the vast tenth-century **palace** of Caliph Abd ar-Rahman III, of the Umayyad dynasty. The other impressive surviving structures are the **army barracks** and the marble-carved **Salón Rico** (Rich Room), a restored hall of the reconstructed palace. Below, the ruins of the **mosque** are correctly oriented toward Mecca. The terraced site, with its sweeping view, cypress trees, palms, and wild cacti, evokes a sense of the power and majesty of Córdoba's caliphate.

Museo Arte sobre Piel

- ✉ Plaza Agrupación de Cofradías
- ☎ 957 05 01 31
- 🕒 Closed Mon.

Palacio de Viana

- ✉ Plaza de Don Gome 2
- ☎ 957 49 67 41
- 🕒 Closed Sat. & Sun. p.m.

Madinat al-Zahra

- ✉ Carretera de Palma del Rio (C431)
- ☎ 957 35 28 60
- 🕒 Closed Sun. p.m. & Mon.
- $ $. Free for E.U. citizens

www.juntadeandalucia.es

Priego de Córdoba

Crowning an outcrop of the craggy Sierra Subbética, Priego de Córdoba is a little known jewel that combines Baroque architecture with a charming Moorish quarter and a flourishing gastronomic sector, olive oil is king. The city's high point comes in May, when every Sunday sees spirited Cruces de Mayo processions, a tradition begun 400 years ago.

Barrio de la Villa, Priego de Córdoba

In the Barrio de la Villa, in the northeast corner of Priego de Córdoba *(visitor information, Oficina Municipal de Turismo, Plaza de la Constitución 3, tel 957 70 06 25, closed Sun., www.turismodepriego.com)*, lanes of whitewashed houses wind past hidden patios and candlelit shrines. This ends abruptly at the **Balcon del Adarve,** a sheer rockface with panoramas over the sierra. On the other side of this quaint quarter looms Priego's medieval **Castillo** *(Abad Polomino, closed Sun. & Mon. p.m., $)*, worth climbing for fabulous views. Opposite, the ornate **Iglesia de la Asuncion** *(Plaza Santa Ana)* epitomizes 17th-century Andalusian baroque. Inside look for the finely sculpted cupola of the sacristy as well as the extraordinary five-level altarpiece. Behind the fortress, the Renaissance **Carnicerias Reales** (Royal Slaughterhouse; *Calle San Luis, closed Sun & Mon p.m., $*) holds historical exhibitions.

Don't miss the unique 16th-century **Fuente del Rey** (King's Fountain; *Calle del Rio*), where 139 spouts feed three pools—a sign of the area's abundant springs.

EXPERIENCE: Off-Road Cycling in La Subbética

La Subbética lies at the center of Andalucía, just an hour from Córdoba, Granada, Sevilla, and Málaga. Spectacularly beautiful, this region is home to rugged hills and deep valleys, traditional towns, and the **Parque Natural de las Sierras Subbéticas,** 76,000 acres (31,000 ha) of craggy peaks and pretty valleys, where eagles, falcons, and kestrals circle the skies.

For a little off-road adventure in this region, join a weeklong bike tour *($$$$$)* with **Joyriders Spain** *(tel 695 25 89 44, www.joy-riders.com)*. Tours can be partly or fully guided, with a midweek rest day. Rides in the foothills of the Subbéticas can be demanding, but you can arrange tours based on fitness level and desire. Luxury accommodation and breakfast are included. Bike rentals are extra.

Úbeda & Baeza

Just 5 miles (8 km) apart in the olive-rich province of Jaén, the once rival towns of Úbeda and Baeza are UNESCO World Heritage sites. Their stunning Renaissance architecture reflects the peak in their fortunes in the 16th century. Úbeda is the aristocrat, Baeza the smaller, poorer, though no less magnificent cousin; both come as surprises in the Andalusian landscape.

Úbeda

Gold and silver from the Americas financed the sober granite buildings of Úbeda, most of which were the work of local architect Andrés de Vandelvira (1509–1575). Sit on a bench on the monumental Plaza de Vazquez de Molina to admire the church of **El Salvador,** with the town hall to the left, and, to your right, Santa Maria, the Palacio del Marqués de Mancero, and the old granary. The grand parador flanking the square was once the residence of the dean of Málaga.

Have a look, too, at the unique local ceramics with cut-out elements, finished in a deep green glaze. On Calle Valencia, just north of the Puerta del Losal, you can visit workshops: At no. 44, Melchor Tito and his son still fire in traditional wood-fueled kilns *(tel 953 75 36 92, www.melchortito.com)*. Older pieces are displayed at the **Museo Arqueológico** in an attractive 14th-century Mudejar house.

Baeza

Baeza's monuments of warm golden stone are better integrated into the modern town than Úbeda's, making it less of a museum. The **cathedral** dominates high ground to the east of the center. Climb the bell tower for views but don't miss the Mudejar cloisters or the 13th-century Puerta de la Luna and rose window.

Just to the west is Baeza's outstanding **Palacio de Jabalquinto,** commissioned by Juan Alfonso de Benavides. No effort was spared in carving this magnificent Flamboyant Gothic facade, and a century or so later the equally exquisite Renaissance cloisters and grand Baroque staircase. The palace now belongs to Baeza University.

West of Baeza, stop at **Puente de Obispo** to learn about olive oil at the **Museo de la Cultura del Olivo** *(Hacienda de la Laguna, tel 953 76 51 42, www.museodelaculturadelolivo.com)*, part of a complex devoted to this age-old product. ■

INSIDER TIP:

Time your visit with Úbeda's music and dance festival *(www.festivaldeubeda.com)* in April–May. The city's stunning Renaissance buildings make the celebration quite unique in Spain.

—PILAR PARRA RUÍZ
Director, Fundación Valparaíso

Úbeda
261 E3
Visitor Information
Oficina de Turismo, Calle Bajo del Marqués 4
953 77 92 04 or 953 77 92 05
Closed Sat. & Sun. p.m.
www.ubedainteresa.com

El Salvador
Plaza de Vazquez de Molina, Úbeda
953 75 81 50

Museo Arqueológico
Calle Cervantes, Úbeda
953 77 94 32

Baeza
261 E3
Visitor Information
Oficina de Turismo, Plaza del Pópulo s/n
953 77 99 82
Closed Sat. & Sun. p.m.
www.baeza.net

Granada

It was in the 19th century that the image of Granada as the quintessential Oriental town first floated into the Western imagination. This was in part thanks to the American writer Washington Irving, whose *Tales of the Alhambra* inspired a succession of writers and artists to try to capture the wonders of Granada's palace, the Alhambra. Behind the city loom the snowcapped peaks of the Sierra Nevada, creating an ethereal atmosphere.

No matter the day, you can always find an outdoor market in Granada.

Granada
261 E2
Visitor Information

Oficina de Turismo, Calle Santa Ana 4
958 57 52 02 or 958 57 52 04

www.granadatur.com
www.turgranada.es

Today the Alhambra is the number one sight for visitors to Spain, so be prepared. You are never alone beside the fountains of its cool patios and verdant gardens, though you can always find a relatively secluded corner in which to muse on the past.

The rest of Granada is also very rich in monuments, and the city has a lively cultural program, partly because of its burgeoning population of 50,000 students and numerous flamenco bars.

How to Visit

You can divide your sightseeing neatly into three areas: first, the hilltop Alhambra; second, the steep, rambling lanes of the Albaicín opposite (sprinkled with restaurants that give huge views); and third, the "new" town that sprawls below. The heart of modern Granada beats here, and is far from lacking in interest between specialist shops, graceful avenues, and a good sprinkling of historical musts. A possible fourth area is Sacromonte, the Gypsy cave dwellers' quarter that stretches north into the hills from the Albaicín.

Flamenco clubs abound throughout the city, but they are not all authentic, so do your research. Don't take valuables with you or leave anything in your car—better still, leave the car itself in a downtown parking lot, using your feet or local minibuses to get you uphill.

History of Granada

Granada was ruled by Moors from 731, but it came into its own in 1031, with the collapse of the Córdoban caliphate. Out of centuries of obscurity emerged a kingdom of splendor, wealth, and poetry, ruled by the Almoravids, then by the Almohads, and, from 1238, the Nazrids. Arts and sciences flourished side by side, in an era of brilliance and religious tolerance that drew together thinkers from Europe, North Africa, and the Middle East. The magnificent buildings of the Alhambra arose, culminating in the magical Nazrid palace.

During this time, the Christian Reconquest was pushing

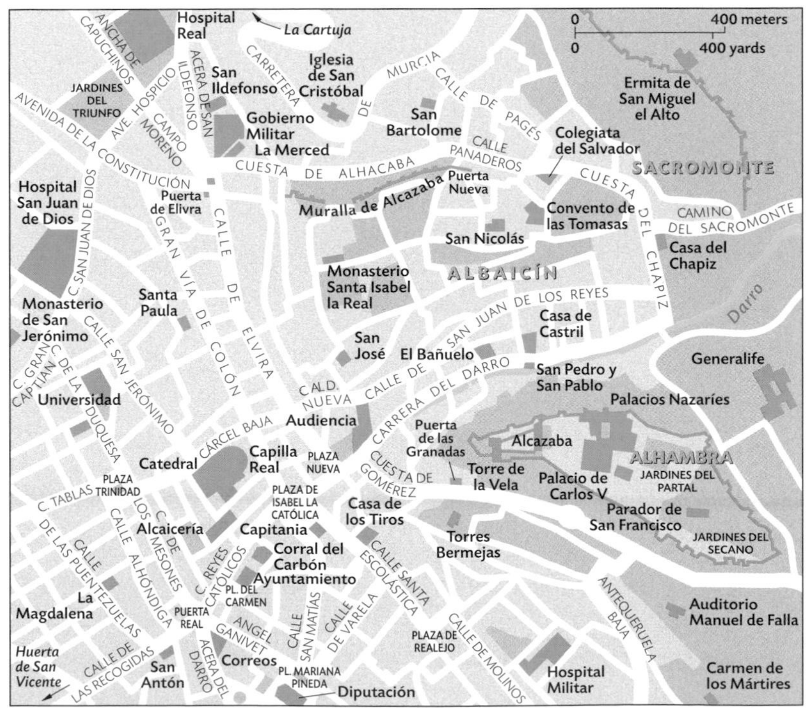

Cathedral
Gran Vía de Colón 5
958 22 29 59
Closed Sun. a.m.
$

www.granadatur.com/DATA/mainMonEN.htm

Capilla Real
Oficios 3
958 22 92 39
$

www.capillarealgranada.com

southward, but Granada held out longer than any other Muslim city in Spain. However, in January 1492, after a six-month siege of the city, the Catholic Monarchs Fernando and Isabel finally rode in victorious. The boy-king Boabdil fled with his mother into exile in the Alpujarras (see pp. 310–312), famously shedding a last tear as he looked back at Granada from the mountain pass now called El Suspiro del Moro ("the Moor's sigh"). Nearly eight centuries of Muslim rule in Andalucía were over, although it was not until the expulsion of the Moriscos (baptized Moors) in 1570 that the city of Granada wholly lost its true creators.

Granada continued to flourish in the Renaissance: Monuments from then include the massive cathedral, monastery of San Jerónimo, and Hospital Real (Royal Hospital). In the 17th century the monastery of La Cartuja was built, and the city produced artists such as Alonso Cano (1601–1667) and Pedro de Mena (1628–1688).

Later the city wove its spell over Eugène Delacroix, the French 19th-century Romantic painter, and inspired musicians such as Manuel de Falla and Andrés Segovia. Granada's greatest 20th-century writer was the poet Federico García Lorca (1899–1936), shot by Franco's troops in the Civil War. Today, this is a sophisticated, vibrant, city, redolent of the past but not buried in it. Ironically, an expanding Moroccan community of about 10,000 is bringing Islam back to the city.

Downtown Granada

The Gran Vía de Colón is the main artery through downtown Granada. The heart of downtown is **Plaza de Isabel la Católica,** a little square with the cathedral and other sights clustered around it.

INSIDER TIP:

Granada is one of the best cities in Spain for free tapas. Visit any of the bars in town, order a drink, and then wait and see what they bring you.

–YUKO AOYAMA
National Geographic grantee

Cathedral: The grandiose cathedral dominates the southwest corner of Granada. The main building is a Renaissance masterpiece, begun under Diego de Siloé (1495–1563) in 1528, with a facade by Alonso Cano, completed in 1667, the year of his death.

The most impressive part of Granada's cathedral, however, is the earlier **Capilla Real** (Royal Chapel) abutting its southern flank. You enter it through the **Lonja** (Exchange). Commissioned by the Catholic Monarchs to house their tombs, the Capilla Real was built in just 15 years, and the result is a harmonious profusion of Isabelline Gothic, fittingly lavish for its royal incumbents.

The superb tombs of Fernando and Isabel are by the Florentine sculptor Domenico Fancelli (1469–1519). Bartolomé Ordóñez (circa 1485–1520) was responsible for those of their daughter Juana ("the Mad") and her husband Felipe. The tombs lie beneath a soaring rib-vaulted ceiling, while their lead coffins lie in the crypt below. Look, too, at the gilded, wrought-iron screen in front, another masterpiece, this one by Maestro Bartolomé de Jaén.

The **sacristy museum** dazzles visitors with its chalices, processional crosses, reliquaries, the crown and scepter of Isabel herself, Fernando's sword, and banners carried during the conquest of Granada. Here, too, is Isabel's impressive collection of Flemish and Italian paintings, including works by Memling, van der Weyden, and Botticelli.

In contrast, the main cathedral seems rather a soulless affair, despite its airiness and height. In the **Capilla Mayor** look for Pedro de Mena's praying figures of Fernando and Isabel. You see Alonso Cano's works throughout.

The cathedral was built on the site of the demolished Great Mosque, a remnant of which stands opposite the Capilla Real. Another relic of this period, tucked away behind Calle de los Reyes Catolicos, is the **Corral del Carbón** *(Calle Mariana Pineda, tel 958 22 11 18)*, an unusually sober courtyard building that functioned as a storehouse and merchants' inn. Between this and the cathedral lies the old Arab souk, the **Alcaicería,** completely rebuilt following a fire and now full of overpriced souvenirs.

South of the cathedral, a succession of animated squares and shopping streets offer a break from sightseeing in the form of tapas bars and restaurants.

Monasterio de San Jerónimo: West of the cathedral, follow Calle San Jerónimo to the 16th-century Monasterio de San Jerónimo

The sacristy of La Cartuja dates from 1727 to 1764.

(Calle Rector López Argüeta, tel 958 27 93 37). This jewel of Spanish Renaissance architecture has a wonderful two-tiered cloister, the work of Diego de Siloé, architect of the cathedral. In the church are beautiful

Huerta de San Vicente

Calle Arabial s/n, Parque Federico García Lorca

958 25 84 66

Closed Mon.

www.huertagarcialorca.org

Alhambra & Generalife

Avenida de los Alixares

902 44 12 21

Open for night visits Fri. & Sat. (winter), Tues.–Sat. (summer)

$$$. Book your visit to Nazrid Palace at 902 88 80 01, +34 934 92 37 50 (from abroad), or at www.alhambra-tickets.es

www.alhambra.org

18th-century frescoes, and the tomb of the Catholic Monarchs' general, Gonzalo Fernández de Córdoba, known as El Gran Capitán. Nuns still live here: You can buy their cakes and jams at the entrance, and occasionally you hear them singing.

La Cartuja: Now take bus No. 18 or Linea C from Gran Vía to the Carthusian monastery of La Cartuja *(Paseo de Cartuja, tel 958 16 19 32)*, by far the greatest baroque monument in Granada. The Carthusians lived austerely but ornamented lavishly, and this monastery takes the cake. Gold leaf, mirrors, stuccowork, marble, Venetian glass, mural paintings, marquetry, and a profusion of sculpted cherubim, flowers, and vines set the tone—and that's just in the church **sanctuary.** This exercise in excess was created by Francisco Hurtado Izquierdo from 1704 to 1720 and is rivaled only by the **sacristy,** which he designed later. Here you find a sculpture of St. Bruno by José de Mora, Alonso Cano's "Inmaculada," and cupola frescoes by Tomás Ferrer. The church glitters with the gilt of Churrigueresque altarpieces, doors inlaid with mother-of-pearl, ivory, ebony, and tortoiseshell—the work of a monk, José Manuel Vázquez. Recover from this visual assault in the peaceful **cloisters.**

Huerta de San Vicente: Poet Federico García Lorca is honored at his family's former summer house, Huerta de San Vicente. He did much of his writing here; at that time the house stood in an orchard, but suburbs have swallowed it up. You see original furnishings, drawings by friends such as Salvador Dalí, manuscripts, and photos. Reserve a place on the guided tour in advance, as numbers are limited.

Washington Irving

He was not the first or last person to be enamored of the Alhambra in Granada, but Washington Irving was the first writer to describe in so humane a fashion the tales and legends of this rambling fairytale palace, bringing to life its silent towers and chambers. It was in 1829 that he installed himself in the governor's apartments overlooking the orange trees and fountains of the garden of Daraxa, and over the next few weeks he penned his tribute to the palace's inhabitants, ***Tales of the Alhambra.***

The Alhambra

Visible from all over the city, the Alhambra reigns in splendor from its hilltop, the simple crenellated towers and walls rising above a cloud of greenery that extends to the Generalife beyond. Walk up the steep incline of Cuesta de Gomérez, through shady pines to the Puerta de la Justicia, or ride in a minibus from the Plaza Nueva. If you are driving, plenty of signs point the way. You can also approach from the Darro riverbank up Cuesta del Rey Chico, where a steep path leads to the main entrance.

The Alhambra encompasses four sections: the military fortress of the Alcazaba (the oldest part); the exquisite Nazrid Palace (the ultimate flowering of Moorish architecture); the summer palace of the Generalife; and the Renaissance Palace of Carlos V.

Between these four areas lies a labyrinthine garden of paradise, or at least a good earthly semblance of heavenly bliss. Every sense is ignited by the subtle combination of light, color, sound, and smell created by trickling fountains, reflective ponds, high hedges, and an abundance of fragrant flowers—roses, plumbago, honeysuckle, jasmine, and bougainvillea.

The color of the walls, built from a durable mixture of red earth and stone, gave the Alhambra its name, derived from the Arabic word for "red." The walls once enclosed a self-contained town with four gateways, 23 towers, seven palaces, workers' houses, workshops, baths, a madrasa (Islamic school), and mosques. Many of these have disappeared, but the surviving palaces continue to exert their magic, just as they did on Carlos V: He built his own imperial palace here but used it only for ceremonial functions, preferring to live with his family in the more congenial Moorish palaces.

The Alhambra gardens were designed to symbolize paradise on Earth.

The Alhambra's overwhelming popularity means that in peak season you have to dodge large guided tours. Ideally, make time for a second daytime visit, and also come back at night when lighting brings to the fore elements that you might have missed by day.

(continued on p. 302)

Moorish Architecture

Although nearly all the mosques of the Moors were demolished after the Christian Reconquest, other structures such as palaces and bathhouses survived. The architectural elements they introduced to Spain became integrated into Hispanic architecture.

Ornate brickwork and blind arches face La Giralda in Sevilla.

Vaults & Domes

Domes were a common feature in Moorish architecture, and they are best seen today in Spain's remaining bathhouses. Developed in the Middle East in the eighth century, these single-story structures had domed and vaulted roofs perforated by star-shaped openings for ventilation and light.

The most luxurious bathhouse in Spain is that of the Alhambra in Granada (see pp. 298–299, 302–305), where white marble columns and floors combine with glazed wall tiles, plaster, and timber. Good examples of public baths can also be seen in Ronda, Girona, and Granada's Albaicín.

Horseshoe Arches

The quintessential Moorish arch is shaped like a horseshoe, its most memorable example being in Córdoba's Mezquita (see pp. 286–287, 290). Although the Mezquita is based on the Great Mosque of Damascus, its superimposed tiered arches are said to have been inspired by Roman aqueducts. Builders recycled Visigothic and Roman columns and capitals, while creating a sensation of infinite space. Alternating bands of stone and red brick in the arch itself add even greater visual dynamism. Repetitive horseshoe arches can also be seen in Toledo's Santa María la Blanca synagogue, and blind horseshoe arches on facades were extensively used by Mudejar craftsmen. Later extensions brought other arch designs: the trefoil, multilobed, pointed horseshoe, and pointed arch.

Minarets

The muezzin's call to prayer came from lofty minarets built next to mosques. Spain's most impressive remaining example is that of Sevilla, the main al-Andalus base for the orthodox Almohad dynasty. This was designed by Ahmed ibn Baso, who repeated its form at the Koutoubia Mosque in Marrakech. The square tower, known as La Giralda, is faced in sebka brickwork, the repetition of small arch forms. Mudejar craftsmen multiplied the same use of brick patterning in the intricately faced towers of Teruel and at Zaragoza's La Seo cathedral.

Stucco

The sculptural quality of plaster combined with powdered marble (stucco) produced acres of walls carved with arabesque and floral patterns, edged by bands of Kufic calligraphy. Stucco's fragility meant that it was applied only to upper walls, archways, and ceilings. The apogee of stucco complexity is found in the Nazrid Palace of the Alhambra, where *muqarnas* (resembling honeycomb and stalactites) dripping from star-shaped domes create a dazzling optical effect.

Sevilla's Casa de Pilatos features a sumptuous display of stuccowork and horseshoe arches.

Azulejos

Glazed tiles were extensively used for surfacing dados (lower walls) in Moorish and Mudejar buildings. Their bold colors and geometric patterns create a strong visual contrast with the more delicate appearance of the stucco-faced upper walls. Geometry was one of the Arabs' greatest skills, and their talent for multiplying basic star forms can be seen in the incredible variations of their *azulejo* designs. Ceramics were also incorporated into Mudejar decorative brickwork.

EXPERIENCE: Moorish Baths

The habit of public bathing came from the Romans, but the Moors elevated it to more sybaritic heights. Ablutions are an integral part of Islam, which maintains that purity of body and spirit are linked. As it says in the Koran, "Hygiene is a sign of faith."

Start your tour of Granada's Moorish baths by stepping back 1,000 years with a visit to El Bañuelo *(Carrera de Darro 31, tel 958 02 78 00, closed Sun. & Mon.)*, the oldest and best preserved Arab bath complex in the city, though Roman and Visigoth columns suggest a longer history. Inside this small neighborhood bath, which was once connected to a mosque, men talked business and politics while women chatted about domestic matters. Three shallow pools—warm, hot, and cold—were fed by the Darro River. (Vestiges of the clay pipes are still visible.) Geometric holes cut in the barrel roof provide the only light.

Then treat yourself to an Arab-style bath and massage at the luxurious Baños Árabes *(Calle Santa Ana 16, tel 958 22 99 78, www.hammamspain.com, $$ for 90-min. bath)*, a modern but evocative complex located at the foot of the Alhambra over the ruins of baths closed in the 16th century. Marvel at the inlaid stone and relax to the sound of North African music.

For the Nazrid Palace you have to reserve a visit (try late in the afternoon when crowds have thinned), but you can soak up the atmosphere of the rest of the Alhambra for as long as you want.

Alcazaba: This is a good place to start. You can climb to the roof of the **Torre de la Vela** for a fantastic panoramic view of the entire site, and of the rest of Granada, the Sierra Nevada, and the endless *vega* (plain) to the west. Dating from the ninth century, the Alcazaba was Granada's first major Moorish structure, though the front two towers were built four centuries later. An often deserted **garden** on the southern side makes a meditative oasis.

Palacios Nazaríes (Nazrid Palace): Called an earthly paradise by the French poet

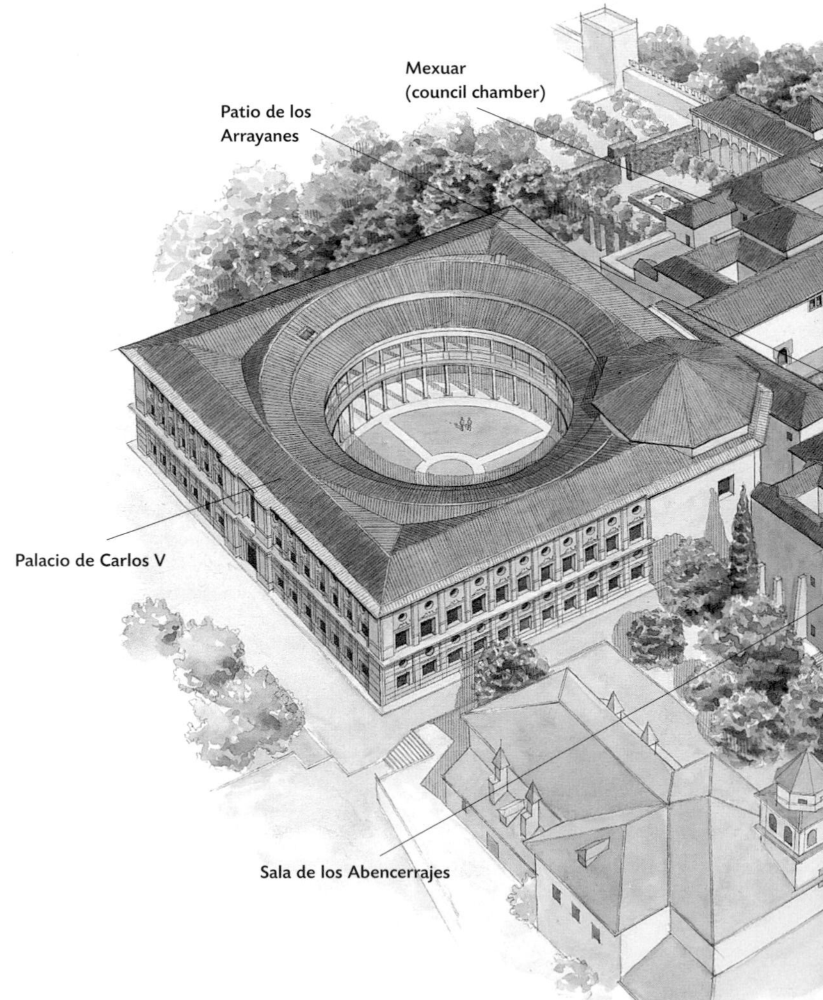

Théophile Gautier, the palace was built for Yusuf I and Mohammed V in the 1300s, and its two patios, intricately carved stucco ceilings, friezes, capitals and archways, geometric mosaics, fountains, and infinite perspectives constitute the zenith of Moorish style in Spain.

From the beautifully tiled **Mexuar** (Council Chamber) you enter the Patio del Cuarto Dorado, then the overwhelming

Despite its popularity with tourists, the Alhambra does have some secluded spots.

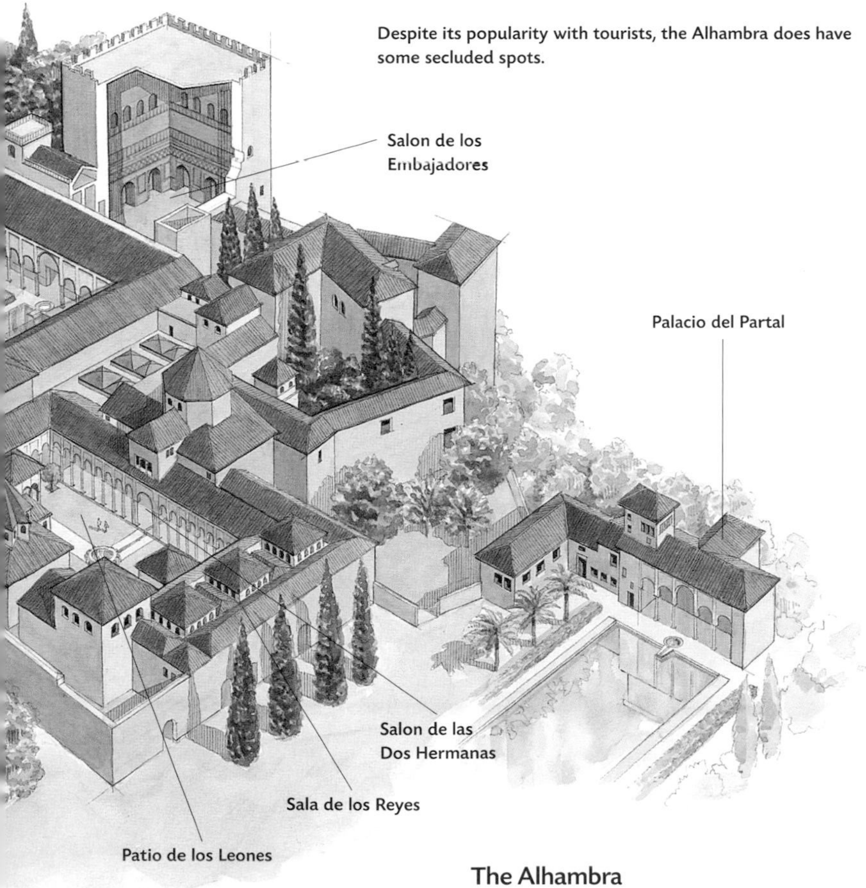

Salon de los Embajadores

Palacio del Partal

Salon de las Dos Hermanas

Sala de los Reyes

Patio de los Leones

The Alhambra

Salón de los Embajadores (Hall of Ambassadors, inside the Comares Tower). Its complex domed marquetry ceiling is said to consist of more than 8,000 polygonal pieces of cedarwood, and the stuccowork of the walls is masterful. Look at the beautiful *muqarnas* (honeycomb stuccowork used in ceiling, archways, and domes), then admire the wonderful views from the windows. Outside, the **Patio de los Arrayanes** (Court of Myrtles) presents one of the finest perspectives in the Alhambra, accentuated by the myrtle hedges flanking the pool.

From here, a passage leads to the **Sala de los Mozárabes,** an anteroom that opens onto the much photographed **Patio de los Leones** (Court of Lions). This rhythmical, colonnaded courtyard is divided into four sections, in traditional Islamic style, accentuating the fountain and water channels, symbols of the four rivers of life. You have to imagine this patio planted with cypresses, palms, orange trees, pomegranates and flowers. Twelve stone lions hold the fountain basin, whose rim is carved with a poem that extols the beauty of the court, the garden, and the play of water. Written by Ibn Zamrak, Mohammed V's chief minister, it is one of many that are inscribed in the Alhambra's surfaces.

Around the patio are three halls, each one a jewel of delicate craftwork. In the most breathtaking, the **Sala de las Dos Hermanas** (to the left as you enter the patio), the domed octagonal ceiling has finely worked muqarnas resembling stalactites, lit by natural light filtered through the windows just below.

Opposite, linked to the Sala de las Dos Hermanas by a water channel, is the **Sala de los Abencerrajes,** with its high domed ceiling and stalactite vaulting.

Generalife

Built on a higher level than the Alhambra, the Generalife is a delightful summer palace that celebrates the outdoors. An oblong pool edged by fountain jets, the Patio de la Acequia is its heart; terraced gardens, pergolas, bowers, and cypress trees provide refreshing shade at the height of summer. Don't miss the Mirador de la Sultana viewpoint at the very top. In late June to mid-July, some of the performances of Granada's phenomenal music and dance festival are held in the gardens.

INSIDER TIP:

The Alhambra is extremely popular, so don't leave your visit to chance. Reserve your tickets in advance of traveling and plan to spend an entire day exploring this beautiful and historic place.

—YUKO AOYAMA
National Geographic grantee

The third hall, the **Sala de los Reyes,** lies behind the main cluster of arches. The ceiling paintings here may be the work of Christian painters commissioned by Mohammed V. North of the Sala de las Dos Hermanas, another hall leads to the **Mirador de Daraxa,** overlooking a lovely garden patio.

Outside the main palace, you come to the **Palacio del Partal,** which was probably the first part to be built. Its arched gallery leads to the Torre de las Damas (Ladies' Tower), reflected in the mirrorlike surface of a large pool. Beyond this, the **gardens** take you through their different levels to cross a bridge to the Generalife (see sidebar opposite).

Palacio de Carlos V

One of Spain's most spectacular Renaissance buildings, Carlos V's palace was designed by Pedro Machuca, a disciple of Michelangelo. The stunning, vast circular courtyard represents the Universal Empire (the globe) and is unlike anything else in the Alhambra, quite stunning in its own right.

Inside you will find the **Museo de Bellas Artes** *(tel 958 22 48 43, closed Sun. p.m. & Mon.)* and the **Museo de la Alhambra** *(tel 958 22 56 40, closed Sun. p.m.–Mon. & p.m.).* The latter has beautiful Hispano-Muslim exhibits, including ceramics, carved screens, and fragments of sculpted stucco. Upstairs, the Bellas Artes' display of Granadino artists (Diego de Siloé, Alonso Cano, Pedro de Mena, Diego and José de Mora) is hard to do justice after the overwhelming artistry of the Moorish palaces and gardens. ■

The Renaissance Palacio de Carlos V is an intruder in the midst of an Arabian Nights setting.

A Stroll in the Albaicín

The Albaicín district flanks the hill opposite the Alhambra and was the site of the first Arab fortress. This walk leads you through its picturesque lanes and past beautiful *cármenes* (houses in walled gardens). Streets are steep and cobbled, so come prepared.

A stroll through the Albaicín promises stupendous views at every turn.

Walk north from the **Plaza Nueva** past Santa Ana, following the Darro riverbed. On your left you soon come to **El Bañuelo** ❶ *(Carrera del Darro 31, tel 958 02 78 00, closed p.m. & Sun.),* 11th-century Arab baths with colonnaded rooms. A little farther on stands the **Casa de Castril,** a Renaissance mansion housing the **Museo Arqueológico** ❷ *(Carrera del Darro 43, tel 958 22 56 40, temporarily closed for renovation).* Continue past the Convento de Santa Catalina, with the walls and towers of the Alhambra looming high above to the right. You come to a large esplanade, **Paseo del Padre Manjón,** packed with bars and cafés. Turn left up Cuesta de la Victoria, left again into Calle San Juan de los Reyes, and then right up steps that plunge you into the Albaicín. Climb to the top, turn left then right up Calle Carrillo, and then take a sharp left into Carril de San Agustín.

NOT TO BE MISSED:

El Bañuelo • Museo Arqueológico • Colegiata del Salvador • Carmen-Museo Max Moreau • Casa de Porras

---

Follow it to the top, passing the 17th-century Convento de las Tomasas, and circle around the church, **Colegiata del Salvador** ❸ *(Plaza del Salvador, tel 958 27 86 44, closed Sun.),* to reach its entrance. Built in 1501 on the foundations of the Albaicín's largest mosque, El Salvador has a magnificent Almohad patio of horseshoe arches. The small museum has beautiful religious paintings and sculptures. Outside, you could stop for a drink on Plaza del Aliatar, then continue by turning right onto Calle Panaderos, which leads to shady Plaza Larga full of local market shoppers. Cross the square to admire the restored Arab house on the corner and the beginning of the Arab walls. Take a look through the arch of the 11th-century Puerta Nueva.

Retrace your steps along Calle Panaderos, then go right on a dogleg turn to reach charming **Plaza Charca.** Walk up steps opposite, then down an alley to emerge at **Plaza San Nicolás** ❹ with its whitewashed 16th-century church *(open only for Mass)*. In front is the quintessential view of the Alhambra with the peaks of the Sierra Nevada behind. This spot is a favorite with guitar-strumming students and castanet-clicking Gypsies. Beside San Nicolás is Granada's brand-new **mosque** *(tel 958 20 25 26)*.

Walk down the steps beside the viewing terrace to Camino Nuevo de San Nicolás, turn right, and then stop to see the **Carmen-Museo Max Moreau** ❺ *(Camino Nuevo de San Nicolás 12, tel 958 29 33 10, closed Sun.–Mon.)*. This house belonged to the Belgian painter Max Moreau (1902–1992) and his wife, Felice. His studio and their home are full of items from their extensive travels. On leaving, turn left down Calle María de la Miel to Placeta del Nevot and keep walking down dilapidated Cuesta San Gregorio to finally take a sharp left into Placeta de Porras. The **Casa de Porras** ❻ *(Placeta de Porras, tel 958 22 44 25, closed Sun.)* is a magnificent example of Renaissance-Mudejar wooden architecture. Return to San Gregorio, turn left, and walk down **Caldería Nueva.** At the bottom, turn left to return to Plaza Nueva.

See also area map pp. 260–261
Plaza Nueva
1.5–2 hours
2 miles (3 km)
Plaza Nueva

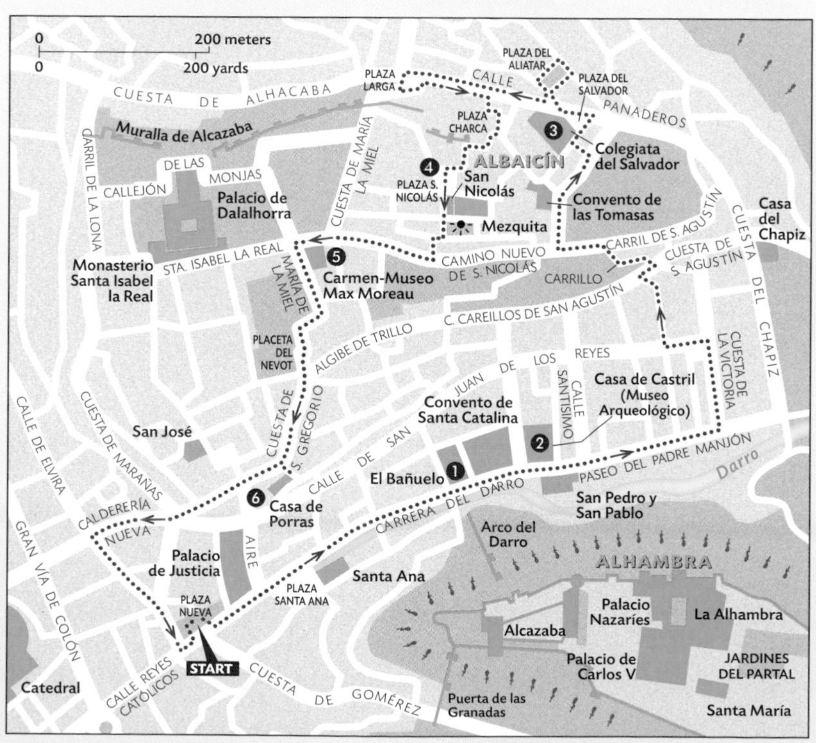

Troglodyte Towns

The arid limestone landscape of Almería and eastern Granada provinces was one of Europe's earliest inhabited areas more than a million years ago. It is still a land of cave dwellers (troglodytes), but today TV aerials, satellite dishes, and even burglar alarms sprout from their pristine, ever expanding houses, snapped up as holiday homes during the real estate boom.

Guadix
261 E2
Visitor Information
Oficina de Turismo, Avenida Mariana Pineda s/n
958 69 95 74
Closed Sat. p.m. & Sun.
www.andalucia.org

Museo de Alfarería
Calle San Miguel, Guadix
958 66 47 67
Closed Sun. p.m.

Cueva Museo
Plaza del Padre Poveda, Guadix
958 66 47 67
Closed Sun. p.m.

Baza
261 F2
Visitor Information
Oficina Municipal de Turismo, Plaza Mayor 1
958 86 13 25
Closed Sat. & Sun. p.m.
www.ayuntamientodebaza.es

Guadix

The distinctive whitewashed chimneys of cave dwellings stud the landscape around Guadix, 34 miles (54 km) northeast of Granada. They extend north and east to the Sierra de Baza, to Orce, and beyond to Cuevas de Almanzora. Guadix is the most accessible of these towns, but be wary of inhabitants who do not always take kindly to ogling tourists. Be sure to keep an eye on your wallet, too.

INSIDER TIP:

Purullena, 4 miles (6 km) west of Guadix, has numerous cave houses, their smooth white chimneys punctuating the outskirts of town. Pottery shops line the main road selling typical Granadino green-and-blue ware.

—FIONA DUNLOP
National Geographic author

Crowned by a dramatic Moorish castle, Guadix has a generous sprinkling of 16th- and 17th-century buildings, but is otherwise pretty ramshackle. You'll find the **Ermita Nueva,** or cave zone, beyond the whitewashed church of Santiago. On your way, stop at the **Museo de Alfarería,** a simple pottery museum in a renovated cave dwelling. Continue to the **Cueva Museo,** a charmingly restored cave dwelling complete with furniture and farming implements. Then wander around this extensive troglodyte area to admire the increasing sophistication of today's dwellings.

Baza

The town of Baza lies 27 miles (44 km) northeast of Guadix across a stark landscape of hillocks and esparto grass. The sculpture known as the "Dama de Baza," now in Madrid's archaeological museum (see p. 70), was found here. Historical sights include the crumbling **Alcazaba,** tenth-century **Arab baths** (Spain's oldest), and the lovely 16th-century church of **Santa María de la Encarnación.** The church was designed by Alonso de Covarrubias and built under the supervision of Diego de Siloé.

Baza's cave district is on the eastern side of town. About 25 miles (40 km) northeast is **Galera,** an Iberian necropolis with an entire valley of cave dwellings at the back of town. ■

Sierra Nevada

The ski season is from November to April, but this spectacular massif is a challenge throughout the year, whether you are traveling on foot, skis, or by car. The tortuous road that runs from Granada into the sierra is Europe's highest and defies even the hardiest drivers.

Whatever the season, the **Parque Nacional de la Sierra Nevada** is awesome, and for most of the year is snowcapped. With Mulhacén peak rising to 11,420 feet (3,481 m) and neighboring Veleta to 11,128 feet (3,392 m), it is the highest massif in Western Europe after the Alps. It is also the continent's southernmost ski resort—barely 25 miles (40 km) from the balmy coast.

The mountains have glacier lakes such as **Laguna Altera** around the 10,000-foot (3,000 m) mark and stark tundra landscapes favored by agile mountain goats. Lower down are pine forests where badgers, beech marten, and wild mountain lions roam. It also boasts more than 2,000 botanical species and is home to butterflies like the rare Nevada blue and Glandon blue. Hoopoes show their flashy plumage, and birds of prey soar overhead. The main **visitor center** *(Plaza de la Libertad, Pampaneira, tel 958 76 31 27, closed Sun. & Mon. p.m., www.mma.es)* is in Las Alpujarras (see pp. 310–312).

The slopes of the main ski resort, **Pradollano** (or Solynieve), are open into May. Buses from Granada stop here, and there is a parking lot at the Albergue Universitario. The road beyond, to the Alpujarras, is only accessible on foot or by bicycle. You can hike to the summit of **Veleta** in about three hours, allowing two hours for the descent, for a stupendous panorama south to the Mediterranean and north across the sierra. Experienced mountaineers take three to four days to cross the Sierra Nevada, starting in Jerez del Marquesado on the north flank and ending in Lanjarón, in the Alpujarras.

The view from Veleta's summit is predictably fantastic.

The two Nasmyth telescopes of the **Observatorio Astronómico** *(closed to the public)* are located at Loma de Dilar at 9,348 feet (2,850 m) above sea level. ■

Sierra Nevada

261 E2

Visitor Information

Centro de Visitantes, Carretera A395 (Granada–Sierra Nevada), km 23

958 34 06 25

www.cetursa.es
www.sierra-nevada.costasur.com

A Drive in Las Alpujarras

This drive twists from west to east through the Alpujarras, the southern foothills of the Sierra Nevada. It passes few specific sights, but the scenery is beautiful, and you may want to allow time for a hike to enjoy the clear air and spectacular views, and to get a close look at the wildflowers.

Start your drive in **Lanjarón ❶**, a popular spa town and source of a renowned mineral water. It was a Roman town, but is more famous for the Moorish population's heroic stand against the troops of Fernando and Isabel of Aragón in March 1500. The Moorish castle, downhill from the main road, has been left to slowly crumble, but the scenic view over the valley is special.

Drive out on the C332 toward Órgiva, and you start to enter the dramatic mountain scenery of Las Alpujarras. In the market town of **Órgiva ❷** stop at the main junction to look at the twin-towered baroque church and rather dilapidated Mudejar mansion across the road.

NOT TO BE MISSED:

Pampaneira • Bubión • Fuente Agria • Mecina Fondales

The castle of the counts of Sástago stands here, but it has been left to deteriorate.

On Thursdays Órgiva's **weekly market** draws northern European expatriates who live in the hills nearby. The large alternative community has spawned a few health-food shops and vegetarian restaurants to join pack mules and tepee as part of the townscape.

Stop to shop for colorful hand-woven rugs in Pampaneira.

Return to the entrance to Órgiva and turn right onto the GR421 in the direction of Trevélez (21 miles/34 km).

Switchbacks immediately take you uphill into an extraordinary landscape of chasms and glowering mountains with tiny white villages clinging to the slopes. A surprising number of people live here. On this northern side of the valley the road passes numerous isolated houses and *fincas* (farms), many of which are now foreign owned, and the hamlets of Carataunas and Soportújar. As the road swings north, you enter the **Barranco del Poqueira** ❸, a deep canyon created by the Poqueira River.

At **Pampaneira** ❹, park the car and walk into the main square behind the church. This picturesque, well-conserved village is a major crafts center, and its shops are draped with hand-woven rugs. Ceramics and jewelry are the other chief attractions. The **Parque Nacional de la Sierra Nevada** (see p. 309) has its main visitor center in the village, and you can pick up detailed trekking maps here—this is one of the best hiking areas. Wander around the pretty streets and enjoy a drink on the little square with its old fountain. From here the road climbs to dizzying heights as you come to a turnoff to the left for **Bubión** ❺ (2 miles/3.2 km) and **Capileira** (3 miles/4.8 km). These spectacularly sited villages cater to visitors with abundant craftshops and other facilities. The Sierra Nevada's highest peaks rise behind them, and Capileira is a well-trodden meeting point for mountaineers. The snow line is just 2 miles (3.2 km) on. It is also on the GR7 hiking trail.

Return to the GR421 and turn left toward Trevélez. Three miles (4.8 km) farther, take a turnoff to the right to visit the traditional villages of **Mecina Fondales** ❻, **Ferreirola,** and

Busquistar. Lying 1 to 2 miles (2–3 km) down in the valley, they still have unspoiled Alpujarras architecture: thick stone walls, often white-washed, flat roofs, and a few covered bridges between the upper stories. Return to the main road to drive through Pitres and Pórtugos, enjoying the views of stark mountains studded with white hamlets, occasional meadows, oaks, chestnuts, and poplars.

One mile beyond Portugos is **Fuente Agria,** a rushing mountain spring of naturally carbonated water. Stop at the roadside chapel to park, cross the road, and walk down the steps beside the waterfall of this iron-rich water.

The road then turns north into another deep gorge with a reservoir far below. This is wilder country, favored by goats and free-roaming pigs. The pigs turn up on your plate at **Trevélez** ❼, the local capital of *jamón serrano* (cured ham), which produces some top-quality brands. In the Renaissance, the town was famous for silk made by Moriscos expelled from Granada. Here you are among pine trees, at a height of 4,820 feet (1,470 m) in Spain's highest village, which spills down the cleft of the mountain to the Trevélez River. The lower part is not particularly picturesque, but it has plenty of watering holes catering to domestic tourism. Walk uphill to see traditional buildings. Trails from here lead up into the mountains or across to Juviles.

The road that you arrived on now backtracks along the opposite side of the gorge, then curves back into the main valley skirting the peak of **Peñabón** (8,310 feet/2,533 m). Ignore turnoffs and follow signs to Bérchules and Ugijar until you come to the attractive village of **Juviles** ❽, also a major silk producer in Renaissance times, an industry started by the Moors. This peaceful place is worth another stop before you make the last push to the neighboring villages of Bérchules and Alcútar, through increasingly barren moor dotted with olive trees. As you reach Alcútar you see the road snaking ahead of you across the Guadalfeo River and up again to give more vertiginous views.

Follow signs to Cádiar, then on to Órgiva (24 miles/39 km), as you turn right down into the valley. **Cádiar** ❾ has become one of the Alpujarras's largest towns because of its strategic setting. Life revolves around the main square dominated by a 16th-century church. During fiestas in February and October, the town's fountain spouts wine instead of water. In February, the slopes of the Sierra de Contraviesa rising to the south are blanketed in terraced almond trees, with clouds of pink and white blossom.

The Creative Draw of Las Alpujarras

Over the years, the savage beauty of Las Alpujarras has magnetized a creative crowd. First of the foreign writers to relocate here was Gerald Brenan (1894–1987), a British Hispanist who moved to the remote village of Yegen in 1919 after serving in World War I. He arrived there by chance, striding over the hills "south from Granada," a romantic adventurer in search of sunshine and cheap living. His prolonged stay led to his best known work, *South from Granada: Seven Years in an Andalusian Village* (1957), a wonderful picture of the sights, sounds, and customs of Andalusian village life. The book was made into a Spanish movie in 2003. Brenan later returned to Andalucía with his American wife, Gamel Woolsey, and was living outside Málaga when the Civil War broke out.

In 1999, Chris Stewart, founder of the rock group Genesis, moved to the region. Now a sheep farmer, Stewart is also the successful author of three ripping reads about Las Alpujarras, *Driving Over Lemons* (2001), *A Parrot in the Pepper Tree* (2009), and *The Almond Blossom Appreciation Society* (2009). Farther north, in the Sierra del Sur, lives Michael Jacobs, author of numerous books on Spanish culture.

Almería

Seen from the eyrie of the immense Alcazaba, Almería resembles North Africa, with a background of yellow ocher desert and a hodgepodge of traditional flat-roofed houses and concrete high-rise apartment blocks. From the harbor, car ferries leave for Melilla, one of Spain's remaining possessions in Moroccan territory.

Almería—which has a thriving immigrant population—was Muslim Spain's most prosperous port.

Soak up the atmosphere in the seafront **Parque Nicolás Salmerón,** with palm trees, fountains, and gardens. Moroccans clad in *djellabas* (loose robes) come here to sip mint tea. You find a more European face to the city in **Paseo de Almería,** the main shopping and social hub. Take a peek at No. 56, the ornate **Círculo Mercantil,** or Traders' Guild *(tel 950 23 11 22).* In the streets to the west is the fortified **cathedral** *(tel 950 23 48 48, closed Sat. p.m. & Sun.),* built in the 17th century. Look out for the Sol de Portocarrero, a large sun carved in the stone facade which symbolizes Almería's privileged climate. A reminder of the port's industrial past is the **Cable Inglés,** a cable-loading relic of the province's former tin exports. Plans are afoot to transform it into a cultural center.

You can't miss the **Alcazaba** (Arab citadel), its crenellated walls and towers soaring over the town. Built in 955, it fell to the forces of the Catholic Monarchs in 1490. Today, little remains within its walls, but wander through three enclosures, partly landscaped with aromatic plants, fountains, and water channels. Climb the **Torre de Pólvora** at the far end to admire the **Muralla de la Hoya,** a fortified wall that dips into the valley. ■

Almería

Map 261 F2

Visitor Information

- Oficina Municipal de Turismo, Plaza de la Constitución s/n
- 950 21 05 38

www.almeria-turismo.org

Alcazaba

- Calle Almanzor
- 950 27 16 17
- Closed Mon.
- $. Free for E.U. citizens

www.visitalmeria.com

Desert Places

The province of Almería has the lowest rainfall in Spain, barely 16 inches (400 mm) annually. Dryness combines with 3,000 hours of annual sunshine to create Europe's only desert. This torrid climate is exploited at Spain's largest solar-energy installation, which lies between Tabernas and Sorbas.

Mini-Hollywood
- 261 F2
- Carretera Nacional 340, Km 138, Desierto de Tabernas
- 950 36 52 36
- Closed Mon.–Fri. Nov.–April
- $$$$

www.minihollywood.es

In the **Desierto de Tabernas,** 19 miles (30 km) northeast of Almería, an undulating lunar landscape is alleviated only by the odd palm tree and cactus. Dramatic hills and canyons, crystalline light, and low production costs have lured many filmmakers to the area. David Lean made *Lawrence of Arabia* here, and Sergio Leone filmed a string of spaghetti Westerns, including A *Fistful of Dollars* and *The Good, The Bad, and The Ugly.* You can visit old film sets of this Spanish Wild West at the theme park **Mini-Hollywood.** Then continue to the village of **Tabernas,** dominated by the ruins of a Moorish castle.

Mini-Hollywood, a film set near Tabernas, comes complete with false-fronted buildings.

INSIDER TIP:

If you want to tour the fantastic caves at the Parque Natural de Karst en Yesos, be sure to plan ahead. Reservations are required.

—MARY STEPHANOS
National Geographic contributor

From Tabernas it is 15 miles (25 km) east to **Sorbas** *(visitor information, Centro de Visitantes de los Yesares, Calle Terraplén s/n, tel 950 36 45 63, www.sorbas.es, map 261 F2),* a dramatically sited village hanging over a dry gorge. This characteristic little village has long been renowned for its pottery, particularly simple glazed terracotta ovenware. Follow signs for *Alfarería* (Pottery) to see potters at work and buy their wares.

Around it unfolds the **Parque Natural de Karst en Yesos,** an eerily white landscape that is the world's largest gypsum karst. Huge subterranean caves with stalactites and stalagmites can be visited on **tours** *(tel 950 36 47 04, www.cuevasdesorbas.com),* which last about two hours and lighted helmets are provided. Alternatively you can walk or drive eastward to **Los Molinos del Río Aguas** for panoramic views. ■

A Drive Around Cabo de Gata

This route takes you from a village renowned for crafts, through arid and rugged landscapes typical of eastern Andalucía. It includes stops at pretty fishing villages and a succession of wonderful sea and mountain views. Most of this area lies in the Parque Natural de Cabo de Gata-Níjar.

The fishing village of Isleta del Moro makes a relaxing spot for lunch.

Allow an hour or so to look at crafts in **Níjar** ❶ *(visitor information, tel 950 61 22 29, closed Sun. p.m.)*, a typical Almerían village of whitewashed houses huddled against the slopes of the Sierra de Alhamilla. Leave the car at the top of the village, dominated by a 15th-century church with a fine Mudejar ceiling. Walk to the **Plaza del Mercado,** or descend to the main street lined with shops selling *jarapas* (woven cotton rugs and blankets), ceramics, and baskets. Most of the items are made in Níjar.

Back in the car, leave Níjar on the main street, turning right at the bottom, then left following signs to Almería and San Isidro. Don't turn onto the highway but drive straight on through an underpass to emerge into an unappealing plain of plastic greenhouses. This lasts for 8 miles (12 km) before the scenic landscapes of the **Parque Natural de Cabo de Gata-Nijar** *(visitor information, Avenida de San José 27, San José, tel 950 38 02 99, http://cabodegata-nijar.com)* begin. Follow signs to San José as the road winds over low sierra through yuccas, aloes, prickly pears, and olive trees. As you drive through **Boca de los Frailes,** look for the igloo-shaped stone oven (formerly used for baking bread) on your left. At **Pozo de los Frailes,** stop to look at the mill and old *noria*

NOT TO BE MISSED:

Níjar • Isleta del Moro • Rodalquilar • Agua Amarga

(water wheel), one of 95 in the park, on your right. When you finally enter San José, turn right at a fork in the road following signs to Playa de los Genoveses.

Drive uphill and circle around the headland. The road soon becomes an easily negotiated dirt road, passing an old windmill on the left before descending to a sea of prickly pear cactuses and other more unusual flora. Turn off to enjoy **Playa de los Genoveses** ❷ or continue 2.5 miles (4 km) to **Playa de Monsul,** signaled by an enormous sand dune on the left. Both beaches are of fine yellow sand, and Monsul has a great view south to the Cabo de Gata lighthouse *(faro)* at Spain's extreme southeastern point. These beaches have been locations for numerous films, including *Indiana Jones and the Last Crusade* (1989) and *The Last Adventures of Baron Münchhausen* (1989). They become packed in high summer.

Retrace your tracks to the largest resort in the area, **San José,** where you can stop for a drink. Continue to more authentic villages where local farmers and fishermen live in traditional houses. Follow the same main road out for 2.5 miles (4 km) as far as Pozo de los Frailes, where you turn right at a sign for Rodalquilar and Isleta del Moro (5 miles/7 km) into yucca- and palm-studded hills. After passing the 18th-century coastal fort of **Los Escullos** (built to fend off pirates) and capriciously eroded cliffs nearby, watch for a turnoff to your right

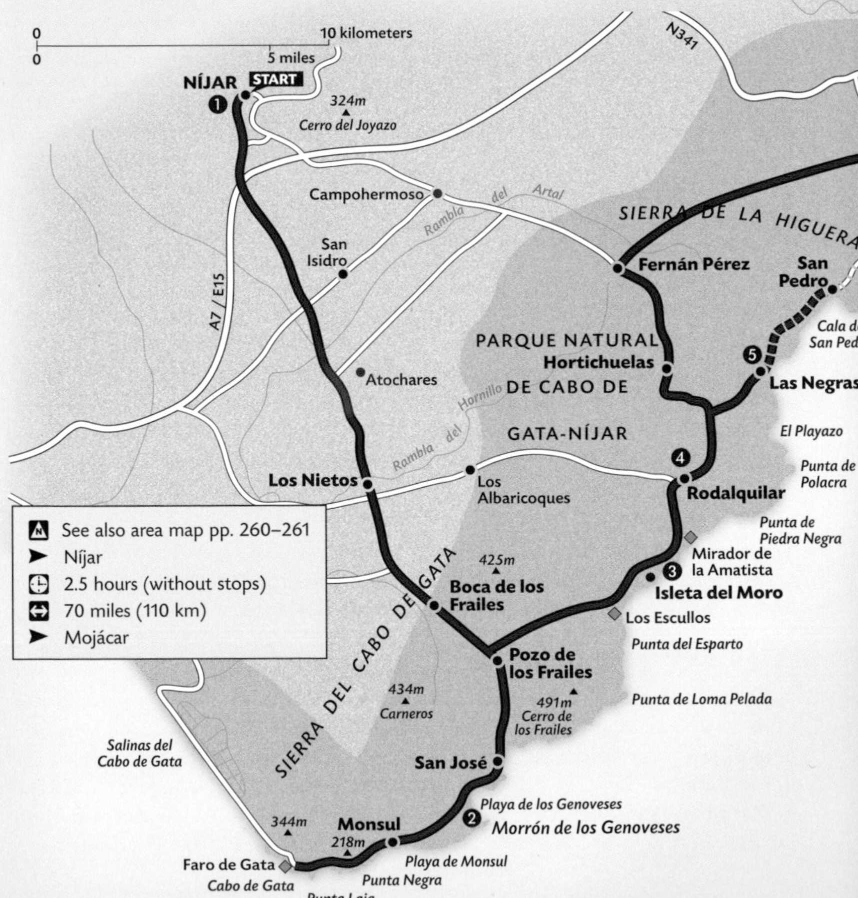

down to the promontory and islet of **Isleta del Moro** ❸, a good spot to stop for lunch.

From here continue north, stopping at the **Mirador de la Amatista** for sweeping views, before arriving in the lovely valley of Rodalquilar. Lost in the hills to the west is the farmhouse of **Cortijo de los Frailes,** scene of the crime of passion that inspired Federico García Lorca's *Blood Wedding,* the story of a bride-to-be kidnapped by her ex-lover on the eve of her wedding. Turn off into **Rodalquilar** ❹ village and drive up to the back, where you can look at the ruined remains of an old gold mine, and then return to the main road. You pass a turnoff to El Playazo, a secluded little beach between volcanic gullies, before reaching a junction. Turn right to the fishing village of **Las Negras** ❺ and drive straight down to the beach, where you can stop for a drink and enjoy the lovely sea view. A walk along a path to the left brings you to **Cala de San Pedro,** a cove containing the only freshwater spring in the entire reserve.

Return up the main road and drive straight on to Fernán Pérez. In the village, watch for a sign on the right to Agua Amarga. This takes you through farmland before entering an area of lime quarries. As you emerge, the sea reappears in the distance. Keep going until you reach a junction with a paved road. Turn right and drive down past scattered white houses to eventually reach the pleasant fishing village of **Agua Amarga** ❻ nestling in its bay. Water sports and dive centers are available.

Return to the main road and turn right up into the hills. As you descend, you are confronted by huge cementworks that introduce the resort of **Carboneras** with its long palm-lined beach and marina. Follow signs for Mojácar (16 miles/26 km) that take you around the village and up into the hills. As you round the headland, the road skirts the beautiful **Playa la Galera** ❼, backed by dramatic clefts of high sierra. Spectacular switchbacks lead to a lookout point with stupendous coastal views. Descending through rugged mountains, the road traverses the pretty village of **Sopalmo,** and soon passes the fort of Macenas. One more headland brings you to the long, built-up sweep of **Mojácar Playa,** and another 5 miles (8 km) leads to the turnoff up to the hill village of Mojácar (see p. 321).

INSIDER TIP:

Watch the sunrise from the Mirador de la Amatista in Cabo de Gata. It offers a superb view of the beautiful coastal landscape, with its mountain ranges jutting out beneath the deep blue sky.

—TINO SORIANO
National Geographic photographer

In & Around Murcia

It is easy to overlook Murcia, sandwiched between vast Andalucía and the coastal region of Valencia, but it does have points of interest. To the north lies the prolific wine-growing region of Jumilla. In the arid south is the old market town of Lorca, which suffered two devastating earthquakes in 2011. Give the overdeveloped coastline a miss: La Manga del Mar Menor is package-holiday heaven, and the airport is nearby, 23 miles (37 km).

The Sierra de Espuña is named after its highest peak, Espuña (5,193 feet/1,583 m).

Murcia

261 G3

Visitor Information

Oficina de Turismo, Plaza Cardenal Belluga, Edificio Ayuntamiento

968 35 87 49

Closed Sun. p.m.

www.turismodemurcia.es

Murcia

Murcia has long flourished on oranges, mining, and industry. Its inhabitants have a proud, independent spirit that dates from its ninth-century status in the kingdom of al-Andalus: The name derives from the Arabic "Murshiya," but it also thrived before that under the Romans. During the Civil War Murcia backed General Franco's Nationalist forces, which did little for neighborly relations with anarchist Almería or republican Valencia. The city of Murcia, the prosperous modern capital, still has a distinctive feel. It shows little concern for the needs of visitors, but stop for lunch, as it is a renowned gastronomical center.

At the heart of the pedestrianized **old quarter** spreading north from the Segura River stands the **Catedral de Murcia** *(Plaza de la Cruz, tel 968 22 13 71)*, notable for the lavish plateresque **Capilla de los Vélez** and Gothic exhibits in the museum. Follow Calle de Trapería north of here to the idiosyncratic **Casino,** now partly a restaurant. It is a 19th-century remake of Moorish style. To the west lies Murcia's main commercial street, **Gran Vía Escultor Salzillo,** named for the Murcian sculptor Francisco Salzillo (1707–1783). The **Museo Salzillo** *(Plaza San Agustín 1, tel 968 29 18 93, closed Sun. p.m. & Mon.)* displays his carved wooden figures for Murcia's spectacular Semana Santa *pasos* (Holy Week floats), carried on the shoulders of penitents.

Lorca

The coastal highway misses Lorca, by tunneling through the chalky hill crowned by the ruins of a Moorish castle. Its refurbished turrets and dungeons are now part of the **Fortaleza del Sol** *(tel 968 47 74 37, $$)*, a medieval theme trail accessed from the **Antiguo Convento de la Merced** *(Puerta de San Ginés)*, one of Lorca's fine baroque buildings. Head uphill from the main street to Plaza de España, with its towering Renaissance **Colegiata de San Patricio** *(tel 968 46 99 66)*, built between 1534 and 1780. The west facade teems with cherubim. Opposite, look at the former Casa del Corregidor with its corner carvings (1750) by Juan de Uzeta.

Downhill, don't miss the wonderful **Casa de Guevara** *(Calle Lope Gisbert, tel 968 46 63 21)*, Lorca's most elaborate example of domestic baroque architecture with an impressive entrance. Inside, a number of reconstructed rooms include a well-stocked, wood-paneled 19th-century pharmacy, and an 18th-century ballroom with Venetian furniture.

Close by, the **Centro Regional para la Artesanía** *(tel 968 46 39 12, closed Sun. p.m.)* is housed in a starkly modern building by the Murcian architect Juan Antonio Molina. Handicrafts of local materials (clay, wood, glass, ceramics, bamboo) are for sale.

If you can't be here for Lorca's sensational Semana Santa processions, you can get an idea of them at the **Museo del Paso Azul** *(Casa de las Cariátides, Calle Nogalte, tel 968 47 20 77, closed Sun. p.m., $)*. It is situated beside the church of San Francisco, which is itself worth a look for its dazzling baroque interior, full of gilded altarpieces. This restored late 19th-century house is the base of the Blue Brotherhood, one of the rival procession organizations. Upstairs is an embroidery workshop and a selection of the most finely worked costumes in silk and gold thread. The White Brotherhood, has an equally rich display in the

Lorca

261 G3

Visitor Information

Oficina de Turismo, Calle Puerta de San Ginés, Antiguo Convento de la Merced s/n

968 44 19 14

Closed Sat. & Sun. p.m.

www.lorcaturismo.es

EXPERIENCE: Lagoon Kayaking

Located about 31 miles (50 km) south and east of Murcia's city center, the Mar Menor is a saltwater lagoon separated from the Mediterranean by a narrow sandbar. Its shallow waters, dotted with islands, are best explored via kayak. Aqua Adicta *(tel 968 54 51 93, www.aquaadicta.co.uk, $$–$$$$$)* offers everything from two-hour paddles suitable for adults and children 8 and older to four-hour adventures around Mar Menor and into the sea. Exact routes depend on weather conditions. Windsurfing and other water sports, as well as classes, are also available.

Sierra de Espuña
261 G3
Visitor Information
Centro de Visitantes "Ricardo Codorniu," Sierra Espuña, Alhama de Murcia
968 43 14 30
www.sierraespuna.com

Alhama de Murcia
261 G3
Visitor Information
Oficina de Turismo, Plaza Constitución 10
968 63 35 12
Closed Sat. & Sun. p.m.
www.alhamademurcia.es

Caravaca de la Cruz
261 G3
Visitor Information
Oficina de Turismo, Calle de las Monjas 17
968 70 10 03 or 968 70 24 24
www.turismocaravaca.org

church of Santo Domingo *(Calle Santo Domingo, tel 689 78 25 04, closed Sat. p.m. & Sun.–Mon.).*

Sierra de Espuña

Rising abruptly from Murcia's plain, this beautiful, remote sierra is best reached from **Alhama de Murcia,** an 11th-century Moorish town with hilltop castle ruins and remains of Arab baths. From here the road twists through the sierra to Aledo and Totana, on the N340. The mountain range represents a miracle of repopulation and reforestation in what had become an arid desert by the 18th century, due to over-logging of the native oak forest.

Cartagena

Thirty-four miles (55 km) southeast of Murcia, the port of Cartagena was named for the Carthaginians from North Africa who captured it in 223 B.C. Their fortifications still look down on Spain's largest naval base. The Museo Nacional de Arqueología Marítima ***(tel 968 50 84 15, closed Sun p.m. & Mon.)*** **has Punic (Carthaginian), Phoenician, and Roman artifacts collected from the seabed, with models of boats.**

Cartagena is between Murcia's main beach resorts of Mazarrón and La Manga and has become a popular summer venue for rock concerts worth checking out.

Hiking trails lead up the slopes to the Sierra's ***pozos de la nieve*** (snow wells). An example of real peasant ingenuity, these 16th-century domed brick structures were built to store snow during the winter months; this was subsequently hammered into crushed ice, and then transported on horseback at night, to keep it cool, to villages below. Just outside Aledo, look for the **hermitage of Santa Eulalia,** a tiny Mudejar chapel entirely covered in 17th-century frescoes by Juan de Ibáñez, a local artist. Traditions run deep, including the local specialty of rice and rabbit.

Caravaca de la Cruz

Thirty-eight miles (60 km) due west of Murcia, lost in the sierra, is this medieval town, much revered by Catholics for allegedly possessing a piece of the holy cross (the "vera cruz"). Caravaca's role kicked off in 1232 with the alleged conversion of a Moorish king. Since then the walled town has attracted streams of pilgrims, resulting in a plethora of convents and churches, including the Renaissance masterpiece, the **Iglesia del Salvador.** At its highest point looms the 17th-century **Santuario de la Vera Cruz** *(Calle Monjas 9, tel 968 70 77 43).* Here, a side-chapel displays the holy relic though it is often mobbed by sick people desperate for a miracle. The museum *(tel 968 70 56 20, closed Mon.)* has an illuminating display on the history of the relic. ■

More Places to Visit in Andalucía & Murcia

Carmona

High on a promontory 24 miles (38 km) east of Seville, Carmona is an atmospheric, easily scaled destination. The main sight is the **Puerta de Sevilla Alcazar** where differing styles of arch point to its former rulers. Moorish Carmona lives on in the maze of narrow streets, a delight to roam around. Watch for the church of **Santa Maria,** built upon the former main mosque, and the noble mansions of the upper town. *www.turismo.carmona.org* 260 C3 **Visitor Information** Oficina Municipal de Turismo, Calle Alcázar de la Puerta de Sevilla 954 19 09 55

Visit any of the cafés in Carmona for a taste of the little town's particularly delicious tapas.

Jaén

Due north of Granada lies Jaén, an unassuming yet prosperous town crowned by the hilltop castle of **Santa Catalina.** In the oldest quarter of La Magdalena is the **Palacio de Villardompardo,** a mansion housing two small museums built over an exceptional complex of Arab baths. Jaén's pride and joy is the massive Renaissance **cathedral.** *www.turjaen.org* 260 E3 **Visitor Information** Oficina Municipal de Turismo, Casa Almansa, Calle Ramón y Cajal 4 953 19 04 55 Closed Sat. & Sun p.m.

Mojácar

Once one of Andalucía's prettiest coastal resorts, Mojácar succumbed to developers and lost much of its charm. Nothing, however, can detract from its spectacular site, high in the shadow of the Sierra Cabrera overlooking the Mediterranean. One mile (1.6 km) separates the pueblo from the *playa* (beach), the latter an unbroken strip of low-rise development. In the village, cubelike white houses pile up the slopes to a main square with craft shops, bars, and restaurants. *www.mojacar.es* 261 G2 **Visitor Information** Oficina Municipal de Turismo, Calle Glorieta 1 950 61 50 25

Montilla

In the undulating hills 20 miles (32 km) south of Córdoba, this little known center of wine production uses similar methods to those of Jérez. The popularity of Montilla's dry *finos,* sweet dessert wines, and Pedro Ximénez vinegar, a favorite with Spanish chefs, is increasing. Tour a bodega and sample its most famous tipple, amontillado, a mellow, aged fino. **Bodega Alvear** *(tel 957 66 40 14),* with its astonishing "cathedral" of 5,000 barrels, is Andalucía's oldest bodega, dating from 1729, although the present buildings are mainly 20th century. Another good tour with tasting is at **Pérez Barquero** *(tel 957 65 05 00).* In the old part of town knock on the door of the **Convento de Santa Clara,** which dates to 1525, for a tour. *www.montilla.es* **Visitor Information** Oficina Municipal de Turismo, Casa del Inca, Calle Capitán Alonso de Vargas 3 957 65 23 54

Osuna

Osuna is one of Andalucía's many inland surprises, lost in agricultural plains north of the Serranía de Ronda. Penetrate the old center and you enter a Renaissance and baroque world of elegant mansions, convents, and churches. The town's aristocratic character stems from the Dukes of Osuna who were among Spain's most powerful nobility. Overlooking the town are the old **university** and the interesting 16th-century **Colegiata,** which you can visit on a guided tour. It is a treasure trove of plateresque decoration and fine artworks, including the "Expiración de Cristo" by José de Ribera (1591–1652) and a superb crucifixion by Juan de Mesa (1583–1627). Best of all is the lavish underground pantheon housing the tombs of the Dukes of Osuna. *www.ayto-osuna.es* 260 C2 **Visitor Information** Oficina Municipal de Turismo, Calle Carrera 82 954 81 57 32 Closed p.m. & Sun.

Sierra de Cazorla

The wild mountains of the Sierra de Cazorla are the source of three major rivers: the Segura, the Guadalquivir, and the Borosa. The very beautiful biosphere reserve **Parque Natural de las Sierras de Segura y Cazorla** lies in Jaén's northwest corner near the border with Murcia. You can use several places as a base to visit the park. One of the nicest is the town of **Cazorla,** a postcard white village nestling in the shadow of a Moorish castle. From there you can take a stunning but dizzying road up to the **Puerto de las Palomas,** then drive north 25 miles (40 km) to Tranco, where you have a choice of onward routes. In between are hiking trails: Cazorla has 2,300 species of plants, and you glimpse wild deer, foxes, or stone marten. Overhead, look for birds of prey, including the royal eagle. *www.turismoencazorla.com* 261 F3 **Visitor Information** Centro de Visitantes, Carretera A319, km 45 953 71 30 17

Vélez Blanco

This village lies in the rocky, semiforested Sierra de Maria, wonderful hiking territory west of Lorca (see p. 319). The towering castle was built for the local marquis in 1515, but to see its main patio (complete with Carrara marble columns) you must visit New York's Metropolitan Museum of Art. It emigrated in 1903 courtesy of George Blumenthal, an American millionaire who bailed out the bankrupt marquis. Other sights are the **Convento de San Luis,** on the opposite side of the village, and the nearby **Cueva de los Letreros.** This prehistoric cave contains faded paintings, including one known as the *indalo*—a figure holding a rainbow, adopted as the region's symbol. 261 F3 **Visitor Information** Oficina Municipal de Turismo, Avenida del Marqués de los Vélez s/n 950 41 53 54

El Rocío

Andalucía's biggest annual pilgrimage takes place in Huelva province in May or June, when more than a million pilgrims embark on El Rocío, as the pilgrimage is known, to the town of El Rocío to pay their respects to the Virgen del Rocío, or Blanca Paloma ("white dove"). This is no solemn religious event, quite the opposite. The weeklong procession is a heady, communal affair of complex ritual mixing music and dance.

A hundred or so confraternities are involved, making their way on foot or on horseback to El Rocío. At the head of each group walks the *tamborilero,* who sets the pace for his followers. Men sport wide-brimmed hats and white shirts, while women wear flamenco dresses. Barrel-top wagons drawn by oxen rattle along behind, all in a cacophony of song and chatter. The pilgrimage culminates on Pentecost Monday in the storming of the chapel of El Rocío to carry the Virgin's statue on a walkabout. Capping it all is the *juerga,* a wild party that lasts deep into the night.

A gentle Mediterranean climate and landscapes long favored by artists and writers

Balearic Islands

Paseo del Born, Palma de Mallorca

Balearic Islands

This jewel-like cluster of islands scattered over the Mediterranean azure draws visitors from Spain and all over Europe. Mallorca, in particular, has been pulling in the package crowds since the 1960s, and Eivissa is now one of the summer nightlife capitals of Europe. Mellow Menorca, after a sleepy existence on the fringe, is favored by more discerning travelers, while tiny, rocky Formentera welcomes those in search of unadulterated nature.

Although widely perceived as a simple sun-and-sea destination, the Balearics have great beauty, and (especially Mallorca) a rich history set against an idyllic, rural interior. Their background is linked with Catalunya's, and the language is a close cousin of Catalan, although Castilian Spanish is also spoken. Carthaginians, Romans, Vandals, Moors, French, and British were all attracted to these indented shores strategically located on Mediterranean trade routes, and they left contrasting historical imprints on the various islands. Mallorca is the most developed, but it is also the largest island and the one with the most varied landscapes and history. In recent years German investment has soared, and the result is a string of villas dotting the beautiful coves of the east coast. Palma, the capital, is cosmopolitan and sophisticated. The island still retains extraordinary beauty and unique points of historical interest, not least are the megalithic structures, also a feature of Menorca.

Crafts have flourished on all the islands since the 1950s, when people came to the Balearics for alternative lifestyles. Eivissa-Ibiza became the hippie capital of Europe in the 1960s and 1970s, and crafts such as pottery and basket-making continue today, despite the islands' popularity, hot clubs, and rising prices. One traditional industry in the Balearics is leatherware, from shoes to bags and belts, and it is a good place to stock up on shoe labels such as

NOT TO BE MISSED:

Palma's cathedral and Almudaina palace at sunset 326

Dining in style in Deiá 328

Pollença's dazzling artisan shops and market 328

Boating across subterranean Lago de Martel at Coves del Drac 329

An afternoon exploring Eivissa's quaint Dalt Vila 330

Snorkeling in translucent waters at Playa Mitjorn on Formentera 331

Horseback-riding past megaliths on the island of Menorca 332

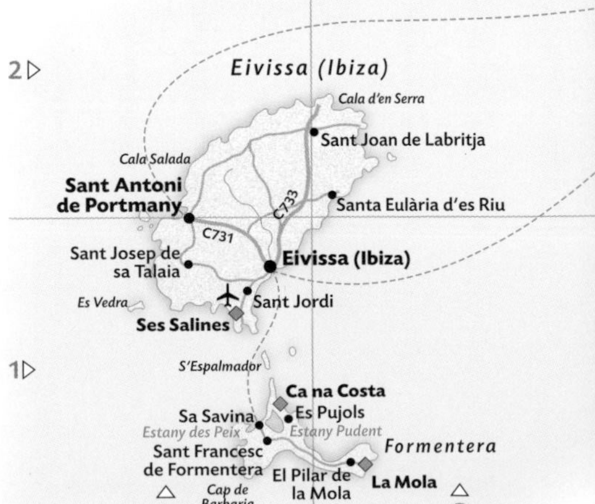

Camper and Farrutx as well as classic *abarcas* (leather sandals).

Artists have left major legacies, especially on Mallorca, which has the foundations of Joan and Pilar Miró, Miguel Barceló (Spain's leading contemporary artist), and Joan March. Military history is explored at length in Menorca, and Eivissa has an excellent archaeological museum. But most visitors come for the great outdoors. The mild Mediterranean climate makes for wonderful hiking and cycling year-round. Swimming and other water sports are popular from May to October, and sailing and scuba diving are widely available. Golf is another major attraction.

The peak season for vacationers is July and August, when beaches are packed with roasting tourists. Try to come outside this time, when the islands are less crowded and wildlife is more visible. Finally, food: It tends to be good, as unusual influences combine brilliantly with innovative Catalan refinement. ■

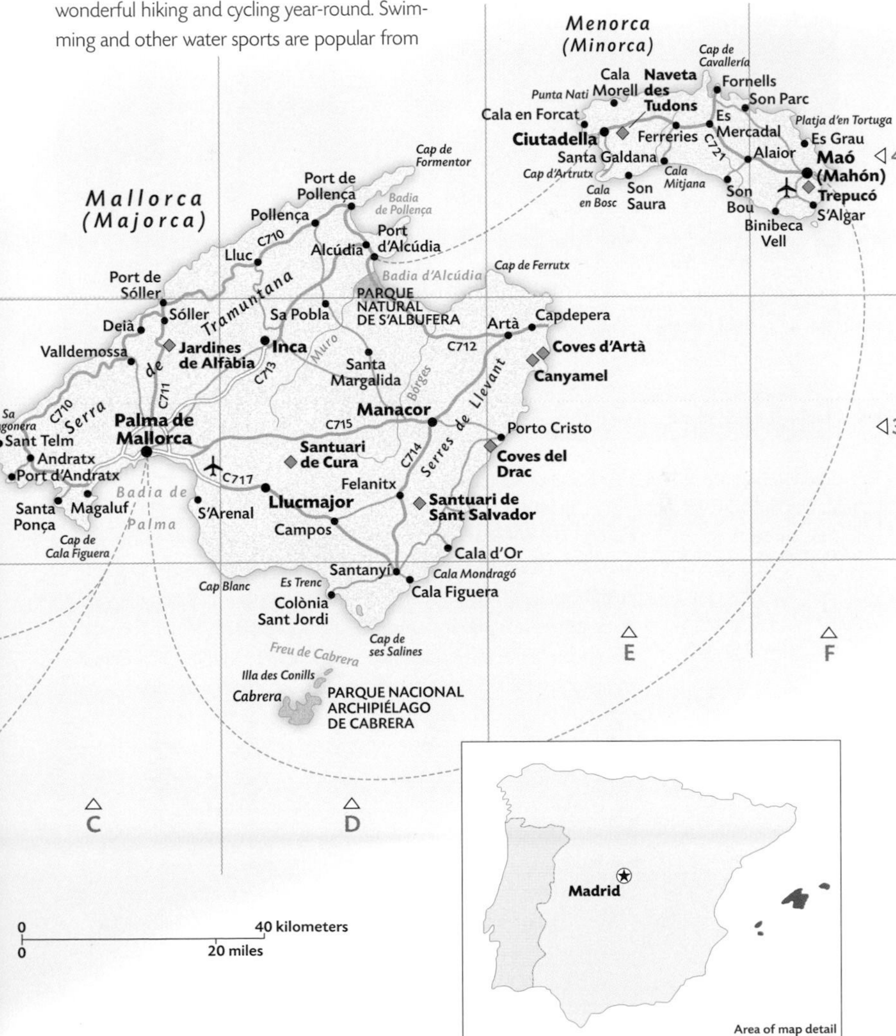

Mallorca (Majorca)

Multifaceted Mallorca is no secret to millions of vacationers. Here you can switch your focus from rugged mountains to coves of crystalline water, white-sand beaches, underground caves, or lively Palma. Mallorca's popularity in summer extends even to the Spanish royal family, so an off-season visit is the best option.

Turquoise waters surround the island of Mallorca.

Palma de Mallorca
325 C3
Visitor Information
Oficina de Turismo, Carrer Sant Domingo 11
971 72 40 90
www.illesbalears.es

La Seu
Carrer Palau Reial 29
971 72 31 30
Closed p.m. & Sun.
$

Palma de Mallorca

More than half of Mallorca's 700,000 people live in Baleric's attractive, upbeat capital. Waterfront palm trees, marinas, and elegant 18th-century mansions create a grand backdrop, while pedestrianized streets around Plaça Major hum with life. Scenically built around the secluded curve of the bay, Palma was founded by the Romans in 123 B.C., captured by the Moors in A.D. 903, and entered the Catalan net in 1229.

Dominating the port is the **Almudaina** *(Carrer Palau Reial, tel 971 21 41 34, closed Sat. p.m. & Sun.)*, the Moorish citadel. It acquired Gothic extensions as the palace of Jaume II, and it is still an official royal residence. You reach it by steps from the breezy **Parc de la Mar,** an elongated lake.

Opposite stands the massive Gothic cathedral, **La Seu.** The ornate southern portal, the **Portada del Mirador,** gives fine sea views. Vast proportions continue in the sober nave overlooked by **rose windows** designed by Antoni Gaudí (see pp. 172–175). One chapel contains an installation by Miguel Barceló. Kings Jaume II and Jaume III are buried in the lovely Mudejar chapel of **La Trinitat.**

Immediately to the east of the cathedral lies the **Museo de Mallorca,** where archaeological exhibits and medieval artworks are displayed in a lovely 17th-century mansion. Just behind are the tenth-century **Baños Árabes** (Arab Baths), Palma's only complete relic of Moorish presence. From here, northward, extends a network of more than 150 patios, the heart of old Palma, also epitomized by a Roman arch and the **Calle Platería.**

Palma has exceptional 20th-century art collections. Northwest of the center, the **Fundació Pilar i Joan Miró** was set up by the artist and his wife to preserve his studios, where he had worked from 1956 until his death in 1983. Some of his works are displayed here; you can see more at the **Museu d'Art Espanyol Contemporani** *(Sant Miquel 11, tel 971 71 35 15, closed Sat. p.m. & Sun.)* alongside other Spanish greats such as Picasso, Juan Gris, and Dalí. Behind the Almudaina, the neo-baroque **Palau March Museu** *(Calle Palau Reial 18, tel 971 71 11 22, closed Sun., www.march.es/arte/ingles/palma)* boasts a panoramic terrace with sculptures by Rodin, Henry Moore, Barbara Hepworth, and Eduardo Chillida. The stunningly designed **Museu Es Baluard,** with a limited international collection, opened in 2004. Views take in the bay, which hosts the prestigious Copa del Rey (King's Cup) regatta every August.

Northwestern Mallorca

Avoid Mallorca's concentrated resort area, west of Palma between Magaluf and Santa Ponça, but don't miss the island's dramatic northern coastline. Backed by the Serra de Tramuntana, the tortuous clifftop road (C710) has vertiginous views. Even when glowering clouds blanket the granite sierra, the mountain villages and rocky cliffs are spectacular.

Just inland from the picturesque **Port d'Andratx,** a fishing harbor and summer yacht haven, is **Andratx** itself, dominated by a fort. From here a secondary road leads down to the extreme

Museo de Mallorca

✉ Carrer Portella 5, Palma de Mallorca

☎ 971 71 75 40

🕒 Closed Sun. p.m. & Mon.

Baños Árabes

✉ Calle Serra 7, Palma de Mallorca

☎ 971 72 15 49

Fundació Pilar i Joan Miró

✉ Carrer Joan de Saridakis 29

☎ 971 70 14 20

🕒 Closed Sun. p.m. & Mon.

http://miro.palmademallorca.es

Museu Es Baluard

✉ Plaça Porta de Santa Catalina, Palma de Mallorca

☎ 971 90 82 00

🕒 Closed Mon.

$ $$

www.esbaluard.org

A Haven for Artists

The dramatic beauty and balmy summer climate of Mallorca have long magnetized creative talents, with Frédéric Chopin and George Sand leading the fray. The long, cold, wet winter they spent together in Valdemossa (1838–1839) was a disaster, but that has not deterred others. British writer Robert Graves (1895–1985) lived in Deia from 1929 until his death, with a break of only ten years. His idyllic house and garden are now a museum *(tel 971 63 61 85, www.lacasaderobertgraves.com).*

More recently, two modern artists have left an indelible mark on the Coll Baix peninsula. The **Fundación Yannick y Ben Jakober** *(tel 971 54 69 15, www.fundacionjakober.org),* an original and compelling art center in a stunning building, features a rose garden, sculpture park, contemporary international art exhibits, and portraits of children by Old Masters. Miguel Barceló (born 1957), an acclaimed Mallorcan painter, continues to maintain a house on the island.

Sóller

325 C3

Visitor Information

Oficina Municipal de Turismo, Plaça Espanya 15

971 63 80 08

www.ajsoller.net/turisme

southwestern cove of **Sant Telm,** where boat tours take you past the island nature reserve of **Sa Dragonera.** Next stop at the Carthusian **monastery of Valldemossa** *(tel 971 61 21 06, closed Sun. p.m. & Mon.)*, nestling in the flanks of 3,490-foot (1,064 m) Tex. Hourly piano concerts recall the romance of French writer Georges Sand and her lover, Frédéric Chopin, who stayed here during the winter of 1838–1839.

EXPERIENCE: Ride the Sóller Railway

While visiting Palma de Mallorca, slip back in time with a ride on the Ferrocarril de Sóller ***(tel 902 36 47 11 or 971 63 01 30, www.trendesoller.com, $)*****, a narrow-gauge train that dates from 1912. Seventeen miles (27 km) of beautiful scenery slip by as the lovely old train, powered by an electric locomotive, winds through mountains, including 13 tunnels, and over bridges and a viaduct to reach Sóller one hour later. From here an hourly tram creaks 3 miles (4.8 km) more down to the resort below. Trains run daily throughout the year.**

Alcúdia

325 D4

Visitor Information

Oficina Municipal de Turismo, Carretera Artà 68

971 89 26 15

www.alcudiamallorca.com

The beautiful hilltop village of **Deiá,** discovered decades ago by writers and artists (including Robert Graves, 1895–1985, the British author of *I, Claudius*), makes a bucolic stop. Its shingly cave below is magical.

Farther north, the market town of **Sóller** is connected by tram with a burgeoning resort in the bay below. Boat tours travel along the magnificent coast. Make the detour from Sóller through the hills to see the palm trees, oleanders, and bougainvillea of the lush **Jardines de Alfàbia** *(Carretera Palma-Sóller, tel 971 61 31 23)*.

The northern stretch of this attractive road wiggles inland to reach **Pollença,** where strong artisan traditions vie with gastronomy. Don't miss the 365 steps up to Monte Calvario for stunning views, or the Sunday market. Down below, the sheltered bay, **Bahía de Pollença,** has seen rampant hotel development, but the port itself is still very scenic. At the very end of the promontory, **Cap de Formentor,** a lighthouse is perched above a sheer 650-foot (200 m) drop down to the waves. From here, sweeping views take in the island of **Formentor.** To reach its white-sand beaches, take a half-hour boat ride from the Bahía de Pollença.

Overlooking the bay from the east is the charming walled town of **Alcúdia,** with extensive Roman ruins and beaches at the resort nearby. Birders should head straight for the **S'Albufera** natural park *(tel 971 89 22 50)*, south of Port d'Alcúdia, where wetlands attract more than 230 bird species.

Southeastern Mallorca

The much flatter southeastern side of Mallorca unfolds in pastoral splendor toward a string of idyllic coves, creeks, and breathtaking caves indenting the eastern coast. Beaches are fewer in the south around Cap de Ses Salines, but salt flats and marshes give good bird-watching, and monasteries and megalithic sites dot the interior.

In the easternmost corner, just 9 miles (15 km) apart, Capdepera and Artà make a good starting point for exploring the nearby cave networks of Coves d'Artà. **Capdepera** is a striking hill town topped by a 13th-century fortress, **Castillo de Capdepera.** Visit the castle for sweeping views. **Artà,** too, rises in medieval fortified splendor from a high rock crowned by the church of **San Salvador.** Both towns have megalithic settlements on their outskirts.

Mallorcan scenic drama returns in the island's 800 limestone caves. Just beyond the **Canyamel,** a landmark 12th-century tower, lie the magnificent **Coves d'Artà.** This cavernous underworld dripping with stalactites is spotlit to highlight the extraordinary formations: The so-called **Sala de las Banderas** (Hall of Flags) soars to an inspiring 148 feet (45 m).

Continue south to the fishing village of **Porto Cristo** to reach the mile-long (1.6 km) chambers of the **Coves del Drac.** To add to its otherworldliness, boatloads of musicians play classical music in this eerie natural theater set.

South of here is **Felanitx,** an important ceramics center. The **main square** is a lovely place to relax and admire the unusually rich church, which mixes Gothic, Renaissance, and baroque decoration. Just south of town, a road switchbacks up through pine trees to the stunningly sited **Santuari de San Salvador.**

Together with Campos and Santanyí, Felanitx creates a triangle of delightful pastoral scenes where dry-stone walls edge fields of wheat, citrus, and olives. **Campos,** the market town, has traditional Mallorcan architecture, as does **Santanyí.** Look for the **talayot of Son Danus,** a megalithic watchtower that stands on the outskirts.

The coastline to the east is a succession of stunning creeks of transparent water edged by white sand, with wooded hills rising above. One of the developed resorts, **Cala d'Or** remains low key compared with those of the west coast. **Cala Figuera** still has the atmosphere of a fishing village. Tops in beauty goes to **Cala Mondragó,** a nature reserve. Off the south coast resort of Colònia Sant Jordí lies the **Cabrera archipelago,** a national park of 19 islets with rich underwater life and bird-watching. Day trips leave from Sant Jordí.

A last leap 28 miles (45 km) inland from the nudist beach of Es Trenc brings you north of Llucmajor to the **Santuari de Cura.** This modernized medieval monastery has conserved its 17th-century church, school, and museum. From the hilltop site you have magnificent views west toward Palma, the bay, and moody Serra de Tramuntana, and north toward the Formentor lighthouse. ■

INSIDER TIP:

A tour of the awesome Coves del Drac includes a boat ride across Lago Martel, the largest subterranean lake in the world.

—FIONA DUNLOP
National Geographic author

Castillo de Capdepera
☎ 971 81 87 46

Coves d'Artà
Map 325 E3
☎ 971 84 12 93
$ $$
www.arta-web.com/cgi-bin/altres/vven.cgi

Porto Cristo
Map 325 E3
Visitor Information
✉ Oficina Municipal de Turismo, Calle Molls s/n
☎ 971 81 51 03
🕒 Closed winter
www.manacor.org

Coves del Drac
Map 325 E3
☎ 971 82 07 53
$ $$
www.portocristo.com

Santuari de San Salvador
☎ 971 82 72 82

Cabrera Archipelago
Map 325 D2
Visitor Information
✉ Ses Salines, Sant Jordí
☎ 971 65 62 82

Santuari de Cura
☎ 971 12 02 60

Eivissa (Ibiza) & Formentera

Eivissa is hot in temperature and mood. It attracts planeloads of hip young things who come here purely for the nightlife. If clubs and street fashion are not your scene, then avoid July and August. Or head for quieter Formentera. Both islands are drier than Mallorca, lack its fertile meadows and mountains, but bask under clear blue skies virtually year-round.

The 19th-century Church of Sant Vincent on Eivissa is decorated for a fiesta.

Eivissa (Ibiza)
324 A1
Visitor Information

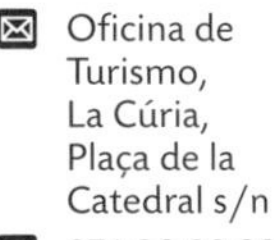

Oficina de Turismo, La Cúria, Plaça de la Catedral s/n
971 39 92 32
Closed Sun. p.m.
www.eivissa.es

Eivissa (Ibiza)

The old capital of Eivissa is perched on a promontory dominating the harbor of Eivissa and defined by the silhouette of the cathedral and Renaissance walls encircling the **Dalt Vila** (old town). Spectacular 16th-century ramparts, steep stone steps, and elegant mansions testify to its history, in contrast with the bars, restaurants, and boutiques that line the narrow streets of the "new town" below. To get an idea of the island's ancient past, look at the Carthaginian and other artifacts at the **Museo Arqueológico de Ibiza i Formentera,** located beside the cathedral. Then take off into the interior of the island.

The traditional rural house of Eivissa is a simple, south-facing *casament,* a composition of whitewashed cubes around a central, communal room, with verandas for storing crops. Beside these North African–looking houses are simple, fortified churches where inhabitants would shelter from pirate attacks, including **Sant Jordi, Sant Antoni de Portmany,** and **Sant Joan de Labritja.**

Some of Eivissa's 56 beaches with transparent warm waters remain unspoiled. Both sandy and rocky **Cala Salada,** near Sant Antoni, is one of the more tranquil beaches in the developed area. (Sant Antoni is the capital of Eivissa's clubbing culture—so beware.) Less accessible Sant Joan to the northeast has **Cala d'en Serra** and **S'Illot des Rencli** along its vertiginous coastline. This wilder end of the island is a haven from the crowds. Santa Eulària des Riu is a booming high-rise resort yet with aging hippies at the Wednesday market. Head south to the nature reserve of **Ses Salines** to find surprising landscapes, extensive salt flats, and endless water sports.

Formentera

Tiny Formentera may seem a mere hiccup in the Balearics: Its 5,000 inhabitants occupy an area of just 31 square miles (80 sq km). But for faithful visitors it represents the last bastion of unadulterated tranquillity in the Mediterranean. Only 11 miles (18 km) from Eivissa, it is easily reached by ferry. Cyclists and hikers revel in its untouched landscapes and well-marked trails; swimmers, snorkelers, and kayakers love the sandy beaches edged by crystalline water.

The Romans grew wheat extensively on Formentera, but constant pirate attacks made it uninhabitable in the Middle Ages, and it recovered only in the late 17th century. The capital, **Sant Francesc de Formentera,** is not much more than a fortified **church,** a small ethnological **museum** *(tel 971 32 26 40)*, and a cluster of hippy-style craft shops.

In summer, culture courses in the form of outdoor cinema. It is just 2 miles (3 km) to the stunning white Ses Illetes beach, a snorkeler's paradise. Rockier Playa Mitjorn, on the south coast, is less frequented so you might find a cove all to yourself.

Sant Francesc and the only tourist center, **Es Pujols,** flank the shores of **Estany Pudent,** a large lagoon that attracts flocks of migrating birds and leads to a skinny promontory of land edged by beaches. To the west is **Estany des Peix,** a smaller lagoon protected as a nature reserve. On the northern bank stands the striking megalithic monument of **Ca na Costa.** At the eastern point of Formentera is **La Mola,** with a lighthouse and a monument to Jules Verne (1828–1905), the French writer who wove the magic of this beautiful spot into a book. Views reach across the island. ■

INSIDER TIP:

Explore the island of Formentera on bike or scooter. They are cheap and easy to rent in La Savina harbor, where the ferries dock.

—ANNIE BENNETT
National Geographic author

Museo Arqueológico de Ibiza i Formentera

- Plaça de la Catedral 3, Eivissa
- 971 30 12 31
- Closed Sun. p.m. & Mon.

Formentera

- 324 B1

Visitor Information

- Oficina Municipal de Turismo, Calle de Calpe s/n, La Savina
- 971 32 20 57

www.formentera.es

Menorca (Minorca)

Long outshone by Mallorca and Eivissa, this peaceful, 274-square-mile (702 sq km) island—declared a biosphere reserve in 1993—is slowly gaining in popularity. A long history of occupation by a series of invaders, including a century of intermittent British rule, has given it a very distinctive flavor and gastronomy. North African couscous meets British puddings here, and Maó (Mahón) is the place where French mayonnaise was first created.

Menorca (Minorca)

325 E4

Visitor Information

Oficina de Turismo, Estación Central de Autobuses, Avenida J. Anselmo Clavé Esquina, Plaza Explanada s/n, Maó

971 36 37 90

www.menorca.es

Maó (Mahón)

Moll de Levant 2, Maó

971 35 59 52

Ciutadella

Plaça de la Catedral 5

971 38 26 93

Fort Marlborough

Cala Sant Esteve, Es Castell

971 36 04 62

Menorca's only drawback is the wind—so be prepared. **Maó (Mahón),** the capital, lies at the end of a 3-mile (5 km) inlet and is one of the safest harbors in the Mediterranean. Life revolves around the cafés and restaurants of **Plaza del Ejercito,** and shops are concentrated in the streets between here and Plaza de España. Signs of sporadic British occupation from 1713 to 1802 are evident in older houses. In the town of Es Castell, 2 miles (3 km) along the inlet, well-conserved **Fort Marlborough** gives you a picture of the period.

Far more memorable are the 500 **megaliths** from the second millennium B.C. dotted over the island (see sidebar this page). Two sites are outstanding: the settlement of **Trepucó** with its 16-foot-high (4.9 m) *taula,* just outside Maó, and the **Naveta des Tudons,** 3 miles (5 km) east of **Ciutadella,** the delightfully scenic former capital. Join a pony trek *(tel 630 60 53 97 or 658 17 75 75)* through the interior to discover more.

The **north coast** beaches are mainly red-ocher sand backed by windy heath. An exception is **Pregonda,** protected by rocky islets. Finer sand lines the **south coast creeks** attracting the majority of visitors, but you can still find solitude at **Son Saura, Cala Mitjana** in the south, and **Platja d'en Torotuga** in the northeast. Tops for transparent turquoise is **Cala Macarella** in the far southwest. ■

Menorcan Megaliths

Menorca's ancient stone monuments can be divided into three categories: *talaiots* (conical stone mounds, rising up to 25 feet/7.6 m); enormous *taules* (T-shaped structures thought to have been temples), and *navetes* (resembling upturned hulls of boats). Their function was spiritual, as either graves or altars, but inevitably their sheer number and scale have inspired countless esoteric theories. The Torre d'en Gaumés is the largest prehistoric settlement in the Balearics, with three striking talaiots surrounded by a defensive wall, pillared naves, and a taula. Nearby is a dolmenic burial chamber, Ses Roques Llises. This lies to the south of Alaior, between the village and beach at Son Bou.

Volcanic landscapes, unique flora and fauna, and picturesque local architecture under year-round sun

Canary Islands

Cactus garden, Lanzarote

Canary Islands

Clustered in the Atlantic Ocean 620 miles (1,000 km) south of mainland Spain, these stark, volcanic islands are only 71 miles (115 km) from the African coast. Today the Canaries' reputation as a budget sun-and-sea destination for northern Europeans tends to eclipse their other charms, but visitors with a bit of initiative find endless corners of astounding beauty and wonderful hiking territory.

Tenerife's volcanic hills rise above pleasant Los Cristianos, the island's tourist mecca.

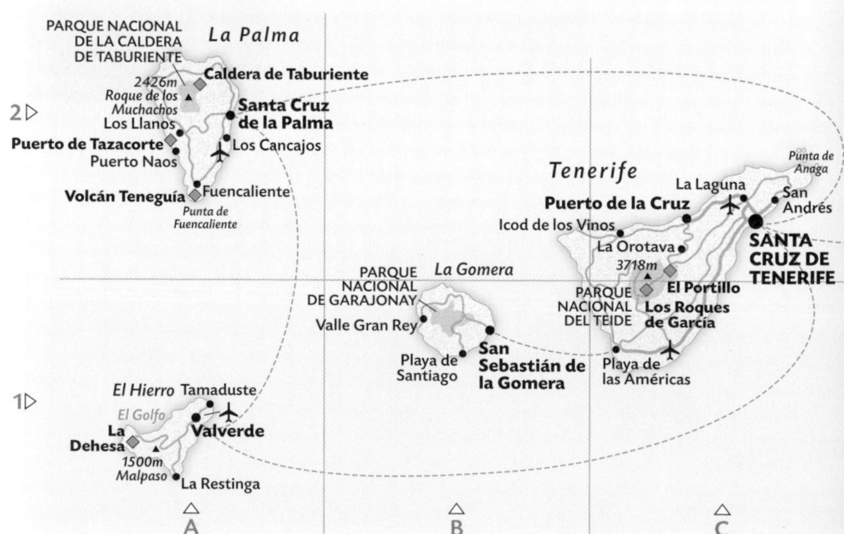

Seven main islands make up this archipelago, each with its own identity. The main bulk of tourists spills out onto the sands of Tenerife, the largest island, dominated by the snow-covered peak of Teide. It is closely followed in popularity by Gran Canaria, the most populated island and the one with the greatest scenic diversity. La Palma has the greenest landscapes, in total contrast to Lanzarote's extraordinary lunar horizons of lava flows or Fuerteventura's desertlike dryness. Idyllic La Gomera has subtropical vegetation of laurel forest and palms, and tiny Hierro's abrupt, windswept slopes end in twisted juniper trees.

Much of the appeal of the Canaries lies in their year-round mild, sunny climate. Temperatures hover between 66°F (19°C) in winter and 77°F (25°C) in summer. The other magnet is the sea. Deep-cobalt waters wash 930 miles (1,500 km) of coastline edged by dramatic cliffs and beaches. Huge high-rise resorts monopolize most Tenerife and Gran Canaria. To escape the hordes, head for the smaller islands. ■

NOT TO BE MISSED:

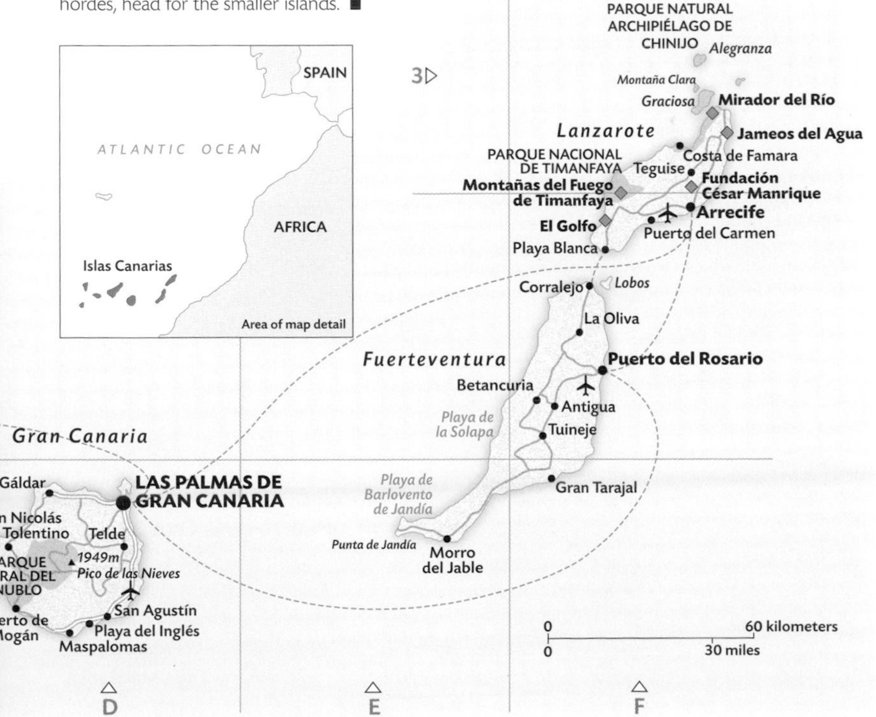

Tenerife

This mountainous, 780-square-mile (2,000 sq km) island divides into the highly developed southern coast with its golden beaches, and the more humid, windier northern coast, where black-sand beaches beneath sheer cliffs remind you of Tenerife's volcanic origins. Between is Spain's highest peak, permanently snowcapped Teide, rising 12,192 feet (3,718 m).

Puerto de la Cruz is the oldest beach resort on Tenerife.

Santa Cruz de Tenerife

334 C2

Visitor Information

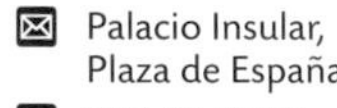

Palacio Insular, Plaza de España

922 28 12 87, 0080 010 01 01 00 (free in Spain)

www.cabtfe.es

www.webtenerife.com

Santa Cruz de Tenerife

The capital and main port lies in the southeastern corner with a dramatic bay setting. Its February **carnival** is the most exuberant in Spain. This is now rivaled by Santiago Calatrava's $90 million **Auditorio** (opera house) with its soaring 200-foot-high (61 m) suspended canopy. The **seafront promenade** is the work of Swiss architects Herzog & De Meuron, also responsible for the gigantic arts center, **TEA** *(www.teatenerife.com),* which houses the Instituto Oscar Dominguez (ca 1906–1957), a surrealist painter and son of the island. Don't miss the excellent **Museo Arqueológico** *(Calle Fuente Morales, tel 922 53 58 16, closed Mon.).* Five miles (8 km) northeast is **Playa de Las Teresitas,** a pretty curve of golden sand, with good seafood at the port of **San Andrés.** For historical background, head inland to the university town of **La Laguna,** Tenerife's first capital.

Puerto de la Cruz

Verdant Puerto de la Cruz, Tenerife's oldest resort, has mushroomed into a high-rise mirage built on black lava-stone rocks. Swim at **Lago Martiánez,** a series of saltwater pools by the Lanzarote artist César Manrique (see p. 339) that harmonize with the lush vegetation and volcanic rock. Enjoy more subtropical plants at **Jardín Botánico de la Orotava,** a botanical garden created in the 18th century.

La Cruz's magnificent surroundings include the **Valle de la Orotava,** a cleft cutting to the water's edge from Teide. A 17-mile (27 km) drive up to the lookout point, **Mirador de Humboldt** (named after the German naturalist Alexander Humboldt), gives you stunning views over banana groves to the sea.

Nearby **La Orotava** is a jewel of traditional timber houses with latticework balconies. Don't miss the baroque church of **La Concepción,** the beautiful **Casa de los Balcones,** actually two 17th-century mansions built of tea (a local pinewood), or the craft museum in a 17th-century monastery, **Museo de Artesanía Iberoamericana.**

Parque Nacional del Teide

Twenty-six miles (42 km) southwest from La Orotava, the road winds up to the spectacular Parque Nacional del Teide, declared a World Heritage site in 2007. The immense Cañadas de Teide are a volcanic plateau and former crater of 50 miles (80 km) circumference. Natural lava-stone sculptures, **Los Roques de García,** stand near the parador (see p. 379), which houses an information center.

Take a cable car from beside the C821 just below the peak or trek for 5 hours. You may see the Teide violet and the conspicuous Teide bluetit. Join daily treks from the visitor center at the pass of **El Portillo** *(reserve at 922 92 23 71, treks start at 9 a.m. & 1:30 p.m., or stay at the simple refuge, tel 922 01 04 40).*

Icod de los Vinos

Fourteen miles (22 km) west of Puerto de la Cruz on the north coast is **Icod de los Vinos,** once famous for the production of Malvasía wine, which is being successfully revived after centuries of oblivion. The town also has traditional architecture, baroque churches, lush vegetation, good traditional restaurants, and a legendary, rare drago tree (see sidebar p. 338). ■

Puerto de la Cruz
- Map: 334 C2

Visitor Information
- Address: Oficina de Turismo, Casa de la Aduana, Calle Las Lonjas s/n
- Tel: 922 38 60 00 or 922 37 01 32

www.puertodelacruz.es

Jardín Botánico de la Orotava
- Address: Calle Retama 2, Puerto de la Cruz
- Tel: 922 38 35 72

Museo de Artesanía Iberoamericana
- Address: La Orotava
- Tel: 922 32 17 76
- Hours: Closed Sat. & Sun. p.m.

Parque Nacional del Teide
- Map: 334 C1

Visitor Information
- Address: El Portillo
- Tel: 922 35 60 00

www.reddeparquesnacionales.mma.es

Mojo

You will be hard pressed to find a Canarian restaurant without little bowls of *mojo* on the table. The basic ingredients of mojo, which can be either red *(mojo rojo)* or green *(mojo verde),* are olive oil, garlic, and wine vinegar. Green mojo generally contains green pepper, cilantro, parsley, and a touch of cumin, while the red variety of mojo (also known as *mojo picón*) adds red pepper, *pimentón* (paprika), and cumin.

Mojo is meant to be spooned over vegetables. The red mojo goes beautifully slathered over *papas arrugadas* (new baby potatoes cooked in saltwater then baked until they are divinely wrinkled), while the green gives a wonderful kick to simple grilled fish.

Gran Canaria

Tourists flock to the most populated island of the Canaries, due partly to 31 miles (50 km) of beaches, but also its dramatic interior, half of which is biosphere reserve.

Gran Canaria
335 D1
www.grancanaria.com

Las Palmas
335 D1
Visitor information
Oficina de Turismo, Plaza de Hurtado Mendoza
928 44 68 24
www.promocionlaspalmas.com

Museo Canario
Calle Doctor Chil 25, Las Palmas
928 33 68 00
Closed Sat. & Sun. p.m.

Volcanic formations dominate the interior, while the most popular beaches fringe the almost desertlike terrain of the south coast. Canyons dominate the west, and the ravines of the central plateau vary from pine forests to stark volcanic rock.

An extensive network of hiking trails runs through these diverse landscapes. Naturalists head for the **Parque Rural del Nublo** on the flanks of Pico de las Nieves (6,393 feet/1,949 m).

Gran Canaria's biggest draw is the immense 5-mile-long (8 km) beach shared by three resorts: **San Agustín, Playa del Inglés,** and **Maspalomas.** Innumerable facilities include water sports and hot nightlife, but the greatest sight is the area of undulating sand dunes and oases of palm trees at **Maspalomas.** Smaller resorts on the west coast include the attractive fishing port of **Puerto de Mogán** and secluded **Playa de Güigüi.**

The sprawling port of **Las Palmas de Gran Canaria,** capital of the Canaries, was founded in 1478. In the historic **Vegueta** district you find the twin-towered **cathedral** and the lovely Renaissance **Casa de Colón** *(Calle Colón 1, tel 928 31 23 84, closed Sat. & Sun. p.m.),* which has exhibits on Colombus's four stopovers on the island and on the importance of the Canaries in the early voyages to America. At the **Museo Canario** you get a picture of the indigenous Guanche culture. The **Centro Atlantico de Arte Moderno** *(Calle Los Balcones 11, tel 928 31 18 00, closed Mon., & Sun. p.m.)* exhibits contemporary art in an 18th-century building. Overlooking the port is the **Castillo de La Luz,** built in the 16th century to fend off pirates. **Playa de las Canteras** is the buzzing city beach. ■

Wealth of Flora & Fauna

The ancient Greeks and Romans knew of the Canary Islands, but no outsiders had settled here before the 15th century. This long isolation preserved an exceptional range of flora and fauna: Of the 2,000 species of flora, 600 are endemic. Only Hawaii and the Galápagos islands have a comparable wealth of native species.

Evergreen laurel forests *(laurisilva)* that disappeared several millennia ago from the rest of the planet still thrive here. Laurisilva depend on specific conditions of humidity, temperature, and altitude, and can best be seen in Tenerife's Anaga highlands, at El Cedro in Gomera, and in La Palma's national park.

Named for its terrifying, gnarled appearance, the drago tree has slothlike growth and a penchant for wild locations. The specimen at Icod de los Vinos (see p. 337), standing right beside the main road on the edge of town, is thought to be the world's largest and oldest. It now rises more than 50 feet (15 m) high, seemingly aloof to visitors.

Lanzarote

Dromedaries, architecture that is sensitive to the environment, and blinding white beaches are just some of the attractions of this 323-square-mile (836 sq km) island, all of which is a biosphere reserve. Lanzarote is special for its otherworldly volcanic cover, the result of momentous eruptions in 1730–1736 and 1824 that buried towns and fertile valleys under lava flows.

These events produced the awesome landscapes of the **Parque Nacional de Timanfaya** *(Calle Laguneta 64, Pinajo, tel 928 84 02 38/40, www.lanzarote.com/timanfaya)*. Don't pass up a bumpy dromedary ride through this extraordinary national park, where the volcanoes still simmer.

The main port and town is **Arrecife,** named for the outlying reefs of this south coast and defended by thc 16th-century **Castillo del San Gabriel.** This houses the **Museo Arqueológico y Etnográfico** *(tel 928 80 28 84, closed Sat. p.m. & Sun.)*. Arrecife's other guardian, **Castillo de San José,** has been converted into the **Museo Internacional de Arte Contemporáneo** *(tel 928 81 23 21)*. The latter was the brainchild of Lanzarote's greatest artist, César Manrique (1920–1992).

You can enjoy more of Manrique's work at the **Jameos del Agua** (a saltwater lagoon in a volcanic cave) and the breathtaking, clifftop **Mirador del Río,** both in the north of the island, and at the **Fundación César Manrique** *(Taro de Tahíche, Teguise, tel 928 84 31 38, $$)*. This intriguing lava-top house was built by Manrique in 1968 to exemplify affinities between art and nature, and it houses a good collection of contemporary Spanish art.

On Lanzarote, ancient volcanic activity shaped the landscape.

On the southern edge of the park lies **El Golfo.** This spectacular emerald-green crater lake is at the base of volcanic cliffs and creates a startling contrast with the black-sand beach. More tormented rockscapes characterize **Los Hervideros,** before the road reaches the **Salinas de Janubio.** This natural phenomenon is formed out of dazzling white salt mounds and salt pans within a crater.

Beaches

Some of Lanzarote's best beaches are the golden sandy coves of **Papagayo** around the southern tip. Best of all are the unspoiled, idyllic sands of **La Graciosa,** an islet off the northern tip. ■

Lanzarote

335 F3

www.turismolanzarote.com

Arrecife

335 F2

Visitor Information

Oficina de Turismo, Parque José Ramírez Cerdá s/n

928 81 31 74

www.arrecife.es

Other Islands to Visit

La Gomera

For decades most visitors who came to this island with its rugged terrain were seeking to escape the rat race. The 40-minute hydrofoil ride from Santa Cruz de Tenerife has changed that, yet Gomera's deep ravines and bad roads have preserved its charms for hikers and cyclists. Terraced farming, date palms, and banana plantations surround the central plateau characterized by its ancient laurel forest often shrouded in mist. This is the **Parque Nacional de Garajonay,** where you'll find around 400 native species of flora that became extinct in Africa and Europe millions of years ago. There are well-marked trails, and guided treks are available. Accommodations are concentrated in the capital of **San Sebastián** (where Columbus prepared to cross to America), **Playa de Santiago,** and idyllic **Valle Gran Rey.** *www.gomera-island.com* 334 B1 **Visitor Information** Patronato Insular de Turismo, Calle Real 4, San Sebastián de La Gomera 922 14 15 12

INSIDER TIP:

A drive from San Sebastián to Valle Gran Rey on La Gomera will give dramatic views of all the island summits.

—FIONA DUNLOP
National Geographic author

El Hierro

This somewhat bleak bump in the Atlantic Ocean has inspired numerous legends. As the westernmost island in the archipelago, for Europeans it was the end of the known world —in fact it was once used by geographers as zero meridian until it was relocated through Greenwich. Fish, sheep, goats, pineapples, and vineyards are the islanders' main resources; tourism is limited to **Valverde,** the tiny capital, and neighboring **Tamaduste** with its lava pool. The rest of the island slopes dramatically down from the peak of **Malpaso.** *www.elhierro.es* 334 A1 **Visitor Information** Patronato de Turismo, Calle Doctor Quintero 4, Valverde 928 55 03 02

La Palma

Teardrop-shaped La Palma attracts hikers, botanists, and nature lovers. The steepest island in the world, it is also home to the Northern Hemisphere's largest astrophysics observatory on the summit of **Roque de los Muchachos** (7,957 feet/2,426 m). At the heart of the island lies **Caldera de Taburiente** *(visitor center, El Paso, tel 922 49 72 77),* the world's largest crater, with a diameter of 5 miles (8 km). Trails lead through the wonders of the surrounding cones. The northwestern flank, around **Puntagorda,** is particularly beautiful.

Cruise ships and ferries from Tenerife, Gran Canaria, and Cádiz dock at the port in **Santa Cruz,** but the east coast capital remains low key. The delightful seafront quarter of Canarian wooden houses with fretwork balconies marks the city's atmospheric restaurant hub. Cobbled streets lead up to the attractive, shady **Plaza Santo Domingo.**

The popular resort of **Los Cancajos,** good for water sports, lies just south of town but it is the warmer west coast that attracts most beach lovers. From **Los Llanos** a stunning road winds down to the palm-studded black-sand beach of **Puerto Naos** and another to **Puerto de Tazacorte,** a beach and fishing harbor.

Don't miss out on La Palma's handmade cigars, embroidery, and silk, and be sure to taste its local tea (pinewood) wine. *www.lapalmaturismo.com* 334 A2 **Visitor Information** Oficina de Información Turística, Avenida Blas Pérez González s/n, Santa Cruz 922 41 21 06

Travelwise

Grand old cars on display in Soria town, Castilla y León

TRAVELWISE

PLANNING YOUR TRIP

When to Go

Unless you wish to bask on busy summer beaches or ski in the Pyrenees or Sierra Nevada in winter, the time to visit Spain is during spring (March to mid-June) or fall (mid-September to November). Spring is perhaps the finest season, when wild flowers burst into life and gregarious locals return to the streets after the short and, in places, severe winter. Fall sees Spain return to life as temperatures drop to a pleasant level and rain ends the summer drought.

Although winter can be cold in some areas, the Mediterranean coast, particularly near Valencia, has some of the highest winter temperatures in Europe. On the other hand, Spain also has some of the highest summer temperatures on the continent, resulting in an exodus from the cities to the coast. In August virtually the entire country is on vacation. Combined with the arrival of millions of (mostly European) foreign visitors, this makes the coasts, particularly the Mediterranean, terribly overcrowded.

Climate

Spain's geographical and geological diversity means that the climate varies greatly. The north coast is battered by the Atlantic over the winter, suffering cold, rain, and mist, but has hot summers marked by thunderstorms. The Mediterranean coast ranges from the deserts of Almería (Europe's lowest rainfall) to a subtropical climate in Granada to the pine-covered hills of Catalunya. To the north, the Pyrenees are permanently snowcapped. The center of the country is occupied by the high *meseta,* "the plain of Spain," that ranges in height from 1,310 feet (400 m) to 3,280 feet (1,000 m). This region bakes in the summer and is swept by freezing winds in the winter. To the west, the meseta stretches to the border with Portugal. In this verdant area of rivers and oak forests, moss and lichen thrive in the damp air.

Average temperatures:
Barcelona
Jan. 40°F/4°C–56°F/13°C
Aug. 67°F/19°C–82°F/28°C
Madrid
Jan. 37°F/3°C–49°F/10°C
Aug. 65°F/18°C–87°F/37°C
Málaga
Jan. 45°F/7°C–62°F/17°C
Aug. 69°F/27°C–87°F/30°C

Main Events

Spain has an enormous number of festivals and fiestas. Probably the best known is **San Fermín,** the running of the bulls in Iruña (Pamplona), July 6–14. Holy Week or **Semana Santa** (the week before Easter, see pp. 272–273) is marked by spectacular processions, most famously in Sevilla (Seville). If it's a party you want, then visit Valencia for **Las Fallas de San José** (March 15–19). More sedate are Madrid's fiestas. During **San Isidro** (centered around May 15), many operas, concerts, and ballets are performed. Other festivals are listed on pp. 388–389.

What to Take

You should be able to buy most things that you need in Spain. Spaniards tend to dress quite formally except at the coastal resorts during the summer. Casual clothing and footwear (such as sneakers) are quite acceptable during the day, but you should dress up when going out at night.

Bring any essential prescription medication; for other medicines, Spanish pharmacy staff are helpful and knowledgeable, and dispense many drugs that in other countries might need prescriptions.

Insurance

Make sure you have adequate travel and medical coverage for treatment and expenses, including repatriation, baggage, and money loss. Keep all receipts. Report losses or thefts to the police and obtain a signed statement *(una denuncia)* from a police station to help with insurance claims.

Further Reading

Publishers are not included as many of these books have been reprinted by different companies.

***South From Granada* by Gerald Brenan.** A fascinating account of life in rural southern Spain between the two World Wars.
***For Whom the Bell Tolls* by Ernest Hemingway.** Perhaps the most famous book written on Spain and the Civil War.
***The Sun Also Rises* by Ernest Hemingway.** This book put the San Fermín festival in Iruña (Pamplona) on the map.
***Voices of the Old Sea* by Norman Lewis.** The author recalls the fishing village he knew in his youth.
***Spain* by Jan Morris.** A good general book on the country.
***The Spanish Temper* by V. S. Pritchett.** Perceptive portrait of Spain's landscape and history.
***Our Lady of the Sewers* by Paul Richardson.** About "the ancient, perverse and eccentric" Spain that is increasingly hard to find.
***Homage to Barcelona* by Colm Tóibín.** Firsthand account of modern life in Barcelona.

HOW TO GET TO SPAIN

Entry Formalities

U.S., Canadian, and E.U. citizens may enter Spain without a visa and remain for up to 90 days. Keep your identity card or passport on you at all times.

Airlines

The national carrier, Iberia, has direct flights from North America to Madrid and Barcelona. U.S. airlines also offer direct flights, and several other European carriers have services to Spain.

Useful Numbers & Internet Addresses

In the U.S. and Canada:
Air Europa, tel 800/238-7672, www.aireuropa.com
American Airlines, tel 800/433-7300, www.aa.com
British Airways, tel 800/247-9297, www.ba.com
Delta Airlines, tel 800/241-4141, www.delta.com
Iberia, tel 800/772-4642, www.iberia.com

In Spain:
Air Europa, tel 902 40 15 01
American Airlines, tel 902 11 55 70
Barcelona, tel 901 11 69 46
British Airways, tel 902 11 13 33
Delta Airlines, Madrid, tel 902 81 08 72; SkyMiles queries, tel 912 71 81 64
Iberia, tel 902 40 05 00
Vueling, tel 807 00 17 17, www.vueling.com

Arrival

By Air

Most intercontinental flights touch down at Barajas airport, Madrid. The airport is 10 miles (15 km) from downtown Madrid, a 20-minute taxi ride (25 €/$34.50). Express buses to the city center (2 €/$2.75) run every 15 minutes, 24 hours a day. The underground train is slower and harder to use than the bus.

If you arrive in Barcelona, a taxi ride into the center (25 €/$34.50) takes about 25 minutes. Buses (5.30 €/$7.35) leave every 5, 10, or 15 minutes from 6 a.m. to 1 a.m. A train service (3 €/$4.15) runs twice an hour from 6:08 a.m. to 11:38 p.m.

By Car

You must choose between the Atlantic or Mediterranean coasts if you wish to travel by highway. Smaller roads cross the Pyrenees, but they may be blocked by snow in winter. The exception is the road through Andorra; it is closed only during extreme conditions.

By Sea

Several ferries sail from the U.K. and France to the northern ports of Santander and Bilbo (Bilbao). Timetables change depending on the season. In the U.K.:
Brittany Ferries
tel 08712 440 744
www.brittany-ferries.com
P&O European Ferries
tel 08716 645 645
www.poferries.com

By Train

You can go by train from the U.K. via the Channel Tunnel, changing trains in Paris and passing the night on a *trenhotel.* The Madrid sleeper leaves Paris Austerlitz train station at 7:45 p.m. and arrives at Madrid Chamartín at 9:10 a.m. The train for Barcelona leaves at 8:33 p.m. and arrives at 9:29 a.m.

GETTING AROUND

By Airplane

Most major cities in Spain have an airport for internal and international flights. The national airline **Iberia** *(tel 902 40 05 00)* has the most frequent internal flights. Other airlines are **Air Europa** *(tel 902 40 15 01),* **Vueling** *(tel 807 00 17 17),* and **Spanair** *(tel 902 13 14 15).*

By Car

Driving in the countryside is often a relaxing experience if you are used to the congested roads of northern Europe, but driving in the cities can be quite the reverse. Dual lane *autopistas* and the *autovías* link many provincial capitals and, outside of major cities and holidays, are relatively free of traffic. Tolls are paid in cash or with credit cards on exiting the autopista or, on short stretches, on entering. In the south, most highways are toll-free.

National roads, or *nacionales,* marked in red on road maps, have been superseded by the highways. Smaller roads marked in yellow are *comarcales,* regional roads, and are often picturesque and quiet, as are local roads, marked white and often without any names or numbers.

Driving Information

European driving permits are valid in Spain. U.S. and Canadian citizens require an International Driving Permit, obtainable at any AAA or CAA office. If your permit does not include a photo, you must carry ID that does—such as a passport. It is compulsory to carry two warning triangles, spare lightbulbs, fuses, reflective jackets, and a spare tire. The minimum legal age for car drivers is 18. You must be over 21 to rent a car. If entering Spain in your own car, make sure that you have appropriate insurance, including the green card available from your insurer. Using GPS/SatNav systems and cell phones, unless fully hands-free, while driving is prohibited.

Breakdown assistance Freeways have emergency telephones at intervals. The nearest garage will send help. You must place a warning triangle behind your vehicle. AAA, CAA, or AA members can get help from RACE *(tel 902 30 05 05, www.race.es)*, Spain's driving organization.

Distances All distances are in kilometers (1 km=0.62 mile).

Drunk-driving The limit for breath alcohol content is 0.25 mg/liter (0.15 for driver's with less than two years' experience) and for blood alcohol concentration is 0.5g/liter (0.3 if less than two years' experience). Fines start at 200 € ($276). Prompt payment secures a 50 percent discount, except in cases of major excess.

Fuel Fuel prices are controlled by the government and are slightly cheaper than in the U.K. but nearly twice those of the U.S.

On-the-spot Fines Failing to wear your seat belt receives a minimum fine of 200 € ($276). Exceeding the speed limit results in a fine of between 100 and 600 € ($138–829). Nonresidents must pay immediately, thereby securing a 50 percent prompt payment discount; make sure you get a receipt *(recibo)*.

Parking A yellow line on the road or curb means no parking. Blue lines denote pay parking. Look for ticket-dispensing machines marked by a sign of a coin being pushed into a slot, and display the ticket in your car. If your car has been towed away, an orange sticker will give details of your car, the time it was taken, and the number to call. In cities it makes sense to use the underground parking lots, which now proliferate.

Seat belts Wearing seat belts is compulsory in the front seats and also in the back if the car is fitted with them.

Speed limits They are: freeways 75 mph (120 kph); nacional roads 62.5 mph (100 kph); C roads 56 mph (90 kph); towns and in built-up areas 31 mph (50 kph) on two-way streets and just over 18 mph (30 kph) on one-way streets. Stay alert: They may change.

Traffic circles Vehicles already in the circle have the right of way unless it is marked otherwise.

Renting a Car

Renting a car in Spain is straightforward and relatively cheap.
Avis, tel 902 18 08 54, www.avis.com
Europcar, tel 902 10 50 30, www.europcar.com
Hertz, tel 902 40 24 05, www.hertz.com
If you start in Madrid, bear in mind that road signs as you leave the city give road numbers rather than destinations.

By Train

RENFE (Red Nacional de Ferrocarriles Españoles) is the mainline national rail network. Outside the main holiday periods (summer and Easter Week), traveling by train is recommended, particularly on the Talgos (Tren Articulado Ligero Goicoechea Oriol) and the high speed AVEs (Alta Velocidad Española). Talgos are fast, comfortable, and reliable. AVEs have telephones and other facilities.

Tickets can be bought at the station up to 15 minutes before the train departs. Reserve your seat for longer journeys. Travel agents that display a RENFE sticker sell rail tickets, and RENFE also has offices in many cities. For a long-distance rail journey in the high season, book well in advance. RENFE *(www.renfe.es)* has a comprehensive website with the latest prices, routes, and timetables in both Spanish and English.

Trains are generally divided into 1st and 2nd class, but standards vary. You can get a 20 percent reduction on a round-trip ticket. There are special rates for those over 60 and children between 4 and 13, and for travelers with disabilities.

Inter Rail *(www.interrailnet.com)* and Eurail *(www.eurail.com)* passes are valid in Spain. Students should get an International Student Identity Card (ISIC), those younger than 26 an International Youth Travel Card (IYTC), and teachers an International Teacher Identity Card (ITIC)—all offer useful discounts *(www.istc.org)*.

Transportation in Madrid

Taxis

Downtown Madrid teems with taxis (white, with a red stripe along their sides), and you rarely have to wait long before one appears. Madrid is a compact city, and taxis are not expensive, which makes them an ideal mode of transport. A supplement is charged between 10 p.m. and 6 a.m. and for passing beyond the city limits.

Metro

The subway system is the most efficient and rapid mode of public transport. The distances between stops are short, so you tend to be near your destination when you exit the station. Punch your ticket as you start your journey. Most major attractions are within Zone A, for which single tickets cost 1 € ($1.38). The Metrobús ticket gives you ten journeys, either by subway or by bus, for 9.30 € ($12.86). The Tourist Travel Pass (Abono Turístico) gives you one day's subway and bus travel throughout Zone A for 6 € ($8.29) or seven days for 25 € ($34.56). To buy it you must show ID, and it cannot be shared. Lines are color coded and the train's direction is indicated by the terminal stations. Hold on to your ticket until exiting the system: Inspectors check for fare dodgers.

Bus

Madrid's bus network is extensive but confusing. On a short stay it may not be worth mastering. The price of a journey is the same as on the metro, and you can use tickets from your pass. If not, pay the driver, using small change rather than bills. Punch your ticket in the machine near the driver.

Transportation in Barcelona

Barcelona has buses, cable cars, trams, and underground trains. If you plan to stay for more than a few days, buy one of the various *targetes* (similar to abonos in Madrid), either the T10 or the Barcelona Card, which work on all forms of public transport. The Zone 1 T10 offers ten journeys, covers all of central Barcelona, can be shared, and costs 8.25 € ($11.40). The Barcelona Card offers unlimited travel for 2, 3, 4, or 5 consecutive days for 27.50, 33.50, 38, and 45 € ($38, 46.31, 52.53, and 62.20, cheaper for under-13s), free entry and discounts at some museums, sights, shows, and restaurants, and cannot be shared. Buy it at the airport or at tourist information offices.

Taxis

Like Madrid, Barcelona abounds in taxis, only here they are black and yellow. They offer a cost-effective way of getting around the city, though much of the center is pedestrianized. The minimum charge is 2 € ($2.77).

Metro

Again, the quickest way of getting around the city is the metro. Smaller than Madrid's system, just five lines, it is open between 5 a.m. and 12 p.m, until 2 a.m. on Friday, and all night on Saturday.

Bus

Barcelona's bus service is reliable and cheap: 1.30 € ($1.80) a trip. Most day buses and all night buses stop at the Plaça Catalunya. The main airport service is the Aerobús.

PRACTICAL ADVICE

Communications

E-Mail

Almost every public library *(biblioteca municipal)* offers free Internet access. Most towns have easy-to-find Internet cafés.

Madrid

Café Comercial Glorieta de Bilbao 7, tel 91 521 5655, metro Bilbao, 8 a.m.–1 a.m. Cost: 1 € ($1.38)/50 minutes.
WORKcenter www.workcenter.es, Plaza de la Castellana 149, tel 911 21 76 30, metro Cuzco, Mon.–Fri. 8 a.m.–10 p.m., Sat.–Sun. 10 a.m.–2:30 p.m., 5–8:30 p.m.; Calle María de Molina 40, tel 911 21 56 80, metro Avenida de América, Mon.–Thurs. 24 hours, Fri. midnight–11 p.m., Sat. 9 a.m.–11 p.m., Sun. 9 a.m.–12 p.m. Access card 1 € ($1.38), 0.65 € ($0.85)/10 minutes.

Barcelona

Acoma Carrer Boquería 21, tel 933 01 75 97, metro Liceu, 9 a.m.–12 p.m. No cost.
Bornet Barra de Ferro 3 (by the Picasso Museum), tel 93 268 15 07, metro Jaume 1, open Mon.–Fri. 10 a.m.–11 p.m., Sat.–Sun. & holidays 12 a.m.–11 p.m. Cost: 2.80 € ($3.87)/hour.
Ciber Condal Basses de Sant Pere 26, tel 93 268 12 00, metro Arc de Triomf, open 10 a.m.–11 p.m. Cost: 1 € ($1.38)/hour.

Sevilla

Internetia Avenida Menéndez Pelayo 43-5, tel 95 453 40 03, open 10 a.m.–11 p.m. Cost 2.20 € ($3.04)/hour.
WORKcenter Buhaira Avenida de la Buhaira 14, open Mon.–Fri. 8 a.m.–9:30 p.m., Sat.–Sun. 10 a.m.–2 p.m. and 5 p.m.–9 p.m. Access card 1 € ($1.38), 0.33 € ($0.42) for 10 minutes.

Post Offices

Most letters and postcards cost 0.65 € to send within the E.U. and 0.80 € to North America. Registered mail *(correo certificado)* costs an extra 2.30 €. Stamps are available at post offices *(correos)*, which in major cities are open Mon.–Fri. 8:30 a.m.–8:30 p.m. and Sat. 9:30 a.m.–1 p.m., and at state tobacco stores *(estancos)*.

Telephones

The country code for Spain is 34 followed by the provincial code, which starts with a 9. Codes to some provinces are: Madrid (91), Barcelona (93), Valencia (96), Sevilla (95), and Vizcaya (94). Many provinces have three-digit codes: Navarra (948) and Granada (958). Call boxes usually allow you to pay in cash or with a card *(tarjeta telefónica)*. Tarjetas are sold at post offices and estancos, and come in various denominations. The access code to make an international call is 00. For a collect call *(llamada a cobro revertido)* within Spain, dial 1009; to Europe, North America, and Turkey, dial 1008; and to all other countries dial 1005. For national directory inquiries dial 11818, for international 11825. Spanish cell phone numbers start with 6. Calls to 900 numbers are free.

Conversions

1 kilo = 2.2 pounds
1 liter = 0.2642 U.S. gallon
1 kilometer = 0.62 mile
1 meter = 1.093 yards

Women's clothing

U.S.	8	10	12	14	16	18
Spanish	36	38	40	42	44	46

Women's shoes

U.S.	6–6.5	7–7.5	8–8.5	9–9.5
Spanish	38	39	40–41	42

Men's clothing

U.S.	36 38 40 42 44 46
Spanish	46 48 50 52 54 56

Men's shoes

U.S.	8	8.5	9.5	10.5	11.5	12
Spanish	41	42	43	44	45	46

Electricity
The electricity voltage is 220 or 225 AC, not 110 V as in North America. Plugs are two pin. Check whether your appliance will need a power converter/transformer.

Holidays
Spain has national, regional, and local holidays. It is not possible to list all of them. The main national holidays are:
January 1 & 6 (Epiphany)
Good Friday
Easter Sunday
Easter Monday
May 1 (May Day)
October 12 (National Day)
November 1 (All Saints)
December 6 (Constitution),
8 (Immaculate Conception),
25 (Christmas)

Media
Newspapers
The most popular dailies are *El País, El Mundo,* and *ABC.* There are many regional English language papers on the Mediterranean coast. In the tourist areas you find same-day *International Herald Tribune* and British newspapers.

Radio
The state-run Radio Nacional de España has four stations covering sports, pop, classical music, and current affairs. The Voice of America can be streamed live online at *www.voanews.com.* The same applies to the BBC World Service, which can be accessed at *www.bbc.co.uk/radio.*

Television
Spanish television has good news coverage but tends to be a mess of game, quiz, audience participation shows, and Latin American soaps. There are two state-run channels, TVE1 and TVE2, with no commercials, four independents, and regional channels. Most hotels are equipped with satellite, cable, or digital television, offering international channels such as CNN, BBC World, Canalt, and Sky.

Money Matters
Take a combination of traveler's checks and credit or debit cards that you can use for cash at ATMs. Major credit cards are accepted in most establishments and all gas stations. Traveler's checks are a secure way to hold money (keep a list of their numbers separate from the checks) and can be changed in banks and exchange offices. Banks give you a better exchange rate but exchange offices are open longer hours.

Spain's currency is the euro (€). The euro comes in coins of 1, 2, 5, 10, 20, & 50 cents *(céntimos)* and of 1 & 2 euros, and notes of 5, 10, 20, 50, 100, 200, and 500 euros. (At the time of printing 1 € = $1.38.)

Opening Times
Most **banks** open 8:30 a.m.–2:30 p.m. Some open on Sat. a.m.

Museums open 9 a.m. –7 p.m. Generally most close on Monday. Shops and pharmacies, open 9:30 a.m.–2 p.m, and again between 4:30 p.m.–5 p.m., closing at 8 p.m.

Restaurants open around midday, close around 5 p.m., reopen around 7 p.m. and often serve food until past midnight.

Bars are open virtually 24 hours. **Cafés** open from 7 a.m. onward. **Music bars** open until between 3–5 a.m., and **nightclubs** often until 7 a.m.

Places of Worship
When visiting churches, remember that they are places of worship and act accordingly.

Restrooms
Public toilets are rare outside tourist spots. Luckily, you are never far from a bar and it would be unusual if the owner did not let you use the toilet. Carry toilet paper with you as this is often in short supply.

Time Differences
Spain runs on CET (Central European Time), one hour ahead of Greenwich Mean Time, six hours ahead of Eastern Standard Time. The Canary Islands run on CET minus one. Noon in Spain is 6 a.m. in New York.

Travelers with Disabilities
In recent years Spain has begun to cater to the needs of people with disabilities. Newer buildings are more accessible than older ones, but there may still be problems. Check with hotels and restaurants before booking. Get advice from:

Disabled Peoples' International (DPI)
Suite 188, 38 Pearson St., St. John's, Newfoundland, A1A 3R1, Canada, tel 709/747-7600, e-mail info@dpi.org

European Disability Forum
35 Square de Meeûs, 1000 Brussels, Belgium, tel 32 2 282 4600, Fax 32 2 282 4609, e-mail: info@edf-feph.org, www.edf-feph.org

Mobility International U.S.A.
132 E. Broadway, Suite 343, Eugene, OR 97401, tel 541/343-1284, e-mail info@miusa.org, www.miusa.org

RADAR (Royal Association for Disability and Rehabilitation)
12 City Forum, 250 City Road, London EC1V 8AF, U.K., tel 020-7250 3222, www.radar.org.uk

Etiquette & Local Customs

The Spanish siesta is not a myth. Almost everything closes from 2 to 5 p.m., even later in summer. Lunch—the day's main meal—begins at 2 and often lasts until 5 p.m. Sunday lunch can go on longer. Dinner is a lighter affair, as it is considered unhealthy to eat a lot before going to bed.

Tipping

Service is included on restaurant bills, so there is no need to tip. However, the Spanish service industry is poorly paid; a tip for good service would not be amiss. The Spanish themselves often leave their small change when paying for a drink and tip about 5 percent at restaurants. Tip taxi drivers and porters 2–3 €, depending on the distance and amount of luggage.

EMERGENCIES

Embassies

Embassies are in Madrid, but larger cities have consulates.

United States
Serrano 75, tel 91 587 22 00, http://madrid.usembassy.gov

Canada
Torre Espacio, Paseo de la Castellana 259D, tel 913 82 84 00, www.canadainternational.gc.ca

United Kingdom
Torre Espacio, Paseo de la Castellana 259 D, tel 917 14 63 00, www.ukinspain.com

Spanish Embassies

United States
2375 Pennsylvania Ave. N.W., Washington, D.C. 20037, tel 202/452-0100, www.spainemb.org

Canada
74 Stanley Ave., Ottawa, Ontario K1M 1P4, tel 613/747-2252, www.embassyincanada.maec.es

United Kingdom
39 Chesham Place, London SW1X 8SB, tel 020-7235 5555, www.maec.es

Emergency Phone Number

The central number for police, fire, and ambulance is 112. Victims of a crime or accident should report the incident to the police *(tel 902 10 21 12, English spoken)* and to their consulate.

Police

Spain has three distinct police forces. The **Policía Local** (or Municipal) is controlled by the local town hall and deal with minor matters such as traffic infringements. The **Policía Nacional** is the main crime-fighting force in the cities (except in Euskadi/Basque Country, where they become Ertzaintza and in Catalunya, Mossos d'Esquadra). The **Guardia Civil** operates in the countryside and on highways, in addition to controlling borders and prisons.

Loss of Credit Cards

American Express España,
tel 902 37 56 37 (24 hrs.)
Diners Club Español,
tel 900 80 13 31 (24 hrs.)
MasterCard,
tel 800/307-7309 (24 hrs.)
VISA International,
tel 900 99 11 24 (24 hrs.)

What to Do in a Car Accident

The Guardia Civil operates special units designed to deal effectively with anything other than minor accidents. If you have an accident call the police at 112. Everyone who leaves the car must wear reflective jackets. Move the car only if necessary for road safety. If so, note the cars' positions and take photographs if possible. Wait for the police. Place reflective triangles 164 feet (50 m) in front and behind. If it is a minor accident involving another vehicle, there is no need to call the police as long as both parties agree how it occurred. In this case, simply fill out the insurance details. For repairs, call from an SOS phone on freeways or call RACE *(tel 902 40 45 45).*

Health

Make sure that your health insurance covers you during your visit to Spain. E.U. citizens should complete and carry the EHIC form available from main post offices. Doctors are listed in the telephone directory, but in an emergency go to the nearest *urgencias,* or call 112 or the Red Cross (Cruz Roja; *tel 913 35 45 45*). A hospital stay can be expensive, so make sure your insurance is valid and up to date.

Tap water is safe to drink though it may have a chlorine taste. Plastic bottles of mineral water are widely available. The primary health concerns are sunburn and dehydration. Make sure to wear suitable clothing and put on sunscreen. During the hottest parts of the day in the summer you will notice few locals about on the streets.

International Association for Medical Assistance to Travelers

(IAMAT; *www.iamat.org*) is a nonprofit organization that anyone can join free of charge. Members receive a directory of English-speaking IAMAT doctors on call 24 hours a day and are entitled to services at a set rate.

United States
1623 Military Rd., Suite 279, Niagara Falls, NY 14304-1745, tel 716/754-4883

Canada
67 Mowat Ave., Ste. 036, Toronto, Ontario M6E IB8, tel 416/652-0137

Hotels & Restaurants

Spain has a wide variety of accommodations, ranging from the humblest of *fondas* or *casas de huéspedes* (guesthouses) to luxurious five-star hotels. A new interest in the countryside is reflected in the number of *casas rurales* (country houses) that have recently opened. Located in some beautiful and wild spots, they may be farm houses, country cottages, or restored palaces, and offer outdoor activities such as horseback riding, hiking, and bicycling. Facilities are reflected in prices, and in cheaper hotels you may not have a private bath. If in doubt check when making your reservation.

HOTELS

A number of hotels offer *media pensión* (includes breakfast and dinner) or *pensión completa* (includes lunch as well) at a competitive price. Inquire upon reservation or arrival. Spain is a noisy country and peace and quiet can be hard to come by. When reserving a room, mention that you would like one away from likely noise.

Paradors

Unique to Spain are the paradors, the nationally owned chain of hotels—some in historic buildings—often in national parks or other places of scenic interest.

Grading System

Hotels throughout Spain are graded with a star system of one to five stars, with five stars given to hotels at the top of the range. *Hostales* or *pensiones* have a different system of one to three stars. Standards may vary from region to region as the autonomous governments are responsible for their own classifications.

Some of the hotels in this guide fall out of the star rating system—this includes the *casas rurales* and the *posadas*.

The following is a selection of hotels throughout the country, listed by location, price, and then alphabetical order. Hotels that are historically, architecturally, or aesthetically interesting have been chosen wherever possible.

Note, unless otherwise stated:

- Breakfast is not included in the price.
- The hotel has a restaurant. A restaurant icon indicates a notable hotel restaurant.
- Smoking is prohibited in bars and restaurants. Hotels can keep 30 percent of their rooms for smokers, but many are entirely smoke-free.
- Price categories are given only as guidance and do not take into account seasonal variations.
- The 8 percent I.V.A. (Value Added Tax) is not included in the price categories.
- Prices are for a double room.

In high season always try to book in advance. You may be asked for a deposit or credit card number.

Credit & Debit Cards

Many hotels accept all major cards. Smaller ones may only accept some, as shown. Abbreviations used are: AE (American Express), DC (Diners Club), MC (MasterCard), and V (Visa).

Hotel Chains & Groups

www.husa.es
(reservations: tel 902 10 07 10)
www.nh-hotels.com
(reservations: tel 913 98 44 00)
www.parador.es
(reservations: tel 902 54 79 79)
www.solmelia.com
(reservations: tel 902 14 44 40)

Hotel groups or chains often have special offers, for example five nights in selected paradors at a fixed price that works out one-third cheaper than the normal price. Ask your travel agent or check their Web sites.

PRICES

HOTELS

An indication of the cost of a double room in the high season is given by **$** signs.

$$$$$	Over $300
$$$$	$220–$300
$$$	$160–$220
$$	$80–$160
$	Under $80

RESTAURANTS

An indication of the cost of a three-course meal without drinks is given by **$** signs.

$$$$$	Over $80
$$$$	$50–$80
$$$	$35–$50
$$	$20–$35
$	Under $20

RESTAURANTS

By law, all restaurants must provide a *menú del día* (starter, main course, dessert, and a drink). Upscale restaurants may also have a *menú degustación* (taster menu) that allows you to try small portions of several courses. At bars and cafés it is common to have tapas with beer and wine. Some restaurants close on public holidays. Check before you go.

Restaurants have been listed by location, price, and then alphabetical order. The price categories are for a meal à la carte, excluding wine.

L= lunch, D = dinner

IN & AROUND MADRID

HOTELS

RITZ
$$$$$ ★★★★★
PLAZA DE LA LEALTAD 5
TEL 917 01 67 67
www.ritzmadrid.com
Built in 1910, this hotel full of beautiful antiques and elegant chandeliers is surrounded by luscious gardens. Breakfast is served in the highly acclaimed **Goya Restaurant.**
167 Banco de España
All major cards

SOMETHING SPECIAL

SANTO MAURO
$$$$$ ★★★★★
ZURBANO 36
TEL 913 19 69 00
www.hotelacsantomauro.com
The interiors of this 1894 neoclassical palace combine original materials with contemporary. An intriguing feature is the basement pool with columns and vaulted ceilings. **La Biblioteca,** the restaurant, occupies the old library and serves innovative, seasonal cuisine.
50 24 Alonso Martínez All major cards

ÚNICO
$$$$$ ★★★★★
CLAUDIO COELLO 67
TEL 917 81 01 73
www.unicohotelmadrid.com
This luxurious and fashionable boutique hotel in a beautiful 19th-century palace has a large and private garden. Enjoy original cooking with a Catalan touch at **Ramón Freixa** *(tel 917 81 82 62, www.ramonfreixa madrid.com, $$$$$)*, the restaurant adjoining the garden.
44 35 Serrano
All major cards

VILLA MAGNA
$$$$$ ★★★★★
PASEO CASTELLANA 22
TEL 915 87 12 34
www.villamagna.es
Surrounded by gardens, this hotel, which was refurbished in 2008, sports a modern facade that contrasts with its Charles IV–style interiors. It also has two fine restaurants: **Villa Magna** gives a 21st-century touch to classic Spanish cuisine, and **Tse-Yang** serves Madrid's highest quality Chinese food.
150 Núñez de Balboa
All major cards

WESTIN PALACE
$$$$$ ★★★★★
PLAZA DE LAS CORTES 7
TEL 913 60 80 00/900 81 12 45
www.westinpalacemadrid.com
Inaugurated in 1912, the Westin has a sumptuous interior, with period decor. Guest rooms are small, but furnishings and bathrooms are impressive. Try Cantonese dishes in **The Asia Gallery,** or eat dinner in **La Rotonda,** named after the spectacular stained-glass cupola that is a distinguishing feature of this palace-hotel.
467 All major cards

ME MADRID
$$$$ ★★★★
PLAZA DE SANTA ANA 14
TEL 915 31 45 00
www.memadrid.com
Once the favored hotel of bullfighters and writers like Ernest Hemingway, the ME Madrid now attracts the hip and ultra-fashionable. Eat dinner in the ground-floor **ME Restaurant & Lounge,** and then head to **The Roof,** the rooftop bar and terrace, for spectacular views.
192 Sevilla
All major cards

REGINA
$$$$ ★★★
ALCALÁ 19
TEL 915 21 47 25
www.hotelreginamadrid.com
Recently redesigned and modernized, this 1918 building is within walking distance of many of Madrid's sights and its rooms are spacious and inviting. The **Aymara Restaurant,** which has its own wine cellar, serves seasonal Mediterranean cuisine with a modern twist.
180 80 Sevilla
All major cards

SOMETHING SPECIAL

VILLA REAL
$$$$ ★★★★★
PLAZA DE LAS CORTES 10
TEL 914 20 37 67
www.derbyhotels.com
Built to blend in with its older surroundings, this modern hotel is decorated in the French style. The wonderful artworks include modern and antique sculptures, paintings, tapestries, and a collection of third-century Roman mosaics. Guest rooms have sitting areas with mahogany furniture and marble bathrooms; suites have balconies and saunas. The **East 47** restaurant and bar serves a creative mix of traditional and modern dishes in a Pop Art setting.
115 Sol
All major cards

LIABENY
$$$ ★★★★
SALUD 3
TEL 915 31 90 00
www.liabeny.es
The large, modern Liabeny is just a two-minute walk from Puerta del Sol and Gran Vía. Guests enjoy marble bathrooms and all the facilities of a four-star hotel.
220 Sol All major cards

BEST WESTERN CARLOS V
$$ ★★★
MAESTRO VICTORIA 5
TEL 915 31 41 00
www.hotelcarlosv.com

Two minutes' walk from the Puerta del Sol, the Carlos V has an art nouveau entrance and its own cafeteria. Rooms are large and simply decorated; ask for one with a balcony. The guest lounge has stucco ceilings and crystal chandeliers.

67 Sol All major cards

INGLÉS
$$ ★★★
ECHEGARAY 8
TEL 914 29 65 51
www.hotelinglesmadrid.com

British author Virginia Woolf and other writers and artists of her time stayed at this no-frills hotel very well situated near Plaza Santa Ana and Puerta del Sol. The hotel does not have a restaurant.

58 Sol All major cards

RESTAURANTS

JOCKEY
$$$$$
AMADOR DE LOS RÍOS 6
TEL 913 10 04 11
www.restaurantejockey.net

The elegantly decorated Jockey is among the top restaurants in Spain, and it boasts an excellent selection of wines and ports. Start with the house aperitif, Gin Jockey, then move on to one of the restaurant's specialties, which include lobster ragout with truffles and fresh pasta, and delicious stuffed young chicken Jockey. Jacket and tie are required.

100 Colón Closed public holidays All major cards

LA TERRAZA DEL CASINO
$$$$$
ALCALÁ 15
TEL 915 32 12 75
www.casinodemadrid.es

La Terraza del Casino features grand dining rooms and a fantastic summer terrace Here, the original cooking of chef Paco Roncero, disciple of Ferrán Adrià, offers a wonderful combination of aromas and textures. Try the wild mushroom risotto with parmesan and king prawn, knuckle of veal, or the *menu degustación* (taster menu). Jacket and tie are required.

65 Sevilla Sat. L, Sun., public holidays & Aug. All major cards

SANT CELONI
$$$$$
LA CASTELLANA 57
TEL 912 10 88 40
www.restaurantesantceloni.com

Sant Celoni serves brilliant modern reinventions of classic cuisine by Óscar Velasco, a star pupil of Santi Santamaría. Specialties include caviar with green beans and razor shells, and knuckle of white veal with creamed potato. The restaurant boasts two Michelin stars and an excellent wine list.

45 Gregorio Marañón Closed Sat. L, Sun., Easter & Aug. All major cards

SERGI AROLA GASTRO
$$$$$
ZURBANO 31
TEL 913 10 21 69
www.sergiarola.es

Sergi Arola is one of Spain's most outstanding chefs, daring and creative, seasonal and straightforward. His restaurant features two Michelin stars and an ever-changing menu, as well as a cocktail and tapas bar. Try slow-cooked mullet with cucumber, mushroom, seaweed coulis, and fennel cream.

45 Rubén Darío Closed Sat., Sun., Easter, last 3 weeks in Aug, & 10 days over Christmas All major cards

LA TRAINERA
$$$$$
LAGASCA 60
TEL 915 76 05 75
www.latrainera.es

This informal restaurant offers the best seafood in Madrid. Dishes are kept simple, generally either grilled or cooked on a hot plate; the *salpicón de marisco* (seafood salad) is particularly popular. Ham is the only meat on the menu.

300 Serrano Closed Sun. & Aug. All major cards

ZALACAÍN
$$$$$
ÁLVAREZ DE BAENA 4
TEL 915 61 48 40
www.restaurantezalacain.com

One of Spain's top restaurants, Zalacaín is a pioneer of *nueva cocina* (see p. 118). Specialties include cold cream of pumpkin with profiteroles, scallops and leeks in Albariño wine, and grilled sea bass with green olive vinaigrette. Reservations are essential here, and jacket and tie are required.

100 Gregorio Marañón Closed Sat. L, Sun., Easter, public holidays, & Aug. All major cards

NODO
$$$$
VELÁZQUEZ 150
TEL 915 64 40 44
www.restaurantenodo.es

Nodo's mix of Japanese and Mediterranean cuisine is so popular that diners must reserve weeks in advance. The red tuna is excellent, or try the cold semi-sweet tomato stuffed with smoked mackerel.

130 República Argentina All major cards

PRÍNCIPE DE VIANA

$$$$

MANUEL DE FALLA 5

TEL 914 57 15 49

This old favorite serves Basque-Navarrese cuisine. Try the famous ham croquettes or one of the house specialties: *menestra de verduras de Tudela* (asparagus stewed with other vegetables) or monkfish with clams in a green sauce. Reservations are essential.

80 Santiago Bernabéu P Closed Sat. L, Sun., Easter, & Aug. All major cards

SAMARKANDA

$$$$

GLORIETA DE CARLOS V

TERMINAL DEL AVE

TEL 915 30 87 21

Between museums, stop for refreshment at Samarkanda, amazingly set in the old Atocha train station, transformed into a tropical garden. The international cuisine includes caramelized duck crepes.

300 Atocha–Renfe P AE, MC, V

CASA LUCIO

$$$

CAVA BAJA 35

TEL 913 65 82 17

www.casalucio.es

Casa Lucio keeps dishes simple and focuses on quality ingredients. Try the Lucío potatoes, Madrid-style stewed tripe, and the rice pudding. The decor reflects the area's traditional Castilian houses.

120 La Latina P Closed Sat. L & Aug. All major cards

LA DOMINGA

$$$

LIBERTAD 16

TEL 915 23 75 89

www.ladominga.es

La Dominga was once the Taberna Carmencita, open in 1850 and frequented by García Lorca, Dalí, and Buñuel. Today it serves fresh Mediterranean cuisine like wild mushroom and white truffle croquettes.

50 Chueca Closed Mon. & Tues. D V

LA VACA VERÓNICA

$$$

MORATÍN 38

TEL 914 29 78 27

www.lavacaveronica.es

Try the spinach, mushroom, and pancetta salad at this atmospheric establishment with antique chandeliers and walls covered with artwork. Homemade desserts include white chocolate tart with raspberries. Reservations are suggested.

55 Antón Martín Closed Sat. L. All major cards

BOTÍN

$$

CUCHILLEROS 17

TEL 913 66 42 17

www.botin.es

Established in 1725, Botín is reputed to be the world's oldest restaurant and, according to Hemingway at least, the best. Legend even has it that Goya once worked here as a dishwasher. Recommended dishes include traditional roast suckling pig and roast lamb.

260 Sol All major cards

CASA MINGO

$$

PASEO DE LA FLORIDA 34

TEL 915 47 79 18/58 45

www.casamingo.es

Founded in 1888, this friendly cider tavern was probably the first in Madrid. It is noted for its roast chicken, Asturian pork and bean stew *(fabada)*, sausage, tripe, and goat cheese. It tends to get crowded so go early.

200 Príncipe Pío

MIRADOR DEL THYSSEN

$$

MUSEO THYSSEN-BORNEMISZA

PASEO DEL PRADO 8

TEL 914 29 39 84

www.elmiradordelthyssen.com

In summer the beautiful garden terrace at the Museo Thyssen-Bornemisza becomes a palm- and magnolia-filled restaurant serving modern Mediterranean cuisine including meatballs in cocoa and port sauce, and turbot in rosemary. The restaurant is open evenings only, and reservations are required.

150 Banco de España Closed Sun., Mon., & Oct.–June All major cards

ARANJUEZ 28300

EL COCHERÓN 1919

$$ ★★

MONTESINOS 22

TEL 918 75 43 50

www.elcocheron1919.com

This small hotel is located near the Aranjuez Palace and its park. Rooms are inviting, and there is a lovely interior patio.

18 All major cards

CASA JOSÉ

$$$$

ABASTOS 32

TEL 918 91 14 88

www.casajose.es

Imaginative and seasonal cuisine has won Casa José one Michelin star. Specialties include pig's feet with stewed peas and mushrooms, and hake belly with chard and vegetables.

50 Closed Sun. D, Mon., & Aug. All major cards

RODRIGO DE LA CALLE

$$$$

ANTIGUA CARRETERA DE ANDALUCÍA 85

TEL 918 91 08 07

www.restaurantedelacalle.com

This celebrated restaurant offers inventive, strikingly fresh

dishes such as large sautéed oysters with coriander and ice plant gazpacho. The gastrobar upstairs is open year-round
30 Closed Mon., July, & Aug. AE, MC, V

CHINCHÓN 28370

PARADOR DE CHINCHÓN
$$$ ★★★★
CALLE DE LOS HUERTOS 1
TEL 918 94 08 36
www.parador.es
Housed in a 17th-century Augustinian monastery, this parador has a landscaped garden and Castilian-style rooms with dark wood and tiles; some have Renaissance murals. Enjoy traditional fare at **El Convento.** The other restaurant, **El Bodegón,** is open weekends and holidays only.
38 130 All major cards

MESÓN DE LA VIRREINA
$$$$
PLAZA MAYOR 28
TEL 918 94 00 15
www.mesonvirreyna.com
On a plaza that doubles as a bullring, La Virreina serves Castilian staples such as roast lamb and suckling pig, as well as the famous local anise. Reserve if you want a table on one of the wooden balconies.
110 No parking on weekends Closed Mon. All major cards

SAN LORENZO DE EL ESCORIAL 28200

BOTÁNICO
$$ ★★★
TIMOTEO PADRÓS 16
TEL 918 90 78 79
www.botanicohotel.com
This beautifully restored mansion set in gardens away from the bustle of town is a peaceful place to spend the night. The **Restaurante Botánico** specializes in rice dishes.
20 All major cards

MIRANDA & SUIZO
$$ ★★★
FLORIDABLANCA 18-20
TEL 918 90 47 11
www.hotelmirandasuizo.com
The interiors of this Victorian building, one of many in town, are functional and well kept. Eat in **El Restaurante Arturo El Escorial** or the wonderful Modernista café.
52 All major cards

NORTHWEST SPAIN

GALICIA

CAMBADOS 36630

PARADOR DE CAMBADOS
$$$ ★★★★
PASEO DE LA CALZADA S/N
TEL 986 54 22 50
www.parador.es
The beautiful rooms in this 17th-century parador have views of the interior patio or countryside. The restaurant serves local dishes like *empanada de berberechos* (cockle pie) and local Albariño wine.
58 130 All major cards

A CORUÑA (LA CORUÑA) 15000

HOTELS

HESPERIA FINISTERRE
$$$ ★★★★★
PASEO DEL PARROTE 2
TEL 981 20 54 00/04
www.hesperia-finisterre.es
Situated on the port, this hotel has wonderful views and a large sports complex. The **Novo** restaurant serves international cuisine with a local twist.
92 All major cards

NH ATLÁNTICO
$$$ ★★★★
JARDINES DE MÉNDEZ NÚÑEZ
TEL 981 22 65 00
www.nh-hotels.com
This hotel in the heart of the old town offers spacious rooms and port views. **Restaurante Abrego** highlights regional dishes and seasonal ingredients.
199 All major cards

RESTAURANTS

CASA PARDO
$$$$
NOVOA SANTOS 15
TEL 981 28 00 21/17 46 78
www.casapardo-domus.com
Enjoy classic Galician food with the freshest local ingredients at

PRICES

HOTELS
An indication of the cost of a double room in the high season is given by **$** signs.

$$$$$	Over $300
$$$$	$220–$300
$$$	$160–$220
$$	$80–$160
$	Under $80

RESTAURANTS
An indication of the cost of a three-course meal without drinks is given by **$** signs.

$$$$$	Over $80
$$$$	$50–$80
$$$	$35–$50
$$	$20–$35
$	Under $20

this restaurant near the port. Try the braised sea bass in a creamed crab sauce or griddled duck liver with roast apple.

65 P Closed Sun., Mon. D, & March All major cards

LA PENELA
$$$
PLAZA MARÍA PITA 12
TEL 981 20 92 00
www.lapanela.com

Housed in one of the finest Modernista buildings in La Coruña, this elegant restaurant offers Galician dishes with class. Try the stuffed mussels, roast beef, or monkfish stew.

110 Closed Sun. & 2 weeks mid-Jan. All major cards

NOIA (NOYA) 15200

LA PESQUERÍA DEL TAMBRE
$$ ★★★
SANTA MARÍA DE ROO
TEL 981 76 94 25
www.pesqueriadeltambre.com

This lovely complex of stone buildings is on the site of an old Cistercian fishery. **La Central** restaurant serves good homemade Galician food. Fishing licences available May–Sept.

16 45 P All major cards

OURENSE (ORENSE) 32000

ARNOIA CALDARIA
$$ ★★★
VILA TERMAL 1, ARNOIA (2 MILES/3 KM FROM RIBADAVIA, 19 MILES/30 KM W OF OURENSE)
TEL 988 49 24 00
www.caldaria.es

This spa hotel along the Miño River offers all types of health treatments and outdoor sports activities.

50 P All major cards

ZARAMPALLO
$ ★
HERMANOS VILLAR 19
TEL 988 23 08 19
www.zarampallo.com

Housed in an old building that has been modernized and elegantly decorated, Zarampallo features rooms that look onto pedestrianized streets. The restaurant's Galician cuisine focuses on vegetables.

14 60 Closed Sun. D All major cards

MARTÍN FIERRO (CASA OVIDIO)
$$
SÁENZ DÍEZ 17
TEL 988 37 20 26
www.restaurantemartin fierro.com

The menu here offers char-grilled Argentine meat and Galician seafood. Specialties are monkfish, beef entrecôte, and homemade chestnut ice cream.

70 P Closed Sun. All major cards

PONTEVEDRA 36000

HOTELS

PARADOR DE PONTEVEDRA
$$$ ★★★★
BARÓN 19
TEL 986 85 58 00
www.parador.es

The interior of this 16th-century palace complements the stone facade with antiques and a hand-carved staircase. Guest rooms look onto a rose garden, and the dining room serves local meat and fish.

47 140 P All major cards

RÚAS
$ ★
FIGUEROA 35
TEL 986 84 64 16
www.hotelruas.net

Most of Pontevedra's hotels are in the business sector, but Rúas looks onto a lovely square. Its simple rooms are quiet, though noise picks up on weekends. Enjoy traditional Galician fare in the restaurant.

22 70 P All major cards

RESTAURANTS

DOÑA ANTONIA
$$$$
SOPORTALES DE LA HERRERÍA 4, 1ST FLOOR
TEL 986 84 72 74

Looking onto the lovely Plaza de la Herrería, Doña Antonia serves Galician cuisine using the freshest regional produce.

35 Closed Sun. & Mon. D, except Aug.–Dec. All major cards

SOLLA
$$$$
AVENIDA SINEIRO 7
SAN SALVADOR DE POIO (ON ROAD TO LA TOJA 2 KM)
TEL 986 87 28 84
www.restaurantesolla.com

Just outside the city, this bucolic restaurant boasts an exciting mix of creative and traditional Galician cooking. Try the razor shells in balsamic citrus juice.

50 P Closed Mon., Thurs. D & Sun. D All major cards

SANTIAGO DE COMPOSTELA 15700

HOTELS

SOMETHING SPECIAL

PARADOR HOSTAL DOS REIS CATÓLICOS
$$$$$ ★★★★★
PLAZA DO OBRADOIRO 1
TEL 981 58 22 00
www.parador.es

Built in 1499 as a hostel for

pilgrims, this parador still boasts an exquisite carved doorway, four superb courtyards, and a Gothic chapel. Rooms have tapestries and antiques. Dine at **Dos Reis** or the less formal **Enxebre.** Reserve well ahead.
128 All major cards

COMPOSTELA
$$$ ★★★★
HÓRREO 1
TEL 981 58 57 00
www.hotelcompostela.es
Reproduction antiques adorn the spacious rooms in this historic building located by two main roads (ask for a quiet room). A breakfast buffet is served in the dining room.
99 All major cards

MELIÁ ARAGUANEY
$$ ★★★★★
ALFREDO BRAÑAS 5
TEL 981 55 96 00
www.araguaney.com
This modern hotel—with a disco, two restaurants, and a shopping center—is just a ten-minute walk from the cathedral.
81 All major cards

VIRXE DA CERCA
$$ ★★★
VIRXE DA CERCA 27
TEL 981 56 93 50
www.pousadasdecompostela.com
The rooms in the old wing of this 18th-century building have sitting areas, while the modern wing has more spacious rooms. Complementary breakfast is served in the restaurant.
43 All major cards

RESTAURANTS

EL MERCADITO
$$$$
GALERAS 18
TEL 981 57 42 39
www.elmercadito.es
Classic Galician fare has been inventively updated with seasonal produce at this spot near the cathedral. Try free-range egg with river spider crab and baby broad beans, or fresh hake in a basil *pil-pil* sauce.
50 Closed Sun. D All major cards

LA TACITA D'JUAN
$$$$
HÓRREO 31
TEL 981 56 20 41/32 55
www.latacita.com
Enjoy hearty Galician food and a good selection of local wines at this restaurant, whose specials include seafood crepes, cod cheeks, and ox entrecôte.
100 Closed Sun. & first 3 weeks in Aug. AE, MC, V

O CURRO DA PARRA
$$
TRAVESA 20
TEL 981 55 60 59
www.ocurrodaparra.com
This welcoming place creatively mixes classic and avant-garde. Try the oxtail ravioli or black rice with scallop. There is a gastrobar on the ground floor.
20 Closed Sun. D & Mon. All major cards

A TOXA (ISLA DE LA TOJA-O GROVE) 36991

SOMETHING SPECIAL

GRAN HOTEL LA TOJA
$$ ★★★★★
TEL 986 73 00 25
www.granhotellatoja.com
Originally constructed in 1907, this luxurious spa hotel has four restaurants and sits right on the waterfront, with access to tennis courts, a nine-hole golf course, and thermal baths.
199 600 All major cards

HOTEL LOUXO
$$ ★★★★
TEL 986 73 02 00
www.louxolatoja.com
Located on the waterfront next to the casino, but less spectacular than the Gran, the Louxo offers sumptuous rooms and opportunities to play tennis or golf (9 holes) and go sailing. The restaurant specializes in seafood.
115 350 All major cards

TUI 36700

PARADOR DE TUI
$$$ ★★★★
AVENIDA DE PORTUGAL
TEL 986 60 03 00
www.parador.es
Built of granite and chestnut wood on the banks of the Mino River, right by the Portuguese border, this large, modern reproduction of a Galician country house offers guests a wide range of healthy activities, from swimming to tennis, as well as hearty regional food in its restaurant.
32 All major cards

O NOVO CABALO FURADO
$$$
PRAZA DO CONCELLO 3
TEL 986 60 12 15/22 63
Excellent fresh fish and shell fish are served in the simply decorated dining room at O Novo Cabaldo Furado, or on the restaurant's small patio in summer. Try the hake and monkfish stew, and, for dessert, why not tuck into the delicious hazelnut mousse?
60 Closed Sun. July–Sept., Sun. D, & Mon. Oct.–June, Christmas–early Jan., & last 2 weeks June All major cards

ASTURIAS & CANTABRIA

CASTRO URDIALES 39700

MESÓN EL MARINERO
$$$$
CORRERÍA 23 - BAJO
TEL 942 86 00 05/15 63
www.mesonmarinero.com
With a fantastic array of tapas and an upstairs dining room overlooking the port, this restaurant is a find. Choose from the selection of fresh fish cooked in the oven or in salt.
140 All major cards

COSTA VERDE

AULTRE NARAY
$$ ★★★
PERUYES 33547, CANGAS DE ONÍS (OFF CTRA N-634, KM 335)
TEL 985 84 08 08
www.aultrenaray.com
This large 19th-century house is located in a beautiful spot that looks out onto the mountains. Inside, the decor combines traditional and modern styles.
10 All major cards

LA CASONA DE PÍO
$$ ★★
RIOFRIO 3, CUDILLERO 33150
TEL 985 59 15 12
www.lacasonadepio.com
This restored stone house in the town center offers comfortable rustic-style rooms. The restaurant serves locally caught fish including the Cudillero specialty, *curadillo* (dogfish).
11 MC, V, AE

CASA CONSUELO
$ ★★
CTRA. N-634 (KM 511), OTUR (3 MILES/5 KM FROM LUARCA)
TEL 985 47 07 67
www.casaconsuelo.com
This family-run hotel is known for its restaurant, which serves traditional Asturian dishes, fresh fish, and great desserts.
36 150 Closed Mon., except in Aug.; closed Nov. All major cards

LOS OSCOS

LA RECTORAL
$$ ★★★★
TARAMUNDI 33775
TEL 985 64 67 60/67
www.arceahoteles.com
Set in an 18th-century rectory with beautiful mountain views, this hotel has a restaurant and offers lots of activities.
18 40 Closed in low season All major cards

CABEZA DA VILA
$
SAN MARTÍN DE OSCOS 33777
TEL 985 62 60 19
www.cabezadavila.com
This restored 17th-century farmhouse features large rooms (no TV) furnished with antiques. A separate house is also available for rent.
5 V

CASA RODIL
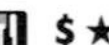
$ ★
AS POCEIRAS
1 MILE/2 KM FROM SANTA EULALIA DE OSCOS 33776 (CRTA. VEGADEO)
TEL 985 62 61 85
www.casarodil.es
Surrounded by green fields and mountains, this idyllically sited hotel has simple rooms (no TV) with large baths. The restaurant offers delicious down-to-earth cooking that relies on local ingredients.
4 All major cards

OVIEDO 33000

DE LA RECONQUISTA
$$$ ★★★★★
GIL DE JAZ 16
TEL 985 24 11 00
www.hoteldelareconquista.com
Formerly an 18th-century orphanage and hospital, this hotel has an arcaded courtyard and spacious, modern rooms.
142 60 All major cards

CASA FERMÍN
$$$$
SAN FRANCISCO 8
TEL 985 21 64 52/97
www.casafermin.com
This glass-ceilinged restaurant located in the old city center has been run by the same family since 1924. It serves excellent Asturian fare, both classic and avant-garde, like monkfish with broad beans in clam sauce and *fabada* (pork and bean stew).
120 Closed Sun. All major cards

PICOS DE EUROPA

HOTEL DEL OSO
$$ ★★★
COSGAYA 39582
CARRETERA DE POTES A FUENTE DÉ, KM 14
TEL 942 73 30 18
www.hoteldeloso.com
Situated in the heart of the Picos de Europa, this hotel has cozy rooms with wooden balconies. The restaurant serves hearty regional fare.
50 90 Closed Jan. MC, V

SANTANDER 39000

HOTELS

SOMETHING SPECIAL

REAL
$$$$ ★★★★★
PASEO DE PÉREZ GALDÓS 28
TEL 942 27 25 50
www.hotelreal.es
Overlooking the bay, this imposing French-style château is surrounded by gardens. The restaurant, **El Puntal,** offers

modern cuisine like venison loin with cauliflower and celery purée and chutney.
123 40 All major cards

CENTRAL
$ ★★★
GENERAL MOLA 5
TEL 942 22 24 00
www.elcentral.com
Everything is blue in this family-run hotel. No restaurant.
41 All major cards

RESTAURANTS

CAÑADÍO
$$$$
GÓMEZ OREÑA 15
TEL 942 31 41 49
www.restaurantecanadio.com
Cañadío mixes classic cuisine with exciting modern touches. Try frittered hake tempura with a light garlic sauce.
65 Closed Sun. All major cards

EL SERBAL
$$$$
ANDRÉS DEL RÍO 7
TEL 942 22 25 15
www.elserbal.com
The imaginative and creative dishes here use the freshest seasonal ingredients. Try the suckling pig with salted peach and lemon verbena.
45 Closed Sun. D & Mon. All major cards

SANTILLANA DEL MAR 39330

PARADOR DE SANTILLANA GIL BLAS
$$$$ ★★★★
PLAZA RAMÓN PELAYO 11
TEL 942 02 80 28
www.parador.es
The dark wood in this 17th- to 18th-century mansion, which has expanded to include a new building across the plaza, are similar in style to the original decor. The restaurant's menu includes a mountain stew.
28 60 All major cards

ALTAMIRA
$$ ★★★
CANTÓN 1
TEL 942 81 80 25/83 09
www.hotelaltamira.com
The rooms in this reconstructed palace feature wood floors and exposed stone walls, while the restaurant has a growing reputation for game, cod, and rice dishes.
32 270 Restaurant only All major cards

NORTHEAST SPAIN

EUSKADI & NAVARRA

BERGARA 20570

ORMAZABAL
$ ★★
BARRENKALE 11
TEL 943 76 36 50
e-mail: ormazabalreservas@infonegocio.com
This 17th-century stone house in the city center is full of period furniture. No restaurant.
14 DC, MC, V

BILBO (BILBAO) 48000

HOTELS

CARLTON
$$ ★★★★★
PLAZA FEDERICO MOYUA 2
TEL 944 16 22 00
www.hotelcarlton.es
This elegant old hotel on one of the city's prettiest plazas has hosted bullfighters and artists like Hemingway and Orson Welles. The restaurant serves haute cuisine.
144 40 All major cards

PRICES

HOTELS
An indication of the cost of a double room in the high season is given by **$** signs.

$$$$$	Over $300
$$$$	$220–$300
$$$	$160–$220
$$	$80–$160
$	Under $80

RESTAURANTS
An indication of the cost of a three-course meal without drinks is given by **$** signs.

$$$$$	Over $80
$$$$	$50–$80
$$$	$35–$50
$$	$20–$35
$	Under $20

ITURRIENEA OSTATUA
$$ ★★
SANTA MARÍA 14
TEL 944 16 15 00
www.iturrieneaostatua.com
The appealing interior decor of this old pension in Bilbo's historic center matches the original facade colors. The rooms have large beds and showcase local art.
21 DC, MC, V

LÓPEZ DE HARO
$$ ★★★★★
OBISPO ORUETA 2
TEL 944 23 55 00
www.hotellopezdeharo.com
A five-minute walk from the Museo Guggenheim, this remodeled 1800s building has a classical English feel. Rooms are luxurious and quiet—some non-smoking. The restaurant, **Club Náutico,** serves modern and classic cuisine.
53 60 All major cards

RESTAURANTS

ETXANOBE

$$$$$

ABANDOIBARRA 4

TEL 944 42 10 71

www.etxanobe.com

The cooking of Fernando Canales is widely rated as Bilbo's best. His cold anchovy sauce has its own fan club. Try the thick fish soup with shellfish or the classic cod *pil-pil.*

90 Closed Sun., Easter, New Year's Eve, & first 2 weeks Aug. All major cards

ZORTZIKO

$$$$$

ALAMEDA DE MAZARREDO 17

TEL 944 23 97 43

www.zortziko.es

Daniel García is one of the Basque region's top chefs. His modern cuisine contrasts with the historic early 20th-century villa. Dishes include baked turbot with *pil-pil* sauce and mustard, and pigeon prepared in five different ways. Zortziko has earned one Michelin star, is located close to the Museo Guggenheim, and features a great wine list.

120 Closed Sun., Mon. D, & first 2 weeks Sept. All major cards

AIZIAN

$$$$

LEHENDAKARI LEIZAOLA 29

TEL 944 28 00 39

www.restaurante-aizian.com

Chef José Miguel Olaza Balaga fuses classic Basque cuisine and avant-garde creativity. Try the foie cooked with sweet-and-sour caramel and salted cherries, or the sliced brisket of Wagyo ox with garlic.

90 Closed Sun., Easter, & first 2 weeks in Aug. All major cards

DONOSTIA (SAN SEBASTIÁN) 20000

HOTELS

SOMETHING SPECIAL

MARÍA CRISTINA

$$$$$ ★★★★★

PASEO REPÚBLICA ARGENTINA 4

TEL 943 43 76 00

www.hotel-mariacristina.com

Named after the queen who opened it in 1912, this luxurious hotel has been restored to its belle epoque glory. The guest rooms overlook the sea and the Urúmea River. The restaurant, **Easo,** is on its way up.

136 All major cards

DE LONDRES Y DE INGLATERRA

$$$$ ★★★★

ZUBIETA 2

TEL 943 44 07 70

www.hlondres.com

This central belle epoque hotel has superb sea views. Its restaurant, **La Brasserie Mari Galant,** specializes in local meat dishes and grilled fish.

148 All major cards

RESTAURANTS

AKELARE

$$$$$

PASEO PADRE ORCOLAGA 56

TEL 943 31 12 09

www.akelarre.net

Pedro Subijana's playful, daring cuisine fully deserves its three Michelin stars. Gems in the tasting menus include red mullet with fusili sauce, razor shell with veal shank, and roast suckling pig with tomato bolao and cured ham emulsion.

140 Closed Sun. D, Mon., Tues. (Jan.–June), Feb., & 1st two weeks Oct. All major cards

SOMETHING SPECIAL

ARZAK

$$$$$

AVDA. ALCALDE ELOSEGUI 273

TEL 943 27 84 65/28 55 93

www.arzak.es

This is one of the very best restaurants in Spain. Chef Juan Mari Arzak and his daughter, Elena, produce innovative cuisine that never loses sight of Basque traditions. The entire menu here is superb. Try the hake in green sauce with clams. Reservations suggested.

80 Closed Sun., Mon., June 17–July 4, & Nov. 4–28 All major cards

MUGARITZ

$$$$$

ALDURA ALDEA 20, RENTERÍA (13 KM FROM SAN SEBASTIÁN)

TEL 943 52 24 55/51 83 43

www.mugaritz.com

Chef Andoni Luis Aduriz is a world famous pioneer of molecular gastronomy. The constantly varied menu includes sautéed scallop with Arbequina olives and chestnut flakes.

50 Closed Sun. D, Mon., Tues. (Tues. L May–Sept.), & Dec. 12–April 12 MC, V

GASTEIZ (VITORIA) 01000

PARADOR DE ARGÓMANIZ

$$$$ ★★★★

CARRETERA N-1, KM 363

TEL 945 29 32 00

www.parador.es

This stone Renaissance palace is only 7.5 miles (12 km) from Vitoria and worth the trip for a peaceful sleep. Spacious and light rooms have pine floors and balconies. The restaurant serves regional dishes like *perretxikos* (mushrooms).

55 All major cards

IKEA
$$$$$
CALLE CASTILLA 27
TEL 945 14 47 47
www.restauranteikea.com
Ikea offers traditional cuisine with innovative twists and a varied menu served in a sophisticated, modernized mansion. Recommended dishes include prawn carpaccio with gazpacho sorbet and lamb magret with broccoli purée and sautéed apricots.
279 Closed Sun. D, Mon., & 3 weeks Aug.–early Sept. All major cards

HONDARRIBIA (FUENTERRABÍA) 20280

PARADOR DE HONDARRIBIA
$$$$$ ★★★★
PLAZA DE ARMAS 14
TEL 94 364 55 00
www.parador.es
This parador, set in a fortified castle built in the tenth century, has made the most of its wonderful building, leaving the beautiful thick stone walls exposed, even in the bedrooms. Some rooms have terraces overlooking the sea. There is no restaurant.
36 All major cards

RAMÓN ROTETA
$$$$
IRÚN 1, VILLA AINARA
TEL 943 64 16 93
www.roteta.com
The inventive Mediterranean fare at Romón Roteta includes shellfish salad and monkfish in gooseneck barnacle sauce.
350 Closed Sun. D, Tues., & Feb. All major cards

IRUÑA (PAMPLONA) 31000

IRUÑA PALACE TRES REYES
$$$$$ ★★★★
JARDINES DE LA TACONERA
TEL 948 22 66 00
www.hotel3reyes.com
This hotel offers spa-baths, a hairdresser, golf, and squash courts in luxurious surroundings. The restaurant serves French Basque cuisine.
160 All major cards

MAISONNAVE
$$ ★★★
NUEVA 20
TEL 948 22 26 00
www.hotelmaisonnave.es
The French founded this hotel a hundred years ago, and since then personalities such as Hemingway, Valle-Inclán, and Ava Gardner have stayed here. Enjoy regional Navarra cuisine made with local ingredients in the restaurant, which also has a wine cellar. The hotel holds occasional art exhibitions and music recitals.
138 All major cards

JOSETXO
$$$$
PLAZA PRINCÍPE DE VIANA 1
TEL 948 22 20 97
www.restaurantejosetxo.com
A sober dining room is the setting for this classic establishment. Try the monkfish with black olive vinaigrette and soy and anchovy mayonnaise, or ox sirloin, pepper, mustard, and vanilla potato balls.
60 Closed Sun. (except San Fermín), Easter, & Aug. All major cards

ORREAGA (RONCESVALLES) 31650

LA POSADA
$
COLEGIATA DE RONCESVALLES
TEL 948 76 02 25
www.laposadaderoncesvalles.com
The restaurant of this restored 16th-century inn, now a historic monument, serves delicious home-style cooking.
19 130 Closed Nov. DC, MC, V

TUDELA 31500

TREINTAITRÉS
$$$$
CAPUCHINOS 7
TEL 948 82 76 06
www.restaurante33.com
Treintaitrés focuses on traditional cuisine using an abundance of vegetables. Specials include lamb stuffed with artichokes.
130 Closed Sun., Mon. D, Tues. D, & first 3 weeks Aug. All major cards

LA RIOJA

HARO 26200

LOS AGUSTINOS
$$$ ★★★★
SAN AGUSTÍN 2
TEL 941 31 13 08
www.hotellosagustinos.com
Situated in a 14th-century convent, this beautifully restored hotel has a good restaurant.
62 All major cards

HOSPEDERÍA SEÑORÍO DE BRIÑAS
$$$ ★★★
TRAVESÍA DE LA CALLE REAL 3, BRIÑAS (2 MILES/3 KM FROM HARO)
TEL 941 30 42 24
www.hotelesconencantodelarioja.com
Set among vineyards, this 18th-century mansion has been restored with flare. No restaurant.
20 Closed 2 weeks Dec.–Jan. All major cards

TERETE
$$$
LUCRECIA ARANA 17
TEL 941 31 00 23

www.terete.es
Specials at this family-run establishment include typical Riojan fare like roast lamb and stuffed peppers.
120 Closed Sun. D, Mon., first 2 weeks July, & last 2 weeks Nov. DC, MC, V

LAGUARDIA 01300

CASTILLO EL COLLADO
$$$ ★★
PASEO EL COLLADO 1
TEL 945 62 12 00
www.hotelcollado.com
This small castle dating from 1920 with an 18th-century chapel makes an enchanting hotel. The restaurant serves refined Riojan cuisine. Be sure to try the desserts.
10 60 All major cards

POSADA MAYOR DE MIGUELOA
$$ ★★★
MAYOR 20
TEL 945 62 11 75
www.mayordemigueloa.com
The rooms in this hotel—which is housed in a 1619 mansion—follow 17th-century Spanish style. Each is different and full of decorative details. Regional cooking includes homemade foie gras and delicious desserts.
8 120 Closed Jan. 9–Feb. 9 All major cards

LOGROÑO 26000

CARLTON RIOJA
$$ ★★★★
GRAN VÍA DEL REY JUAN CARLOS I, 5
TEL 941 24 21 00
www.hotelcarltonrioja.es
This modern building with a glass facade is centrally located but not in the old town. Its rooms are spacious, and dining options include a restaurant and snack bar.
116 All major cards

SAN MILLÁN DE LA COGOLLA 26226

HOSTERÍA DEL MONASTERIO DE SAN MILLÁN
$$$ ★★★★
MONASTERIO DE YUSO
TEL 941 37 32 77
www.sanmillan.com
The restored wing of the 17th-century Yuso Monastery offers warm, inviting rooms and a comfortable restaurant.
25 All major cards

SANTO DOMINGO DE LA CALZADA 26250

PARADOR DE SANTO DOMINGO DE LA CALZADA
$$$$ ★★★★
PLAZA DEL SANTO 3
TEL 941 34 03 00
www.parador.es
Part of the parador is in the 12th-century pilgrims hospital, next to the cathedral. Try the Riojan style cod offered in the restaurant.
61 85 All major cards

ARAGÓN

ALBARRACÍN 44100

CASA DE SANTIAGO
$$ ★★
SUBIDA A LAS TORRES 11
TEL 978 70 03 16
www.casadesantiago.net
The colorful rooms in this small hotel feature cane furniture and baked clay floors. The building dates from the 16th century.
9 Closed 3 weeks Feb. & Sept. 13–17 MC, V

DAROCA 50360

POSADA DEL ALMUDI
$$
GRAJERA 7
TEL 976 80 06 06
www.posadadelalmudi.es
Warm yellows and patterned textiles enliven the rooms of this intimate hotel in a renovated 15th-century mansion. Enjoy the beautiful Renaissance courtyard. The restaurant serves complementary breakfast.
30 All major cards

HUESCA 22000

HOSPEDERÍA DE LOARRE
$$ ★★★
PLAZA MAYOR S/N, LOARRE
(19 MILES/30 KM FROM HUESCA)
TEL 974 38 27 06
www.hospederiadeloarre.com
The restaurant in this 16th-century palace in the center of town serves seasonal cuisine. The building looks to the church tower.
12 MC, V

LILLAS PASTIA
$$$$
PLAZA DE NAVARRA 4
TEL 974 21 16 91
www.lillaspastia.es
In the old casino, the dining room is Modernist and the cuisine is modern Aragonese.
170 Sun. D, L, & Mon. All major cards

JACA 22700

GRAN HOTEL
$ ★★★
PASEO DE LA CONSTITUCIÓN 1
TEL 974 36 09 00
www.granhoteljaca.com
This popular hotel is located in the town center. The wood, stone, and glass exterior conceals simple warm rooms.
165 All major cards

LA COCINA ARAGONESA

$$$$

CERVANTES 5

TEL 974 36 10 50

www.condeaznar.com

La Cocina Aragonesa serves regional cuisine with Basque influences and seasonal game like stuffed partridge.

150 All major cards

SOS DEL REY CATÓLICO 50680

PARADOR DE SOS DEL REY CATÓLICO

$$$ ★★★★

SAINZ DE VICUÑA

TEL 948 88 80 11

www.parador.es

Set in the historic area of town, this parador is in the characteristic Aragonese style. Spacious, light rooms have views of the countryside. The restaurant features Aragonese lamb.

66 All major cards

TARAZONA 50500

LA MERCED DE LA CONCORDIA

$$ ★★★

PLAZA LA MERCED 2

TEL 976 19 93 44

www.lamerced.info

The restaurant in this stylishly restored palace, built in 1501 in the old town center, offers good regional cooking.

7 90 Closed first week Sept. AE, MC, V

TERUEL 44000

REINA CRISTINA

$$ ★★★

PASEO DEL ÓVALO 1

TEL 978 60 68 60

www.hotelreinacristinateruel.com

On the edge of the old town, this hotel has balconies with views and spacious corner rooms. Hotel specialties include Teruel ham.

83 All major cards

ZARAGOZA 50000

BOSTON

$$ ★★★★★

CAMINO DE LAS TORRES 28

TEL 976 59 91 92

www.hotelboston.es

The rooms here are comfortable, and the lobby and panoramic elevator are positively futuristic. Dine at the café or **Amaranto** restaurant.

313 All major cards

NH GRAN HOTEL

$$ ★★★★

JOAQUIN COSTA 5

TEL 976 22 19 01

www.nh-hotels.com

Celebrities prefer this elegant hotel in Zaragoza. Its restaurant, **La Ontina,** conjures up dishes such as truffled mash potato with squid tempura, and Aragonese beef in bechamel sauce with cheese chunks.

134 75 All major cards

BARCELONA

HOTELS

ARTS BARCELONA

$$$$$ ★★★★★

MARINA 19–21

TEL 932 21 10 00

www.hotelartsbarcelona.com

Occupying one of the Olympic towers in Port Olímpic, this hotel offers superb views of the sea and city. Dining options include Sergi Arola's **Arola** restaurant and **Enoteca.**

483 322 All major cards

CLARIS

$$$$$ ★★★★★

PAU CLARIS 150

TEL 934 87 62 62

www.derbyhotels.com

Claris is set in a palace with more than 400 works of art and archaeological artifacts. Three restaurants serve Mediterranean cuisine with flare.

120 All major cards

LE MÉRIDIEN

$$$$$ ★★★★★

LA RAMBLA 111

TEL 933 18 62 00

www.lemeridienbarcelona.com

The top hotel occupies a 1900s building with a neoclassical facade and modernized interiors. Enjoy Catalan dishes in the **CentOnze** restaurant.

233 All major cards

PALACE

$$$$$ ★★★★★

GRAN VÍA DE LES CORTS CATALANES 668

PRICES

HOTELS

An indication of the cost of a double room in the high season is given by **$** signs.

$$$$$	Over $300
$$$$	$220–$300
$$$	$160–$220
$$	$80–$160
$	Under $80

RESTAURANTS

An indication of the cost of a three-course meal without drinks is given by **$** signs.

$$$$$	Over $80
$$$$	$50–$80
$$$	$35–$50
$$	$20–$35
$	Under $20

TEL 935 10 11 30
www.hotelpalacebarcelona.com
Since it opened in 1919, this grand hotel (formerly the Ritz) has been offering elegance and luxury. The suites have bathrooms inspired by Roman baths. Its **Caelis** restaurant has received one Michelin star.
125 All major cards

AVENIDA PALACE
$$$$ ★★★★
GRAN VÍA DE LES CORTS CATALANES 605
TEL 933 01 96 00
www.avenidapalace.com
This distinguished hotel near Gaudí's monuments has two restaurants and exudes an old-fashioned elegance.
151 All major cards

THE MIRROR
$$$$ ★★★★
CÒRSEGA 255
TEL 932 02 86 86
www.themirrorbarcelona.com
This boutique hotel on a quiet tree-lined street is chic and modern, with white walls and mirrors everywhere. In the restaurant, chef Paco Pérez offers contemporary cuisine with an emphasis on the freshest fish and seafood.
63

CONDES DE BARCELONA
$$$ ★★★★
PASSEIG DE GRÀCIA 73–75
TEL 934 45 00 00
www.condesdebarcelona.com
In central Eixample, this is one of the city's best hotels with light, modernized rooms. Its two magnificent 19th-century buildings face each other across Carrer de Mallorca. In the excellent restaurant, **Lasarte** *(tel 934 45 32 42, www.restaurantlasarte.com, closed Sun., Mon., Aug. & Easter)*, chef Antonio Sáez combines Martín Berasategui's signature classics with his own innovative cooking.
235 35 All major cards

GAUDÍ
$$$ ★★★
NOU DE LA RAMBLA 12
TEL 933 17 90 32
www.hotelgaudi.es
Gaudí features modern rooms with views of the Palau Güell roof as well as a café.
73 All major cards

GRAN VÍA
$$$ ★★★
GRAN VÍA DE LES CORTS CATALANES 642
TEL 933 18 19 00
www.nnhotels.com
For old-fashioned charm and elegance, this 19th-century town house with an elaborate Modernista staircase and high ceilings is a good central option.
53 All major cards

ESPAÑA
$$ ★★
SANT PAU 9–11
TEL 935 50 00 00
www.hotelespanya.com
This hotel is famous for its Modernista dining rooms designed by Lluís Domènech i Montaner. Rooms facing the interior patio are quieter.
82 All major cards

RIALTO
$$ ★★★
FERRÁN 40-42
TEL 933 18 52 12
www.hotel-rialto.com
The birthplace of painter Joan Miró, the Rialto offers simple rooms with pine floors and dark wood furniture. Interior-facing rooms are quieter.
207 All major cards

RESTAURANTS

ABAC
$$$$$
AVENIDA TIBIDABO 1
TEL 933 19 66 00
www.abacbarcelona.com
The young prodigy chef Jordi Cruz offers original and creative cooking in elegant minimalist surroundings, Try the macaroni with lobster bolognese or suckling pig with mango tatin.
56 Avenida Tibidabo Closed Sun. & Mon. All major cards

ALKIMIA
$$$$$
INDÚSTRIA 79
TEL 932 07 61 15
www.alkimia.cat
Jordi Vilà's calm and creative seasonal Mediterranean cooking has been rewarded with a Michelin star. Try his pickled oysters with glazed pork cheek and spinach sauté, or the baked chicken cannelloni with almond bechamel and fresh salad. The lunch menu is very well priced.
40 Sagrada Familia Closed Sat., Sun., Easter, & 3 weeks Aug. DC, MC, V

CA L'ISIDRE
$$$$$
LES FLORS 12
TEL 934 41 11 39
www.calisidre.com
This charming restaurant on the edge of the Raval district serves traditional Catalan dishes using local ingredients.
35 Paral.lel Closed Sun., Sat. June–Aug., Christmas, Easter, & 3 weeks Aug. AE, MC, V

COMERÇ 24
$$$$$
COMERÇ 24
TEL 933 19 21 02
www.comcerc24.com
The creative avant-garde

cuisine offered by chef Carles Abellan, inspired by Ferran Adrià, includes tapas-style dishes like soup-salad of tiger nut milk, quail, and soy, lollipops, and cuttlefish black rice.
50 Arc de Triomf Closed Sun., Mon., Christmas, & 1 week Aug. All major cards

LA DAMA
$$$$$
AVENIDA DIAGONAL 423
TEL 932 02 06 86
www.ladama-restaurant.com
Enjoy modern Catalan cuisine in a wonderful Modernista building in Eixample. The pastries made here are excellent.
80 Diagonal All major cards

GAIG
$$$$$
ARAGÓ 214
TEL 934 29 10 17
www.restaurantgaig.com
Four generations of the Gaig family have run this classic restaurant, now in the Hotel Cram. Chef Carlos Gaig has developed a modern approach to traditional recipes. Try the cannelloni with truffle cream and fantastic desserts.
60 Passeig de Gràcia Closed Sun., Mon. L, Easter, Christmas, & 3 weeks Aug. All major cards

NEICHEL
$$$$$
BELTRÁN I RÓZPIDE 1–5
TEL 932 03 84 08
www.neichel.es
Chef Jean Louis Neichel uses the freshest ingredients at this top Barcelona restaurant, serving modern Catalan–French haute cuisine. Desserts and cheese are superb. Reservations are suggested.
60 Maria Cristina Closed Sun., Mon., first week Jan., Easter, & Aug. All major cards

SANT PAU
$$$$$
NOV 1, SANT POL DE MAR (34 MILES/54 KM FROM BARCELONA)
TEL 937 60 06 62
www.ruscalleda.cat
Chef Carme Ruscalleda's delicious fusion of classic Catalan cuisine with inspired creative touches includes Cod brandade with peppers and black olives, and boneless pig's feet with almonds, alfalfa, and spicy oil.
35 Closed Sun., Mon., Thurs. L, 1st 3 weeks May, & 1 3 weeks Nov. All major cards

VIA VENETO
$$$$$
GANDUXER 10
TEL 932 00 72 44
www.viaveneto restaurant.com
Via Veneto is noted for its elegance. Try the scampi tartare with salmon or roast duck.
94 La Bonanova Closed Sat. L, Sun., & Aug. 1–20 All major cards

JAUME DE PROVENÇA
$$$$
PROVENÇA 88
TEL 934 30 00 29
www.jaumeprovenza.com
Chef Jaume Bargués offers Catalan–French haute cuisine, such as sea bass with fennel confit and *cava* sauce, or duck breast filet mignon à la orange. Reservations suggested.
60 Hospital Clinic Closed Sun. D, Mon., Aug., & Christmas All major cards

SET PORTES
$$$$
PASSEIG ISABEL II, 14
TEL 933 19 30 33
www.7portes.com
This popular early 19th-century establishment near the waterfront serves generous portions of traditional Catalan cuisine. Reservations are suggested.
300 Barceloneta All major cards

TICKETS
$$$$
PARAL.LEL 164
TEL 933 19 30 33
www.ticketsbar.es
Founded by Albert and Ferran Adrià, Tickets offers imaginative dishes like rabbit ribs with foamed garlic mayonnaise or quail eggs with almogrote crumbs. Their cocktail bar, **41°**, is in the same building.
50 Poble Sec Usually closed Sun., Mon., Tues.–Sat. L, Easter, last 2 weeks Aug., & last week Dec. All major cards

EASTERN SPAIN

CATALUNYA

COSTA BRAVA

MAS DE TORRENT
$$$$$ ★★★★★
TORRENT D'EMPORDÀ 17123
TEL 972 30 32 92
www.mastorrent.com
Enjoy fantastic views of the coastline in this 18th-century farmhouse. The decor is a mix of sophisticated Catalan and rustic elements. The excellent restaurant offers traditional dishes such as crispy foie gras and a notable wine list.
30 All major cards

DIANA
$$ ★★
PLAÇA D'ESPANYA 6, TOSSA DE MAR 17320
TEL 972 34 18 86
www.diana-hotel.com
This early 20th-century building offers views of the sea and Platja Gran. No restaurant.
21 All major cards

DURÁN
$$ ★★★
LASAUCA 5
FIGUERES 17600
TEL 972 50 12 50
www.hotelduran.com
This low key, central hotel is owned by a friend of Dalí and has a reputable restaurant.
65 All major cards

PORT LLIGAT
$$ ★★
SALVADOR DALÍ S/N,
CADAQUÉS 17488
TEL 972 25 81 62
www.port-lligat.net
Some rooms at this hotel next to Dali's last home have terraces and views of the sea. The mixture of furnishings adds to the general charm.
29 MC, V

SOMETHING SPECIAL

EL CELLER DE CAN ROCA
$$$$$
CAN SUNYER 48
TEL 972 15 04 57
www.cellercanroca.com
The three Roca brothers create cutting-edge Catalan dishes like grilled Palamós prawn with amarita mushroom juice, lemon caviar, and ginger. The restaurant boasts outstanding wines. Reservations are essential.
30 Closed L except Sun. Apr.–June, Oct.–Mar., & Mon. & Tues. Apr.–June All major cards

GIRONA (GERONA) 17000

CARLEMANY
$$ ★★★★
PLAÇA MIQUEL SANTALÓ
TEL 972 21 12 12
www.carlemany.es
This good-value modern hotel with large rooms in the new part of town is only a five-minute walk from the old and has a good restaurant.
82 All major cards

COSTABELLA
$$ ★★★
AVENIDA FRANÇA 61
TEL 972 20 25 24
www.hotelcostabella.com
Located just five minutes from the old town, this welcoming new hotel serves superior breakfasts.
49 All major cards

MONTBLANC 43400

FONDA BOHÈMIA RIUOT
$ ★★
PLETA 21–23
TEL 977 87 51 45
www.fondariuot.com
This friendly, artistic stone-built hotel in the center of this medieval town offers nine rooms and five studio apartments.
14 MC, V

SANT CELONI 08470

CAN FABES
$$$$$
SANT JOAN 6
TEL 93 867 28 51
www.canfabes.com
Sample Santi Santamaría's exquisite cuisine with the taster menu at this restaurant situated in an old stone farmhouse near the Hotel Can Fabes.
50 Closed Sun. D, Mon., 2 weeks Feb., & 2 weeks June–early July All major cards

SITGES 08870

CELIMAR
$$ ★★★
PASSEIG DE LA RIBERA 20
TEL 93 811 01 70
www.hotelcelimar.com
This Modernista hotel sits right on the seafront, but it doesn't have a restaurant.
25 All major cards

TARRAGONA 43000

FARISTOL
$$ ★★
SANT MARTÍ 5, ALTAFULLA
43893 (7 MILES/11 KM FROM TARRAGONA)
TEL 977 65 00 77
www.faristol.es
The rooms in this 18th-century mansion have been furnished with period furniture, while the restaurant serves grilled meats in its cool interior courtyard.
5 All major cards

IMPERIAL TARRACO
$$ ★★★★
PASSEIG DE LES PALMERES
TEL 977 23 30 40
www.hotelhusaimperialtarraco.com
The semicircle of this large block reflects the ruins of the Roman amphitheater. Rooms have balconies, but ask for a sea view. Eat meals at the cafeteria.
170 All major cards

AQ
$$$$
LES COQUES 7
TEL 977 21 59 54
www.aq-restaurant.com
Right next to the Cathedral, AQ mixes classic and creative. Try roast strips of Wagyu beef with cucumber and apple salad.
44 Closed Sun., Mon., first 2 weeks July, & 2 weeks Christmas MC, V

TORTOSA 43500

PARADOR DE TORTOSA
$$$ ★★★★
CASTILLO DE LA ZUDA
TEL 977 44 44 50

www.parador.es
This impressive tenth-century fortress has views of the Ebro plains and Beceite Mountains. Enjoy local eel in the restaurant

72 All major cards

VIC 08500

PARADOR DE VIC-SAU

$$$ ★★★★
PARATGE BAC DE SAU
(9 MILES/14 KM FROM VIC)
TEL 93 812 23 23
www.parador.es
Some rooms in this parador resembling a Catalan *masía* (farmhouse) overlook the Sau reservoir. The restaurant serves regional Osona cuisine.
34 All major cards

VALENCIA

ALACANT (ALICANTE) 03000

HOTELS

MELIÁ ALICANTE

$$$ ★★★★
PLAZA DEL PUERTO 3
TEL 965 20 50 00
www.meliaalicante.com
Enjoy traditional shellfish dishes in the **Terra** restaurant at this large centrally located hotel. All rooms have balconies and sea views.
544 All major cards

TRYP GRAN SOL

$$ ★★★★
RAMBLA MÉNDEZ NÚÑEZ 3
TEL 965 20 30 00
www.solmelia.com
This is the only high-rise in the center of Alacant near the sea. Enjoy Mediterranean cuisine and views of the city in the **Mirador** restaurant.
123 All major cards

RESTAURANTS

NOU MANOLÍN

$$$$
VILLEGAS 3
TEL 965 20 03 68
www.noumanolin.com
Eat at the bar or in the dining room. The *montaditos,* typical of Alacant, are mini sandwiches with fillings of your choice. The rice dishes are delicious, as is the *jamón ibérico.*
315 All major cards

TABERNA DEL GOURMET

$$
SAN FERNANDO 10
TEL 965 20 42 33
www.latabernadelgourmet.com
Traditional and creative cooking mix in this welcoming setting. Try black rice with cuttlefish, prawns, and artichoke.
100 All major cards

ALCOI (ALCOY) 03803

MAS DE PAU

$$ ★★
CARRETERA ALCOY-PENÀGUILA, KM 9
TEL 965 51 31 11
This 18th-century farmhouse is a quiet retreat in the Penàguila Valley. The terrace offers fine views, though rooms are somewhat cramped.
18 All major cards

ALTEA 03590

OUSTAU

$$
MAYOR 5
TEL 965 84 20 78
www.oustau.es
Once a convent, the Oustau offers French-influenced food in beautiful surroundings. Try the roast fillets of sea bass in shrimp and white-wine sauce. Reservations are essential.
80 Closed Mon. (Oct.–June) & Feb.–mid-March All major cards

PRICES

HOTELS
An indication of the cost of a double room in the high season is given by **$** signs.

$$$$$	Over $300
$$$$	$220–$300
$$$	$160–$220
$$	$80–$160
$	Under $80

RESTAURANTS
An indication of the cost of a three-course meal without drinks is given by **$** signs.

$$$$$	Over $80
$$$$	$50–$80
$$$	$35–$50
$$	$20–$35
$	Under $20

CALP (CALPE) 03710

VILLA MARISOL

$$ ★★★★
URBANIZACIÓN MARISOL PARK 1A
TEL 965 87 57 00
www.marisolpark.com
This quiet, friendly, and well-appointed hotel lies away from the hustle and bustle of the town center.
17 AE, MC, V

GUADALEST 03517

CASA PATRICIO

$$
ARRIBA 37, EL ABDET (6 MILES/9 KM FROM GUADALEST)
TEL 965 88 53 10
Casa Patricio offers good local cuisine such as roast lamb.

55 Closed Mon., & 3 weeks July MC, V

VALENCIA 46000

HOTELS

AD HOC MONUMENTAL
$$ ★★★
BOIX 4
TEL 963 91 91 40
www.adhochoteles.com
The restaurant in this 1880s house, which combines modern and antique, serves Mediterranean cuisine.
28 40 All major cards

REINA VICTORIA
$$ ★★★★
BARCAS 4
TEL 96 352 04 87
www.husareinavictoria.com
The rooms at the Victoria, still the most elegant hotel in Valencia, are classically decorated. Queen Victoria may have stayed here.
96 All major cards

SH VALENCIA PALACE
$$ ★★★★★
PASEO DE LA ALAMEDA 32
TEL 96 337 50 37
www.hotel-valencia-palace.com
The modern facade of this hotel opposite the Palau de la Música encloses a state-of-the-art interior and a restaurant where the menu changes daily.
248 All major cards

RESTAURANTS

LA SUCURSAL
$$$$$
GUILLEM DE CASTRO 118
TEL 963 74 66 65
www.restaurantelasucursal.com
Inside the Institute of Modern Art (IVAM), chef Jorge Bretón offers innovative contemporary cuisine, such as risotto of ribs, snails, and wild mushrooms.
50 Closed Sun., Sat. L, Easter week, and first 2 weeks Aug. All major cards

ALBACAR
$$$$
SORNÍ 35
TEL 963 95 10 05
www.restaurantealbacar.com
The modern setting provides the atmosphere for innovative dishes like honeyed lamb loin with rosemary and trinxat.
60 Closed Sat. L, Sun., Easter, 3 weeks Aug., & 1 week Sept. All major cards

ARROP
$$$$
ALMIRANTE 14
TEL 963 15 52 87
www.arrop.com
In this futuristic restaurant set into the city walls, Ricard Camarena has transformed traditional Valencian cooking.
50 Closed Sun. & Mon.; holidays vary AE, MC, V

RÍAS GALLEGAS
$$$$
CIRILO AMORÓS 4
TEL 963 52 51 11
www.riasgallegas.es
This restaurant has its ingredients, and wines, sent from Galicia. Sample the scallops and Galician-style turbot.
77 Closed Sun., Mon. D, & Aug. All major cards

LA PEPICA
$$$
PASEO NEPTUNO 6–8, PLAYA DE LA MALVAROSA
TEL 963 71 03 66
www.lapepica.com
La Pepica been dishing up exquisite seafood and rice dishes since 1898, either inside or out on the breezy terrace.
450 Closed Sun. D & last 2 weeks Nov. All major cards

XÀBIA (JÁVEA) 03730

EL RODAT
$$$ ★★★★
LA MURCIANA 9
CARRETERA CABO DE LA NAO
TEL 966 47 07 10
www.elrodat.com
Surrounded by gardens, this elegant hotel offers views of the Montgó mountains and the coast. You can enjoy Mediterranean fare made with fresh local ingredients in the restaurant.
42 All major cards

XÁTIVA (JÁTIVA) 46800

HOSTERÍA DE MONTSANT
$$ ★★
SUBIDA AL CASTILLO S/N
TEL 962 27 50 81
www.mont-sant.com
A garden surrounds this restored 1320 monastery. Rooms are simple but elegant, and the restaurant has a wine cellar. Breakfast is included.
16 All major cards

CASTILLA Y LEÓN

ÁVILA 05000

PALACIO DE LOS VELADA
$$ ★★★★
PLAZA DE LA CATEDRAL 10
TEL 920 25 51 00
www.veladahoteles.com
The rooms in this 16th-century palace are airy and attractive. Dining options include **El Tostada** restaurant and a café.
145 All major cards

HOSPEDERÍA DE BRACAMONTE
$ ★★
BRACAMONTE 6
TEL 920 25 12 80
www.hospederiade bracamonte.com

This charming 16th-century mansion close to the cathedral has a good-value restaurant, where lamb roasted in a wood-burning oven is a specialty.

23 200 DC, MC, V

EL ALMACÉN
$$$
CARRETERA DE SALAMANCA 6
TEL 920 25 44 55

On the outskirts of town, this restaurant may serve the most refined cuisine in Ávila. Try the gil-head bream filet.

75 Closed Sun. D, Mon., & Sept. All major cards

BURGOS 09000

LANDA
$$$$ ★★★★★
CARRETERA N1 MADRID-IRÚN, KM 235
TEL 947 25 77 77
www.landahotel.as

For luxury and the best food in Burgos, stay in this former palace. The restaurant serves seasonal specialties, tasty rice dishes, and delicious desserts.

42 MC, V

LA POSADA
$ ★★★
LANDELINO TARDAJOS 3, CASTROJERIZ 09110 (25 MILES/ 40 KM FROM BURGOS)
TEL 947 37 86 10

This quiet 16th-century inn on the Camino de Santiago offers rustic furniture, medieval bodegas, and a glass-covered patio.

21 Closed 2 weeks late Sept.–early Oct. MC, V

CIUDAD RODRIGO 37500

PARADOR DE CIUDAD RODRIGO
$$$$ ★★★★
PLAZA CASTILLO 1
TEL 923 46 01 50
www.parador.es

Well-kept gardens surround this 14th-century castle on the banks of the Águeda River. One of the rooms is circular with a domed ceiling. Check the tower views, and enjoy Iberian ham in the restaurant.

35 All major cards

MESÓN LA ARTESA
$
RÚA DEL SOL 1
TEL 923 48 11 28
www.mesonlaartesa.com

In the historic center, this restaurant serves reasonably priced Castilian fare, specializing in grilled meats.

60 Closed Sun. All major cards

LEÓN 24000

PARADOR DE LEÓN
$$$$$ ★★★★★
PLAZA SAN MARCOS 7
TEL 987 23 73 00
www.parador.es

This stunning parador, built in the 16th century, has an ornate plateresque facade and is filled with antiques and works of art; ask for a room in the medieval wing. The splendid dining room serves regional dishes such as frog legs, river eel stewed with potatoes, and *cecina* (cured beef).

226 All major cards

LA POSADA REGÍA
$$$ ★★★
REGIDORES 9–11
TEL 987 21 31 73
www.regialeon.com

The rustic rooms in this small hotel in a 14th-century town house have wooden floors and beamed ceilings. The restaurant, **Bodega Regía,** serves regional cuisine.

19 120 DC, MC, V

VIVALDI
$$$$
REYES LEONESES 24 (INSIDE CONTEMPORARY ART MUSEUM)
TEL 987 26 07 60
www.restaurantevivaldi.com

The creative modern cuisine offered her uses local produce. Specials include toasted cubes of suckling pig with citrus sauce.

65 Closed Sun. D, Mon., Tues. D, & when exhibitions change All major cards

SALAMANCA 37000

HOTELS

RECTOR
$$$$ ★★★★
PASEO RECTOR ESPERABÉ 10
TEL 923 21 84 82
www.hotelrector.com

This grandiose 1940s stone building has elegant rooms. The breakfast here is excellent, but there is no restaurant.

13 All major cards

SAN POLO
$$$ ★★★
ARROYO DE SANTO DOMINGO 2
TEL 923 21 11 77
www.hotelsanpolo.com

Many rooms in this modern hotel, built among the ruins of an 11th-century Romanesque church, look over the old town.

37 All major cards

PALACIO DE CASTELLANOS
$$ ★★★★
SAN PABLO 58–64
TEL 923 26 18 18
www.nh-hotels.com

The **Trento** restaurant at this stylish hotel near the Plaza

Mayor serves international and Spanish cuisine. The original cloister is a fantastic example of Hispanic–Flemish architecture.
62 P All major cards

RESTAURANTS

VÍCTOR GUTIÉRREZ
$$$$
SAN PABLO 66–80
TEL 923 26 29 73
www.restaurantevictorgutierrez.com
This Peruvian chef with one Michelin star offers fresh and inventive dishes like roast pigeon with quinoa stew and baked sea bass with creamed peas and Iberian ham.
25 Closed Sun., Tues. L, second & third weeks Jan., & first 2 weeks July All major cards

COCINA DE TOÑO
$$$
GRAN VÍA 20
TEL 923 26 39 77
www.lacocinadetono.es
Cocina de Toño serves inventive and unpretentious highland cooking with a Basque touch. Dishes include mille feuille of beef sirloin and foie gras in wine sauce, and San Sebastián–style sole with chili pepper.
40 Closed Sun. D & Mon. (Sept.–June), & Sun. & Mon. L (July–Aug.) All major cards

EL BARDO
$$$
LA COMPAÑÍA 25
TEL 923 21 90 89
www.restauranteselbardo.com
Just off Calle Mayor, this small place has a lively ground floor tapas bar and a first-floor dining room. Recommended dishes include lamb cutlets with vegetables and cod cooked with honey.
50 All major cards

SEGOVIA 40000

HOTELS

PARADOR DE SEGOVIA
$$$ ★★★★
CARRETERA DE VALLADOLID
TEL 921 44 37 37
www.parador.es
This modern parador filled with contemporary art and furniture boasts stunning views of Segovia but is far from the city center. Its restaurant serves some of the city's best roast suckling pig.
113 P All major cards

LOS LINAJES
$$ ★★★
DOCTOR VELASCO 9
TEL 921 46 04 75
www.loslinajes.com
This quiet hotel occupies part of a medieval palace within the city walls. Some of the older rooms have views of the Eresma Valley.
62 P All major cards

RESTAURANTS

MARACAIBO–CASA SILVANO
$$$$
PASEO EZEQUIEL GONZÁLEZ 25
TEL 921 46 15 45
www.restaurantemaracaibo.com
Chef Óscar Hernando mixes traditional Castilian dishes with the latest creative cooking. Try the wild mushrooms with foie gras and grated black truffle.
70 All major cards

MESÓN DE CÁNDIDO
$$$
PLAZA AZOGUEJO 5
TEL 921 42 59 11
www.mesondecandido.es
Under the *aqueducto* these quaint dining rooms—now a national monument—have functioned since 1786. The cuisine is traditional Castilian.
420 All major cards

SORIA 42000

PARADOR DE SORIA
$$$$ ★★★★
FORTÚN LÓPEZ S/N
TEL 975 24 08 00
www.parador.es
The rooms in this modern parador have wood floors and furnishings; ask for one overlooking Soria and the Duero River. The restaurant offers pheasant pâté and suckling pig.
67 P All major cards

TORDESILLAS 47100

LOS TOREROS
$$ ★
AVENIDA VALLADOLID 26
TEL 983 77 19 00
www.hotellostoreros.com
This family-run hotel in a former country house has small but cozy rooms.
27 P All major cards

TORO 49800

JUAN II
$$ ★★★
PASEO DEL ESPOLÓN 1
TEL 980 69 03 00
www.hoteljuanii.com
The spacious rustic rooms in this good-value hotel feature tile floors and views over the plains of Zamora. Enjoy hearty stews and soups made from fresh regional ingredients in **Los Bocoyes** restaurant.
42 P All major cards

VALLADOLID 47000

MOZART
$$$ ★★★
MENÉNDEZ PELAYO 7
TEL 983 29 77 77
www.hotelmozart.net
Some of the ample-size and

functional rooms in this 1872 house in the city center have attractive wood balconies. There is no restaurant.
38 P AE, MC, V

RAMIRO'S
$$$$
MONASTERIO NUESTRA SEÑORA DE PRADO 2 (CENTRO CULTURAL MIGUEL DELIBES)
TEL 983 38 48 12
www.ramiro.es
Innovative young chef Jesús Ramiro has won a Michelin star for his fresh and seasonal cooking, with delicious dishes such as butterfish carpaccio with black olive sorbet and pine nuts, and Iberian pork cheeks with potato and vanilla confit and stewed apples.
35 P Closed Sun. D AE, MC, V

ZAMORA 49000

HOSTERÍA REAL DE ZAMORA
$$ ★★★
CUESTA PIZARRO 7
TEL 980 53 45 45
www.hosteriasreales.com
This delightful hotel occupies the Palacio de la Inquisición, a historic monument on a quiet street with a walled garden. The small rooms open onto the 16th-century interior patio.
26 All major cards

LA POSADA
$$
BENAVENTE 2
TEL 980 51 64 74
www.restauranteposada.com
The *menú turístico* is a good choice at this classically decorated restaurant.
50 Closed Sun. D, Mon., & first week July All major cards

CASTILLA-LA MANCHA & EXTREMADURA

ALARCÓN 16214

PARADOR DE ALARCÓN
$$$$$ ★★★★
AVENIDA AMIGOS DE LOS CASTILLOS 3
TEL 969 33 03 15
www.parador.es
Once Moorish, then a fortified medieval castle, this parador features turret rooms with narrow slits for windows. In the restaurant, dine on typical local fare including *morteruelo* (a hash of mixed meats).
14 80 P All major cards

ALMAGRO 13270

SOMETHING SPECIAL

PARADOR DE ALMAGRO
$$$ ★★★★
RONDA SAN FRANCISCO 31
TEL 926 86 01 00
www.parador.es
This 16th-century Franciscan convent, built around 14 courtyards, is decorated with paintings and beautiful old tiles. The restaurant serves traditional Manchegan fare such as *mojete* (cold roasted onions and peppers) and *tiznao.*
54 P All major cards

EL CORREGIDOR
$$$$
JERÓNIMO CEBALLOS 2
TEL 926 86 06 48
www.elcorregidor.com
At this delightful restaurant in an old house with original tiling, the food is modern Manchegan; try hake in puff pastry with red pepper sauce.
130 P Closed Mon. (except July) & last week July All major cards

PRICES

HOTELS
An indication of the cost of a double room in the high season is given by **$** signs.

$$$$$	Over $300
$$$$	$220–$300
$$$	$160–$220
$$	$80–$160
$	Under $80

RESTAURANTS
An indication of the cost of a three-course meal without drinks is given by **$** signs.

$$$$$	Over $80
$$$$	$50–$80
$$$	$35–$50
$$	$20–$35
$	Under $20

BADAJOZ 06000

HOTELS

SOMETHING SPECIAL

MONASTERIO DE ROCAMADOR
$$$ ★★★★
CARRETERA NACIONAL BADAJOZ-HUELVA, KM 41.1, ALMENDRAL
TEL 924 48 90 00
www.rocamador.com
Some of the rooms in this 16th-century monastery are built into the rock. Dine on Basque–Extremaduran cuisine in the former chapel.
30 P All major cards

HUSA ZURBARÁN
$$ ★★★★
GÓMEZ DE SOLÍS 1

TEL 924 00 14 00
www.hotelhusazurbaran.com
Service is attentive at this hotel overlooking Castelar Park and the Guadiana River.
213 All major cards

RESTAURANTS

ALDEBARÁN
$$$$
AVENIDA ELVAS S/N
URBANIZACIÓN GUADIANA
TEL 924 27 68 37
www.restaurantealdebaran.com
Elegant and charming, this is the city's best restaurant, where Fernando Bárcena uses the freshest local produce to create the Basque-influenced menu of Extremaduran haute cuisine. Dishes include fresh anchovies marinated with truffles and melted Casar cheese salad.
100 Closed Sun. & Mon. D & 2 weeks Aug. All major cards

LA TOJA
$$$
SÁNCHEZ DE LA ROCHA 22
TEL 924 27 34 77
www.restaurantelatoja.com
On the outskirts of town, this classy restaurant provides Galician seafood, including *pulpo a la gallega* (octopus stewed with potatoes, parsley, and paprika) and (on Sundays) paella.
75 Closed Sun. D, & first 2 weeks Feb. AE, MC, V

CÁCERES 10000

HOTELS

PARADOR DE CÁCERES
$$$$ ★★★★
ANCHA 6
TEL 927 21 17 59
www.parador.es
This 14th-century palace in the heart of medieval Cáceres has a small, pretty interior patio that leads to reception. The restaurant, **Torreorgaz,** offers fine local fare including frog legs and Iberian pork tenderloin with Casar cheese.
33 All major cards

NH PALACIO DE OQUENDO
$$ ★★★★
PLAZA DE SAN JUAN II
TEL 927 21 58 00
www.nh-hotels.com
The guest rooms in this renovated 16th-century palace in the old town are modern and spacious. The restaurant, bar, and some rooms have beautiful brick-vaulted ceilings.
86 All major cards

RESTAURANTS

ATRIO
$$$$$
PLAZA DE SAN MATEO 1
TEL 927 24 29 28
www.restauranteatrio.com
In this brand-new restaurant in the medieval town center, chefs Toño Pérez and José Polo offer inventive classical/modern cooking. Dishes include roast scallops with creamy *bolefus* and truffle, and roast pigeon with lime and cardamom. An excellent hotel is attached.
60 Closed Sun. D, & first 2 weeks Sept. All major cards

CHEZ MANOU
$$$
PLAZA DE LAS VELETAS 4
TEL 927 22 76 82
This small cozy place specializing in French cuisine and regional dishes is one of the few restaurants in the historic walled town near the museum.
50 Closed Sun. D & Mon. MC, V

CUENCA 16000

HOTELS

PARADOR DE CUENCA
$$$$ ★★★★
SUBIDA A SAN PABLO S/N
TEL 969 23 23 20
www.parador.es
This parador sits in the Hoz del Huécar gorge, its building a restored 16th-century monastery. The restaurant in the old refectory has an interesting menu that includes *morteruelo* (Cuencan game gruel), *pisto con lomo de orza* (ratatouille with pork loin), and *alajú* (almond, walnut, and honey dessert).
63 150 All major cards

LEONOR DE AQUITANIA
$$ ★★★
SAN PEDRO 60
TEL 969 23 10 00
www.hotelleonordeaquitania.com
An 18th-century hanging house overlooking the gorge in the old town, this hotel combines traditional design with contemporary decor. The restaurant serves regional far.
46 All major cards

SOMETHING SPECIAL

POSADA DE SAN JOSÉ
$$ ★★
JULIÁN ROMERO 4
TEL 969 21 13 00
www.posadasanjose.com
The antique-filled rooms in this rambling 17th-century hanging house in the heart of the old town are simple (no TVs or telephones), and not all have bathrooms. A bar-dining area serves breakfast and tapas, but there is no restaurant. Reserve early.
22 All major cards

RESTAURANTS

RAFF
$$$
FEDERICO GARCÍA LORCA 3
TEL 969 69 08 55
www.restauranteraff.es
Chef José Ignacio Herraíz Gil serves up some of the freshest and most delicious food in Cuenca. Try his cannelloni of cod cooked in olive oil, garlic, and peppers, the roast rack of lamb, or sardines marinaded in raspberry coulis.
30 Closed Sun. & July 15–Aug. 15 MC, V

MESÓN CASAS COLGADAS
$$$
CANÓNIGOS S/N
TEL 969 22 35 09
www.mesoncasascolgadas.com
Enjoy the magnificent panorama from this 14th-century hanging house next to the Museum of Abstract Art. The restaurant serves game and Manchegan specialties. Worth sampling are the *ajo arriero* (a paste made from salted cod, garlic, parsley, and paprika), venison, and roast suckling pig. Reserve ahead.
100 Closed Mon. D & Tues. All major cards

GUADALUPE 10140

PARADOR DE GUADALUPE
$$$$ ★★★★
MARQUÉS DE LA ROMANA 12
TEL 927 36 70 75
www.parador.es
This 15th-century building was a palace, hospital, and noted medical school. Orange and lemon trees in the courtyard enhance the Moorish atmosphere. The restaurant serves simple local dishes.
41 All major cards

HOSPEDERÍA DEL REAL MONASTERIO
$$ ★★
PLAZA DE JUAN CARLOS I S/N
TEL 927 36 70 00
www.hotelhospederiamonasterioguadalupe.com
Comfortable rooms surround the cloister of this imposing 16th-century building. The restaurant serves hearty fare such as tomato soup and goat *caldereta* (stew). For weekends reserve two months ahead.
47 Closed Jan. 15–Feb. 15 MC, V

JARANDILLA DE LA VERA 10450

PARADOR DE JARANDILLA DE LA VERA
$$$ ★★★★
AVENIDA GARCÍA PRIETO 1
TEL 927 56 01 17
www.parador.es
The restaurant in this elegant 15th-century building offers a good selection of typical Extremaduran dishes.
52 50 All major cards

JEREZ DE LOS CABALLEROS 06380

LOS TEMPLARIOS
$$ ★★★
CARRETERA DE VILLANUEVA
TEL 924 73 16 36
www.hotellostemplarios.net
This is a simple three-star hotel in a town with few choices.
48 All major cards

MÉRIDA 06800

PARADOR DE MÉRIDA
$$$ ★★★★
PLAZA CONSTITUCIÓN 3
TEL 924 31 38 00
www.parador.es
Some rooms in this 1900s building in the heart of Mérida give onto a pretty interior courtyard. The restaurant serves reliable regional dishes like gazpacho and *caldereta extremeña* (stewed lamb with red peppers, fried bread crumbs, and sausage).
82 All major cards

NOVA ROMA
$$ ★★★
SUÁREZ SOMONTE 42
TEL 924 31 12 61/31 12 01
www.novaroma.com
Only two-minute walk from the Roman ruins, this modern building has a white marble reception area and cafeteria. Breakfast is expensive.
55 AE, MC, V

RUFINO
$$
PLAZA DE SANTA CLARA 2
TEL 924 31 20 01
Rufino has wide selection of tapas and solid Extremaduran fare such as partridge stew.
45 Closed Sun. & 3 weeks Sept. All major cards

SIGÜENZA 19250

MOLINO DE ALCUNEZA
$$ ★★★
CARRETERA DE ALBORECA, KM 0.5 ALCUNEZA
TEL 949 39 15 01
www.molinodealcuneza.com
A 15th-century flour mill on the banks of the Henares River has been converted into a comfortable hotel.
17 All major cards

TOLEDO 45000

HOTELS

PARADOR DE TOLEDO
$$$$ ★★★★
CERRO DEL EMPERADOR S/N

TEL 925 22 18 50
www.parador.es
This fine example of a *cigarral,* a Toledan country home, built beside the River Tagus, has spacious rooms, some with magnificent views of the city.
78 All major cards

ALFONSO VI
$$$ ★★★★
GENERAL MOSCARDÓ 2
TEL 925 22 26 00
www.hotelalfonsoVI.com
Probably the most luxurious hotel in Toledo, the Alfonso is situated opposite the Alcazar.
83 All major cards

SOMETHING SPECIAL

HOTEL DEL CARDENAL
$$$ ★★★
PASEO DE RECAREDO 24
TEL 925 22 49 00
www.hoteldelcardenal.com
Built as a summer palace in the 18th century, this beautiful hotel features rooms decorated in Castilian style with dark wood headboards, big old mirrors, and hand-painted bathroom tiles. Reserve early. The restaurant serves local dishes like baked sea bass and roast suckling pig.
27 200 All major cards

PINTOR EL GRECO
$$ ★★★★
ALAMILLOS DEL TRÁNSITO 13
TEL 925 28 51 91
www.hotelpintorelgreco.com
In the heart of the old Jewish quarter next to El Greco's house-museum, this pretty 17th-century bakery became a hotel in 1989. The interior courtyard and facade are well preserved. Airy rooms have ironwork, tiles, and lanterns.
60 All major cards

RESTAURANTS

ADOLFO
$$$$$
HOMBRE DE PALO 7
TEL 925 22 73 21/25 24 72
www.adolfo-toledo.com
This classic establishment, in a beautiful building with Mudejar workmanship, offers innovative and traditional dishes and has an excellent wine cellar. Try the grilled venison or rice with lobster and manchego cheese.
100 Closed Sun. D All major cards

HIERBABUENA
$$$$
CALLEJÓN DE SAN JOSÉ 17
TEL 925 22 39 24
www.restaurantehierbabuena.com
The food here is served on a bright but covered Moorish patio. A seasonal menu includes saltboar and venison sirloin with mango/raspberry sauce.
80 Closed Sun. D, Sun. in summer, & Aug. All major cards

ALFILERITOS24
$$$
ALFERITOS 24
TEL 925 23 96 25
www.alfileritos24.com
Located off the tourist trail, but close to Plaza de Zocodover, stylish, friendly Alferitos has a tapas tavern and an upstairs restaurant serving classic food with a creative touch. Try the seasonal venison.
179 All major cards

TRUJILLO 10200

PARADOR DE TRUJILLO
$$$ ★★★★
SANTA BEATRIZ DE SILVA 1
TEL 927 32 13 50
www.parador.es
The old town's only hotel occupies the 16th-century convent of Santa Clara. Rooms lead onto the glassed-in cloister and courtyard. Try the restaurant's wild boar.
50 All major cards

FINCA SANTA MARTA
$$
CARRETERA TRUJILLO-GUADALUPE, KM 89.5
TEL 927 31 92 03
www.fincasantamarta.es
Once an olive farm, this hotel with a rustic feel is still surrounded by acres of trees. Order your meals in the restaurant in advance.
13 MC, V

MESÓN LA TROYA
$$$
PLAZA MAYOR 10
TEL 927 32 13 64
The chaotic but friendly atmosphere is reason enough to dine here, though huge portions and low prices also make it popular. You will be served a tortilla, salad, and sausage to start whether you order them or not! Have tapas at the bar.
250 All major cards

ZAFRA 06300

PARADOR DE ZAFRA
$$$ ★★★★
PLAZA CORAZÓN DE MARÍA 7
TEL 924 55 45 40
www.parador.es
This 15th-century castle has nine towers. Its rooms are rather somber, but the marble bathrooms are luxurious. Enjoy local cuisine in the restaurant.
51 All major cards

HUERTA HONDA
$$ ★★★
LÓPEZ ASME 30
TEL 924 55 41 00
www.hotelhuertahonda.com
Decorated with differing colors and textiles, the rooms here evoke the style of a country

manor. The restaurant serves regional and national cuisine with a strong Basque influence. Specials include cod loin with baby squid risotto and tomato oregano broth.
49 40 All major cards

LA REBOTICA
$$
BOTICAS 12
TEL 924 55 42 89
www.lareboticadezafra.com
Set in a lovely mansion in Zafra's old quarter, this restaurant offers the freshest local produce in traditional dishes such as Iberian pork tenderloin with figs and brandy sauce.
28 Closed Sun. D., Mon., & first 2 weeks Aug. AE, MC, V

ANDALUCÍA & MURCIA

ALMERÍA 04000

AC ALMERÍA
$$ ★★★★
PLAZA FLORES 5
TEL 950 23 49 99
www.hotelacalmeria.com
This is the most comfortable place to stay in Almería. The roof terrace with a pool affords wonderful views of the sea. Dining options include two restaurants and a bar.
97 All major cards

LA ENCINA PLAZA VIEJA
$$$
MARÍN 16
TEL 950 27 34 29
www.restuarantelaencina.es
Set in an 1860 town house, with an 11th-century well within, La Encina offers both traditional and creative cuisine. Try zucchini-wrapped prawns in roast pepper sauce, or quail's egg, ratatouille, and potato pie.
40 Closed Mon. (Sept.–June), Sun. (July–Aug.), first 3 weeks July, & third week Sept. AE, MC, V

CASA PUGA
$
JOVELLANOS 7
TEL 950 23 15 30
www.barcasapuga.es
Open since 1890, this bar in the old town center serves excellent tapas and *raciones* (larger portions), including *jamón de jabugo* (ham from acorn-fed pigs), smoked cod with roasted peppers, and fried fish of the day. Good wine list.
50 Closed Sun.

ALPUJARRAS

ALQUERÍA DE MORAYMA
$$ ★★★
CÁDIAR 18440
TEL 958 34 32 21
www.alqueriamorayma.com
This hotel has nice rustic rooms with fantastic views of the Sierra Nevada. The restaurant serves local food.
24 50 V

CASA MEZCUA
$
CUESTA SAN MIGUEL
184391 CÁSTARAS
TEL 958 85 55 26
www.casamezcua.com
This delightful guesthouse in a tranquil village boasts superb views. It has two self-catering apartments (sleeping four) and two guest rooms. Excellent meals with advance notice.
4 All major cards

ANTEQUERA 29200

PARADOR DE ANTEQUERA
$$$ ★★★★
PASEO GARCÍA DEL OLMO, S/N
TEL 952 84 02 61
www.parador.es

PRICES

HOTELS
An indication of the cost of a double room in the high season is given by **$** signs.

$$$$$	Over $300
$$$$	$220–$300
$$$	$160–$220
$$	$80–$160
$	Under $80

RESTAURANTS
An indication of the cost of a three-course meal without drinks is given by **$** signs.

$$$$$	Over $80
$$$$	$50–$80
$$$	$35–$50
$$	$20–$35
$	Under $20

Quiet and surrounded by gardens, this modern parador has luminous rooms with wood floors and leather furnishings.
58 All major cards

CASTILLA
$ ★★
INFANTE DON FERNANDO 40
TEL 952 84 30 90
www.castillahotel.com
This hotel occupies a restored building in the historic center. Dine in the restaurant.
18 All major cards

EL ANGELOTE
$$$
PLAZA COSO VIEJO S/N
TEL 95 270 34 65
El Angelote offers traditional cooking in a restored 17th-century building opposite the Nájera Palace.
70 Closed Sun. D., Mon., & last 2 weeks Aug. All major cards

BAEZA 23440

PUERTA DE LA LUNA
$$ ★★★★
CANÓNIGO MELGARES RAYA
TEL 953 74 70 19
www.hotelpuertadelaluna.com
Next to the cathedral, in the old town, this noble mansion is spacious and well-priced, with a good restaurant.
44 40 All major cards

CABO DE GATA 04150

CORTIJO EL SOTILLO
$$ ★★★★
ENTRADA DE SAN JOSÉ S/N
TEL 950 61 11 00
www.cortijoelsotillo.es
This 18th-century ranch-style building with large rooms and marble floors was used in the film *A Fistful of Dollars*. The restaurant serves seasonal dishes. Horseback riding is available.
20 45 All major cards

LA OLA
$
ISLETA DEL MORO
TEL 950 38 97 58
www.restaurantelaola.es
You can dine year-round on the terrace over the water at this simple restaurant. The menu depends on the day's catch.
35 Closed Tues. & Sun.–Thurs. D (Dec.–June), Oct., & Nov. No credit cards

CÁDIZ 11000

PLAYA VICTORIA
$$$ ★★★★
PLAZA INGENIERO LA CIERVA
TEL 956 20 51 00
www.palafoxhoteles.com
This well-equipped hotel has direct elevator access to Victoria beach. Even-numbered rooms enjoy sea views.
188 All major cards

EL FARO
$$$
SAN FÉLIX 15
TEL 956 21 10 68
www.elfarodecadiz.com
You'll find a fantastic spread of *raciones* at the bar in this chic spot specializing in seafood.
215 All major cards

CARMONA 41410

PARADOR DE CARMONA
$$$$ ★★★★
ALCÁZAR S/N
TEL 95 414 10 10
www.parador.es
Built within the 14th-century fortress walls, this parador has spectacular views of the Corbones plains. Some of the spacious rooms have balconies; others have large windows. You can dine in the impressive medieval refectory.
63 All major cards

CASA DE CARMONA
$$$ ★★★★★
PLAZA DE LASSO 1
TEL 95 419 10 00/414 41 51
www.casadecarmona.com
This elegant 16th- to 17th-century Mudejar house has three interior courtyards, a couple of regal sitting rooms, and antique-filled rooms. The hotel's restaurant serves fresh local dishes.
34 60 All major cards

SAN FERNANDO
$$
SACRAMENTO 3
TEL 95 414 35 56
Set in a grand house on one of Carmona's plazas, San Fernando serves very good seasonal game. Try the cod with garlic.
60 Closed Sun. D, Mon., & Aug. All major cards

CÓRDOBA 14000

HOTELS

HOSPES PALACIO DEL BAILÍO
$$$$$ ★★★★★
RAMÍREZ DE LAS CASAS DEZA 10–12
TEL 957 49 89 93
www.hospes.com
This luxurious hotel in a 16th-century palace boasts a beautiful internal courtyard. The ruins of an ancient Roman villa are visible through the restaurant's glazed floor.
53 All major cards

AMISTAD CÓRDOBA
$$$ ★★★★
PLAZA DE MAIMÓNIDES 3
TEL 957 42 03 35
www.nh-hotels.com
This stylish hotel at the entrance to the Judería is really two beautifully restored 18th-century mansions plus an annex. The informal bar/café serves Cordoban fare.
83 All major cards

ALBUCASIS
$$ ★★
BUEN PASTOR 11
TEL 957 47 86 25
www.hotelalbucasis.com
This hotel off a quiet street is centered on a pretty courtyard. Rooms are simple and the tile bathrooms spacious.
15 DC, MC, V

MEZQUITA
$ ★★
PLAZA SANTA CATALINA 1
TEL 957 47 55 85
www.hotelmezquita.com
Opposite the mosque, this mansion has two patios. The rooms and halls have antique furniture and paintings. Each is different, but all are spacious

with white-marble floors.
31 All major cards

RESTAURANTS

SOMETHING SPECIAL

ALMUDAINA
$$$$
PLAZA CAMPO SANTO DE LOS MÁRTIRES 1
TEL 957 47 43 42
www.restaurantealmudaina.com
This beautiful 16th-century house is now Córdoba's top restaurant, where elegant dining rooms lead off the covered interior patio. The cuisine puts a modern twist on local recipes. If you are up to it try the *rabo de toro* (bull's tail).
182 Closed Sun. D & Sun. mid-June–Aug. All major cards

BODEGAS CAMPOS
$$
CALLE DE LOS LINEROS 32
TEL 957 49 75 00
www.bodegascampos.org
Founded as a bodega in 1908, this complex of typical Córdoba courtyards features rustic decor and leafy patios for summer dining. The menu includes local dishes with modern touches.
600 P Closed Sun. D All major cards

GRANADA 18000

HOTELS

PARADOR DE GRANADA
$$$$$ ★★★★
REAL DE LA ALHAMBRA S/N
TEL 958 22 14 40
www.parador.es
This exquisite parador—a 15th-century convent in the Alhambra gardens—offers privileged views and a good restaurant. The old wing has rooms with antiques and rugs. Reserve a year in advance.
40 P All major cards

ALHAMBRA PALACE
$$$$ ★★★★
PLAZA ARQUITECTO GARCÍA DE PAREDES 1
TEL 958 22 14 68
www.h-alhambrapalace.es
Most rooms at this over-the-top imitation of the Alhambra have fine views. Traditional dishes meet modern creativity in the restaurant.
126 P All major cards

AMÉRICA
$$$ ★
REAL DE LA ALHAMBRA 53
TEL 958 22 74 71
www.hotelamericagranada.com
This old house has a pretty Andalusian patio and rooms set within the Alhambra precincts. Reserve months in advance.
17 Closed Dec.–Feb. All major cards

CARMEN DE SANTA INÉS
$$ ★★★
PLACETA DE PORRAS 7
TEL 958 22 63 80
www.carmensantaines.com
This quiet old Arab house on the Alcazaba wall in the Albaicín has antique-filled rooms and views of the Alhambra. There is no restaurant.
9 P All major cards

PALACIO DE SANTA INÉS
$$ ★★★
CUESTA DE SANTA INÉS 9
TEL 958 22 23 62
www.palaciosantaines.com
Some rooms in this small 16th-century palace (with Plateresque facade) in the Albaicín have an Alhambra view. There is no restaurant.
35 All major cards

REINA CRISTINA
$$ ★★★
TABLAS 4
TEL 958 25 32 11
www.hotelreinacristina.com
Once the home of poet Luís Rosales, this grand 19th-century town house has traces of an interior patio and simple rooms. Dining options include a restaurant and café.
56 150 P All major cards

RESTAURANTS

HORNO DE SANTIAGO
$$$$
PLAZA DE LOS CAMPOS 8
TEL 958 22 34 76
www.hornodesantiago.com
This restaurant serves modern cuisine based on regional recipes and market availability. Try the venison medallions with rosemary and quince sauce.
120 Closed Sun., & Aug. All major cards

CUNINI
$$$
PLAZA DE LA PESCADERÍA 14
TEL 958 25 07 77
www.marisqueriacunini.es
Reservations are needed at this popular place near the cathedral. Try the superb seafood spread at the tapas bar.
45 Closed Sun. D, & Mon. All major cards

RUTA DEL AZAFRÁN
$$$
PASEO DE LOS TRISTES
TEL 958 22 68 82
www.rutadelaazafran.es
This friendly, relaxed spot along the Darro River offers modern twists on Andalusian classics.
71 All major cards

GUADIX 18500

HOTEL COMERCIO
$$ ★★★★

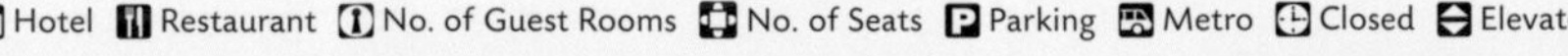

MIRA DE AMEZCUA 3
TEL 958 66 05 00
www.hotelcomercio.com
The Comercio features simple, comfortable rooms and a prize-winning restaurant that serves regional dishes.
42 All major cards

JAÉN 23001

PARADOR DE JAÉN
$$$ ★★★★
CASTILLO DE SANTA CATALINA
TEL 953 23 00 00
www.parador.es
Built in the style of the nearby 13th-century Arab fortress, this parador offers rooms with fantastic views. The restaurant serves local dishes; try the pipirrana salad or spinach and egg Jaén-style, with the local red wine—Duque de Bailén.
45 All major cards

JEREZ DE LA FRONTERA 11400

JEREZ SPA
$$ ★★★★★
AVENIDA ALCALDE ÁLVARO DOMECQ 35
TEL 956 30 06 00
www.jerezhotel.com
One of the city's few hotels, Jerez Spa has an unusual tropical garden.
127 All major cards

PALACIO GARVEY
$$ ★★★★
PLAZA RAFAEL RIVERO
TEL 956 32 67 00
www.sferahoteles.net
In old town, by the casino, this 1850s mansion was built for the Garvey sherry dynasty. It has an exclusive feel and is well modernized, arty, and light. Enjoy meals in the restaurant.
16 All major cards

LA MESA REDONDA
$$$$
MANUEL DE LA QUINTANA 3
TEL 956 34 00 69
This antique-filled restaurant serves Andalusian specialties and seasonal game. Try the Iberian pork fillets with foie gras. Reservations are essential.
45 Closed Sun., Easter weekend, & mid-July–mid-Aug. All major cards

MÁLAGA 29000

PARADOR DE MÁLAGA GIBRALFARO
$$$$ ★★★★
CASTILLO DE GIBRALFARO S/N
TEL 95 222 19 02
www.parador.es
The best place to stay in Málaga is the parador, a stone building with a view of the city and bay. Reserve well ahead.
38 All major cards

DEL PINTOR
$$ ★★★
ÁLAMOS 27
TEL 952 06 09 80
www.hoteldelpintor.com
Near the Picasso Museum, this modern hotel was decorated in red, white, and black by the local painter Pepe Bornoy.
17

MOLINO DE SANTILLÁN
$$ ★★★★
CARRETERA DE MACHARAVIAYA, KM 3, RINCÓN DE LA VICTORIA 29730 (12 MILES/20 KM FROM MÁLAGA)
TEL 952 40 09 49
www.molinodesantillan.es
Reached via a dirt road from the coast, this idyllic colonial-style villa nestles in the hills. Its small rooms are comfortable and quiet. The restaurant uses produce from its own greenhouse and organic garden.
21 All major cards

MARBELLA 29600

CALIMA
$$$$$
JOSÉ MELIÁ S/N
TEL 952 76 42 52
www.restaurantecalima.es
Chef Dani García offers creative, modern Andalusian cooking in beautiful surroundings. Try the pipirrana salad with cod.
55 Closed Sun., Mon., Tues.–Thurs. L All major cards

SOMETHING SPECIAL

ANTIGUA CASA DE GUARDIA
$
ALAMEDA PRINCIPAL 18 (CORNER OF CALLE PASTORA)
TEL 95 221 46 80
www.antiguacasadeguardia.net
Packed with locals, Málaga's oldest bar is a lively place. Try local wines dispensed from large wood barrels. No tables.
Closed Sun. except Easter week & Dec. No credit cards

MOJÁCAR 04638

CORTIJO DE LA MEDIA LUNA
$$
PARAJE DE LAS MARINAS 36
TEL 950 47 88 13
www.cortijodelamedialuna.com
Enjoy great views at this peaceful farmhouse between the village and the beach.
8 All major cards

MURCIA 30000

ARCO DE SAN JUAN
$ ★★★★
PLAZA CEBALLOS 10
TEL 968 21 04 55
www.arcosanjuan.com
In a restored 18th-century building by the cathedral in the old town, this well-equipped

hotel has a good restaurant.
94 P All major cards

MORALES
$$$$
AVENIDA DE LA CONSTITUCIÓN 12
TEL 968 23 10 26
This popular intimate dining room serves Murcian fare such as roast kid goat and fresh-caught seafood.
60 Closed Sat. D, Sun., & last 2 weeks Aug. All major cards

RONDA 29400

PARADOR DE RONDA
$$$ ★★★★
PLAZA DE ESPAÑA
TEL 952 87 75 00
www.parador.es
Ask for a room overlooking the spectacular Tagus gorge at this central hotel with a fine restaurant.
79 P All major cards

DON MIGUEL
$$ ★★★
VILLANUEVA 4 & 8
TEL 952 87 77 22
www.dmiguel.com
Don Miguel sits on the edge of the gorge, with spectacular views, particularly in the restaurant, which serves local dishes.
30 100 P All major cards

SEVILLA (SEVILLE) 41000

HOTELS

ALFONSO XIII
$$$$$ ★★★★★
SAN FERNANDO 2
TEL 954 91 70 00
www.alfonsoxiii.com
Inaugurated in 1929, this neo-Mudejar building built around a large courtyard is Sevilla's grandest hotel. The salons are ornately decorated with Moorish lamps and Sevilla tiles. Dining options include three restaurants and a bar.
151 P All major cards

SOMETHING SPECIAL

HACIENDA BENAZUZA
$$$$$ ★★★★★
SANLÚCAR LA MAYOR
(10 MILES/15 KM FROM SEVILLA)
TEL 955 70 33 44
www.haciendabenazuza.com
A beautiful tenth-century Moorish farmhouse has been restored and recreated as a luxury hotel and restaurant by the irrepressible Ferran Adrià. **The Alma,** led by chef Rafa Zafra, reinterprets and develops Adrià's cuisine, offering dishes such as rabbit shoulder with warm apple jelly and foie gras.
44 60 P Restaurant closed L, Sun., Mon., & Nov.–Mar. All major cards

---

EME CATHEDRAL
$$$$ ★★★★★
ALEMANES 27
TEL 954 56 00 00
www.emecatedralhotel.com
This stylish boutique hotel, created from 14th- to 16th-century homes in the heart of the city, offers seven bars and restaurants, and rooms and terraces with spectacular views of the cathedral and Giralda.
60 P All major cards

LAS CASAS DE LA JUDERÍA
$$$$ ★★★★
CALLEJÓN DE DOS HERMANAS 7
TEL 954 41 51 50
www.casasypalacios.com
In the heart of the Barrio de Santa Cruz, this magical hotel is made up of 27 homes in the old Jewish quarter, with wonderful courtyards. The rooms are spacious and quiet.
112 P All major cards

TABERNA DEL ALABARDERO
$$$$ ★★★★
ZARAGOZA 20
TEL 944 50 27 21
www.tabernadelalabardero.es
The popular and elegant restaurant in this early 1900s house, a pure Andalusian place around a central patio, serves modern Mediterranean cuisine.
7 225 P Closed Aug. All major cards

DOÑA MARÍA
$$$ ★★★★
DON REMONDO 19
TEL 954 22 49 90
www.hdmaria.com
All the rooms in this large stately mansion opposite the cathedral and Giralda have a different decor. There is a top

PRICES

HOTELS
An indication of the cost of a double room in the high season is given by **$** signs.

$$$$$	Over $300
$$$$	$220–$300
$$$	$160–$220
$$	$80–$160
$	Under $80

RESTAURANTS
An indication of the cost of a three-course meal without drinks is given by **$** signs.

$$$$$	Over $80
$$$$	$50–$80
$$$	$35–$50
$$	$20–$35
$	Under $20

floor terrace but no restaurant. 64 All major cards

LOS SEISES
$$$ ★★★★
SEGOVIAS 6
TEL 954 22 94 95
www.hotelhusalosseises.com
This 16th-century palace is now a smart, stylish hotel incorporating the Renaissance, Roman, and Moorish materials discovered during restoration. It has airy rooms, a roof terrace, and a restaurant serving cuisine with Arabic touches.
42 200 All major cards

RESTAURANTS

LA ALBAHACA
$$$$
PLAZA SANTA CRUZ 12
TEL 954 22 07 14
www.andalunet.com/la-albahaca
Right in the center of the Barrio de Santa Cruz, this restaurant occupies a lovely old Andalusian house.
60 Closed Sun. All major cards

EGAÑA ORIZA
$$$$
SAN FERNANDO 41
TEL 95 422 72 54
www.restauranteoriza.com
This simple, elegant restaurant backs on to the old city walls. Basque-influenced recipes include game in season. Try the delicious lobster in salad with truffle vinaigrette. Reservations are needed.
150 Closed Sat. L, Sun., & Aug. All major cards

SANTO
$$$$
ARGOTE DE MOLINA 29
TEL 954 56 10 20
www.emecatedralhotel.com
Chef Baltasar Díaz Corbacho has won a Michelin star for his creative Mediterranean flair. Try the roast sole with clams, citrus butter, and foamed potatoes in salsa verde, or the chocolate souffle with iced cream of caramel and cinnamon.
50 Closed Sun. & Mon. All major cards

AZ-ZAIT
$$$
PLAZA SAN LORENZO 1
TEL 954 90 64 75/65 15
www.az-zaitrestaurantes.com
Emerging chef Antonio Conejero offers creative avant-garde cuisine in a beautiful setting. Try scallops with strawberry caviar, or noodles with poached eggs and king prawns. Reservations by telephone only.
50 Closed Sun. (except Easter & Christmas) & Aug. All major cards

SIERRA NEVADA 18196

EL LODGE
$$$$ ★★★
MARIBEL 8, MONACHIL
TEL 958 48 06 00
www.ellodge.com
Log cabin interiors with cozy, warm rooms covered in Finnish pine. Ski to the hotel in winter.
20 All major cards

TARIFA 11380

SOMETHING SPECIAL

HURRICANE HOTEL
$$ ★★
CARRETERA N-340 CÁDIZ-MÁLAGA, KM 77
TEL 956 68 49 19
www.hotelhurricane.com
Close to Tarifa, the Hurricane stands in a luscious palm-filled garden. The modern building has a design in keeping with local architecture. The candlelit restaurant is known for modern cuisine with eastern influences. Try the fish of the day. Horseback riding is available.
33 All major cards

ÚBEDA 23400

PARADOR DE ÚBEDA
$$$$ ★★★★
PLAZA DE VÁZQUEZ MOLINA
TEL 953 75 03 45
www.parador.es
Sporting high beamed ceilings, the rooms in this grand 16th- to 17th-century Renaissance palace are arranged around two interior patios. The restaurant is comfortable.
36 All major cards

SOMETHING SPECIAL

PALACIO DE LA RAMBLA
$$$ ★★
PLAZA DEL MARQUÉS 1
TEL 953 75 01 96
www.palaciodelarambla.com
This exclusive, peaceful hotel in the center of Úbeda is a 16th-century palace with a Renaissance cloister. Each of the rooms has palatial dimensions, some four-poster beds, and all contain interesting antiques. No restaurant. Breakfast included.
8 Closed Jan. 10–28 & mid-July–mid-Aug. AE, MC, V

MARÍA DE MOLINA
$$ ★★★
PLAZA DEL AYUNTAMIENTO
TEL 953 79 53 56
www.hotelmariademolina.es
This 16th-century mansion in the heart of Úbeda has a lovely covered and colonnaded central courtyard.
27 All major cards

VEJER DE LA FRONTERA 11150

V
$$$
ROSARIO 11-13

TEL 956 45 17 57
www.hotelv-vejer.com
You can see Morocco from one of the three rooftop terraces at this well-equipped, minimalist hotel in a strikingly converted 17th-century manor, which also has in internal courtyard.
12 All major cards

ESCONDRIJO
$$
CALLEJÓN OSCURO 3
TEL 956 44 74 38
www.escondrijo.com
This lovely guesthouse with Moorish touches in the old quarter features an internal courtyard and views from the ample terrace. The large rooms have character and style.
5 Closed Dec.–mid-Feb. MC, V

TRAFALGAR
$$$
PLAZA DE ESPAÑA 31
TEL 956 44 76 38
www.miraalsur.com/trafalgar
A rather sophisticated establishment for Vejer, the dining room here is decorated in warm colors, with lovely old floor tiles. Specialties include Mediterranean cuisine using fresh local produce.
100 Closed Mon. & Dec.–Jan. All major cards

BALEARIC ISLANDS

MALLORCA (MAJORCA)

PALMA DE MALLORCA 07000

HOTELS

CAN CERA
$$$$ ★★★★★
SAN FRANCISCO 8
TEL 971 71 50 12
www.cancerahotel.com
This spacious 13th-century mansion in Palma's old quarter is now a boutique hotel with a fine courtyard, roof terrace, and spa. The restaurant serves creative Mediterranean-Asian fusion cuisine.
12 All major cards

CONVENT DE LA MISSIÓ
$$$$ ★★★★
CARRER DE LA MISSIÓ 7A
TEL 971 22 73 47
www.conventdelamissio.com
This stunningly converted 17th-century monastery in the heart of the old town includes an art gallery and some of the rooms have terraces. The restaurant serves seasonal cuisine.
14 All major cards

MELIÁ DEL MAR
$$$$ ★★★★★
PASEO DE ILLETAS 7, ILLETAS (5 MILES/8 KM FROM PALMA)
TEL 971 40 25 11
www.melia-demar.com
This elegant modern hotel by the sea and conveniently close to Palma is fun and peaceful—and closed to guests under the age of 15. Its temptations include Mediterranean and Far Eastern food in the restaurant, a cocktail bar, and a spa.
144 All major cards

SOMETHING SPECIAL

HILTON SA TORRE MALLORCA
$$$ ★★
CAMÍ DE SA TORRE (KM 8.7), LLUCMAJOR (20 MILES/32 KM SE OF PALMA)
TEL 871 96 37 00
www.hotelsatorremallorca.com
A rural manor house dating back to the 14th century, surrounded by olive and almond trees, this charming and peaceful Hilton boasts a working windmill, a large private chapel, a spa, and the Zaranda restaurant, where chef Fernando Pérez Arallano has won a Michelin star for dishes such as fresh baby squid with bean stew and Mallorcan pork sausage, and rack of suckling pig with oriental sauerkraut.
90 35 Restaurant closed L & Mon. All major cards

SAN LORENZO
$$$ ★★★★
SAN LORENZO 14
TEL 971 72 82 00
www.hotelsanlorenzo.com
A 17th-century mansion with each room unique. There is no parking nearby.
9 All major cards

RESTAURANTS

BACCHUS
$$$$
CARRETERRA VIEJA SANTA MARÍA-ALARÓ (KM 4, 12 MILES/20 KM FROM PALMA)
TEL 971 14 02 61
www.readshotel.com
In a 16th-century room within the Read's hotel, this restaurant offers inventive dishes. Try the sea bass with broccoli puree, fried shrimp and beetroot, or fillet of suckling pig with white asparagus, squash, and broad bean and pea ragout.
30 Closed Sun., Mon., & L (Tues.–Sat.) All major cards

CELLER SA PREMSA
$$
PLAZA OBISPO BERENGUER DE PALOU 8
TEL 971 72 35 29
www.cellersapremsa.com
A tavern full of old-wood wine barrels and walls covered in faded *feria* posters. Basic food in a great setting.
200 All major cards

NORTHWESTERN MALLORCA

L'HERMITAGE

$$$$ ★★★★
ORIENT, CARRETERA ALARÓ BUNYOLA, KM 8
TEL 971 18 03 03
www.hermitage-hotel.com

This peaceful 17th-century convent features a grand tower and baroque cloister. Four rooms are in the convent itself; others are in a terraced building. The restaurant, located in an old olive oil mill, serves meals inside or out on the patio.

20 P All major cards

ES RACÓ D'ES TEIX

$$$$$
SA VINYA VELLA 6E, DEIÀ
TEL 971 63 95 01
www.esracodesteix.es

In this beautiful setting in an old house at the foot of Teix Mountain, chef Josef Sauerschell has won a Michelin star for his fresh and inventive Mediterranean cuisine. Try his Mallorcan lamb with tomato, fennel, and olives, or hake and lobster in shellfish sauce.

35 P Closed Mon., Tues., & mid-Nov.–early Feb. AE, MC, V

NORTHEASTERN MALLORCA

PETIT HOTEL CASES DE PULA

$$
CARRETERA SON SERVERA-CAPDEPERA, KM 3
TEL 971 56 74 92
www.pulagolf.com

Warm and full of character, this little hotel occupies the Finca de Pula (1581). Modernized rooms feature Internet connections. Suites are spacious with Italian marble floors and rustic decor.

10 P All major cards

EIVISSA (IBIZA)

EL CORSARIO

$$$ ★★
PONIENTE 5
TEL 971 30 12 48
www.ibiza-hotels.com/corsario

At the highest point inside the city walls, this lovely hotel occupies a 17th-century corsair's palace. The best rooms overlook the town and harbor; although some lack air-conditioning. The restaurant offers a short and expensive menu, but the food is superb.

15 45 All major cards

LA VENTANA

$$$
SA CARROSSA 13
TEL 971 39 08 57
www.laventanaibiza.com

This small hotel has simple rooms. For a quiet night ask to be as far from the terrace as possible. When reserving, you are asked for a 50 percent deposit on a credit card.

13 AE, MC, V

MENORCA (MINORCA)

MAÓ (MAHÓN) 07700

PORT MAHÓN

$$ ★★★★
FORT DE L'EAU 13
TEL 971 36 26 00
www.sethotels.com

A colonial-style building decorated with reproduction furnishings and a terrace looking onto the sea. Quiet, well-equipped rooms.

82 All major cards

JÁGARO

$$$$
MOLL DE LLEVANT 334
TEL 971 36 23 90
jagaromenorca@hotmail.com

On the port shore, with excellent seafood. Menorcan lobster is famed: try the *caldereta* (stew) or *fritada de pescado* (fry-up of assorted fresh fish).

200 Closed month before Easter All major cards

LA CARABA

$$$
CAMÍ D'ES BALIACS 1, SANT LLUÍS
TEL 971 15 06 82

This restaurant in a lovely old Menorcan house offers inventive Mediterranean cooking and a friendly local atmosphere. Fine terrace and garden. Reserve in high summer.

60 Closed L & Nov.–May

CANARY ISLANDS

GRAN CANARIA

LAS PALMAS 35000

SANTA CATALINA

$$$ ★★★★★
LEÓN Y CASTILLO 227
TEL 928 24 30 40
www.hotelsantacatalina.com

Set in the palm park, this is Las Palmas's classiest hotel with the air of another era. Dining options include a restaurant and two bars.

202 P All major cards

LA HACIENDA DEL BUEN SUCESO

$$ ★★★
CARRETERA ARUCAS-BAÑADEROS (KM 1)
TEL 928 62 29 45
www.haciendabuensuceso.com

Find rural peace in an elegant 16th-century hacienda, surrounded by banana trees and only a short drive from Las Palmas. The hotel is well-equipped and with a fine restaurant.

18 P All major cards

EL REFUGIO
$$
CRUZ DE TEJEDA
(VEGA DE SAN MATEO)
TEL 928 66 65 13
www.hotelruralelrefugio.com
At the foot of volcanic rocks this hotel offers views of the native pine trees. Breakfast includes homemade bread.
17 All major cards

EL CUCHARÓN
$$$
MARINA 5
TEL 928 33 13 65
This simple restaurant serves typical local food mixed with modern touches.
50 Closed Sun. D, Mon., & mid-Aug.–mid-Sept. All major cards

LANZAROTE

FINCA DE LA FLORIDA
$$
EL PARRAL 1, SAN BARTOLOMÉ
TEL 928 52 11 24
www.hotelfincadela florida.com
This rural hotel is a traditional whitewashed farmhouse with an attractive garden and simple but comfortable rooms. Ask for directions when reserving.
16 All major cards

FINCA DE LAS SALINAS
$$
LA CUESTA 17, YAIZA 35570
CARRETERA YAIZA-ARRECIFE
TEL 928 83 03 25
www.fincasalinas.com
Restored grand 18th-century mansion with elegant, spacious interior and quiet bedrooms. Breakfast included.
19 All major cards

TENERIFE

PARQUE NACIONAL DE LAS CAÑADAS DEL TEIDE 38300

PARADOR DE LAS CAÑADAS DEL TEIDE
$$$ ★★
LAS CAÑADAS DEL TEIDE, LA OROTAVA
TEL 922 37 48 41
www.parador.es
The parador is unattractive but has views of the Pico del Teide. Some rooms have balconies.
37 All major cards

PUERTO DE LA CRUZ 38400

MONOPOL
$$ ★★★
QUINTANA 15
TEL 922 38 46 11
www.monopoltf.com
This long-established hotel in a 1742 building has stylish rooms and a leafy courtyard.
92 DC, MC, V

SANTA CRUZ DE TENERIFE 38000

HOTELS

MENCEY
$$$ ★★★★★
AVENIDA DOCTOR JOSÉ NAVEIRAS 38
TEL 922 60 99 00
www.iberostargrandhotel mencey.com
The most expensive hotel in town occupies a grandiose marble and stucco building in a quiet residential section. It features colonial-style interiors and wonderful gardens. You can enjoy Canarian and international cuisine in the restaurants and bar.
286 All major cards

PRICES

HOTELS
An indication of the cost of a double room in the high season is given by **$** signs.

$$$$$	Over $300
$$$$	$220–$300
$$$	$160–$220
$$	$80–$160
$	Under $80

RESTAURANTS
An indication of the cost of a three-course meal without drinks is given by **$** signs.

$$$$$	Over $80
$$$$	$50–$80
$$$	$35–$50
$$	$20–$35
$	Under $20

RESTAURANTS

EL COTO DE ANTONIO
$$$$
EL PERDÓN 13
TEL 922 27 21 05
This restaurant uses local produce to create Basque and Canarian cuisine with modern influences. Try kid goat in almond sauce.
40 Closed Sun. D, & first 2 weeks Sept. All major cards

SOLANA
$$$
PÉREZ DE ROZAS 15
TEL 922 24 37 80
e-mail: solanarestaurante@ hotmail.com
Showcasing modern Spanish cooking with an emphasis on local produce, Solana also boasts an excellent wine list.
32 Closed Sun., Mon., & last 3 weeks Aug. DC, MC, V

Shopping

A number of goods are particularly associated with Spain, such as leather, ceramics, embroidery, fans, and foods like olives, almonds, hams, honey, wines, and sherry. Try to shop for these items in their place of origin, where often prices are lower and the quality is higher. Spain is still full of fantastic old-fashioned shops, with service to match, where everything from cheese to apple liquor to dish detergent is beautifully laid out. However, chain stores are encroaching.

Markets

Everywhere, from the smallest village to the largest city, there's at least one weekly market where you can find everything from clothes to pottery and food. Markets usually start early in the morning and last until around 2 p.m. For the pick of the produce go early, although you won't find it really bustling until around 10 a.m. Often there will be a stand where you can buy freshly made churros (fritters) accompanied by coffee for breakfast. A lot of the produce on sale is locally grown and you can recognize local farmers by the woven baskets they use for weighing produce. Buy things that are in season and that are more expensive at home, such as almonds, strawberries, avocados, and wonderful red and green tomatoes. Look also for local delicacies like cheeses, honey, olives, dried peppers and tomatoes, hams, and herbs. When buying cheeses it is quite acceptable to ask to taste a small portion first.

Spain has few secondhand markets *(rastros)* or flea markets *(mercadillos)* and you are more likely to come across them, apart from Madrid and Barcelona, in places where there are communities of other nationalities, for instance on the Costa Blanca and Costa del Sol.

Opening Hours

Apart from bakeries *(panaderías)* that open at 8 a.m., other shops open at 9:30 a.m. or 10 a.m. They close for lunch between 1:30 p.m. or 2 p.m. and 4 p.m. or 5 p.m., and then stay open until 8 p.m. or 8:30 p.m. Supermarkets and stores like El Corte Inglés stay open all day, often until later than 8:30 p.m. Some shops close on Mondays, and bakers are open on Sunday mornings.

Payment

Supermarkets, El Corte Inglés, and other chains accept credit cards backed by ID, which you should carry. Check the signs on the door before you go in and always ask before paying.

Exports

Eighteen percent VAT (value-added tax), known as IVA in Spain, is included in the price of most goods. Non-E.U. visitors can claim back the IVA if more than 90.15 € ($118) has been spent in any one shop and the goods are taken outside the E.U. within three months. Make sure you receive an invoice *(factura)* identifying the vendor and the purchaser's name and passport number (you must show your passport) and fill in the required form. When leaving Spain, the invoice must be stamped by Customs *(aduana), before* check-in if at an airport, and the goods available for inspection. Refunds can be claimed at major airports (at a bank or Bureau de Change), or the invoice mailed to the vendor, who will send you the refund. Some shops are members of tax-free shopping schemes (often not indicated, so ask). They will give you a "Tax Free Cheque," with instructions on reclaiming, which also must be stamped by Customs on departure. From these shops, goods can also be sent home by delivery service.

Returns

If you have any complaints about a purchase, return it to the shop as soon as possible with the receipt as proof of purchase. Anything bought in a sale *(rebaja)* is usually not refundable.

■ IN & AROUND MADRID

Cake Shops & Delis

Casa Mira Carrera de San Jerónimo 30, tel 914 29 88 95. Excellent handmade turrones, marzipans, and other pastries. Open since 1842.

Lhardy Carrera de San Jerónimo 8, tel 915 21 33 85, www.lhardy.com. Open since 1839. You can buy pastries, cakes, cold meats, and cheeses. Restaurant.

La Mallorquina Puerta del Sol 8, tel 915 21 12 01. Incredible selection of delicious cakes to take away, or eat upstairs with a coffee.

Cigars

Cava de Puros Barquillo Barquillo 22, tel 915 22 02 22. Excellent selection of cigars.

Clothes & Shoes

Agatha Goya 6-8, tel 915 77 63 11 or Arturo Soria, tel 917 59 13 15. Contemporary jewelry.

Camper Gran Vía 54, tel 915 47 52 23, www.camper.com. Trendy shoes for men and women. All over Spain, 45 shops in Madrid.

El Corte Inglés Preciados 3; Plaza Callao 2; Goya 76 & 87; Princesa 42; Serrano 47; and others. Madrid's largest department store, found all over the country.

Purificación García Serrano 28, tel 914 35 80 13, www.purificaciongarcia.com. Designer clothes for women.
Zara Serrano 48, tel 915 76 95 58; Gran Vía 34, tel 915 21 12 83. Stylish clothes and accessories chain with reasonable prices. All over Spain, 25 shops in Madrid.

Embroidery

Artesanía Reyes Preciados 11, tel 915 31 81 48. Embroidered shawls, sheets, and tablecloths.
Gil Carrera de San Jerónimo 2, tel 915 21 25 49. Beautifully embroidered silk shawls and fans, plus flamenco dresses and accessories. Open since 1880.

Hats & Umbrellas

Casa de Diego Puerta del Sol 12, tel 915 22 66 43; Mesoneros Romanos 4, tel 915 31 02 23; www.casadiego.com. Opened in 1858, this shop specializes in umbrellas of every design.
Casa Yustas Plaza Mayor 30, tel 913 66 50 84, www.casayustas.com. Specializes in hats.

Markets In Madrid:

Cuesta de Moyano Claudio Moyano, metro Atocha. New and used books.
El Rastrillo Marqués de Viana, Sun., metro Tetuán.
El Rastro Ribera de Curtidores, metro La Latina, Tirso de Molina. Sun.
Mercado de Monedas y Sellos Plaza Mayor, metro Sol, Ópera. Sun. Stamps and coins.
Mercado de San Miguel Plaza de San Miguel, Permanent covered food market. Mon.–Sat.
Mercado de Tetuán Avenida de Asturias, metro Tetuán. Food, antiques, ceramics.

Around Madrid:

Alcalá de Henares Mon.
Aranjuez Sat.

NORTHWEST SPAIN

Cheeses

La Barata Av. de Covadonga 15, Cangas de Onís, tel 985 84 33 13, www.la-barata.com. Mountain cheeses, fabada kits, pork produce, and white fava beans.
La Casa de los Quesos Artesanos Rúa Bautizados 10, Santiago de Compostela, tel 981 58 50 85. All types of Galician cheeses: Arzúa-Ulloa, Tetilla, Cebreiro, and San Simón da Costa.
La Masera Párroco Camino 29, Luarca, tel 985 47 09 47. Cheeses from the region, and vacuum-packed ingredients for making the famous *fabada* (Asturian bean stew).

Chocolate & Candy

El Metate Preguntoiro 12, Santiago de Compostela, tel 981 58 19 16. The best chocolate in Santiago. Located in what used to be a chocolate factory.

Jewelry

Marín y Durán Orfas 11, Santiago de Compostela, tel 981 58 17 83. Silver and jet stone jewelry.
Regueira Rúa da Azabachería 9, Santiago de Compostela, tel 981 58 36 27. Jet stone jewelry.

Lace & Embroidery

Bolillos Rúa Nova 40, Santiago de Compostela, tel 981 58 97 76. Handmade lace and embroidery made by several women in the shop, using traditional methods.

Markets

Cudillero	Fri.
A Coruña (La Coruña)	Tues., 2nd & 3rd Sat. each month
Luarca	Wed.
Noia (Noya)	Thurs. & Sun.
Ourense (Orense)	7th & 17th each month (if Sun., nearest Mon.)
Oviedo	Thurs. & Sun.
Pontevedra	Sat.
Santander	Mon.–Sat.
Santiago	Mon.–Sat.

Pottery & Ceramics

De Cotío Rúa Xelmírez 26, Santiago de Compostela, tel 981 56 07 96, www.decotio.com. Locally made handicraft including traditional Galician pottery.
Sargadelos Rúa Nova 16, Santiago de Compostela, tel 981 58 19 05, www.sargadelos.com. Modern designs and traditional blue-and-white pottery.

NORTHEAST SPAIN

Antiques

Eduardo Borrás Barriocepo 44, Logroño, tel 941 20 10 83.
A Través del Espejo Iturrioz Leza Portales 7, Logroño, tel 941 25 33 63.

Food

Aitor Lasa Aldamar 12, Donostia (San Sebastián), tel 943 43 03 54. Specializes in cheeses and all varieties of mushrooms (fresh, dried, and frozen). Also walnuts and Tolosa beans.
La Koxkera Fermín Calbetón 34, Donostia, tel 943 42 45 99. Famous old deli, specializing in salted and unsalted cod, cheeses, pâtés, and Basque specialties.

Markets

Bilbo (Bilbao)	Mon.–Sat. food; Sun. books, coins, crafts
Calahorra	Thurs.
Daroca	Thurs.
Donostia (San Sebastián)	Sun.
Gasteiz (Vitoria)	Thurs. & Sat., first Sat. each month
Haro	Tues. & Sat.
Hondarribia (Fuenterrabía)	Wed. food, Sun. fleamarket

Huesca	Mon. & Tues. clothes market; Thurs. flower market
Iruña (Pamplona)	Sun. & first Sat. each month (secondhand)
Jaca	Fri.
Laguardia	Tues. & Fri.
Logroño	Sun.
Nájera	Thurs.
Oñati (Oñate)	Sat.
Santo Domingo de la Calzada	Sat.
Teruel	Thurs. & Fri.
Zaragoza	Wed. & Sun

Pottery

Arte y Artesanos León XIII 18, Zaragoza, tel 976 21 20 51. Pottery from all over Spain.

Wine

Bodega Nuestra Señora del Romero Carretera Tarazona 33, Cascante (4.5 miles/7 km from Tudela), tel 948 85 14 11. Wines from Navarra.

Bodega Vinícola Real Carretera de Nalda, Km 9, Albelda de Iregua, Logroño, tel 941 44 42 33. Regional wines and foods. Also functions as a 12-room hostel.

C.V.N.E. (Compañía Vinícola del Norte de España) Barrio de la Estación, Haro, tel 941 30 48 00, www.cvne.com. Rioja wines.

Mi Bodega Santo Tomás 13, Haro, tel 941 30 40 03. Rioja wines and other regional products.

Vinacoteca Ezquerra Beato Tomás de Zumarraga 27 bajo, Vitoria-Gasteiz, tel 945 24 95 51, www.vinocaezquerra.com. A wide selection of Rioja wines, and their own wine from Leza.

BARCELONA

Cakes & Pastries

Farga Diagonal 391, tel 934 16 01 12, www.farga.barcelona.com. Delicious pastries that you can sample in the tearoom. Many other stores.

Chocolates

Petit Plaisir Ganduxer 33, tel 934 14 41 93, www.petitplaisir.com. Belgian chocolate.

Xocoa Vidriería 4, tel 933 19 79 05, www.xocoa.es. Catalan chocolates and homemade candies.

Food

Cafés el Magnífico Argenteria 64, tel 933 10 33 61, www.cafeselmagnifico.com. Open since 1919. More than 30 freshly toasted coffees.

Fira Artesana Plaça del Pi 1, metro Liceu. First Fri.–Sat. of each month 10 a.m. to 10 p.m. Homemade cheeses, pâtés, and various candies with honey and almonds.

La Cansaladería Alsina Canalejas 29, Sants. Open since 1883. Honors the pig in all its edible forms.

Semon Ganduxer 31, tel 932 40 30 88, www.semon.es. Excellent smoked fish, caviar, and pâtés.

Gadgets

Beardsley Petritxol 12, tel 933 01 05 76. Kitchen utensils & gadgets.

El Corte Inglés Plaça de Catalunya 14, Diagonal 471–473 & 617, Portal de L'Angel 19, and more.

Konema Rambla Catalunya 43, tel 934 88 33 25. Designer stationery and gift shop.

Vinçon Passeig de Gràcia 96, tel 932 15 60 50. Sophisticated designer store, from sofas to kitchen knives.

Jewelry

Puíg Doria Diagonal 612, tel 93 201 29 11; Rambla Catalunya 88. tel 932 15 10 90.

Markets

Feria Nova Artesanía Rambla Santa Mónica, metro Drassanes. Sat. 5–10 p.m. & all day Sun. Arts and crafts.

Mercat Gotic Metro Jaume I, Liceu. All day Thurs., closed Aug. Antiques in the Plaça de la Seu opposite the cathedral.

Mercat de Sant Josep or de la Boquería. Rambla de Sant Josep, metro Liceu. Mon.–Sat. all day. One of Spain's best food markets.

Mercat dels Encants Plaça de les Glories Catalanes, metro Glories. Mon., Wed., Fri., & Sat., 8:30 a.m.–7 p.m. Used and new (and sometimes antique) items, from furniture to fabrics.

Mercat de Sant Antoni Comte dUrgell, metro Saqnt Antoni. Mon.–Sat., 7 a.m.–8 p.m. Old-style food market. Old books, collector cards, movie posters, and comics on Sun. a.m.

Mostra D'Art Plaça del Pi and Plaça Sant Josep Oriol, metro Liceu. All day and Sat. & Sun. morning. Art on show and on sale at reasonable prices.

Wine

Celler de Gelida Vallespir 65, tel 933 39 26 41, www.cellerdegelida.com. A wide selection of Catalan wines and cavas, Rioja, Rueda, & armagnacs. Opened in 1895.

Lafuente Juan Sebastián Bach 20, tel 932 01 15 13, www.lafuente.es. Wines from all over Spain including rare Reservas. Open since 1905.

Vila Viniteca Agullers 7, tel 932 68 32 27, www.vilaviniteca.es. An outstanding collection of Spanish wines, also wines from France, and port from Portugal.

EASTERN SPAIN

Food

La Garriga Espalter 9, Sitges, tel 938 94 19 72. Hams & meats.

La Granadina Girona 7, Alacant (Alicante), tel 96 521 11 51. Cheeses, hams, pâtés, and caviar.

Markets

Alcoi (Alcoy)	Wed.,Thurs., Sat., & Sun.
Alacant (Alicante)	Thurs., Sat. a.m.
Altea	Tues., Sat., Sun.

Bégur	Wed. a.m. & Tues., Thurs., & Sun. p.m. (July–Sept.)
Cadaqués	Mon.
Calp (Calpe)	Sat.
Dénia	Mon.
Elx (Elche)	Mon. & Sat.
Girona (Gerona)	Tues. & Sat.
Montblanc	Fri.
Palafrugell	Sun. & summer evenings all week
Ripoll	Sat.
Sagunt (Sagunto)	Wed., Thurs., & Sat.
Sitges	Thurs. & Sat.
Tarragona	Fri. & Sun.
Tortosa	Mon.
Tossa de Mar	Thurs.
Valencia	Sun.
Xàtiva (Játiva)	Tues. & Fri.

CASTILLA Y LEÓN

Basketwork & Antiques

Antiquaria Rúa Mayor 47, Salamanca, tel 923 26 72 99. Antiques and reproductions.

Food

Artesa Ordoño II 27, León, tel 987 25 18 55. Regional meats, sausages, Bierzo wines, cheeses, and chocolates from Astorga.
La Casa de los Quesos Plegarias, León. Cheeses from Spain and abroad.
La Despensa Ramos Carrión 6, Zamora, tel 980 53 68 16. Local products.
La Quesería Alcalde Miguel Castaño 1, León, tel 987 26 44 24. Spanish cheeses.

Leather Goods

Calzados San Luis Plaza Mayor 5, Ciudad Rodrigo, tel 923 46 03 65. Shoes and leather wine bottles.

Markets

Ávila	Fri.
Burgos	Wed., Fri., & Sun.
Ciudad Rodrigo	Sat.
El Burgo de Osma	Sat.
León	Sun.
Peñafiel	Thurs.
Salamanca	Sun.
Segovia	Thurs.
Soria	Daily; flea-market Thurs.
Tordesillas	Tues. & 1st weekend Oct.
Valladolid	Tues., Thurs., Sat., & Sun.
Zamora	Tues.

Pottery

Luisa Pérez Fermoselle 79, Zamora, tel 980 53 06 02. A traditional pottery workshop.
MJ Cerámica Balborraz 13 Zamora, tel 980 53 44 45. Traditional with modern influences.

Cake & Candy

Convento de las Dueñas In front of Iglesia San Esteban, Salamanca. Cakes & marzipan made by nuns.
Convento de Santa Teresa Plaza Santa, Ávila. Spain's best *yemas* (yellow cakes).

Wines

Bodegas Fariña Camino del Palo s/n, Toro, tel 980 57 76 73, www.bodegasfarina.com. Toro wines. Guided tour & tasting.
Bodegas Protos Bodegas Protos 24–28, Peñafiel, tel 983 87 80 11, www.bodegasprotos.com. Wines from the Ribera del Duero region.
Pecados Originales Pasaje Gutierrez 6, Valladolid, tel 983 39 23 26. Regional, national, and international wines.

CASTILLA-LA MANCHA & EXTREMADURA

Food

Gabriel Mostazo San Antón 1, Cáceres, tel 927 24 28 81. Regional products and Extremaduran wines, including those from the Monasterio de Tentudia.
La Almazara Plaza Mayor 4, Trujillo, tel 927 32 28 56. Regional hams, wine, cheeses, and honey.
Santo Tomé Santo Tomé 3, tel 925 22 37 63; Colombia 17, tel 925 25 42 96; & Plaza de Zocodover 7, tel 925 22 11 68, Toledo. Marzipan makers since 1856, and cakes, too.

Knives

Cuchillería Gómez La Feria 52, Albacete, tel 967 22 01 61. Traditional family cutlery business, near the bullring.
Simón Cuchillería Marqués de Molíns 14, Albacete, tel 967 21 03 67. Old-fashioned cutlery & hardware in the center of town.

Markets

Albacete	Sun.
Belmonte	Mon.
Cáceres	Wed.
Cuenca	Tues.
Mérida	Tues.
Plasencia	Tues.
Sigüenza	Sat.
Toledo	Sat.
Trujillo	Thurs.
Zafra	Thurs.

Pottery

Centro de Artesanía Iglesia Santa Cruz Santa Catalina s/n, Cuenca, tel 969 23 31 84, closed Mon. Very good arts and crafts.
Cerámica Rosi Padre Juan de Mariana 15, Talavera de la Reina. Traditional and imaginative ware.
DAM–Diseño–Decoración Adarve del Padre Rosalio 14, Cáceres, tel 927 24 46 92. Furniture and pottery.

ANDALUCÍA & MURCIA

Books & Antiques

Antigüedades Juan Carlos I Real 47, Úbeda, tel 953 75 76 37.
Librería Atlántida Gran Via de Colón 9, Granada, tel 958 22 44 03. Stocks books in English.

Carpets & Arts & Crafts

ACA Zoco–Artesanía Cordobesa Judíos s/n, Córdoba, tel 957 20 40 33. Locally made jewelry, leather crafts, and ceramics.

Lorca Artesana Río Guadalentín 9, Lorca, tel 968 46 61 97. Traditional carpets and rugs from Lorca.

Food & Wine

Monasterio de Santa Paula Santa Paula 11, Sevilla (Seville), tel 954 54 00 22. Jams, marmalades, sweet-meats, and candies.

COVAP Barqueros 2, Córdoba, tel 957 49 85 05. Ham, sausages, and cheeses.

Galería de Vinos Caldos Cerón 12, Jaén, tel 953 23 59 99. Wide selection of wines, including Duque de Bailén from Jaén.

La Flor de Toranzo Jimios 1, Sevilla, tel 954 22 93 15. Very good quality cheeses, ham, and cod. This is also a popular bar.

Las Campanas Plaza del Socorro, Ronda 17, tel 952 87 22 73. *Yemas* (small sweet yellow cakes).

Rincón de Baco Madre de Dios 9, Murcia, tel 968 22 34 40. Local wine and food to go with it.

Hats

El Sombrero de Tres Picos Plaza de Cuba 8, Sevilla, tel 954 28 34 58. Sombreros, bags, and belts.

Sombreros Padilla Crespo Avenida de la Constitución 2, Sevilla, tel 954 22 24 55. Stylish selection of Sevilla sombreros since 1935.

Leather Goods

Curtidos Varo Alfaros 5, Córdoba, tel 957 47 87 03. Boots and everything to do with horseback riding and hunting. Open since 1917.

Guarnicionería López Cuna 34, Sevilla, tel 954 21 69 23. Saddles, boots, belts, and bags.

Markets

Almería	Mon., Tues., Fri., Sat., & Sun. (airport)
Antequera	Daily except Sun., Tues. flea market.
Baeza	Tues.
Cádiz	Thurs. & Sun.
Carmona	Mon. & Thurs.
Córdoba	Sun. & Mon.
Granada	Wed. & Sat., Sun. flea market.
Guadix	Sat.
Jerez de la Frontera	Sat. & Sun. flea market, Oct.–June
Lorca	Thurs. & 2nd Sun. of month
Málaga	Sat. & Sun. flea market
Mojácar	Wed. & Sun.
Murcia	Thurs. & Sun.
Níjar	Wed.
Sevilla	Arts & crafts Mon.–Sat.; antiques & paintings Thurs.; general Fri. & Sat.; secondhand & antiques Sun.

Olive Oil

La Tienda del Aceite Avenida de Castro del Río 96, Baena, tel 957 69 20 31. Quality regional oils.

Pottery & Tiles

Alfarería Melchor Tito Valencia 44, tel 953 75 36 92; Fuenteseca 17, Úbeda, tel 953 75 33 65.

Azulejos Santa Isabel Alfarería 12, Sevilla, tel 95 434 46 08, www.azulejosantaisabel.com.

Cerámica Fajalauza Fajalauza 2, tel/fax 958 20 06 15. Famous Granada pottery.

Cerámica Triana Antillano Campos 14, Sevilla, tel 95 433 21 79, www.ceramicatriana.com.

Diego Lozano Jiménez Arco de las Escuelas 2, Baeza., Jaén, tel 953 74 14 71. Baeza's green designs.

La Tienda de los Milagros Callejón del Artesano 1, Níjar, Almería, tel 950 36 03 59, www.latiendadelosmilagros.com. Colorful original designs. Higher prices but better quality than many.

Sherry Bodegas

Domecq San Ildefonso 3, Jerez de la Frontera, tel 956 15 15 00, www.bodegasfundadorpedrodomecq.com. Reserve for a tour.

González Byass Manuel María González 12, Jerez de la Frontera, tel 956 35 70 16, www.gonzalezbyass.com. Call ahead.

BALEARIC ISLANDS

S'Alambic Andén de Poniente 33-36, Maó (Mahón), tel 971 35 03 03. Local pottery and clothes.

Colmado la Montaña Jaime II 27, Palma de Mallorca, tel 971 71 25 95, www.colmadolamontana.com. Local cheeses and *sobrasada* (raw, red pork sausage with paprika).

Markets

Eivissa (Ibiza Town)	Daily
Maó (Mahon)	Tues. & Sat.
Palma	Mon., Tues., Fri., & Sat. arts & crafts (daily summer & Christmas); Sat. flea market

CANARY ISLANDS

El Rincón del Fumador Albareda 23, Las Palmas de Gran Canaria, tel 928 27 82 15, www.elrincondelfumador.es. Immense selection of tobacco and cigars from Canaries, Cuba, and Philippines; pipes, and other smoking accessories.

Mercado de Nuestra Señora de África Avenida San Sebastián 51, Santa Cruz de Tenerife. Cheeses and other food.

Kiosco Artenerife Plaza de España, Santa Cruz de Tenerife, tel 922 29 15 23. Goods made by local artisans.

Market

Santa Cruz de Tenerife	Sun. flea market

Entertainment

Madrid and Barcelona are packed with bars, cafés, and things to do in the evenings. Madrileños tend to stay up the latest, often until sunrise, and really know how to enjoy themselves. Barcelona is very good for classical music and avant-garde theater and designer bars. You can usually pick up information on entertainment and events from visitor information centers, and this is often in English.

For tickets all over Spain and phone/online reservations:
Caixa Catalunya tel 902 10 12 12, www.telentrada.com
El Corte Inglés tel 902 40 02 22, www.elcorteingles.es
Entradas.com tel 915 70 07 50, www.entradas.com
ServiCaixa tel 902 33 22 11, www.servicaixa.com
GeneralTickets www.generaltickets.com
Ticketmaster tel 902 15 00 25, www.ticketmaster.es

■ MADRID

Flamenco

Café de Chinitas Torija 7, tel 915 47 15 02/01, www.chinitas.com, metro Santo Domingo. Shows at 8:30 & 10:30 p.m. Reserve ahead.
Cardamomo Ecchegaray 15, tel 913 67 07 57, www.cardamomo.es. Metro Sol.
Corral de la Morería Morería 17, tel 913 65 84 46, www.corraldelamoreria.com, metro Ópera. From 9:30 p.m.
Casa Patas Cañizares 10, tel 913 69 04 96, www.casapatas.com, metro Antón Martín, Tirso de Molina, Sol. Flamenco at 9 or 10:30 p.m., Fri. & Sat. midnight. Top performers. Reserve ahead.

Theater

Madrid's Theater Festival, from mid-May–early June features all forms of theater including dance.
Teatro de Bellas Artes Marqués de Casa Riera 2, tel 915 32 44 37, metro Banco de España, Sevilla.
Teatro Pavón Embajadores 9 (Plaza de Cascorro), tel 915 28 28 19, metro La Latina. Compañía Nacional de Teatro Clásico currently performs classic drama.

Opera & Classical Music

Auditorio Nacional de Música Príncipe de Vergara 146, tel 913 37 01 40, www.auditorio nacional .mcu.es, metro Cruz del Rayo. Classical music.
Teatro de la Zarzuela Jovellanos 4, tel 91 524 54 00, www.teatrodelazarzuela.mcu.es, metro Banco de España, Sevilla. Spanish genre of light opera, *la zarzuela.*
Teatro Monumental Atocha 65, tel 914 29 12 81, metro Antón Martín. Classical music.
Teatro Real Plaza Isabel II, tel 915 16 06 60, www.teatro-real.com, metro Ópera. Opera and ballet.

Pop, Rock, World & Jazz

Advance tickets online or from Halcón Viajes, Viajes Carrefour, and the FNAC store, Calle de Preciados. Cash. Venues include:
Café Central Plaza del Ángel 10, tel 913 69 41 43, www.cafecentralmadrid.com, metro Sol & Antón Martín. Live jazz nightly.
Clamores Alburquerque 14, tel 914 45 79 38, www.salaclamores .com, metro Bilbao. Jazz, world music, flamenco, pop.
Honky Tonk Covarrubias 24, tel 914 45 61 91, www.clubhonky.com, metro Alonso Martínez. Rock, funk, pop. Restaurant. All week.
La Boca del Lobo Echegaray 11, tel 914 29 70 13, www.labocadellobo.com, metro Sevilla & Sol. Reggae, flamenco, rumba.
Moe Club Alberto Alcocer 32, tel 914 58 33 48, www.moeclub.com, metro Colombia, Cuzco. Jazz, funk, soul, blues, rockabilly.
Populart Las Huertas 22, tel 914 29 84 07, www.populart.es, Metro Sevilla & Antón Martín. 10:45 p.m.–midnight. Jazz.

Cinema

These central cinemas show films in their original language:
Cine Doré (Fllmoteca Nacional) Santa Isabel 3, tel 913 69 25 18, metro Sol. Closed Mon.
Cines Renoir Locations throughout Madrid, www.cinesrenoir.com.
Círculo de Bellas Artes Alcalá 42, tel 913 60 54 00, www.circulobellasartes.com, metro Sevilla.
Golem Martín de los Heros 14, tel 915 59 38 36, www.golem.es, metro Ventura Rodríguez, Plaza de España.
Verdi Bravo Murillo 28, tel 914 47 39 30, www.cines-verdi.com, metro Bilbao, Quevedo.
Yelmo Cines Ideal Doctor Cortezo 6, tel 913 69 25 18, www.yelmocines.es, metro Tirso de Molina.

Casino

Casino Gran Madrid Carretera de La Coruña, Km 29, Torrelodones, tel 918 56 11 00, www.casinogranmadrid.es, open 4 p.m.–5 a.m. (6 a.m. Fri. & Sat.). Passport or driver's license required to get in.

Bullfighting

Plaza de Toros Monumental de las Ventas Alcalá 237, tel 913 56 22 00, www.las-ventas.com, metro Ventas. Largest bullring in Spain. Main season starts in mid-May (San Isidro feria). Must reserve; best seats are in the shade. Tickets: bullring, tel 902 15 00 25 (credit card), or www.taquillatoros.com.

Cafés & Bars

Café de Oriente Plaza de Oriente 2, tel 915 41 39 74, metro Ópera. An elegant old-fashioned café-bar and restaurant.

Café Gijón Paseo de Recoletos 21, tel 915 21 54 25, metro Banco de España, Colón. Regional fare.
Círculo de Bellas Artes Alcalá 42, tel 913 60 54 00, metro Banco de España. Elegant surroundings.
La Chata Cava Baja 24, tel 913 66 14 58, metro La Latina. Great tapas bar and restaurant.
La Venencia Echegaray 7, tel 914 29 73 13, metro Sevilla. A dusty old bar dedicated to sherry.
Viva Madrid Manuel Fernández y González 7, tel 914 29 36 40, metro Sevilla. Gets crowded so go early.

BARCELONA

The monthly *Agenda,* available from tourism offices, carries listings of all types of cultural events.

Theater

Barcelona theater is mainly in Catalan, sometimes Spanish. Some groups mix miming, special effects, and modern theater such as La Fura dels Baus, Els Joglars, and Els Comediants. These show modern work unless otherwise indicated.
Mercat de les Flors Lleida 59, tel 934 26 18 75, www.mercatflors.org, Metro Poble Sec. At foot of Montjuïc, this venue shows drama, dance, and concerts.
Teatre El Molino Vilà i Vilà 99, tel 932 05 51 11, www.elmolinobcn.com, metro Paral•lel. Cabaret.
Teatre Llantiol Riereta 7, tel 93 329 90 09, www.llantiol.com, metro Sant Antoni & Paral•lel. Concerts, comedy, musicals.
Teatre Lliure Passeig Santa Madrona 40–46, tel 932 89 27 70, metro Fontana; Montseny 47, tel 932 38 76 25, metro Plaça Espanya; www.teatrelliure.com. Musicals and dance.
Teatre Poliorama La Rambla dels Estudis 115, tel 933 17 75 99, www.teatrepoliorama.com, metro Plaça Catalunya. Theater, opera, flamenco, and more.
Teatre Romea Hospital 51, tel 933 01 55 04, www.teatreromea.com, Metro Liceu.
Teatre Tívoli Casp 8, tel 902 33 22 11, www.grupbalana.com. Musicals and dance shows.
Teatre Victòria Paral.lel 67, tel 933 29 91 89, www.teatrevictoria.com, metro Paral.lel. Ballet, modern dance, and musicals.

Opera & Classical Music

Gran Teatre del Liceu La Rambla 51–59, tel 934 85 99 98, www.liceubarcelona.com, metro Liceu. Opera and dance.
Palau de la Música Catalana Palau de la Música 4–6, tel 932 95 72 00, www.palaumusica.org, metro Urquinaona. Classical and choral music, and more.

Pop, Rock, World & Jazz

Apolo Nou de la Rambla 111–113, tel 934 41 40 01, www.sala-apolo.com, metro Paral.lel. Rock, flamenco, reggae, jazz, movies.
Bikini Deu i Mata 105, tel 933 22 08 00, www.bikinibcn.com, metro Les Corts. Rock, funk, hip hop.
Harlem Jazz Club Comtessa Sobradiel 8, tel 933 10 07 55, metro Jaume I. Jazz, Latino, rock, African, blues, and more.
Jamboree Plaça Reial 17, tel 933 01 75 64, metro Liceu. Mainly jazz, plus pop, rock, and hip-hop.
Moog Arc del Teatre 3, tel 933 19 17 89, www.masimas.com, metro Drassanes. Techno, rock, disco.
Razzmatazz Almogavers 122, tel 932 72 09 10, www.salarazzmatazz.com, metro Bogatell, Marina. Five clubs offering pop, rock, techno, disco, house, and more.
Tarantos Plaça Reial 17, tel 933 01 75 64, www.masimas.com/tarantos, metro Liceu. Historic flamenco joint.

Cinema

The following cinemas show films in their original language with Spanish subtitles:
Cines Renoir Floridablanca 135, tel 934 26 33 37, metro Sant Antoni, Universitat; Eugeni d'Ors 12, tel 934 90 55 10, metro Les Corts; www.cinesrenoir.com.
Cines Verdi Verdi 32 or Torrijos 49, tel 932 38 79 90, www.cines-verdi.com, metro Fontana.
Filmoteca de Catalunya Avinguda de Sarrià 33, tel 934 10 75 90, www.gencat.cat/cultura/icic/filmoteca, metro Hospital Clinic.
Girona Girona 175, tel 931 18 45 31, www.cinemasgirona.cat, metro Diagonal.
Maldá Carrer del Pi 5, tel 933 01 93 50, www.cinemamalda.net, metro Liceu.
Méliès Villarroel 102, tel 934 51 00 51, www.cinesmelies.net, metro Urgell.
Yelmo Icaria Salvador Espriú 61, tel 932 21 75 85, www.yelmocines.es, metro Ciutadella, Vila Olímpica.

Casino

Casino de Barcelona Marina 19–21, Port Olímpic, tel 932 25 78 78, www.casino-barcelona.com. Gaming 4 p.m.–4 a.m. (5 a.m. Fri. & Sat.); slots from 10 a.m. Passport/driver's license needed.

Cafés & Bars

7 Sins Mutaner 7, tel 934 53 64 45, www.7sinsbar.com, metro Universitat.
Bar Marsella Sant Pau 65, tel 934 42 72 63, metro Liceu. Opened in 1820 and known for its absinthe.
Bar Pastis Santa Mónica 4, tel 933 18 79 80, metro Drassanes. Live music at 10:30 p.m.
Boadas Tallers 1, tel 933 18 95 92, metro Catalunya. Hemingway haunt. Dress well.
Café de l'Òpera La Rambla 74, tel 933 17 75 85, www.cafeoperabcn.com, metro Liceu. Classy.
El Paraigua Pas de l'Ensenyança 2, tel 933 02 11 31, www.elparaigua.com, metro Jaume I. Cocktails and tapas in a former convent.
Els Quatre Gats Montsió 3, tel 933 02 41 40, www.4gats.com, metro Catalunya, Urquinaona. Striking place.
El Xampanyet Montcada 22, tel 933 19 70 03, metro Jaume I. Excellent *cava* and tapas.

Activities

Spain is a large mountainous country with huge tracts of land turned into national parks. It also has thousands of miles of coastline. Consequently it is a delight to anyone seeking outdoor activities. Below are various central federations and some individual venues for a variety of activities, but it is by no means a complete list. For comprehensive information on local activities and events, contact the local tourist offices.

Golf
Real Federación Española de Golf tel 915 55 26 82, www.rfegolf.es

Horseback Riding
Real Federación Hípica Española tel 914 36 42 00, www.rfhe.com

Polo
Real Federación Española de Polo tel 954 99 93 65, www.rfepolo.org

Mountaineering
Federación Española de Deportes de Montaña y Escalada tel 934 26 42 67, www.fedme.es

Sailing
Real Federación Española de Vela tel 915 19 50 08, www.rfev.es

Scuba Diving
Scuba Schools International tel 961 52 22 97, www.divessi.com

Thermal Springs
Asociación Nacional de Balnearios tel 915 49 03 00, www.balnearios.org

MADRID

Climbing
Federación Madrileña de Montañismo tel 915 27 38 01, www.fmm.es

Hiking
Espacio Acción tel 913 26 72 92, www.espacioaccion.com

Horseback Riding
Federación Hípica de Madrid tel 914 77 72 38, www.fhdm.es

Paragliding
De Madrid al Cielo Escuela de Parapente tel 915 52 84 33, www.madridalcielo.com

NORTHWEST SPAIN

Festivals
Feast of St. James July 25, Santiago de Compostela.
Festival Internacional de Santander Aug., tel 942 21 05 08, www.festivalsantander.com

General
Los Cauces Av. de Covadonga 23, Cangas de Onís, Asturias, tel 985 94 73 18, www.loscauces.com.

Golf
Real Club de Golf de La Coruña La Zapateira, A Coruña (La Coruña), tel 981 28 52 00, www.clubgolfcoruna.com
Real Golf de Pedreña Pedreña, tel 942 50 00 01, www.realgolfdepedrena.com

Horseback Riding
Benjamín Cobrana Valle de Lago, Somiedo, Asturias, tel 985 76 39 52

Scuba Diving
Buceo Galicia A Coruña, tel 981 21 22 06, www.buceogalicia.com

NORTHEAST SPAIN

Festivals
Festival de Cine de San Sebastián Sept., tel 943 48 12 12, www.sansebastianfestival.com
Fiesta de San Fermín www.sanfermin.com. Running of the bulls in Iruña (Pamplona).
Fiestas de San Mateo Around Sept. 21. Grape harvest (Logroño).
Festival de Jazz Late July in Donostia (San Sebastián), tel 943 48 19 00, www.heinekenjazzaldia.com

Golf
Club de Golf Larrabea Legutiano, Álava, tel 945 46 54 82, www.larrabea.com

Horseback Riding
Hípica del Zaldiarán Armentia, Vitoria-Gasteiz, tel 945 14 53 67, www.hipicadelzaldiaran.com
Rancho Bocalarroca Benabarre, Huesca, tel 609 35 98 13, www.equipirineo.com

Kayaking & Climbing
TT Aventura Avenida Pirenaica 10, Ainsa, Huesca, tel 974 51 00 24, www.ttaventura.com

Water Sports
Aguas Blancas Avenida de Sobrarbe 11, Aínsa, Huesca, tel 974 51 00 08, www.aguasblancas.com. White-water rafting.
Buceo Euskadi Puerto, Mutriku, Guipuzkoa, tel 943 19 50 88, www.buceoeuskadi.com. Scuba.

BARCELONA

Climbing & Trekking
Spanish Trails Ronda Sant Pere 23, tel 935 00 16 16, www.spanish-trails.com.
Travessa Galileu 64, tel 93 491 49 98, www.travessa.net

Golf
Real Club de Golf El Prat Plans de Bonvilar 17, Terrassa, tel 937 28 10 00, www.rcgep.com

EASTERN SPAIN

Festival

Las Fallas Valencia, March 15–19. Fireworks, bonfires, and music.

Golf

Golf Girona Sant Julià de Ramis, Girona (Gerona), tel 972 17 16 41, www.golfgirona.com

Hiking & Biking

Tururac Canónigo Sendra, Orba, Alacant (Aliccante), tel 965 78 23 60, www. tururac.com

Horseback Riding

Club Hípic Lloret Urb. El Condado del Jarnco, Lloret de Mar, tel 972 36 86 15, www.clubhipic lloret.com

Rafting & Kayaking

Deportur Camping Cauarca Les, Lleida (Lérida), tel 973 64 70 45, www.deportur.com

Scuba Diving

Dive Paradís Port de la Clota, L'Escala, Girona, tel 972 77 31 87, www.diveparadis.com

Sotamar Diving Center Avenida Caritat Serinyana 17, Cadaqués, tel 972 25 88 76, www.sotamar.com

Skiing

Estación Baqueira-Beret Vielha, Lleida, (Lérida), tel 973 63 90 10, www.baqueira.es

Skydiving

Skydive Empuriabrava Sector Aeroclub Empuriabrava, Girona, tel 972 45 01 11, www.skydive empuriabrava.com

CASTILLA Y LEÓN

Golf

Club de Golf Villar de Olalla Villar de Olalla, Cuenca, tel 969 26 71 98, www.villardeolallagolf.es

CASTILLA-LA MANCHA & EXTREMADURA

Festivals

WOMAD (World of Music, Arts, and Dance) Cáceres in mid-May. www.womad.org/caceres

Festival de Teatro Clásico Mérida, Badajoz, in July & Aug. Classics staged. Tel 924 00 94 80 www.festivaldemerida.es

Golf & Paragliding

Aerofly Andrés Sánchez, Badajoz, tel 656 65 65 62, www.aerofly.es

Norba Club de Golf Urbanización Ceres Golf, Cáceres, tel 927 23 14 41, www.norbagolf.com

ANDALUCÍA & MURCIA

Festivals

Carnaval in Cádiz Month before Easter. www.carnavaldecadiz.com

Feria del Caballo (Horse Fair) April or May, Jerez de la Frontera, Cádiz. Expect crowds. www.jerez.es

Festival de la Guitarra de Córdoba Early July in Córdoba. www.guitarracordoba.com

Corridas Goyescas Early Sept. in Ronda, Málaga. Matadors in 19th-century costumes. www.rmcr.org

Semana Santa Easter processions in Sevilla (Seville)

Golf

La Manga Club Los Belones, Cartagena, Murcia, tel 968 33 12 34, www.lamangaclub.es

Mijas Golf Mijas, Málaga, tel 952 47 68 43, www.mijasgolf.org

Real Club de Golf Las Brisas Nueva Andalucía, Marbella, Málaga, tel 952 81 30 21, www.lasbrisasgolf.es

Real Club de Golf Sotogrande Sotogrande, Cádiz, tel 956 78 50 14, www.golfsotogrande.com

Hiking, Skiing, Climbing

Nevadensis Guías de Montaña Plaza de la Libertad, Pampaneira, Granada, tel 958 76 31 27, www .nevadensis.com.

Horseback Riding

Club Hípico de Cordóba Carretera de Trasierra Km 3.2, Córdoba, tel 957 27 16 28, www.clubhipicodecordoba.com

Club Hípico Málaga Camino de los Almendrales, Málaga, tel 952 26 85 09, www.clubhipico malaga.es

Scuba Diving

Buceo La Herradura Puerto Deportivo Marina del Este, La Herradura, Granada, tel 958 82 70 83, www.buceolaherradura.com

Buceo Petuba Puerto Deportivo El Candado, Málaga, tel 952 20 37 98, www.petubo.com

BALEARIC ISLANDS

Golf, Horseback Riding, & Scuba Diving

Aqua Diving Center Puerto, Santa Eulàlia, Eivissa (Ibiza), tel 971 33 84 59, www.aquadiving center.com

Federación Hípica Uruguay s/n, Palma de Mallorca, tel 971 75 67 54, www.fhbalear.com

Golf de Club Ibiza Santa Eulàlia, Eivissa (Ibiza), tel 971 19 60 52, www.golfibiza.com

CANARY ISLANDS

Golf, Horseback Riding, & Scuba Diving

Club Hípico La Atalaya San Cristóbal de la Laguna, Santa Cruz de Tenerife, tel 922 25 14 10, www .clubatalaya.com

Golf Costa Teguise Avenida Golf, Teguise, Lanzarote, tel 928 59 05 12, www.lanzarote-golf.com

Ocean Deep Dive Marina Sur, Las Galletas, Arona, Tenerife, tel 658 83 28 02, www.oceandeep dive.com

Real Club de Golf Las Palmas Santa Brígida, Las Palmas, tel 928 35 01 04, www.realclubdegolfdelas palmas.com. Also has horses.

Language Guide

Excuse me *Perdón*
Hello *Hola*
Goodbye *Adiós*
Please *Por favor*
Thank you *Gracias*
You're welcome *De nada*
Good morning *Buenos días*
Good afternoon/evening *Buenas tardes*
Good night *Buenas noches*
today *hoy*
yesterday *ayer*
tomorrow *mañana*
now *ahora*
later *más tarde*
this morning *esta mañana*
this afternoon/this evening *esta tarde*
Do you speak English? *¿Habla inglés?*
I am American *Yo soy americano*
I don't understand *No entiendo*
Where is...? *¿Dónde está...?*
I don't know *no sé*
At what time? *¿a qué hora?*
when? *¿Cuándo?*

Do you have...? *¿tiene un...*
a single room *una habitación individual?*
a double room (double bed) *una habitación con cama de matrimonio?*
a double room (twin beds) *una habitación con dos camas?*
for one night *para una noche?*

I need a doctor/dentist *Necesito un médico/dentista*
Can you help me? *¿Me puede ayudar?*
hospital *hospital*
police station *comisaría de policía?*

I'd like *Me gustaría*
How much is it? *¿Cúanto es?*
Do you accept credit cards? *¿Se aceptan tarjetas de crédito?*
cheap *barato*
expensive *caro*
post office *el correo*
visitor information center *la oficina de turismo*
open *abierto*
closed *cerrado*
every day *todos los días*

Menu Reader

breakfast *el desayuno*
lunch *el almuerzo/la comida*
dinner *la cena*
I'd like to order *Me gustaría pedir*
Is service included? *¿Está incluido el servicio?*

la carta **menu**
menú del día **fixed priced three-course meal including a drink**
a la carta **ordering anything other than** *menú del día*
lista de vinos **wine list**
la cuenta **check**

tapa **small snack taken with a drink**
ración **portion, helping**
a la parrilla **grilled**
a la plancha **grilled on a hot plate**
crudo **raw**
ahumado **smoked**
estofado **stew**
frito **fried**
horno **oven**
empanada **savory pastry**
tortilla **Spanish omelet made with potatoes and often served cold**

un agua mineral **mineral water** *sin gas* **(still)** *con gas* **(sparkling)**
el azúcar **sugar**
un café americano **large black coffee**
un café con leche **large white coffee**
un café descafeinado **decaffeinated coffee**
un café solo **short black/ espresso**
una cerveza **beer**
cubiertos **knives and forks**
la leche **milk**
el pan **bread**
la sal **salt**
un té **tea**
un vino tinto **red wine**
un vino blanco **white wine**
vino de la casa **house wine**
un zumo de naranja **fresh orange juice**

cerdo **pork**
chorizo **spicy sausage**
conejo **rabbit**
cordero **lamb**
hígado **liver**
jamón **ham**
lomo **loin (usually of pork)**
pato **duck**
pavo **turkey**
perdiz **partridge**
pollo **chicken**
salchichas **sausages**
ternera **beef**

atún **tuna**
caballa **mackerel**
lenguado **sole**
lubina **sea bass**
rape **monkfish**

almejas **clams**
calamares **squid**
camarón **shrimp**
cangrejo **crab**
chipirones **small squid**
gambas **prawns**
langosta **lobster**
mejillones **mussels**
ostra **oyster**
pulpo **octopus**
vieira **scallop**

arroz **rice**
berenjena **eggplant**
cebolla **onion**
champiñones **mushrooms**
col **cabbage**
espárragos **asparagus**
espinacas **spinach**
guisantes **peas**
habas **broad beans**
judías **beans**
lechuga **lettuce**
patatas fritas **french fries**
pepino **cucumber**
puerro **leek**
seta **wild mushroom**
zanahoria **carrot**

albaricoque **apricot**
cereza **cherry**
frambuesa **raspberry**
fresa **strawberry**
limón **lemon**
manzana **apple**
melocotón **peach**
naranja **orange**
uva **grape**

INDEX

Bold page numbers indicate illustrations. CAPS indicates thematic categories.

ILLUSTRATIONS CREDITS

All photographs by Tino Soriano unless otherwise noted.

4, Natursports/Shutterstock; 8, Vinicius Ramalho Tupinamba/iStockphoto; 11, Jorg Greuel/Getty; 17, Gonzalo Azumendi; 33, Dioscoro Teofilo de la Puebla Tolin/Getty; 34, Visual Language/Fotosearch; 38, Hulton Archive/Getty; 42, James Blair/National Geographic; 47, Marianne Greenwood/Getty; 59, Quim Llenas/Getty; 69, Guy Vanderelst/Getty; 97, Juan R. Fabeiro/Getty; 148, MILOSZ WILCZYNSKI/National Geographic My Shot; 273, Alan Crawford/iStockphoto; 299, Jean Gill/iStockphoto; 326, Slow Images/Getty.

National Geographic

TRAVELER

Spain

Prepared by the Book Division

Hector Sierra, *Senior Vice President and General Manager*
Anne Alexander, *Senior Vice President and Editorial Director*
Jonathan Halling, *Design Director, Books and Children's Publishing*
Marianne R. Koszorus, *Design Director, Books*
Barbara Noe, *Senior Editor*
Carl Mehler, *Director of Maps*
R. Gary Colbert, *Production Director*
Jennifer A. Thornton, *Director of Managing Editorial*
Susan S. Blair, *Director of Photography*
Meredith C. Wilcox, *Director, Administration and Rights Clearance*

Staff for This Book

Mary Stephanos, *Project Editor*
Kay Kobor Hankins, *Art Director*
Linda Makarov, *Designer*
Matt Propert, *Illustrations Editor*
Galen Young, *Rights Clearance Specialist*
Michael McNey and Mapping Specialists, *Map Production*
Connie Binder, *Indexer*
Jane Herman, *Contributor*

Manufacturing and Quality Management

Phillip L. Schlosser, *Senior Vice President*
Chris Brown, *Vice President, NG Book Manufacturing*
George Bounelis, *Vice President, Production Services*
Nicole Elliott, *Manager*
Rachel Faulise, *Manager*
Robert L. Barr, *Manager*

First edition: Edited and designed by AA Publishing (a trading name of Automobile Association Developments Limited, whose registered office is Norfolk House, Priestley Road, Basingstoke, Hampshire, England RG24 9NY. Registered number: 1878835).

Area map illustrations drawn by Chris Orr Associates, Southampton, England
Cutaway illustrations drawn by Maltings Partnership, Derby, England

National Geographic Partners, LLC
1145 17th Street NW
Washington, DC 20036-4688 USA

The Library of Congress catalogued the first edition as follows:
Dunlop, Fiona, 1952-
The National Geographic traveler. Spain/Fiona Dunlop.
p. cm.
Includes index.
ISBN 0-7922-7922-0
1. Spain--Guidebooks. I. Title: Spain. II. Title.

DP14 .D86 2001
914.604'83--dc21

00-052681

CIP

National Geographic Traveler: Spain
(Fourth Edition)
ISBN: 978-1-4262-0955-0

Printed in Hong Kong
16/THK/2